A COLLECTION OF 24 STOCK SPECULATION CLASSICS

Volume I, 1880 - 1922

By
Robert B. Kirkconnell, III

READINGCOPY.COM
2007

ISBN-13: 978-0-9794415-2-3
ISBN-10: 0-9794415-2-8

Library of Congress Catalog number: 2007925074

CONTENTS
(Volume 1)

CONTENTS (Volume 2)

SPECULATION AS A FINE ART AND THOUGHTS ON LIFE
Dickson G. Watts – 1880

Contents
I – Speculation as a Fine Art
II – Life
III – Business
IV – Society
V – Language

Speculation as a Fine Art - What is Speculation?

Before entering on our inquiry, before considering the rules of our art, we will examine the subject in the abstract. Is speculation right? It may be questioned, tried by the highest standards, whether any trade where an exact equivalent is not given can be right. But as society is now organized speculation seems a necessity.

Is there any difference between speculation and gambling? The terms are often used interchangeably, but speculation presupposes intellectual effort; gambling, blind chance. Accurately to define the two is difficult; all definitions are difficult. Wit and humor, for instance, can be defined; but notwithstanding the most subtle distinction, wit and humor blend, run into each other. This is true of speculation and gambling. The former has some of the elements of chance; the latter some of the elements of reason. We define as best we can. *Speculation is a venture based upon calculation. Gambling is a venture without calculation.* The law makes this distinction; it sustains speculation and condemns gambling.

All business is more or less speculation. The term speculation, however, is commonly restricted to business of exceptional uncertainty. The uninitiated believe that chance is so large a part of speculation that it is subject to no rules, is governed by no laws. This is a serious error. We propose in this article to point out some of the laws in this realm.

There is no royal road to success in speculation. We do not undertake, and it would be worse than folly to undertake, to show how money can be made. Those who make for themselves or others an infallible plan delude themselves and others. Our effort will be to set for the great underlying principles of the "art" the application of which must depend on circumstances, the time and the man.

Let us first consider the qualities essential to the equipment of the speculator. We name them: Self-reliance, judgment, courage, prudence, pliability.

1. *Self-Reliance.* A man must think for himself, must follow his own convictions. George MacDonald says: "A man cannot have another man's ideas any more than he can another man's soul or another man's body." Self-trust is the foundation of successful effort.

1

2. *Judgment.* That *equipoise,* that nice adjustment of the faculties one to the other, which is called good judgment, is an essential to the speculator.

3. *Courage.* That is, confidence to act on the decisions of the mind. In speculation there is value in Mirabeau's dictum: "Be bold, still be bold; always be bold."

4. *Prudence.* The power of measuring the danger, together with a certain alertness and watchfulness, is very important. There should be a balance of these two, Prudence and Courage; Prudence in contemplation, Courage in execution. Lord Bacon says: "In meditation all dangers should be seen; in execution one, unless very formidable." Connected with these qualities, properly an outgrowth of them, is a third, viz: promptness. The mind convinced, the act should follow. In the words of Macbeth; "Henceforth the very firstlings of my heart shall be the firstlings of my hand." Think, act, promptly.

5. *Pliability,* the ability to change an opinion, the power of revision. "He who observes," says Emerson, "and observes again, is always formidable."

The qualifications named are necessary to the make-up of a speculator, but they must be in well-balanced combination. A deficiency or an over-plus of one; quality will destroy the effectiveness of all. The possession of such faculties, in a proper adjustment is, of course, uncommon. In speculation, as in life, few succeed, many fail.

Each department of life has its language, expressive if not elegant, and in dealing with the subject we must perforce adopt the language of the Street. The laws given will be found to apply to speculation of any kind. They are universal laws; but for the sake of clearness we assume the case of speculation as conducted in one of our exchanges, where they can be best demonstrated.

Laws Absolute

1. *Never Overtrade.* To take an interest larger than the capital justifies is to invite disaster. With such an interest a fluctuation in the market unnerves the operator, and his judgment becomes worthless.

2. *Never "Double Up";* that is, never completely and at once reverse a position. Being "long," for instance, do not "sell out" and go as much "short." This may occasionally succeed, but is very hazardous, for should the market begin again to advance, the mind reverts to its original opinion and the speculator "covers up" and "goes long" again. Should this last change be wrong, complete demoralization ensues. The change in the original position should have been made moderately, cautiously, thus keeping the judgment clear and preserving the balance of the mind.

3. *"Run Quickly,"* or not at all; that is to say, act promptly at the first approach of danger, but failing to do this until others see the danger, hold on or close out part of the "interest."

4. *Another rule is, when doubtful, reduce the amount of the interest;* for either the mind is not satisfied with the position taken, or the interest is too large for safety. One man told another that he could not sleep on account of his position in the market; his friend judiciously and laconically replied: "Sell down to a sleeping point."

Rules Conditional

These rules are subject to modification according to the circumstances, individuality and temperament of the operator.

1. *It is better to "average up" than to "average down."* This opinion is contrary to the one commonly held and acted upon; it being the practice to buy, and on a decline to buy more. This reduces the average. Probably four times out of five this method will result in striking a reaction in the market that will prevent loss, but the fifth time, meeting with a permanently declining market, the operator loses his head and closes out, making a heavy loss - a loss so great as to bring complete demoralization, often ruin.

But buying at first moderately, and, as the market advances, adding slowly and cautiously to the "line" - this is a way of speculating that requires great care and watchfulness, for the market will often (probably four times out of five) react to the point of "average." *Here lies the danger. Failure to close out at the point of average destroys the safety of the whole operation.* Occasionally a permanently advancing market is met with and a big profit secured. In such an operation the original risk is small, the danger at no time great, and when successful, the profit is large. The method should only be employed when an important advance or decline is expected, and with a moderate capital can be undertaken with comparative safety.

2. To "buy down" requires a long purse and a strong nerve, and ruin often overtakes those who have both nerve and money. The stronger the nerve the more probability of staying too long. There is, however, a class of successful operators who "buy down" and hold on. They deal in relatively small amounts. Entering the market prudently with the determination of holding on for a long period, they are not disturbed by its fluctuations. They are men of good judgment, who buy in times of depression to hold for a general revival of business - an investing rather than a speculating class.

3. In all ordinary circumstances our advice would be to buy at once an amount that is within the proper limits of capital, etc., "selling out" at a loss or profit, according to judgment. *The rule is to stop losses and let profits run.* If small profits are taken, then small losses must be taken. Not to have the courage to accept a loss, and to be too eager to take a profit, is fatal. It is the ruin of many.

4. Public opinion is not to be ignored. A strong speculative current is for the time being overwhelming, and should be closely watched. The rule is, to act cautiously with public opinion; against it, boldly. To go with the market, even when the basis is a good one, is dangerous. It may at any time turn and rend you. Every speculator knows the danger of too much "company." It is equally necessary to exercise common caution in going against the market. This caution should be continued to the point of wavering - of loss of confidence - when the market should be boldly encountered to the full extent of strength, nerve and capital. The market has a pulse on which the hand of the operator should be placed as that of the physician on the wrist of the patient. This pulse-beat must be the guide when and how to act.

5. *Quiet, weak markets are good markets to sell.* They ordinarily develop into declining markets. *But when a market has gone through the stages of quiet and weak to active and declining, then on to semi-panic or panic,* it should be bought freely. When vice versa, a quiet and firm market develops into activity and strength, then into excitement, it should be sold with great confidence.

6. In forming an opinion of the market, the element of chance ought not be omitted. There is a doctrine of chances - Napoleon in his campaigns allowed a margin for chance - for the accidents that come in to destroy or modify the best calculation. Calculation must measure the incalculable. In the "reproof of chance lies the true proof of men."

It is better to act on general than special information (it is not so misleading), viz., the state of the country, the condition of the crops, manu-facturers, etc. Statistics are valuable, but they must be kept subordinate to a comprehensive view of the whole situation. Those who confine themselves too closely to statistics are poor guides. "There is nothing," said Canning, "so fallacious as facts, except figures."

"When in doubt, do nothing. Don't enter the market on half convictions; wait till the convictions are fully matured."

We have written to little purpose unless we have left the impression that the fundamental principle that lies at the base of all speculation is this: *Act so as to keep the mind clear, its judgment trustworthy.* A reserve force should therefore be maintained and kept for supreme movements, when the full strength of the whole man should be put on the stroke delivered.

It may be thought that the carrying out of these rules is difficult. As we said in the outset, the gifted man only can apply them. To the artist alone are the rules of his art valuable.

LIFE

Compensations do not always compensate. A common deception, — self-deception.

Hold in time, or take the jump.

A danger known is half overcome. A fault recognized is half conquered.

A great insult, — tell a man he can't take a joke.

Fools try to prove that they are right. Wise men try to find when they are wrong.

That writer is the greatest who says the least and suggests the most.

Follow the vague and intangible, and it will become definite and tangible.

A man's good qualities are often, at bottom, only pride.

Two standards, — one for yourself and one for your neighbor. The first should be fixed, the second flexible.

That man is greatest who quickens most the lives of other men.

All see; few observe, fewer still compare.

The finished fabric of science is the raw material of philosophy.

Destruction must often precede construction, most men stop at the former.

Common sense is sense men have in common.

Better capital in a man's head than capital in a bank.

Look after the principal; the interest will look after itself.

In the business world, as in the physical and moral world, plasticity is life, rigidity is death.

To be "too greedy" is as bad in business as in morals.

Learn principles. Facts will then fall into their relations and connections.

Quick decisions are the best decisions. When you begin to doubt, begin to "get out." Thought and act should be hyphened.

If a speculation keeps you awake at night, sell down to the sleeping point.

MEN

Some men are so mellow that they are rotten. Little men talk of people; great men, of things.

The self-important man is seldom important to others.

No man is as good as he is thought to be; no man as bad.

A tiresome man, — a man with a theory.

Money adds nothing to an extraordinary man, but it is the "saving grace" of an ordinary man.

The able man compares himself with the known and is proud. The great man compares himself with the unknown and is humble.

The vain man is laughable; the proud man is insufferable.

An able man disdains the wisdom of other men; a great man uses the wisdom of other men.

Two kinds of men, — men who see things as they are, and men who see things as they ought to be. The former are practical, the latter reformers. The wise man accepts the position of the former, and works to accomplish that of the latter.

Against flattery women are on guard. Men can be flattered into doing almost anything.

Men excuse their vices by enumerating their virtues.

The great man is little, the little man great. The difference between them lies in that the great man knows his littleness, but the little man does not comprehend his greatness.

The little man demands to be understood; the great man is content to be misunderstood.

The man who talks of his grand acquaintances is never a grand man.

Some men are icebergs, — they never had any heat; others are burned-out volcanoes, — only the ashes remain.

Men who go straight to the point either see very little or see very much.

Many men have the "courage of their opinions," few the courage to abandon opinions.

A real man has no "appearances" to "keep up."

The man who stands on his dignity has nothing else to stand on.

The "self-made man" is proud of a very poor job.

Strong men are silent. When a strong man begins to talk, he is losing his power.

The talented man must live to be appreciated. The genius must die to be appreciated.

The most complete man is he who touches life at the most points.

The man who monopolizes the conversation has a monopoly himself.

The mistake of an able man is that he thinks others are as able as he.

SOCIETY

THE least "manner" the best manners. Second-class people, — those just below us.

The Hobgoblin of Society, — "What people will say?"

The world is not deceived; it distinguishes between that which is "put on" from that which grows on.

Men wear masks and the world takes them seriously; when a man shows his real face, the world laughs.

Nondescripts, — "nice people."

Disturbers of society, — people who are aggressively intellectual, and people who have prominent consciences.

Man seeks society because he can't endure his own companionship.

Society is one organism. Life the race and the individual is lifted. Life the individual and the race is lifted.

"Make believe" is a game society plays as well as children.

Better talk good sense than good English. Public opinion is the scarecrow of society.

Society people order their clothes, but get their opinions "ready made."

What sap is to the tree, blood to man, money is to society.

LANGUAGE

Language is an evolution, and has its roots in the ground.

Words are counters in the game of life. Use them carefully; they must be redeemed.

Words burn like fire and heat like balm.

Words are coins. Stamp them with your own image.

The language of sorrow is tears; the language of despair, silence.

Thoughts are vitalized blood.

We can say things we can't write; write things we can't say.

Brevity is the soul of — language.

To know when to speak is rare; when to be silent, rarer still.

Not what others have written, but what you think.

There is a language of science, a language of diplomacy, a language of commerce, a language of spirit.

To understand a man, you must know the language spoken.

A *word* in times saves nine.

FINIS

DUNCAN ON INVESTMENT AND SPECULATION
William W. Duncan - 1895

Contents

PREFACE – In presenting this work to the public our object has been to explain the technicalities of the Stock Exchange, and to clear up such difficulties as have hitherto lain in the paths of inexperienced investors.

We show the principles upon which a capitalist, large or small, can obtain the highest return for his money, and point out the comparative risks he runs in investments of various qualities.

Without expressing our own views or indicating any particular securities as suitable for investment, we have endeavoured to place a capitalist in the position to judge for himself and employ his money according to his means, his requirements and his intelligence. We hope we have succeeded. - *DUNCAN'S, Stock and share dealers, (est. 1867)*

Chapter I - The Principle of Investment

A farmer once asked a banker, "Shall I invest my money in English Railway Debentures or in Argentine Government Bonds? The answer given was, "If you want to sleep soundly buy the Railway Debentures; if you prefer good living to a good night's rest buy the Argentines."

In this fragment of conversation lies the whole philosophy of investment.

Capital embarked in a well-selected security, such as English Railway Debentures, means, practically, safety of the principal; but naturally the interest on this class of investment is but small. Still, to some people, the confidence that their money is secure is more valuable than a larger revenue; they can "sleep o' nights" without fear of waking up poorer than they laid down. On the other hand, big interest is supposed to mean corresponding risk; and it is true that various causes operate upon securities which are not of the very highest description.

But it must by no means be accepted as an infallible rule that small interest ensures safety, or that large interest means that the capital is in jeopardy. This is a popular fallacy that keeps money idle and moneyed people poorer than they need be.

It is obviously the duty of everyone, both for his own sake and the sake of those dependent on him and who may come after him, to obtain for his capital the largest possible return compatible with safety. He should invest on the best terms; and investments, if properly understood, can be made to produce large interest. When danger is known it can be provided against. There are safeguards in the investment of money, and these being properly applied, a capitalist will find himself able to sleep soundly, although he has no Railway Debentures to represent his money.

Capital is lost and income wasted by people who do not take the trouble to acquire the art of investment. So many have thought the subject too easy to necessitate study; so many have not learnt to discriminate between one investment and another; they follow either the suggestions of others no wiser than themselves or venture in whatever may happen to be the prevailing fashion of the moment. They pride themselves on being remarkably clever because their capital has not shrunk, and they have received regularly their dribbling installments of interest.

Or, in search of high interest, they have rushed into ventures the particulars of which they have barely digested, and think themselves unlucky when the roseate promises remain unfulfilled.

As in every other business there is a happy medium in investment. Lethargy and disinclination to move with the times have brought as many prosperous houses to grief as even speculation. And the secret of success is to thoroughly understand a business before embarking on it.

To obtain a fair revenue with reasonable safety is not difficult, and there is no business in life more important than that of investing money. Therefore our object is primarily directed to teaching those with capital, not how to invest—for that is a matter of individual judgment—but how to learn to exercise in his investments the judgment with which every ordinary person is endowed.

Chapter II - Investment and Speculation

Investment and speculation are twin sisters, and so nearly alike that it is almost impossible to discriminate between them.

There are investors, that is to say, people with money laid out to produce income, who would be horrified at the idea of being classed with speculators. Yet what are speculators if they too are not people with money laid out to produce income? Where is the difference?

An "investment" is supposed to mean absolute safety, but where is absolute safety to be found?

And the so-called speculator? Does not he consider that his ventures in the aggregate are absolutely safe to bring him a fair return for the capital embarked?

All investments of money are more or less speculations as surely as that all speculations are investments of money. Both methods call them what we will, have the same object in view, to be achieved by similar means; namely, to put out money to the best advantage.

The very people who are most shocked at speculation and gambling are often themselves the most inconsistent gamblers. They invest, and perforce take a chance of losing. But what they do not see is that in their forms of investment the chances are against them; their chance of loss greatly exceeds their chance of gain. If the unforeseen should happen they might make heavy losses, but no combination of circumstances could make them heavy winners. On the other hand they would contend that speculation implies large chimerical gains with possible loss of the whole capital. This also is an unfair explanation.

As a matter of fact, investment and speculation are words with but slightly different meanings.

INVESTMENT, strictly speaking, is the placing of capital in a security which does not vary in value, and which offers a certainty that interest upon the same will be regularly paid.

SPECULATION is the placing of capital in a security not selected so much with a certainty of regular interest as with the idea of the value of such security increasing. And a good speculation is one in which the chance of decrease in value is smaller than the chance of increase. The investor receives his interest; the speculator his profit. Again a distinction without much difference. We may take it therefore that there are three ways of laying out money to produce income, by:

Investment—Speculative Investment—Speculation.

To appreciate the difference between these three is a most important lesson to be learnt. To know how to adapt each to one's personal circumstances, to become master of the art of employing money in investment, in speculative investment, or in speculation according to the probabilities of the moment will follow in due course if proper attention be paid to the subject.

And unless a capitalist is prepared to take the very slight trouble necessary to teach himself to invest, he had better be satisfied with the tiny return which high class investment offers him. If, on the other hand, he is sensible enough to want the most he can get for his money, then he must calculate what risks he runs and employ his capital where the contingencies are in his favour. When he knows them he can provide for them and fortify himself against them. If he thinks he holds the one class of security when really he has the other he is in danger that he may not realize until it is too late to save himself and his money. So the prime point is to know whether his property consists of investments, of speculative investments, or of speculations.

Chapter III - Investment

Money has frequently to be put out at interest in cases where it is desirable that no change should take place in the value of the amount laid by.

This is the case with trust money. Trustees who have the administration of money which is not their own, owe a prime duty to those interested in the fund, and that is, that at the end of their time they shall deliver up the property in as nearly as possible the same condition as they received it.

It is, of course, praiseworthy of trustees to increase the amount of capital placed under their charge. But they must not speculate, no matter how honorable their intentions may be or how fully they may be conversant with financial matters. Their duty is quite clear; it is laid down by law; and the Acts of Parliament relating to their rights and privileges regulate the securities in which they are entitled to invest.

Naturally, the selections in the statutes have been most carefully made, and they have been considered more with regard to safety of capital than with the idea of large revenue. They have been chosen as non-varying in value and regular in interest paying. Any that do not answer these requirements, or which would probably, in the future, not answer these requirements, are not available for the investment of trust funds.

Now, private investors who deal with their own money are of course unfettered by any regulations except their own desires. That they would like to make the most they could of their capital is pretty obvious. The question of non-varying value and regular interest need be of no moment to them provided they can do better. But some do not take the trouble to do better; some are afraid to approach the subject of profitable investment. Very well, let them follow the example of trustees. They need not bother their brains or use their intelligence; they need only find a security such as the Acts of Parliament have indicated as fit for the investment of trust money; they can purchase this and rest assured that their capital is practically safe. There is always money forthcoming for this class of investment. People die and leave money to be dealt with in the future; marriage settlements provide for the almost permanent investment of funds; public institutions find it advisable to place a reserve capital in the safest of securities, and hosts of temporary causes necessitate that cash shall be put away for the moment in something that pays interest, is non-varying in value and is immediately realisable. So the demand for trustee securities is out of proportion to the supply. Hence the price is high, and it follows that the rate of interest is small, almost infinitesimal. It ranges between 2 ½ and 3 ¼ percent per annum. But this is the only form of real investment in existence apart from that in which there is an element of speculation.

Many people having invested in lower class securities, and having regularly received a substantial return, may be inclined to doubt the accuracy of these observations. But however satisfactory their essays may have been outside the "Trust Range," they cannot find a security which is not liable to fluctuation or uncertainty.

We know that foreign government funds are sometimes excellent investments; but not only do they vary on political rumours and domestic intrigues, but appertaining to properties outside our Majesty's dominions, they might easily diminish in value or delay in payment of interest. Therefore they do not affect our contention. There are, of course, investments outside of stocks and shares which are perfectly secure, such as mortgages on freeholds to half the value of the property mortgaged, ground rents, &c., but these bring with them certain responsibilities, and besides we are not concerned in this class of security.

A real investment, then, in the purest meaning of the word must be free from all contingencies. In return for the absence of risk, those who invest must be content with the smallest possible interest. People who do not understand risks, and do not care to learn to provide against them, should not expose themselves to the possible chance of losing part of their capital for the sake of additional income. If without experience and without knowledge they endeavour to improve their financial position they will certainly find themselves poorer for their pains.

But it is easy enough to learn where there are risks and what are the nature and extent of such risks. People of ordinary intelligence can without technical knowledge learn to weigh the chances of gain against the probabilities of loss, and take their places amongst investors who reap the full benefit of their capital.

There is no magic in successful investment; the subject is open to all who choose to investigate it. And the knowledge is worth acquiring since it enables a shrewd capitalist of common business capability to get two pounds where his lethargic colleague accepts one, and practically he incurs no further risks.

Chapter IV - Speculative Investment

The range of the investments discussed in the last chapter is necessarily limited. There is a definite list of them, and it may be said to never vary. On the other hand, the range of speculative investments is very large, embracing as it does the ordinary stocks of all Railway Companies, most of our commercial and industrial joint stock enterprises, and also stocks with uncalled capital, in which last category are comprised Banks and Insurance Societies.

To those unversed in the first principles of finance it may seem strange that such sought after securities as Railway and Bank stocks should be included in a list of speculative investments. But a mere cursory examination will prove the accuracy of the description. We admit that there is a difficulty in determining where "investment" ends and "speculative investment" commences, but the distinction is most important, and is better treated of by example than by theory. In dealing with speculative investments, the chief questions to be considered are:—

(1). Safety of capital.

(2). Safety of interest.

(3). Contingent liability.

To fairly judge anything with the "speculative" qualification the main point is to ascertain if the chances of gain outweigh the chances of loss. If they do, then it may be deemed a good speculative investment; if the contrary, it is surely a bad speculative investment.

I – Safety of Capital

There are no stocks the price of which does not vary from time to time. English Railway Debentures and Consols are admitted to be *par excellence,* the acme of perfection of the investing world. Yet they fluctuate considerably.

So while Consols stood as high as 101 in the year 1894, they sold in 1890 at 94, or 7% lower. And this in a security representing the purest and safest form of investment! It would therefore be absurd to imagine that a "speculative investment" should remain stationary in value. Nor is it desirable, from an investor's point of view, that it should be so. The main consideration is to buy it when it is low in price, not when it is high.

In order to illustrate our meaning let us take an example; say Egyptian Unified Stock. When the fluctuations in this stock come to be compared, it will be found that it sold as low as 91 in 1891, and reached its maximum of 104 in 1894, the time of writing these lines. A further rise can hardly be expected, and it is apparent that Egyptian Unified Stock is now being sold at 12 per hundred dearer than it was, while the interest payable, and all other attendant circumstances, have remained the same. In all probability, then, if the stock moves at all it should be in a downward direction. We do not mean to imply that the stock, having reached a high price will immediately begin to fall, and continue to do so until it has again touched its lowest at 91. We merely indicate with confidence that it will go down more points in the next few years than it is likely to go up. The history of the fluctuation, proves this, and therefore the chances of a present investor in Egyptian Unified are that his capital will diminish, not increase; so this is not a stock to be selected at the moment as a good speculative investment.

As an instance in the other direction, let us consider Great Northern Deferred Stock. In August, 1894, the price was 63, and during the five preceding years it was once as low as 50. On the other hand, however, in 1889 the price rose to 116, or 53 higher than in August, 1894.

During the whole period of contemplation, then, this stock has been 13 percent lower and 53 higher than it was in August, 1894. The deduction is obvious. The chances of a rise as against a fall are 53 to 13, and it follows that an investment in Great Northern Deferred Stock would seem to offer practical safety of capital.

As with Egyptian Unified and Great Northern Deferred, so with other Stock Exchange securities.

In order to make a similar analysis to that above it is necessary to know the range of fluctuations of any investment over a number of years. To save our readers the trouble of investigation we have compiled a table showing the highest and lowest prices of the principal stocks dealt in on the market. Should any stock have been inadvertently omitted we shall be happy to send particulars to enquirers free of charge.

Our table affords simple opportunity for calculating chances of a rise as against a fall, and no investor should omit to refer to it before making his purchases. We have taken a range of five years in the example of Great Northern A, but the most careful investor can if he likes go further.

There are instances in which the rule of history repeating itself may not be applied in safety. But when an investor opposes such rule and buys when the tables point against him he embarks on a "speculation" with which we shall deal later on. A dealing according to the indications of the tables is a "speculative investment."

Some stocks are not yet five years old. How are they to be considered? In our opinion they are not suitable for "speculative investment." There are, of course, exceptions; but we have known so many instances where capital has been lost in new ventures, which looked as safe as the Bank of England, that we do not intend to deal with them further than to say that so far as safety of capital is concerned they must be relegated to the ranks of "speculations."

II - Safety of Interest

While "investments" must bear an unvarying rate of interest, this is not necessarily the case with "speculative investments." But the chance of the interest ceasing altogether or being reduced to a minimum should be remote.

It will be noticed that in most "speculative investments," although the rate of interest does not vary, the market value of the stock alters considerably from time to time. Advantage can be taken of this, for there are two methods of getting a return for capital invested; one is in the form of dividend and the other by way of increased capital value; and therefore it is possible that an investment which pays but little or no dividend may be made to return a good rate of interest. This, which seems paradoxical, can be shown by examples, as follow:—

TURKISH GOVERNMENT BONDS (*Group 1 to 4*) pay only 1 percent dividend on their nominal value. Therefore most capitalists would regard them as an investment best left alone. But there are certain conditions for the redemption of this stock, which, if carefully studied, will show that there is reason for their capital value increasing considerably.

In 1889 these "Turks" sold at about 37; now their price is 64. A purchaser at the former date would have obtained only 2 percent dividend on his outlay—very small interest indeed considering the nature of the security?

This is the theory.

Practically he would have made a remarkably good deal. Supposing he had bought 1,000 of these Turks in 1889 at the price of £370, he could have realized in 1894 £640 for the property. So the capital value would have increased £270. Add to this £50 received in interest during the period, and in five years his revenue on the investment would have been £320, or £64 per annum on his capital of £370. This is equal to about 17 percent. And our paradox is proved true. Turks which pay 1 percent dividend have actually returned 15 percent and the capital has been safe all the time!

As we have dealt with the safety of capital, so can we regard safety of interest.

It is the nature of a "speculative investment" that it should fluctuate more considerably than an "investment" pure and simple. The additional risk there-fore should be compensated for by some substantial probability. And while an "investment," as we have said, does not produce more than 3 percent, a considerably larger return must be expected from well selected "speculative investments."

Supposing an investor wanted 4 1/2 percent for his money, and selected South Metropolitan Gas shares. The average dividend paid on this stock as shown by our table may reasonably be taken as the rate of interest likely to be returned. Let us examine how it would work out.

The present price of South Metropolitan Gas shares is about £315 for each £100 nominal value. The dividend now being paid is about £15 percent, so that it returns, on an outlay, just under 5 percent per annum. This would be most satisfactory if the rate were stable. But can it always be depended on? From the subjoined table it would appear so.

In 1888 it paid.........15 7/8 percent per annum
In 1889 it paid.........14 3/4 percent per annum
In 1890 it paid.........14 3/8 percent per annum
In 1891 it paid.........15 1/2 per annum
In 1892 it paid.........15 1/2 per annum
In 1893 it paid.........15 1/2 per annum

Should the dividend recede to the lowest figure that has been paid the interest would still amount to over 4 1/2 percent per annum. So this is a stock which an investor wishing for that rate of interest could safely select.

Against this we find that North British Preferred Railway stock would not be suitable for a person seeking safety of interest.

The price was about 60, the dividend in 1893 was 3 percent which produced about 4 ½ on the capital invested.

On looking at a table of interest paid during the past five years we find that in:

1889 it paid...........3 percent per annum
1890 it paid...........2 1/4 percent per annum
1891 it paid...........2 percent per annum
1892 it paid...........2 3/4 percent per annum
1893 it paid...........3 percent per annum

Obviously then, from some cause or other, the dividend is liable to great fluctuations, and a steady income could not be relied on.

All stocks should be tabulated and considered in this manner as regards both their safety of capital and safety of interest.

There are plenty of good speculative investments always on offer which pay even more than 6 percent and there are pitfalls into which the unwary can tumble. Therefore those people who desire a high rate of interest for their money should use the utmost caution, and never embark upon an investment until they have fully investigated its past history and formed an opinion as to its future probabilities.

III - Casualties and Contingent Liabilities

Most important points for the consideration of speculative investors are the risks of casualties and contingent liabilities. To thoroughly weigh these, and to appreciate their chances and their effect, require a certain knowledge of finance and business generally. Each case as it arises demands an investigation on its own merits, and so for the guidance of those who do not profess special knowledge, we offer the following suggestions:

(1.) Do NOT invest in small companies, say those with under £100,000 capital. The smaller the ship the more easily it can be turned over by the ordinary motion of the sea; the smaller the company the more likely is its success to be dependent upon one individual member of its board of management. Large companies with over £500,000 capital are safer in every way.

(2.) Do NOT invest in companies whose business is liable to be affected by competition. Undertakings based upon an Act of Parliament or a Government concession must be infinitely more stable than those unprotected by legislative enactments.

(3.) Do NOT invest in a new or unknown country which is liable to changes in its own government, or to erratic alterations in its conditions of business. The crises in Australia and New Zealand show that even the apparently most prosperous colonies are not always reliable.

(4.) Avoid companies with uncalled capital, unless a. very large return for money is obtainable. Through the custom prevailing in the construction of the London banks and Insurance societies, investors, have become used to regarding uncalled capital as no drawback. And no more it has been where business has been sound and prosperous. But now and then one of these institutions collapses, and a ruined investor sees his folly. There are numerous instances in our own knowledge where shares, which formerly realized £50 would not now be accepted by solvent persons if they were offered £10 bonus to transfer them into their own names and hold the vendors free from further liability. Not only is the capital invested lost, but the unfortunate investor has to sell good securities to pay up his share of the further losses.

A complete book might be written upon each of the four foregoing paragraphs, but space permits us only to hint at the dangers incurred by investors who do not appreciate the difficulties in their paths.

As a general principle they should select, large companies, with a fully-paid capital, situate in England, and as far as possible free from competition.

Those who have the necessary experience for gauging the extent of the risks ahead of them should provide for such risks. They should proceed on the lines of a Fire Insurance Company which charges for ordinary household insurance a rate of 1/6 per £100, but increases up to 30 percent for mills, theatres, and other places where there is exceptional danger. If an investor is satisfied with 4 percent for his money he can take in the less speculative properties such as English Railway stock, but he has a right to expect infinitely more from a trading company, the extra percentage being by way of insurance against possible contingencies.

Chapter V - Speculation

Speculation is a two-edged sword, an invaluable weapon in the hands of those who know how to use it, an instrument of stupendous danger when wielded by those who are ignorant. The mere word speculation inspires many people with a feeling of dread; and not unnaturally, since so great a number of prosperous men of business and men of science have been ruined by recklessly embarking their money in things they did not fully understand.

There are few who appreciate where speculation begins and investment ends. People who have speculated all their lives, probably with infinite risk, would be indignant if they were told that they ever speculated at all. Yet, when investigated, their investments, with which they have been peacefully contented, would turn out to be purely speculative. This condition of matters we shall explain in succeeding chapters.

In order to conveniently discuss the subject we shall divide speculation into two classes (1) Permanent Speculation. (2) Temporary Speculation. Every purchase of stocks and shares, where the money has been paid and the stocks or shares transferred, and which cannot be classed as an investment or speculative investment, as previously dealt with, must be called a PERMANENT SPECULATION.

Every purchase or sale where the money has not been paid and no delivery made must be called a TEMPORARY SPECULATION.

Many of our readers will doubtlessly cavil at our definitions; they will, for example, suggest that if the prospectus of a new company appears, and they take shares in it, the transaction will not be a speculation but an investment. Probably it is with that intention that they have subscribed to the undertaking, but we shall be able to show that buying shares in a new venture is one of the very worst forms of speculation.

If anyone wishes to insure a life he will find that the premium payable on the lives of children under five years old is very small compared with those between the ages of five and ten. The reason is simple; statistics show that there is a high degree of mortality among children of that age, owing to the usual diseases of infancy.

Joint stock enterprises show analogous results. They too suffer terribly from the diseases of infancy. Since the Limited Liability Acts have been passed, up to January 1st, 1893, 39,911 companies have been registered, and of these only 17,555 survive. The remainder 22,356 or nearly two-thirds of the whole have died a natural—or, perhaps, an unnatural—death! And of these which have survived only 8,692 are more than ten years old; but 2,309 are between five and ten, and there are 6,554 which have not yet attained the age of five!

The immediate result of these figures is to show that only one company out of five lives to see its tenth birthday, and only one in three passes its fifth birthday. So an applicant for shares in each of ten new companies must be prepared to lose four-fifths of his capital. Of course he may make up his deficit with the small balance remaining, but it is indeed a venturesome spirit which could hope for such good fortune.

These facts and figures are better than all the argument in the world. By means of our "Investment Register" we have been able to follow the transactions of hundreds of investors. We find one unvarying result; namely, that those who are in the habit of applying for shares in new companies lose 70 percent of their capital. It is not a pleasant subject; we will pass it over lightly for fear to reopen old wounds, but we unhesitatingly lay it down as a valuable maxim that *"applying for shares in new companies is the worst form of gambling"*.

Chapter VI - Permanent Speculation

A prudent person wishing to buy anything would presumably find the cheapest market, that is, where he could obtain the best value for his money. Yet when seeking for investments many rush blindly and stupidly to the dearest market. They see a prospectus of a new venture, holding out hopes that may or may not be realized. Now an investor having decided that this is the class of investment he wishes to put his money in should ask himself, "could I purchase a similar investment at a lower price?"

If he has no personal knowledge on the subject he should ask his stockbroker, and most likely he would find that shares in established companies on the same lines were procurable and at a cheaper price. Sometimes of course they might be at a premium, but as the tables of mortality regulate the amount of premium charged by insurance companies, so should the tables of mortality of joint stock enterprises show the shrewd investor that such premium is worth paying.

It must be more advantageous in the long run to pay a little extra for an established property than a little less for one whose hopes and chances have yet to be realized. If, on the other hand, he can find some shares at a discount, all the better for him and the greater the profit he will eventually make either by increased interest on outlay or augmented capital value.

It will naturally occur to our readers that if everyone acted upon the maxim we are promulgating, there would be no joint stock enterprises, since no one would apply for shares in them. But we are writing for the information of those who do not pretend to have mastered the mysteries of finance.

Shrewd and experienced investors may understand how to appreciate prospectuses and weigh the chances of the hopes set out in them. They may hit upon the one in five which realizes its promises, and by buying the shares when they are issued eventually make a profit by selling at a premium. But the would-be clever person, the investor who cannot read between the lines of an enticing prospectus, who cannot distinguish between possibilities and probabilities, will assuredly get himself into serious trouble if he subscribes for shares in a newly established company.

Another form of permanent speculation is every kind of investment which pays large interest, but where the capital is not altogether secure.

In this class are conspicuous shares in trading companies, which are liable to competition or which depend upon fashion or any other cause, which may reasonably be foreseen as acting upon their prosperity.

A study of the list of prices will show that frequently, while a company is commercially sound, has existed several years and always paid large dividends, its shares do not stand at a premium. The reason is that the capital is not adequately secured. So that when purchasing speculations of this sort, the question, as to whether the dividends returned are sufficiently large to compensate for probable loss of capital, should be seriously considered.

If any one tried to borrow money upon the terms that he should pay interest at 10 percent for eight years and then be under no obligation to repay the principal or *any* more interest he would be laughed at by a money lender. But investors frequently part with their cash to companies on similar conditions. They receive a fine return for a period, then it ceases and the capital will be found to have disappeared also.

As, for instance, when the Manchester Ship Canal was bought the promoters-guaranteed 5 percent interest for five years, upon the subscribed capital. Where is that interest now? And where indeed the money invested?

Then again Eastman's Meat Company began its career by paying dividends at the rate of 10 percent. Since this short season of prosperity it has paid nothing, so a very easy calculation will show how disastrous was a speculative purchase of the shares.

It comes to this: A man buys 10 shares at £10 each thereby investing £100. For five years he receives 5 percent, that is in all £25. The price dwindles then from £10 to £3 10s per share, so he sells out and realizes £35. He has had in all £25 in interest and £35 capital returned, that is £60 in all for his output of £100 and the interest on it for five years. Therefore, instead of having received any interest at all he has been out of his capital for five years and lost £40 percent of it!

Such a class of speculation must be dangerous to the highest degree; it should not be entertained for a moment because not only is the money always in jeopardy but the investor lives in a fool's paradise while he receives what he treats as interest, but what really is merely an installment repaid of his own capital.

In dealing with permanent speculation we must consider shares on which there is a liability for uncalled capital. We have already mentioned the subject under another heading, but cannot too strongly impress upon our readers that when investing in such securities, however sound, they should leave a margin as compensation for the liability.

And an investor should also calculate upon a proper basis what interest he is receiving. Take for instance the City Bank. If an investor holds a forty pound share, of which only ten pounds has been paid up, he ought not to reckon his dividend as though it were paid upon the ten pounds. He must remember that he might at any time be asked for the thirty pounds not called up.

In such an institution as the City Bank this is not probable: but it is possible. And when reckoning a risk the difference between possibility and probability is only in degree. All sorts of the most prosperous institutions have been known to fail, and the prudent investor will bear in mind that if uncalled-for capital was not a real liability then there need be no other sort of shares than those fully paid up.

But all this only brings us back to the point we started from. People who apply for shares in new companies, who purchase stocks paying large interest, but where the capital is not quite safe, or who take up securities with liabilities, are embarking in transactions which are rash and hazardous.

A long time may elapse before it dawns upon a person who thinks he has safely invested that he is poorer than he was, that his figs are thorns, and that he has built his financial house upon a foundation of sand. But the painful awakening is sure to come, and it is no consolation to know that he erred through childish ignorance and not through vanity or avarice.

There are people who never like parting with an investment when once they have purchased it; a dangerous practice, since it is by holding on that money is lost, and by judicious changing of investments that money is made.

On the other hand, there are investors who like to see their money grow faster than it would under ordinary circumstances; they like compound interest. And it is to be obtained. But before entering into a speculation the chances of gain as against the chance of loss must be carefully considered, and no proposal entertained unless the chances seem in favour of the operator.

Naturally, if these chances arrive as predicted, the permanent speculator cannot gain so great an advantage as the temporary speculator.

Hazardous as a temporary speculation may seem at first sight, its result is easier to foresee than that of a permanent speculation, and, therefore, if people wish to speculate at all their transactions should be of a temporary nature, as we shall show by our discussion of the subject in the next chapter.

Chapter VII - Temporary Speculation

Only about one-twentieth of all the transactions which take place upon the London Stock Exchange are completed by the actual payment for, and delivery of, the stocks bought and sold.

As every purchase or sale which is not so completed must be deemed a temporary speculation, it is obvious that nineteen-twentieths of the business must be included in this category. The reason is that the public have found out that temporary speculations offer better chances of profit than permanent speculations or investments.

And this is explicable primarily by the fact that a smaller capital is required for a temporary than for a permanent speculation, so that if a good chance presents itself a comparatively large gain and in a shorter space of time can be secured. For example:

An investor hears from a source he can rely on that the dividend, say, on the Caledonian Railway Company is likely to be higher than it was. Naturally he argues that the stock must go up in price. The stock stands at 114 and the capital he wishes to employ is £600. If he works his money on the system of permanent speculation and buys as much of the stock as he can pay for he acquires £500 stock and pays for it £570. All goes as he expected, the stock rises to £120, and he sells out for £600. The profit on the transaction will be £30.

Bought 500 Caledonian Railway stock at 114.........£570 Profit brought down............<u>30</u> £600	Sold 500 Caledonian Railway stock at 120...........£600

If, on the other hand, he works on the system of temporary speculation, he would act quite differently. He would know either from experience or as the result of enquiry that he could always borrow at a fair rate £100 on every £100 nominal value, or £114 actual value, of stock in such a sound concern as the Caledonian Railway.

Therefore with, say, £15 he could, without incurring any hazardous risk, buy £100 stock; his capital would be practically as safe as if he had paid the whole of the purchase money. It follows that with his £600 cash he could become master of £4,000 stock. Supposing he wished to be doubly cautious, of course he need acquire only half the amount, say, £2,000 stock.

Now compare what the result of this temporary speculation would be with the permanent speculation. Let us make out another account:—

Bought £4,000 Caledonian Railway stock at 114........£4,560 Profit brought down............240 £4.800	Sold £4,000 Caledonian Railway stock at 120........£4,800

Now the stock has only risen six points, as in the former instance, the capital utilised would also be the same, and even the most cautious person would be fully justified in having provided this sum for all contingencies. Yet the profit on the transaction would be £240 as against £30!

We have instanced Caledonian as a substantial and desirable concern, but of course any other stock on similar lines could be applied just as well to our argument.

Thus it is shown that those who want to speculate can do so to infinitely greater advantage in temporary than in permanent speculations, and also that it must be more beneficial to deal in this class of security than to apply for shares in new companies, or in companies where the capital is not fully secured, and where £100 stock cannot with absolute safety be acquired with a cash outlay of £15.

To thoroughly understand the system of temporary speculation and to fully realize its advantages and its dangers, a fundamental knowledge is essential, not only of what stocks and shares really are and what they represent, but also of the customs and usages of the London Stock Exchange and the various methods of working accounts.

Only by acquiring this knowledge is it possible for an investor to judge properly for himself, which is the best plan for operating when the golden opportunities offer, and when the risk of loss exceeds the chances of profit.

One of the chief objects of this work is to put investors in the position of acting warily upon their own opinions without recourse to the advice of others, and therefore we shall in succeeding chapters thoroughly explain the rules and regulations of the Stock Exchange, and analyse the mode in which business there is conducted.

Part II. Chapter VIII - Companies and Stocks and Shares

Joint Stock enterprise may be said to have had its origin in the South Sea Bubble. From the date of that gigantic fraud to the present day there have been an enormous number of schemes constructed on similar, if more honest, lines. In fact, all the greatest undertakings, like Railway Companies, Canal Companies, Gas Companies, all industrial and trading companies are joint stock concerns, and representing as they do a huge slice of the invested capital of the world, the subject must be explained and considered.

A Joint Stock Company is a partnership formed for certain purposes, but in which, as a rule, the partners are not limited to any particular individuals. Portions of the partnership are sold on the money market to whomsoever like to buy them; such portions are called shares.

This is a simple definition which, however, admits of innumerable qualifications. To more easily place before our readers the practical effect of a Joint Stock Company we offer an example:—

If ten persons join together to purchase the apples in an orchard for the sum of £200 each of them contributing £20, this is a simple company whose capital is £200 divided into ten shares of £20 each. The purchase of the fruit is a temporary venture and the capital with the profit can be divided as soon as the apples are sold. There is nothing more to be done and the partnership or company is dissolved.

But supposing the orchard itself, the land, trees, &c., had been bought? Then the venture would be of a permanent nature, the property would require maintaining, business arrangements would have to be made and wages paid. In fact, the concern would have to be run just as if one person only had been interested, with the exception of course that profits would have to be divided, after payment of all outgoings, between the ten copartners.

There is no difference between a partnership between Brown and Jones and a partnership between five thousand people, except that in the latter case the venture is termed a company, and the partners shareholders. As between Brown and Jones most likely a deed defines the positions and relative interests of Mr. Brown and Mr. Jones; the positions and interests of the holders of the five thousand shares are also defined by a deed which is called "Articles of Association."

As against the outside public a partnership is in the same position as a company. All the partners are jointly and severally responsible for the due fulfillment of the engagements of the partnership; all the shareholders are jointly and severally responsible for the acts and liabilities of the company. No matter how many shares a person may hold, whether one or a thousand, he might be called upon to make good the whole indebtedness which the directors of the company may have incurred.

This at least was formerly the condition of affairs, and it remains so to this day, except in the case of Limited Liability Companies, Twenty years ago we had a cruel example. The City of Glasgow Bank failed and ruined thousands of shrewd hard-headed business men, for they were all called upon to fulfil the obligations of the Bank to its creditors. Naturally many went through the bankruptcy court, so the burden fell more heavily upon those who had anything left to pay with. But so general was the devastation that the commercial worlds of Scotland and England were completely paralysed for the time.

To obviate such a state of affairs had previously occupied the attention of the Legislature. In 1862 the Limited Liability Act was passed, and it provided that if the general public were warned by the publication of the word "Limited" appended to the name of the company, it was understood that each partner or shareholder was responsible only to the extent he had subscribed for.

No one could lose more than he originally agreed to put into the concern. The total amount of such subscription is called the "nominal capital."

Any one who desired to do business with a Limited Company could satisfy himself as to its position; for a complete record of particulars as to capital, articles of association, and contracts entered into have to be periodically furnished to the Board of Trade. This record is filed at Somerset House, and is open for the inspection of all who choose to pay a small fee.

Naturally enough almost every company which is formed, and which invites the public to subscribe, takes advantage of the Limited Liability Acts. Even Railway, Dock, Canal and other companies which have been created by Parliament for the working of certain monopolies have clauses in their special acts limiting the liability of their members.

Some companies are limited by guarantee, the shareholders being liable only for the amount they guarantee to it—a penny or a thousand pounds. And it is obvious that if a number of persons band together to work a certain scheme they can do so on any conditions they may agree amongst themselves; in other words, Articles of Association can contain any terms the signatories desire. As for instance, the Costbook Mining Companies in Cornwall have arranged that each member should pay up primarily what he agreed. Should occasion demand further capital he is entitled to pay or refuse payment, but if he elects the latter course he forfeits all his interest in the concern, and frees himself from future responsibility.

All these intricate clauses, and the unlimited liabilities which have brought ruin on so many shareholders in companies which are not "limited" have led to the almost universal adoption of the protection offered by the Limited Liability Acts. But whether limited or not a company is a company, and its shares can be and are bought and sold every hour of the day on the London Stock Exchange.

It is a question whether the majority of those who buy and sell really know what they are dealing in—whether they are acquainted with the actual significance of the words "Stocks" and "Shares."

Let us go back to our example of the orchard: The original £200 was divided into ten parts. If each part were held by an investor agreeable to divide equally all the profits made, these parts would be termed ORDINARY SHARES. But suppose one holder would not embark in the enterprise without being certain of a profit and the others agreed to guarantee him 5 percent he would be the holder of what is known as a GUARANTEED SHARE.

Or, another one might demand that his share of the profits must be paid before the others receive anything, but in return for this concession he would accept 4 percent in full satisfaction of his interest. This would be called a PREFERENCE SHARE. On the other hand there might be some speculative spirit who said "I will wait until the Ordinary shareholders have received 5 percent and the Preference shareholders have had 4 percent and will take what is left." He might get nothing or lie might get 10 or 20 percent; his share would be a DEFERRED SHARE.

These four classes of shares are dealt with every day. Founders' shares are not so common and are not worth discussing.

It is within the power of companies, as with private firms or individuals, to borrow money when required. Suppose an Orchard Company were in need of further cash to develop its property or its trade, it would offer as security a mortgage upon the undertaking. Such mortgage might be divided amongst several partners, who would thereby become owners of what are called DEBENTURES or DEBENTURE STOCKS. These also could rank as different grades, or might be split up into portions of various values.

In fact a company, limited or not, can carry on its business precisely as any tradesman can, provided of course it does not exceed the powers agreed to in the Articles of Association. It can even go into liquidation, voluntarily or by process of law set in motion by a creditor. The whole affair can be sold as a going concern, or wound up gradually as assets can conveniently be realised. From the sums received the amount due on the Debentures would be paid first; then all trade liabilities would be discharged, after which the Guaranteed and Preference shares would be paid off. The balance in hand would be divided amongst the holders of Ordinary and Deferred shares. A company going out of business acts in an almost similar way to a tradesman giving up his shop.

Often a member of a company desires to sever his connection therewith. In Stock Exchange parlance, he wishes to sell his shares. He must find some one who wants to buy them, and they must agree as to price.

This is the object of the Stock Exchange,—to have a permanent market where all dealings are concentrated and prices rule according to the ordinary doctrine of supply and demand.

Sometimes a vendor cannot find a purchaser to give him as much as the shares cost, they have sunk below their NOMINAL VALUE. He must either put up with the loss or keep his shares. On the other hand, the company may have been prosperous, and a purchaser will buy at a bigger price than the nominal value. In either case the figure at which the shares change hands constitutes the ACTUAL VALUE of the shares.

Chapter IX - The Stock Exchange

In the latter part of the 18th Century, soon after stocks and shares came into existence, it was found necessary to have a meeting place where buyers and sellers could assemble to transact their business, and the parlour of the Bank of England was utilised for that purpose.

It was, however, soon found that the number of people who attended was so large that they encumbered the routine of the bank, and, being turned out from there, they selected Change Alley as a place of general assembly. There bargains in stocks and shares were arranged, until in the year 1801 the foundation stone of the present Exchange was laid in Capel Court. This building was enlarged until it assumed its present magnitude.

The Stock Exchange is practically a private institution, and is governed by a committee of its members. The members are divided into two classes, viz., jobbers and brokers.

A BROKER is an agent who buys and sells shares for his clients presumably on the best terms he can get. He charges them a commission for so doing, and this is his only permissible profit.

A JOBBER is a capitalist who keeps a quantity of stocks and shares upon his books. He buys and sells them as occasion offers, carrying on his business much after the same manner as any other trade is conducted. He makes his profit out of the difference between buying and selling price. That is to say he buys at one price and sells at a higher. So does a butcher who gives 1s per lb. for meat and retails it at 1s. 2d.

If there were no jobbers, brokers could not execute their clients' commissions unless they just happened to come across someone who had the very stocks to dispose of they were instructed to buy, or who wanted to purchase the identical stocks they were instructed to sell. Jobbers ensure an almost unlimited market in the principal stocks, while brokers are merely middle men who act between the public and the jobbers.

If the public were allowed to go upon the Stock Exchange, as they are upon every other market, they would establish direct communication with the jobbers (merchants) and save brokers' (agents) commission; in fact brokers would cease to exist. For a jobber is practically a permanent buyer or seller. He will buy at a price whether he wants the stock or not, and he takes his chance of being able to sell it again later on. Or he will sell whether or not he possesses the stock on the chance of being able to buy it cheaper as the markets fluctuate.

What on earth, then, is the use of a broker?

That is a question which can only be answered by the Committee of the Stock Exchange, who by excluding the public from within its portals enable a number of useless individuals to get a slice of all transactions which take place within the sanctified enclosure.

Naturally enough the general public have begun to appreciate their position in this regard, and as they do not care to be mulcted in small sums every time they desire to purchase or change an investment, many dealings are now conducted outside the Stock Exchange, and brokers' unnecessary services are dispensed with.

Dealing in stocks and shares is like dealing in any other kind of merchandise. But it differs in one important respect. While of most classes of goods the general public are buyers only, and the manufacturers and producers sellers only (the dealer, of course, buying from the manufacturer or producer) of stocks and shares they are both buyers and sellers. The public know only the buying price of most articles; it never comes in their way to sell. A butcher would indeed look amazed if a customer offered to sell him a leg of mutton. A stock jobber expects his customers to sell him stock; sometimes they buy, and sometimes they sell, and if he wishes to procure the confidence of his connection he must be prepared to deal either way. But he does not stand to be shot at; he must have a profit. Therefore stocks and shares always stand at two prices, one at which a jobber will sell, another at which he will buy. Out of the difference between these two prices, usually merely fractional, he earns his living.

Stocks and shares are two distinct classes of security, and as a general rule they have different nominal or face values. "Stock" is always priced at so much per £100, while "shares" are many different nominal values and proportionately vary in price. Some shares may be nominally £1, their market value may be 2s. 6d. or £5; others may be £10; in fact the nominal value of a share is the price at which it was originally issued, and it never varies. The market value is what it will realise if sold, and it fluctuates from day to day, frequently varying several times during business hours.

But the jobber or dealer always makes two prices, one at which he will buy and one at which he will sell, and a cautious customer who desires to deal does not say at first whether he means to buy or sell. He asks the jobber to make him a price in, say, a thousand Brighton A's. The jobber will reply 160 1/2 to 160 3/4. This means that the jobber will buy £1,000 Brighton A Stock for £1,605 or he will sell £1,000 Brighton A Stock for £1,607 10s. And the enquirer can accept the bargain either way he wishes and either buy or sell at the price named.

The jobber may prefer selling to buying or buying to selling, but once having opened his mouth with an offer he is bound to deal whichever way the investor chooses.

Of course if a jobber knows that his customer wishes to sell, and this does not quite suit his own book, he offers a lower price with a larger margin, and so an experienced customer who goes to deal endeavours not to indicate his intention until the jobber has bound himself.

Sometimes jobbers get landed with what they do not want.

A jobber may have a large quantity of Uruguay Unified; a customer asks him for a price: wishing to sell at the highest price he names a high figure and the customer sells him some stock. He has made a bad bargain, but it serves him right for overvaluing his stock.

In dealing in most of the recognised stocks there is no difficulty in getting a jobber to make a price, but in securities not frequently dealt in a jobber will refuse or will state that he is a buyer at a certain figure or a seller at a certain figure for he is not bound to buy when he would rather sell or to sell when he wants to buy. In securities not constantly dealt in the business becomes a matter of negotiation, as would occur with any other article of merchandise.

Thus, it is clear that the jobber is the important person in the Stock market. He makes the price, the broker is merely the hired mouthpiece of his own client.

But it is obvious that the jobber must not make prices arbitrarily; he must be guided by supply and demand at the moment, otherwise, he would find himself in the unpleasant position of being proprietor of a lot of stock he could not get rid of advantageously, or of having sold a lot that he did not possess. So that, in reality, it is the investor who regulates the prices of stocks and shares.

Chapter X - Prices of Stocks

In order to acquaint the public with the prices ruling in the principal stocks, the Committee of the Stock Exchange publish an official list of quotations. This purports to give, not only quotations, but also the prices at which business has actually been done. If this list were carefully compiled and properly superintended, it would form an absolute guide to the public as to what their stocks and shares were really worth. Unfortunately, however, this is not the case. One important particular must be absent, for there is no rule to regulate the difference between buying and selling prices. That there ought to be is shown by the following example:

On the 10th September, 1894, this quotation appeared in the official list: "Allsopp's Ordinary Stock, 108 to 110. Marks of business done: 107 7/8, 110, 110 3/8, 109 1/2."

In the special edition of the *Evening Standard* of the same day we find the following, which is certainly more explanatory:

Time	Selling price	Buying Price
10.57	107 1/2	108 1/2
11.42	110	111
12.10	109 1/2	110 1/2
3.45	109	110

Now a great and palpable flaw in the official quotations is that they need not be accurate. There is no rule of the Stock Exchange which forces a broker or jobber to register or "mark" his bargain. Why should he do so? To assist the public? Is it to his advantage that the outside world, should know exactly the price of this stock or that?

We do not desire to impute improper motives to a body of men who may be most honourable in their dealings, but it is apparent that if a broker by error of judgment gives too high price for stock from, or sells at too low a figure to, a jobber, and he takes the trouble to "mark" his deal on the official quotation list he can show such quotation to his client as evidence that it was the current price at the moment. To make official quotations of any value it should be compulsory that all bargains should be "marked."

Then again the margins; that is to say the difference between the jobber's buying and selling prices. The official list quoted Allsopps at 108 to 110; they would buy at the former or sell at the latter and make a profit of £2 on each £100 stock.

The *Special Standard* quotes the margin at the more reasonable figure of £1, the difference between 109 and 110. And even this is above the mark; for in an active market when Allsopps were being freely dealt in, a smaller margin would be accepted, since the jobbers can make any number of in-and-out, purchase and sale, deals during the day. Practically when things are lively they can keep on turning over their capital and so do well enough with a small profit each time.

And the official quotation is insufficient.

It does not give the two prices, and it does not show whether the outside investor— who we have shown regulates the price by virtue of supply and demand—bought or sold. It does not show if the jobber bought or if he sold, or if he wanted to buy because the markets looked like going up, or if he wanted to sell because circumstances foreshadowed depression. A study of margins and a knowledge of the details of bargains-made, would indicate this.

It is impossible, by giving one daily quotation, to enable the public to gauge the state of the market in any particular stock.

Frequently prices go up and down two percent in the course of half an hour; they may be high in the morning, droop in the afternoon, and rally to the original quotation before business is over for the day. It is of paramount importance to the investor to know the exact price of a stock at any hour, for how otherwise is he to ascertain whether his broker or jobber has done his business in a fair and straightforward manner?

As there are many honest and honourable stock brokers and jobbers, so there must be black sheep, and the most pleasant and lasting business relations are those in which neither party has a chance of getting the better of the other.

It is a broker's or a jobber's business to carry out an order directly he receives it and at the price then prevailing. If such order is remitted by post and arrives at the office the first thing in the morning, it should be executed when the markets open; should it be sent by telegram, the customer can calculate pretty accurately what time it should arrive, and a subsequent reference to the tape will show him that he has been fairly dealt with.

An unscrupulous broker might receive an order to sell stock. He does so at the opening price. During the day the stock goes down, say 1 percent. Thereupon, he invoices the stock to his customer at the lower price and keeps the balance for himself—in fact, steals the difference which he has obtained from the jobber.

On the other hand, should the stock have increased during the day he will simply invoice the real price he obtained. If he were instructed to buy stock and did so at a low price, which afterwards improved, he might pretend he had bought at the highest, instead of the lowest, and again defraud his client. And with comparative safety; for he is under no compulsion to put upon his contract the hour he did the job, and his client must be content with the explanation that he did his best according to his judgment.

A customer is justified in regarding with suspicion any broker or jobber who does not execute his commission directly it is received. The failure to do so is more often than not to be accounted for by sinister motives.

Investors should invariably consult the tape of the Exchange Telegraph Company. It can be found in most of the London evening and provincial papers. The prices are invariably to be relied on, as they are collected constantly throughout the day by creditable agents in the Stock Exchange. Any change is immediately recorded and transmitted through the machines to the offices of the principal brokers, jobbers and merchants.

Even if an error creeps in it is immediately challenged and checked by some one interested in the stock, and who naturally desires that a correct account be kept.

So, those who are dealing have before them, when they choose to look for it, a positive report from which they can ascertain that their broker or jobber dealt at the price ruling at the time the order was received.

Chapter XI - Stock Exchange Bookeeping

For every Stock Exchange transaction effected by the public a written contract is issued specifying the details of the bargain made. Brokers and jobbers do not issue contracts to each other but make entries in the books they habitually carry, and their clerks at their respective offices to check such entries and avoid discrepancies.

Between a broker's and a jobber's contract there is an important distinction. A jobber "buys of" or "sells to" his customer; a broker buys or sells on behalf of his client, as a commission agent.

If a customer buys of a jobber the contract would be in the following form:

London, Sept. 20th, 1894.

Sold to Thomas Smith, Esq.
£1,000 Brighton Deferred @ 158 1/8..............£1,581   5   0
For settlement 28th Sept., 1894.
John Jones & Co., Stock and Share Dealers.

If a customer sells the jobber's contract will read:

London, Sept. 20th, 1894.

Bought to Thomas Smith, Esq.
£1,000 Brighton Deferred @ 158.................£1,580   0   0
For settlement 28th Sept., 1894.
John Jones & Co., Stock and Share Dealers.

A broker's contract would read conversely. Thus, if the customer bought through a broker he would receive a contract as follows:

London, Sept. 20th, 1894.

Bought for Thomas Smith, Esq.
£1,000 Brighton Deferred @ 158 1/8..............£1,581   5   0
Commission 1/8..............£1,581   5   0
For settlement 28th Sept., 1894.
Robert Robinson & Co., Stock Brokers.

Had the customer sold this would be the form of contract:

London, Sept. 20th, 1894.

Sold for Thomas Smith, Esq.
£1,000 Brighton Deferred @ 158 ....£1,581   5   0
Commission 1/8.................   1   5   0
For settlement 28th Sept., 1894.
Robert Robinson & Co., Stock Brokers.

An important difference between the jobber's and broker's contracts is that when buying or selling to a jobber an investor pays or receives the *nett* price of the stock. When he employs a broker he pays an addition to the price, by way of commission, if he buys, and sacrifices a portion of the receipts when he sells. The broker, is, as we have pointed out, a middleman, and is entitled to "sweat" any money that passes through his hands.

As a protection to the public against those brokers who would retain more than they are entitled to, there is a rule that they should disclose on their contracts the names of the jobbers with whom they have dealt. The customer can then, if he be suspicious, refer to such jobbers and check the transaction. That this is not often clone is accounted for by the fact that the rule is not generally known by investors and that all brokers do not, although they should do so, give the names of the jobbers upon their contracts.

If all contracts were checked as indicated it is more than possible discrepancies would be discovered. It might be found that as well as the commission he has a right to, a broker has defrauded his client by not returning the real price at which he dealt. A buoyant market and an insufficient method of recording prices give him a chance of returning the price which is most advantageous to himself. Of course he is not entitled to any profit beyond his commission; to take one is distinctly dishonest, but according to practice the risk of discovery is remote.

A system which offers no opportunity for speculation is preferable. Under existing circumstances, it must be safer to deal direct with jobbers than through the intermediary or broker.

According to the rules of the London Stock Exchange, bargains are settled about once a fortnight, upon days fixed by the Committee.

If all bargains were made for immediate cash payment, selling would be as simple a matter as any other sale of goods for "cash on delivery." But a large majority of transactions are not done for investment, but for speculative account. It would not always suit a speculator to pay for and take up stocks, so arrangements can usually be made for "carrying over," that is, for postponing the completion of the purchase or sale.

This is a matter of mutual agreement, which is so general on the Exchange that a special carrying over day is fixed before each settling day. When such an agreement has been arrived at, the postponement does not take place at the actual purchase price of the stock, but at the price ruling at noon on carrying-over day. These prices are called "making-up prices," and are fixed by officials appointed for the purpose by the Committee of the Stock Exchange.

As for instance: If an investor bought £1,000 Brighton Deferred at 159 for settlement on the 13th September, and did not wish on that day to pay for and take a transfer of the stock, he would "carry it over," not at the price of 159 but at the price of 158, that being the "making-up" price on the 13th September. A broker would deliver the following account:—

Sept. 8th, 1894 –				Sept. 11th –			
£1,000 Brighton				£1,000 Brighton			
A, 159 ½ £1,595	0	0		A, 159 ....£1,590	0	0	
Commission..1/8	1	5	0	(next a/c)			
Commission..1/16	0	12	6	Balance	£9	7	6
Contango £1,000							
Brighton A, ¼	2	10	0				
£1,599	7	6			£1,599	7	6
Balance down	£9	7	6				

Thus the customer would have to pay £9 7s. 6d. to his broker to make the account even. This would not necessarily be a loss, simply an adjustment, and actually part payment off the original purchase-money. In the next account the stock would be charged not at the purchase price of 159, but at the "making-up" price of 158. If the investor had ultimately sold his stock before the next settling day at the price of 161, he would receive the subjoined account:—

Sept. 11th, 1894 –				Sept. 16th –			
c/o £1,000				£1,000 Brighton			
Brighton A, 159..£1,595	0	0		A, 161 ½.............£1,615	0	0	
Commission..1/8	1	5	0				
Balance	23	15	0		£1,615	0	0
Balance down	£1,615	0	0	Balance down	£23	7	6

And the broker would send him the balance of £23 15s.

Analysing the transaction we find that: The investor bought £1,000 Brighton Deferred Stock for £1,595, and sold them ultimately for £1,615, apparently making a profit of £20.

He did not get it.

All he actually received was £14 7s. 6d., for he paid out £9 7s. 6d. and got back £23 15s. The difference, £5 12s. 6d., was retained by the broker for his charges and commission; surely a substantial slice of £20, more than 27 percent of the investor's profit!

Had he dealt with a jobber instead of a broker, the commission would not have been incurred, and he would have received his full profit of £20.

There is, however, one item in the account which an investor would have to pay, whether he dealt with a broker or a jobber. This is "contango," a perfectly reasonable and proper charge, as will be seen by an explanation of what it is.

Money always commands some rate of interest. When an investor desires to postpone completing the purchase of his stock, it is clear that some one must find the money necessary to pay for it, take it up, and hold it during the investor's convenience.

The interest charged for so doing is called CONTANGO.

The rate of contango varies from time to time according to the fluctuations in the Bank rate. When interest on money ranges high, naturally contango will be high; when money is cheap and interest low, then contango will be proportionately reduced.

Contango is charged, according to the custom of the London Stock Exchange, for the exact number of days of the "account" succeeding the date of carrying over. So unless an investor sells out precisely on account day he is charged interest for a longer period than he has used the money. As for instance: If an investor purchase, say, £1,000 Milwaukee stock at the price of £675 on the day preceding the account, and sells it again three days after the account, he must nevertheless pay 14 days' interest. Suppose contango rules at the rate of 6 percent per annum, he is really paying at the rate of about 26 percent for he has only used the money for three days.

This is manifestly unfair; but it is the rule, and Stock Exchange rules naturally incline more to benefit its own members than the outside public, who year after year timidly submit to unnecessary charges.

In English Rails contango is quoted at percent per account; thus, in the account contango 1/4 means 5s. for every £100 stock per fortnight. In most other stocks the quotation is at so much percent per annum; while in mining stocks and a few other fugitive stocks contango is reckoned at so much a share.

If we make a close calculation we shall find that on the average the contango on high class stocks ranges between 3 percent and 8 percent and on more speculative securities it varies between 10 percent and 30 percent.

It must not be supposed that the contango is always fixed according to the rate of interest ruling at the time, as the rate of contango largely depends upon whether purchasers or sellers are in the majority in the market, that is to say, whether the stock is scarce or otherwise.

In cases where stock is scarce, or where more has been sold than can be delivered, then premiums are offered for the right to postpone delivery. Such premiums are called BACKWARDATIONS, and wherever backwardations exist on a stock it may always be known that a great deal more of this stock has been sold than the public is desirous of delivering; these backwardations are, however, of comparatively rare occurrence.

We have therefore shown how accounts are made up in case stock is not taken up.

Wherever stock is taken up, the name, address and description of the purchaser has to be given to the seller, in order that he may prepare when necessary the transfer documents. The names are written on slips of paper called TICKETS, and made up in the Stock Exchange Clearing House.

Ultimately, when all these formalities have been gone through, and it is finally settled whether stocks are taken up or carried over, the whole accounts are settled, stocks delivered, and purchase-money paid.

There are therefore three distinct formalities to be gone through. Each requires a good deal of time, and as it would be impossible to accomplish the whole in one clay, arrangements have been made to allow three days for the settlement of each bimonthly account.

The first day is called "carrying over day," and on this day only carrying over arrangements, as indicated by the name, are made. The second day is called "ticket day," on which, as also the name indicates, the tickets bearing the names and addresses of the parties taking up stock are passed by the brokers and jobbers. The third day is called "pay day," on which stocks are delivered and accounts paid. As, however, large amounts change hands on these pay days, and as a broker or jobber might have hundreds and thousands of pounds pass through his account, whilst only a few hundreds remain with him as difference or profit, it is a matter of paramount importance that all Stock Exchange accounts should be settled with punctuality.

Supposing a broker bought for his client £120,000 of stock, and the client did not provide the funds punctually on pay day, the broker might find himself greatly embarrassed, as he would have to pay to the parties from whom he bought the stock, although he had not received the cash from his customer. The total profit on his transaction might only be a hundred or two, and he might find himself in the position of being unable to carry out his bargain with the party from whom he bought the stock on behalf of his client. Investors should always remember this, and endeavour to send their money for stocks or difference of account prior to settling day, if possible, but never later than the settling day.

All stocks to bearer must be delivered on the actual settling day. All stocks which pass by transfer have 10 days' grace allowed, in order to enable the transfer documents to be prepared and signed.

This is a fact but little known by the general public.

They think their broker or jobber unpunctual if he does not transmit the transfers on settling day, whilst this is really impossible, so a necessary custom prevails providing 10 days for delivery.

The whole system of Stock Exchange bookkeeping is very simple when once understood, and it is of the greatest importance that investors should thoroughly master it an order to be able to check their accounts. That there should be so many settling days is an irritating rule of the Stock Exchange. One in every fortnight is surely to many, as the constant examination of accounts may become embarrassing, and so to both investors and speculators it would come as a boon if a longer period were allowed to elapse between the settling days.

Chapter XII - Another Mode of Settlement

The foregoing explanation shows that according to the prevailing system of Stock Exchange bookkeeping fortnightly settlements do not affect ultimate results, but they keep an investor constantly on the move. Of course, it makes no difference whether a profit made is received by instalments, or if a loss made is paid by instalments, or whether profits or losses are adjusted by receipt of a profit one fortnight and the payment of a loss the next, provided that eventually the account is on the right side.

Still some system which saves both jobber and investor trouble, and which also saves expense to the latter, must naturally be preferable.

A person who enters into a speculative investment or a speculation does not care to be constantly bothered with accounts; he would rather do his deal, let it take its course, and settle at a reasonable time, after having had proper notice and having been able to provide for a contingency.

Supposing he had purchased £10,000 Spanish 4 percent. Bonds on the 2nd of June, at the price of 65. He intended to go for a profit of 3 percent. For a long time there was hardly any movement in this security until the beginning of August, when it gradually rose, and on the 1st September he sold at 68. His profit was £300. But as there were five "accounts" intervening between the 2nd of June and the 1st September, such accounts had to be adjusted five times, and he had to send three cheques to his broker for differences, while the broker had sent him two.

Here, in simpler form, is the transaction which the investor entered into, and which he intended to enter into:—

Sept. 1st	Sold	£10,000	Spanish 4% at 68 = 6,800
June 2nd	Bought	£10,000	Spanish 4% at 65 = 6,500
			Profit £300

Had the account been rendered like this a great deal of correspondence, the writing of five cheques, and other inconveniences, would have been saved. We shall show later on how much more complicated and expensive is the ordinary mode employed by brokers.

It has always appeared to us that an ideal system would be to render accounts when they are actually concluded, by either delivery of the stock or by the stock being resold. To effect this, however, is hardly possible, as payments on account would have to be made from time to time if the difference between purchase and sale had reached a certain amount. But we have very nearly approached the desired end, for a method of settling accounts every three months has been inaugurated by the firm of W. W. DUNCAN & Co.

Such system obviates constantly recurring settlements; it arranges for a suitable rate of interest on the purchase-money, not for an imaginary period like ordinary contango, but for the time the money is actually employed in the operation.

We have shown above how the transaction in Spanish Stock would have come out if no recognised modes of settlement were in vogue. We will proceed to show how it would work according to the prevalent fortnightly Stock Exchange practice, and we will show how it would appear had it been transacted according to DUNCAN'S three-monthly system.

The advantage of this last-named over the preceding example is so obvious that the system has naturally become highly popular; in fact, few shrewd and clever investors now receive accounts rendered on the old fashioned fortnightly plan, nearly all have adopted the three-monthly system.

This is an important subject which all investors should master. Here then are the conditions and advantages of this new system:

Settling days are appointed at definite dates always three months in advance, therefore investors know beforehand how much time they have for the development of their operations. Seven days prior to the actual settling day, a carrying over day is appointed, on which the stocks are revalued on the same principle as the London Stock Exchange accounts. When the post-ponement of settlement is not desired all stocks are delivered. Instead of the ever varying rate of contango, a uniform rate of 4 percent per annum is charged, and this from the date of opening until the date of closing or delivery of the stock, so the operator pays interest only for the exact time during which he had the use of the money.

On settling day the accounts are adjusted, and balances handed over. During the account, the investor is entirely unfettered, open to buy back what he has sold, or sell what he has bought, either with his jobbers or with any other firm. He can arrange his accounts in such a way that even his jobber does not know what he is doing.

Supposing at any time, he should not be able to deal with the firm of DUNCAN, then he could effect the transaction with another firm, and this firm would make up the account with Duncan's, by the actual delivery of the stock.

Stock Exchange accounts are thus brought down to their utmost simp-licity, and can be understood by anyone, and this is why the three-monthly system has proved to be such a grand success.

The "Cover" system also obviates the necessity of Stock Exchange settling days. But as dealings on this system are somewhat similar to gambling on horse races we do not desire to explain it further than by saying that it is merely betting as to whether the price of a stock will go up or down. No purchase or delivery of stock is ever contemplated and the speculator limits his loss to the actual amount lodged in the hands of the broker.

A point we must again urge upon readers who examine the examples we are about to give is this: although a broker may be employed, the investor and the jobber are the real parties to a bargain. A broker is a middleman, an unnecessary, and as the accounts will show, an expensive luxury who charges an investor certain fees to do that which he could perfectly well do for himself free of charge. The fees may seem small, merely fractional, but they mount up and take a good slice off any profits that may be made.

If the profit should be but small, it frequently happens that over a term of years the broker gets it all, and the investor has worked and risked his capital for the broker's benefit.

Now let us look at accounts. This is the position. Thomas Smith on the 2nd of June bought through Robert Robinson & Co., stock brokers, £10,000 Spanish 4 percent bonds at the price of 65 and sold them at the end of August following at 68. He would have received every fortnight accounts as will be found on the following pages.

To those not versed in Stock Exchange accounts we offer the following explanation.

On the right side of the account will be found all *credit* items, viz., everything that the client is entitled to receive; on the left side all debit items, viz., all that the client has to pay.

If the credit side be larger than the debit, the client receives money on balance, and on the other hand if the debit be larger than the credit, he has to pay.

Stocks are carried over from one account to the other at making up prices (see ABC).

Thomas Smith, Esq. in a/c with Robert Robinson & Co. Mid - June 1894

1894.							
Bought for Thomas Smith				Deferred Deliver to next a/c			
June 2 -	£	s.	d.	June 1	£	s.	d.
£10,000 Spanish 4 pc.......6,500	0	0		£10,000 Spanish 4 pc 6,475	0	0	
Commission..1/8	12	10	0	Balance...................60	3	8	
Commission..1/16	6	5	0				
Contango £10,000 Spanish				£6,535	3	8	
@ 4 p.c., 15 days...............16	8	8					
£6,535	3	8		June 14th -			
				Cheque paid by investor to			
				broker.......................£60	3	8	
Balance down.................£60	3	8					

End June Account, 1894

June 12th	£	s.	d.	June 26	£	s.	d.
c/o from last a/c £10,000				Deferred delivery to next			
Spanish 4 pc 64	6,475	0	0	a/c of £10,000 Spanish			
Commission..1/16	6	5	0	4 pc 65 1/8	6,512	10	0
Contango £10,000 Spanish							
@ 3 ½ pc 14 days	13	8	4				
Balance.........................17	16	8		£6,512	10	8	
£6,512	10	0					
June 28th –				Balance due to investor from			
Cheque received from broker				broker.......................£17	16	8	
By investor...................£17	16	8					

Thomas Smith, Esq. in a/c with Robert Robinson & Co. Mid - July 1894

June 26th	£	s.	d.	July 10th	£	s.	d.
c/o from last a/c £10,000				Deferred delivery to next			
Spanish 4 pc 65	6,512	10	0	a/c of £10,000 Spanish			
Commission..1/16	6	5	0	4 pc 64 3/8	6,437	10	0
Contango £10,000 Spanish				Balance	92	15	0
@ 3 pc 14 days	11	10	0				
				£6,530	5	0	
£6,530	5	0					
				July 12th –			
Balance down.................£92	15	0		Cheque paid by investor to			
				broker.......................£92	15	0	

End July Account, 1894

June 10th	£	s.	d.	June 25th	£	s.	d.
c/o from last a/c £10,000				Deferred delivery to next			
Spanish 4 pc 64	6,437	10	0	a/c of £10,000 Spanish			
Commission..1/16	6	5	0	4 pc 64 1/4	6,425	0	0
Contango £10,000 Spanish				Balance	39	5	10
@ 5 pc 15 days	20	10	10				
					£6,464	5	10
	£6,464	5	10				
				July 27th -			
				Cheque paid by investor to			
Balance down £39		5	10	broker.......................£39		5	10

Thomas Smith, Esq. in a/c with Robert Robinson & Co. Mid - Aug 1894

June 25th	£	s.	d.	Aug 13th	£	s.	d.
c/o from last a/c £10,000				Deferred delivery to next			
Spanish 4 pc 65	6,425	0	0	a/c of £10,000 Spanish			
Commission..1/16	6	5	0	4 pc 65 3/8	6,562	10	0
Contango £10,000 Spanish							
@ 3 ½ pc 19 days	18	4	4		£6,562	10	0
Balance 113		0	8				
	£6,562	10	0	Aug 15th –			
Aug 15th –				Balance due from broker to			
Cheque received from broker				investor....................£113		0	8
By investor...................£113		0	8				

End July Account, 1894

Aug 13th	£	s.	d.	Aug 26th	£	s.	d.
c/o from last a/c £10,000				Sold for "A. B" £10,000			
Spanish 4 pc 65	6,562	10	0	Spanish 4 pc 68	6,800	0	0
Commission..1/8	12	10	0				
Contango £10,000 Spanish					£6,800	0	0
@ 4 pc 15 days	18	9	10				
Balance.......................206		10	2	Aug 28th -			
	£6,800	0	0	Balance due from broker to			
				investor....................£206		10	2
Aug. 28th-							
Cheque received from broker							
By investor £206		10	2				

Total Results

June 14th	£	s.	d.	June 28th	£	s.	d.
Thomas Smith has paid	60	3	8	Thomas Smith received	17	16	8
July 12th				Aug 15th			
Thomas Smith has paid	92	15	0	Thomas Smith received	113	0	8
July 27th				Aug 28th			
Thomas Smith has paid	39	5	10	Thomas Smith received	206	10	2
Total paid	£192	4	6	Total received	£337	7	6
				Nett profit on whole	£145	3	0

These accounts are made out strictly in accordance with the custom of the Stock Exchange, and in pursuance of its rules with regard to the dealings between brokers and their clients. It shows that an investor's net cash profit on a successful transaction effected through a broker amounted to £145 3s. 0d.

Now, suppose that Mr. Thomas Smith, instead of employing a broker, had dealt directly with jobbers, say, Messrs. W. W. DUNCAN & Co., and this not on the system of fortnightly settlements but on the system of three-monthly accounts. However, accounts on both systems are made out in similar manner. Here is an account to show how Mr. Thomas Smith would have fared with Duncans:—

Sept. 8th, 1894 –				Sept. 11th –			
£1,000 Brighton				£1,000 Brighton			
A, 159 ½ £1,595	0	0		A, 159 ....£1,590	0	0	
Commission..1/8	1	5	0	(next a/c)			
Commission..1/16	0	12	6	Balance	£9	7	6
Contango £1,000							
Brighton A, ¼	2	10	0				
	£1,599	7	6		£1,599	7	6
Balance down	£9	7	6				

There is no difference actually between Mr. Smith's intention in the first instance and his intention in the second. He meant to buy £10,000 Spanish on the 2nd of June, and sell them at the end of August. In both instances he has done so, and at the same price all round. But, whereas, through a broker he received £145 3s. 0d., when he dealt with Messrs. DUNCAN he received £240 3s. 5d. Can there be a question as to which is the more beneficial system?

The risk was the same in both cases; the transactions were absolutely identical, and yet, a dealing with a jobber produced something like a 40 percent better profit!

It is really almost superfluous after these examples to expatiate further on the advantages of the three-monthly system, or on the benefits which an investor experiences in dealing with a jobber instead of a broker. And it is but

Certainly. For the person who allows his money to lie fallow, without taking advantage of the opportunity of increasing it, risks some of his capital, sacrifices income and gives himself no chance of making up the deficiencies which may arise. Supposing one's fortune in 1890 had consisted of £9,400, and with this money at that date £10,000 Consols had been purchased. There is no "snugger" investment than British Consols; they pay 2 3/4 percent interest, so the income would have been £275 per annum. The investor might have been content to live on this; it might have supplied all his wants.

Well, after four years, namely, now in 1894, the value of Consols has increased. The £9,400 originally invested are now worth £10,100. Our so-called prudent investor is actually worth £700 more than he was; yet he does not sell, he still holds on, he still receives his £275 per annum.

The increment of £700 is no use to him; he has not turned it into cash and re-invested it, and he receives no increased income from it. In short, he has wasted it, wantonly allowed it to lie fallow.

If this man with an income of £5 10s. a week were told that he is practically throwing away £700 he would laugh at the idea. His friends would sententiously refer to his "snug" investment, and he would doubtlessly consider himself a shrewd, cautious, prudent fellow. Where the shrewdness, caution and prudence come in it is difficult to say, for if £9,400 produced the "snug" income of £275 a year it is pretty apparent that £10,100 ought to produce more.

Lethargy must not be confounded with prudence. People ought to make money if they safely can do so. And the method to be employed is to keep capital active, to turn it over when profitable occasion arises.

If the man with £9,400 in Consols finds his property worth £10,100 he should sellout and reinvest in some other security producing as good a rate of interest, and in which there is again a probability of an increase in value.

This is how capital grows and how increased incomes are obtained.

We do not suggest that a person unversed in the art of investment should be constantly watching for changes and altering his securities at every turn in the market, but he should certainly take the opportunity to reap the benefits which favourable fluctuations place within his grasp. If he is too lazy to do so he does not deserve the profit accruing, but he must not flatter himself that he is shrewd and cautious when he is idle and wasteful

Another argument against allowing securities to rest permanently where they were, is the probability of loss of capital. If an investor does not make use of a profit that offers itself when his capital increases in value, how can he make up the deficit if it decreased?

Supposing today one invests £10,100 in Consols and in a few years they have sunk again to the value of £9,400, as in 1890, the purchaser would have lost £700, in other words all his interest would have been swallowed up, and his capital have dwindled into the bargain. Still he would pride himself on his "snug" investment, and fancy he was receiving a "snug" income. In reality he would have been living on his capital.

There is a good deal of humbug about permanent investments.

People who hold high-class securities are in the habit of disparaging others. In their self-satisfied vanity they consider that they, and they only, do the right thing. Forgetting that where they are not taking advantage of opportunities offered they are positively wasting money, they regard those who do as speculators and adventurers, and while believing themselves the acme of substantiality forget that perfect safety of capital and interest can be obtained in combination with occasional variation in investment.

And the man who gets the most he can for his money will find in the long run that his fortune is just as "snug" and a good deal larger than that of his apathetic neighbour who foolishly prides himself on having held the same investment for a quarter of a century.

Chapter XV - Profits versus Dividends

Every investment should be regarded from two aspects. From one it should be looked upon as capital; from the other as a profit earning power.

The majority of investors, while taking the most intimate concern in the latter, are content to ignore the former view, and the result, anomalous as it may appear, is that the best chances of the latter are lost.

People are so wrapped up in the question of dividends that, as a rule, they miss grand opportunities of making profits. So long as an investment brings in a good return, it cannot matter much to the holder of a security whether his profits are derived from the dividend earning power of the concern or from cautious manipulation of his holding.

What his object ought to be is, to get the most he can out of his investment, and we say once for all that the best method of accomplishing this end is not to sit quietly on his holdings and wait for his dividends.

To bring our meaning forcibly to the minds of our readers, we cannot do better than refer to Allsopp's Ordinary Stock.

What do the holders of it expect to get? What are they hoping for?

The best rumours that reached us in the summer of 1894 on anything like authority were that a dividend of 6 percent might be paid.

Very satisfactory no doubt. A person who possessed £1,000 stock might, if hopes were realised, have succeeded in benefiting to the extent of £60 for the year. Not bad as things go; but those who were jubilant or even content because of such success, might have calmed their emotions when they learn that in the month of April 1894 alone £180 might have been made by a judicious use of a £1,000 stock! And this without altering the position of the holder, and without sacrificing the ultimate dividend.

Nor is there anything magical in the system which might have been pursued to this desirable end. The plan was simplicity itself, and founded upon the principles we are always laying down; namely, by selling when the stock was up, and buying it back when a sufficient profit had been made for the moment.

To make the matter perfectly plain, here is a table showing what might, and what, indeed, ought to have been done in the months of March and April, 1894, by a holder of £1,000 stock:

Sold on	Price	Bought back on		Price
Profit on £1,000				
Mar. 20th ..	107 ½	Mar. 22	104	£35
Mar. 28th ..	106	Mar. 31	104	£20
Apr. 2 ..	105	Apr. 11	97	£80
Apr. 14th ..	100 ½	Apr. 17	96	<u>£45</u>

Total profit without parting with stock................. **£180**

Now, supposing these dealings terminated the transaction, the holder would still retain his stock, he would have received £180 cash, and could wait patiently, if he chose, for any dividend that might be declared. More, he need never have parted for one moment with his holding, and as matters turned out he would have seen several more profits.

Simply, he would have had sense enough to have taken advantage of the frequent fluctuations and have turned the vivacity of the market to his own profit.

And one of the principal advantages of dealing in a lively stock, that is, in a stock which is continually going up and down, is that similar opportunities offer themselves.

In stagnant securities these chances do not present themselves, and if an investor makes no use of market movements he may just as well purchase at the onset dead-and-alive stocks, and leave profitable securities for his more enterprising neighbours.

We may be met with the observation that it was impossible to know when to buy and when to sell; that of course if we can buy at one price and sell higher we can make money, but that there is no royal road to accurate prophecy.

None of these remarks apply, for the simple reason that unless such fluctuations do take place; that unless the market is busy a holder can sit quietly on his stock and draw his dividend when it comes payable.

This at least cannot be taken from him, and in sporting parlance "he stands the rest to nothing."

Again, we do not pretend to prophesy; we merely imagine that what has been, will be again. It is pretty safe to foretell that when a stock is abnormally high it will drop, and that when it is unusually low it will rise.

But in such a deal as we have indicated in Allsopps, neither very highest nor very lowest price need be waited for.

A holder is satisfied to accept a profit of say 2. He waits until he can realise this and then sells; if a fall succeeds the rise he can buy back again, pocket his margin and then wait again.

What occurred in Allsopps during March and April 1894, might not occur every month with equal celerity, but similar opportunities do offer in lively markets several times in each year, and when once an investor has bought and paid for his stock he is master of the situation and need only deal when it serves his purpose to do so; that is, when he sees a profit.

People imagine that to carry out such transactions as these they must devote a lot of time and attention to watching the market. Some of them even think that they further their ends by hanging about Stockdealers' offices and assiduously watching the tape every time the machine clicks forth a fresh quotation.

Nothing of the sort is necessary; in fact this feverish anxiety, this element of excitement is bad for business, it warps the intelligence of the investor and impedes the business of the dealer.

Those who live in the country and carry out their stock transactions by correspondence, can do as well, or even better, than those who spend so much time over their investments. They have only to give their instructions to a respectable dealer and the bargains are carried out.

A man knows perfectly well what his stock has cost him; if he wants a profit of 2 on it he has only to send to the jobber he deals with and say he wishes to sell at the price registered on the tape, and he can repeat his orders, or give others as those fluctuations occur that seem advantageous to him.

In dealing as we do, strictly at tape prices, no opportunity is offered for getting the better of the investor, as our customers are fully aware by this time.

Bargains are accepted at the price of the moment they are submitted, and so profits are easily made if our customers happen to be intelligent enough to take advantage of the prevailing markets.

It must not be understood that it is in Allsopps only that opportunities present themselves.

Investors and holders of stocks should notice all securities in which the market is active, they should conduct their transactions a little in advance of the fluctuations, and to do so is not difficult if they study the ordinary doctrine of probabilities. By so doing they give themselves the fullest chances of making the most of their capital and not remaining quiescently satisfied by merely receiving the dividends which this or that enterprise may earn.

And the fact that after the month of April, 1894, there was another big rise in Allsopps, strengthens considerably all our arguments. In the first place it proves the buoyancy of the market, and further it increases the investor's profit something like £240. But our example was taken haphazard, and merely shows what could have been done in March and April, 1894.

Chapter XVI - How to Make Your Own Dividend

The large fortunes which have been made upon the Stock Exchange have been derived from the fluctuations from time to time of stocks and shares.

High-class stocks paying ascertained dividends do not fluctuate largely. Therefore the money must have been made out of a different class of securities, namely, those which have a speculative rather than definite value. And whether we draw five percent on our capital by way of interest or by way of profit the result is the same. But with this distinction; that interest is annual and comes but once a year, while by judicious buying and selling we may make half a dozen profits of five percent each in the course of the same period.

It is the duty of everybody to get the most he can for his money; more, it must conduce to the comfort of the moderate capitalist to increase his income.

People do not always understand how to keep their expenses within their means. They would reason that because four percent upon their invested money is not sufficient for their requirements they must look out for a five percent security.

That such investments can be found is undoubted.

The difficulty is where to look for them. And the persons who are not in the habit of earning money, who have not been brought up with business qualifications are the last people in the world to be able to exercise the ingenuity necessary for the selection of appropriate investments. They trust to other people; their orders are precise. "Invest my money to bring me in five percent and do not let me be bothered."

Uninspired professional men carry out these instructions honestly and to the best of their ability.

But their lack of knowledge stands in their way, and frequently their efforts result in a total collapse. Investments are badly chosen and principal and interest both get lost.

A shrewd man can obtain five percent for his money. An inexperienced investor ought to be satisfied with three percent or four percent. Still, the wants of both are equal, and their capital the same. How are they to be brought on a level?

There is a way out of the difficulty; and that is not to invest at all, as we understand the word investment, but to earn one's own dividend.

Nor is this beyond the scope of the most ordinary intelligence.

By buying and selling stocks that fluctuate in the market advantage can be taken of low prices and a percentage of profit earned far in excess of the usual rates of interest. Of course, a certain amount of common sense must be brought to bear upon dealings with money as it must upon all other affairs of life. But with capital it is not difficult to earn money.

To buy a thing at a low price and sell it at an advance is the essence of all commerce.

And there can be no class of goods so easy to deal in as stocks and shares, since there exists a practically unlimited market, and official prices of them are quoted from day to day—almost from hour to hour.

The man who wants to earn a dividend for his money has therefore a fine field open to him. He should look out for a low-priced security, the history of which shows that it has been at a much higher price than that at present quoted. He should select a security of which he can purchase the largest amount of nominal capital for the smallest outlay of cash. Then he will find himself in this enviable position. He has a chance of the largest possible profit with a possibility of infinitesimal loss.

One example is worth a dozen columns of theory. And we can find a dozen examples. Take for instance securities like Chatham & Dover Ordinary, Sheffield "A," Atchison & Topeka, Central Pacific, Erie Ordinary, Northern Pacific Preferred, Ontario & Western, and hosts of others. All these are non-dividend payers; all might be described as "rubbish." Naturally an investor will ask, "how can I get an income if I buy such securities as these?" It is simple enough.

Now on the 1st of March, 1894, Sheffield "A" stood at 26, that is to say 3,500 stock could have been purchased for £910. On the 13th March the stock stood at 27, and would therefore have realised £945, making a profit of £35 in 13 days. If we pursue the calculation to the end we shall find that the rate of interest made as profit comes out at something like 95 percent per annum!

Similar opportunities occur every day, but even if the investor could only make four such bargains in the year he would be getting over 15 percent for his outlay! Yet all this time Sheffield "A," the stock he had invested in, would be paying no dividend at all.

Supposing instead of Sheffield "A" the capitalist had selected Atchison and Topeka, the proportionate profit is still more striking. From the 1st March, 1894, till the 13th this stock rose from 12 7/8 to 14 1/2, a profit of one pound twelve and sixpence on every twelve pounds seventeen and sixpence laid out, over 12 percent profit in 13 days.

Why, in this case the investor would have made almost two and a-half years' interest on his money in less than a fortnight, and out of a stock that pays no interest at all! This is indeed earning one's own dividend.

The cautious reader may remark that he runs a risk. That Sheffield "A" or Atchison and Topeka might have gone down and he might have lost. Quite so! But by exercising a little judgment the chances are largely in favour of an increase, as against a decrease. Merely a little thought is necessary in selecting the stock, and discretion would have pointed to Sheffield "A" as a likely stock to deal in.

By even a casual study of the table of highest and lowest, it will be seen that this security was quoted at 53 in 1890, that the lowest price it touched was 20 in 1894. The price at which we suggested the purchase was 26, that is to say six points higher than the lowest, and 23 lower than the highest. It does not require an accomplished mathematician to calculate that the odds were about four-to-one in favor of the purchaser.

Do not let it be supposed that we advise every capitalist who lives upon his dividends to risk and invest his all in non-dividend paying stocks. He must walk before he can run. Common prudence would suggest that provision must be made for absolute daily wants.

If a man has £5,000 paying him at most 5 percent he would be drawing an income of £250. Probably he would like more, and it is easily managed. Let £4,000 remain for the present where it is and pay him his £200 a year.

The other thousand can be well employed in earning his own dividend. With this he should purchase some low priced security and wait for a rise. It may come in a few days, it may take a month.

But with ordinary discretion and judicious selection of stocks, he ought to be able to make a five percent profit on his capital, four times in the year. In other words, he would make 20 percent per annum out of his one thousand pounds, so that one fifth of his capital would produce him the same income as his remaining four-fifths.

His safe high-class interest paying investment would be one-fifth of the value of his investment in rubbishing stocks that pay nothing! But he would by a little care and intelligence be earning his own dividend, and a very substantial one too!

Chapter XVII - No Permanent Investments

So many capitalists pride themselves on the possession of what they call "permanent investments." They purchase Consols, or Indian Government Stocks, or Railway Debentures; they draw the dividends as they accrue, and think that having got outside the pale of speculation they have done something very clever indeed.

While not wishing in the least to detract from the value of these most excellent gilt-edged securities, we cannot admit to any wonderful admiration for the people who have found no better investment for their capital.

From the point of safe security, of course nothing could be better than the stocks, well known and justly well trusted, which we have indicated; but a stupid person can invest in them, in fact many stupid persons do, not because they are afraid to venture their capital in better paying investments, but because they have no idea how to make the best income out of their money, and they are naturally timorous of trying.

We do not blame them for their want of knowledge, but we suggest that they might take the trouble to acquire some, and having got it without much difficulty, they could apply it to increasing their incomes.

Consols, Indian Government Stock, Railway Debentures and other high class stocks of the same calibre have their uses.

Persons in positions of trust, who have no personal interest in the dividends; minors under age, whose property must be controlled with the utmost jealousy; married women, whose husbands are not to be trusted with capital; these are the sort of people for whom the gilt-edged securities come as a boon and a blessing. The income derivable from them is secure if infinitesimal, and its amount is accurately ascertained from the moment of investment.

But for sensible persons of even the lightest business aptitude such forms of investment should not for a moment be considered, as the instant that capital is embarked in them so much per annum income is wasted.

Legislation which provides for the protection of the property of minors, married women and lunatics, has settled that this class of security is proper for the investment of the funds belonging to those unable to guard their own interests.

This in itself, an ascertained fact, acted upon every day by the Chancery Division of the High Court, shows that people who are neither minors nor married women nor lunatics can do something better than tie up their capital in stocks which produce the minimum rates of interest.

When Lord Beaconsfield in one of his novels extolled "the sweet simplicity of the Three percents," he might have gone further and allotted a modicum of criticism to the "sweet simplicity" of those who invest in the Three percents.

For they are simple indeed, since by the most ordinary exercise of intelligence they might get more, and after all interest for money, in other words income, is what we strive for.

Since, however, the statesman novelist wrote "Sybil," the three percents have dwindled down and Consols do not return so much. In fact, it is a constant cry that money produces hardly any interest, but with this cry we have no sympathy, for nobody of sense is bound to accept absolutely gilt-edged securities such as the Chancery Courts select, and a little careful manipulation can always make capital return reasonable income.

It may be a sort of satisfaction to own Consols and such like; to possess money in the "funds," and leave it there to stagnate, yielding the smallest possible return.

But this is the satisfaction which sensible men could hardly share.

Yet many of them are proud of permanent investments. They do not speculate, they will tell you; what they have is secure, and the income it produces suffices for their wants.

No doubt this is an enviable position to be in, but it is rather stupid, for who on earth possessing sense wants to accept three for what they can get four? And this is the sum total advantage accruing from permanent investments.

There really ought to be no such thing.

Naturally there are moments when the Money market is not in an inviting state, when stocks are too dear all round.

There are moments when a man receives or inherits a large sum of money for which he has no immediate use, and for which no desirable investment at once presents itself.

Rather than leave the money actually idle at one's bankers it may be advisable to buy Consols and wait until the turn in the financial tide invites profitable dealing. But normally there are opportunities for the purchase of this security or that, which, practically possessing all the attributes of the safest stocks, returns a much larger income. Even with these it is well to be active; they should be bought when cheap, not to sit upon permanently, but to sell when dear.

Now Consols, Government Stocks and Railway debentures do not fluctuate sufficiently to make them any use, except as income producers, and we have explained that in this capacity they are so small as to be hardly worth holding. Other securities differ in this very substantial respect; that there always arrives a time when money can be made out of them.

The true secret is to buy them when their history shows that they are too low; in the ordinary course of things they must rise; then the prudent investor will sell, and with the money and with his profits he can buy something else that seems cheap.

A tradesman who gets the reputation for selling cheap, who is content with small profits, achieves his popularity and makes his fortune by constantly turning over his money. He buys a quantity of attractive wares, lets the public know he has them, and they walk in to secure their bargains. What is the result? This long-headed shopkeeper turns his money over, say once a month. If he only makes a profit of five percent this comes to sixty percent per annum. And what usurer asks for more?

Supposing, on the other hand, he buys a line of goods which he knows are very cheap, and which he will not sell except at what he considers their fair retail value? He may be left with them on his hands for six months, and then if his view is proved correct, and he makes his 15 percent profit, he has not done so well as with the other lot.

And as with goods so with money; the great secret of stock dealing success is to turn the money over frequently. A little profit here and a little there mounts up at the end of the year, and shows a much better return by way of income than the frittering dividends paid for gilt-edged securities.

To allow money to lie fallow is the greatest mistake a capitalist can make; it shows his laziness when he boasts of his permanent investments, and his ignorance when he proclaims himself satisfied with Government income.

However, if an investor chooses to take advantage of the rules laid down for married women, children and lunatics he has only himself to blame when he sees his neighbours flourish and grow great while he stagnates beneath the restrictions of what are called trustees' securities.

Chapter XVIII - Second-Hand Shares

If you fancy an investment see that you get it.

Quite so; but that is no reason why you should buy it at a higher price than it is worth.

Yet, strangely enough, this is a point that generally seems to escape the consideration of applicants for shares in new companies, a point that if carefully investigated at the right time would lead to an immense saving of capital.

People get dazzled with the promises of prospectuses. New commercial enterprises are launched from time to time that certainly seem likely to do well. Old established businesses, whose names are household Words, suddenly emerge in joint stock form, and it is no wonder that investors should wish to take advantage of the promised profits in notoriously sound and wholesome concerns.

But what is remarkable is that they never pause to think whether they are paying too much for the desired privilege—they do not look round the market in similar shares and calculate whether they cannot find an analogous security at a lower price.

It is the feverish anxiety to be in first that assists to feather the nest of the promoter.

Shares are offered in the first instance at par, investors apply, get their allotment, and before a blow is struck to develop the property concerned, the price dwindles to a discount.

No matter how good the enterprise may seem, no matter how flattering the prospectus there usually comes a moment of reaction and the share price is reduced. Had the investor waited for this he must have found himself in a superior position; he would at least have been able to buy for nine that which cost him ten, and this means that he could have bought ten shares for the price of nine, truly a substantial difference.

These remarks are prompted by our observation of the several firms or tradesmen who have recently formed themselves into companies and offered to the public any advantage there may be in subscribing for shares.

We do not for a moment suggest that all or any of them are undesirable for investment. What we do most emphatically say is, that an undue hurry to apply for shares must be more beneficial to the promoters than to the investors.

Companies are like children; there are certain diseases of infancy that must be got over; or let us compare them with puppy dogs, "over the distemper preferred."

We prefer a company that has a history, that has seen the juvenile ups and downs inherent in all businesses—a company which has sobered down in its maturity and of whose prospects a sound opinion can be founded" on facts rather than on roseate estimates.

Do not let it be understood that we disapprove of investments in what is termed the Miscellaneous market.

On the contrary, there are frequently very nice chances of money-making and dividend-earning in this department. What we want to impress upon our readers is that we can show them the best chances, whereas, when left to their own devices they too frequently take the worst.

And we are of opinion that, as a general rule, those investors who apply for shares at par directly a promising new company is advertised put themselves in an unenviable position, for it stands to reason that what is so freely offered may not be worth accepting.

In these days of joint stock enterprise there are so many opportunities of investing in almost every class of trade that capitalists can afford to take their time and look about them for the cheapest securities. Supposing, for instance, one's taste and judgment lead to a desire to participate in a drapery concern. Several have been floated lately and to an extent subscribed for. Well, why should we rush in to take shares at the issue price in any particular company?

The prudent person would look round the market; he would say, for instance, "I would like to invest in D. H. Evans & Co., Limited, but before doing so I will enquire whether there are not other shares in a drapery business or in Stores that have realised their prospects or that are at a discount."

If he did not want to take much trouble he might communicate with W. W. DUNCAN & Co., and ask for a list of shares in similar concerns. We should be happy to send one along, and show which companies had overcome their infantile troubles, on which a definite opinion could be formed and which looked cheap.

It may be taken for granted that the shares in a new company offered to the public are never particularly cheap in the first instance, no matter how good the speculation or investment may eventually turn out.

On the other hand, shares in tried and established companies may often be picked up at less than their value.

At least investors can form a sound judgment as to the future by investigating the past; and it goes without saying that a new company which has no past must be relegated to the category of speculation— usually speculation at the worst—for the price of the shares is fixed, and has been carefully considered by vendors and promoters, whose business it is to charge the public just as much as it will pay.

Second-hand shares are, as a rule, better worth buying and better worth dealing in than those only just issued. There is a market in them; they have found their level; if they are at a discount, and the business they refer to is progressing favourably, the investor who comes in second-hand is certainly better off than the one who in his hurry to acquire them paid full price. If they be at a premium, it is fair to presume that the dividend and prospects warrant the price; so the purchaser can know what he is paying for.

It is to our advantage to encourage our customers to buy shares, but we cannot see any particular object in their being over anxious to buy shares in new companies. The supply of old ones is by no means exhausted, and much better value is to be obtained in the second-hand market than by the more fashionable manner of becoming original shareholders.

We will assist our customers to obtain a gratification of any desire to join in this business or in that; to become shareholders in Breweries, or in Draperies, or in Stores, or in anything else they fancy; but we urge them strongly to apply to us for advice before embarking their capital, and we will show them which particular company in the line they like offers the best chances and are the cheapest at their respective current prices.

Chapter XIX - Fluctuations in Prices

The prices of stock vary. Now, here is an observation that would seem to be hardly worth while making, since it is evident that, out of the fluctuations in prices, money is made or lost upon the Stock Exchange. Yet it would appear absolutely necessary for us to call attention to the apparently obvious fact and to emphasize it upon the minds of our customers.

Our Market Report is issued at the end of each week. At the back of the report will be found a Table of Prices, showing the current value of the principal stocks up to the time we go to press. Some hours must necessarily elapse before this, our Official List, reaches the hands of the public; and in the meanwhile there must be dealings in stocks. Highly as we might approve of such a plan it is clear that the Stock Exchange will not suspend operations for our convenience, and so our quotations must be accepted as recording the prices up to the time when the report leaves our offices.

Why we find it incumbent upon us to impress this upon the public is that would-be purchasers or vendors send us orders from time to time that it is impossible to execute. They read our articles, study our table of quotations, take a day or two to consider what they will do, and then send on an order to buy or sell at a price that exists no more!

Other people have also read our report, and have acted more promptly, but whether they had clone so or not we could not guarantee that Tuesday's price is the same as, that quoted on the previous Thursday; in fact, we would much more conscientiously guarantee the other way; for as long as there is business there must be fluctuation. And a good job, too, since it is upon the rise or fall that our customers depend for their profits.

By sending orders with fractional limitations as to price investors frequently miss their best chance. Either a stock is worth buying or selling; it should go up or go down. If the question of an eighth or a quarter percent weighs down the opinion of the investor, then it is clear that he has selected a stock hardly worth dealing in. And by such finicking instructions he wastes our time and his own.

A dealer who transacts business on our conditions is practically a machine; we must obey orders to the letter, and not exercise any discretion at all.

If a customer writes "Buy 500 Erie Ordinary Shares at 17 1/2" that is a definite mandate. The dealer must not reply "I have sold you 500 Erie Ordinary Shares at 17 5/8 or 17 3/4," though this may be the market price when the order is received.

Should we take upon ourselves to do this it would be at our own peril; the purchaser could repudiate the bargain. He told us he wanted to buy at 17 1/2, and we did not comply with the order! So time would be wasted and unpleasantness occur.

Of course in such a case as that put we could write asking for further instructions, but before the answer could arrive a still further fluctuation might have occurred in the stock. This is how the course of business gets arrested and fair bargains frequently missed.

To limit a dealer as to price is the most foolish procedure possible.

As a rule the question only turns upon a fraction, which hardly influences the operation either way. And in stock dealing, a dealer, even if he desired to take advantage of his customer, is not in a position to do so. We could not charge a fancy price; there is no such thing as a fancy price for stocks. Whatever is the market price at the time we receive the order, we are bound to deal at, if the bargain be accepted by us. If a customer should feel aggrieved and think he has been charged too much, he can by the most simple method of enquiry discover that he is wrong; if he found he was right he could insist on an immediate reduction to the proper figures.

Beyond this, *Duncan's absolutely guarantee that the price they charge shall always be correct.*

A customer can always check us if he deals in the stocks quoted upon the Exchange Telegraph Company's tape. This is afterwards reprinted in the special edition of the *Evening Standard,* together with the precise time that the fluctuations, if any, have taken place, so that anyone who desires to deal can do so in perfect confidence that his stock has been bought or sold at the ruling price at the hour his order reached us.

There may be unscrupulous dealers who would charge their customers the highest price of the day, but with such persons we have no concern.

It is evident that if an investor found himself charged the highest price on two or three occasions, he would justly become suspicious, and would cease his transactions with the dealer who treated him in such a manner. In a quickly moving stock a dealer can cheat his client out of, say, £2 10s. to £5 in £1,000, but a trick of this sort is so easily discovered that it would not be worth the risk. It is simple to find out if you are being fairly dealt with, and if you are not, to shift your patronage to some other and more righteous dealer.

We cordially invite the strictest investigation into any transaction we do. We guarantee to deal at the exact market price, no more, no less, and we are happy to say that our customers for the most part thereof, instruct us to buy this stock or that, leaving the price, not to our discretion, but to the official quotation.

Investors who desire to deal, but who have not previously dealt with us, will do well to follow this example, to tell us what they wish to do without any restriction, and they cannot fail to find themselves fairly treated, for in the first place it is our earnest desire to make friends, and in the second place it is out of our power to cheat them, even if we wanted to.

Chapter XX - No Haggling

One great advantage that presents itself in dealing on the Stock Exchange above dealing in any other market is that the prices paid for stocks and shares are definitely ascertained. There can be no bargaining between a customer and a respectable jobber. Each stock has its two prices at every hour of the day, a buying price and a selling price. And yet occasionally people unversed in business try to beat down a vendor or squeeze a little extra out of a purchaser.

A waste of time, purely.

The plain fact is that men of commercial instincts who are used to dealing in some commodity or other apparently labour under the impression that they can do the same with stocks largely dealt in.

No doubt in dealing in ordinary articles of merchandise, where buyer and seller meet together to try and beat each other down, some sort of success may reward their efforts. For rather than miss a deal a seller will often accept the lowest margin of profit, and sometimes a purchaser having a special market for certain goods will give a larger price than he would normally.

But all this trouble is wasted when they come to deal in stocks of magnitude.

These have a certain definite quotation from time to time, and no amount of acumen or finesse will make a man give mere than the official price or sell at less. Both vendor and purchaser are on equal terms, inasmuch as every hour, almost every minute, prices are quoted for dealers in either direction.

Every stock is quoted at two prices; one at which a purchaser can buy if he pleases, the other at which a vendor can sell. The difference between the two prices—generally merely fractional—is jobber's profit.

Now this is so simple that it seems absurd for any mistake to be made or for any misapprehension to exist. Yet our correspondence shows that the fact is hardly understood. So many of our correspondents are ignorant, or pretend to be ignorant, that their letters occasionally border on the humourous. An attempt is made to reverse the ordinary course of proceeding; to offer the loss of margin to the jobber and to gain it for the would be investor.

If we carried on our business from a purely philanthropic point of view we might be accommodating; but strange as it may appear, we keep open our office and pay our clerks and assistants with a sordid desire to make money. Goodness knows the margin between buying and selling prices is small enough; anyhow, we mean to have it, and not to allow our customers, however greatly we respect them, to divide it amongst themselves.

We will deal at either of two prices; both are quoted on the tape; both are published in the papers. We will buy at the lower price or sell at the higher.

And we claim that our business is more straightforward than that of any class of merchants or tradesmen. In dealing with them the consumer does not know the profit the dealer makes; with us he knows exactly, for the registered quotations tell him.

Supposing, for instance, a customer wishes to deal in London and Chatham Ordinary stock. The quoted price may be 15 3/4—16. This means that if a person wishes to buy, he must pay 16; if he wish to sell he must accept 15 3/4. The difference between the two prices is the profit which the dealer or jobber makes on the transaction.

Naturally enough if a person wants to buy he would prefer paying the lowly figure; if to sell he would prefer the higher. But his desire in this regard cannot possibly be gratified, and the sooner this is understood once and for all the better for all parties interested in stock and share dealings.

It is easy to sympathise with the shrewd man of business, who, accustomed to get the better of most bargains he makes, would like to carry his close-fisted habits into the Stock Exchange. Unfortunately they are wasted there. He would, of course, like to get 16 for his London and Chatham Ordinary, and to buy them for 15 3/4; but it is so clear that this cannot be, for if investors could come and deal *against* the jobbers, there would soon be no Stock Exchange and no markets.

Buy as cheaply as you can certainly; but do not attempt to buy below the market price, or you will make yourself ridiculous, and never carry out a deal with honest people able to fulfil their obligations.

A simple arithmetical sum will show the absurdity of the attempt.

Take ourselves, for instance, we are jobbers or dealers, we will buy or sell any description of stocks or shares. Naturally we do so for profit. If we bought 1,000 London and Chathams at 16 and sold them at 15 3/4, we should lose £2 10s. on the transaction, and this in addition to our office expenses, &c. If on the contrary we bought at 15 3/4 and sold at 16, we should make £2 10s., out of which our expenses are paid.

Customers, or intending customers, must please consider this fundamental principle of stock dealing, and then we shall not have to answer so many letters that really ought never to have been written.

Chapter XXI - Moral from a Baby Panic, Oct. 1894

It is extraordinary how attractive to the public an announcement of "panic on the Stock Exchange" is. There seems to be a sort of general idea that a panic is something decorative and amusing, something between a riot and the Lord Mayor's show.

Certainly Throgmorton Street was full of spectators, newspaper reporters rushed wildly around, anxious operators whispered together in corners, and investors consulted earnestly with brokers, who, under the unusual demand upon their brain-powers, pushed their hats on the back of their heads and looked wiser than roosting owls.

Yet we only had a baby panic after all. And it amused us considerably. For in the first place such a *bouleversement* does not affect us or our customers, and in the second there was hardly any justification for the scare.

Of course there was bound to be a foundation, such as it was. The foundation selected was that a Cabinet Council had been suddenly summoned to consider how the interests of British inhabitants in China could be protected.

A very proper subject indeed to occupy the attention of Her Majesty's Ministers. But perhaps some one will inform us what the position of British subjects resident in China has to do with the South Eastern Railway? Yet it was the Deferred Stock of this which suffered most materially during the tiny panic of October, 1894.

People who want to go to China, or people who are coming back from China, would probably travel a few miles on the South Eastern Railway, therefore the stock, if affected at all, ought to incline upwards, not downwards.

Why, then, is it that such rumours as were rife should send down stocks like Great Northern A, South Eastern, South Western, Lancashire and Yorkshire, and Great Eastern?

The Emperor of China and all his mandarins with their yellow waistcoats and peacocks' feathers have surely no effect, directly or indirectly, upon such properties. There is no connection between the one subject and the other.

The explanation is simpler than it would seem.

Any sudden turn in public events can be utilised to affect the Money Market, always sensitive and impressionable.

Certain shrewd investors knowing that particular stocks are good for a substantial rise want to acquire them as cheaply as possible. They take advantage of a momentary scare, loudly proclaim that things are going to the devil, and solemnly declare that there is no knowing where the panic may end. And this before the so-called panic has really commenced!

Timid holders of stocks and weak speculators get frightened. They do not pause to consider the position for themselves, but rush in to sell at whatever price they are offered. They turn their investments into money, and leave the clever people chuckling at the success of their scheme and in possession of good stocks acquired at panic prices.

It is extraordinary how a feeling of uneasiness spreads without adequate cause.

The near approach of a settlement day is used as a lever to force sales.

Brokers get afraid that their clients may let them in for differences, so they despatch alarming telegrams announcing the panic, stating that stocks will carry over at dreadfully low prices, suggesting that there may be difficulties in continuing, and that the differences may be much larger if accounts, are not immediately closed.

Naturally investors are terrified and fall into the traps; and the general desire to sell forces stocks down to low prices.

At anxious moments like these we may justly claim to be proud of our system of doing business. While there is excitement all round us, while troubles seem to be imminent, our customers and ourselves are as calm and contented as if things were in their normal state of smoothness.

A temporary panic has no effect upon our business, and it does not endanger the accounts of our customers. We do not rush about with alarming telegrams, and urge those who confide, in us to sacrifice their holdings. There is no occasion to do so.

The customers of other firms may be panic-stricken; they are prepared to sacrifice something for fear of losing all. DUNCANS' customers are not flurried or excited or even anxious. And for this simple reason—they have time to look about them, and are offered opportunities of taking advantage of a scare instead of allowing the scare to take advantage of them.

Other firms expect their customers to settle on the next Stock Exchange settling day.

Now, should there be any hitch in the Money Market, should money be tight, or a general feeling of uneasiness prevail, ordinary jobbers might refuse to carry over stocks. Investors and speculators would then have to find large sums of money to protect their bargains. This they might be unable to do at a moment's notice, and a pretty muddle would ensue to the detriment of the stock, and may be to the ruin of many a solvent person.

The knowledge that a panic may force such a position influences an excited operator to act against his own interests, and encourages, the wire-puller to frighten holders into parting with their stocks at whatever prices may be offered.

Nothing of this sort can take place according to our system of doing business.

There is no feeling of insecurity, no forcing the hands of holders of stocks; affairs with us and our customers work smoothly, even in tempestuous times, because we do not settle and carry over at an early date.

There is no racing to obtain a result within a few days. We settle every three months, not every fortnight.

Panics, such as occurred in October, 1894, are one-day flies; they come, do their mischief, disappear, and are forgotten, and things, gradually assume their pristine quietness.

People who are not forced out on account of frequent settling days do not suffer in the least from a two-day scare on the Stock Exchange. They wait until it has passed, and our customers have been altogether untouched by the recent depression,

The quotations on the back page of our Market Report show how every stock fluctuates between a highest and lowest price. Investors who buy for a fortnightly settlement may be caught, and be bound to sell at the lowest, especially in panic times. Those who deal on the three-monthly system can snap their fingers at a momentary scare.

What occurred in October, 1894, was that stocks fell. Almost immediately they rose again. Here is a table giving instances of fall and recovery:

Name of stock	Price before panic	Fell during panic to	Recovered after panic to
Brighton A's....	156 ½	154 ½	156 ¼
Eqyptian Unified	104 ¼	101 ¾	103 ¾
Great Northern "A"	62 ¼	59	62
Great Western	166 ¾	164 ½	166 ¾
Lancashire & Yorks	115	112	114 ½
North Eastern	163 ¾	161	163
Dover "A"	84 ½	80 ¾	83 ¾
Peruvian Debenture	49	46 ¾	48 ¾
Mexican Second Pref	39	35	39

From this it can be clearly seen that our customers' tranquility was justified.

The hungry inside clique who wanted to buy cheap got no slices off the loaves of our, customers. And why? We answer unhesitatingly, because our three-monthly system affords an insurance against panics, and we think we may fairly be permitted to point with pride to the success of our business arrangements, and to congratulate those who deal with us on their safe delivery from the dangers of the little panic of October, 1894.

Part IV - Chapter XXII - The Clever Investor

From the theories promulgated, verified by the examples given, it will be evident to those who have read the foregoing pages that the rules by which capitalists, large or small, should be guided are simple and easy to be learnt.

Investors must know what they possess and what they want.

They are in danger if they think they have investments when in reality they hold speculative investments, or worse still, speculations.

Almost any desired result can be arrived at. A large rate of interest can be practically assured if the capitalist chooses to study the subject of investment and put out his money as the index of history points. He will not succeed by holding investments which pay a large rate of interest, but where the capital is in jeopardy; nor by applying for shares in new companies on the strength of roseate promises of directors, which are rarely fulfilled. The key which unlocks the golden casket will be found by distributing capital in a scientific manner over various investments. How this is to be done we have already shown, but we now propose to summarise and explain tersely and concisely the best method a person with money can adopt to increase his capital and his income and to protect both.

Chapter XXIII - Ideal Management of Capital

To put all your eggs in one basket is traditionally foolhardy. Distribute them amongst as many as you can conveniently carry, and take care, if you can, that each of them is secure.

If an investor wants absolute safety he must be satisfied with, say, 3 percent for his money. He can buy trust investments only; he may consider himself clever and prudent, but he will be sacrificing half the income his capital might bring.

If he wants to be a gambler instead of an investor, and desires to make a fortune in a few months, let him rush wildly into speculation. He *may* succeed; but with inexperience it is long odds on his losing whatever he possesses.

These are the two extremes. To investors who adopt either course we admit this book and what we have written are of no use.

Capital requires management. The greatest income with the smallest risk is what all ought to try for. Here, then, is how to obtain this desirable consummation:

Divide your capital into four equal parts, and invest each part in a different quality of security.

Supposing the fund to be dealt with be £20,000.

Let £5,000 be put into some absolutely safe and permanent security, which need not be easily negotiable, for instance, mortgages, or freehold houses, or land which pays, or in any first-class stock to return about 3 percent per annum. Such an investment can always be found. This £5,000 should be considered as "locked up" capital, and ought not to be disturbed on any account whatever. Another part, £5,000, should be invested in Consols, Railway Debentures, or any other class of trust security which will return about 3 percent and which is immediately at any time convertible into cash. This fund is the "Reserve or Contingent Liability Capital," available in case of panics or unforeseen troubles which might crop up.

The third £5,000 should be employed in permanent speculation, that is to say, in the purchase of stocks which should increase in capital value and thereby return a large rate of interest like the example of Turks. It is imperative that when dealing with this third portion of the fund no shares in new companies should be applied for. We have shown that these are not permanent speculations but temporary speculations of the most alluring and dangerous character.

With the fourth part of the fund, the remaining £5,000, temporary speculation should be indulged in. In Chapter VII we have demonstrated that capital can be judiciously employed to much greater advantage in this than by any other means. Statistics of transactions on the Stock Exchange show that nineteen-twentieths of all business is done in temporary speculation, and this shows that the large majority of those who deal, and presumably find dealing profitable, prefer the temporary speculative method. It must be done with judgment, and our chapter on the subject will teach how such judgment is to be acquired and exercised.

Now let us consider the advantages of the proposed system of dividing capital into four different qualities of investments.

In the first place, the investor can never be "broke." One half of his capital is absolutely safe; whilst the other half is very nearly safe, because being used in so many different channels it is hardly likely that they will all fail. Where one is disappointing the profit on the others will compensate for it. And, besides, with the half of capital invested on sound securities, there is a permanent protection against being cornered or driven to sacrifice the investments representing the other half, if markets should be affected by a panic, or other unforeseen event.

It will also be found that the dividend which the whole fund returns will be considerable. Some of it will pay only a small rate, but the remainder may pay a very big rate indeed, and the average, with common caution and prudence, will surely be high.

An investor who adopts this true system of prudent investment will find that he is acting upon the same lines as banks and sound commercial houses, whose business is primarily finance.

In our experience we come across thousands of investors who apply for shares in new companies, who speculate with their whole capital, and are guilty of other follies, with the idea of getting the biggest rate of interest for all their money.

They invariably fail.

It is the system of averaging which succeeds and is likely to prosper.

We have given our example as though a fund of £20,000 were available. But the principle we promulgate is the same, no matter how much or how little is to be invested. To follow the system a capitalist need only master what we have written above, together with a few technicalities of the Stock Exchange, all of which are described fully in this book.

Dealings must be conducted economically; money must not be wasted in unnecessary fees or brokerages.

Though these may appear at first glance to be merely fractional and unimportant, they actually make a most serious onslaught into profits and reduce the average rate of interest that capital is making.

All this we have shown by figures and comment, but we make no excuse for impressing on investors the fact that the cheapest and most satisfactory method of dealing is with a substantial and honourable jobber on the three-monthly system of settling accounts.

Chapter XXIV - A Good Jobber

Be careful at the outset and prevent ultimate disappointment.

In order to deal with confidence, and in the assurance that he will receive the full benefit of his judgment and his capital, an investor must be very careful in the selection of the jobber with whom he does his business.

He must not deal with mushroom firms only lately established.

He should deal only with those whose standing is recognised, and whose experience is evidenced by the fact that they have conducted their business for a considerable period.

An investor should make the most searching enquiries concerning the stability and honesty of the jobber he proposes to deal with. He should ask for a banker's or solicitor's reference before he opens his account, and also satisfy himself from all sources at command that the jobber is in a position to carry out any bargains he may make.

We do not wish to unduly blow our own trumpet, but with all modesty we call attention to the following facts:

We are the authors of this book; and in it we claim, not only to have explained all the mysteries of Stocks and Shares, but to have pointed out where the pitfalls of investors lie. It cannot be said that we have concealed anything, for we have shown investors how to check their accounts and how to protect themselves against the attempts of unscrupulous brokers and dealers to get the better of them. Our motives, we admit, have been to demonstrate the difference between dealing with the ordinary broker and with ourselves. Those who have tried both will appreciate our methods, and hundreds of old and valued customers will testify to our advantage.

That we have been established since 1867, and for the past 15 years traded in the same building, is some sort of guarantee as to our stability. Every week we publish and issue a MARKET REPORT, with the names of our Bankers on it, and we desire that they shall be referred to by those who intend to do business with us.

In addition, we are prepared to disclose the name and standing of the proprietor of the firm, and the name of his private bankers to those who apply to us *bonafide* with a view of becoming large customers.

Our terms of business are perfectly clear. We leave nothing to chance, no loophole for any misunderstanding between our customers and ourselves. Every one who honours us with custom will be deemed to do so according to the following terms and rules:

1.—The Firm acts as Principal or Jobber in all transactions. It buys from or sells to its customers direct; and does not act as Broker or Agent, and no commission, brokerage or fees are charged. All orders received by the Firm will, if accepted, be carried out (except in the case of limits) at the quotation appearing on the tape of the Exchange Telegraph Co., at the time of receipt of the order.

2.—Instructions, given to the Firm, should be in writing, and free from ambiguity. Written contracts will be issued in respect of every transaction, and complete statements of accounts will, when practicable, be rendered prior to settling days. These contracts and accounts will be delivered to customers, at the office of the Firm, or transmitted by post at the customer's option, but the Firm is not to be responsible for any delay in delivery or posting of any contracts or accounts

3.—Every purchase or sale contracted by the Firm is for completion on a specified settling day. The Firm is always prepared to deliver or take delivery of any stock it may at any time have bought or sold, and any customer wishing to postpone completion of a purchase or sale (carry over) must, 7 days prior to settling day, make arrangements, satisfactory to the Firm, for such postponement of completion.

4.—On all sales to customers the Firm charges such rate of interest (contango) as may be current, or if so agreed upon at the outset, a fixed rate of 4 percent per annum on the purchase-money from the date of purchase until completion. The buyer to receive from the seller all dividends falling due from the date of purchase until completion. All expenses incidental to the transfer of stock to be paid by the buyer.

5.—The completion of all purchases and sales shall take place at the offices of the Firm, or such other place as the Firm may appoint, at or before noon on the day specified in the contract. All customers shall, not less than seven days prior to the settling day, give to the Firm notice in writing stating what quantity of stocks they wish to deliver or take up, as also all information necessary for such completion, and they shall (if required by the Firm to do so) at the same time give a Banker's or other guarantee approved of by the Firm that the purchase-money will be paid or the stock duly delivered on the settling day.

6.—Should the Firm at any time be of opinion that any customer is or may be unable to fulfil any contract entered into by him, the Firm shall have the right to call upon such customer to deposit cash security for the due performance of all contracts then existing between them, and in the event of the customer not providing the Firm with the security so asked for within 3 days from the date of application, the Firm shall have the right to close such contracts at the then ruling tape prices.

7.—The Firm shall have a lien until the account is closed and properly settled upon all stocks, shares, monies or securities in its possession belonging to customers, for the due performance of any contract or engagement which they may have entered into, and should any customer fail to fulfil any such contract or engagement the Firm shall have the right to forthwith buy back from or resell to such customer at the then ruling tape price any stock undelivered or unpaid for, and appropriate any monies, stocks, shares or securities in its possession, or such part thereof as may be necessary for the liquidation of the account without prejudice to its right to recover from the customer in default any balance which may still remain due to the Firm after such realisation.

8.—Any suggestions or advice given by the Firm are to be accepted by customers on their own responsibility, and the Firm will not be liable in any way for such advice or suggestions or for any result that may occur in consequence thereof. Attention is particularly called to this as, the Firm acts as Principal, not Agent or Broker, and is therefore an interested party.

9.—It is agreed between the Firm and its customers that any dispute arising between them shall be referred to two arbitrators, one to be appointed by each party or their umpire, in accordance with the provisions contained in the "Common Law Procedure Act, 1854," and the decisions of the arbitrators or their umpire, under such provisions appointed, shall be final, and. this agreement may be made a rule of the High Court of Justice.

Now of course these foregoing rules have been framed as the result of our experience and to meet the views of those who have dealt with us.

But the circumstances of certain investors might incline them to deal upon somewhat different plans. Very well; let them deal on the rules of the London Stock Exchange and we shall try to accommodate them.

We do not charge any commission; we are jobbers or principals and deal direct with our customers.

Always anxious to do business and to assist our customers, we are prepared to give at all times any information we may be in a position to impart. We will answer letters when we deem it necessary, and we publish every week a MARKET REPORT explaining that which has occurred and predicting that which we have reason to believe may occur.

From the MARKET REPORT, which we send gratuitously, we have reprinted in this book many valuable articles which have appeared from time to time.

Our Investment Register is also maintained for the information of our customers, and for the furtherance of business. The following chapter has been devoted to explaining this system, and the boon it confers upon investors whose names are inscribed on it.

Chapter XXV - An Investment Register

There are moments when Stocks and Shares rise rapidly; at other times they fall with great celerity. Out of fluctuations money is made, and those who are holders of the securities with which the markets are playing battledore and shuttlecock are in the best position to deal profitably.

To be well informed as to the causes of a rise or fall is a safeguard for an investor.

Sometimes unfounded rumours cause a stock to decline; sometimes the impending issue of a satisfactory report causes stocks to rise. People who know what is going on can take advantage of their information and their holdings, and secure profits with hardly any risk or trouble.

Investors should sell when the markets are good and buy back when they are depressed, and this they can do without parting with their holdings.

Supposing there is a boom in a certain stock; it rises three or four points. A holder having satisfied himself that nothing substantial has occurred to increase the intrinsic value of the stock, takes advantage of the temporary craze and sells what he has. He does not deliver it but holds on until the excitement has subsided and the stock has dropped to its normal price, then he quickly buys back and remains in the position he was, plus the profit of three or four points.

Or, having heard before the general public that a forthcoming report will not be satisfactory and that the stock will go down he can sell his holding; presently the news is known everywhere, and, as anticipated, the decline comes. He can then, if he still fancies the investment, repurchase at the decreased price, and so make a profit although his holdings have shrunk in value.

There is, in fact, no limit to the various turns which can be made by those who hold stocks and shares, who are well-informed from time to time as their probable fluctuations, and who have the sense and energy to reasonably utilise their knowledge.

The staring question is how are they to know in advance what is going to happen.

To a great extent we have solved the difficulty.

We do not profess infallibility, or to be able to tell always at any moment what is going to occur in any stock. But it stands to reason that large dealers like ourselves, moving about every day in financial circles, connected with officials of various enterprises and having correspondents all over the investing world, must be able to acquire information which the individual investor does not receive so soon, if at all.

To place such information at the disposal of customers is to benefit them and increase our business.

With these objects in view we invented OUR INVESTMENT REGISTER.

This is a list kept on a system of double entry, wherein we register in the first place the names of our customers and a description of all the stocks or shares each one holds together with the date of purchase and the price paid. On the other side we write down the description of every stock and a list of our customers who are holders of it.

Now see the advantage of this. Directly we hear a rumour on which we can rely concerning any particular stock we turn to our register. At a glance we can see who holds any, in other words whose property will be affected by any movement in such stock. Then we communicate with him stating what, we have heard and what in our opinion will be the ultimate outcome.

Of course a holder need not coincide with our views. He is under no compulsion to sell because we think he will be able to repurchase at a profit, nor need he buy if we have grounds for anticipating a rise. But at least he is in a better position than his neighbours who do not hear what is going on until it is too late to take full advantage of the movement.

The record which we keep is private and confidential as between ourselves and every individual customer whose name is inscribed. No one will have access to it or know its contents, and we shall use it only when we consider we have information beneficial to the holders of this or that stock. In short we will watch our clients' investments for them, and place at their disposal anything we know concerning them.

All we ask is that investors shall send in their names and we will forward them a form as follows. This specimen we have filled in as a model.

JOHN SMITH, 727, Belgrave Mansions, Victoria Street, S.W.

The following is a list of my present holdings, which I wish you to file. I shall be glad of any information concerning the securities which you may communicate from time to time.

Name of stock	No. of Shares	Pref. or Ord.	Price paid
Great Eastern Railway	800	Ord.	93
Mexican Railway	1,100	Ord.	12
Pennsylvania	50	Ord.	50 ½
Russian 4%	2,000	-----	93 ¾
United States Brewery	150	Pref.	10
San Francisco Brewery	50	Ord.	6 ¼
Dover "A"	84 ½	80 ¾	83 ¾
Gen Hydraulic Power	30	Ord.	8 ¾

It is obvious that the larger the number of shareholders on our register, the more powerful we become, so we cordially invite everybody to immediately send us their list of investments, and participate in the advantages to be derived from this sound and solid scheme.

We make no charge whatever for registration. Investors need not follow our suggestions unless they feel inclined to do so, and all we ask as a recompense for our time, trouble and expense is that if they do or do not follow our advice they will in any case give their business to DUNCANS.

THE GAME IN WALL STREET, AND HOW TO PLAY IT SUCCESSFULLY
"Hoyle" – 1898

Part I

If you, my dear sir, were to join a first-class Whist Club you would be expected to know something about the game would you not? Some of the elementary principles of the play you should understand at least, otherwise you have no business to be in the game with experienced players.

What is true of the game of Whist is not less true of the game in Wall Street. In this latter game the amateur who goes into it without study or knowledge, whether he guesses as to the course prices will take, or whether he be influenced by the "tips" and "points" and "gossip" put forth in financial papers and brokers' letters, is almost sure to lose in the end.

"But," I hear you say, "speculation in Wall Street is not a game of chance or skill as in cards. The ups and downs in the prices of stocks depend on economic laws, on crops, on wars and rumors of wars, on high and low money rates, on a thousand and one factors that no man can absolutely foresee." You say, perhaps, that "the price of stocks is regulated by the laws of supply and demand, just as is the price of cloth or flour or any other commodity. That the trading in stocks is as legitimate and honorable as trading in anything else. In any branch of commerce one tries to buy when prices are low, and sell when they are high, and this is just what one does in stock trading."

We reply to your argument that there is a little truth and much sophistry in it. The factors that you mention as determining the prices of stocks have an undoubted influence, but, as you will see before you finish these pages, these commercial factors are not *the* determining influences directing the course of the stock market.

The people who run the game allow for these factors and arrange their plans in accordance with them, but the general course of prices on the Stock Exchange is determined by human intelligence and not by chance or natural conditions.

Let us consider for a moment the argument put forward by the apologist for trading in stocks, by which he seeks to show that the business is a legitimate one, and one which is governed by the same economic laws as is commercial trading in general.

There is, to be sure, a legitimate trading in stocks. If A buys one hundred shares N. Y. C., or W. U., or St. Paul as an investment, in order to receive a dividend, then that is legitimate buying. If, after a time, he wishes to use his capital in some other field, and he sells his one hundred shares of stock, then that is commercial selling. If he gets a higher or lower price than he paid for the stock, then the difference is legitimate profit or loss. Stock exchanges originated undoubtedly to facilitate such transactions as these.

But as at present carried on, such trading as the above does not constitute *five percent* of the business done on the Stock Exchanges. Ninety-five percent of the trading there is purely speculative, and has no relation to the investment demand for stocks.

Let us touch upon a few facts that may serve to throw some light on this point. Take the trading in two of the leading "pool" stocks, Sugar and St. Paul for instance.

The whole of the common stock of the American Sugar Co., is bought and sold on the New York Stock Exchange every six to ten days on an average *throughout the year.* There are only three hundred and sixty-nine thousand shares of the Sugar common stock, and yet, in fifty business days, between February 16 and April 16, 1898, *three million two hundred and twenty-three thousand three hundred shares of this same stock* were bought and sold on the floor of the New York Stock Exchange alone. The actual cash value of the Sugar Common stock traded in there on these fifty business days was about *four hundred million dollars.* If this rate of trading were continued throughout the year, *two billion four hundred million dollars' worth* of this one stock would be bought and sold on one New York Exchange. The total issue of this same stock is only *thirty-six million dollars.*

The peculiar thing is that no matter how many times the capital stock of this company has been bought and sold in the last four years on the floor of the Exchanges, there has been no change in the management of the Company.

And such manipulation of prices and betting on quotations is dignified by the name of "business;" and the managers of the game, the manipulators, are spoken of as "business men" and "eminent financiers," and "our well-known bankers and brokers." "It is a mad world, my masters."

The average number of shares of St. Paul common stock that is bought and sold *every month from one year's end to another,* equals twice the whole number of these shares. Do investors, those who carry their stocks for the dividends they yield, or for voting purposes, change their investments twice a month?

Take another fact that throws light on the subject. There are about one hundred and thirty stocks traded in on the New York Stock Exchange. The year around two-thirds of all the trading will be confined to six or seven leading stocks. Some days manipulation in two stocks, Sugar and Tobacco, makes up two-thirds of the total trading.

Now if any one can explain in the nature of things, and as a result of a legitimate demand, why these facts are so; why for instance, less than one hundred shares of Chicago and Alton, a sound "Granger" stock should be bought and sold on a certain day, and on the same day *seventy-one thousand shares of St. Paul,* a similar stock, should be traded in and, if, furthermore, one will explain why about this same proportion continues in the trading of these stocks every day in the year; if we say, any one will explain this on *business principles,* then we will be ready to admit that the mass of trading in Wall Street is a legitimate, honorable business, governed by the same laws of supply and demand that controls the trading in potatoes and cotton cloth. Until this explanation is made we shall adhere to our opinion that ninety-five percent of the business in Wall Street is part of a game.

We shall show later that it is NOT A GAME OF CHANCE, but a game of skill.

Certificates of stock have no more value than waste paper except as they represent dividend possibilities or voting power in the management of the company. All buying and selling of stocks not based on these two features is simply betting on future up and down quotations. Ninety-five percent then of the business done on the exchanges is simply for the purpose of making up and down quotations for betting purposes.

We dwell upon this point at the outset because the public who play the game should understand that it is a game when they enter it. We shall show that the game has well-defined principles and rules that the public would do well to study.

The game is not a game of chance but a game of skill, directed by shrewd men who control millions of dollars. Just how much money can be commanded by the Sugar Trust Pool, for instance, we would not undertake to say.

It is not uncommon, as we have said, for from twelve to fifteen million dollars' worth of this stock to be bought and sold during one day on the New York Stock Exchange. While of course the Sugar Trust Pool does not do all the trading in their stock, yet it is evident that at all times the pool regulates and controls the price of this stock.

We think we are conservative when we say that the seven big pools that control the movements of the seven most active stocks on the exchange command a capital of not less than SIXTY MILLION DOLLARS in ready cash.

Sixty million dollars is a largo sum you say to be put into any game. Who puts up the backing?

Of course the pool managers will not tell you this. But if you should guess that the "insiders" in the industrial and railroad companies whose stocks are manipulated by these pools, together with certain parties close to the management of our big life insurance companies; and also certain Wall Street banks, furnish a large part of the funds, your guess would not differ from that of some of the shrewdest observers in the Street. Certain it is that people who can command millions are the silent partners in the game.

Now capital is naturally conservative, and the larger the capital the more conservative it is. The shrewd capitalists who control these pools do not put their millions into a game of chance. The Wormsers, the Flowers, the Keenes, the Havemeyers, the Hoffmans and other pool managers, do not risk their own and their associates capital on an uncertainty. Far from it. Neither are they playing "give away."

These men absolutely control the game. They see the finish from the beginning, and they have the capital and the ability to reach the object they aim for in spite of the accidents and happenings that to the superficial observer seem to influence the course of the stock market. There is no chance but that these men will win, and hardly any chance but that the public, in the end, will lose.

There is no use, then, in mincing matters by calling a pack of cards a bundle of tracts. When in later pages you will have seen by the records how the movement of prices on the Stock Exchange goes through a certain well-defined course each year, you will be ready to acknowledge, we think, that human intelligence, and not chance, controls the course of the market, and that prices do not go up and down at haphazard as the public suppose.

If, then, ninety-five percent of the trading in Wall Street is purely speculative, a mere betting on quotations, and if the course of prices is controlled by a few shrewd minds, what kind of a game is it these men are playing? We know that the men who control the pools in Wall Street and who live in uptown mansions and belong to uptown churches think themselves to be, and wish the world to consider them, as "financiers." But before we are through we will show that these men and their silent partners are the managers of *the most stupendous gambling game* the world has ever seen.

It is a game where gains and losses are from one to two million dollars a day: a game that in New York City alone employs more than ten thousand smart men as brokers, clerks, and assistants.

A game that has its daily doings reported free of charge and at great length in every prominent newspaper in the country under the head of "Financial Markets or Wall Street Doings" or some other dignified heading.

A game where the "rake-off" to the brokers and the pools is more than one *hundred million dollars a year,* all of which must come out of the pockets of the public.

Does this latter statement seem extravagant?

Consider that there are eleven hundred members of the New York Stock Exchange and eighteen hundred members of the Consolidated Exchange. Not all are members to be sure, yet on the other hand many of these men employ a small army of clerks and assistants in their offices.

Consider that last year *one hundred and forty-three million seven hundred and ten thousand* shares of stock were bought and sold on these two exchanges, par value of this stock was *fourteen billion three hundred and seventy million dollars.* Commissions on these transactions must have been a pretty sum.

Now trading one hundred shares of stock back and forth adds nothing to the intrinsic or dividend value of the stock, because such trading adds nothing to the earning power of the company whose stock is traded in. But at every trade the broker has received a commission, and in every ten trades ten commissions have come from somewhere and gone into the broker's pockets. Whose pockets do these commissions come from? They do not come out of the ground, as do the profits received from producing wheat and corn and coal and gold.

The broker's commission then must come directly from the pockets of the public who trade in stocks. These commissions are a "rake-off" in other words, and *the public must lose what the brokers gain.* But this is not all the public loses. There are three groups considered in the trading in Wall Street, namely the "Pools," the Brokers, and the Public. We have just shown that the brokers must get a very considerable sum each year. Now how much do the pools or insiders get in addition?

There is no way of estimating the amount the pools make each year, as far as we know. We do know that these men are shrewd and successful and are not there for their health. We believe that we were far within the truth when we claimed that the pools and the brokers together must take more than one hundred million dollars a year out of the pockets of the public. Thus an amount equal to the total yearly loss by fire in the United States is annually swallowed up, as far as the general public is concerned, in "the game in Wall Street."

Isn't this a magnificent gamble then? All the Monaco's and government lotteries in the world are not to be mentioned in the same day nor the same week with this game.

Consider these matters fully. Stock trading is unproductive. The farmer who sells his wheat, and pork, and cotton, gives the world something tangible for the money he gets. The miner adds something to the world's real wealth. The mechanic gives the world added power. The merchant has made it more convenient for the public to obtain the products of the earth. The professional man tries to remedy mankind's physical, or business, or spiritual ills. These men are engaged in legitimate businesses.

But the stock speculator adds nothing to the world's wealth. He is engaged in a betting or gambling game. He is simply a parasite. In the final analysis the rugged "granger" with his trousers tucked into his boots and his patched clothing, is a far nobler figure, and an infinitely more useful citizen than the smug "kings of finance" who manipulate the game in Wall Street.

We have no prejudice against stock speculation and the pools generally. We simply believe in calling a spade by its right name. We think, too, it is important, if you are to go into the game at all, that you should understand the character of the business.

We will presently tell you how to play the game, but before doing so let us consider for a moment what the losses in Wall Street mean. You should first consider your chances of a loss and what that loss will mean to you.

Do you ever stop to think how much ruin the yearly loss of one hundred million dollars spells to those who lose it? How much anxiety and despair to some one? How many sleepless nights? How many broken banks and broken hearts? How many suicides' graves?

Those who have studied the subject know that there is no such prolific cause of suffering and despair in society today as is Wall Street and Chicago Board of Trade speculation.

Take the ruin caused by the Sugar Pool manipulation as an illustration. If one could get the statistics so as to know how many hundreds, yes thousands, of poor fellows have been crushed under the wheels of that Juggernaut Car it would be simply appalling. Every broker can tell you the names of scores who have lost everything betting on the flights of that "Will o' the wisp," "Sugar." We are not prejudiced against the Sugar Trust Pool. Their game is a nice little Klondike for us, as working on the "scale system" with a large margin makes us money easily and safely. We refer to this pool so frequently simply because it is the leading and the largest and most active pool.

The methods used by the other pools are the same in principle, and the ruin caused by them is as great in proportion to their size.

How to Avoid Loss

How can the public avoid losing money in Wall Street? will be asked. A good way for the public to avoid losing money there would be for it to keep out of the game.

We are afraid, however, that no warning will avail to prevent the public gambling in Wall Street, and therefore the only way to save the lambs is to show them some of the pitfalls in this business, and teach them some of the principles of play, so that as little loss as possible may fall upon these innocents.

Bear in mind, as we said before, that we are not taking ground for or against speculation. This is not a moral essay. We are simply giving you facts in cold blood, so that if you propose to trade in stocks you may know exactly what you are doing. You should clearly understand that you are entering a game, where, if you are not sharp, *your* hard-earned dollars will go toward the one hundred millions a year that is lost in the Street. If you lose your money you lose not that alone, but your health and your happiness as well. There is no business in the world that, win or lose, is so sure to wreck soul, mind, and body, as is Wall Street speculation.

Who Takes Part in the Game?

One might ask who does not?

We have a friend who had a broker's office in Washington. His firm had close connections with the Senate chamber. He assured us solemnly that more than half the senators at one time or another were the firm's customers. Whether his statement was true or false we do not know.

It was common talk both in the Street and in the financial and other newspapers when Mr. Cleveland was president that he speculated largely in stocks through his friend, Mr. C. E. Benedict, the broker. The large fortune Mr. C. retired with from the presidency is supposed to have been brought to him principally through Mr. B., from stock transactions. We have no opinion about this matter. We believe, however, that sooner or later the people will demand a law to prevent members of legislatures and of Congress from speculating in stocks, for the reason that *every* important question brought before Congress has a direct and oftentimes very large influence on the prices in the stock market. That the pools and trusts use Congress and our State Legislature, directly or indirectly, as aids in the game there can be no question.

After a very wide and cautious investigation we feel safe in saying that more than one-half the professional men in our larger cities try this game. We know that a still larger proportion of business men take a turn at it. To tell the truth we have never yet questioned *one man in well-to-do circles of business or professional life who did not admit knowing, by personal experience some-thing about this game.*

It is openly stated that there are more than seven thousand "bucket shops" alone run in this country, in addition to ten or fifteen thousand brokers' offices all outside of New York City, *all trading in quotations put out by the New York Stock Exchange and the Chicago Board of Trade, and all for the most part supported by the business and professional men of this country.* We may well ask who does not take part in this game?

Now then if after considering the above facts about this business you still desire to take a hand in it we will first call your attention to certain general principles, and then give you special rules that will aid you to play the game successfully.

Part II

One of the first things to notice is that only SEVEN OR EIGHT TRUMP CARDS are used for the most part in playing this game.

Seven or eight stocks out of more than a hundred and thirty on the board contribute three-fourths of the transactions on the exchanges. You had better confine your attention to these and hold only these cards in your hand. These are the stocks that are manipulated by the big pools. If you will run your eye down the column of "numbers of shares sold" in the daily report, you will at once pick out the stocks that are handled by these pools.

For the last five years Sugar has been the leading card on the board. To-bacco at times comes next, and St. Paul is a good third; Burlington and Rock Island come next. Manhattan, Chicago or Peoples' Gas and Union Pacific preferred. All of these constitute the principal pool cards today. Time was when Atchison and Reading and Lackawanna and Missouri Pacific and other favorites were used; but these have been discarded for the most part, and the list given above are the ones today.

New cards may be taken up from time to time and old ones thrown aside, but take the year through only seven or eight cards are used as trumps, and nine-*tenths of the transactions* will be in these particular stocks. Toward the end of the campaign, either on the bull or bear side, the outside stocks will be made use of more prominently.

To succeed you must study the manipulation of the pool cards. Confine your transactions to these.

Pool Stocks and Specialties

As we have said there are six or eight stocks handled by the big pools; the rest of the stocks may be called "specialties."

Should one deal in the pool stocks or the "specialties?"

At the beginning and during the first half of both the bull and bear campaigns, stick to the big pool stocks. These stocks are the first to move and will make by far the most rapid progress up or down. These stocks are the leaders, the active fighters, both in the advance and the decline, and the others are the reserves.

When Sugar and the "Grangers" have advanced ten or fifteen points the "specialties" will be up only three or five. When, however, the leaders are near the top then the laggards come up with a rush and a hurrah. Invest in the leaders first, then with the profits made in them you can make a turn in the "specialties later in the campaign. Don't invest in anything that is not active as shown by the volume of daily transactions.

There are certain good stocks that while not exactly specialties are late movers: Missouri Pacific, Louisville and Nashville, and Western Union are such stocks. When after a week's advance you see Missouri Pacific suddenly get active and come charging up you may know that, for the present, there will be a rest and a reaction in the leading stocks; and when late in the campaign, either on the bear or the bull side, Missouri Pacific becomes *very* active and makes a big move, then you may be sure the end is not far away. This is a never-failing sign. Missouri Pacific is the "Black Horse Cavalry" that gallops to the front to cover the retreat of the leaders.

The Pools

We find many people who are disposed to doubt our statement that the pools direct and control the grand movements on the stock exchanges. We shall show later by our diagrams that every year movements in the stock market are the result of deep laid plans, and that the general direction of prices follows a course or chart laid out six months or a year in advance. *We shall show that the same or similar plans are followed year after year,* and that the close student may form a tolerably accurate idea of what the general direction of the market will be for a period of time.

It is not claimed that one can tell just how prices will move for any particular day by this study, but one will learn the object the pool managers are aiming for, and as these men control ample capital and are the shrewdest financial generals in the world, one may feel sure that their campaign will be brought to a successful termination sooner or later.

A Campaign

Any person who takes a broad view of Wall Street speculation will be struck by the resemblance between the campaign in the Street each year and the course of a war campaign when directed by some great general. Take a "bull campaign" as an illustration.

There are at least two campaigns each year in the street, a bull and a bear campaign. The bull campaign begins after the bear campaign has been brought to a successful close. The bull campaign begins when prices are low, when the general public are bearish. All the news at such times seems to favor a decline. (The pools can manipulate news and newspapers as well as prices.) There are wars, or rumors of wars; there are foreign complications; there are high money rates, and general dullness. There are numerous clouds in the financial sky. Yet if one notices closely, he will see that after these conditions have existed for some time, the prices on the Stock Exchange, in spite of the continual bad news, do not go any lower. The prices fluctuate day by day up and down over a narrow range, but for some reason, in spite of the continued short selling of the chronic bears, the decline is checked. Although there is no advance in the market and may not be for weeks the bull campaign has already commenced.

At these times the pool generals are quietly and steadily mobilizing their forces. In other words *they are accumulating their stocks* and locking them up in their strong boxes.

These men act on the principal that the time to buy stocks is when prices are low; and the time to sell is when prices are high. The pools buy when times are bad, and sell when everything looks good. *The bull campaign begins in gloom and ends in glory.* It begins at the *bottom* and ends at the *top*.

When this period of low prices that we have mentioned has lasted two or three months and the pools have secured their stocks, the word is given out to commence the advance. A battle takes place, the bears are defeated, and prices advance. Then there may be a retreat to encourage more short selling. Again an advance takes place and this time it goes a little further. So the contest wages, the prices going up and down, but on the whole advancing. Finally toward the end of the campaign, after four or five months of gradually advancing prices, the advance begins to be rapid and continuous, the bears are then routed "horse, foot and dragoons," prices are booming, the public, and even the bears, are madly buying, all the news and indications are favorable for a continued advance, *the volumes of transactions are very heavy,* and right then—the bull campaign ends.

Take the course of prices in the year 1897 as an illustration. In the Winter and early Spring, St. Paul and Burlington, for example, were selling under 70, and sugar at 110 to 112; other stocks in proportion. Those were dark, dull days and the bears seemed to have everything their own way. For three months prices moved up and down sluggishly over a narrow range. The public were decidedly bearish. At this time we published that Sugar, which was selling then at about 112, would sell as high as 137 in the summer. We drew this from the study of the records of the fluctuations of this stock. Of course we were laughed at. In May the advance commenced and continued slowly and steadily. Up and down prices went, but each month saw them a little higher. Take the high and low prices of Burlington from April to October as an illustration.

	April.	May.	June.	July.	Aug.	Sept.
Low,	69	72	77	81	87	96
High,	73	77	85	89	99	102

By the middle of September both St. Paul and Burlington were selling at 102, an advance of 30 points, and Sugar was above 155. (We venture to say that the very people who were on the short side of Sugar at 112 in the spring, and laughed at our prediction then, were on the long side at 150 in August, and predicting that the price would go to 175. It went to 109 instead.)

Those were bright days last fall and everyone was bullish; yet that was the end of the advance. Why? Because the pools who bought St. Paul and Burlington around 70, and Sugar around 110, when things looked bad, sold out at an advance of from 30 to 40 points in these stocks when things looked good. Could there be any better explanation for the sudden ending of the advance?

Whatever the excuses and reasons put forth for the check in the upward movement in prices last Fall, the real reason was that, in the early Spring the pool held the stocks and the public was short. In the Fall the public held the stocks and the pools took the short side of the market.

The course of prices in 1897 was not an exception but the rule. In 1896, "Presidential Year" there were two distinct bull campaigns and two bear campaigns. The first bull campaign commenced in January and ended in June. The second commenced in August and culminated in November.

As a rule there is but one bull campaign and one bear campaign each year and approximately speaking each campaign lasts six months.

This is one of the most important facts to remember if you are thinking of embarking on the stormy sea of Wall Street speculation. We do not mean that each bull and each bear campaign will last just six months to a day. We do not mean that a campaign will commence and end at exactly similar dates each year. We are laying down principles and general rules now so that, by their aid, you can study the philosophy of speculation for yourself.

Take the history of prices on the Stock Exchange for the last year and a half to make this point clear.

The first week in November, 1896, prices reached top. Now in March, 1897, after a six months' decline, they were dragging on the bottom, bobbing up and down, but making no further decline and likewise no advance.

In April, 1897, prices began to sneak up. When did they get to the top? About the middle of September, or, practically speaking, in about six months. From this time on prices declined and in February, 1898, another six-month period, they struck bottom and dragged along on a low level until about the last of April. At the present writing, May, 1898, they have commenced an advance that ought to culminate in September or October this year. Leaving out 1896, which, on account of its being a Presidential Year, had two distinct campaigns, you will find that prices on the Stock Exchange have gone through similar movements to those mentioned above every year for the last twenty years.

An examination of the course of prices for the last four years, starting after the panic of 1893, will show this: 1894 Low point was in March; high point in August.

1895, Low point in March; highest in September.

1896, two distinct campaigns; campaign No. 1, Low point in January; high point in June. Campaign No. 2, Low point in August; high in November.

1897, Low point in April; high in September.

1898, Low point in March; high——?

From this you will see that all these campaigns but one lasted about six months.

Bear in mind as we said before, that you cannot lay down a hard and fast rule in this matter. There are exceptions to all rules and there are, to a certain extent, exceptions to this. But if the following pages and especially the records are carefully studied, you will get suggestions that will aid you in judging the trend of the market so that you will know when to keep out, when to take the bull, and when the bear side.

We will give you a hint now, based on the preceding statements.

Hint Number One

After prices have been *declining for four or five months* and then come, comparatively speaking, to a standstill, simply moving up and down over a narrow range, *do not be tempted to take the bear side of the market.* Everything will look bad at such times. The financial papers and the brokers will all be bearish. There will be every apparent reason why stocks should be sold short, but *don't sell.* Depend upon it the next marked move in prices will be upward.

The pools at such times are accumulating stocks and they aim to buy without putting up prices. They buy quietly and slyly. High rates for money does not deter them, as they can pay for their stocks and lock them up. The worse the outlook the more the bears sell and the cheaper the pools get the stocks. After two or three months of such trading the pools decide to open the campaign and then the advance begins.

How shall one know when the advance will commence? This question will be answered now.

Hint Number Two

After the market has gone on for some time in the manner above mentioned, *there will come a day or two of almost complete stagnation in the market.* Perhaps only fifty or sixty thousand shares of stock will be traded in on the exchange. Everyone will be talking of "the deadly dullness of the stock market." *Then you can buy stocks with safety and hold them for a good rise.*

On April 27 of this year (1898), the stock market had become so dull that only seventy-two thousand shares of stock were traded in on the New York Stock Exchange, and half that amount on the Consolidated Exchange.

We said then that the advance would commence in a few days and we advised our friends to buy stocks to hold. Within two days the advance was under way, and in a week the average trades on the New York Stock Exchange alone amounted to three or four hundred thousand shares a day.

For several weeks previously the price of St. Paul had been moving up and down between eighty-four and eighty-seven. On the 27th the price was still eighty-five. The next day it opened at eighty-five and began to rise. On May 9 the price of St. Paul was ninety-six and seventy-one thousand shares of this stock alone was traded in on that day.

In ten business days the price of this stock had advanced eleven points. In the same length of time Sugar had advanced eighteen points, Rock Island sixteen points, Burlington & Quincy twelve points.

"Oh," but it will be said, "this advance was due to a special cause, Admiral Dewey's victory at Manila." The *rapidity* of the advance was due to this cause, but not the advance itself. The real cause was that the pools had been buying the stocks for two months and were ready to advance prices.

The same phenomena, namely, a period more or less long of nearly stationary prices, then a day or two of dullness and *almost complete stagnation* has preceded every bull campaign for the last ten years to our knowledge.

The explanation of this phenomena is simple enough. As has been said, the pools have bought stocks and the bears have been selling them for weeks. The bears at length got tired of selling them. When they stop there are no more trades. Of course then there comes stagnation, followed by a rising market.

Hint Number Three

If it is important to know when to enter the market on the bull side it is just as important to know when to get out and take the other side.

We have hinted at this in the explanation that "a bull campaign begins in gloom and ends in glory." We mean that the bull campaign ends when prices are rising rapidly, and the volume of daily transactions is enormous. The volume of transactions should put one on his guard.

After five or six months from the time when stocks were at the lowest point, after there has been a good advance and now the bull market is under way with great enthusiasm, then there will come *three days of rapidly advancing prices all along the line with great excitement and an enormous volume of business.* The universal cry is "now we have an old-fashioned bull market," and there is an unanimous scramble for stocks; this marks the culmination of the campaign. The pyramids of stocks that have been built up on the bull side are ready to tumble and great will be the fall thereof. Remember this advice applies only if the bull campaign has lasted five or six months after prices touch bottom. At such times sell out and go into the country to cool off. If you are near the scene you will be hypnotized by the enthusiasm and tempted to make one more turn on the bull side.

Now to illustrate the truth of "Hint Number One" and "Hint Number Three" by statistics. Read those hints again and then consider the following facts.

For two months before the bull campaign of 1897, commenced (the months of March and April), there were in round numbers eight million shares of stocks traded in on the New York Stock Exchange. This was at a time when prices were low and the pools were quietly accumulating stocks.

Six months later the transactions on this same exchange for the months of August and September amounted to about twenty-five million shares, worth at par two billion five hundred million dollars. This was at a time when prices were high, and the public were obligingly taking the stock off the hands of the pools at an advance of twenty to forty points.

Accumulation—Disribution

The whole philosophy of the game in Wall Street is summed up in two words.

The pools first accumulate stocks. We have explained when and how they do it.

Having accumulated they must hold on and gradually manipulate the prices upward. They cannot unload on the public suddenly or the prices would tumble before the stocks were peddled out. It takes a month or two after prices have been worked up near the top to get the public to take the stocks off the hands of the pools. The public have to be stimulated to buy by all the means known to shrewd managers.

As a rule the public has more money and consequently more courage in the *Fall* than in the Spring, and, hence, as a rule, the bull campaign begins in the *Spring and ends in the Fall;* when the public take the stocks.

As we said before, the pools after accumulating the stocks must put the prices up and *hold them up* until they can get out.

They must use the financial columns of the press, market letters, business and crop reports, every artifice that will tend to put a bright outlook before the public. Then the pools can distribute their stocks. When once this distribution has taken place nothing can prevent prices from sagging. Increased earnings of railroads, glowing reports of crops are still put out. Slowly at first, but surely, the tide goes out. After a time the news and reports that were erstwhile so roseate, seem to be a little doubtful. Bills will be introduced into Congress that threaten to interfere with railroad traffic or to unsettle the currency. These bills are introduced by the agents of the pools and are not expected to pass. They have the intended effect, however. The pools' financial papers are used at this time to spread distrust as to the future of the market. The financial columns of the daily press reflect, mirror like, these views; and so after some months prices will be brought down to the point where the pools can begin to accumulate stocks again.

Such a movement as this *must take place every year of necessity.* If the market kept advancing all the time prices would in a year or two be literally "out of sight." Prices *must* come down so that the pools can buy again.

Do not understand, however, that the prices will necessarily come back on the decline to the low points of the previous year. Since 1893, most stocks have been and still are on the up grade. Every year sees both the low point and the high point higher than the previous year. This is particularly true of Sugar stock, as will be seen from the following illustration:

1894 $75 Feb.............................	$114 Aug.
1895 $86 Jan............................	$121 June
1896 1st campaign $79 Jan..................	$125 June
2nd campaign $95 Aug................	$125 Nov.
1897 $110 April...........................	$159 Sept.

The country itself has been on an up grade since 1893, and the pools have taken advantage of that fact in arranging their plans of campaign.

The lowest point reached is not the accumulation point, or the price at which the pools buy the most of their stock. On the final break when the pools bring the stocks down to where they can afford to gather them in, the downward rush carries prices temporarily below the buying-in price.

And in the final upward rush, at the end of the bull campaign, the price is carried temporarily above the distributing point. This will be seen on an examination of the records of the fluctuations on a later page.

Accumulation and Distribution

This is the keynote of the movements of the prices on the Stock Exchange. When once this point is clear in your mind all the mysteries will become plain to you. The game in Wall Street is a GAME OF HUMAN NATURE.

The pool generals are men who study crops and politics, both domestic and foreign, and legislation and finance. They know when the time is ripe to start a bull or a bear campaign, and when they can afford to end it. They know when natural conditions will warrant an extended movement, and, on the other hand, when only a moderate one will be accepted, and they lay their plans accordingly. They take a long look ahead; they study all these facts, but specially they study human nature. They play upon the hopes and fears of the public through their agents of the press and on the exchanges and in the legislative halls, as the organist plays on his instrument. It is not a difficult game for them to play so as to win *with the means they have at their command.* The cards they use are both "marked and stacked," and they take no chances. They can use, and must use, the same tactics to a great extent each year, because the principles of the game must of necessity be always the same, *Accumulation and Distribution.* Beside, there is not much need of their changing their plans and traps, as the speculative public is so short-sighted that the same bait can be used year after year. On a later page we will give a diagram entitled "Sugar traps," that will illustrate this point.

Now that the principles underlying the game are understood by you, we will give some practical hints that will enable you to be as safe as it is possible to be in playing this game.

Speculation A Scientific Study

One ought not to play this game at haphazard. One ought to make as careful a study of it, if he plays at all, as the expert whist player makes of that game. One ought to keep a record of the movements in prices of the big pool stocks, the ones whose transactions are the largest day by day in the manner mentioned, and illustrated further on in this work. This record will tell what the pool in any particular stock is doing. "Actions speak louder than words," and the fluctuations in price are a record of the acts of the pools.

The pool generals do not, as a rule, take the public into their confidence. Personally we would not believe any statements they might make as to the course of prices, simply because we have too high an opinion of the shrewdness of these men. While they might and do at times give a true "tip," yet the "outsiders," who get these "tips" and profit by them once or twice or three times, will be brought low in the end. The "tips" to buy will be profitable at the beginning or middle of the bull campaign, but *still stronger "tips" to buy will be put out at the end,* to aid the pools to unload on the public, and then all that has been made by taking the previous "tips" together with the original capital will be lost. The very fact that the first "tips" were good will give one confidence to "plunge" in the last fatal "tip."

While on the subject of "tips" we wish to say that we have no confidence in those advertising tipsters who for ten or twenty dollars a week will tell you the names of stocks that are going to move ten or twenty points up or down.

The whole thing is absurd. If they know so much why don't these fellows trade for themselves and make their own fortunes. It is guesswork on their part, while you take the risk in the trading and pay for the guessing. Furthermore we happen to know that these forecasters are often used by the pools. The pools give them certain true "tips" at first only to be able to use these tipsters to fool the public with in the end.

But if, as we have said, you keep an accurate record of the fluctuations in prices, and remember that these fluctuations are not due to chance but are *the result of design,* you will have a fairly good idea of what the pools are doing. These records are circumstantial evidence. Now if you will act with the pools, irrespective of what the general public is doing or saying, you will be on the safe side.

If it seems to you too much trouble to keep records and to study this subject, then you have no business in it. It requires study and time and patience to make a success in a mercantile business or in a profession, but it seems to be the general opinion that any one can rush into stock speculation and make a fortune. Stop and think a minute. If this theory were true, if the amateurs could win as a rule, or if even *one-half of them* could win, there would not be any game in Wall Street in two years. If the public in general should take away more money from the Street than it brought, who would pay the expenses of the game? Someone must lose, and if it were the brokers and the pools they would shut up shop after a season or two. If you are not to be one of the losers, then you must be smarter than your neighbor or the public in general; you must look further ahead. You must get in when the majority think prices are going down, and you must get out when they think the market is going higher. Remember that every time you sell one hundred shares of stock there must be some person with like aims and hopes as yourself to buy it. The "clearing house" does not buy your stock, nor does the "market." When you buy a hundred shares of stock you do not buy it for its dividends, or to leave it to your grandchildren, but to sell again at an advance. The fellow who buys from you also expects to sell it at an advance, or at least he thinks the price is going higher. The party who buys from him expects the price to advance. No one will buy if he thinks the price is going down. Now if you expect to unload your purchase *you must sell when the public want to buy.* If you hold till the price goes to what you think is top, and the general public think as you do, no one will be foolish enough to buy your stock. Prices cannot go up all the time. As a matter of fact the records show that in the course of a year the price goes down as often as it goes up. Some one must be left with stocks on their hands bought at top prices each year. See to it that it is not you. This is a game of "beggar your neighbor." In Wall Street it is you against your neighbor, wherever and whoever he may be, and you must beat him to win. This is the cold-blooded truth about the game, and if you have any sentimental compunctions against playing such a game you had better keep out of the Street.

Panics

The one fear that haunts the mind of the amateur trader in Wall Street is panics. A few words on this point may not be amiss.

A real, thorough panic comes only once in about twenty years. Witness 1837, 1857, 1873, 1893. After a panic such as 1893, there will be two or three years of uncertainty and then confidence will be restored and the financial barometer will commence to rise. Between each big panic there are about two smaller cycles, or distinct periods of prosperity, followed by depression. A period of prosperity and advancing prices lasts about three years. Then the pendulum swings the other way and prices gradually decline for four or five years.

We are now in the era of increasing good times and advancing prices, commencing from the spring of 1897. The high point for prices on the stock exchanges will be higher each year than the preceding high point until top prices will be reached, probably in 1899.

The following diagram gives a very good idea of the ebb and flow of prosperity.

It will be noticed that the big panic years each commenced after the top of a rise (Nos. 1, 3, 5, 7, 9), and one of the smaller rises at that. It will also be noticed that the period of prosperity that followed a panic reached a higher level than the preceding period of prosperity (Nos. 2, 4, 6, 8, 10). It will also be noticed that this period was not followed by a real panic but by a decline, while the *second* period of prosperity preceded a panic.

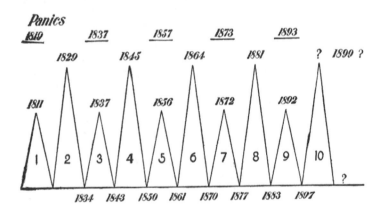

History will repeat itself just as long as human nature remains as it is. Panics are a disease of the public mind. There was just as much sunshine and rain and good land and good crops, and just as much money, and the same men and women, in this country in the years 1893, 1894, and 1895 as in the three years preceding the panic. Nature's condition had not changed; the change was in the public mind.

Short-sighted people attribute panics to some particular cause, such as tariff laws, or Clevelandism, or the Gold Standard, or Free Silver, or Free Trade agitation.

The cause lies deeper. The above are only the foam of the wave. The real reason for panics is in the character of the American mind; the American tendency to rush to extremes; to carry prosperity into inflation, and inflation to what is called a "boom."

Then there comes the inevitable collapse of the irridescent soap-bubble in the form of a panic.

There will be no panics in the business world, even small ones, for several years at least from this date; and no large panics for fifteen or twenty years.

Panics on the Exchange

There will be no panics in the stock market except artificial ones for many years. *But every year when the pools want to buy back stocks an artificial panic will be gotten up.* Take the present year for instance. There was a panic among the speculators over the outbreak of the Spanish-American war. Was there any reason for it? Did any sane man believe that such a war would injure this country? Did the panic extend to any other line of business than the stock market?

We did not hear that there was any panic among the holders of New York real estate, or owners of bank stocks at the time.

But prices of stocks, good dividend railroad stocks, tumbled as if the country was on the verge of ruin. What proved that this was an artificial panic was the fact that prices began to advance as soon as war was declared and have been steadily advancing ever since while the war continues.

There are no panics on the stock exchanges except when the pools are out of stocks. When the pools have the stocks there can be no panic, for the real owners of stocks can lock them up and take them off the market. Stocks then are as firm as real estate. The above is our theory and the facts seem to accord with it.

When a bull campaign is commenced you will be safe from panics if you keep on the long side of the market with a good margin. If you are trading in stocks on a small margin you will be liable to panics every day.

When the pools sell out then you should be working your system on the short side and in that case you need not fear panics, but rather welcome them.

Every big fall in prices that we have noticed on the exchanges has not come until after a big rise.

We give our theory for what it is worth. So far as the records go it is correct. What the future may bring forth we do not know, but we take it that human nature does not change materially from century to century.

Fluctuations

A study of the fluctuations or records of the daily ups and downs in the prices of stocks furnishes the key to an understanding of this whole business.

Take any of the big pool stocks and you will notice that the price at which a certain stock is selling changes from a dozen to a hundred times a day the year through. Now the intrinsic or dividend value of this same stock may not change for years.

Sugar Common is a noteworthy illustration.

This stock has paid its three percent dividend in each quarter since the beginning of 1894 as steadily as the seasons succeed one another. The real or dividend value *has not changed one dollar a share for four years.* But the selling price on the exchanges has not been thus constant. The price in actual sales varies every hour the year through on an average more than one hundred dollars on each hundred shares of stock, or three million seven hundred thousand dollars an hour on whole number of shares. In 1897 Sugar stock sold at one hundred and ten dollars a share in the Spring. A few months later at one hundred and fifty-nine dollars; then still, a few months later, at one hundred and ten dollars again. The latter price being in the Spring of 1898. Yet during the whole twelve months of changing prices it was the same old Sugar stock, earning and paying its regular dividends, and really worth as much at one time as another.

Between these extremes there were how many *thousands* of fluctuations in the price do you suppose?

Were these fluctuations a matter of chance or was there design running through them all?

While the large majority of the small variations may undoubtedly have been partly due to the struggles of the three thousand brokers on the two exchanges to scalp a profit out of each other on the changing quotations, yet when you take a broad view of these changes you will see that a master hand, or head rather, controlled the fluctuations, and led the price through seeming chaos to a predetermined end.

If you know anything about the Sugar Trust Pool you know that the "insiders," had it in their power to put the price from $110 to $159 in six days instead of taking six months to do it as they did. But the Sugar Trust people were not born yesterday. Mr. Havermeyer and his friends prefer to milk their cow (the public) rather than kill her. By manipulating the stock market carefully and with patience, they not only get their regular twelve percent per annum dividends, on refining sugar but they also get two hundred percent per annum from the pockets of the speculative public.

Now you can see what the constant fluctuations in the prices of the pool stocks mean. These fluctuations are the smoke and dust of battle that hides the plans of the general from the men in the thick of the fight. Turn to the records of the one-half point fluctuations in sugar on last pages, and see if we have misrepresented or misjudged the Sugar Trust Pool and their methods. You will see that there are hundreds of fluctuations around a certain low point. This was the laying of the foundation of the building; the greater the number of fluctuations near the bottom the higher the building, that is, the higher prices go.

The movements of all the pools as shown by the fluctuation records are similar to those of the Sugar Trust Pool. A study of the fluctuation record of St. Paul and Burlington is particularly interesting, and we refer you to their records.

System in Speculation

Many "Sure and safe systems" for playing the game in Wall Street have been advertised from time to time.

Most, if not all, of these systems seem plausible enough until one looks into them carefully. Then weakness will be found.

Every system if it is worthy the name of a system at all, must be absolutely automatic and machine-like, that is, the one working it must have no opinion about the market, or at least he must not let his opinion influence his actions. If he begins to be guided in his transactions by his views as to the future course of the market then he ceases to follow a "system" and is guided by his judgment. Again, a "system" to be "safe" must be safe at all times and in all emergencies. "A chain is no stronger than its *weakest link.*" If a system is to be followed it must be *absolutely* safe so that one can venture his last dollar if necessary without fear of losing it.

After a pretty careful study of the different systems put forth we are of the opinion that unless one has almost unlimited capital every system will break down at times, unless one uses some judgment in directing and managing it. In other words, no "system" is to be absolutely and solely relied on by the man who has only a moderate capital.

In our opinion a "system" should be the engine that does a certain work and does it economically and safely. *But every engine requires an engineer, or, at least, an intelligence, to start it in the right direction and stop it at the right time.* Some one who knows when to send it ahead and when to reverse it.

So it is with speculative "systems" in Wall Street. We believe that every amateur should follow to a certain extent a "system" in trading, but he should use his judgment in directing that system. That is, *"system" and brains must go together.*

There are undoubtedly several good systems if rightly handled. An Irishman once applied to us for advice to get him out of a difficulty. We told him that there were two or three plans by which he could be relieved. Quick as a flash he said:

"Try the *best* one first, sor, and if that succeeds we'll not need the rest."

So in our remarks about "systems" we will discuss the one we think to be the best for amateurs first, and then may not consider the others at all.

The "Simple Scale System" is our preference. The "Scale System" means simply buying or selling a certain number of shares of stock at every point or half-point up or down as the prices advance or recede, and then taking profits on every individual transaction when the profit shows. We will explain this more fully on a later page. Now for the dangers of this "system" when one relies on it fully without using his brains.

Suppose A says, "I will buy one hundred shares of St. Paul at every point up or down from a certain price, and sell each purchase at a point and quarter advance, so as to net one hundred dollars profit on the transaction. After any one hundred shares of stock is sold out, if the price recedes to the original buying price, I will buy again."

Suppose he commenced this "system" last fall in September, and bought his first one hundred shares of stock at par; bought another one hundred at one hundred and one, sold the first one hundred at one hundred and one and one-quarter, and then as the price touched one hundred and two bought another hundred. Then if you will look on the records you will see that the prices went down. He buys at par again, at ninety-nine, at ninety-eight, and so on down to ninety-six. Then, the price advances and he sells out such lots as show a point and a quarter profit and has a good profit on these. But the price goes down again and continues to go down until by March 15 he will have sixteen hundred shares of St. Paul on hand, some bought at one hundred and two. At this time he will have had to put up a margin of twenty-eight to thirty thousand dollars with his broker to protect these purchases. Of course he made many hundred dollars' profit on the fluctuations meantime. Now when St. Paul goes back on the next bull campaign, all his purchases made on the decline will show him splendid profits. But there are two points to consider here. Suppose his broker should fail when the market is at bottom. What becomes then of his chance to get back his twenty-eight thousand dollars. Suppose the market should continue to decline. Or suppose that St. Paul should suspend paying dividends for a time as Missouri Pacific did, when it was selling at eighty-four, and like Missouri Pacific go down ultimately to ten dollars a share; how much margin would have been required in that case? This is the weakness of the "scale system," or any other system worked, as we have said, automatically and without using intelligence.

Now on the other hand suppose A had commenced buying St. Paul on the "scale system" in the *Spring* of 1897, instead of the *Fall*, when the price was around seventy and the bull campaign was just commencing. If he had bought his one hundred shares of St. Paul at seventy and again at seventy-one and so on, taking advantage of the fluctuations to buy back the shares sold out at a profit, by fall he would have had some thirty thousand dollars profit. Thus the system if started right would have been safe and profitable at all times until the end of the bull campaign. Now having worked this "scale system" on the long side of the market during the bull campaign, at the end of that time if he could have reversed the system, turned his engine around, and commenced selling short every point up or down until the Spring of 1898, he would have had another twenty-five thousand dollars profit, and been safe at all times.

This so called "scale system," with *brains to direct it* is the safest and most favorable plan the amateur can follow, if he has only a moderate capital to work on, and we unhesitatingly recommend and advise it. So long as one knows the general trend of the market and goes with it, he need never fear any ups and downs if he has a sufficient margin at the start.

Let us make this system so clear that even a child can understand it.

The first requisite is to select one or two good dividend-paying, active stocks, that is, one or two of the big pool stocks.

The essential thing is to first determine, as we have said before, whether a bull campaign or a bear campaign is in progress, so as to know whether to start your system on the long or short side of the market.

We have tried in the preceding pages to give you suggestions for determining in which direction the market will go. Having settled this point in your mind put in your orders to your broker.

Let us suppose, for instance, you started the "scale system" on the long side of the market in Rock Island in April, 1897.

You send your broker an order as follows:

"Buy me ten Rock Island at market (say sixty-five) and ten more every point up or down. Hold only one lot at a time at any particular quotation.

"Sell each purchase one and one-half points advance. Buy back at original buying price any lot that has been sold. Continue until further orders."

Now this order is very comprehensive and covers the whole ground. Your broker buys ten shares at sixty-five: the price advances and he buys ten more at sixty-six: then the price declines and he buys ten more at sixty-four. As he already has ten at sixty-five he does not fill the order again there. At sixty-three he buys ten more shares. Now the price advances to sixty-five. He sells the lot bought at sixty-three at one and one-half points profit. Each purchase, remember, *is to be treated by itself as if it was the only lot of stock you had in the market.* Now the market declines again, he buys ten shares a second time at sixty-three and ten more at sixty-two. Then the market turns and advances to sixty-six. As it goes up he sells the lots bought at sixty-two, sixty-three, sixty-four, each at one and one-half points profit, and you still have the lots bought at sixty-five and sixty-six. Take a paper and pencil and work this out as given above. You will see that you have *closed* five transactions at a net profit on the closed transactions of about seventy-five dollars and you still have two transactions open, one of which shows you a profit of ten dollars and the other is even. Now the price advances to sixty-nine and your broker buys at sixty-seven, sixty-eight, sixty-nine, but he sells meantime three lots each at a profit of fifteen dollars.

Of course if you knew beforehand that the price was going down to sixty-two and then up to sixty-nine, you could have waited til it touched sixty-two before buying and then waited until it got to sixty-nine before selling, and thus have made a very large profit. *But you cannot know beforehand just what the market will do.* All you can determine is the general trend of the market, and, knowing this, the "scale system" will make your transactions safe at all times if your margin is fair, and will make a steady profit. The more ups and downs, the more profits you round up. So long as it is a bull campaign and you are working this system on the long side of the market you are safe, no matter how great the fluctuations.

In May, 1897, Rock Island played all the month between sixty-one and a half and sixty-six and a half, moving up and down frequently. In June the price fluctuated up and down, finally getting to seventy-six. In July it wabbled up to eighty-three.

In August to ninety-seven; and in September to ninety-seven.

Now this "scale system" as given above was always in the market: you always had stock to sell on every advance and on every decline your system bought.

The proper time to buy is when the prices decline and the proper time to sell is when the prices advance. The amateur, working by guess, usually sells on the decline and buys on the advance.

The profits in the six months' working of a "scale system," between April and September, 1897, would not have been less than one hundred percent on five hundred dollars, and the system would have been absolutely "safe" during this time. Most of the time your broker would not have needed more than one hundred dollars to protect your transaction. All the time too your profits taken in would have been increasing your margin. In order to be absolutely safe, however, you should have had five hundred dollars at least up with your broker at all times, and then your trades would have been protected even through a ten point straight fall, something that will never occur in a good dividend paying granger stock after the bull campaign has commenced.

You have now, let us say, worked the "system" on the bull side up to September 1, 1897. The hints given you in the preceding pages tell you that the end of the bull campaign cannot be far off. You can wait awhile and when you find that the market, is getting top-heavy, turn your system around and commence selling on the short side of the market, every point up or down. No matter if it gees against you two or three points, it will come back again. In giving your orders to the broker in working the "scale system" on the short side of the market, simply substitute the word *sell* where the word *buy* occurs in the preceding order.

It will require nerve to turn your "system" at the end of the bull campaign, for the press, and the public, and the brokers, and the "tipsters," will all be against you at this time. Remember, however, that when the pools have sold out, stocks *must* go down sooner or later, no matter how favorable general conditions may be for an advance.

All this requires some intelligence on your part. Well, it requires intelligence to make money in any line of business, and this is as true or truer in Wall Street than in other places. An extract from a circular just received contains some very pertinent remarks on this point.

"A great many unreliable brokerage firms are flooding the country with catchpenny literature of how to make a fortune in three months with a one hundred dollar investment, and similar fairy tales, which *although* ridiculous on the face of it, still often deceive the innocent, and frequently rob quite

A man puts a thousand dollars into a Real Estate loan and is contented to wait a year to get sixty dollars for the use of his money. This same party will go into Wall Street with a thousand dollars and expect to make two or three or five hundred dollars a week on his capital. Of course he usually loses. By studying the principles laid down here and working on a "scale system" with plenty of reserve margins he can with safety make five percent to ten percent or fifteen percent a month on his capital. This will not satisfy the speculator, however. One hundred percent a month is the least that will content him.

An old book, not greatly in vogue in Wall Street, says somewhere, "A fool and his money are soon parted." Solomon would have no difficulty in understanding from whose pockets must come the one hundred million dollars a year that is lost by the public in the street.

The one thing essential for success then, *after you understand the principles laid down in this work, is* that one should not overtrade. If you are carrying too much stock for the amount of your capital, a two or three-point decline in prices makes your broker call on you for more margin, and you are compelled to sell at a loss. If you are right in your views as to the general course of the market you should *buy more stock on the decline,* instead of selling. If you do this, within a day or two prices go up again, and then what promised to be a loss turns out to be a profit. If you work on the right side of the market, starting with a ten or fifteen-point margin so that you can buy more on reactions, you will not need to take a loss during the whole campaign.

Hint Number Five

This is very important. *As a rule do not sell stocks on the third day of a decline* (unless you are working on the "scale system") and *do not buy on the third day of a rise.* We cannot explain why prices move practically three days in one direction and then react, but this is the case. There seems to be about two waves a week, one upward and one downward. If it is a bull campaign the upward wave will be longer than the downward, so that the tide gradually creeps in. If it is a bear campaign the downward wave will be longer than the upward, and the tide gradually recedes.

Hint Number Six

After stocks have advanced three days and close at top and open high the next morning there is almost sure to be a reaction of a point or two.

After they have declined three days and close at bottom they are almost sure to advance the next day.

In a bull market when you are waiting to get in on the reactions do not wait any longer than two full reaction days. On the third morning commence buying on a scale. Sometimes the market reacts only a little, *simply resting for two days* after its rise.

This will be the time when conditions, such as cheap money and business confidence, are favorable.

At these times buy on the *third day* of the resting period.

Hint Number Seven

In a bull market the largest volume of transactions are on the advance. The reactions are marked by smaller volumes. The reverse of this is true during the bear campaign. Closely watch the volumes of transactions and they will give a true indication as to the trend of the market.

Hint Number Eight

During a bull campaign never try to make a turn on the short or bear side of the market. No matter how straight the information may be that a reaction is due, do not allow yourself to get on the wrong side of the market for a day. You may succeed three or four times in cutting out a profit on the short side at such times, and then the next time you try it the market will run away from you and wipe out your margins.

If you wish to be safe stick to the bull side during a bull campaign. If you think there is going to be a temporary reaction then sell out if you like and wait for the reaction, and commence buying again. Do not go short.

During the bear campaign do not go long of the market, even for a time. If you think a rise is due, wait for the rise, and then commence selling short on a scale up. The market must come back sooner or later.

Hint Number Nine

If you start in at the beginning of a bull campaign it is a good plan to "pyramid" for a time, that is, hold your purchases and add more stocks as the prices advance and your margins grow. For instance, you buy fifty St. Paul at eighty-five, and fifty more every two points up for a rise of ten points. Your profits are then fifteen hundred dollars. If you study the St. Paul fluctuations in the records on a later page, you will see that once or twice in the year St. Paul makes a move of this kind.

In order to succeed in this you must commence at the beginning of the bull campaign. At a later stage more money will be made by playing the "scale system" so as to take advantage of the reactions.

Hint Number Ten

We advise studying two or three pool stocks closely. Keep accurate records of their fluctuations and movements. After a time you will be able to read the minds of the managers of these pools.

Hint Number Eleven

Do not let London quotations influence your views as to the course of the market.

Hint Number Twelve

After any decided general rise of six to ten points with *great excitement at the close of the advance,* then even if the market is ultimately going higher, the advance will stop for a time, and, of course, there will be more or less reaction. There will then be a number of up-and-down fluctuations, extending over two or three points in the grangers and more in the industrials. (See fluctuation record.) In other words we might say that the market after such a rise has had a "gorge" and must wait to digest its meal. Here is a time that the "scale system" picks up the profits. Here is the time, too, that "scalping" gets in its best work.

The same law holds true of a sharp fall in prices.

Hint Number Thirteen

The "tips" and "points," and "they say" and "we hear," and the "gossip" of so-called financial papers, as well as the letters of advertising brokers, ought not to be allowed to influence your views as to the course of the market. If these "tips" agree with indications furnished by your records, well and good. If not, pay no attention to them. In the long run one will be safer and make more money if he does not read the financial papers and financial gossip.

Hint Number Fourteen

One must take broad views and look ahead, in order to succeed in Wall Street. There everything is anticipated. If bad news is expected, do not sell after the worst is known, but buy. If favorable news is looked for, buy in advance, and sell out when the good news becomes a fact and is known to the public. Anticipate. The public said, "If war is declared then we will sell out and take the bear side of the market." All the pools had sold out long before and were waiting for an opportunity to get back their stocks. Prices began to *go up* as soon as war was declared.

If you wait until the uncertainties are all removed and the clouds all gone from the financial skies before buying, then prices are up ten to thirty points and those who "anticipated" are ready to unload on you. If you sell when the worst has been told and hope is dead then the pools are ready to buy, because a change is at hand. In Wall Street as in Nature. It is darkest just before the dawn. Anticipate! Anticipate!! Anticipate!!!

Hint Number Fifteen

Keep away from the brokers' offices and do not watch the "ticker." To succeed in Wall Street one must form independent judgments and have the courage to act on his views.

Now if you are hanging around a broker's office listening to the talk and opinions of the "Wall Street Wrecks," who congregate in such places, your mind will be influenced by such talk in spite of yourself. The "ticker" is the worst thing you can study. When prices are rushing up, the "ticker" whispers, "buy, buy;" when prices are going down a panic seizes you if you are watching the "ticker," and you sell when you should buy instead.

The "scale system" buys and sells exactly contrary to the whisperings of the "ticker."

The only amateurs who make money in Wall Street are those who keep away from the brokers' offices.

Hint Number Sixteen

Keep large margins. With a capital of one thousand dollars it is not safe for the amateur to trade in more than twenty-share lots of two or three good stocks. It is for this reason that we advise the amateur to work through the consolidated rather than on the New York Stock Exchange. Unless one is a desperate gambler he cannot afford to work one-hundred-share lots of stock with a smaller capital than from five to ten thousand dollars. Work on the "scale system" and trade on the Consolidated Exchange if your capital is moderate.

Hint Number Seventeen

"Second tops and bottoms." Mr. C. B. Greene, a very shrewd broker, has put forth a theory that has considerable truth in it. We will state this theory in his own words and just as published.

"When a market has gone through the stages of quiet and weak to active and declining, then on to semipanic and panic causing extremes on unexpected news beyond the power of any one to anticipate, Watch for the day to arrive when Volumes of transactions Increase Largely over all proceeding days. You will find purchases made at previous low Chart records or on a Scale Down on This Day on Ample Margin will bring very profitable results contrary to appearances or what your judgment advises. Should you wish to act more conservatively. Wait until the Large Volume Day Closes, showing a reaction of a few Points from bottom figures. Do Not Fail then to send orders immediately to Buy on the next or second Downward Movement At Or Near the lowest previous bottom figures touched on the first downward movement of the large volume day. You will observe the Greater the Volumes and the Bear Excitement the more certain of the lowest figures being touched a second time. Then purchases should be made without relying on lower quotations because you will not be able to buy from this point on a scale down for the reason that on the second decline prices seldom go over a few fractions below first lowest movement before a strong advance sets in.

The reverse is true on an upward movement of the same character.

Rule to Observe

At this Time You Must Lose Your Individuality and become an Automaton, Paying No Attention to News Gossip, and Act on the Second Movements.

Nerve and Patience is needed.

"These purchases should be held for marked advances because excited bull movements always follow on the heels of bear movements in proportion to the extent of the Volumes and Excitement at the extreme decline."

There is much truth in this suggestion, and this truth applies to both the selling and buying movements accompanied by great excitement and large volumes. We indorse everything Mr. Greene says on this point unhesitatingly, but in acting on this suggestion we caution you to keep the campaign in mind.

If it is a bear campaign and you buy for a turn do not hold for too big a reaction.

Hint Number Eighteen

Don't let your desires influence your judgment. The usual speculator if he is long of stocks can only appreciate arguments on the bull side of the market.

The chronic bear has his eyes shut as to the most patent signs of a bull market.

In both cases the desire or hope blinds the judgment.

There is no room for partisanship or politics or patriotism or religion in stock speculation, any more than there is in a game of whist or chess.

A habit of keeping the records of the fluctuations will soon teach one that this is a game of skill based on the eternal laws of human nature.

Do not however, neglect a study of natural conditions and the way they may influence the public mind. The pool generals do not neglect these facts.

Hint Number Nineteen

There are always one or two leaders even in the big pool stocks. The leader or leaders start first and get to the top first, and then are unloaded on the public while the other stocks are advancing. The one that gets to the top first will be the first to start on the downward course. Remember, however, that the price usually makes top a second time before going down and the price must fluctuate up and down just below the top for some time.

During the bear campaign the leaders will get to the bottom and begin to rise while the slower ones are tumbling. There will be second bottoms as well as second tops. Study your chances and while stocks are coming down rapidly wait until the second bottom on big volume days.

Hint Number Twenty

Don't be either a "chronic bull" or a "chronic bear." It ought to be plain to you from the preceding pages and from a study of the diagrams and records that there is a time to take the bull side of the market, and a time to take the bear side. You should change about every six months, when the pools change.

If you must be a "chronic," that is, a person on the same side of the market the year around, stick to the bull side *for the next two years.* It is far better, however, to go with the tide each year.

Hint Number Twenty-One

As a general rule get on the bull side in the late Spring and stay there until Fall. Then reverse and take the bear side. There is usually, however, after a decline in the Fall, a small bull campaign, *starting about the middle of December and lasting til the middle or latter part of January.* Then a decline until April, when the grand yearly campaign starts. This is a general rule, but your records if carefully kept will be your best guide.

Hint Number Twenty-Two

A bull campaign may be divided into three periods. 1st Period.—A sneaking bull market. 2d Period.—A creeping bull market. 3d Period.—A final grand rush.

The first upward move in the campaign comes as a surprise to the bears and the public.

Everything has looked so favorable for lower prices, there were so many clouds in the financial sky, that the sudden advance in prices is looked upon as a temporary move only. "The market was oversold," is the cry, and nearly everyone expects it to go back to the old prices again. After the bears have recovered from their confusion they commence putting out short sales, the bull leaders draw back a little to encourage them, and there is a slight recession in prices, sometimes equal to half of the advance.

Then comes the second period—"a creeping bull market." Here the pools take hold of one stock after another in succession, or one or two at a time, and advance them without any excitement and only a moderate amount of business. Many stocks are quiet during this period, some may recede a little temporarily, but from week to week the prices creep up. There is no excitement during this period. There are many plausible reasons put out to show that prices should go down at least a few points. One of the most prominent financial papers every year tells the public at this period that "there is going to be a bull market later, but it will start from a lower level," and so the public wait for reactions that do not come. The public at this time is very suspicious; they do not really have confidence in the bull market until prices are up twenty to thirty points and rapidly advancing. A rather dull market with one or two stocks at a time advancing and the public waiting for reactions to get in, or selling short to average up past losses, are the characteristics of the second period in the bull campaign.

Then comes the third period, "the final grand rush," the "old-fashioned bull market," fortunes made in a week—on paper: rapidly advancing prices all along the line; specialties and outsiders, "wild-cat and red-dog stocks" galloping to the front; great excitement; *an enormous volume of daily transactions* and then—

What Comes Next?

Well you ask your friends who loaded up with stocks in September, 1897, and November, 1896, and September, 1895, and September, 1894, what came next in their experience.

Hint Number Twenty-Three

On a dull advancing market after the foundation for a bull campaign has been formed, do not play for reactions. If everyone is waiting for reactions so as to buy back short stocks, or to start in on the bull side "from a lower level," be sure there will be no material reactions. *What everyone expects does not happen in Wall Street.*

Play the active stocks one after another as they commence to move. Remember the pools have got to put prices up and *hold them up* before they can unload.

Hint Number Twenty-Four

A bear campaign is not so easily characterized as is the bull campaign. After the big excitement at the close of the bull campaign there is of course a sharp reaction and then prices rush up again to make a second top. Then there is a dull, slow, sullen retreat in prices. The public who have brought stocks at the top, grit their teeth, put up more margins with their brokers and hold on. Hope springs eternal in the human breast: but during the bear campaign prices sag and sag until hope gives way to despair. After about three months of the sagging market, generally in late December or in January, there is a bull campaign lasting four or five or six weeks, and then a still further decline until the real period for accumulating stocks, which will be shown by the records of the fluctuations.

The bear campaign offers as many and as safe chances for making money as the bull campaign, some years better chances, but, as we have said before, for *the next two years we will be in the cycle of advancing prices* and the advances will greatly exceed the declines.

Hint Number Twenty-Five

When you have seen any stock lay a broad foundation for a rise, as shown by the records of the fluctuations, and then this stock advances *beyond the former stopping point of each advance, accompanied with large volumes of transactions,* you may be sure that this particular stock is in for a big rise. The height of the rise may be measured by the breadth of the foundation. Govern yourself accordingly.

Remember that fluctuations mean something. They are the result of design not chance.

Hint Number Twenty-Six

During the bull campaign, stocks generally sell lowest for the week on Thursday afternoon; on Fridays and Saturdays they advance and reach top either on Monday or Tuesday morning. In the bull campaign buy Thursday night and Friday morning; sell Monday and Tuesday morning. Reverse this rule for a bear campaign.

THE A B C OF STOCK SPECULATION
S. A. Nelson - 1903

Following the publication of The A B C of Wall Street there were many requests for a book dealing with the principles governing stock speculation. If there is one man better qualified than another to produce such a book that man is Mr. Charles H. Dow. Several attempts were made to have him write the desired volume but they were unavailing. From time to time in his Wall Street career, extending over a quarter of a century, Mr. Dow has carefully evolved his theories of successful stock speculation. They are to be found in Chapters IV to XX, inclusive, and can be commended to any one interested in stock speculation as remarkable for their grasp of a subject about which so little has been written and so much misinformation is gratuitously offered the public. In the preparation of this little volume thanks are also due to the Wall Street Journal, the Evening Post, the Dow, Jones & Co.'s News Agency, Mr. Alexander Dana Noyes, Mr. Daniel Kellogg, Mr. E. W. Harden, and a number of brokers and speculators. The reader of course understands that there is no royal road to success in speculation. It would be fallacy to undertake to show how money can be made. No infallible plan has yet been discovered. Experience and observation when intelligent, however, are valuable, and we are of the opinion that the average speculator will find a study of the following pages to be useful and profitable.

Chapter I - Origin of Brokers, Exchanges and Speculation

Etymological authorities are not in entire accord respecting the origin of the word "Broker." Jacob's Law Dictionary says: "The etymology of the term Broker has been variously given. By some it has been derived from the Saxon *broc,* misfortune, as denoting a broken trader; the occupation being formerly confined, it is said, to unfortunate persons of that description (Tomlins). According to others it was formed from the French *broieur,* a grinder or breaker into small pieces; a Broker being one who *beats* or draws a bargain into particulars (Termes de la Ley, Cowell). The law Latin from *obrocator,* however, seems to point distinctly to the Saxon *abroecan* (to break), as the true root, which in the old word *abbrochment* (q.v.) or *abroachment,* had the sense of breaking up goods or selling at retail. A Broker, therefore, would seem to have been originally a *retailer,* and hence we find the old word *auctionarius* (q.v.) used in both these senses (Barrill's Law Dict., tit. "Broker"). Wharton gives, as the derivation of the word the French *broceur,* and the Latin *tritor,* a person who breaks into small pieces (Whar. Law Dict., tit. "Broker"). Webster gives as its derivation, the old English *brocour,* Norman French *broggour,* French *"brocanteur.* Under the word "broke," to deal in second hand goods, to he a Broker, Webster says it is probably derived from the word *brock.* Worcester derives it from the Anglo-Saxon *brucan,* to discharge an office; brocian, to oppress; and the French *broyer,* to grind. See "Broke" and "Broker." The word "Broker" seems first to occur in literature in

Pier's Ploughman, "Among burgeises have I be Dwellyng at London. And gart Backbiting be a brocour. To blame men's ware." It clearly means here a *fault finder,* as in Provencal brae is refuse. The Broker was originally one who inspected goods and rejected what was below the standard (Wedgwood). Crabb's Dig. of Stat., tit. "Brokers," 261, says, "There were a class of persons known to the Romans who were deemed public officers, and who united the functions of bankers, exchangers, Brokers, commissioners and notaries all in one under the description of *proxe netae."*

As early as 1285, in England, the term Broker occurs in an Act of Parliament. It enacts that "there shall be no Broker in the city (London), except those who are admitted and sworn before the warden, mayor or aldermen."

John E. Dos Passos, an authority on stock exchange law, says: "The next statute passed in the reign of James the First, more than 300 years later (1604) regulates the calling of Brokers with greater detail than the first act and clearly shows, by the use of the words 'merchandise and wares' that down to this period the Broker in money, stock, and funds had no legal existence. It was not until the latter part of the seventeenth century, when the East India Company came prominently before the public, that trading or speculating in stock became an established business in England; and the term 'Broker' which had then a well-understood meaning was promptly transferred to those persons who were employed to buy or sell stocks or shares, and who thenceforth became known as 'stock-brokers.'"

In 1697 owing to the "unjust practices and designs" of Brokers and Stock-jobbers in selling tallies, bank stock, bank bills, shares and interest in joint stock, a stringent act was passed permitting only sworn appointees to act as Brokers. In the reigns of William III., Anne and George, statutes were passed regulating the practice and trade of Brokers.

An early legal writer describing Stockbrokers, said: "Stockbrokers are persons who confine their transactions to the buying and selling of property in the public funds and other securities for money, and they are employed by the proprietors or holders of the said securities. Of late years, owing to the prodigious increase of the funded debt of the nation, commonly called the stock, they are become a very numerous and considerable body, and have built by subscription, a room near the Bank, wherein they meet to transact business with their principals, and with each other; and to prepare and settle their proceedings before they go to the transfer offices at the Bank, the South Sea and India houses, thereby preventing a great deal of confusion at the public offices, where the concourse of people is so great during the hours of transferring stock that if the business was not prepared beforehand it would be impossible to transact it within the given time."

The advantage of having a Broker as an intermediary was recognized by merchants many centuries ago. A sixteenth century writer on the law says: "It is an old proverb, and very true, that between *what you will buy?* and *what you will sell?* there is twenty in the hundred differing in the price, which is the cause that all the nations do more effect to sell their commodities with reputation by means of Brokers than we do; for that which seems to be gotten thereby is more than double lost another way. Besides, that by that course many differences are prevented which arise between man and man in their bargains or verbal contracts; for the testimony of a sworn Broker and his book together is sufficient to end the same."

Dealings in Stock certificates constitute the main business of Stock-brokers, but the origin of stock certificates has not been satisfactorily traced beyond the middle of the seventeenth century. Property in this form was not known to the ancient law. While mercantile or commercial corporations existed among the Romans, history gives us no information regarding their character or methods of conduct.

Ang. & Ames on Corporations (10th ed.) Ch. 18, Sec. 26, says: "A *Collegium Mercatorum* existed at Rome 493 B. C., but the modern bourse from the Latin *bursa,* a purse, originated about the fifteenth century. Bourges and Amsterdam contend for the honor of having erected the first bourse."

"The Roman law," says John R. Dos Passes, "required three persons to organize a corporation; and as each body had at least that number of members, if not more, it would seem but natural that a certificate, or some other sub-stantial muniment of title, should have been issued by the corporation to its respective members, in which the proportion of interest of each in the capital or corporate property of the association appeared. But whether a certificate was, in fact, issued, and, if so, was regarded as property capable of sale or other negotiation, and of vesting in the representatives of the owner, on his decease, or whether the corporations were all of the nature of guilds conferring upon the members mere *personal* rights—all of these questions seem now to be incapable of solution; and the Roman law, which sheds such floods of light upon commercial subjects apparently leaves the above matters in total darkness."

In England, in 1770, Lord Mansfield in a case wherein it was contended that stock certificates were *money* decided against that view, saying: "This is a *new* species of property *arisen within the compass of a few years.* It is not money."

The Stock Exchange or Bourse in its present use is a modern creation. Brokers and dealers in stocks and merchandise dealt together in an exchange in Cornhill, London, in 1670, or thereabouts. In 1698, the Stockbrokers of London obtained quarters for their exclusive use.

The first Stock Exchange formed in the U.S. was that of Philadelphia, where a Board of Stock-brokers formally organized and adopted a constitution in the early part of the eighteenth century. The New York Stock Exchange, framed on the plan of the one in Philadelphia, was organized in 1817, but curiously enough this institution is in possession of a document bearing date May 17, 1792, signed by a number of Brokers, in which it is stated: "We, the subscribers, Brokers for the purchase and sale of public business, agree to do business at not less than one-fourth of one percent." Medberry, in his "Men and Mysteries of Wall Street," describes early stock speculation in this country as follows: "When Washington was President, and Continental money was worth a trifle more as currency than as waste paper, some twenty New York dealers in public stock met together in a Broker's office and signed their names in the bold, strong hand of their generation, to an agreement of the nature of a protective league. The date of this paper is May 17, 1792. The volume of business of all these primitive New York Brokers could not have been much above that of even the poorest first-class Wall Street house in our time (1870). The Revolutionary shinplasters, as the irreverent already styled them, were spread over the land in such plenty that there were $100 to each inhabitant. Something was to be made, therefore, from the fluctuations to which they were liable. Indeed, one of the greatest Broker firms of subsequent years derived its capital from the lucky speculations of its senior member in this currency.

"The war of 1812 gave the first genuine impulse to stock speculation. The Government issued sixteen millions in Treasury notes, and put loans amounting to one hundred and nine millions on the market. There were endless fluctuations and the lazy-going capitalists of the time managed to gain or lose handsome fortunes. Bank stock was also a favorite investment. An illustration of one of the sources of money-making to Brokers at this period is found in the fact that United States 6's of 1814 were at 50 in specie and 70 in New York bank currency.

"In 1816 one could count up two hundred banks with a capital of $82,000,000. One day in 1817, the New York stock dealers met in the room of an associate and voted to send a 'delegate' over on the stage line to investigate the system adopted in the rival city (Philadelphia). The Philadelphia visit was successful; and the draft of a constitution and by-laws, framed from that of the Philadelphia Board, received the final approbation of a sufficient number of Brokers to enable the New York Stock Exchange to become a definite fact. Three years after, on the 21st of February, 1820, this preliminary code of rules received a thorough revision and the organization was strengthened by the accession of some of the heaviest capitalists in the city. Indeed, with 1820, the real history of the Exchange may properly be said to commence."

In Europe stock speculation historically was marked with white stones by the "Tulip Craze," the South Sea Bubble, the John Law inflation in France, and later by the wild speculation in Kaffirs.

In this country for more than half a century stock speculation had its basis in the securities of the steam railroad. It has ebbed and flowed with the promotion, construction, decline, and reorganization of that industry.

In the last decade speculation has been fostered by the "industrial proposition," which has resulted in offering to the public shares of industrial corporations. Not an industry has been passed by. Like the railroad the industrial corporation is destined to have its periods of promotion, construction, decline and reorganization. It will not be difficult for the reader to determine which period he has under immediate consideration.

Chapter II - Stock Speculation

For many years stock speculation has been of national and absorbing importance. During the period from 1896 to 1902 investment and speculation in corporate securities attained an unprecedented importance, owing to the general movement to combine and incorporate industrial companies with a consequent change of ownership. Ownership which had been vested in small groups of individuals now became widely distributed. Where an industry had been controlled and owned by 10 persons the number multiplied and increased by 10 and 1,000-fold through the medium of share ownership. The mine and the factory owned by the individual were merged into a joint corporation, the shares of which were listed on the Stock Exchange, and offered to the public for investment or speculation. The U.S. Steel Corporation has more than 40,000 stockholders; the American Sugar Refining, 11,000; while other corp- orations, notably those representing the railroad, are relatively as widely distributed. Stock speculation in the U.S. in the period named was also inspired by the rehabilitation of the railroad industry, the stocks of which have always been favorite speculative fuel, and the basis for the intense public interest and activity was the general prosperity and wealth of the country. A variety of causes contributed to the tremendous increase in national wealth. Today, speculation in the shares listed on the New York Stock Exchange is not only confined to New York but extends to California on the West, Canada on the North, Texas on the South and London, Paris and Berlin on the East. The telegraph, telephone and cable wire transmits quotations to facilitate specu- lation today with a speed and perfection of method that would have been regarded as marvelous by the founders of the New York Stock Exchange, and quite impossible by the great manipulators who dominated the arena a quarter of a century ago. Millions of dollars are consumed annually in order to keep the machinery of Wall Street in working order. It is estimated that the annual expenses of 300 leading Wall Street stock firms approximate $15,000,000. In view of the commercial and economic tendencies of the times, the indications are that stock speculation will continue to play a highly important part in the country's trade. In 1901 there were days when dealings on the Stock Exchange exceeded 3,000,000 shares and the machinery of speculation threatened to break down under the intensity of the strain to which it was subjected. Whether the records of that year will ever be broken no man can foretell, but it is reasonable to say that not for a long time will interest in the daily changes of the stock market be confined solely to the ranks of the professional stock speculator who conducts his operations within stone's throw of the Stock Exchange, for there has arisen a vast army of investors and speculators who are deeply interested in the day's price fluctuations.

Chapter III - Stock Speculation and Gambling

Is there any difference between speculation and gambling? The terms are often used interchangeably, but speculation presupposes intellectual effort; gambling blind chance. Accurately to define the two is difficult; all definitions are difficult. Wit and humor, for instance, can be defined; but notwithstanding the most subtle distinction, wit and humor blend, run into each other. This is true of speculation and gambling. The reform has some elements of chance; the latter some of the elements of reason. We define as best we can. Specu- lation is a venture based upon calculation. Gambling is a venture without calculation. The law makes this distinction: it sustains speculation, and condemns gambling. All business is more or less speculative. The term speculation, however, is commonly restricted to business of exceptional uncertainty. The uninitiated believe that chance is so large a part of speculation that it is subject to no rules, is governed by no laws. This is a serious error.—Unknown writer.

Is a broker a trader, a speculator or a manipulator a gambler? Or are all four gamblers? An old speculator takes this somewhat humorous view of the question: "I am not a gambler—the broker is the gambler—I am the lamb, unshorn it's true, but nevertheless the victim of a bad habit. If I enter a gambling house and make a few wagers I would resent the imputation that I was a gambler. I am not a gambler or at the worst only an amateur at the game and then for a few minutes only. The man who backs the game and runs the gambling house is the professional gambler. Now the broker occupies much the same relationship to the stock gambling game that the man with the cards and wheel does to his peculiar trade. Of course behind the stockbroker there is the manipulator and the game itself. The broker does not lose out his own money unless he 'buckets' his orders (when he is a gambler as is every bucket shop operator) so he is only a 'croupier' so to speak, for the game. A stock speculator whose only source of income is stock speculation on a margin may fairly call himself a gambler."

Speculation and gambling, as the words are used today, are substantially interchangeable, but nevertheless there is a marked distinction between the two. All speculators are not necessarily gamblers, although all stock gamblers (traders) are speculators. When speculation in stocks becomes gambling in stocks, the operations are usually confined to transactions made on a margin.

For example: A walks in a broker's office and asks: "What do you think of the market?" "We hear," is the reply, "that St. Paul is a purchase at the opening for a rise of several points." "Very well, buy me 100 shares, sell at 2 points profit and stop the loss at 1 point." Obviously this is a wager in which the gambling factor is very strong and the maker regards himself as a gambler.

Example No. 2. B enters the same office, asks the same question, receives the same reply and says: "Very well, buy me 100 shares, send the certificate to my office and I will give you a check for it." B buys his stock outright and would not buy a single share on a margin. He will admit that he is a speculator, but will be insulted if you call him a gambler.

Example No. 3. C is a trader and an Exchange member. Ask him his business and he will reply that he is a trader. Ask him to define a trader and he will say: "As far as I am concerned a trader is a gambler. I never go home long or short a share of stock. I take advantage of the smallest changes in the market limiting my losses to the minimum—1/8s and 1/4s—and take equally small profits, although I am glad to get larger ones. I excel at calling the successive changes, trade on either side, and have no pronounced views as to whether it is a bull or bear market."

All bucket shop operators and traders are gamblers. Investors are not gamblers.

Brokers and manipulators are not necessarily gamblers, the circumstances governing individual cases.

The case of B will doubtless cause discussion, but his view is that he is no more a gambler than the man who buys a parcel of real estate on a 10 percent equity or the merchant who buys and sells goods in expectation of a rise or fall.

But stock speculation does not owe its importance to the classes of speculators enumerated as closely allied to the gambler. On the contrary they are in the minority. Gambling may at times be an unavoidable accompanyment of stock speculation, but stock speculation is so interwoven with the money market and the commerce of the country that to eliminate it from the world of business would be for civilization to take a long backward step.

Criticism of stock speculation as of other trades, arts and sciences, to be intelligent, should be discriminating. Pulpit and press at times denounce stock speculation as if the Stock Exchange and Wall Street were hotbeds of corruption.

No well-informed man questions the usefulness of the Stock Exchange or stock speculator. Stock Exchange prices register values and the state of trade, precisely as a thermometer registers heat or cold. The stock market is the most highly organized and delicately adjusted market in the world. It offers to the public at large securities which are good collaterals at any bank and securities which on any business day can be sold for cash. It gives the money market great elasticity. It is a safeguard provided for unexpected demands upon the money market, and furnishes a medium of exchange that minimizes the use of gold in international operations. It is a most important part of the modern system of credit. Eliminate the stock market and transferable securities from the life of the county today and contemplate if good can be the result of a demand from Europe for its credit balances to be paid in gold. The result would paralyze industrial progress. The Stock Exchange facilitates the employment of capital, adds to its productiveness, is an accurately registering machinery of credit indispensable to the banks of the country, and is a guiding force for the merchant and financier.

Chapter IV - The Morality of Wall Street

A leading newspaper, commented (1902) editorially on the morality of Wall Street. Part of the burden of its comment was that it was different in some respects from morality elsewhere. Taking the word "morality" to mean in this instance the general law or code of ethics obtaining in Wall Street and elsewhere, it does not appear that there is any essential difference between Wall Street morality and general business morality.

The object of all business is the "making of money" and nothing else. Wall Street is certainly no different from any other place or center of business activity in this respect. Where one business center or group of industries differs from another in the matter of morality is probably only in the details of its code. Now, in the details of its code Wall Street will compare to advantage with most other business centers. As has been pointed out, its machinery is predicated upon rigid observance of bargains made and word passed. While it is true that this kind of honor is absolutely necessary for the smooth conduct of business as it is carried on in Wall Street, it is also true that the high standard required is lived up to by the Street, and breaches thereof are extremely rare.

Perhaps one reason why there is so much disposition to question the morality of Wall Street and contrast it unfavorably with the morality of other business centers is the fact that in Wall Street probably to a greater extent than elsewhere the primal passions and instincts of acquisitiveness and self-preservation wear less disguise than they do in the other channels of industry and money making. A Stock Exchange anywhere is a theatre in which these primal passions battle as gladiators in the arena without concealment or pretense. Every one who goes down into the arena knows that it is a battle wherein his hand must keep his head, and the penalty of failure will be exacted against him to the utmost. *"A la guerre comme a la guerre"* is a proverb that very well describes the conditions under which business is done in Wall Street. Elsewhere, it may appear to be different. The only difference is that in Wall Street there is no pretense, no disguise; the essential struggle is the same everywhere. In Wall Street, there has been and unfortunately still is at times fraud in detail peculiar to Wall Street, but it is not of Wall Street nor inherent in the laws of the game.

It is true that speculation in Wall Street is looked upon as being especially immoral by comparison with speculation elsewhere. It is, however, part of almost every manufacturer's business or of every merchant's business to speculate in raw materials or goods, and nobody thinks of finding fault with either for doing so. In Wall Street speculation stands alone, without any business disguise, for all men to see. There is no difference between one kind of speculation and another so far as essence is concerned; the only difference is that one is disguised and the other is not. It may be noted, moreover, that where the speculation is not disguised it is apt to be more honest than where it hides under a cloak of business enterprise. All men are gamblers and always will be more or less for the "get rich quick" idea, and the chances of "something for nothing" will always prove irresistibly attractive to human nature. The plain fact of the matter is that the general suspicion of and hostility toward Wall Street find their root in the fact that the race for money is carried on simply, openly in the light of day, without pretense or hypocrisy of any kind, and without attempt to cloak the passions that have existed since man first came upon the earth. If gambling be wrong, the principal charge that can be levied against Wall Street is that it is there carried on openly, under simple but rigid rules, and Wall Street does not care who knows it. Elsewhere it goes on in essence just the same, but disguised in a multitude of ways. In these days most forms of business must of their very nature contain a large element of speculation. We do not see that speculation becomes more immoral by being openly carried on.

Wall Street has rather less use for a habitual liar than have other places. It has no use at all for a man who does not keep his word. It may be true that honesty is the best policy in Wall Street, simply for reasons of convenience, but that it is the best policy no one can deny. In fact, it is the only policy that in the long run is successful. We do not think that this is necessarily an argument against the morality of Wall Street.

Chapter V - Scientific Speculation*
The question whether there is such a thing as scientific speculation is often asked. Various answers of a somewhat affirmative character have been given but they have generally been hedged about with so many qualifications as to be nearly useless for practical purposes. The experiences of operators have, however, crystallized into some general rules worth heeding.

The maxim "buy cheap and sell dear" is as old as speculation itself, but it leaves unsolved the question of when a security of a commodity is cheap and when it is dear, and this is the vital point.

The elder Rothschilds are said to have acted on the principle that it was well to buy a property of known value when others wanted to sell and to sell when others wanted to buy. There is a great deal of sound wisdom in this. The public, as a whole, buys at the wrong time and sells at the wrong time. The reason is that markets are made in part by manipulation and the public buys on manipulated advances and after they are well along. Hence it buys at the time when manipulators wish to sell and sells when manipulators wish to buy.

In some commission offices, there are traders who, as a rule, go against whatever the outside customers of the house are doing. When members of the firm say, "all our customers are getting long of stocks," these traders sell out; but they buy when the firm says, "the customers are all short." There are of course, exceptions to this rule. If there were no exceptions, the keepers of bucket shops would all get rich. When the market has an extraordinary rise, the public makes money, in spite of beginning its purchases at what would ordinarily be the wrong time, and this is when the bucket shops either lose their money or close out in order to keep such money of customers as they have in hand.

All this points to the soundness of the Rothschild principle of buying a property of known value when the public generally is disposed to sell; or of selling it when the general public thinks it a time to buy.

Daniel Drew used to say, "cut your losses short, but let your profits run." This was good preaching, but "Uncle Dan" did not, in his later years, practice his rule, when it would have been better for him if he had. The thought here is unquestionably one of the sound principles in trading. It means that if a stock has been purchased and it goes up, it is well to wait; but if it goes down, it is well to stop the loss quickly on the ground that the theory on which the purchase was made was wrong.

The public, as a whole, exactly reverses this rule. The average operator, when he sees two or three points profit, takes it; but, if a stock goes against him two or three points, he holds on waiting for the price to recover, with, oftentimes, the result of seeing a loss of two or three points run into a loss of

---

* Dow Theory

ten points. He then becomes discouraged and sells out near the bottom to protect the margin in which he has left.

How many operators in looking over their books find a considerable number of small profits swept away by one large loss? When a trader finds by his accounts that his profits have been relatively large and his losses relatively small, he can make up his mind that he is learning how to trade.

The trouble with carrying out this plan is that a series of losses of from 1 1/2 to 2 points are very discouraging. A trader who sees that he has taken twice or three times a loss of two points when, if he had waited a few days he need not have taken any loss, is very apt to decide that he will not cut his losses short any more, but will wait, and this is the time when the recovery does not come.

Mr. Jay Gould said his policy was to endeavor to foresee future conditions in a property and then, having made his commitments carefully, to exercise great patience in awaiting results. This also is sound doctrine, but proceeds along very different lines. Assuming the ability to foresee the future, it is the wisest of all courses; but many who have tried this method have found that the omission of essential factors made their forecast valueless, and both their courage and their patience of little avail. Nevertheless, this method should not be discarded on account of the difficulties involved. Within limitations, the future can be foreseen. The present is always tending toward the future and there are always in existing conditions signals of danger or encouragement for those who read with care.

Chapter VI - Two General Methods of Trading*

There are two general methods of trading. One is to deal in active stocks in comparatively large amounts, relying for protection upon stop orders. In this method of trading it is not necessary to know much about the values. The point of chief importance is that the stock should be active enough to permit the execution of the stop order at the point selected so as to cut losses short. The operator, by this method, guesses which way the stock will move. If he guesses right, he lets his profits run. If he guesses wrong, he goes out on the stop order. If he can guess right as often as he can guess wrong, he is fairly sure of profits.

The other system is an entirely different proposition. It starts with the assumption that the operator knows approximately the value of the stock in which he proposes to deal. It assumes that he has considered the tendency of the general market; that he realizes whether the stock in which he proposes to deal is relatively up or down, and that he feels sure of its value for at least months to come.

Suppose this to exist: The operator lays out his plan of campaign on the theory that he will buy his first lot of stock at what he considers the right price and the right time, and will then buy an equal amount every 1 percent down as far as the decline may go,

---

* Dow Theory

113

This method of trading is the one generally employed by large operators. They know the value of the stock in which they propose to deal, and are therefore reasonably secure in following a decline. They feel about a stock as merchants feel about buying staple goods. If an article is cheap at $100, they know it is cheaper at $90, and will strain a point to buy at $80 or at $70, knowing that the price must recover. This is the way a large operator looks at his favorite stocks and this is why he generally makes money in them.

The disadvantage of the small operator in following this method is two-fold. He does not absolutely know the value of the stock. That is, he may know the truth up to a certain point, but beyond that is an unknown factor which interferes with the result. When the price of a stock declines considerably, the small operator always fears that he has overlooked something of importance, and he is therefore tempted to sell instead of averaging his holdings.

The second disadvantage of the small operator in following this policy is that he seldom provides sufficient capital for his requirements. Thousands of speculators believe that because 10 percent is a common speculative margin, that $1,000 justifies them in trading in hundred share lots. This impression produces losses continually.

The man who has $1,000 for speculation is not well equipped for trading in even 10 share lots, if he proposes to deal on a scale. A comparison of high and low prices of active stocks shows frequently a difference of 30 points in a year. Any operator proposing to follow a stock down, buying on a scale, should make his preparations for a possible fall of from 20 to 30 points. Assuming that he does not begin to buy until his stock is 5 points down from the top, there is still a possibility of having to buy 20 lots before the turn will come.

If, however, an outsider will provide $2,500 as his speculative capital and will trade in ten-share lots in a thoroughly good railroad stock, beginning his purchases only after a decline of five points in a rising market, and ten points in a bear market, following the decline with purchases every point down, and retaining all the stock bought, he seldom need make a loss.

Such campaigns require time, patience, and the pursuance of a fixed policy, but whoever will follow this policy will find himself able to get a high rate of interest on the capital invested. It is an old saying in Wall Street that the man who begins to speculate in stocks with the intention of making a fortune, usually goes broke, whereas the man who trades with a view of getting good interest on his money, sometimes gets rich.

This is only another way of saying that money is made by conservative trading rather than by the effort to get large profits by taking large risks. After allowing for all the risks involved, we think the outsider who wants to trade in stocks has a better chance working in small lots on a scale than in any other way, provided he will pay attention to certain essential points, which for convenience of reference we will enumerate in order.

1.—Bull markets and bear markets run four and five years at a time. Determine by the average prices, which one is under way.

2.—Determine the stock or stocks to trade in. They should be railroad stocks, dividend payers, not too low, nor too high, fairly active, and for the bull side below their value; for the bear side above their value. Values are determined roughly by the earnings available for dividends.

3.—Observe the position of your stock with relation to recent fluctuations. In a bull market, the time to begin to buy is when a stock has had four or five points decline from the last previous top. In a bear market, the time to begin to sell is when such a stock has had three or four points rally from the bottom.

4.—Stick to the stock bought until a fair profit or until there is good reason for deciding that the first estimate of value was wrong. Remember that an active stock will generally rally from 3/8 percent to 5/8 percent of the amount of its decline under adverse conditions and more than that under favorable conditions.

5.—Have money enough to see a decline through without becoming uneasy or over-burdened. $2,500 ought to take care of a ten-share scale every point down—that is to say, supposing the first lot to be bought five points down from the top, $2,500 ought to carry the scale until the natural recovery from the low point brings the lot out with a profit on the average cost. It will not do to expect a profit on every lot, but only on the average. In a bull market it is better to always work on the bull side; in a bear market, on the bear side. There are usually more rallies in a bear market than there are relapses in a bull market.

6.—Do not let success in making money in ten-share lots create a belief that a bolder policy will be wiser and begin to trade in 100-share lots with inadequate capital. A few hundred-share losses will wipe out a good many ten-share profits.

7.—There is not usually much difficulty in dealing in ten-share lots on the short side. If one broker does not wish to do it, another probably will, especially for a customer who amply protects his account and who seems to understand what he is doing.

Chapter VII - Three General Lines of Reasoning*

We have spoken in a preceding article of the fact that the experience of great interests in the market seems to have crystallized into three general lines of reasoning.

The first is that the surface appearance of the market is apt to be deceptive. The second is that it is well in trading to cut losses short and let profits run. The third is that correctly discounting the future is a sure and easy road to wealth. The problem is how these rules which are undoubtedly sound, can be operated in a practical way.

---

* Dow Theory

Let us take first the action of the general market with reference to the time to buy. The market is always to be considered as having three movements, all going on at the same time. The first is the narrow movement from day to day. The second is the short swing, running from two weeks to a month or more; the third is the main movement covering at least four years in its duration.

The day to day movement should be disregarded by everybody, except traders, who pay no commissions. The medium swing is the one for ordinary consideration. The outside trader should not attempt to deal in more than two or three stocks at a time. He should keep a chart of the price movements of these stocks so as to know their swings for months or years, and thus be able to tell readily where in the general swing his particular stocks appear to be.

He should keep with his price movement a record of the volume of transactions and notes of any special facts bearing on that property, such as increases or decreases in earnings, increases in fixed charges, development of floating debt, and above all the actual dividend earnings as shown from month to month. He should observe the movement of the general market as indicated by the averages published daily, as this shows the market more clearly than it is shown by any one stock.

The main purpose of this study is to enable the trader to determine, first, the value of the stock he is in; whether it is increasing or decreasing and, second, when the time to buy seems opportune. Assuming the thirty day swing to be about 5 points, it is in the highest degree desirable not to buy when three of these points have passed, as such a purchase limits the probable profits to about two points.

It is therefore generally wise to look for a low point on a decline. Suppose, for instance, that Union Pacific was the stock under consideration; that it was clearly selling below its value, and that a bull market for the four-year period was under way. Assuming further that in a period of reaction Union Pacific had fallen four points from the previous highest. Assume earnings and prospects to be favorable and the outlook for the general market to be about normal.

This would be the time to begin to buy Union Pacific. The prudent trader, however, would take only part of his line. He would buy perhaps one-half of the stock he wanted and then give an order to buy the remainder as the price declined. The fall might go much further than he anticipated. It might be necessary to wait a long time for profit. There might even be developments which would make it wise to throw over the stock bought with the hope of replacing it materially lower.

These, however, are all exceptions. In a majority of cases this method of choosing the time to buy, founded upon clear perception of value in the stock chosen and close observation of the market swings under way will enable an operator to secure stock at a time and at a price which will give fair profits on the investment.

Chapter VIII - Swings Within Swings*

A correspondent asks: "For some time you have been writing rather bullish on the immediate market, yet a little bearish in a larger sense. How do you make this consistent?"

We get this question in one form or another rather frequently. It denotes a lack of familiarity with fluctuations in prices when viewed over considerable periods. Many people seem to think that the change in prices in any one day is complete in itself and bears no relation to larger movements which may be under way. This is not so.

Nothing is more certain than that the market has three well-defined movements which fit into each other. The first is the daily variation due to local causes and the balance of buying or selling at that particular time. The secondary movement covers a period ranging from ten days to sixty days, averaging probably between thirty and forty days. The third move is the great swing covering from four to six years.

In thinking about the market, it is necessary to think with reference to each of these periods in order to take advantage of opportunities. If the main move is up, relapses are speculators' opportunities, but if the main move is down, rallies furnish these opportunities.

Losses should not generally be taken on the long side in a bull period. Nor should they generally be taken on the short side in a bear period. It is a bull period as long as the average of one high point exceeds that of previous high points. It is a bear period when the low point becomes lower than the previous low points. It is often difficult to judge whether the end of an advance has come because the movement of prices is that which would occur if the main tendency had changed. Yet, it may only be an unusually pronounced secondary movement.

The first thing for any operator to consider is the value of the stock in which he proposes to trade. The second is to determine the direction of the main movement of prices. We know of nothing more instructive on this point than the course of prices as printed daily. The third thing is to determine the position of the secondary swing.

Assume for instance that the stock selected was Union Pacific; that the course of prices afforded clear evidence of a bull market under way; that the high point in Union Pacific thirty days ago was 108; that the price had slowly declined in sympathy with the market and without special new features to 98. The chances would be in favor of buying a part of the line wanted at that price with the intention of buying a little more if the stock had further decline or if the price showed a well defined advancing tendency. It would then be wise to watch the general market and wait for an advance.

A 10-point decline under such conditions would be almost certain to bring in a bull market more than 5 points recovery and full 10 points would not be unreasonable; hence if the general market maintained a good tone, it would be wise to wait for 5 points and then begin to think about stop orders.

Even in a bear market, this method of trading will usually be found safe, although the profit taken should be less because of the liability of weak spots breaking out and checking the general rise.

Chapter IX - Methods of Reading the Market*

A correspondent writes: "Is there any way of forecasting the course of the market from the tape, from your records of transactions or from the summarized movement of prices? Transactions must mean something, but how can a trader tell what they mean?"

This is an old question. There have been a variety of answers but it is doubtful if any have been or can be wholly satisfactory. Several methods, however, are in practical use and at times afford suggestions.

There is what is called the book method. Prices are set down, giving each change of 1 point as it occurs, forming thereby lines having a general horizontal direction but running into diagonals as the market moves up and down. There come times when a stock with a good degree of activity will stay within a narrow range of prices, say 2 points, until there has formed quite a long horizontal line of these figures. The formation of such a line sometimes suggests that stock has been accumulated or distributed, and this leads other people to buy or sell at the same time. Records of this kind kept for the last fifteen years seem to support the theory that the manipulation necessary to acquire stock is often times detected in this way.

Another method is what is called the theory of double tops. Records of trading show that in many cases when a stock reaches top it will have a moderate decline and then go back again to near the highest figures. If after such a move, the price again recedes, it is liable to decline some distance.

Those, however, who attempt to trade on this theory alone find a good many exceptions and a good many times when signals are not given.

There are those who trade on the theory of averages. It is true that in a considerable period of time the market has about as many days of advance as it has of decline. If there come a series of days of advance, there will almost surely come the balancing days of decline.

The trouble with this system is that the small swings are always part of the larger swings, and while the tendency of events equally liable to happen is always toward equality, it is also true that every combination possible is liable to occur, and there frequently come long swings, or, in the case of stock trading, an extraordinary number of days of advance or decline which fit properly into the theory when regarded on a long scale, but which are calculated to upset any operations based on the expectation of a series of short swings.

A much more practicable theory is that founded on the law of action and reaction. It seems to be a fact that a primary movement in the market will generally have a secondary movement in the opposite direction of at least three-eighths of the primary movement. If a stock advances 10 points, it is very likely to have a relapse of 4 points or more. The law seems to hold good

---

* Dow Theory

no matter how far the advance goes. A rise of 20 points will not infrequently bring a decline of 8 points or more.

It is impossible to tell in advance the length of any primary movement, but the further it goes, the greater the reaction when it comes, hence the more certainty of being able to trade successfully on that reaction.

A method employed by some operators of large experience is that of responses. The theory involved is this: The market is always under more or less manipulation. A large operator who is seeking to advance the market does not buy everything on the list, but puts up two or three leading stocks either by legitimate buying or by manipulation. He then watches the effect on the other stocks. If sentiment is bullish, and people are disposed to take hold, those who see this rise in two or three stocks immediately begin to buy other stocks and the market rises to a higher level. This is the public response, and is an indication that the leading stocks will be given another lift and that the general market will follow.

If, however, leading stocks are advanced and others do not follow, it is evidence that the public is not disposed to buy. As soon as this is clear the attempt to advance prices is generally discontinued. This method is employed more particularly by those who watch the tape. But it can be read at the close of the day in our record of transactions by seeing what stocks were put up within specified hours and whether the general market followed or not. The best way of reading the market is to read from the standpoint of values. The market is not like a balloon plunging hither and thither in the wind. As a whole, it represents a serious, well considered effort on the part of farsighted and well-informed men to adjust prices to such values as exist or which are expected to exist in the not too remote future. The thought with great operators is not whether a price can be advanced, but whether the value of property which they propose to buy will lead investors and speculators six months hence to take stock at figures from 10 to 20 points above present prices.

In reading the market, therefore, the main point is to discover what a stock can be expected to be worth three months hence and then to see whether manipulators or investors are advancing the price of that stock toward those figures. It is often possible to read movements in the market very clearly in this way. To know values is to comprehend the meaning of movements in the market.

Chapter X - The Operation of Stop Orders*

A correspondent inquires: "My brokers advise me to protect my transactions by stop orders. It seems to me that stop orders may he good for brokers by giving them commissions, but they make customers take unnecessary losses. Do you advise speculators to give stop orders?"

Proof on this point is afforded by taking a large number of fluctuations and seeing how the average works out. We believe that for the margin trader, and especially the trader who operates rather more largely than he ought on the

---

* Dow Theory

margin that he has, stop orders are wise. There are, however, many qualifications which should be kept in mind.

If a man is trading as a semi-investor, using 50 percent margin, depending on values for his profit and operating in harmony with the main tendency of the market, we do not think a stop order desirable. To explain this a little more fully: Suppose the movement of averages shows that the market is in a rising period, such periods usually covering several years with only temporary reversals in direction. Suppose that an operator finds that a certain stock is earning an abnormal percentage on its market value, or, in other words, is intrinsically cheap. Suppose on the occasion of a temporary setback this stock is bought to be carried for months if necessary until the price has risen to approximately the level of the value. A stop order is folly in a case of this kind with anything like fair margin.

But, suppose a trader, having a margin of two or three thousand dollars, wants to trade in and out of stocks without regard to values, but being governed by points or by impressions of what the general market is going to do. Experience has shown that such a trader will, in the end, profit by putting a stop order about 2 points from the price at which he goes in. If there is advice that a stock is going up and it instead goes down 2 points without some obviously good reason for such a decline, the advice was not good, and the quicker the speculator lets go the better.

It often happens that when a stock moves two points it moves more, and it is a peculiarity of the human mind to disregard a small loss, but to get frightened and take a large loss just when wisdom would call for averaging a purchase.

Thousands of traders have said at two points loss that they would see that particular transaction through if the stock went to nothing, only to decide after it had declined ten points that there was good reason for believing that it would decline ten more and acting accordingly. The experience of most traders is that the small losses occasioned by stop orders have a tendency to check their trading with a small aggregate loss, while the practice of letting a loss run not infrequently makes a loss so large that trading comes to an end because the speculator has no more mangy. The maxim "let your profits run, but cut your losses short" has received the approval of most of the great stock operators. The authorship of the maxim has been credited to a dozen people, and most of them would have been willing to father it, although the great stop orders were wise was based on their observation of people who tried to trade with insufficient capital, to whom stop orders especially apply.

The great profits in stocks have almost invariably been made by people who saw the tendency of events clearly, and who then bought a large amount of stock which they thought certain to get the results of great increase in prosperity. Such stock has either been paid for outright or very heavily margined, and then it has been held for months or years until great profits accrued.

Take the opportunities that have occurred in the last six years, or since 1896. Any one of from twenty to forty stocks could have been bought around 20 and sold above 80, and in at least half the cases above par, within that time.

Such great opportunities do not come every year, but there are few times when some stocks cannot be pointed out as being lower in price than in value and as entitled to advance.

In a close speculative sense, a stop order is often useful. Stocks may be bought just when a reaction is setting in. In this case, it is frequently wise to take a quick loss on the theory that the reaction is likely to be 5 or 6 points, and that the stock can be recovered with a net saving of two or three points. A stop order is of use to out-of-town customers, because sometimes the market moves a good deal before a broker can communicate with his client and get an order to act. Stop orders are often valuable on the short side of the market, because a scare of shorts after considerable decline sometimes brings a very rapid rise, which runs away with all the profits that have accrued.

Customers who give stop orders should, however, understand exactly what they mean. A customer who, being long of Union Pacific at 105, should give an order to stop at 103, would in effect be saying to the broker: "Whenever Union Pacific sells at 103, sell my stock immediately at the best price obtainable."

If the best price obtainable were 102 or even 101, the broker would still be within his rights in executing the order. Hence, in giving stop orders, thought should be taken as to the size of the market in the stock. In Union Pacific, for instance, a stop order ought to be executed within 1/8 or 1/4 percent of the stop order price, except in cases of panic, but a stop order in Lackawanna or Chicago & Eastern Illinois or in some industrial stock would be very dangerous, because no approximate idea could be formed as to what price would have to be accepted.

Stop orders should not be given in any case in stocks of very limited market. In other stocks, their value will be found to depend largely upon the methods employed by the trader himself.

Chapter XI - Cutting Losses Short*

We have spoken in previous articles of methods of trading. Experience proves that every operator should adopt one of two methods: Either cut losses short, or take an investment position. We propose to point out today some of the advantages of cutting losses short.

The buyer of any stock has some reason for his action. He has heard that the stock is going up; he believes that it is selling below its value, he sees that a bull market is under way and believes that this stock will go up as much as any other. These and similar reasons lead to buying.

It is obvious that in all but one of these cases the buyer does not profess to know anything definitely about the stock he buys. He acts on the suggestions or advice of others. Points are good when they are good, and under some conditions can very wisely be followed. There is nothing better in trading than to know that a great operator or a great syndicate intends for good reasons to move the price of a stock from a lower to a higher figure.

But almost everybody learns by sad experience that the "best laid plans of mice and men gang aft agley." Great operators change their minds about the expediency of market movements and most of them have learned that it is one thing to will and another to do in stock speculation.

Hence the trader who takes a point, even from good sources, has only partial assurance of profitable results. His true protection in such a case lies in a stop order. If the price advances, well and good, but if it declines his stop order cuts his loss short, while those who do not stop the loss, but who listen to assurances that the market is all right, often see larger losses in the end.

The general rule is to stop losses within a range of two or three points from the purchase price. All purchases on points, tendencies and rumors should be regarded as guesses and protected by stop orders. Traders, looking over their accounts, seldom lament the losses of $200, which they find scattered through their books as the result of stops, but they deeply lament the $1,500 or the $2,500 losses which reflect over-confidence in a position which proved unsound.

The difficulty with stop orders is that they are frequently exercised when the event shows that the loss need not have been taken. There is no help for this, but the placing of a stop order can be wisely varied by the circumstances of a given case. Suppose, for instance, that the 5-year movement showed a bull market to be in progress; that there has come in this advance a 5-point reaction in a stock like Union Pacific and that a purchase had been made 5 points from the previous highest.

If the price declined 2 points more in such a case, it would probably be wise to exercise the stop order as the fall would suggest a down swing of larger proportions than had been anticipated. It might be such a move as occurred in December, 1899, when stop orders proved exceedingly profitable in bull accounts. If the price subsequently recovered the 2 points, and the stock was repurchased at about the original price, it would probably be wise to put the stop order the next time about 3 points away, under a belief that the stock would not go quite so low as it went before and that the stop order would therefore not be executed.

If this reasoning proved sound, and the price advanced, the stop order could wisely be kept 3 points below the market price until the stock had advanced several points and showed signs of what is called "toppiness." Then it might be well to advance the stop order to 2 points and await developments. The stop order is of primary importance when a purchase is first made and when its wisdom is in doubt. It is also of primary importance in pyramiding; that is, where stock is being bought on an advancing market every point up, because in such a case the stop order is relied upon to prevent the turning of a profit into a loss. It is of importance when a stock has had its normal swing for the purpose of saving most of the profit if a reaction comes, while leaving a chance open for further advance. It is of least importance when a stock has been well bought and is slowly advancing. It should be set further away from the market at such a time than any other so as to avoid being caught on the small setbacks which occur in an advancing period.

By means of a stop order, an operator can trade freely in active stocks of uncertain value, which he would not venture to touch as an investment. By it, he can trade in much larger amounts than he could otherwise undertake to protect. The stop order is the friend of the active speculator, who wants to make a quick dash for a large profit and who is willing to make small losses in the hope of getting a good run once in four or five attempts. It is the friend of the small operator, the out-of-town operator and the timid operator. It should be applied, however, only in active stocks where there is a large market. Stop orders should not be given in inactive stocks, as the seller may be slaughtered in their execution.

A stop order to sell 100 shares of Union Pacific at 75 means that the stock must be sold at the best price obtainable as soon as there has been a transaction at 75. If the best price were 74 or 73, it would still be the duty of the broker to sell. Hence the importance of not giving such orders in stocks where wide differences in quotations may be expected.

Chapter XII - The Danger in Overtrading*

A frequent inquiry is: "Can I trade in stocks on a capital of $100, buying on a scale up and stopping my loss so as to protect my original capital?"

There are a great many people in the U.S. who think about trading in stocks on a capital of $100 or $200. Many of them believe that if a thousand dollars is a proper 10 percent margin for trading in 100 shares, $100 must be a fair margin for trading in 10 shares. We regard this reasoning as sound, but dissent from the conclusion that $1,000 justifies trading in 100 share lots.

The reason is that nobody can hope to buy at the bottom or to sell at the top; or to be right all the time or to avoid losses. Making money in stocks for most people resolves itself into a series of transactions in which we may say there are six profits and four losses, resulting in a net gain. The experience of good traders shows that the operating expenses in trading, that is to say, the ratio of losses to profits, run from 50 to 65 percent of the total profits.

A man who may have made $10,000 gross in trading in a specified time will be very likely to have lost from $5,000 to $6,000 gross in the same time, leaving a net profit of from $4,000 to $5,000. Profits and losses run in streaks. There will be times of all profit and no loss, and times of all loss and no profit. But the average even for those who have learned to trade in stocks and who have abundant capital for their operations works out less than half of the gross profits as net profits.

What chance is there for 10 percent to carry a speculator and especially a beginner through the losses which are almost certain to come before he can accumulate any substantial profit? It is possible to say that if an operator had done this or that, buying at the right time and selling at the right time, 10 percent would have been ample. But, there is a great difference between seeing what might have been done in the past and undertaking to do something for the future.

The man who wishes to trade in stocks and who has only $100 to lose, should, in our opinion, adopt one of two courses. He should buy outright one

---

* Dow Theory

share of some stock below par and below its value and wait until the advance in that stock to its value gives him a profit of 5 or 10 percent as the case may be. This is probably the surest way.

The other way is to buy two or three shares on margin, protecting the account by a stop order at about two points from the purchase price. Brokers generally are not anxious to take such small lots, but if a broker believes that a customer is trading on right lines, and is likely to make money, he will go out of his way considerably to serve that customer under a belief that he will be worth something in the future. Nine brokers out of ten would say that an attempt to trade in stocks on a capital of $100 was absurd. But, it would not be absurd if the trading basis were made two shares, as that would give the trader time in which to recover from his losses as well as some confidence in acting at the proper time and would be a sort of school in which experience could be gained.

We think exactly the same reasoning holds good with regard to trading in 100-share lots on a basis of $1,000. Brokers accept such orders readily enough, but it is nonetheless overtrading, and nonetheless likely to result in the loss of the trader's capital. The man who buys 100 shares on a 10 percent margin and stops his loss at 2 percent has lost nearly one-quarter of his capital. He tries again and perhaps makes 1 percent net. His third venture results in a loss of 3 percent more and in a nearly total loss of confidence, leading him probably to sell short just when he ought to have averaged, thereby completing the sacrifice of his money.

If the same man with a capital of $1,000 had begun with 10 shares he could have stood his loss; he would have had courage to average or to buy something else at a low point and would very likely come out ahead.

Almost any man can show profits in stock by assuming that he would do so and so at various conditions of the market. He succeeds theoretically in this way because there is nothing at risk and his judgment is clear. The moment, however, that he has a risk which is very large in proportion to his capital, he consults his fears instead of his judgment, and does in practice exactly opposite what he would have done had his transactions been purely academic.

The remedy for this is to keep transactions down to a point, as compared with capital, which leaves the judgment clear and affords ample ability to cut loss after loss short; to double up; to take hold of something else, and generally to act easily and fearlessly instead of under the constraint which inevitably comes from a knowledge that the margin of safety is so small as to leave no room for anything except a few anxious gasps before the account is closed.

If people with either large or small capital would look upon trading in stocks as an attempt to get 12 percent per annum on their money instead of 50 percent weekly, they would come out a good deal better in the long run. Everybody knows this in its application to his private business, but the man who is prudent and careful in carrying on a store, a factory or a real estate business seems to think that totally different methods should be employed in dealing in stocks. Nothing is further from the truth.

*Chapter XIII - Methods of Trading**

A correspondent inquires: "How can a man living at a distance from Wall Street hope to follow the market closely enough to make any money trading in stocks?"

This question comes to us in different forms frequently, and shows misapprehensions as to what is involved in successful trading. Many people seem to think that if an operator is in Wall Street, he can tell what the market is going to do. Nothing is further from the fact. The more a man really knows about speculation, the less certain he becomes in regard to any market movement, except as the result of general conditions.

The distinction to be made between trading in the Street and trading from out of town is clear in one point. The operator who watches the ticker or blackboard can turn at very short notice, but the ability to turn quickly often proves a great disadvantage, because it leads to many turns at the wrong time.

The out of town speculator should not attempt to make quick turns, unless by private wire connections he is able to watch the market as a matter of business. The out of town operator should trade on broad lines and from an investment standpoint. He should deal not in stocks that happen to be active, and not on points but almost wholly on well considered convictions as to the probable course of the general market and the relative position of price to value of the special stocks in which he proposes to deal.

The first question to consider is what constitutes a speculative investment. We should say it meant in most cases a railway stock paying regular dividends, publishing earnings gross and net, at regular intervals and giving full particulars of its financial and physical condition as often at least as once a year. If oftener so much the better.

It is possible to derive fairly accurate knowledge of the value of such a stock. It should be considered essentially with reference to its ability to maintain or increase its dividends. If the stock seems likely to continue a current rate of dividend, and the return on the cost is such as to make it fairly satisfactory as an investment, it is a good stock to buy when, in sympathy with decline in the general market, it has fallen below its normal price.

Take, for instance, Union Pacific common. A few months ago this stock was selling between 50 and 60. It was paying 4 percent dividends, and the company was known to be earning over 8 percent. Here was the case of a stock obviously selling below its value. It has since risen more than 30 points. There were other stocks, perhaps not as cheap in point of value, but of which, much that was favorable could be said. Three months ago the values of railway stocks generally were above their prices.

Now, this can be said of very few stocks, and this fact ought to make an outsider slow to buy. The chances are that there will come, as there seems to be coming, declines which will carry prices back to a level where it will again be prudent to buy. Suppose that time to arrive. The wise course for an outsider will be to buy of a good railroad stock, an amount he can easily purchase

---

* Dow Theory

outright, and which he would be willing to hold as an investment in case the price should decline. Should it then decline considerably it would probably be prudent for him to buy more, lowering his average, but only after careful revision of the facts bearing upon the value and upon the general market.

This stock should be held without regard to current fluctuations, until it showed a satisfactory profit. Then it should be sold and the operator should wait weeks or months if necessary for an opportunity to take it or some other stock back upon favorable terms.

The outsider who tries to follow the market from day-to-day, is not likely to have very marked success. The operator who selects investment properties carefully and buys after the market has had general declines, and who exercises a good deal of patience both in waiting for the time to buy and for the time to sell—who, in short, treats his speculation as an investment, will be likely to make money in stocks as a rule.

A correspondent writes: "Is there any way by which an outsider who cannot watch fluctuations of the market hourly can trade in stocks with a fair chance of making money?"

We think there are two methods by either of which an outsider has a fair speculative chance. The first is to buy stocks for investment; that is, to pay for them outright when they are selling below value and wait until they are up to value, getting the difference for a profit.

Value is determined by the margin of safety over dividends, the size and tendency of earnings; the soundness of the balance sheet and of operating methods, and general prospects for the future. This sounds rather complicated, but is not especially difficult to work out.

For instance, a year ago we almost daily pointed out that earnings had greatly increased during the year past; that fixed charges had not increased, hence that the actual value of stocks had advanced while prices had in most cases declined. It was obvious that this could not last; that net earnings must decrease or prices advance. There were then many stocks cheap on their earnings and this was easily a matter of demonstration.

In the same sense it can now (1902) be said that most stocks are dear on their earnings. It is true that earnings have increased somewhat over last year, but prices of many stocks have advanced from 50 to 100 percent and in whatever form the yardstick is applied the result is unfavorable to value as compared with prices in a large number of the active stocks.

When a stock sells at a price which returns only about 3% percent on the investment, it is obviously dear, except there may be some special reason for the established price. In the long run, the prices of stocks adjust themselves to the return on the investment and while this is not a safe guide at all times it is a guide that should never be laid aside or over-looked. The tendency of prices over a considerable length of time will always be toward values. Therefore, the outsider who by studying earning conditions can approach a fairly correct idea of value has a guide for his investments which will, as a whole, be found safe.

Most people, however, when they talk about making money in stocks do not mean the slow road through investments but the short cut by way of speculation. We think here again there is one rule worth all others on this subject. It is a rule which is carried out with greater or less precision by a majority of successful traders. It has been approved by the great masters of speculation and it is indorsed by the practical experience of almost everybody who has dealt at all freely in stocks.

This rule is to cut losses short but let profits run. It sounds very easy to follow, but is in reality difficult to observe. The difficulty arises from the unwillingness of an operator to take a small loss when experience shows him that in many cases such a loss need not have been taken. Furthermore, the practice of this rule suggests that having, for instance, bought a stock and taken a loss, the stock should be bought again, and this may have to be done three or four times before an advance finally comes. These three or four losses prove very burdensome and lead people oftentimes to decide not to cut the loss short and that is generally when a large loss ensues.

The question will of course be asked whether there should be a uniform stop loss, or whether it should vary with varying conditions. Experience indicates that two points is the wisest place to stop a loss. If a stock goes two points against the buyer, it is very liable to go more, and it suggests that the expected move has either been delayed or is not coming.

Suppose, for instance, that an operator believes from information, study of values, experience in markets and the tendency of the period that Union Pacific ought to be bought at 107. If he buys at that price and the stock falls to 105, theoretically he should cut his loss, buying it again when the indications are again favorable.

Extended records of trading show that this policy, blindly followed, with, blind following also of the plan of letting profits run, would give better results than most people are able to obtain by the exercise of judgment. At the same time, judgment can sometimes be wisely employed in cutting a loss.

It is not, for instance, necessary in all cases to take a loss because the price is suddenly jammed down 2 points. If the market shows a tendency to rally, wait a little. If a decline in the stock bought is obviously due to a collapse in some other stock, and that collapse seems to have spent its force, it would be unnecessary to execute the stop. The idea is to stop the loss when the market has legitimately declined to that extent.

In letting profits run there are two ways of determining when to close. One is to wait until the general market shows a decided change of temper. The other is to keep a stop order about 3 points behind the high prices on the advance and close on that stop. Here, again, experience has shown that when a stock starts on a manipulated advance, it is seldom allowed to react as much as 3 points until the move is completed. If it reacts 3 points, it may mean trouble with the deal, although there are cases where such reactions are allowed for the purpose of shaking out following. Here, again, something can be left to judgment.

But the great thing is having bought a stock and having got fairly away from the purchase price, not to be in too great a hurry about selling, provided that the general market is bullish. In a bear market, the whole proceeding ought to be reversed, the operator taking the short side instead of the long, but in other respects applying the same rule.

We do not wish to be understood as saying that there is any sure way of making money in stocks, but the principle of buying after a period of steadiness in prices, stopping losses and letting profits run will, as a matter of statistical record, beat most people's guessing at what is going to occur.

Chapter XIV - The Out of Town Trader[*]

A correspondent asks: "How can a man living at an interior city, where he sees quotations only once or twice a day, make money by trading in stocks?"

This question touches a point which seems to find widespread acceptance, namely, that proximity to Wall Street is a special advantage in trading. It certainly is for some kinds of trading. If a man owns a seat on the Stock Exchange and pays no commissions, he can probably do best by operating for his own account on the floor of the exchange, although not every man with these facilities is able to make his profits exceed his losses.

For practical purposes, it may be said that most traders in or out of Wall Street are handicapped by the commission of $25 for buying and selling 100 shares of stock. There probably are some evasions of the commission rule, but as far as individual operators are concerned commissions are not much evaded.

A commission of $12.50 for buying and as much more for selling 100 shares of stock is insignificant if there are ten or even five points difference between the buying and selling price. But the commission is serious if the difference between the buying and the selling price is only one point. A man who started in to trade for one point profit and pays 1/8 commission would inevitably give all his money to his broker in the course of time.

The ordinary operator must always endeavor to get comparatively large profits. He should not buy unless he feels warranted in believing that the stock which he selects will go up four or five points, so that when he makes he will get double his loss when he loses. In trading for five or ten point turns, the operator at an interior city has one advantage. He does not hear the rumors and see sudden movements in prices which are the bane of the office trader.

Wall Street is often full of people today who have been long of the market for a month, but who have made little or no money, because they have been scared out by rumors and by small relapses. The man who does not see the market escapes this. The greatest advantage resting upon the out of town operator is the fact that sometimes the market will change its character so rapidly as to convert a profit into a loss or establish a loss larger than he intended to take before he knows it. This, however, does not occur as frequently as most people seem to suppose.

It is rather exceptional for the market, having run several points in one direction, to reverse the movement suddenly and without considerable fluctuations near the turning points. Such cases do occur, but they are unusual. After a 5-point rise, a stock usually has a period during which fluctuations are

---

[*] Dow Theory

narrow and which are maintained long enough to give the out-of-town trader plenty of time to get out if he dislikes the appearance of the trading. Stop orders are the special protection of the out-of-town trader, who, if he will stick to stable stocks, can almost always cut his loss or save his profit at any spot where he deems wise.

The out-of-town trader wants to begin his campaign with a conviction that the stock which he buys is selling below its value. This should not only be a conviction, but a demonstrated conviction, which cannot be shaken if, at the outset, the price declines instead of advances. Having determined on his stock from the viewpoint of value, he should, if possible, wait about buying until the general market has had its normal setback from a high point.

If twenty active stocks have advanced 10 points, a normal setback would be four points, and then, in an extended period of rising prices, would be the time to make the initial purchase. The operator should then take in a great stock of patience. He will see other stocks go up and his stock stand still. He will see and hear daily that something else is making riches for traders, but he must shut his ears to these statements, even if they are right as far as fluctuations go. He must just sit on his stock, which is intrinsically below its value, until the other people observe that it is selling too low and begin to buy or manipulate it.

The tendency with most people holding a stock which does not move for a time is to sell the stock about as soon as it begins to move, through fear that it will again become dull. This is just the time not to sell, but, if anything, to buy more on the idea that other people have discovered that the price is below value. After the price has moved up two or three points, it is well to put in a stop order perhaps two points back from the top and follow the rise in the stock with the stop order disregarding current reports and waiting until the price is either up to the value or until market conditions make taking a profit judicious, provided always that a sudden setback does not close out the transaction.

An out-of-town operator can do all this just as well as an office trader and in some respects better. Some of the large operators like to go away from the market and work from Newport or Saratoga or other distant points in order to look at the trading with an unbiased mind and without being unsettled by the rumors that always grow out of any special move. The outsider who will wisely study values and market conditions and then exercise patience enough for six men will be likely to make money in stocks.

Chapter XV - The Short Side of the Market[*]

A correspondent writes: "You demonstrate that an operator in stocks ought to work on the short side of the market during about half of almost every decade. I feel some hesitation about selling property which I do not own. Will you not make it clear how the short side of the market is normal trading?"

---

[*] Dow Theory

It is quite true that in each of the past four decades it would have been wise to have worked on the short side at least half of the time. It is also true that the public as a whole does not like short selling. It is true that corners occur at long intervals and are destructive to those caught therein. But they occur so seldom as to make them a very remote danger. There is about one in ten years.

We have explained the principle of short selling many times, but will state the process once more. A customer X directs Broker A to sell short 100 shares of Union Pacific at par. Broker B buys it. A, not having the stock goes to Broker C, and borrows from him 100 shares of Union Pacific, giving as security $10,000 in cash. This stock is then delivered by A to B, who pays A $10,000 therefore. Matters then rest until Union Pacific advances or declines enough to make X wish to close his account, He then directs A to buy Union Pacific, say at 95, and A gets the stock from Broker D; The stock thus obtained is delivered to C, who thereupon returns the money which he has had as security and $9,500 of the amount goes to D, leaving $500, less expenses, as the profit of X on the transaction.

While X is waiting to see what the market is going to do C has the use of A's $10,000, and under ordinary conditions, pays interest on this money. This interest is called the loaning rate on stocks and is usually a little below the current rate for loans on collateral.

The lower these rates are, compared with the rate for money, the more demand there is to borrow that particular stock, and the loaning rate is the point to be watched by those who may be short, to see whether the short interest is large or small.

In case the demand to borrow a certain stock is very large, the loaning rate will be quoted flat, which means in the case cited that C would get the use of A's $10,000 without paying any interest. If the demand for the stock should be still greater, A might have not only to give C the $10,000 without interest, but pay C a small premium in addition. When the loaning rate of a stock is quoted at 1-32 it means that C gets his $10,000 from A, without interest, and in addition a premium of $3.12 a day for each 100 shares, which has to be paid by X, who must also pay all dividends that may be declared on the stock.

In ordinary lines of business, selling short with the idea of borrowing for delivery would be impossible. In the stock market it is impracticable to sell distributed bonds or investment stocks short because such securities are held by investors, and are not carried in quantity by brokers, hence, could not be readily borrowed. But, in active stocks, there is no difficulty whatever in borrowing.

The reason is this: Every broker who carries many stocks employs a great deal more money than he possesses. In theory, a broker carrying for a customer 100 shares of Union Pacific at par would make up the money for the purchase by using $1,000 belonging to the customer, $1,000 of the money of the brokerage firm, and then borrow $8,000 from a bank on the security of the 100 shares of stock purchased.

An active broker, consequently, is always a large borrower of money, and when he borrows from a bank he is expected to put up 20 percent margin on his loan. But if he can lend stocks he gets the full value of the stock and does not have to put up any of his own money or of his customer's money. Hence, every broker is willing to lend stocks, particularly when the demand for stock is sufficient to make the rate of interest lower than the market rate, as the broker in this case makes a profit by charging his customer who is long 5 or 6 percent interest, while he perhaps secures his money without any cost through lending the stock flat.

This, from the standpoint of the short seller, is what makes his operation practically safe. Ordinarily, it is just as easy to borrow active stocks as it is to borrow money, and squeezes of shorts through inability to borrow are little if any more frequent than squeezes of "longs" through the difficulty of brokers in borrowing money.

Squeezes of shorts sometimes develop themselves and are sometimes manipulated. When friends of a property see a large short interest they sometimes try to persuade holders of the stock to agree not to lend it for a day or two and thus scare shorts to cover by difficulty in borrowing. If this under-taking is successful brokers are notified to return borrowed stock, and when they try to borrow elsewhere they find little offering. The loaning rate possibly runs up to 14 percent a day, or perhaps higher.

Shorts are alarmed and cover, advancing the price of the stock and enabling holders to sell at a profit. Such a squeeze usually lasts only two or three days, as by that time the advanced price leads those who have the stock to either sell it or lend it, and the price then usually goes lower than before. Sometimes there is a short interest so large and so persistent as to keep a stock lending at a premium for some time. This is usually almost certain evidence of decline, but the expenses of premiums and the necessity of paying dividends sometimes eat up the profits so that but little remains even after considerable fall in price. Mr. Gould is said to have once remained short of New York Central over four years, and to have had a large profit as between his buying and his selling price, but to have had the greater part of it eaten up in dividends.

In picking out a stock to sell short, the first consideration ought to be that the price is above value, and that future value appears to be shrinking. It should be an active stock and, if possible, a stock of large capital. It should be an old stock by preference, which means having wide distribution instead of concentrated ownership. By preference it should be a high priced stock with a reasonable probability that dividends will be reduced or passed. Such a stock should be sold on advances and bought in on moderate declines, say 4 or 5 points, as long as the market seems to be reasonably steady. But, if the market becomes distinctly weak, only part of the short stock should be bought in with the hope that some short interest may be established at a price so high as to be out of reach of temporary swings. The best profits in the stock market are made by people who get long or short at extremes and stay for months or years before they take their profit.

*Chapter XVI - Speculation for the Decline**

The question is frequently asked whether in taking a bearish view of the general market it is expected that all stocks will go down together or that some will fall and others not.

The answer to this question takes two forms—the first is the speculative movement; the second the effect of values. When the market goes down, especially if the decline is violent or continued, all stocks fall; not perhaps equally, but enough to be regarded as participating fully in a general decline. Indeed, it often happens that a stock of admitted large value will fall more in a panic than a stock of little value.

The reason is that when people have been carrying various stocks, some good and some bad, and a time comes when they are obliged to suddenly furnish additional margin or reduce their commitments, they try to sell the stocks for which they think the market will be best, namely, their best stocks. But the very merit of such stocks prevents the existence of a short interest, hence when considerable amounts are offered in a panic there is no demand for covering purposes, and, in fact, no demand except from investors who may not know of the decline or who may not have money for investment at that particular moment. Consequently the good stock drops until it meets an investment demand somewhere. This condition was illustrated by the action of Delaware & Hudson in the panic of May 9, 1901. It had nearly, if not quite, the largest decline of any stock on the list, falling in half an hour from 160 to 105, chiefly because people generally did not know the price at which stock was being offered.

It may be accepted, therefore, that in a general decline merit in a stock will not count for the time being. Good and bad will decline measurably alike. But here comes in a marked distinction. When the recovery comes, a day or a week later, the good stock will recover more and hold its recovery better than the poor stock. Delaware & Hudson is again a good illustration. After the quotation of 105 was printed on May 9 orders to buy the stock came from all sections, and in another hour the price was in the neighborhood of 150.

Value will always work out in the course of time. A stock intrinsically cheap and a stock intrinsically dear may be selling at the same price at a given time. As the result of six months' trading they may have presented the appearance of moving together in most of the fluctuations, but at the end of the period the good stock will be 10 points higher than the poor one, the difference representing a little smaller decline and a little better rally in each of five or six swings.

This exactly describes what will occur all through the market during the next bear period, whenever that period comes. There will be a sifting of the better from the worse, visible enough at a distance, but not conspicuous at any particular stage in the process. Where there is a great change in the value of a stock it will advance in a bear period. The market as a whole declined from

---

* Dow Theory

1881 to 1885, but in that period Manhattan, while participating in most of the market swings, went from the neighborhood of 30 to the neighborhood of par because the increased earnings of the company increased value steadily and largely during that time.

The practical lesson is that a stock operator should not deal in stocks unless he thinks he knows their value, nor unless he can watch conditions so as to recognize changes in value as they come along. He should then have at least a conviction as to what stocks are above their value and what are below their value at a given time. If the main tendency of the market is downward, he should sell stocks which he believes to be above their value when they are very strong, taking them in on the next general decline. In buying for a rally, he should invariably take the stocks that are below their value, selling them also when a moderate profit is shown.

When the market appears in a doubtful position it is sometimes wise to sell short a stock that is conspicuously above its value and buy a stock which is conspicuously below its value, believing that one will protect the other until the position of the general market becomes clear. It was formerly very popular for traders to be long of Northwest and short of St. Paul, usually with good results.

During the past year (1901-2) there have been operators who have aimed to be long of Manhattan and short of either Metropolitan or Brooklyn on the same line of reason. The general method of operating such an account is to trade for the difference; that is, supposing a transaction to have been started with the two stocks 10 points apart—the account is closed when they are, say, 15 points apart, assuring 5 points net profit. It is all, however, a part of the same general law. Stocks fluctuate together, but prices are controlled by values in the long run.

Chapter XVII - Concerning Discretionary Accounts *

A correspondent writes: "I enclose herewith a circular in which the sender asks me to give him a discretionary account promising large returns and claiming great success in past operations. A man in the market ought to be able to do better for me than I could do for myself at a distance. Is this party reliable, and do you consider his scheme safe?"

We get this letter in some form very often and have answered it many times, but it is difficult to make people see the truth. Outsiders want to make money and they believe that people in Wall Street know what the market is going to do, hence that the only question involved in discretionary accounts is the honesty of the men who run them.

The fact is that people in Wall Street, even those who get very near the center of large operations, do not know what the market is going to do with any regularity or certainty. The more they actually know, the less confident they become, and the large operators who try to make markets are, in most

---

* Dow Theory

cases, the least confident of anybody because they know so well the variety and extent of the difficulties which may be encountered.

People who trade in stocks can set down as a fundamental proposition the fact that any man who claims to know what the market is going to do any more than to say that he thinks this or that will occur as a result of certain specified conditions is unworthy of trust as a broker. Any man who claims that he can take discretionary accounts and habitually make money for his customers, is a fraud; first, because he knows when he makes such statements that he cannot do it regularly or with certainty, and, second, because if he could, he would surely trade for himself and would scorn working for 1/8 commission when he could just as well have the whole amount made.

The governors of the Stock Exchange will not permit a member of that body to advertise that he will take discretionary accounts, and any Stock Exchange member who stated that he was endeavoring to build up a business by discretionary trading for customers would lose caste with his fellow-members. It would be considered that he was either lacking in honesty or in judgment.

We do not say that Stock Exchange houses never take a discretionary account. They sometimes do, but they take them unwillingly in very limited amounts, only for people with whom they have very confidential relations and who understand speculation sufficiently to expect losses and failures quite as frequently as profits. It is safe to say that Stock Exchange houses regard the acceptance of a discretionary account as a rather serious demand upon personal friendship, and this not because they do not wish to see their friends make money, but because they know too well that a discretionary account - of ten means the loss of both money and friends. When, therefore, men of little or no capital and little or no reputation advertise boldly in the Sunday papers that they desire discretionary accounts from strangers and will, for a commission of 1/8 percent, guarantee profits ranging from 25 to 250 percent per annum, commission houses have but one word with which to describe the proposition and people of practical experience in Wall Street are amazed at the credulity of those who send their money to be placed in such accounts and who subsequently appear in the company of those who wail in the outer rooms of closed offices over the rascality which has robbed them of their hard earnings.

The head of a discretionary concern which was very prominent a year or two ago frequently said that if the U.S. Government would let his mails alone and deliver to him the money forwarded by his dupes he would ask no better occupation and no quicker road to wealth. Evidence presented in court has shown repeatedly that swindlers who have advertised to make money for the public in speculation have received thousands of letters containing money; that none of this money was ever invested in stocks; that the advertisers were not members of any exchange and did not even pretend to have any business other than receiving and keeping the bulk of the money entrusted to their care. A small amount of the money received was usually returned to senders as profits on alleged transactions.

This is substantially, we believe, the general practice. If a man sends $100 to one of the concerns, he is notified, after a little time, that he has made $10 and, a little later, that his share of a pool profit is $15. At this point he is usually advised to send $100 more on account of some extraordinary opportunity which has just arisen. If this money is sent, he is told that profits have accrued and still more money is called for. Persons who call for some of their profits are occasionally given money in order that the receiver may induce others to join the list of future victims.

The end, however, is almost, if not quite invariably, a communication stating that by some adverse and utterly unexpected fatality operations have been unsuccessful and the money invested has been lost. It is usually thought wise to make the victims appear somewhat in debt in order to induce them by not having to pay the alleged debt to accept as a mysterious dispensation of Providence the loss of their capital and previous alleged profits.

Speculation is not at its best a simple and easy road to wealth, but speculation through people who advertise guaranteed profits and who call for participation in blind pools is as certain a method of loss as could possibly be discovered. The mere fact that a man openly asks for such accounts is the most ample and exhaustive reason possible for declining to give them.

Chapter XVIII - The Liability for Loss *

Of a number of inquiries lately the following is a sample: "I was long of stocks May 9, 1901, and was sold out. The broker now asks me to pay a loss in excess of my margin. Am I liable therefore?"

This question has never been definitely settled as a matter of law. There have been a good many decisions in cases of this kind but they have generally been sufficiently dissimilar to make each decision rest upon that particular case, and not as establishing a principle of law, bearing thereon. The courts have shown a disposition to rule that in such cases trade customs must be considered and that such customs while not making the law, affect the bearing of the law thereon.

Cases of this kind generally fall under one of two general divisions. Either the broker notifies his customer that his margin is nearly exhausted, or he does not. It is probably good law to assume that where a stock is bought on margin and, on a fall in the price, the broker calls on the customer for more margin and there is no response within a reasonable time, the broker is justified in selling the stock without a positive order to do so from the customer. The courts have held in such cases that the broker gave ample notice and the customer should have responded in time to protect his interests. The broker could not be expected to wait more than a reasonable time. In cases of this class it sometimes happens that the customer does not think it wise to put up more margin and orders the stock sold. It may be sold at a loss on account of a rapid decline in prices. In this case, there seems to be little doubt of the liability of the customer, because the broker is executing an order to sell for the account and risk of that customer. Here, however, might enter special questions as to whether the broker was or was not negligent in notifying the

---

* Dow Theory

135

customer that margin was needed, or in the execution of the order when it was received, or in some other respect, whereby the interest of the customer was allowed to suffer.

The other general class of cases is where margin on accounts is swept away by a sudden decline and the broker faces the question whether it is better to sell his customer's stock without an order or to endeavor to carry the customer through the decline with the expectation that the loss, if there is a loss, will be made good by the customer. The tendency of decisions in these cases is toward holding the broker to rather close accountability for his actions. The point has been made that the broker in such a case is acting in a double capacity. First, as a broker executing an order for a customer for a commission. Second, as a banker in making a loan to this customer, being protected therein by the security of money deposited and the possession of the stock purchased. As a broker, the equity might be one way, while as a banker it might be exactly opposite. Generally speaking, a banker has no right to sell out a loan without notifying the borrower, except where there has been a special agreement permitting such action. This fact leads banks and institutions in nearly all cases to make loans with a formal agreement authorizing them to sell the collateral at their option in case the loan ceases to be satisfactory. As a matter of practice, banks call for more collateral when prices decline. But in cases of panic, or the inability of brokers to furnish more collateral, loans are frequently sold out, under the special agreement to that effect.

Some commission houses protect themselves by a formal agreement with customers similar to that required by banks. When a customer opens an account, he signs an agreement authorizing the broker to sell the stock bought at his discretion in case the margin runs down to the danger line.

This is undoubtedly a wise method, as it removes all doubt as to the position of each party in the premises. Such agreements are not invariably made because in the competition for business brokers do not like to impose restrictions which are not universal and which may have a tendency to drive away custom. Nevertheless, experiences like those of the 9th of May have a decided tendency toward defining the relations between broker and customer.

The action of the market May 9 was so rapid as to make it impossible for a broker to notify a customer of the need of more margin and get a response in time to be of any use. A 10-point margin was of no use at a time when stocks were falling 10 points in five minutes. There were many cases that day in which wealthy commission houses saw a large percentage of their capital disappear in customers' accounts between 11 and 11.30. The rapidity of the recovery was all that saved multitudes of customers and many commission houses. Loans, small and large, were unsound and sound again before lenders had time to sell even if they had been disposed to do so.

There were, however, many cases where stocks were sold entailing large losses and the location of these losses is in a number of cases still in legal controversy, with the probability that the decision will turn more or less upon the circumstances peculiar to each case. The 9th of May was a very extraordinary day and allowance must be made for its unusual character. Stock Exchange rules based on the occurrences of the 9th of May would prohibit doing business under ordinary conditions, but such days come and on this account brokers and customers should make provision for the unexpected by a clear understanding as to what shall be done in emergencies.

It is often difficult to say what shall be done when a loss has occurred through unusual conditions and under circumstances which made the action taken largely discretionary. This fact in its application to the May panic has led brokers and customers in cases to adopt a policy of trying to divide the loss equitably and with due reference to the facts involved in that particular case. A jury familiar with Stock Exchange business would be very likely to render a decision along somewhat similar lines.

Chapter XIX - The Recurrence of Crisis *

A correspondent writes: "Is it true that commercial or stock exchange panics are approximately periodic in their occurrence?"

The facts point distinctly in that direction, and there is reason back of the facts. The reason is that the business community has a tendency to go from one extreme to the other. As a whole, it is either contracting business under a belief that prices will be lower or expanding under a belief that prices will be higher. It appears to take ordinarily five or six years for public confidence to go from the point of too little hope to the point of too much confidence and then five or six years more to get back to the condition of hopelessness.

This ten-year movement in England is given in detail by Professor Jevons in his attempt to show that sun spots have some bearing upon commercial affairs. Without going into the matter of sun spots and their bearing upon crops, commerce, or states of minds, it may be assumed that Professor Jevons has stated correctly the periods of depression as they have occurred in England during the last two centuries.

The dates given by him as the years in which commercial crises have occurred follow: 1701, 1711, 1712, 1731-2, 1742, 1752, 1763, 1772-3, 1783, 1793, 1804-5, 1815, 1825, 1836, 1847, 1857, 1866 and 1878.

This makes a very good showing for the ten-year theory, and it is supported to a considerable extent by what has occurred in this country during the past century.

The first crisis in the United States during the nineteenth century came in 1814, and was precipitated by the capture of Washington by the British on the 24th of August in that year. The Philadelphia and New York yanks suspended payments, and for a time the crisis was acute. The difficulties leading up to this period were the great falling off in foreign trade caused by the embargo and non-intercourse acts of 1808, the excess of public expenditures over public receipts, and the creation of a large number of state banks taking the place of the old United States bank. Many of these state banks lacked capital and issued currency without sufficient security. There was a near approach to a crisis in

---

* Dow Theory

1819 as the result of a tremendous contraction of bank circulation. The previous increases of bank issues had promoted speculation, the contraction caused a serious fall in the prices of commodities and real estate. This, however, was purely a money panic as far as its causes were concerned.

The European crisis in 1825 caused a diminished demand for American products and led to lower prices and some money stringency in 1826. The situation, however, did not become very serious and was more in the nature of an interruption to progress than a reversal of conditions.

The year 1837 brought a great commercial panic, for which there was abundant cause. There had been rapid industrial and commercial growth, with a multitude of enterprises established ahead of the time. Crops were deficient, and breadstuffs were imported. The refusal of the government to extend the charter of the United States Bank had caused a radical change in the banking business of the country, while the withdrawal of public deposits and their lodgment with state banks had given the foundation for abnormal speculation.

The panic in Europe in 1847 exerted but little influence in this country, although there was a serious loss in specie, and the Mexican war had some effect in checking enterprises. These effects, however, were neutralized somewhat by large exports of breadstuffs and later by the discovery of gold in 1848-9.

There was a panic of the first magnitude in 1857, following the failure of the Ohio Life Insurance & Trust Company in August. This panic came unexpectedly, although prices had been falling for some months. There had been very large railroad building, and the proportion of specie held by banks was very small in proportion to their loans and deposits. One of the features of this period was the great number of failures. The banks generally suspended payments in October.

The London panic in 1866 precipitated by the failure of Overend, Guerney & Co., was followed by heavy fall in prices in the Stock Exchange here. In April there had been a corner in Michigan Southern and rampant speculation generally, from which the relapse was rather more than normal.

The panic of September, 1873, was a commercial as well as a Stock Exchange panic. It was the outcome of an enormous conversion of floating into fixed capital. Business had been expanded on an enormous scale, and the supply of money became insufficient for the demands made upon it. Credit collapsed and the depression was extremely serious.

The year 1884 brought a Stock Exchange smash but not a commercial crisis. The failure of the Marine Bank, Metropolitan Bank and Grant & Ward in May was accompanied by a large fall in prices and a general check which was felt throughout the year. The Trunk Line war, which had lasted for several years, was one of the factors in this period.

The panic of 1893 was the outcome of a number of causes—uncertainty in regard to the currency situation, the withdrawal of foreign investments and the fear of radical tariff legislation. The anxiety in regard to the maintenance of the gold standard was undoubtedly the chief factor, as it bore upon many others.

Judging by the past and by the developments of the last six years, it is not unreasonable to suppose that we may get at least a stock exchange flurry in the next few years. This decade seems to be the one for the small crisis instead of the large one—a type of 1884 rather than a recurrence of 1837, 1873 or 1893.

Chapter XX - Financial Criticism

The stock market and its relation to newspapers is a much misunderstood subject. With the great increase in speculation and public interest, the news-papers have responded to a demand which, all things considered, is filled most creditably. It is only a few years ago that opening, high, and low quotations were considered sufficient to satisfy those interested in the stock market and for forty years there had been no improvement. This primitive method was superseded by a careful compilation of the day's trading, printed in tabulated form and including every sale made or transacted from the ticker, reproduced in an afternoon paper and sold on the street for a penny twenty minutes after the closing of the Stock Exchange. This remarkable development in the way of newspaper enterprise was made possible by the present owner of *The Sun* and *The Evening Sun* of New York, who was quick to realize the value to the public of such a service at the astonishing cost of the country's smallest coin. And so accurate has that service been that it has been accepted in courts of law as official in lieu of any better or as good service from the Stock Exchange itself.

Each newspaper supports a staff in Wall Street and the Street itself is represented by two reputable news bureaus a number of daily financial newspapers and several weeklies.

Stock market criticism is dependent largely upon the individual point of view of the writer and the policy of the newspaper itself. An afternoon news-paper market review may be an academic study of the money market, with the Stock Exchange subordinated to its relative position in the perspective, or it may be a simple review of the influential news factors that caused market fluctuations, and explanations reduced to common sense. Or it may pursue a middle course, indulging in economic speculations and at the same time not losing sight of the important fact that the reader wishes to know why particular stocks advanced or declined. A writer may be ultra-conservative and pessi-mistic as distinguished from the majority who are given to prophecy and inclined to optimism. And again he may be honest or corrupt, moral conditions that are governed by the individual and his environment.

The reliable critic usually endeavors to avoid the field of prophecy. It is almost invariably the fact that in reviewing the factors governing the situation he will endeavor to make bullish deductions; that is to say, he is prejudiced in favor of advancing security prices and the prosperity of those who own them. This is a natural position and one which meets with the approval of the reader. He is from necessity committed to the constructive side.

There are times, though, when his judgment enables him to detect the approaching financial storm and sound a note of warning. There are writers who see so many dangers in stock speculation and in the tendency to human excesses that scarcely a day passes that they do not justifiably condemn the market in one phase or another. And there are others, corrupted by their own speculations or the gratuities of stock manipulators, who pen grossly inaccurate and deceptive articles for pecuniary gain.

A market review is entitled to consideration to the extent that it is reasonable and accurate. If it is unreasonable, inaccurate and perhaps too radical in departing from established rules and customs it should be ignored. Per contra the opposite qualities should make it worthy of consideration.

Corrupt and inspired articles are readily detected. Should the alleged facts not be verified; should the prophet prove to be a false prophet; should the hand of the press agent be in plain view, know then that you are following an unreliable and dishonest guide.

The usual method employed in corrupting the financial critic is for a stock manipulator to offer the disseminator of news, views and tips, a "Call" on a specified number of shares. Should a pool have a deal in view intending to advance a particular stock it will endeavor to obtain the support of those newspaper writers who will lend their columns and their newspapers to the legitimate or illegitimate movement, as the case may be, for a speculative opportunity to participate in a small way in the profits.

The representative of the pool proceeds in one of two ways. He will send (1) for the individual writer and offer him a "Call" on the stock under manipulation at a price. This price is usually above the market. In return the writer agrees to "boom" or "apply the hot air method" as it is required; or in simpler terms print misleading statements to facilitate the sale of stocks to its readers. A "Call" in such a proposition would mean that the writer received the privilege of calling upon the manipulator for a specified number of shares of stock at a certain price. If the stock declined the privilege would have no monetary value. If the stock advanced the writer could sell the stock against the "Call" and receive the difference between the price written on the "Call" and the price at which the stock was sold or the transaction would be closed in the manner most acceptable to the man who had paid the bribe.

Or (2) the manipulator may send for one newspaper writer who in turn represents a combination of writers and give the newspaper man complete charge of the transaction and the power to distribute the "Calls" as in his judgment he considers that the best results can be obtained. Some of these "Calls" are very profitable and others quite worthless. They may be repudiated at any time and their holders have no redress or claim. Their owners are powerless to antagonize the interest which deceived them, for publicity means exposure, and exposure ruin.

It must be conceded, however, that where this form of corruption exists it is readily detected and that all things considered the newspaper protects the public better than the public are at times willing to acknowledge. The majority of the Wall Street financial writers are honest men and will freely sacrifice the "main chance" in order to state the facts.

Stock market critics endeavor to find a reason or explanation for the day's fluctuations. The price movement may be uniform—up or down—or it may be irregular, one stock or group of stocks advancing, others declining and others remaining dull and passive. He must search the field for the primary cause. At times this cause may be plain to everyone, again it may be concealed from the outsider's view and yet again the superficial factors may be written down as the cause when the true facts are completely hidden. The speculator can form his own conclusions regarding the merits of each critic by a study of the latter's work.

The criticism has been frequently made by speculators that nine out of ten newspapers are bullish at all times and through all markets. This is true, and the following story will partially explain why: The editor of a financial journal was a bear on the market. He believed in lower prices. He was committed to short contracts in the market and from day to day he gave his readers the benefit of his convictions, honestly and with enthusiasm. The market declined. Day by day, however, he lost subscribers, until finally the losses became too serious to be ignored. An important commission house among others notified him to discontinue its subscription of three copies. He first sent his business manager to the house in question for an explanation. A member of the firm said: "Your paper is bearish on the market. All our customers are hulls. Your paper is on file in our offices and our customers find a great deal of fault with it. It makes some of them very angry."

"But we have been right on the market?" "I can't help that; we can no longer ignore the complaints, for they are too numerous."

"If you continue to run a bear paper," reported the business manager to his editor, "you will ruin yourself."

The conclusion appears to be that the public will buy a newspaper that is bullish and wrong in its judgment, and desert a paper that is bearish and correct in its judgment.

The value of a newspaper writer's market views may depend to some extent on whether he is a speculator or an onlooker. Most newspaper writers speculate, although a minority do not. Undoubtedly the one who does not speculate is in a better position to advise than one who is prejudiced in favor of his own ventures just as the advice of the non-speculating broker is to be preferred to that of the speculator.

The field of prophecy is invaded to a greater or less extent by all financial critics. The more experienced the writer the less positive he will be in making predictions regarding price movements. It will also be observed by the speculator that the newspaper critic will carefully state two sides of a proposition and leave the reader in complete and illuminating possession of the fact that if "the market (or a special stock) does not go up it will go down." This is the easiest way out of a complicated situation and the reader can hardly dispute the accuracy of the conclusion.

Wall Street is served by two news bureaus with great energy. They print and distribute daily a mass of facts, figures, comment, prophecy and rumor. There are traders who find the compilation at times so confusing and contradictory that they ignore everything except definite newt-statements. Nevertheless, Wall Street would find it exceedingly difficult to get along without its news service, and it is a fact that each bureau strives with energy and intelligence to be accurate. At the conclusion of each day each bureau has a method of so analyzing the day's work that misstatements are accounted for by the reporters responsible.

The speculating student of the news bureau service should learn to differentiate between the varying statements. It is the desire of the bureau to print all rumor and gossip that it can gather and the relative values as market factors are very wide apart. For example, a statement made by the president of a bank of acknowledged authority is entitled to more consideration than an interview with "a leading banker." Then again a review of business conditions by a railroad officer under his name is more to be relied upon than the prophecies of a speculator along the same line. And to judge of the value of a statement regarding the copper, iron, or any other industry one must know something about the man, his reputation and his associates. Crop reports and opinions are notoriously misleading. Financial statements and statistical tables must be accepted with conservatism. The tendency is always to exaggeration rather than the opposite direction. The news bureaus do their work well and in this respect Wall Street ranks ahead of Lombard Street. If the speculator is to derive value from their service he must learn to classify the various items in the same spirit in which they are printed.

The genesis of a Wall Street rumor is a curious thing in itself. It is the function of the news bureau and the newspaper to print rumors whenever they appear to have foundation in fact. A rumor should always be verified before it is spread broadcast, but this sound rule of the newspaper is as often ignored as it is followed. Rumors are thickest regarding coming events which, according to the old adage, cast their shadows before.

For the purpose of illustration we will say that the Alphabet Mining Company is to have a dividend meeting on the 15th of the month. A change is to be made in the dividend as the company is doing a poor business. The rate of dividend had been 6 percent per annum. It is reasonable to say that between the 10th and the 15th following will be some of the rumors:

(1) The dividend will be passed.

(2) The dividend will be reduced to 4 percent.

(3) A director says that the present dividend will be maintained as the situation is not as bad as represented.

(4) The dividend will be reduced to 5 percent.

(5) The directors will postpone their meeting.

And so on others suggest themselves as even more commonplace. Or it may be a railroad meeting when it is intended to advance the rate of dividend and the company has been subjected to rumors of change of control. Prior to such a meeting the rumor maker is a very busy man.

Again, in times of panic, the writer has found it difficult to walk a few blocks in the Wall Street district without being stopped and "confidentially" informed that such-and-such a house is "in trouble." It is then that great mischief and injury can be accomplished by the newspaper writer, who must use tact and discretion in "killing" such rumors as they arise, for they are rarely based on facts. When failures occur, they are frequently unheralded and rarely preceded by rumors.

When private wires between New York, Boston and Chicago become commonplace the two latter cities become responsible for many Wall Street rumors. Chicago in particular seemed to keep a stereotyped line which read: "It is reported that ———— is dead." The blank space was filled in with the name of the President of the United States or that of any other person who would attract speedy attention. Boston's fancy ran to the creation of beautiful stories of mining, industrial and railroad deals. At times they have been worthy of an Indiana novelist for power of imagination and gift of expression.

The newspaper writer acquires the knack of almost knowing offhand the truth or falsity of a rumor. If it originates with a man who prefaces his statement with "I hear," "They say," "It is said," "A man I don't know says," or any other source of information equally unreliable, it is well to disbelieve the rumor. If a definite authority is named for the rumor, and it is not received at second or third hand, then you may have something worthy of investigation. A rumor is known by its father. A speculator should study the relative values of rumors and learn to take advantage of their market effects, always remembering that 90 percent of them are not true, but that fiction as well, as fact prevails in price making.

In conclusion, it can be said that the financial writer does not expect his reader to accept his views as final. It is not the function of the financial writer to win or lose money in speculation for the reader as so many small speculators believe. It is rather his duty to discuss as they arise those factors which govern the financial and economic situation, giving to each its proper place, and considering each with common sense, even temper and mature judgment.

The speculator will do well to remember that the financial writer has his own theories and prejudices; good, bad or indifferent judgment, and is only the doctor in so far as he endeavors to diagnose the case. He differs from the doctor in that he does not prescribe for the patient. Should he prescribe and become a prophet of prices, he is then like the doctor and also the lawyer in that he is not responsible for mistakes of judgment. The speculator pays the bill.

A writer in the *Wall Street Journal* discusses this question as follows:

A correspondent asks: "I notice that practically all the financial articles in the daily newspapers and most of the discussions of financial matters in other financial papers are always bullish in character. Why is this? I have been reading financial articles for many years, and, with very few exceptions, this has always been so. Can you explain it?"

In order to understand what is involved in the answer to the above query, it is necessary to have a clear idea of what a "bull" is. A bull is a man who has something to sell and is desirous of selling it at a good price. Consequently he is anxious for prices to go up in order that he may sell. A bear, on the contrary, is a man who wishes to buy at a low price.

Now, the end and object of all Wall Street finance is just one thing, namely, the gathering up of public money in exchange for securities distributed to the public. A Wall Street banker in active business is engaged in a process that may be called the manufacture and sale of securities. Much the largest part of his work consists in turning securities into cash, either for his own account or for the account of other bankers, in return for a commission. There are times when the financial community needs the public's money less than at other times, but, taking it all in all, anything that tends to whet the public's appetite for securities so that it is in a mood to exchange its cash for securities is satisfactory to what are commonly called the large financial interests.

Consequently these large financial interests are always, or almost, always, concerned in keeping the public in proper disposition toward the security market. They are always anxious to prevent the public from becoming alarmed, and they are usually willing to assist in stimulating the public's speculative desires. This is probably one reason why the published articles in the daily papers are so generally optimistic in character alike through good and bad times. It has become a maxim in Wall Street that the public, or, rather, Wall Street, will endure any amount of inaccuracy, and even misrepresent-ation, as long as its effect is bullish at least for the time being.

The public does not realize, and probably never will realize, that it is the court of last resort in all important financial operations. It is its custom to regard itself as helpless, at the mercy of shrewd financiers and unscrupulous speculators. If it could only once get it into its head that it holds the key to the situation in its own hands and that without its money the large financial interests could of themselves do little or nothing, and if, in addition to this, it would take a little pains to inform itself as to actual facts, figures and values, very much less money would be lost in Wall Street and a great many enterprises would never be undertaken. Stocks and bonds are never sold until they are sold to the public. Manipulators may move prices up and down on the Exchange and may make fictitious transactions to an enormous extent, but unless the public comes with its money and buys the securities, the work is unavailing.

Of course, it is not fair to suggest that the generally bullish character of financial comment at all times is the result of prearranged plans in behalf of the large financial interests as against the public. The hopeful and even the optimistic side of things is necessarily the more popular of the two sides. Moreover, as a rule, the conditions that make for higher prices of securities are conditions favorable to the business world and to the public. Consequently it is pleasanter to look at the cheerful side of things than at the other side. Nevertheless, it is perhaps true to say that, on the whole, there is somewhat too much of this kind of thing and too little of its opposite. Only too often it has happened that the public has been pretty generally encouraged up to the last minute, and when trouble has come and the public's money has been lost, the only consolation that it gets is usually in the form of a mild scolding for not having foreseen the trouble before it came.

A healthy skepticism is seldom out of place in Wall Street, so far as speculation is concerned. Money is very seldom lost thereby. People who have had experience covering one or two panics know very well that the first lesson that has to be learned by the successful speculator is the avoidance of the disaster always caused by a panic. The very essence of a panic is that it sweeps away every one who is overtrading—whether it be to a large or to a small extent. Of what use is it to pile up imposing paper profits if they are all to be swept away when the tidal wave strikes? The only way whereby people can avoid being caught in a panic is by the exercise at all times of great conservatism and considerable skepticism. The successful speculator must be content at times to ignore probably two out of every three apparent opportunities to make money, and must know how to sell and take his profits when the "bull" chorus is loudest. When he has learned that much, he has learned a great deal.

Chapter XXI - Physical Position of the Speculator

It is a habit with some active speculators to attribute their own lack of success to advantages of physical position; that is to say, the outside trader believes that the member of the Exchange is in a relatively more advantageous position to make money. The broker is "on the spot," and is in such close relationship to the market that he commands greater opportunities and less risk than the outsider, according to the latter's conclusion, which is not always true. As a fact, however, they occupy distinctly different positions and employ radically different methods, although having the same object, viz., money making.

It is reasonable to hold that the member of the Exchange who trades for his own account, occupies a relationship to the market which gives him substantial advantages—independent of commissions—as compared with his position were he an outside trader, located in New York, Chicago or elsewhere.

As an illustration we can use the case of a young Chicago Hebrew, who had been graduated from Harvard, and who selected stock trading as a vocation. His father, a successful trader, was in complete sympathy with his ambition. The young man started to trade in the New York Stock Exchange market over a Chicago wire. He lost money. He figured that as a trader he was handicapped by certain conditions which he could eliminate. His view was that he lost several minutes in the transmission of the quotations from the floor of the Exchange over the ticker, more time in the transmission of the quotations from New York to Chicago, additional time in their distribution throughout that city and fresh delay in the transmission of his order to New York, thence to the Exchange, and in its execution. Although the machinery required in the processes enumerated has been perfected in a high degree and narrowed down to seconds, the trader who sought to make "quick turns" undoubtedly clearly comprehended the disadvantages or handicaps under which he labored.

He therefore left Chicago for New York, and trade from the office of a Stock Exchange house, alternately watching and studying the ticker or the blackboard quotations as his fancy dictated. The real or imagined advantages did not result in substantial profits and after a fair trial of trading from the outside he bought a Stock Exchange membership and became a daily trader.

He was now free to roam as he pleased, study the habits and methods of individual brokers and groups of brokers in the execution of orders, the tricks of the trade, the relative value of gossip designed to make fluctuations. His early speculations were by no means entirely successful; parental assistance being required to help the young trader carry a block of stock with which he became entangled in a brief period of great mental excitement.

At the expiration of a year, however, the trader had become a practical money maker who derived his livelihood from daily hazards in the stock market. He is, as might be expected, of the opinion that as an active trader he is free from disadvantages with which the outsider has to contend.

But it may be held that not all traders may become members of the Stock Exchange and that to become a "trader-broker" requires qualities of temperament not always to be found in successful speculators who are not Exchange members. And the outsider may hold that, given capable brokers, a quiet office, a ticker and the news of the day, and his advantages will more than offset those of the Exchange member. In the first place he will prefer a quiet office to the babel of voices and confusion of the Exchange floor. Absolute quiet may be to him a foremost consideration. Secondly, he sits alongside the ticker from which position he can study purchases and sales, supply and demand and market tones, factors that call for careful study by the professional trader. The time lost in the execution of his order he regards as more than offset by the condition which enables him to calmly read the tape and draw rapid conclusions as to the significance of the transactions so quickly printed.

Yet another consideration is that which comes from trading in an office receiving good market gossip, calculated to influence prices. Thus one office may possess very substantial advantages over another. It may be represented on the floor by brokers clever enough to keep the office informed of the Board Room gossip and news; it may possess superior sources of news information, such as newspaper financial writers occupying desk room therein or close relationship with this or that powerful speculative or banking faction or clique. The successful outside trader knows that market activity on his part must be accompanied by quick decision, the possession of correct market judgment and the entire day at his disposal.

Men rather than markets differ. The experience of traders suggests the conclusion that as each trader has a different temperament, arriving at conclusions from entirely different points of view, and calling for different conditions, each position (1) trading on the Exchange floor and (2) trading from a New York office in a favorable environment, has advantages and disadvantages which almost balance.

In this consideration of the questions involved the point of view prevails that each of the two brokers is an Exchange member. One executes his own orders, after which it costs him $1.12 to clear each 100 shares of stock, while the other entrusts the execution to another member and the net cost is $3.12 per 100 shares. The floor trader, therefore, has a $2 advantage on each 100 share trade. Should the outside trader not be a member of the Exchange his commission bills will place him in this position: The board member holds a

$75,000 membership. Money is, say, worth 5 percent and therefore his initial expense is $3,750 per annum. To be even with the game he must net that sum in any one year, plus his clearance bills. The outsider starts without any fixed charge of this character. Should, however, the outsider be a very active or heavy trader his commission bills would soon exceed the expenses of the Exchange member. The average trader, however, does not pay $3,750 a year in commissions. This question of expense is one to be determined by the individual trader, who should have no difficulty in arriving at the proper course to pursue.

To compare the number of successful outside traders with the number of successful Exchange member traders does not lead to accurate conclusions. The number of traders in the 1,100 membership of the Stock Exchange is of necessity limited, and the number of outside traders is many times greater, consequently the outsiders can point to superior numbers. But in comparing the accounts of 25 members and 25 outside traders the figures would favor the members.

Consideration of the questions involved will lead to the conclusion that the outside daily trader, dealing from a branch office in New York or in another city, is at a round disadvantage as compared with the floor-trading member or the office-trading member.

The experience of Wall Street men, legitimate brokers and bucket shop proprietors, is that the outside daily trader (not an Exchange member) is rarely successful. He is reduced to the position of a bettor, heavily handicapped, and obliged to pay a fee of $25 on each guess, plus the interest on his account. It must be conceded, however, that the chances of failure of the occasional trader, who deals from a distance, are obviously not so great as those of the trader making daily ventures. Where the latter is almost absolutely certain to fail in the long run, the occasional trader occupies a very much safer position.

Chapter XXII - Temperament and Equipment

The man of phlegmatic temperament, who can lose without feeling mental depression and who can win without corresponding elation, is the man who is best adapted for speculation, provided he possesses the other necessary qualifications. It should not be understood, however, that the nervous temperament is not represented by many successful speculators; in fact the majority of speculators are very nervous men. Many of them are troubled with nervous diseases. The most successful stock speculators of the day are sufferers from nervous indigestion, attributable to worry and irregular habits in eating and drinking during periods of active speculation. There are speculators, who are unable to eat during the Stock Exchange session; others can digest only the lightest and most digestible foods; others smoke and drink freely and do not eat, and still others, win or lose, eat heartily with unimpaired digestive organs. The advantage is naturally with the latter group, for such a temperament, with regular habits, makes far stronger vitality than is possessed by the extremely nervous man. A sound body makes a sound mind, and good health is a factor of importance with the speculator. One of the cleverest of the younger speculators on the Stock Exchange inherited his membership from his father, also a successful speculator, and who died of a nervous disease which was in all probability attributable to the uncertainty of his trade. The son, who is essentially a moneymaker, rivaling his father, suffers from nervousness to a greater degree than his father, and at frequent intervals is obliged to leave Wall Street and travel for rest and recreation.

An unknown writer, considering the qualities essential to the equipment of a speculator, names them in this order: (1) self-reliance; (2) judgment; (3) courage; (4) prudence; (5) pliability.

"1. *Self-reliance.* A man must think for himself; must follow his own convictions. George Macdonald says: 'A man cannot have another man's ideas any more than he can have another man's soul or another man's body.' Self-trust is the foundation of successful effort.

"2. *Judgment.* That EQUIPOISE, that nice adjustment of the faculties one to the other which is called good judgment, is an essential to the speculator.

"3. *Courage.* That is, confidence to act on the decisions of the mind. In speculation there is value in Mirabeau's dictum: 'Be bold, still be bold, always be bold.'

"4. *Prudence.* The power of measuring the danger, together with a certain alertness and watchfulness, is very important. There should be a balance of these two, prudence and courage; prudence in contemplation, courage in execution. Lord Bacon says: 'In meditation all dangers should be seen; in execution none, unless very formidable. Connected with these qualities, properly an outgrowth of them, is a third, viz., promptness. The mind convinced, the act should follow. In the words of Macbeth: 'Henceforth the very firstlings of my heart shall be the firstlings of my hand.' Think, act, promptly.

"5. *Pliability.* The ability to change an opinion the power of revision. 'He who observes,' says Emerson 'and; observes again, is always formidable.'

"The qualifications named are necessary to the make-up of a speculator, but they must be in well-balanced combination. A deficiency or an overplus of one quality will destroy the effectiveness of all. The possession of such faculties in a proper adjustment is, of course, uncommon. In speculation, as in life, few succeed; many fail."

Chapter XXIII - The Broker and his Client

There are two classes of brokers dealing with the public: (1) the speculating stockbroker, and (2) the non-speculating stockbroker.

Preferably, the broker who does not speculate is to be employed. He occupies an unprejudiced position toward the market, and his opinion is therefore more valuable than that of the broker who is a speculator, and is swayed this way and that by every turn in the market. What is more natural than that he should advise his customer to trade as he is trading in the conviction that his judgment is right and in the belief that the customer's trade will help his own?

A physician will not prescribe for himself or his family treatment that he will successfully prescribe for others. Some brokers acknowledge, without hesitation, that while they can successfully advise and conduct the market operations of other persons they are dismal failures in conducting ventures for their own account. Many firms of brokers—and they are to be preferred in the selection of a broker—on signing articles of copartnership stipulate that no firm member shall be permitted to speculate. Experience has taught them that in this way only are the risks of the stock commission trade minimized. Large operators select houses of this class for the execution of manipulative orders whenever it is possible to do so. By so doing they increase the margin of safety from the points of view of non-interference and financial stability.

There are traders who believe that the chances of success are increased when they trade with a firm which is identified with the operations of a leading manipulator. At times doubtless this selection is to be commended, provided the trader always remembers that his interests are distinctly a secondary consideration and that in an emergency the operator in question will protect himself even at the expense of the customers.

A trader in stocks should, when possible, make a study of his broker. He will find that brokers vary as much in mental habit and conscience as they do in appearance. There are brokers who will ascertain what their customers are desirous of doing in the market and advise them accordingly. The writer on more than one occasion has heard brokers offer advice that was absolutely contradictory in the effort to influence trading. For example: A was advised to buy a certain stock, having expressed belief in the view that it would advance, while B, ten minutes later was advised to sell the same stock short, having informed his broker that he believed in a decline. The singular result was that both customers lost money, each trader closing out at a loss on the minor fluctuations. The broker encouraged "trading" and profited by his commissions. There are brokers who will strain their consciences to the point of spraining to encourage trading, but they should not be difficult to detect.

In opening an account the reputation of a broker should carry weight. Is he an old or a new hand? Has he been successful? Are his customers of the permanent or transient class? Does he advise frequent or occasional ventures?

The exigencies of his trade require that the broker should preserve an impassive demeanor. He must not be disturbed by his clients' losses. If he were thus swayed by sentiment he would be in as dangerous a position as the too sympathetic nurse at the bedside of a precariously sick patient. The broker is navigating a craft that calls for a cool head at all times, especially in times of panic. If he were to sympathize with every client who loses, he would soon be a nervous wreck, retire from business or find an exhausted bank account. A successful broker of twenty years' experience has on his books small accounts aggregating $100,000, which he made good with his personal check. "I doubt," said he, in discussing the subject, "that I would pay those losses had I to do it again. The men were ungrateful in almost every instance. As a practice to be followed in trade I have no hesitation in condemning it. It is bad for the broker and bad for his client."

The honest and capable broker wants to have his client make money. A successful following is the best advertisement a broker can have. He will try to advise his clients so that they will make money. His advisory attitude to his client will be determined by the mental and financial capabilities of his client and the latter's attitude to the market and particular stocks.

Chapter XXIV - The Bucket Shop

A bucket shop is a place where bets can be made on the advance or decline of stocks. The bettor deposits his margin, which may be 1 to 10 percent and "buys" or "sells" a specified stock. The dealer accepts the margin and nominally "buys" or "sells" the stock in question. There is no actual sale or purchase, as the dealer simply "buckets" the order, which is to say, that he agrees to pay any losses that he may sustain should his customer make a winning wager, and on the other hand if the customer loses, the dealer or bucket shop operator, profits by the exact amount of the bettor's loss.

The theory of the bucket shop operator is that four speculators out of five, and even a greater percentage, lose money in the long run if they become steady traders. They aim to obtain the money thus lost, and are willing to back their belief that the stock market is "unbeatable," by the average speculator.

Bucket shops have been engaged in business for more than twenty-five years. Many unsuccessful attempts have been made to suppress them. Since their early days the bucket shop system has expanded to tremendous limits; in the aggregate a large sum of money is invested in the trade, and the statement that millions of dollars are annually lost and won in this form of stock gambling is moderate and conservative. Twenty years ago the only important bucket shop in Wall Street and New York was that of Louis Todd, a New England man, who conducted a large establishment at 44 Broad, which extended through to and had an entrance on New Street. Hundreds of impecunious, broken down speculators and clerks gambled there, and Todd, the backer of the game, waxed fat and rich, building two Broadway hotels—the Marlborough and Vendome—on part of his profits. When he became a millionaire he retired from business. In the meantime, dozens of little bucket shops sprung up in lower New Street, until certain buildings in that neighborhood were regarded as little better than pest holes by the Wall Street community. Those bucket shops were conducted by cheap gamblers who, after running a week, would fail, the proprietor closing the doors and absconding with the money, while the "customers" were out the amount of their ventures. In a week or two the defaulting bucket shop operator would have no hesitation in resuming business in another office under another name. There may have been occasional honest failures, where the bank account was legitimately lost to the concern's bettors, but they were very few. Except at rare intervals those engaged in this trade have never been disturbed. Dishonest failures are so frequent that it seems strange that the criminal law is not more actively engaged in punishing those so plainly employed in this form of robbery.

Since 1890 the bucket shop system has advanced to such an extent that it now plays a very important part in the trade of stock speculation. It has been perfected so that many speculators are unable to distinguish the legitimate from the illegitimate firm and is now closely, interwoven with stock speculation wherever it exists. There are bucket shops of the following types:

(1) One which caters to a local trade on a limited capital.

(2) One which poses as a banking firm, advertising extensively, has no Exchange memberships, and seeks a local mail order and private wire trade with the large cities.

(3) One which operates and holds an Exchange membership.

(4) One which operates a private wire system, but has no local trade, and depends for profits on the losses of country town investors.

(5) An outwardly respectable firm which buckets its trade when necessity arises.

The bucket shop represented by the first type is conducted by men of no responsibility. It will open with a cash capital of $100, $1,000 or nothing at all if the operator is desperate. It will remain open just so long as bettors lose money to it, for the operators rarely remain long enough to pay out all the margins that have been deposited. The favorite lot traded in is one of 5 shares, while ten share trades are the limit. Margins of 1 percent are required and 2 percent is usually the limit. The commission is 1/8 or 1/4. When margins are about to be exhausted, the bettor can remargin his venture if he so elects,

From 1895 to 1902, owing to the advancing market, there wore many large failures of bucket shops transacting business in the group designated as type No. 2. There are many in operation today, and in the number there are several which are very strong financially. Their customers are pleased with their methods and are unable to distinguish them from legitimate firms. They maintain elaborate offices, they spend thousands of dollars in advertising and disseminate expensive books and pamphlets to prospective losers.

In group 3 are found bucket shops which consider that an Exchange membership cloak is a valuable asset in obtaining business. They are the concerns which "match orders" on an exchange and consider themselves to be somewhat better than their competitors.

The private wire bucket shop has a central office in Wall Street. It leases a system of private wires, transmits quotations and employs agents on a profit sharing or salary basis. Usually the identity of the owner or backers is concealed under such a title, as for example, The New York Stock Commission Co. At times they employ as many as a dozen telegraph operators and deal not only in stocks, but also in grain and cotton. Members of this group are believed to have conducted highly profitable operations. Their customers are inexperienced, and the out-of-town speculator is regarded in this trade as a swift loser.

Those included in group 5 will resent the indignity, as they can hardly be classed as bucket shops, although resorting to bucket shop methods when the financial sky threatens disaster. Firms in this class are Exchange members. The members of such a firm may be carrying a large line of stocks. A decline is inevitable. The firm requests its customers to liquidate and the advice is unheeded; on the contrary the speculators may insist on buying more stocks. In order to escape the fury of the storm, the firm decides to jettison part of the cargo, and so with self-preservation in view, rather than assume further risks, the firm sells part or all of its customers' line of stocks, and stands in the position of having "bucketed" its customers' accounts. As soon, however, as the storm has passed, they are rebought. The brokers, it is true, have profited by their customers' losses. All the rules governing Exchange trading are complied with in this operation, for when the stocks were sold, they were sold for the individual account of one of the members of the firm and stand as a short sale, for which he or the firm is responsible on the books. Money made is credited to this account just as money lost is debited. The broker simply wagers that his customers will lose, and rather than jeopardize his own position, he pursues this course. When you read that a brokerage concern has failed because its customers did not respond to "margin calls," you will know that the suspended firm succumbed to the conditions which the "bucketing" broker wished to avoid when he sold his customers' stocks.

The bucket shop appeals to several speculators, notably

(1) The small trader whose account is refused by legitimate concerns;

(2) The trader who believes that he can more advantageously trade on board quotations than on open market quotations, and

(3) The trader who deals in a bucket shop rather than in the New York market by mail or telegraph order.

The small speculators supply the bulk of the bucket shop profits. Speculators of the second class are in error for the dealer overcomes his seeming advantage with tricks peculiar to the trade. Those in group 3 would be richer in pocket if they refrained absolutely from trading.

Some of the theories and views of bucket shop operators are:

That $5,000 is sufficient capital with which to open for business.

That four out of five speculators lose money in stock speculation and that the steady player is sure to lose.

That the most certain losers are the small speculators, and those who operate on a margin.

That the smaller the margin the greater the chance of loss by the speculator, hence the preference for small margins.

That to encourage a speculator to pyramid on his success and enlarge the scope of his transactions is to win all his money in the long run.

That it is policy to pay out winnings promptly to new customers, who once satisfied of financial responsibility are forever after credulous.

That speculators rarely draw down their profits, but persist invariably in wanting more, and in this fact exists the bucket shop operators' safety.

"Of course," explained a bucket shop broker to the writer, "this is a gambling game. There are thousands of tricks to it. The average speculator is a fool in believing that he can guess a game which he knows nothing about. For example, suppose a large bucket shop has persuaded its customers to buy in the aggregate 10,000 shares of Sugar on small margins. It is short just that much on the books. The operator will then make a play in the open market. He will send in a broker he employs to the Sugar crowd, and there are times when he has his own representative on the Exchange, to sell the market off a couple of points in order to wipe out his customers' accounts. He is willing to lose $1,000 to make $10,000. This has been done many times. And then again, I have known clever adventurers to work precisely the same game with the bucket shops. They have planted orders in all the bucket shops and then have hastily manipulated the stock market to successfully execute a heavy winning play.

"When Gov. Flower died in 1899, there was hardly a solvent bucket shop in the country. They had paid out all their own capital, and all their customers' margins, and millions more were liabilities on their books. Had their customers made a concerted demand for their money, not one could have kept its doors open. The smash came and in one day every bucket shop account was wiped out; the operators had all the money, and they started afresh without a liability.

"In conducting a large bucket shop, it is almost impossible to make a big winning on a bull market such as the one of recent years. Almost all bucket shop traders are bulls. In a rapidly shifting two-sided market with broad fluctuations, the bucket shop will always reap a harvest. The bucket shop has no use for customers who trade and take small losses and attempt to scalp the market. They want speculators who will 'guess' the market for 'big money,' the fellows who 'buy 'em when they are strong and sell 'em when they are weak.'

"There are concerns engaged in the business of bucketing trade who have never been suspected of such a thing and so elaborate are their precautions that they will never be suspected. With an abundance of capital and knowledge of the business, a bucket shop operator knows that he stands behind one of the best money-making gambling institutions in the country.

"When a bucket shop secures an undesirable customer— one who can make money—it will try to freeze him out. A few years ago $5,000 was regarded as a fair amount of cash with which to embark in this trade. Today the amount required is larger. A bucket shop starting with $100,000 will pay out to its backers as dividends the first $100,000 that comes in the office and trust to luck to continue in business on the margins of its customers. Should this plan 'go wrong,' the custom is to assess the backers of the game, and if an assessment plan is rejected by them, the bucket shop suspends or 'welches' as you please to call it. One of the singular things about the bucket shop speculators is that as a class they will return and do business with a concern which has failed and resumed.

"Experience teaches a bucket shop operator that the average speculator will play the game in this way: He is a bull and buys stocks. He is successful and runs $100 into $1,000. He then writes for, or demands in person, his principal and profits. The money is promptly paid. The successful speculator then concludes that the firm is financially sound. He believes that he is the one man in 1,000 who can call the turns of the market. Fortune is in his grasp. Success makes him conceited, less careful and more daring. He returns the $1,000 and possibly more. He may interest one or two friends to try the same rapid road to fortune. He resumes trading on the bull side.

"Giving him the best luck possible, we find that he has increased his $1,000 to $2,000. The chances are that he is now overtrading, or scattered all over the board—trading in too many stocks—and so extended that any sharp set back in the market will wipe him out. Along comes an unfavorable development. The market breaks 1, 2, 3, 4 or 5 points and our speculating country customer is wiped out.

"The lesson does not prove to be a valuable one. The speculator try's again. He has abandoned his idea that he is going to make a fortune. He now humbly aspires to "get even," or in other words, to recover his lost money. In the attempt to "get even," he loses more money, and then sensibly quits gambling in stocks or becomes a confirmed 'piker' and a victim of the gambling habit. Once acquired by a poor man, it is as hard to shake off as a taste for strong drink. It will pauperize him and make it almost impossible for him to take up genuine work and become a useful citizen in the community."

The bucket shop speculator injures his own chances of success the very minute that he gives an order. Supply and demand are the basic factors influencing the price of stocks. When demand exceeds supply, prices advance and opposite conditions result in declines. The bucket shop purchase is shorn of power to influence prices, for the order has not been executed in the open market. Assuming that 50,000 shares of stocks are bought in the bucket shops of the U.S. in a single day—and the estimate is conservative—it will be observed that this buying power is absolutely a negative factor in influencing enhancement of stock values which would mean profit to the speculative buyers. On the other hand, such a buying demand, with the orders actually executed on the floor of the Stock Exchange, would at times stimulate an advance, check a decline or exert an otherwise important influence. It will therefore be perceived that the bucket shop speculator is a force arrayed against himself; that he enters the game with many handicaps and penalizes himself by reducing his venture to a wholly negative value as a price maker.

It has been argued that precisely the same conditions prevail with orders executed on the Consolidated Exchange, but this is an erroneous view, for in all such transactions the actual delivery of stock balances is contemplated and made. Where there remains at the expiration of any day or week a balance to be received or delivered in stocks, and the stocks are not available on the Consolidated Exchange, then its brokers resort to the primary market— the Stock Exchange—and purchase any stocks that may be required to balance their accounts, or sell if the circumstances call for sales.

The writer has heard occasionally of individuals who have made winnings in bucket shops. He has never heard of any man who became rich as a bucket shop speculator or even had the common sense to take down substantial winnings and retire from the contest. While conceding that there are times when the purchase or sale of stocks, even in a bucket shop, results in profit to the speculator, an examination of bucket shop accounts shows conclusively that in the long run the bucket shop speculator is certain to become bankrupt; while they are also suggestive of the belief that the average bucket shop speculator fails to understand the first principles of the game.

A contemporary writer says: "The large number of gambling places in the country known as bucket shops, with their frequent failures and resultant disclosure of their unscrupulous methods, yet with a train of victims which seemingly is larger after each new exposure, is causing a great deal of moralizing these days, provoking troubled inquiry whether the American people are more foolish and ignorant than they are usually thought to be, and whether this folly and ignorance is growing.

"There is no doubt that among the customers of these bucket shops there are many of the gullible sort who spend their lives and what little cash resources they possess in attempting to extract wealth from one visionary project after another. But the fundamental reason why bucket shops flourish is that the American people as a people are irresistibly fond of financial speculation. While our countrymen can in no wise be called a nation of gamblers, and while great speculative manias, such as the South Sea bubble, the John Law scheme, or the tulip craze have never possessed the whole country, as each in turn swept over parts of Europe in the last two centuries, there exists a strong element in our national character wherein the love of venture and the dominance of a lively imagination hold full sway. This tendency, of course, is most noticeable in a period of great prosperity like that which so happily exists at present; and the most natural direction of this manifestation is in the shares of the great railway and industrial corporations through which the country's prosperity chiefly pulsates.

"The bucket shop offers the readiest road of speculation. The man in a country village who would hesitate to put $10 upon a roulette wheel would willingly buy ten shares of a railway stock in the office of one of the numerous 'investment companies' or bucket shops of similar high names which are located in his town. Stock speculation through the regular channels of a Stock Exchange house is costly and complicated. The commissions and interest charges are large and most of these houses do not care to accept small amounts or to deal in less than one hundred shares of stock, save for very well-known customers. It is carried on with difficulty by a speculator living in a small town where he does not have frequent access to market reports. And the customer of a Stock Exchange house may, if the market goes heavily against him, lose not only the margin of his investment, but find himself heavily in debt to his broker besides. Bucket shops do business on a very different principle. They neither buy nor sell the stocks upon orders given to them by their customers, and in very many instances they make no pretence of assuming to do this, nor do their customers have any idea that their "orders" to buy and sell are obeyed. Both parties to the operation look upon it in its true light of a simple bet made that a stock quoted upon the New York Exchange will go up or down within certain limits. The commission charged by the bucket shop keeper is much less than that of a Stock Exchange firm. The bucket shop man is willing to deal in very small lots of stock, accepting very small margins. He charges his customer no interest for the money which, if the business was done in the usual way, would have to be borrowed to pay for the stocks actually purchased. Moreover, the bucket shop keeper allows his customer to begin or close his trade at a definitive quotation as it appears upon the ticker of the Stock Exchange operations, and he closes the customer's account instantly upon the exhaustion of the margin, so that the customer is assured that no further claim is to be made upon him in case the market still continues to go against him. The bucket shop keeper however, for his part, often declines to allow an accumulated profit in certain stocks to run beyond a certain figure, and he generally is willing to deal in but small lots of stock. His whole system of doing business is one which presents very great inducements to the small speculator, and if these inducements could be offered by any responsible house having a membership in the Stock Exchange, that house would very soon have a monopoly of speculative operations conducted by the outside public in Wall Street. Where, then, does the bucket shop keeper make his money? In this simply, that, as his operations are, in reality, those of a series of bets with his customers, the bets, so far as the customers are concerned, taking the form of guesses as to which way the stock market will go, experience has demonstrated that such guesses of the general run of people are in the main incorrect and that there is a steady, average profit to be had in miscellaneously accepting, or as the slang of Wall Street has it, 'coppering' them. As most of the outsiders are 'lambs' as they are called in Wall Street, they buy stocks, rather than sell them, so that the customers of bucket shops find their greatest profit and the keeper of the concern his greatest loss, in periods of prosperity and advancing markets such as we have just seen. Then if the bucket shop man is a dishonest individual, as he usually is, he finds it convenient to fail at the proper time, sweeping into his own pockets all the margins and paper profits of his patrons. Many of these patrons, indeed, are very far from being innocent and unsuspecting lambs. They have no illusions on the score of the game they are playing, and they know that the bucket shop keeper is probably a pretty 'crooked' person. They are apt to belong to that unhappy class of individuals known as the 'ghosts' of Wall Street, that is, men who once did business there on a large scale, but have lost the money they won and are forced to gamble, if they gamble at all in a very humble way. The question, on which these men concentrate most of their attention is the possibility of the bucket shop failing, and after a prolonged 'bull' market when they know that the proprietor of the concern is probably losing heavily, they take their profits in cash, if they have any, and beware the shop as a very dangerous locality.

"It is very clear, therefore, that the business of trying to speculate by means of bucket shops is an extremely hazardous thing. If man feels he must speculate, he ought to become a customer of a house having membership in the Stock or Consolidated Exchanges. And it is still as true as it ever was that the best way to make money is not to speculate at all."

Chapter XXV - The Speculator and the Exchange

The speculator should have a clear idea of the Consolidated Exchange, its advantages and disadvantages and relation to the Stock Exchange. This is necessary inasmuch as the Consolidated Exchange has at times afforded a market for many thousand small speculators in stocks, particularly those living out of town. The Consolidated Exchange is generally advertised as the "N. Y. Con. Stock Exchange." It is a consolidation of a mining exchange and an oil exchange. In the '70's and '80's it was the scene of violent speculation in mining stocks, and certificates representing crude oil in lots of 1,000 barrels. Accompanying the decline of speculation in mining shares and oil certificates, the members decided to trade in the active stocks dealt in on the Stock Exchange. Today the trading in mining shares is on a nominal basis only, while the pipe line certificate as a speculative factor has been entirely eliminated, hence the name New York Consolidated Stock and Petroleum Exchange is a misnomer, and the substitution of the assumed title—"N. Y. Con. Stock Exchange." Almost the entire floor of the Consolidated Exchange is now devoted to dealing in Stock Exchange shares. In the main, the dealings are confined to fractured lots; in fact the bulk of the trading is in 10 share lots. Certain members of the Consolidated Exchange are accustomed to say that their Board is the "primary market" for speculation in fractional lots. This is not so. The Stock Exchange is the primary market for the sale of each and every stock dealt in thereon. On its quotations, questions before courts of law are decided and its prices are recognized as official in any legal dispute involving the price of 1 share or its multiple. Then again, inasmuch, as it is impossible to deal on the Consolidated Exchange in many inactive stocks listed on the Stock Exchange, the limitations of such a market obviously make the claim to a "primary market" absurd. And again, it is possible to conceive of the complete elimination of the Consolidated Exchange, without thereby affecting investors, speculators, or those corporate interests which have listed their securities on the Stock Exchange after compliance with the rules of the latter institution.

Whether the Consolidated Exchange is or is not a useful public institution are questions which will not be answered here. Membership on the Consolidated Exchange is nominally quoted at $2,500. Stock Exchange memberships (in 1902) commanded $83,000. The disparity in values is also calculated to cheapen the "primary market" claim. In connection with the Consolidated Exchange there have been many scandalous failures in which credulous investors have in the aggregate been robbed of a large amount of money. Bucket shops have secured representation in the institution, and the later-day management has not yet been able to overcome the corruption which was fostered in the early '90's.

Of all Consolidated Exchange assets and possessions figuratively the most valuable is the "blackboard." This "blackboard" is the largest in the country. Its length is almost that of a city block. Two men are employed from 10 A.M. to 3 P.M. to post thereon the quotations received by a telegraph operator who calls them off as rapidly as they are received. Where the quotations come from no one knows, as the Stock Exchange does not recognize the Consolidated Exchange and would not permit it to use the official prices if any means could be devised to exclusively hold them. It is reasonable to believe, however, that the Consolidated Exchange has at some remote point secured a Stock Exchange ticker or connection with a telegraph wire on which Stock Exchange quotations are transmitted. There are two stock quotation telegraph companies. One supplies tickers transmitting quotations to Stock Exchange members exclusively. That is the fastest ticker service. The other, and slower ticker, by perhaps one or two minutes, can be obtained by Consolidated Exchange firms, hotels and public places generally, provided two members of the Stock Exchange will indorse the application of the person who wishes to rent one or more. On the floor of the Consolidated Exchange there are two of the slower tickers separated from and apart from the blackboard. Many efforts have been made by the Stock Exchange to have those tickers removed, but in the legal contests resulting from such attempts the Consolidated Exchange has successfully maintained its right to possession and use. How the two tickers on the Consolidated Exchange floor are used by the members will hereafter be explained. The Consolidated Exchange has a small ticker service of its own, but to it no particular importance is attached. Now Stock Exchange quotations are also received by Consolidated Exchange members in one other way, although this fact is not generally known, and certainly not by the public. It requires no explanation to understand that inasmuch as the Consolidated Exchange must rely on its two slow tickers on its floor, and its posted blackboard quotations which are slower than the ticker (because they are probably transmitted from a similar ticker) that the speculator who can get Stock Exchange prices through the medium of the fast ticker or by telephone from the floor of the Stock Exchange can trade at a substantial advantage over his competitors. Taking advantage of his "quick" prices he can, when there is a broad market, undersell or outbid his fellow members by 1/8's, 1/4's or even full points, provided they are dependent on the slower quotation facilities.

Trading on the Consolidated Exchange is conducted by the following dealers:

(1) The legitimate commission firm which executes and closes out its customers' transactions without departing from the recognized rules.

(2) The illegitimate commission firm, which is in fact a bucket shop, and which evades the rules.

(3) The speculator who trades for his own account to save commissions and expenses that trading through a Stock Exchange house would necessitate.

(4) The room-trader who scalps fractions and "evens up" his business at the end of each session.

(5) The trader who relys upon quick quotation service in order to make profitable ventures.

(6) The arbitrage trader who trades between the New York, Philadelphia and Boston markets.

(7) The broker who executes orders for other brokers, Total membership in the Consolidated Exchange is limited to 2,400 and about one-fifth of that number are active members.

Legitimate commission firms are not few and transact a very respectable volume of business. Their customers, as a rule, are 10-share traders, although many firms have customers who deal in 100 share lots and more. Up to 1902

the commission charged for a fractional share trade —50 shares or under—
was 1-16 of 1 percent or one half the Stock Exchange commission, but the rate
was increased by vote of members to 1/8 of 1 percent, thus placing the two
Boards on a parity; but on lots of 50 shares or more the charge is 1-6 of 1
percent each way or 1/8 of 1 percent for the round transaction. In the three or
four most active stocks on the Consolidated Exchange the commission broker
contends that he can always give his customer the Stock Exchange price or
one approximating it 1/8 or 1/4 percent. On the other hand, he holds that the
fractional lot trader—as distinguished from the 100 share trader—is at a disadvantage on the Stock Exchange inasmuch as custom compels him to accept
or pay 1/4, 1/2, 3/4, 1 percent or even more on 10 shares as it is offered or
bought. There are also times when he can give his customer the advantage of
fractions, as during an excited rising market the Consolidated Exchange prices
will rise faster than those on the Stock Exchange, but it is obvious that in such
an instance that which works to the advantage of the seller must be the
disadvantage of the buyer, while the proposition is exactly reversed if the
speculation is for the decline, as distinguished from the rise. The Consolidated
Exchange member will at times when he does not find a broad market execute
large orders on the Stock Exchange paying the regular commission of 1/8.
This latter fact proves that his own market has clearly defined limitations as
distinguished from the primary market, and also that he has telephonic—
almost instantaneous—connection with the floor of the Stock Exchange. The
following conclusions regarding the facilities of the Consolidated Exchange
commission firm which executes its orders are fair:

(1) The market for fractional lots in the favorite and most active speculative stocks is an excellent one and a trader in 10 share certificates
can usually buy and sell closer to Stock Exchange 100 share lot prices
than he can on the Stock Exchange itself.

(2) The market for large blocks of stocks is too narrow for traders of the
100 to 500 share class.

(3) There is no market, or at least only a nominal market for inactive
stocks. Thus, it frequently happens that a stock will become the center
of speculative activity on the Stock Exchange. If it is maintained, the
Consolidated Exchange may take it up for a brief period, when with a
cessation of activity on the Stock Exchange holdings of small
amounts must make concessions on the Consolidated Exchange.

(4) A few Consolidated Exchange houses charge 6 percent interest
throughout the year from the day of purchase. Among others the rate
is usually higher than the Stock Exchange rate. During the period
when the weekly settlement was in practice, there were no interest
carrying charges for stocks from Monday until Saturday. Stocks
carried over Saturday also carried one week's interest. The Exchange
having unwisely adopted the daily clearing plan, interest is charged
from the day of purchase. The plan of clearing stocks is identical with
that of the Stock Exchange—balances in stocks are received and
delivered each day.

There are fewer bucket shops on the Consolidated Exchange today than there have been in the past. Certain firms of this description find that they can secure more business through an Exchange connection than without one. Their business is transacted under the cloak of respectability. Such a house, for example, receives your order to buy 10 or 100 shares of stock. It employs on the Exchange five or ten brokers as necessity may require. The order to buy at a price is transmitted over the telephone to the Exchange and at the same time an order to sell at the same price is also transmitted. The two brokers then "come together" if they can and "match" or "bucket" the order. They know each other and endeavor to trade with each other, whenever possible. When this is not possible the buying and selling order is executed as near the first purchase or selling price as the market will permit. This is called "getting names." Having executed such a transaction, the firm in question finds itself in the position of a bucket shop—it has no liability on the Exchange. If the customer loses, the firm takes his margin; if the customer wins, the firm pays the loss. Another reason for this awkward method of conducting a bucket shop is that a customer of an Exchange firm can demand the names of the brokers to his transaction, and failing to get them, could complain to the Exchange. If the Exchange demanded them and they were not furnished, the firm would be liable to expulsion from membership. And again, the customer might insist upon the return of money lost on the plea that no transaction had been effected. The brokers executing such orders comply with the rules to all intents and purposes and the details of the complicated bookkeeping involved are worked out with great ingenuity. The business of this character on the Consolidated Exchange has reached proportions that have been responsible for much complaint. "Matched" or "bucketed" orders injure rather than help an exchange. Others, trading legitimately, are placed at a disadvantage and the value of such trade is best represented by a cipher. The speculator trading through such a firm takes serious chances on its financial responsibility, although a half dozen of them have weathered many financial storms. In closing out trades through such concerns, the customer frequently has to accept prices that are wide of the market, and when this is so, the broker has no hesitation in placing the fault —not with himself—but with the facilities of the Exchange which enables him to carry on his trade.

Young men—and older ones—who wish to speculate with the least possible expense buy Consolidated Exchange memberships, and trade for their own account. They have retired as clerks from Stock Exchange houses, are sons of Stock Exchange members or may be men of limited capital. They pay nothing in commissions. If they are "bears" on a "bear" market, they make money on their commitments by "carrying" stocks for the interest charges which they receive. If they care to lend money on stocks as collateral, they can average 6 percent or better through the year, owing to the demand from brokers with small capital to have their stocks "taken up" and "carried" by someone else.

The trader is a speculator of the same type as the one described above. He, however, closes up his accounts each day. He returns to his home, neither "long" nor "short," and says that he sleeps better than if he were deep in the market. He trades for small profits—and small losses. His usual loss is 1/8 and he rarely assumes more than a 1/4 loss. He has made a study of the demands arising from each group of brokers on his Exchange and he can usually "guess" the "next" quotation" instinctively. He lives on the money lost through the legitimate commission houses, or his fellow traders and is a "gambler." He has no market opinions and simply follows the two Stock Exchange tickers, guided by the volume of Stock Exchange transactions and his knowledge of the same. He detests the bucket shop firms for the reason that when they match their orders it means that less money will be lost on the Exchange by the outside public than if the orders were actually transacted instead of "matched." He has the same feeling toward the trader who relies upon quick quotations. The trader who relies upon quick quotations gets them in one of two ways. He has private and secret telephone connection with a fast Stock Exchange ticker or with a member of the Stock Exchange. There are few of these "wires." Such a broker will stand in a crowd and receive "finger" signals from the telephone boy of the rise and fall of prices and will buy or sell on the changes, slightly in advance of the blackboard and ticker quotations. At times traders of this type—who are very unpopular with other traders on the ground that they are taking an unfair advantage—have conducted profitable operations. They operate spasmodically, for a "wire" may be suddenly discontinued and as unexpectedly open up. Other traders who have not the advantage of these special facilities try to trail behind them. The work itself is hard on the nerves and few men stand it very long.

There are Consolidated Exchange houses which affect to transact an arbitrage business between New York, Philadelphia and Boston. They do not, however, appear to make very earnest bids for business in either city. The arbitrage business between the Consolidated Exchange, Boston and Phila-delphia is not large at best. There are members of the Consolidated Exchange who say that they would like no better proposition than to be able to pay for a Stock Exchange membership, put a representative in that institution and arbitrage through the possession of superior quotation transmission facilities between the Consolidated and Stock Exchanges. An arbitrage house, such as the one described, must own at least several Exchange memberships and command comparatively large capital.

The risk is great, for, if a member of the Stock Exchange were found guilty of conducting such a trade he would be promptly expelled from that institution. It is nevertheless true that there are brokers who risk their repu-tations in this way.

Chapter XXVI - The Tipster

The novice in stock speculation, among his first inquiries, before making ventures, asks: "Is there any information that I can buy which will help me to make profitable deals?" The reply is in the negative, without qualification. There are two types of tipsters before the public.

(1) The advertising tipster, man or woman, who advertises under fictitious names or assumes pretentious "information bureau" titles, and offers for sale advance information regarding stock market movements, and,

(2) The tipster news bureau appealing to private subscribers and distinguished from the first group only by the fact that it does not advertise.

The tipster is a comparatively new figure in Wall Street. Ten years ago he would have been an impossibility. The amazing increase in wealth, the love of speculation peculiar to every people and a foolishly credulous public combined to open a field for the adventurer. His development has been rapid. Reputable newspapers have freely sold him their advertising columns. The U.S. Government not only fails to prohibit the use of the mails to him but in New York he has no difficulty in renting post-office boxes, and transacting business from a post-office box under an assumed name. Naturally many of these rogues had no wish to see their patrons, and so they were safeguarded by their post-office box connections, which rendered it unnecessary to advertise street and number addresses. This in itself should have been sufficient to warn sensible persons that the tipsters were disreputable thieves, but, strange to say, individuals and so-called "bureaus" at times obtained as many as 1,500 subscribers who paid $5 and $10 a month each for illiterate market letters.

A Brooklyn youth of the name of Miller, employed as a tool by a group of gamblers, organized on paper, what he called the "Franklin Syndicate." With the aid of shabby stationery and advertising from a 2-story frame house in a remote and poor section of Brooklyn, this young man succeeded in collecting more than $800,000 on his simple promise that he had discovered a successful method of speculating in the stock market and one which would enable him to pay his clients 520 percent per annum. He was exposed as a fraud by the daily newspapers, and sentenced to a term of imprisonment in the State penitentiary, while those behind him succeeded in escaping to Europe with the bulk of the money. Men, women and children were among Miller's clients, while, curiously enough, the number of physicians was large. The desire to gamble at this time (1900) was intense. Many persons confessed that they knew Miller to be a fraud and that he could not honestly keep his promise, but they had hoped to be among the early investors who would have received all their original capital back and a profit, to, in weekly installments, before the crash arrived. Another man who had a commonplace Irish name and was in every respect a most commonplace person, advertised under a high-sounding English name for subscribers to his tips. To each subscriber he sent a wonderful telegraphic code, which he used as a medium in telegraphing his tips. His methods were so original; his advertising so specious, and the gambling fever so prevalent, that on the eve of the second election of McKinley he had 1,500 to 1,600 subscribers to his so-called "service." He notified his subscribers prior to Mr. McKinley's re-election that stocks were a "short sale," as, in his opinion, Bryan would be the victor as the result of a landslide. His subscribers were compelled on the election of the Republican candidate to buy back their commitments at figures which represented losses, and the wail of condemnation was so great that the Irish tipster retired from the field with from $75,000 to $80,000 and later engaged in the then profitable business of selling worthless oil stocks.

Still another representative of this type was the man who having 100 subscribers advised 50 to sell a certain stock having 100 subscribers advised 50 to sell a certain stock short and the remaining 50 to buy the same stock. If 50 lost, his argument was that 50 had to win—an erroneous deduction—but he did not experience long life in the trade.

Another type included "confidential stenographers" "private wire telegraph operators," and "bookkeepers," who advertised inside information for cash in advance. Some of the tipsters were so crude and fraudulent in their methods that their advertisements became the laughing stock of Wall Street and yet many persons were and are today deceived by them. All "information" disseminated by group one is valueless. It is nothing more nor less than haphazard "guessing" by men absolutely lacking in self-respect.

Upon one occasion a Western adventurer, on coming to New York, was exposed in the newspaper with which the writer was identified as a member of its financial staff. He called with a letter of introduction from a broker and a very earnest request that he be allowed to live in peace as he had reformed and had engaged in no illegitimate business since his arrival in Wall Street. He had been one of the most audacious of the Western men who coined money from "tip" and "discretionary brokerage" operations. He was a fine looking, amiable fellow, and his statements were so ingénuous, and his letter of introduction so strong that there was no hesitancy in informing him that he would get no further publicity if he lived up to his promises. Profuse in his thanks he was about to depart when the writer remarked that if he fancied there was any obligation, it could easily be repaid by imparting some information about his old business.

"There is very little to tell," explained the tipster. "It is such a simple proposition. You see it is like this: Assume that I offer the public a sound, safe and absolutely reliable 6 percent investment in the form of stocks or bonds for sale. I could advertise it through the newspapers or through the mails until I grew grayheaded before I could get rid of it to small investors the class with which we do business, and always, preferably the man in the small town or the country. But, let me offer the public 40, 50 or 100 percent, give me a good start and the use of the mails, and I assure you that I would have to hire a wagon in which to cart down Broadway my money-laden mail. Appeal to the cupidity of the small investor and you can get his money and in no other way. And I don't mind telling you that one reason why I have reformed is that I can no longer use the mails, having been shut out by order of the authorities."

In less than nine months a private detective who operates a bureau that is supposed to expose frauds called on the writer and made the statement that he represented the reformed tipster and had a proposition from him. He said: "Mr. —— has been engaged in a legitimate brokerage business, not under his own name, but with another man. It is a discretionary business, 'mail order,' and no one has been robbed. Reporters have told him that he is going to be written up in tomorrow's paper. I will pay you $1,000 now if you will agree to stop the story."

The detective was requested to depart and invited not to call again, in which event he was promised that he too would be "written up." The editor of the newspaper interested was informed of the proposition, and the exposure was published the following day. The reformed tipster defaulted with profits estimated to exceed $100,000 and two "firms" closed up—(1) the "discretionary pool" brokerage house he directed and (2) the exchange brokerage house through which the tipster alleged he transacted his orders. The money was secured from out-of-town speculators on promises of dividends at the rate of 40 percent annually and which, in the early stages of the game, are always paid regularly.

The tipster in group one is a "guesser" who has not even the advantages possessed by a first-class brokerage house. He is as far removed from the avenues that lead to desirable information as he is from those which lead to Paradise.

It is, indeed, a great pity that New York City has not produced a district attorney of force sufficient to break up this trade and bring the offenders within reach of the criminal law.

Type two is a somewhat different proposition. Tipster bureaus (called news bureaus) must be differentiated from the two excellent news bureaus which supply Wall Street with news. The most charitable thing that can be said about them is that they do the best they can; that is to say, if their owners, by diligent work, gain early knowledge of manipulation in stocks they do not fail to make it known to their subscribers. They are also employed at times by manipulators, through the distribution of "Puts" and "Calls" to "boom" certain stocks and freely delude their subscribers to the best of their limited ability. It can be concluded without fear of contradiction that such information—as is all stock market information—must be very dangerous to the buyer.

A successful broker, watching a customer reading the market letters of one of the tipsters, remarked: "Why do you read that stuff? Don't you know that to follow that fellow regularly a trader would go broke if he had the wealth of the Bank of England behind him?" A Hebrew tipster, who has a considerable following, upon one occasion explained his business and his following in this way: "I occupy the same relation to the stock market that the doctor does to the patient. I diagnose the case, or in other words, with 20 years' experience and some knowledge of speculation, I investigate market conditions and draw conclusions. I try to obtain information whenever I can get it. I examine the fluctuations and volume of trading with care and govern myself accordingly. I am at my office early and late studying the market. It is true that I am almost always a bull. All my subscribers are bulls. I could not exist without them. I never predict declines unless we are on the verge of a panic or a bad break. If I think that a certain stock will decline I advise my clients to 'take profits.' Such advice sounds well. I rarely advise 'short' sales, for experience teaches me that my clients will not make them. I am always positive—more positive when I am in doubt than when I am reasonably certain. No man can succeed in my business unless he is positive. Men who play this game want to follow a leader. They wish to be told to do things. They know that they cannot rely upon their own judgment. In a 'bull' market I can do better for them than many of them can do themselves. Am I often wrong? Yes. But I overlook my errors of judgment, as do my clients in constantly directing their attention and gaze to my successful tips. If a man wants to speculate let him do so. If he wants to buy and has a fancy, advise him as he wishes to be advised. If he buys and loses he will forget and forgive; but, if you advise him not to make the venture on which he had concentrated his mind, and the market movement favors his conception, then he will never forgive you for, in a majority of cases, he will hold you responsible for the loss of so much money. The stock speculative public is constantly changing. Novices today and veterans tomorrow. 'Flush' this year and 'broke' the next. The best we can do is to entertain them while they are here and try to give them a run for their money."

The cheerful humbug responsible for the above views disposes of his typewritten opinions for in round figures about $22,000 a year. That buyers are to be found for the product of the tipsters does not speak well for the intelligence of the buyers. Wall Street regards them with impatience and contempt and would suppress them if it could.

Chapter XXVII - *Conclusions of a Speculator*

A close student of speculation in all its forms as conducted on the exchanges of this country has arrived at the following conclusions, which, he says, in application to speculation are "universal laws." He divides his conclusions into two groups, laws absolute and laws conditional.

Laws absolute. *Never overtrade.* To take an interest larger than the capital justifies is to invite disaster. With such an interest, a fluctuation in the market unnerves the operator, and his judgment becomes worthless.

1. Never "double up"; that is, never completely and at once reverse a position. Being "long," for instance, do not "sell out" and go as much "short." This may occasionally succeed, but is very hazardous, for should the market begin again to advance, the mind reverts to its, original opinion and the speculator "covers up" and "goes long" again. Should this last change be wrong, complete demoralization ensues. The change in the original position should have been made moderately, cautiously, thus keeping the judgment clear and preserving the balance of mind.
2. "Run quick" or not at all; that is to say, act promptly at the first approach of danger, but failing to do this until others see the danger hold on or close out part of the "interest."
3. *Another rule is,* when doubtful *reduce the amount of the interest;* for either the mind is not satisfied with the position taken, or the interest is too large for safety. One man told another that he could not sleep on account of his position in the market; his friend judiciously and laconically replied: "Sell down to a sleeping point."

Rules conditional. These rules are subject to modification, according to the circumstances, individuality and temperament of the speculator.

1. *It is better to "average up" than to "average down."* This opinion is contrary to the one commonly held and acted upon; it being the practice to buy and on a decline buy more. This reduces the average. Probably four times out of five this method will result in striking a reaction in the market that will prevent loss, but the fifth time, meeting with a permanently declining market, the operator loses his head and closes out, making a heavy loss—a loss so great as to bring complete demoralization, often ruin.

   But "buying up" is the reverse of the method just explained; that is to say, buying at first moderately and as the market advances adding slowly and cautiously to the "line." This is a way of speculating that requires great care and watchfulness, for the market will often (probably four times out of five) react to the point of "average." *Here lies the danger. Failure to close out at the point of average destroys the safety of the whole operation.* Occasionally (probably four times out of five) a permanently advancing market is met with and a big profit secured. In such an operation the original risk is small, the danger at no time great, and when successful the profit is large. This method should only be employed when an important advance or decline is expected, and with a moderate capital can be undertaken with comparative safety.

2. To *"buy down"* requires a long purse and a strong nerve, and ruin often overtakes those who have both nerve and money. The stronger the nerve the more probability of staying too long. There is, however, a class of successful operators who "buy down" and hold on. They deal in relatively small amounts. Entering the market prudently with the determination of holding on for a long period, they are not disturbed by its fluctuations. They are men of good judgment, who buy in times of depression to hold for a general revival of business—an investing rather than a speculating class.

3. In all ordinary circumstances my advice would be to buy at once an amount that is within the proper limits of capital, etc., "selling out" at a loss or profit, according to judgment. *The rule is to stop losses and let profits run,* If small profits are taken, then small losses should be taken. Not to have the courage to accept a loss and to be too eager to take a profit, is fatal. It is the ruin of many.

4. Public opinion is not to be ignored. A strong speculative current is for the time being overwhelming, and should be closely watched. The rule is, to act cautiously with public opinion, against it, boldly. To so go with the market even when the basis is a good one, is dangerous. It may at any time turn and rend you. Every speculator knows the danger of too much "company." It is equally necessary to exercise caution in going against the market. This caution should be continued to the point of wavering —of loss of confidence—when the market should be boldly

encountered to the full extent of strength, nerve and capital. The market has a pulse, on which the hand of the operator should be placed as that of the physician on the wrist of the patient. This pulse-beat must be the guide when and how to act.

5. *Quiet, weak markets are good markets to sell.* They ordinarily develop into declining markets. *But when a market has gone through the stages of quiet and weak to active and declining, then on to semi-panic or panic, it should be bought freely.* When, vice versa, a quiet and firm market develops into activity and strength, then into excitement, it should be sold with great confidence.

6. In forming an opinion of the market the element of chance ought not to be omitted. There is a doctrine of chances—Napoleon, in his campaign, allowed a margin for chances—for the accidents that come in to destroy or modify the best calculation. Calculation must measure the incalculable. In the "reproof of chance lies the true proof of men." *It is better to act on general than special information* (it is not so *misleading), viz.: the state of the country, the condition of the crops, manufactures, etc. Statistics are valuable, but they must be kept subordinate to a comprehensive view of the whole situation.* Those who confine themselves too closely to statistics are poor guides. "There is nothing," said Canning, "so fallacious as facts except figures." *"When in doubt do nothing." Don't enter the market on half conviction; wait till the convictions are full matured.*

7. I have written to little purpose unless I have left the impression that the fundamental principle that lies at the base of all speculation is this: *Act so as to keep the mind clear, its judgment trustworthy.* A reserve force should therefore he maintained and kept for supreme moments, when the full strength of the whole man should be put on the stroke delivered.

Chapter XXVIII - Successful and Unsuccessful Speculators

Speculators may be divided broadly into two classes— those who are successful and those who are unsuccessful. The successful speculator when compared with the total number of speculators is in the small minority. This is a statement that can be established by an examination of any broker's books of accounts. Even in a bull market, the only market in which the outside speculator will trade freely, speculators for the rise lose money.

Almost all speculators are amateurs. They approach the market with confidence, score an initial success and then cast prudence to the winds. Failure is the result. It takes time to make a successful speculator, except under extraordinary circumstances. While simple purchases and sales are in themselves extremely easy, knowledge of stock speculation can only be acquired by experience. A 55-year-old Stock Exchange broker who won and lost three fortunes and yet managed to retire on a competency, remarked on one occasion: "A man usually quits this business at the time when he should begin to make money." This broker won his early successes in the days of Vanderbilt and Gould. Later he was unsuccessful, and in the markets of 1896 to 1902 his winnings were not notably heavy. Just prior to his retirement he said: "The market has changed since I was a young man. It is a much larger proposition. As I grow older I find that I lack the nerve of my youth. The younger men have the nerve and vitality which I lack. I love to trade and can make money in any market as a trader, provided the fluctuations are wide enough, but my judgment of prolonged price movement can no longer be relied upon, although I know men who are as correct in their market conclusions today as I was 15 and 25 years ago. I suppose that I am too much inclined to measure events by my old yard stick; in other words, I am behind the times."

A successful Hebrew speculator, a young man of 35, said during a discussion of stock speculation: "I started out in the dry goods business and recall the time when a dry goods merchant who speculated in stocks was regarded as an unsafe man by his friends and creditors. He was the exception, and yet today the merchant who does not speculate is probably the exception. The introduction of industrial stocks doubtless has had much to do with the changed conditions. In my opinion the man who comes to Wall Street without experience in stock speculation and in possession of a large sum of money will become bankrupt or crazy or both. Wall Street is no place for a man with money. The only man entitled to consider himself the possessor of hard common sense and the right attitude toward this business is the one who is satisfied to risk a very little money in an experiment to ascertain if he has the right temperament for a speculator, and, reasoning powers that can be successfully applied to market movements."

It would appear therefore that the successful speculator should have the knowledge gained through experience, a condition which is suggestive of a period of experimentation and losses. Judging from the view of the retired broker a man may have too much experience, but this experience will be an advantage to him in gaining a livelihood as a trader. From the Hebrew's point-of-view the speculator must experience the up-and-downs of victory and defeat before he can consider himself to be other than a novice.

It must not be concluded, however, that all experienced Wall Street men are successful speculators. Quite the contrary is true. Many of the most successful brokers never speculate, experience having taught them that they do not possess those mental faculties required in the successful speculator. Other Stock Exchange firms, in their articles of co-partnership, require that no partner shall be permitted to speculate. It is also true that the financial critics, who write so knowingly and cleverly of market movements, are not successful speculators, insomuch as they are rarely men of wealth. If their market judgment were as sound and accurate as they would lead one to believe from a perusal of their articles, there is no reason why they should not be millionaires in fact, and yet, strange to say, financial journalism has not yet produced a millionaire speculator.

It is hardly reasonable, therefore, for the amateur speculator to expect to make successful ventures until he has had some experience, and this experience presumably will cost money. It certainly seems wise for the novice to reduce his early speculations to the minimum limit. If he contemplates trading in 100 shares, the preliminary ventures should be reduced to 10 when his theories of market movements and judgment may have ten tests at the cost of one 100 share venture. Undoubtedly one of the great roads to failure in stock speculation is the one which leads a speculator to trade on small margins, with no reserve; to score early success, and to enlarge his operations until he is so extended that the first serious decline turns profit into loss.

It has been said often enough that Wall Street—meaning the stock market—is reasonable; that in "the end reason prevails." What is meant is that after a prolonged period of fluctuation the price of a stock approximates its real money earning value. This value, however, fluctuates also with bad and good times. Values ultimately determine prices. Values are often hard to ascertain. They are more attainable in the railroad than the industrial quarter. The more obscure they are the more violent the fluctuations and the more violent the fluctuations the greater the risk of the speculator, and especially the one who trades on a margin.

It may be asked by the seeker for principles, Can safe and definite rules be formulated through known methods of reasoning by the speculator? Unquestionably the man with a logical mind, who can analyze all the factors governing price movements, has an immense advantage over the most common type, known as the "guesser." The successful speculator, however, must not only reason logically regarding transpired events, but he must anticipate the results of those that are coming. A man's reasoning may be accurate and even then his speculations are at the mercy of the "unexpected development" which has been the Waterloo for more than one unfortunate taker of chances.

If "the basis of inductive reasoning is the natural inclination of the mind to believe that whatever is true of a considerable number of individuals, will be true of the whole class to which these individuals belong," then the simple inductive reasoner will not succeed as a speculator, and yet in this class must be included most speculators. Their conclusions are hasty and not subjected to the test of further reasoning.

And if the speculator is to rely upon deductive reasoning on the belief that "whatever can be affirmed of an entire class can be affirmed of every individual of that class," he will find that he has many associates who have been flat failures.

Nor can the stock market be unerringly judged by "demonstrative" or "probable" reasoning. It is true that the speculator does at times form premises that lead to accurate conclusions. The premises are the "mathematical or other self-evident truths."

In the practical work of the stock market premises are formed on statements and beliefs that may be called "probable truths"; they are supposed to be true and are believed. The conclusions in all such syllogisms, like the premises, however, are only "probable" truths, and so the "probability" factor becomes very important. The successful speculator can only accurately rate Wall Street statements of "probable truths" when he has acquired knowledge of stock market manipulators, and the speculative public. Most stock market speculative ventures are based on "loose reasoning" or bold guess work, hence the speculator contends not only with his own tendency to fallacious reasoning but with the sophistry of the manipulators and manufactures of stock. There has been discussion of speculators who possess "intuitive judgment." The idea that the market will undergo a change becomes an impulse, and straightway the impulse becomes a venture. In speculation their theory is that "he who hesitates is lost," but the trader who possesses intuitive stock market judgment of value can be counted upon the fingers of one hand.

"Reasoning rests upon the ultimate basis of immediate and intuitive judgments," and the average stock speculator must stand or fall on the accuracy of his own conclusions. His powers of reasoning should be nicely balanced and adjusted. He should be a shrewd judge of "men, money and things." Reasoning, born of his own experience, is of the most permanent value. It is direct evidence. As a matter of fact, however, he is a trader generally on "circumstantial evidence," for which he has formed rules and which are chiefly remarkable for missing links. Reasoning by analogy must also be employed by the speculator who will find in all probability that like his fellow, he prefers others to do his reasoning for him when it becomes difficult.

In the stock market, as elsewhere, men love to follow a leader. They will take desperate chances on the opinions of others; on the merest hearsay, the most absurd rumor. They are as easily frightened as a flock of sheep and credulous to the point of stupidity. Men who are contemptibly mean in the matter of expenditures on themselves and their families will lose thousands of dollars in betting on a tip, and others who in their ordinary walks of business are sane and reasonable lose all their powers of reason on coming in contact with the "chance" to make "something for nothing."

"If," said a wealthy business man and a losing speculator, "I would be satisfied with the profits and losses I make in my own business I could become rich in Wall Street; but no, I am too greedy. That is the trouble with almost all men who speculate."

"My speculations," said a successful speculator, "would be more successful if I kept faith with myself. In the morning I come down town promising myself to carry out a certain plan of campaign. I depart from it on a snap judgment. The sound conclusion was the one I should have adopted every time."

There is a type of speculator who has been making imaginary ventures based on the daily quotations. He is invariably successful. This is the same man who always tells his friends what to do, and what he and they might have made had his "judgment" been followed. The writer has met this man as he was about to test his judgment in the market itself—and after. Needless to say he has made no distinction between the two propositions, in one of which he is "out" of the market and the other "in." He ascertains that it is quite one thing to have his money in his pocket and another to have it staked upon the rise and fall of a stock. With his money up, he is swayed by the passions of the gambler. He is deluded by the sophisms uttered by the manufacturers of "news," he is impatient, stout and weak-hearted in succession, a creature beset by worry in a new form, and torn by a conflict of emotions that were absolutely foreign to him when he traded on paper and made money. A good stock market advisor may be a very poor speculator, as is frequently the case. The man who contemplates embarking upon the sea of speculation should carefully consider the psychological side of speculation.

A man may place a wager on a horse or a card. The decision is almost instantaneous or at the most requires but a few minutes. The mental strain and worry incidental to the decision that you win or lose is not of long or serious duration. In stock speculation the duration of your venture may be weeks or months. This factor of uncertainty and suspense, inducing worry and impairment of reasoning powers, increases or decreases in keeping with the temperament and capital of the speculator. He may be a "good loser" or a "bad loser." He may be rich and can afford the loss when his judgment will not be impaired or he may be relatively poor or unduly extended when his judgment becomes utterly worthless. Here we have the crux of the speculative proposition—a man may embark on his ventures backed by accurate powers of reasoning; but on making his hazard the suspense is unexpectedly prolonged or his margin is tested to the extreme point of elasticity, or there is some other unlocked for adverse influence when he succumbs to loss of nerve.

"Loss of nerve" is an expression often used in Wall Street. A man may be accurately diagnosing the stock market fluctuations and yet "lose his nerve" on the day or the week prior to the successful fruition of his commitment. But, having lost his nerve, he retires defeated and perhaps a loser. "Loss of nerve" is frequent among professional, but more common among amateur speculators, and it may be accompanied by a still worse symptom— loss of power to act— leaving the victim irresolute, undecided and the prey to hundreds of whims and fancies. In his observations the writer has known old and successful speculators to lose their nerve and liquidate their stocks on the "twaddle" of a loud-voiced, irresponsible reporter who talked of possible disasters during a temporary period of distress.

And again, it has been observed that a room can be crowded with small, happy, talkative speculators during a rising market and be succeeded by the same room crowded with gloomy, discontented, silent speculators during a slight decline. Enter the same room, during the decline, a "bear," vigorously outspoken, and the equanimity of the room and the nerve of the speculators is lost to the point that the manager of the office has difficulty in keeping his customers from needlessly sacrificing stocks, while the interval may be one of natural reaction.

The manager of a large commission office, where many hundred thousand dollars are lost annually, says: "I hate to see men lose money; but if they did not lose it here they would go somewhere else. This is the only business that I understand. I have made and lost a fortune in it. Now, although I am a young man (42), I would willingly sell out my chances for an annuity of $5,000 a year. Do I speculate? No. I prefer a good appetite, and sound sleep to a poor appetite and broken sleep. My friends think I am pretty clever, and so I am, but I am no cleverer than the large majority of speculators, although there are times when my judgment is much better than theirs. Disinterested advice, under the circumstances, is better than their own judgment. Yes, of course the majority are losers. Most of them are unable to acquire the most simple and essential principle of the game, i.e., taking a small loss. In this contest men are not their normal selves. I refer now to the margin speculator who is gambling and governed by passion and excitement. He is far removed from myself, for example. I am cold and impassive, even during a panic, for I am not risking money. I must see to it that the firm does not lose money and we must sacrifice the gamblers with a strong hand—not because we like to, but because we have to. The successful speculator in the time of stress I take it, should have the same control of himself as I have and I know very few speculators who are outwardly and inwardly calm when they are steadily losing and perhaps threatened with serious losses or even bankruptcy. I have not that control over myself, and that is why I lost my money.

"Then again, the average speculator buys stocks when they are 'strong' and sells them when they are 'weak.' This is a common principle with them and shows fallacious reasoning. In stock fluctuations, prices advance and decline, or vice versa, as it is a bull or a bear market. Therefore when a stock is 'strongest,' to the superficial eye, it is really 'weakest,' for then it should be sold for a reaction, just as it is sold by the so-called insiders. When outside buying orders are most numerous, a decline usually follows, and in the case of a bear market the conditions are precisely reversed."

During normal markets, brokers have observed that the psychological factor is so strong that speculators are not disposed to trade as freely and confidently in wet and stormy weather as they are during the dry days when the sun is shining, and mankind cheerful and optimistic. The average stock speculator is an optimist, and usually an enthusiast. He is on the constructive side of the account; he speculates for the rise. He is easily influenced—it may be by the weather or it may be by idle gossip, and frequently his cause of failure is due to temperamental shortcomings of his own with which his broker only is acquainted and to which he is absolutely blind.

The average man prides himself on his judgment. He is an egotist, a vain creature and places an exaggerated value on his own acumen. In the study of several hundred speculators the writer has observed that the amateur speculator, when he makes a winning on his broker's suggestion or advice, calmly and unhesitatingly compliments himself on his own excellent judgment. Per contra if the venture is a losing one he has no hesitation in blaming his broker for the error of judgment. He is always reluctant to acknowledge that the loss may have been due to his own error; in fact he places so high a value on his own judgment that in seeking for excuses for the loss the idea of blaming his faulty methods or reasoning capacity is the last idea which occurs to him. There is no broker of experience who is not familiar with this type.

Conceit in this form is probably responsible for the inability of the average speculator to accept small losses. Now the average speculator will take a 1 to 3 percent profit and a 5 or 10 percent loss. A speculator who pays 1/4 commission for the round turn and interest charges— say 1/8 more—or 3/8 net on every hundred shares must make 1 percent at least on every four transactions to be even with the game. That is his handicap, and it is a severe one. But it is a well-known fact that the penalty is not considered in this light. If, therefore, it is calculated along with the traders' tendency to take small profits and large losses, it will at once be acknowledged that the amateur who backs his "raw" judgment has a precarious foothold in the quicksand which has overtaken him.

The speculator will purchase a stock on, say, a 10 percent margin. If it advances 1 1/2 points he will likely take his profit. If it declines 1 1/2 points he will hang on in the hope that he made no error of judgment, although he is somewhat doubtful. Should the decline be continued he will become even more doubtful, but as the loss is a substantial one, he is determined not to take it but to "hang on," as he is a fighter. Should the decline become more extensive, he, to use his own expression, becomes "obstinate." He "knows" that he is "right" and is determined to see "the thing through." And finally he probably closes the trade when his broker advises him to sell out or deposit more margin.

A successful speculator must make 1 percent on every four trades to be even with the game, and he must exactly reverse the novices' usual procedure of taking large losses and small profits. If he finds on testing his capabilities that he cannot do so, then he should abandon the speculative field to others, as there is no profit in it for him.

Upon more than one occasion the writer has known of two persons trading through a commission house in this way. One would buy a stock at a price and the other sell it short at the same price and yet both lose money. For example, A bought 100 shares of Sugar at 124 7/8 and B sold short 100 shares of Sugar at 124 7/8, and for the moment this was the high price. Sugar the following day declined to 123, at which point A, becoming nervous, sold and lost $212.50 plus one day's interest. B, elated over the keenness of his judgment and his beautiful foresight, made his trade with the idea of securing a 1 percent profit, but success emboldened him and he changed his plan and determined to hold on. Two days later Sugar had not only recovered its loss but had advanced to 128 1/2, where the short stock was bought in at a loss of $362.50. So much for the judgment of the amateur speculator.

Again, it is to be observed that a manipulated stock breaks sharply. The object of the break may be to force out margin traders—to dislodge their holdings when the advance will be resumed. The margin trader will grimly contemplate the decline and finally, when a serious loss confronts him, will sell out. He has too much "company," for other speculators in the same predicament are doing precisely the same thing—selling out at a loss, which is exactly what the manipulators playing with known conditions want. The manipulators having secured the desired stock and resumed the advance the speculator reasons with himself after this fashion: "There, I told you so. I knew I was right about that stock. Didn't I say to myself that it would sell up to —— ? Wasn't I convinced by what I knew that I had the right idea? Just my infernal luck. If I had only held fast and sat through the decline I would have been all right." Delusions again. There were many others who bought and sold under the same conditions. The decline would have been continued until all or most of the stock in question had been liquidated. The purchases of the margin speculators caused the manipulated decline. Their forced liquidation was necessary before the rise could be resumed. His sale of the stock induced the rally, or was at least a prerequisite. His purchase at the "top" helped check the rise and furnished fuel for a decline profitable to the manipulators. And yet in his own reasoning he has not considered himself as a factor contributing to the decline and aiding the subsequent recovery. In other words his judgment is wholly at fault; his conclusions were in error when the commitment was made and again following its consummation. He deceives himself so cleverly that the sophism of the manipulator is hardly necessary to add attractiveness and fascination to the struggle for money.

To land in the office of a commission firm all day and hear the market opinions expressed and the reasons for making commitments is to understand why so much money is lost. The man who "guesses," who has a "fancy for a particular stock," "who wishes to make a bit," who has "a tip," is in the majority. He has the speculative fever, and having contracted the disease he has not the time nor the mood to adopt the reasoning dictated by ordinary common sense.

"Buy," says a customer to his broker, "100 shares of Metropolitan at 150."

The stock is bought at a cash cost of $15,000. The customer's equity in the stock is $1,000. The stock is capable of wide fluctuations.

"What did you buy it on?" the customer is asked.

"My friend Smith told me that it is going up."

"Who is Smith?"

"Oh, a neighbor of mine. He heard it was a good thing from Jones, whose cousin is a director in the company."

Would this man, who is a type, have invested $15,000 (equity $1,000) in his own business (mercantile) without a most careful investigation of conditions, and consequences, profits and losses, present and prospective? Would Smith and Jones influence him in such a transaction? Certainly not. And yet thousands of stock market ventures are made annually without any more justification.

Therefore if about to speculate in stocks, it behooves you to ask yourself if you possess the temperament and accurate and swift reasoning powers necessary to cope with the ablest money getters in the world. If you do, you will find that hardly a day passes that Wall Street does not present, great opportunities for your skill in money making.

Chapter XXIX - An Interesting Inquiry

A correspondent asks for an explanation in detail of the meaning of "a large short interest" "a squeeze of shorts," "loaning rates for stocks," etc.

This inquiry implies some lack of comprehension of the principles involved in short selling, and as it comes from a banker, it is possible that others may be interested in a statement of how it is practicable to operate for a fall. The present form of operating for a fall is a modern device. It was preceded by a system of "buyers and sellers options" by means of which a buyer or seller acquired a right to deal at specified prices at dates more or less distant from the date of the contract. This, however, was a rather awkward method of trading and has ceased to exist in this market, except when it is unusually difficult to borrow stock.

In operating for a rise, only two parties are necessary for the contract. One buys and one sells. Delivery of the stock is made by the seller to the buyer; payment is received and the transaction is closed.

An operation for a fall as carried on in the New York Stock Exchange require three parties for its completion. Let us suppose that People's Gas is selling at par. A, although not the owner of any People's Gas, believes that the price will go lower. He, accordingly, offers a hundred shares of the stock at par. B accepts this offer and acquires the stock. A thereupon goes to C, who owns People's Gas, and borrows 100 shares, which A then delivers to B. B pays A $10,000, the price of 100 shares, and the transaction, as far as A and B are concerned, is at an end. But A, in order to obtain the use of the stock owned by C, has to deliver to C $10,000 as security for the return of the borrowed stock. Time elapses when it may be supposed that People's Gas has fallen to 95. A then buys of D 100 shares at 95, and, receiving the stock from D, returns it to C, the previous lender, and receives back from C the $10,000 deposited as security for the loan of the stock. A has, therefore, made $500 as the result of the operation for a fall begun with B.

A number of questions may be anticipated. Can A with certainty borrow stock from C? If C has the stock, and some one always has it, he is willing to lend it because there is little risk in so doing and because C gets the use of A's money, deposited as security, at lower rates of interest than C would have to pay for the use of the same amount of money if borrowed from a bank. Furthermore, if C borrowed $10,000 from his bank, he would be obliged to give as collateral securities valued at perhaps $12,000, whereas by loaning his stock to A he, in effect, procures a loan of $10,000 from A by the use of only $10,000 collateral.

The practice of borrowing and lending stocks is so universal that it is as much a part of the business to borrow stocks as it is to borrow money at the banks. The customer of an office has no trouble or difficulty on this account. He merely gives the order to sell, margins his account, and the broker arranges the terms of borrowing with his fellow brokers.

If there is a general impression that a stock is going to fall many people may sell it short at the same time. In this case, the borrowing demand may exceed the current supply. When this occurs the loaning rates fall. That is to say, A gives C the $10,000 as before described; but, on account of the demand for the stock, C does not pay as much interest. Assuming the money rate to be 4 percent, the rate on borrowed stock under normal conditions might be 3 1/2 percent, but if the demand to borrow were quite large, the lender of the stock would have to pay only 2 percent or even less for the money received as security. If the demand to borrow were still greater, the stock would loan at what is called "flat," which means that no interest would be paid on the money deposited; or, with a still greater demand, A would be compelled not only to give C the use of the $10,000 without interest, but would have to give C an arbitrary sum, called premium, in addition for the use of the borrowed stock. Premiums range all the way from 1-256 up to 1 percent or more a day—the latter, of course, only in very extraordinary cases. A premium of 1-16 of 1 percent per day is as high as premiums often go even in a bear market. This means that A not only gives his money without interest, but pays C $6.25 per day for the use of 100 shares of stock. This premium is, of course, charged by the broker to the customer who is short of the stock.

Generally speaking, it is cheaper to operate on the short than upon the long side of the market. The interest account always runs against the operator for a rise, while the operator for a fall, selling a non-dividend stock, has no interest to pay, unless the short interest creates a premium. Some houses allow customers a part of the interest received on account of short sales. Traders usually operate more heavily upon the short than upon the long side, as it does not take as much capital, the money required in borrowing stocks being furnished by the buyer.

All this suggests the meaning of the term "squeeze of shorts." If a large number of people are borrowing stocks, those who lend the stocks know who the borrowers are, and in a general way, something of the amount which is being borrowed. The rules provide that the borrower can any day return the stock borrowed and receive back his money. The lender can any day return the money deposited and get back the stock loaned, in which case some other lender must be found.

When a bear campaign is under way, the owners of stocks see their property depreciate in value. They then sometimes form combinations for the purpose of calling in a large part of the stock loaned in some one day. The consequence is that the borrowers, being notified to return stock, look about for other lenders, and, finding the supply insufficient, are obliged to buy stock in order to get it for delivery, and this buying, coming suddenly, is apt to make a rapid advance in prices, especially as the bulls who have called in the stock usually join in advancing quotations.

This would seem to be a very dangerous position for the bear, but in practice squeezes do not usually last very long or cause very great fluctuations. There have been cases where a squeeze of shorts has sent the price of a stock up 30 or 40 points in one day. There have been a considerable number of squeezes which have advanced prices as much as 10 points in a day. Ordinarily, however, the total advance, in a squeeze is not more than 4 or 5 points because the owners of stock, who understand the reasons for decline as well as, anybody, take advantage of the rise to sell and the bulls, therefore, supply their bear friends with stock enough to make the required deliveries. The possibilities of this kind always make the short interest watched with more or less attention as containing the germs of advance not founded on value, but on the necessity of having stock to deliver.

A corner is a disastrous affair, very seldom occurring. It means that the bears in over confidence have sold more of a certain stock than there is in existence. It is, therefore, impossible for some of the bears to obtain stock for delivery and the bulls therefore are able to bid the price up to any figure which they like. It is theoretically possible for a bear to be absolutely ruined in a close corner, but such a thing is almost impossible in these days of large capitalization. The last close corner in the market was in Northern Pacific. A corner usually inflicts great loss upon the people who make one as well as upon the bears who are caught, and knowledge of this fact has led the great market leaders time and again to refuse to permit corners when the oversold condition of the market would have justified it. Mr. Gould could undoubtedly have made a close corner in Missouri Pacific in 1884, but he absolutely refused to permit anything more than a well sustained squeeze of shorts.

Broadly speaking, there is no more danger in being short of the market than in being long, although care should be taken to sell only stocks of large capital, which are known to have been distributed and in which trading is active. There is a little more difficulty in selling fractional lots short on account of the fact that it is sometimes necessary for the broker to borrow 100 shares in order to deliver 20 or 30 shares. Ordinarily, however, this is arranged with the odd lot dealers without difficulty.

The public as a whole avoids the short side, partly through not under-standing it and partly through what seems to be a natural feeling against operating for a fall. Even among professional traders, there are many who have an instinctive feeling against the short side of the market. This, however, should be overcome by anyone dealing in stocks, inasmuch as the bear period is usually longer than the bull period and, in recent years an operator should have been a bear through at least half of every decade.

It has been said occasionally that bears never make fortunes. There are exceptions to this rule, and, so far as it is a rule, it is due to the fact that the general development of the country has had a tendency to bring out whole people who stayed long of securities even through a reorganization. This will probably be true to a certain extent in the future. Nevertheless a great deal more money has been lost on the long side of stocks than was ever lost on the short side. There is no sound reason against operating for a fall, when a bear period is under way.

Chapter XXX - Stock Market Manipulation

The machinery of a "pool" in stocks and the process of "working" the market is described as follows by an experienced manipulator.

"It is only fair to say that the public rarely sees value until it is most markedly demonstrated to them, and the demonstration comes generally at a pretty high price. It is easier for them, as experience shows, to believe a stock is cheap when it is relatively dear, than to believe it is cheap when it is more than cheap. A Stock Exchange operator or group of operators decides, we will say, that a certain stock is selling cheap—that is, below value. Value means, in Stock Exchange speculation, intrinsic value, plus future value, plus the additional Stock Exchange value. A large holder of the stock begins by going around to other large holders. Ownership is counted, and the outstanding stock in public hands fairly estimated.

"The first necessary detail is to 'tie up' in a pool these known holdings, in order to prevent realizing sales by larger interests. If such large holdings cannot be kept off the market, hands are joined in certain direction, and a long and patiently worked-out plan of accumulating the stock at low prices, before tying it up, is devised. This takes the form of manipulation within a certain range of prices. It may be assisted by natural stock market conditions, which encourage sales by outsiders at a sacrifice. Frequently persistent attacks on the stock by the people who wish to buy it are undertaken, which bring out miscellaneous public holdings, and which, if carried sufficiently far, dislodge even important inside holdings. To accomplish the decline, matched orders are frequently used, whereby the pool really sells to itself. Large offerings of the stock are also continually placed on the floor with no takers, resulting in the gradual lowering of commission-house selling limits, and the securing of cheap stock thereby.

"The question of borrowing money is important. A pool can rarely do the whole thing with its own capital. It is assumed that the money-market outlook favors a stable condition, for it is idle to suppose such operations would be conceived were conditions pointing otherwise. Money brokers have, of course, been employed by the house handling the pool, to borrow from the banks large amounts of time and short-time call money, termed 'special loans,' on which the collateral is largely to be the security in question, and on which loans a liberal rate is paid and liberal margins given.

"The 'publicity department' must also have been covered. Practically all important pool operators keep on hand this appendage to their work. The 'gossip' affecting the stock must be printed, and this department is systematized to a degree few suspect. It is generally in charge of a man intimately connected with newspaper channels, covering every important city, if need be, and this person receives a large compensation for the duty performed of distributing for circulation, when the managers of the pool see fit, items of news and gossip affecting the stock. The 'insiders' being in the pool, every item of news is carefully bottled up, and distributed only at what is thought to be the right time. The need for this will be apparent when it is observed that ᵢexplanation must be made for advances and excuse for declines in all manipulated stocks. The fact that insiders and the pool own the news, so to speak, and can thus discount its effect ahead of those which get it through 'publicity' channels, involves a moral point of view which has often been the subject of Wall Street discussion.

"The machinery of Stock Exchange work varies little. Orders are given to different sets of brokers from time to time to buy the stock, sometimes carefully and quietly, sometimes by openly and aggressively bidding for it, and vice-versa on the selling side. Barely is one broker alone allowed to remain - conspicuous on either side for any considerable length of time. All these transactions are 'cleared' by the brokers filling the orders; that is, instead of 'giving up' the names of their principals in the trades, they take in and deliver the stocks themselves, and then receive and deliver them from and to their principals,

"Market conditions now being favorable to the 'deal,' and emission of favorable news facts having resulted in public interest, the commission-house broker, who represents the 'public,' begins to be in receipt of many requests for opinion on the stock made active. The commission-house broker is a pretty good judge of the situation generally, and has spent his life studying values and watching manipulation. He thus assists in the operations by advising purchase. As a general rule, the advice falls flat, and few orders come out of it. But the pool continues; they are at present really buying stock and selling little. Some of these are actual trades, some are matched orders, but it is impossible, even for the brokers in the crowd, to tell which of such orders they may be. The result, however, is a marked stimulation of public interest, and commission-house buying orders begin. More news is published, and the deal becomes public talk.

"When this condition is created, the stock is up several points, and the pool begins to figure on selling. The machinery of the publicity department is then worked to its utmost extent, and the following morning finds a general demand for the stock from all commission houses. This is the time when a 'widespread' opening is figured on. Orders by the thousands are put in on the selling side, distributed to many brokers, with, of course, some buying orders also put in to a limited degree to 'take it as offered' at the opening. The 'high opening' is effected, and stock sold by balance sufficient to warrant pool support and renewed buying, after the overnight public orders have been filled. Then follows bold, aggressive buying by the pool in large quantities, aided by matched selling orders, and the volume of the business done attracts attention everywhere, and leads to enormous absorption by the public.

Given favorable conditions, the public buying thenceforward controls the market, and the pool places only 'supporting' orders in the stock from time to time, when outside interest flags. This public buying will continue until it has carried the price so much, beyond value that the pool can afford to liquidate freely. From then on, the operation proceeds to its profitable close, the various official, semi-official, and 'inside' announcements of news and suggestions covering the outlook in the immediate and near future — affecting the value of the stock, dividends to be paid, bond conversions, new alliances, consolidations — are the only necessary machinery."

Discussing "manipulation," Mr. Charles H. Dow says: "In a broad sense, trading on the Stock Exchange represents the operation of supply and demand as applied to securities. Ordinarily, however, a comparatively small part of the business is done by investors. The larger part is the outcome of professional trading and of the manipulation that is carried on by large interests to accomplish desired results.

"Trading in stocks can ordinarily be divided into professional and public dealings. There is a great difference between the two. Professional trading includes manipulation and the operations of those who make trading in stocks a considerable part of their daily business. Trading by the public covers investment business and a form of dealing which is partly speculative and partly investment. The professional operator trades all the time. Public trading is variable and very uncertain.

"The two extremes in the market are occupied by manipulators who either wish to buy or to sell in considerable quantity, and the public which, in the end, wishes to invest wisely. The manipulator, therefore, looks to the public to buy the stocks which he wishes to sell, or to sell those which he wishes to buy. A large proportion of all manipulation is aimed at the public, and professional traders are merely the middlemen who try to take profits out of the movements which manipulators appear to be trying to make.

"Suppose that a syndicate finds itself with a profit in the form of $10,000,000 worth of stock. The way to convey this profit into cash is to sell the stock. The syndicate, therefore, makes an arrangement with some skilled manipulator, who undertakes to induce the public to buy this stock. He begins by seeing that the merits of the case are stated as fully and as widely as possible.

"Whether the stock is intrinsically valuable and the enterprise sound or unsound makes a great difference as to the class of men which undertake the manipulation, but it makes but little difference as to the methods which are employed to secure public buying. In any event, the first thing is to have the property known about and talked about. The way to obtain this result is to have the stock do something which makes brokers and speculators and writers try to find out what is causing the movements which are recorded on the tape.

"Manipulators in such cases usually tell friends that the stock in question is to be made active and advanced. This brings buying of a professional class, because it is understood that a deal of the magnitude proposed cannot be accomplished without sustaining the market for the stock for a considerable time during which trading in it will be comparatively safe. Manipulators know, furthermore, that one of the best ways of getting a stock talked about is to have people tell friends that they have made money by buying it. Accordingly, there is almost always money to be made with a minimum of risk in the early stages of such a campaign.

"The manipulator must keep the stock active, buying and selling from ten to twenty thousand shares a day in order to keep traders confident of a market on which they can sell, if at any time they become alarmed. It is characteristic of the public to buy on advancing prices rather than on declining prices. A stock which is to be sold is therefore kept strong and advanced moderately if the general market will permit this to be done.

"The larger the manipulation, the larger will be the volume of professional trading, and the greater the likelihood of the public taking an interest in the stock. Usually in such cases the public buying is at first small; then it becomes more confident, and finally there is full confidence and the stock is rapidly unloaded upon the public buying. Then the activity dies out, professional trading becomes less, and the public is satisfied or dissatisfied with its bargain, as the case may turn out.

"This occurs to a greater or less extent in the market all the time. There is always some large interest which would like to have the public buy or sell, and manipulation is going on with that end in view. Large interests know that if the public can be induced to trade freely in stocks which are of unquestioned value, they can generally be led into other stocks; therefore, an attempt is often made to get the public into the market by advancing three or four leading stocks. If the public comes in, the market is widened. If the public does not come in, the manipulators discontinue their efforts to make a market after a few days and wait for a more opportune time.

"The rule for the public ought to be essentially the rule which is followed by professional traders. When a stock is made active, consider it first with reference to its value. If it is intrinsically cheap, it can ordinarily be traded in as long as it is kept active. But it is generally wise to sell when activity ceases. If the stock is apparently above its value, a good deal more caution ought to be exercised about going in, and stop orders should be used to guard against severe drops.

"Generally speaking, manipulation in a new property is for the purpose of selling; in an established property, bull manipulation is usually discounting some favorable news which insiders are holding back. Bear manipulation in perhaps eighty percent of cases is the discounting of something which is unfavorable. In twenty percent perhaps, it is for the purpose of accumulating stock with reference to a succeeding rise.

"As a whole, however, bear manipulation is founded on knowledge that the stock under treatment is intrinsically dear. It is not, as a rule, good judgment to buy stocks which are under attack until the attack ceases and there are indications of a rally on the short interest which may have been made by those who followed the decline." And again discussing a campaign in stocks, Mr. Dows:

"The stock market alternates between periods of activity and periods of rest. Its periods of activity are usually started by manipulation and continued by a mixture of manipulation and public buying. Professional traders and the public usually try to follow the lead of some individual or clique which is apparently advancing some particular stock or stocks.

"The main difference between manipulators and general traders is that the manipulator endeavors to take advantage of conditions which he thinks will exist in the future. He believes that the condition of money or change in the value of a particular stock or something else will cause a given security to be worth more three months hence than it is now. He buys stocks quietly and then advances the price slowly or rapidly, as the case may be, with the expectation that the public will take his stock off his hands when it sees what he saw at the beginning. Whether the public does this or refuses to do it determines the success of the campaign.

"In a majority of cases, a well sustained advance supported by large trading will bring enough outside buying to enable a manipulator to unload a substantial line of stock. The speculative public always buys on advances and seldom on declines, in which respect it differs from the investing public which buys on declines and sells on advances. One of the most skillful manipulators in Wall Street says that any stock possessing merit and having some influential fact to be made the basis of a campaign can be marketed at an advance in price, if the manipulating interest is willing to pay the cost of such a campaign, which would perhaps average $250,000.

"This cost is chiefly applied to the creation of a market. The rules of the Stock Exchange do not permit A to tell B to buy stock from C at a given price, but it does not prohibit A from telling B to buy 10,000 shares of a given stock and at the same time telling C to sell 10,000 shares of the same stock. The results of such an operation would show that many brokers had participated in the trading, through a wish to take either the buying or the selling side, and that on the whole the market, although artificial in one sense, had been legitimate in the sense that anybody had a chance to step in and buy or sell at the price established.

"A bull campaign in the market is a far bigger undertaking than a campaign in one stock, because many stocks have to be moved. On the other hand, it is sometimes easier because it invites cooperation from many sources, and sometimes a very small amount of encouragement in a stock is sufficient to induce its friends to do all that is required to promote an active speculation.

"The general progress in a bull market is for the manipulating interest to take two or three prominent stocks, and by making them active and higher attract attention to the fact that a campaign has been started. It is customary to take stocks of the best class, in which there is a large investment interest and where the supply of floating stock liable to come on the market is known not to be large. This is why St. Paul is so often used as a leader, and why closely held stocks like Rock Island, Northwest and others of that class are frequently advanced materially at the beginning of a bull campaign. "After stocks of this kind have been put up from 5 to 10 points, it is customary to shift the trading to stocks of the middle class on the idea that the public will not buy where there has been very large advances or where prices are very high, but will buy the cheaper stocks, even if they are intrinsically dearer. After stocks of this kind have been carried up a few points, it is customary to take up stocks of still lower price. It was considered for many years that when manipulators moved Erie, the end of a period of rising prices was at hand, because Erie was regarded as of next to no value and putting it up was considered diversion of the public, while other stocks were being sold.

"In a prolonged bull campaign, after the manipulators have moved the low priced stocks, they sometimes go back and move the others all over again, following the same order—the high priced stocks first, stocks of the middle class next, and then the cheapest on the list."

Chapter XXXI - The Record of Five Panics

Recorded below are the movements of a few active stocks in the panics of 1873, 1884, 1893, 1895 and 1901. The figures include the high prices prevailing shortly before the panic, in some cases those the day previous, and in others several days prior thereto. The low prices are the low points in the panic. The recovery given is to prices established within a week or the low point in the panic, coming in some cases within a few days and others not until nearly a week afterwards.

We are accustomed to think of the panic of 1873 as a very serious event. It was sufficiently serious to compel the closing of the Stock Exchange, but the decline outside of Lake Shore and Western Union, seems singularly small in view of losses which have been seen since. The panic itself was the culmination of a feverish market which had lasted all the week, the final break coming on Saturday. The average decline in that panic for nine active stocks was 10.32 percent. Figures follow:

1873 Panic	High	Low	Decline	Recov'y
N.Y. Central	**95**	**89**	**6**	**6**
Erie	**56 1/8**	**50 ¾**	**5 3/8**	**2 3/8**
Lake Shore	**88**	**68**	**20**	**11**
Wabash	**50**	**42 ½**	**7 1/2**	**7**
Rock Island	**95**	**86**	**9**	**10 1/4**
St Paul	**37 ½**	**30**	**7 1/2**	**5 1/2**
Lackawanna	**92 ½**	**86**	**6 1/2**	**7 1/8**
Western Union	**76**	**54 ¼**	**21 3/4**	**19 1/4**

The panic of 1884 reflected a larger average movement of prices, the losses of May 13-16 running from 8 to 15 points. The panic proper covered two days, while the recovery for ten stocks amounted to about five-eighths of the loss. Details follow:

1884 Panic	High	Low	Decline	Recov'y
Lake Shore	**94**	**81**	**13**	**8 7/8**
Rock Island	**116 1/4**	**109 1/2**	**6 3/4**	**6 1/4**
St. Paul	**77**	**65**	**12**	**7 5/8**
Burlington	**118**	**114 1/4**	**3 3/4**	**3 3/4**
Louisville	**44**	**30 1/4**	**14 3/4**	**5**
Missouri Pacific	**80**	**65**	**15**	**7 1/4**
Union Pacific	**50**	**41 1/2**	**8 1/2**	**3 7/8**
Western Union	**60**	**51 3/4**	**8 1/4**	**5 7/8**

The panic of 1893 was not very severe in the extent of the losses. The average fall in 13 stocks was 7.34 percent and in only a few cases did the loss exceed ten points. In the leading stocks quoted the losses were from 7 to 9 points, while the recovery was in nearly every case larger than the panic decline.

1893 Panic	High	Low	Decline	Recov'y
Burlington	**74**	**69 1/4**	**4 3/4**	**10 3/4**
St. Paul	**52**	**46 3/8**	**5 5/8**	**9**
Rock Island	**58**	**53**	**5**	**8 1/4**
Louisville	**53**	**47 1/2**	**7 1/2**	**10 1/8**
Missouri Pacific	**23**	**16 1/2**	**6 1/2**	**6 1/2**
Sugar	**73**	**66 3/4**	**6 1/4**	**8 3/8**

Chicago Gas	53	43 1/2	9 1/2	8 3/4
Western Union	75	67 1/2	7 1/2	10 5/8

The Venezuela panic of 1895 was about equal in intensity to the panics of 1873 and 1884. The average of 15 stocks fell 9.72 percent and a considerable proportion of the losses exceeded 10 points. The recovery was normal, about two-thirds the amount of the decline.

1895 Panic	High	Low	Decline	Recov'y
Burlington	199 7/8	178	21 7/8	14 1/2
St. Paul	72 3/8	60 1/2	11 7/8	7 1/2
Rock Island	72 1/2	59	13 1/2	10
N.Y. Central	98	90 1/2	7 1/2	7 1/4
Louisville	49 1/8	39	10 1/2	6 1/4
Missouri Pacific	27 5/8	19 1/2	8 1/8	6 1/4
Jersey Central	105 1/2	93	12 1/2	8 1/4
Sugar	100 1/2	92	8 1/2	7 7/8
Chicago Gas	68 1/2	57 1/2	11	7 7/8
Western Union	88 1/4	82 1/2	5 3/4	4 1/4

The following shows the fluctuation in a few stocks in the panic of 1901:

1901 Panic	High	Low	Decline	Recov'y
Atchison com	199 7/8	43	47 1/4	33
Burlington	72 3/8	178	21 5/8	14 1/2
St. Paul	72 1/2	134	54	29 1/2
Rock Island	98	125	44 7/8	28
Louisville	49 1/8	76	35 1/2	27 3/4
Manhattan	27 5/8	83	48 3/4	32 3/4
Missouri Pacific	105 1/2	72	44 3/4	36 1/2
N.Y. Central	100 1/2	140	30	15
Union Pacific	68 1/2	76	57	47 1/2
Amalgamated Copper	88 1/4	90	38 1/2	32
Tobacco	130 7/8	99	31 7/8	25 3/4
Union Pacific	119 1/2	98 1/2	21	13 1/4
Union Pacific	55	24	31	22

The declines are amazing when compared with the losses in other panics. Drops exceeded 40 points each in Atchison, St. Paul, Rock Island, Manhattan, Missouri Pacific and Union Pacific. The figures showing the high point were in some cases a week or more before the low point, but the drop as between the close, May 8th, and the low point, May 9th, covered in most cases a large proportion of the total decline.

The recovery was equally noteworthy. Union Pacific fell 57 points and rose 47% points within one week. Missouri Pacific fell 44% points and recovered 36% points in the same time. Other changes were almost as pronounced, going to show that in the extent of the fluctuations the panic this month was not to be named in the same breath with any panic record in the past.

It came and went so swiftly as to leave onlookers almost dazed. The speed and the extent of the recovery was all that saved the panic from being a financial catastrophe.

A long train of ills followed the smaller declines in panics past. The ills would have been a calamity had the low prices of May 9, 1901, continued for twenty-four hours.

The fluctuations of the May 9 panic show that while investment stock was not greatly disturbed and while commission houses proved to be strong enough to endure the strain without failure, the large trading which had been the feature of the market that year resulted in a rush to sell which carried prices far below what the decline would have been under normal selling pressure.

In other words, a great market represented by transactions of from two to three million shares a day, carries with it the possibility of movements in prices as much greater than normal as is the volume of trading greater than normal. There is a relation between the volume of business and the movement of prices. Great activity means great movements whenever the normal balance between buyers and sellers is violently disturbed.

Chapter XXXII - End of Several Booms

The 1902 autumn collapse of numerous stocks, inflated in the progress of the crazy "boom" of that season to the highest prices on record, suggested reminiscences. There are many of such reminiscences in point.

The first half of 1881 was a period much resembling the first four months of 1901. Burlington and Quincy had risen 22 points, St. Paul 28, Northwestern 23, Lake Shore, 17, Louisville 59, New York Central 27, Panama Railway 60, Western Union 57. This is the account of the period by a conservative reviewer of the time: "In the present era, consolidation is the word, and nothing in the financial world has now such charms for investors and capitalists as this magic term. Let the stocks of two non-competing companies each he selling at 20, with few buyers; let a consolidation be proposed, share for share, and immediately the stocks are run up to 30—40— 50—as the case may be. Add one more element to the transaction—water—in the shape of a stock distribution of 100 percent or more, and the original amount of stock, selling for only 20, is found to be worth par. This illustration may present an extreme view of the case in the details mentioned, but the general fact is indisputable that a large number of stocks on roads that have never paid a dividend, nor have any prospect of paying one for some years to come, are now selling at 60 to 100, which last year were considered dear at 20 to 40."

There was a somewhat familiar ring to the description when applied to markets of 1901-2.

President Garfield was shot on July 2. A railroad rate-war broke out almost the next week; following which, the hot winds ruined the corn crop. All these occurrences were described, as usual, as "thunderclaps from a clear sky." The markets collapsed, with intervals of support from "inside interests." By autumn, stocks were down as a rule 10 to 20 points, the intervening decline having been much more severe.

In most respects, 1882 resembled 1902 exactly as 1881 resembled 1901. The "boom" of 1882 occurred later in the year. Up to midsummer, advances of more than 10 points or thereabouts were not numerous. September's high level, however, showed upward movements such as 33 in New Jersey Central, 24 in St. Paul, 34 in Lackawanna, 23 in Illinois Central, and 58 in Manitoba. From then until November, prices hung fire; they even scored "marked advances," with the help of rumors from Mr. Vanderbilt. On November 18 money was described as "easy and in a normal condition." On Monday, November 20, it rose to 20 percent; it touched 30 later on. The surplus bank reserve had vanished, and a deficit of $3,000,000 took its place. It was said in a contemporary journal on November 25:

Stock market fluctuations have been so violent that feeling has almost verged on panic. The two points are the railroad war and the condition of the steel trade. Production of steel rails was enormously stimulated by rapid railroad building and the high tariff, and profits of manufacturers for a time were fabulous. It was a foregone conclusion (this was written long after the event) that mills could not keep up these profits.

They certainly did not keep them up, and depression was very severe, with a number of leading mills closed down during the autumn. The close of the year showed some such declines from the earlier autumn prices as 19 in Burlington and Quincy, 23 in Lackawanna, 11 in New York Central, 18 in Union Pacific, 22 in Manitoba, 23 in Pullman, 25 in Oregon Navigation. This was the last of the "big booms" of the period.

Passing over a long series of minor "booms," such as those of 1885, 1886, 1890, and 1895—nearly all of which were upset by the money market's rebellion against the excesses of the speculators—we come to 1899. The famous "Flower boom" was one of the most hollow in the entire series. It now appears laughable that the hopes of a great market should have been pivoted on such a stock as Brooklyn Rapid Transit, but so it was. The genial atmosphere of the commission office where stock-jobbing "tips" were distributed to the unwary had its effect on the whole community and on the whole stock list. "Brooklyn" itself rose not quite 60 points; but there were other advances like the 25-point rise in Burlington, New Jersey Central's advance of 25, Lackawanna's 22, Manhattan Elevated's 36, Metropolitan's 81, and New York Central's 20. The chief manipulator died suddenly on May 13. None, or practically none, of the windbag stocks were found in his vaults by his executors. He at least had sold out what he had; but the public was left to sell the rest. The bell-weather stock of the entire list fell 37 points within a day, and has never touched its high price since. Manhattan Elevated dropped off 28 points of its recent inflated price, Metropolitan 54, and the standard railway shares some 15 to 20 points. The new-fledged industrials, which had shared in the happy movement, tumbled in similar proportion. The interesting fact of the "boom" of 1899 was that the money market played little part in tripping up the Stock Exchange.

Chapter XXXIII - Dealing in Unissued Stocks

Trading in unissued securities, in advance of their actual distribution, started in this country in connection with the issue of the new Government 4 percent bonds, which were bought by the Morgan-Belmont syndicate on February 19, 1895. A somewhat similar practice had previously been in vogue in Europe, having originated in the desire of investors to arrange for the purchase of bonds or stocks in advance, when new issues were expected to come out. They naturally appealed to their banker to put through the transaction, and it came to be a common thing to fix upon the price which investors were to pay. This naturally led to trading in contracts for the new securities, based upon the estimated value which different persons thought they were worth.

Messrs. Morgan and Belmont had so arranged the terms for the flotation of the $62,315,000 of new Government 4's —so they thought—that those placed abroad would not be resold to this country right away, which would tend to defeat the purpose for which they were issued. But the foreign bankers were experts at disposing of securities before they were issued. Before the Secretary of the Treasury had put out the first lot a large number had changed hands at a sharp advance in price, and in many instances the original buyers never saw the securities which they had turned over. What they were really dealing in were contracts to deliver United States Government 4's, "when, as, and if issued." The syndicate got the bonds at 104 and offered them to the public at 112 on the next day. On February 25, only 5 days after the offer to the public, trading in the new bonds, "when issued," began in the unlisted department of the Stock Exchange, the initial sale being at 118, or 5% above the price at which they were offered to the public. The price ran up to 119 before the end of the week. On March 14, when the first bonds appeared, the price did not go above 120.

While there was much of a speculative character about the trading in the new bonds, most of the buying above 118, before the securities were issued, represented the execution of orders for investors who had failed to get any when they were offered at 112, and who thought they might have to pay still higher prices after the certificates came out. In this case they did not gain much by buying the "when issued" contracts.

The trading in Government bonds before issued opened up to American traders visions of great possibilities in getting an early start in new securities, and when the reorganizations of Northern Pacific, Reading, Atchison, and other railroad properties came along a little later dealing in contracts became a common thing on the Broad Street curb. For a long time the foreign bankers, who are experts in figuring out the niceties of "arbitrage" and of exchange transactions, did most of the business in the "when issued" contracts. One of their number says that profits of from $25,000 to $50,000 were sometimes made in a single security before the certificates came out. They made large amounts out of Northern Pacific, but some of them came out with a small loss on Atchison bonds and stocks, because they had made a mistake in not allowing enough margin for interest. Interest is a very important item. The method of operators consists in buying the old shares and selling the prospective new ones against the former. In determining the price at which to sell the new the interval of time before the new are issued is taken into consideration, since interest must be paid on the shares which have been bought, and they must be carried until they can be exchanged. The trouble in the case of the Atchison was that the new securities did not come out until a later time than had been expected.

The important part which contracts for securities "when issued" may play was perhaps best illustrated by the first transactions in those of the U.S. Steel Corporation on the Broad Street curb. These prices really determined the movements of Federal Steel, Steel and Wire, and other subsidiary shares on the Stock Exchange. For several days it was not known just what the old shares ought to be worth in the exchange for new, and they fluctuated wildly until the relationship was determined by watching the prices of U.S. Steel shares when issued. The common started on the curb at 38, and the preferred at 82% in the second week of March, last year. That an investor benefited by buying before issued seemed clear from the fact that when the new shares came out and they were introduced on the Stock Exchange, on March 28, the common started off at 42 and the preferred at 92. From the standpoint of the person who wanted to buy the old shares and sell the new against them it was a difficult task, because of the restrictions placed upon the exchange of securities. Some of the traders tried a little of what was termed "arbitraging" between the Stock Exchange and the curb, figuring out, as they thought, a profit of 4 or 5 points, but they gave it up when they realized how completely the syndicate controlled the situation.

The dangers sometimes incident to trading in unissued securities are illustrated by the San Francisco bond case (1902) and that of the United States Steel bonds, which it was proposed to issue, partly for the retirement of preferred stock and partly for betterments. Syndicate agreements provide, as a rule, that the participants shall take their proportion of the new securities issued, and find a way to dispose of them. It has been a common habit for syndicate members to make contracts for the sale of the securities "when, as, and if" issued so as to get them off their hands as soon as possible. In the case of most of the companies promoted or reorganized by Mr. Morgan, the syndicate members were expected to take their proportion of the securities, unless it was specifically agreed that the managers were to dispose of them. No negotiable certificates were issued permitting of the transfer of subscriptions, as in the case of the San Francisco Street Railway Company, financed by Brown Brothers & Co. The subscriptions of the latter are dealt in on the curb; exactly like stocks.

The trouble in the case of the 'Frisco bonds doubtless arose from the fact that the agreement provided that the members should take the stock to which they were entitled. They might also be compelled to take the new bonds unless the bankers were able to sell them to better advantage—or such part as the bankers did not sell. It was possibly inadvertence on the part of the subscribers that caused them to sell the new 'Frisco bonds, not knowing whether they would have the certificates to deliver; or, they may have thought there would be "enough to go around" when $20,000,000 were issued. The small amount of San Francisco bonds that came out at the start, as well as the possibility that only $50,000,000, instead of $250,000,000 of U.S. Steel bonds might have been issued, illustrate two of the dangers that may arise from selling securities in advance. In the one case a temporary scarcity rendered it possible to run the price up to a fictitious figure, assuming that the contract was literally enforced which compelled the seller to deliver them the moment they were issued. In the second instance, a smaller issue of U.S. Steel bonds would render it necessary for the seller to deliver a really more valuable security than he thought he had sold, and he might have to take a loss.

Of course, there is always the risk that plans may be changed and the securities will not be issued at all. A notable instance which caused quite an uproar was the announcement of a new issue of India stocks by the British Government some years ago. These were extensively traded in "when issued," but the Government changed its mind, and all of the transactions had to be declared off.

Chapter XXXIV - The Tipsters Point of View

The stock market from the tipster's point of view is not uninteresting. As a guide, however, he is invariably less valuable than an honest broker, and is usually very clever in "calling" market movements after they have run their course.

The following "study" of stock speculation is the work of an advertising tipster, and the reader will be his own judge of its value.

Wall Street's Great Game

Over 90 percent of the transactions on the Exchange are purely speculative—mere betting on quotations. So, likewise, 90 percent of the fluctuations are based on manipulation, and not on the values of the properties or outside conditions. Good or bad crops have a very close relationship with the country's actual prosperity, and should be the paramount factor in stock market values; but the insiders are supreme in Wall Street, and manipulate prices up and down without much regard for crops, earnings or any outside factors. Nobody can scut his eyes to the fact that in a bull market (that is, when insiders are long), stocks go up in the face of bad news, and in a bear market (insiders short), prices go down, no matter how rosy the outlook. Every extended movement is planned in advance and controlled throughout by the shrewdest financial generals in the world. They know the actual—not the published—conditions of the properties whose stocks are to be handled. They know when natural conditions warrant a bull or a bear campaign. They leave nothing to chance, but their trump card is the weakness of human nature.

When the plans have been arranged for a bull campaign, or extended upward movement, every sort of bear argument imaginable is used to induce the public to sell; elections, war scares, stringent money, damaged crops, gold exports, etc., etc., are resurrected and used effectively year after year. Meanwhile, the insiders are quietly accumulating stocks and checking every advance at certain figures. Finally, when all is ready, and the vast majority of speculators bearish, and declines seem inevitable, the bull market commences—often upon the actual happening of some anticipated bad news. The advance is at first very gradual; some stocks rise, others remain stationary while a break is made in one or two, to encourage the bears in putting out more "short lines." Presently the "leaders" advance more rapidly, and the others begin to move up. Each stock has its individual range and peculiarity in moving, though toward the end of a campaign those stocks which have been lagging behind come forward with a rush. The importance, therefore, of confining your attention to the leaders during the first half of a campaign, can readily be seen. The money made on them can be transferred to the "specialties" before the latter have had their advance.

During all this time there have been thousands of fluctuations, like surface waves, but the tide is on the flood and prices steadily rise. Every one becomes enthusiastic over improving business. The "sneaking" bull market has developed into a "creeping" bull market and the "lambs" are at last making money. Finally there comes a grand rush to buy, accompanied with great excitement and the wildest optimistic rumors. Enormous quantities of stocks are handled, and this is the finish, for a time, at least, of the bull campaign. Insiders are "unloading"; and although newspapers, financial writers, news bureaus, and every bull artifice that can be devised, are used to "jolly" the public into buying, though everything looks rosy and there is not a cloud in the financial horizon, the market comes to a stand. Spite of good news prices sag. Gradually but surely and with many false upward starts, the market falls.

Once the insiders have distributed their stocks, absolutely nothing can keep prices up. Before long, excuses are found to force down the market; and then the same old game is played over again. It all resolves itself into two grand divisions: Accumulation—or buncoing marginal and investment owners out of their stocks at less than actual value; and Distribution—or selling the same stocks, by means of false pretenses, at vastly more than actual value.

The details are changed, but the same general tactics are employed year after year. The lambs never learn to buy stocks when everything looks darkest. They never learn that a bull campaign begins in gloom and ends In glory.

Pool Methods

Human nature is such that it is almost impossible to buy stocks at the bottom, with nothing but bad news pouring in. It is still harder to sell at the top when the market looks strong and only goods news is heard, and personal friends tell you of some Insider who has assured them of a 15 or 20 points advance in such and such a stock. People generally buy at these times. The manipulators' game is to play on this phase of human nature, and they pull the wires so as to get everybody full of financial optimism Just at the time when they are ready to sell. Surely anyone can see that the big fellows are not here for their health, or for glory, but to make money, and the largest amount possible, with absolute disregard of whose pocket it comes out of. SOME-BODY must lose the money which they make. See to it that YOU are not one of those somebodies.

In accumulating stocks preparatory to a bull campaign, the usual pool method is to depress prices as far as possible with a view of catching stop orders, etc., then to quickly buy without bidding up prices until the market has advanced three or four points, then work it down again as far as circumstances will permit. After some weeks of feverishness and narrow fluctuations, during which time the pools are quietly gathering in all the stock possible without bidding up prices, the market is allowed to run up five to ten points, and the pools take profits on a portion of their holdings, as a kind of feeler. Then prices are worked down about half the advance, and their sales repurchased. The next advance may carry the market up ten or fifteen points, and so on. There may be a dozen pools at work all this time in different stocks, but they are all playing the game on practically the same lines.

Before the upward move is fairly under way, and sometimes after the move starts, sudden breaks will be made in a stock to shake out "company" and induce short selling; for if outside traders can be made to think the stock is a sale whenever it "puts its head up," a large and weak short interest can be fostered, which makes upward manipulation easy. A common method, not only by the pools, but by many professional operators, is to divide their holdings into three equal lots; holding one lot perhaps two or three years, for the extreme movement of say 80 points. The second lot is sold at the culmination of each minor bull campaign, perhaps in three or four months, at a profit of twenty to thirty points, and bought back on a reasonable decline. Profits of five to ten points are taken on the third lot, which is also bought back in due course. This method, with but slight variations, was employed by the Insiders from August, 1896, to March, 1899. Some operators divide their purchases into four lots instead of three, using the fourth lot entirely for scalping purposes.

When the larger pools are preparing for a bear campaign, they usually begin by holding the market strong, and if possible advance two or three showy, attractive stocks with great ostentation, to fool the public with stories of "Vanderbilt buying," "Standard Oil buying," etc., while they sell the general list at the highest possible prices. The smaller pools, however, and individual professional bears, often cover with as little loss as they can if their short selling and manipulation fail to bring about a decline; and then they help to bid up stocks a few points to where they can again commence selling, and so on until finally a break is forced. Whether the pool be big or little, when at last the market commences going in their favor, they hammer it on the way down, and as the decline continues, liquidation of long stocks is induced, and outside short sellers invariably come in about the time bottom is reached.

Almost every important play which the pools make in stocks is in anticipation of some event. Often the movement culminates just after, and occasionally just before, the happening of this event. When, however, there is a strong element of uncertainty, and even the insiders themselves are not sure of the result, then the movement will probably continue after the anticipation becomes an accomplished fact.

Hints on How to Win

"In all the stupendous works of nature there is nothing more sublime than the egotism of the man who expects to win when he plays at a game of skill which he does not understand, and has for an opponent an expert who uses marked cards."

But a study of the following facts and suggestions should enable you to play this game with at least a chance of success.

1st.—When a dull, weak market has become active and declining, then panicky, and enormous quantities of stock are changing hands, prices are most likely very near the bottom, and a rally of several points may be expected. After this rally, there is usually a second downward movement to about the previous low figures touched before; but this is not invariable. Stocks bought at such times should be held for good advances, provided other signs indicate that it is the end and not the beginning of a bear campaign.

2nd.—If after a dull, sagging market, when everybody is bearish, or after a decline, there comes a rally of 3 or 4 points, and then certain stocks lose 1/2 to 3/4 of this rally, after which they rally again, and this time lose only about half of the latter rally, the next upward move of about a point makes it certain that insiders or pools are accumulating those stocks, which will indicate higher prices. The same movements reversed, when market is at top, indicate lower prices.

3rd.—If, after a pronounced general advance, there comes a day of large transactions, excitement and enthusiasm, the advance will suddenly stop and the market react, even if it goes higher ultimately. Then will ensue a period of 2 to 5 points fluctuations, that is, a "traders' market"—just the thing for the "scale" and "fluctuation" systems.

4th.—Keep accurate charts and records of the most active stocks, and endeavor through them to learn what the insiders are doing. When your charts show a great many fluctuations over a narrow range in a certain stock after a decline, and finally the stock advancing beyond this range on heavy transactions, it will be a fair assumption that the insiders or pools have been accumulating that security and intend advancing the price. If your records show that several leading stocks are acting in a similar manner, it is very good evidence that a bull market is ahead.

5th. — After the market has been dragging along a low level for some weeks, with only small fluctuations in prices, then a day or two of extreme dullness, it is safe betting that a bull campaign will soon be under way. When the bears get tired of selling and there are no more stocks offered, the market of course comes to a standstill, and the insiders conclude the time has arrived to advance prices.

6th. — When everything appears to favor lower levels and everybody is bearish, when every possible reason is given why you should sell, when continued bad news comes in — and yet stocks still fluctuate over a narrow range, without going materially lower in spite of short selling by chronic bears — you may be sure the insiders are accumulating, and the next pronounced move should be upward.

7th.—The volume of transactions is an, excellent indicator as to the general trend of prices. When the largest volumes are on the advances and trading falls off on the reactions, you can be pretty sure it is a bull market.

8th.—It's usually dangerous to buy stocks on the third day of an advance. The market generally moves two or three days in one direction and then either rests or reacts. If stocks close at top after a three days' advance and open strong next morning, four times out of five they will react a point at least. But if after a three days' rise the market halts, and there is no decided movement either way for a couple of days, the reaction is not likely to occur. The advance will probably be resumed on the third day of this resting period; vice versa after a three days' decline.

9th.—A three days' rampant advance after a prolonged bull market, coupled with enormous transactions, great excitement and enthusiasm— especially on the culmination of expected good news—is an infallible indication that the campaign is over, for a time at least.

10th.—When a stock advances for three days, and on the third day of the advance the total transactions in that stock foot up an enormous total, the move is very likely over. But when, after a period of dullness, a stock begins to advance on heavy transactions, buy it for a three days' rise.

11th.—There are only two ways to trade—either take small losses, or else never take a loss at all. This is a very old rule, but a good one. If a stock goes against you, limit your loss at from half a point to 2 points; especially so in the case of "tips." Or else buy on scale down, first taking very good care to find out that the shares you propose buying are intrinsically worth the current market price. Unless you deal in small lots, or are a capitalist, the limited loss plan is preferable. Another old rule and a good one, is to buy when everybody wants to sell, and sell when everybody is clamoring to buy.

A Few DONT's

DON'T "go short for a turn" in a bull market, or "long" in a bear market, no matter how certain you may be that a reaction is due. It is poor policy to run the risk of losing ten points to scalp one. If you have good profits and expect a reaction, close out if you choose, and buy back cheaper—but DON'T "go short." DON'T shut your eyes to the bear elements in the situation because you are long of stocks. And DON'T be a "chronic bear," blind to all signs of higher prices. DON'T allow your desires and hopes to obscure your judgment; the wish should not be father to the thought. Keep posted on all the elements in the situation and how they are likely to influence public sentiment, but DON'T forget that this is of less importance than acknowledge of how the insiders are working. DON'T be a bull when the public have the stocks, and DON'T be a bear when the floating supply of securities is held by insiders.

DON'T attach importance to the weekly "Bank Statements" or to London quotations; they are often "doctored," and are usually misleading. DON'T read the gossip or "news" in financial papers, brokers' letters, etc. Insiders manipulate the press as they do values, and very little goes into public print that they want to keep out. Don't live over the ticker, unless you are an expert at tape reading; it will only mislead you"; nor will you learn anything from the old "rounders" and "tapeworms" who study it. DON'T handle stocks not easily traded in; and DON'T try to get the last fraction when you already have good profits. DON'T fight the course of the market, rather follow it; but if you have been bearish in a bull campaign, DON'T reverse your position and become a bull when the advance is over; if you have been bullish when prices were falling, DON'T become a bear when the bull campaign is about to begin. "Run quickly or not at all." DON'T trade in one stock exclusively, as something might happen; divide your trades over 5 or 6 sound stocks. DON'T overtrade, or carry a larger number of shares than your capital justifies. And DON'T buy on bulges nor sell on breaks.

Systems

The two following systems, or rather methods, are as good as any: Use the first toward the end of either a bull or bear campaign, and continue until an extended movement is indicated; then switch over to the second.

Catching the Fluctuations. —During a 'traders' market," or a market without any pronounced trend one way or the other, any active stock will move over certain points dozens of times. The plan is to place a net that will catch these daily fluctuations. Buy 100 shares of, say, St. Paul, at the market price, and 100 more every half point up or down, but don't hold more than 100 at a time at the same figure, and don't accumulate more than 600 shares altogether. Treat every purchase as a separate transaction, and whenever a profit of one point net is shown, sell that 100 shares, buying back on a one point reaction. When a purchase and sale are both indicated at the same figure, do nothing—simply hold that 100 shares, but for convenience assume that 100 has been sold and 100 bought. If St. Paul should keep on going up without a reaction, you would thus always be long of 200 shares. Don't get frightened because of a temporary downward tendency. The fluctuations are what bring you profit. Great care must, of course, be taken not to work this system on the bull side if the general trend is downward, or on the bear side if the trend is upward.

Limited Pyramiding.—When the rules and indications already given show that a pronounced upward movement is not far off, buy on weak spots such quantities as your means justify. Do nothing more until the bull campaign gets under way. Then buy small lots with your profits on recessions of half a point, and as much more every half point down. Such recessions are continuous, two or three a day, even in the strongest bull market. Continue these tactics until there come two or three days of rapidly advancing prices, general enthusiasm, and heavy volume of transactions; in other words, when the public are rushing in to buy, and the pools are feeding out some of their stock. Then sell about half your holdings; wait for a reaction of at least a point, and begin buying back every half point down. When the upward movement is resumed follow same plan as before, until the signs and principles laid down in preceding pages show the whole bull market as about to culminate. Then sell out everything on the "bulge." Wait for the third day of a reaction and buy moderately for the "second top." When you get out this time, either take a rest, or return to the "Fluctuation System," playing it on the short side.

Further Remarks on How to Play the Game Successfully

Though the same general tactics are pursued year after year, insiders constantly scheme out new tricks to deceive their opponents. If you propose, therefore, to win money instead of losing it, you must not only master the ordinary complications of the game, but also keep up to date, the same as in any other business. Good judgment, both of conditions and men, is necessary. If you keep charts, keep them properly, and learn how to read them. Do you think a farmer who had never seen the ocean before, could navigate a ship by means of charts? I believe in charts only when other indications point the same way. Watch the volumes of daily transactions. Both bull and bear campaigns culminate in large volumes. By large volumes I mean large as compared with the preceding daily volumes. Don't mistake for this, those times when, after a long period of dullness, certain stocks begin to advance on heavy buying. Time and seasons are to be considered. Four months is the usual length of time for a bull campaign. As a rule, there is also a minor bull campaign in midwinter. The position on the market of the public and small traders is of great importance. No bull campaign ever started with the public long of stocks, and no bull campaign ever yet ended with the public short. Rates at which stocks are carried on the Exchanges give a clue to the public's position; but as loaning rates on stocks are easily manipulated a better way is to find out from bucket Shops or brokerage houses which side their customers are on. If outsiders are all selling, it is pretty safe for you to buy, and vice versa.

When heavy volumes begin to come out the old trader knows there is 'something doing.' There are times when it is comparatively easy to discern whether activity in a stock will be followed by an advance or a decline. Don't try to trade every day, and don't chase fractions. Unless playing some good scale system, take a quick loss if a purchase or sale goes against you, and start over again. If it goes in your favor, try to get 5 to 20 points, according to what the stock is. One trade closed at a profit of 10 points will more than make up for five losing trades of one point each. As to the usual scale system (that is, buying small lots every point or half point down, and taking profits of one point net on any separate lot), it is all right; but you must first be sure that the stock you propose buying is worth approximately its current market price; then you must put up each big margins In order to be absolutely safe, that your percentage of profit on the investment will usually look very email.

Chapter XXXV

A collection of Wall Street aphorisms, maxims, truisms, proverbs, opinions and points of view, follows: Hearsay is half lies. Talk little and well. Control your temper. Enough is great riches. No one is always right. The first loss is the best. All players cannot win. Press luck to the finish. There is luck in leisure. Cheap advice is plentiful. A true word needs no oath. Done leisurely—done well. Negotiate before slaughter. When in doubt do nothing. After one loss comes many. Wall Street easily forgets. Great vaunters, little doers. Learn to take a loss quickly. Information makes a market. Nothing risked, nothing won. For a lost thing care nothing. Losses make us more cautious.

Little and often fills the purse. All is not lost that is in peril. When wisdom fails, luck helps. Punctual pay gets willing loan. Let profits run; limit all losses. Some men learn only by failing. Losers are always in the wrong. Cut a loss and let a profit run. A thing well bought is half sold. A plunger gets but seldom holds. Interrogate before you negotiate. Money is most valued when lost. Everyone is wise after the event. At a great bargain make a pause. Don't buy an egg until it is laid. Under fair words beware of fraud. Liberal hands make many friends. Novelty always appears handsome. Business neglected is business lost. After extreme weakness buy stocks. More sheep than lambs are sheared. Better lose the wool than the sheep. It is fortune, not wisdom that rules. Fraud is built on misrepresentation. Don't put all your eggs in one basket. Better lose the saddle than the horse. The market will be here tomorrow. Small losses often prove great gains. Men often seem rich to become rich. Inspiration often means perspiration. By the husk you may guess at the nut. Hear the other side and believe little. Beware of one who has nothing to lose. Speculation begins when certainty ends. The rich buy in a hurry when they buy. In a traders' market buy low—sell high. Delay overmuch is oftentimes great risk. An old man's sayings are seldom untrue. Get an investment that will let you sleep. They who lose today may win tomorrow. Opportunity is often lost by deliberating. Illusions ruin all those whom they blind. The maxims of men disclose their hearts. The poorer the sheep, the harder it bleats. A little loss frightens—a great one tames. Where something is found there look again. He that will have eggs must have cackling. The best is always the cheapest in the end. Liberality is not giving largely, but wisely. Get information before you invest, not after. Thrice happy they who have an occupation. Wisdom adorns riches, and shadows poverty. No lock will hold against the power of gold. Begin to buy when prices are dull and weak. Satisfy the rich and they will pay your price. He is a wise man who wears poverty decently. Great minds have purposes; others have wishes. An ounce of luck is worth a pound of wisdom. Great undertakings require great preparations. Of what use is a 10 percent margin in a panic?

is not invariable. The lowest prices are usually made on the second day. From those prices there is a recovery amounting usually to more than half the amount of the decline from the level of prices prevailing before the panic. This recovery culminates within a week and sometimes not for thirty days, but in all cases prior to the May 9, 1901 panic, within thirty days. After that comes a slow decline during which prices lose at least half of their recovery and in case of a bear market all the recovery and more is lost.

Nothing is more common than to hear people say that the big bankers can do what they please with the stock market, and yet nothing is further from the truth. The stock market is in the end made by the public and by no one else, if the smaller fluctuations and minor "swings" be disregarded. Traders can move prices within narrow limits; bankers can move them within wider limits, but without the public the market tends constantly to equilibrium. Stocks go off when traders sell and rally when they cover; stocks advance when bankers bid them up, but decline unless the public buys on the advance. Both traders and bankers can and generally do anticipate the public in its operations, but if the public does not do what is expected of it nothing is gained thereby.

The investor determines the prices of stocks in the long run. This statement is sometimes disputed by those who point to the fluctuations which are confessedly made by manipulators without regard to value. It is true that such fluctuations occur, but when the manipulation is over; the voice of the investor is again heard. If he decides that a given stock is worth only so much, the manipulator will ultimately be compelled to accept that valuation because manipulation cannot be kept up. The object of manipulation is to buy below value and sell above value. The experience of all traders will afford many illustrations of how stocks have recovered after artificial depression and relapsed after artificial advances to the middle point which represented value as it was understood by those who bought or held as investors.

The evident uncovering of many stop-loss orders on a decline moved an old trader to belittle their use for speculative protection. "When a man," said he, "gives his broker a stop order he thinks that only he and his broker know it. But the broker, being a busy man, turns the stop over to some two-dollar specialist in that particular stock. In the course of a week, or two weeks, the principal specialists in any active stock accumulate a large number of such orders. Then the manipulating interests go to them and say: 'What have you got in the way of stops?' The specialists disclose what they have, and if the stops are abundant enough the manipulating interests say: 'Shake them out.' That's why it so often happens that a stock moves just far enough against you to catch your stop and then moves back again."

Daily fluctuations in the stock market are influenced by sentiment. There are perhaps 400 men who trade more or less on the floor of the Exchange. They are not generally the class of operators who try to forecast the somewhat distant future, but their object in their daily trading is to act promptly on such news and developments as come to them hour by hour. Practice in this has made the professional traders extremely skillful in detecting signs of changes in the market and in reading anything that is likely to affect trading. The result is that the attention of these operators is apt to be fixed on one or two prominent facts and the trading of all hinges more or less on developments at those points. If the market is declining and it begins to rally on some special news or special buying, traders all want to buy at the same time, causing the speed of the recovery. Or, if news is unfavorable, the room wants to sell all at the same time, causing the rapidity and the extent of decline. Value has little to do with temporary fluctuations in stock prices, but is the determining factor in the long run. Values, when applied to stocks, are determined, in the end, by the return to the investor, and nothing is more certain than that the investor establishes the price of stocks. The manipulator is all-powerful for a time. He can mark prices up or down. He can mislead investors, inducing them to buy when he wishes to sell, and to sell, when he wishes to buy; but manipulation in a stock cannot be permanent, and in the end the investor learns the approximate truth. His decision to keep his stock or to sell it then makes a price independent of speculation and, in a large sense, indicative of true value. It is so indicative because the price made is well known to insiders, who also know better than anyone else the true value of the stock. If the price is too low, insiders will buy; hence stability in the price of a stock means that insiders do not think the stock especially cheap or dear.

Early information affecting stock market fluctuations is dangerous to trifle with and the story of the "Minister and the Stock Exchange," as told in the following letter to the *London Spectator,* illustrates the point:

Sir: Permit me to impart to you the substance of a family legend. My grandfather was a city man, a Member of Parliament, and an adherent of the Grenville party. On matters connected with "the city" the politician was in the habit of consulting the city man in question. On one occasion when the subject of conversation was the possibility of realizing large profits from early information, Lord Grenville asked my grandfather whether he thought all the stories told of these large profits were founded on fact. My grandfather answered that he was not a stockjobber, still less a political authority, but that he could easily test the matter if Lord Grenville wished it. His Lordship then said: "I will give you the earliest information obtainable in the position I hold as Prime Minister, and you shall try your fortune and mine in dealing on the Stock Exchange."

At the end of a year the statesman and merchant met again to study the account after the earliest information given by the Prime Minister to the city man bad been acted on. My grandfather rendered the account, and showed that, had the information led to transactions on a large scale, all parties connected with them would have been utterly ruined.

When the battle of Waterloo was fought it was not the Government which told the news to Rothschild, but Rothschild who told it to the Government.

In my own experience I have known the man with the most brilliant prospects granted to any one utterly disgraced and ruined by attempting to deal in the manner suggested. His own description of what occurred will suffice. He had not a minute's peace all the morning till the evening paper came in with the news obtained by its editor, not by the speculator's exclusive information. H. B. G.

If the public would realize one thing, and realize it so that it never forgot it, its chances in Wall Street would be materially improved. From the Wall Street point of view—meaning thereby the sentiment prevailing as a whole, and on an average on the part of the speculative and financial community—the public has money which Wall Street desires that it shall exchange for securities. It is true that so far as a large section of the Street is concerned there is not the slightest desire to knowingly sell worthless securities to the public. The essence, however, of the matter is that Wall Street is always in the position of selling securities to the public for money, sometimes being able to sell easily and in quantity, and at other times not being able to sell much, and that only with difficulty. The public should remember that all the manipulation of Wall Street has but one end, namely, to exchange securities for money. For in the long run the public does not sell securities. What it buys and pays for it generally keeps. Once stocks have been sold to the public they seldom or never return in any quantity to the Street, Jay Gould said once that the first requisite for successful speculation was patience. Most operators realize that they have cut short their profits, frequently and needlessly, by the lack of patience. A great movement in the market does not usually come suddenly. The market, while manipulated in a narrow sense, is in its large sense created by conditions. The prices of stocks act as a sort of skirmish line, out in front of the developments that have actually occurred, and in the direction of those which are expected to occur. When they get too far out, they have to fall back. Then, when the facts become clear, they move for a time with a rush. When the tide is nearly in or nearly out, there is a period of slack water. When the business tide is nearly in or nearly out, there is a period when it is impossible to say definitely that conditions have changed in a large way either for better or for worse. Some conditions may have changed and others not, with the balance doubtful. This makes a corresponding situation in the stock market. Prices go off on that which is unfavorable and recover again on that which is favorable. The net change during such a time may be small even if the market is fairly active and the gross changes are quite large.

"Addison Cammack, a great bear trader in his day, believed in Napoleon's famous dictum: 'The Lord is on the side of the heaviest battalions.' That is, he would start to sell the market; if it yielded, he would follow up the advantage with an avalanche of selling orders; he overwhelmed his opponents. The simple question was could he sell more stock than the other side was able to or willing to buy. If the heavier battalion happened to be on the other side and the market continued to advance he quickly beat a retreat so as to be able to fight another day. And this is the difference between the big, wise bear and the foolish little bear. The big bear knows that some time conditions will be ripe to hammer the market. He tries it occasionally. Frequently he makes a mistake, but he withdraws from the field with his resources practically intact. His opportunity surely comes, and then there is dismay among the bulls. The cub specimen, however, does not know enough to run away from danger. He continues to fight when there is no fighting chance. That is why Addison Cammack retired from the field with the reputation of having been a very big and dangerous bear, while so many cubs with bear instincts never grew up into fearsome objects."—Schuyler West.

Question—In answer to an inquiry, you say $1,000 is the proper margin for trading in 10 shares. In most stocks listed $1,000 would more than pay outright for 10 shares. In many stocks listed $1,000 would pay outright for 20 shares. Will you, therefore, be good enough to explain your meaning? Should not the size of the margin be governed by the nature of the security bought, and by the purchase value, rather than by any arbitrary rule?—Z.

Answer—There is a general impression that $1,000 is a fair margin for 100 shares of stock. Perhaps no one idea in speculation has cost traders more money. If a man buys 100 shares, with 10 percent margin, he is in no position to average his account, and moderate losses absorb his capital so rapidly as to leave him little option except to lose money. The man who looked upon $1,000 as the proper margin for dealing in 10 shares would, as you say, buy outright in some cases. But, supposing his first purchase to have been made on an estimate of value, he would be able to buy a second lot, and even a third lot, if it should become necessary and his opinion of value was unchanged. The ability to stay and to average wisely would mean a profit in the end. The great curse of speculation is overtrading. If operators would work on a basis illustrated by the relation of $1,000 to 10 shares, they would be very much surer of making money than they are now. The amount of margin is not to be considered with reference to the initial purchase, but as bearing upon the ability of the trader to stay in the market and to turn and take advantage of such opportunities as may occur. This cannot be done without a large factor of safety.

"There is always a disposition in people's minds to think that existing conditions will be permanent. When the market is down and dull, it is hard to make people believe that this is the prelude to a period of activity and advance. When prices are up and the country is prosperous, it is always said that while preceding booms have not lasted, there are circumstances connected with this one which make it unlike its predecessors and give assurance of permanency. The one fact pertaining to all conditions is that they will change. This change follows modifications of the law of supply and demand. The cycle of trade is well known. Beginning with a period of depression, the small dealer finds himself unable to buy the amount of goods required for hand-to-mouth trading quite as cheaply as when the previous purchase was made. He, therefore, buys a little more. The aggregate of this buying increases the business of the jobber and this swells the output of the manufacturer, who is enabled to employ more labor, resulting in larger purchases by labor of manufactured goods and agricultural products, which brings the circle round to the producer. At each step in the proceedings, rising prices bring increased purchases and increased confidence, until the retailer buys without hesitation many times the amount of goods which he would have dared to take at the beginning of the cycle of improving trade. This multiplied by millions makes the demand which at times seems inexhaustible, which supplies the railroads with tonnage, and which in its ramifications creates the investment fund which finally seeks employment in Wall Street. The declining period is accompanied by steady reversal of these varied transactions. When the retailer and the jobber find that goods cost less than before they shrink purchases.

When purchases in advance of requirements bring loss and not profit, they bring also loss of confidence and curtailment of demand. As the process of shrinkage goes on, it touches all points of trade. It is a kind of flame which creates the fuel which is burned. Experience has shown that it takes about five years for one of these cycles to complete itself. It takes approximately five years for the country bare of stocks to become the country filled with stocks, and it takes about five years, more for the over-stocked markets of the country or of the world to become practically bare. As the stock market is always an effect and never a cause, it must respond to these conditions. As, however, the stock market, while an effect, is also a discounted effect, the decline in prices of stocks usually anticipates decline in commodities, because operators "for a fall sell in anticipation of the changes which they foresee in business conditions."—Dow.

"It is true in finance as it is in philosophy or in any subject of mortal thought, that the general tendency of weak human nature is to believe what one wants to believe rather than what is so. The judgments formed by the great mass of people are apt to be those of idiosyncrasy, passion or temperament, rather than of calm and poised reflection. Few men are so constituted that they can look facts and facts alone in the face and form conclusions uncolored by native optimism or pessimism. A corollary proposition is that few people, as a rule, take pains in their investigation of financial matters or go cautiously from general belief to a specific position. In buying or selling securities it is the vague and glittering that is apt to determine their action rather than the detailed and the substantial. And there is no part of human activity, looked at from the mere worldly point of view, in which just these qualities of accurate and balanced thinking are so necessary as in the financial world. If a man has a bond does he know exactly what is its lien? If he is interested in a company as a stockholder, does he look carefully into the company's annual report and make up his mind accurately is to the wisdom of the dividends paid and the true significance of the various amounts charged for operating expenses and depreciation? An incident which may fairly be called a part of recent financial history, and which should be adverted to because of the lesson it carries of this need of rigorous scrutiny in financial matters, is the story told of those bondholders of the Chicago, Milwaukee and St. Paul Railway who allowed a valuable privilege to lapse because of their ignorance concerning the meaning of the obligation possessed by them. Too late they discovered that they must receive payments upon their bonds at par, when a few weeks before they could have converted the bonds into preferred stock worth nearly double the sum received. Nothing could be plainer than the declaration contained in the bond that the privilege of conversion it offered should be exercised only at a certain time and in a certain way. Yet many of the bondholders were wholly inappreciative of it. Nor is carelessness in such matters confined to people who are untrained in finance. It is trustworthily stated that a great man in one of the banking houses having much to do with the great Northern Pacific fight for control, admitted that not until he had so far engaged in the battle for the possession of the Northern Pacific shares that he could not retreat from it, had he read the certificate of the preferred stock, upon whose disputed construction the question of defeat or victory in the struggle depended. A very much surprised man he was when he found that there were clauses in the certificate of which he was not aware."—Daniel Kellogg (Philip King). A correspondent writes: I have several points' profit in Atchison and in Missouri Pacific. I cannot see the market more than once a day and I am afraid that my profit will run away before I know it. At the same time I hope for more profit by holding on. What can I do?

The thing to do in this case is to put a stop order in your stock and keep it about two points below the highest price. Missouri Pacific has sold at 117. Tell your broker to sell if Missouri Pacific falls back to 115. If Missouri Pacific goes to 118 raise your stop order to 116. Keep this up until the stop order is executed or until you are satisfied to take the profit which you have. For an out-of-town operator, no method of trading, once a profit has been established, is any more satisfactory than this. When a bull campaign is fairly under way in a stock, the price frequently advances a greater part of the movement without a reaction of two points. Some operators think 2 1/2 points a little safer, as sometimes a two point stop is just sufficient to spoil a handsome profit. In a large percentage of cases, however, if a stock drops back two points it will drop more than two points. An operator running a bull campaign likes to see reactions of about a point, because they enable him to test the market frequently and to see if the public is following his manipulation. But he does not like to see reactions go much further, because they would have a tendency to chill the bull enthusiasm which he wishes to create. Success, from his standpoint, means a growing public interest which will gradually absorb the stock which he has to sell. This interest can be kept up only by a comparatively large market, a well sustained tone and a gradual rise. Hence, the reason for putting a stop about two points from the highest. The manipulating interest, as long as the campaign lasts, will be certain to have a good volume of buying orders in a stock after it has had about one point decline unless there is some special reason for a change of tactics. Ordinarily a stock which has had a 10 point rise is kept for some time around the upper level of prices. It takes a little time to accumulate stock and a little time to market it, and during the marketing process, the price has to be kept strong and given the appearance of going higher. An operator who wishes to sell 10,000 shares of stock at an advance would usually have to be a large buyer at the higher prices in order to be able to sell. His hope would be that for every thousand shares of stock bought he would be able to sell twelve or fourteen hundred, and that this process would gradually exhaust his line. The follower in a campaign has the advantage that he can sometimes see evidences of this realizing and obtain therefrom a hint as to when it is best for him to sell. If not, the stop order is apt to prove his best friend. He loses two points that he might have made, but by waiting for the stop order to be executed he often makes more than two points which he would not have obtained had he relied upon his judgment as to the best time to sell.

It is an article of faith with many operators that dullness is always followed by decline. The basis for this belief is that during certain periods this occurs, and the repetitions are regarded as establishing a rule. The fact is, however, that the action of the market after dullness depends chiefly upon whether a bull market or a bear market is in progress. In a bull market, dullness is generally followed by advances; in a bear market, by decline. As bear markets as a rule last longer than bull markets, dullness is followed by decline rather oftener than by advance. There are exceptions, but they do not alter the general rule. The reason why in a bull market, dullness is followed by advance, is that a bull market is the exponent of increasing values. Values go on increasing, while the market rests, and prices start up because it becomes apparent to cliques or individuals that values are above prices, and that there is margin for rise. Exactly the reverse argument applies to declines after dullness in a bear period. Prices fall because values are falling, and dullness merely allows the fall in values to get ahead of the fall in prices. The start after a period of inactivity is generally due either to some special event or to manipulation. In the former case, the reason for acting is obvious. In the latter case, manipulators begin by studying the situation and reach a conclusion that it will pay them to move prices. They then scrutinize the speculative situation, and learn something of the position of traders; whether they are carrying a good many stocks or not; whether they seem disposed to deal; whether margins appear to be large or small; and whether specialists have large scale orders to either buy or sell. This gives a basis on which manipulation begins. The public often follows the lead given, sometimes to its own advantage and sometimes to the advantage of the manipulators. All this, however, is merely an incident in the main tendency of prices, which, as a whole, is in accord with the values which grow out of changes in earnings. Temporary movements in the market should always be considered with reference to their bearing on the main movement. The great mistake made by the public is paying attention to prices instead of to values. Whoever knows that the value of a particular stock is rising under conditions which promise stability, and the absence of developments calculated to neutralize the effect of increasing earnings, should buy that stock whenever it declines in sympathy with other stocks, and hold it until the price is considered high enough for the value as it is believed to exist. This implies study and knowledge of the stock chosen, but this marks the difference between intelligent trading and mere gambling. Anybody can guess whether a stock will go up or down, but it is only guessing and the cost of guessing will eat up most of the net profits of trading on pure guesses. Intelligent trading begins with study of conditions, and a justified opinion that the general situation is either growing better or worse. If general conditions are improving, ascertain if the particular stock to be dealt in is having a fair share of that general improvement. Is its value rising? If so, determine whether the price of the stock is low or high with reference to that value. If it is low, buy the stock and wait. Do not be discouraged if it does not move. The more value goes on increasing, the greater the certainty that rise in the stock will come. When it does come, do not take two or three points profit and then wait for a reaction, but consider whether the stock is still cheap at the advance, and if so, buy more, rather than sell under the assumption that the expected rise is underway. Keep the stock until the price appears to be up to the value and get a substantial profit. This is the way the large operators make their money; not by trading back and forth, but by accurate forecasts of coming changes in value, and then buying stocks in quantity and putting the price up to value. The small operator cannot put prices up, but if his premises are sound, he can hold stock with assurance that large operators and investors will put the price up for him.

WALL STREET SPECULATION – ITS TRICKS AND ITS TRAGEDIES

Franklin C. Keyes – 1904

Part I —It's Tricks - Chapter I

Wall Street speculation is the most stupendous game known to the world of chance; as compared with it, the game at Monte Carlo pales into utter insignificance; in no other game are the stakes so high, is success so transitory and failure so overwhelming. It is a game in which the wealth of Croesus changes hands in a single hour, a game in which a few manipulators behind the scenes pile up millions on top of more millions year after year; but in which the vast majority of the outside public, who tamper with it, go to financial and often to physical and moral ruin.

Many, who are unacquainted with Wall Street methods, regard speculation in stocks, on a margin, as legitimate business; this however is an error, which we may as well acknowledge first as last; it is, as I say, a game, run by Wall Street's millionaires and multimillionaires, who since the organization of the Stock Exchange have succeeded in niching from the pockets of the general public, without giving any equivalent whatever, untold millions.

The public's annual average of loss to Wall Street has usually been estimated in former years, at $100,000,000 per annum; but owing to the more recent enterprising methods of the "Street," in manipulating the game, this estimate is now far too small, as we shall see.

Beginning with September, 1902, we witnessed for over a year thereafter an almost continuous decline in the stock market, a decline manipulated by the Standard Oil party and largely superinduced and made possible by the dishonest organization and overcapitalization of trust properties by the so-called great captains of industry. These corporations were not only over-capitalized, until the ciphers ran out, but were bled of vast sums, generally by their organizers, for underwriting their securities or, in other words, for unloading their stocks and bonds, at inflated prices, upon the unsuspecting public.

On this decline, the shrinkage in market value of stocks and bonds on the various exchanges amounted to the unprecedented sum of approximately three billion dollars; and the proportion of this vast amount fleeced from the public in cold cash is so large, that the public's annual average of loss is now certainly far beyond the one hundred million dollar mark.

The general public seldom have any opportunity to become familiar with the inside workings of Wall Street speculation, as it really is, except through an expensive personal experience; but by the time most people have learned enough through personal experience to make money in Wall Street, their experience is all the capital that they have left, and this alone makes rather a light margin, with which to operate in stocks.

Those who have had experience and lost, invariably keep the lamentable matter as quiet as possible. To disclose their losses would injure their credit and their business standing and would be a reflection upon their sagacity, so you do not learn anything from them. Those who have been fortunate enough to make money, also keep perfectly quiet; they prefer to have you think that their wealth was accumulated in some legitimate business, and so you learn nothing from them.

A candid statement of the facts, therefore, and an honest disclosure of the wiles employed in Wall Street to ensnare the general public would not seem uncalled for. This will appear the more expedient, when we consider the demoralizing and ruinous effects of stock gambling upon the country at large, when we recall the prosperous business houses forced to the wall by "outside speculation" or by the embezzlements of speculating clerks, when we remember the banking institutions wrecked by speculating officials, and the many honest men who have been converted into thieves and forgers and driven to despair and suicide through their losses in Wall Street.

Chapter II

There is of course a legitimate side of Wall Street; it is here that great enterprises may be honestly financed; it is here that the surplus money of the country, unemployed in general business, may find a quick and often profitable investment, in railroad and industrial stocks and bonds; it is through Wall Street that public bond issues have been quickly floated to relieve the Federal government, in times of financial distress. The legitimate side of Wall Street, therefore, is nearly as great a necessity, in our financial system, as the U.S. Treasury; it serves as a propelling center, through which the financial life blood of the nation courses.

It is not this side of Wall Street, however, that we shall consider here, but the speculative side, in which too many of the general public are more or less interested and infatuated; the side that wastes its life, in trying to chase the flying fractions up and down the fluctuations of the market; the side that buys stocks, not outright for investment but on margin for speculation; the side, as some one has expressed it, that tries to take a shoestring and run it into a shoe store.

Some great fortunes, we must admit, have been made in stock speculation; but this is possible only for a few insiders, and not for the general public; their fortunes are lost, not made here. With the public, money acquired in marginal transactions, if at all, is sooner or later lost in the same way, and generally much move with it. Brokers' books show that only about one speculator in ten ever makes anything, the other nine lose, and of this one-tenth who make, not one in ten keeps his profits.

You have, therefore, about one chance in a hundred to beat the game. Now wouldn't you consider that rather desperate gambling! It certainly is and the reason why the public ever become involved in stock speculation is because, at the start, they know nothing about it.

Jay Gould, in the management, wrecking and development of great railroad properties, rigged the stock market up and down, to his vast profit; but as he was in a position, through his connection with these corporations, to virtually control the market price of their stocks, with him it was scarcely a speculation at all, but rather, a certainty; and bear in mind that what he alone made, in stock speculation, pure and simple, the general public had to lose, since he won fortune from the ruin of thousands.

What may be said of Gould as to the element of chance, may also be said of the "Standard Oil crowd" today, for with this powerful faction, the most powerful and dangerous ever in Wall Street, stock speculation is much more of a certainty than it could be with Jay Gould.

Chapter III

If there was ever an *Ignis fatuus,* a delusion and a snare, the speculative side of Wall Street is one. If the speculator, by any chance, should at first blunder into making money rapidly, as is sometimes the case, his days are numbered; for this first success is, almost surely, the precursor of his untimely fall; and the larger his first profits, the greater will be the shock of that fall.

There can be nothing more stimulating, more exhilirating, more intoxicating, than these first successes in Wall Street speculation, seeming to open up a smooth and easy path to great wealth, power and happiness. With the coming of these first profits, the speculator begins to dream dreams and see visions. What appears to him, in these dreams, naturally depends upon his temperament and tastes, his early education and environment.

One man, perhaps, sees a fine stable of horses and the excitement and enthusiasm of the race course; he sees his favorites win the victory and hears the shouts of excited thousands; another man dreams of abundant leisure and freedom from distracting care; he sees an easy chair before a cheerful fire, and surrounding him his splendid library, the choice literature of all the ages, through which he may commune with the great souls of earth; another dreams himself the owner of a grand mansion, standing amid stately parks; he sees its velvet lawns, its verdant shrubbery and beautiful flowers, he sees its walls hung with the rich tapestries of the East and with the rare paintings of genius, he hears strains of sweet music and the laughter of convivial feasts — here shall be boundless hospitality and here shall be endless delight; another sees a panorama of travel in foreign lands, and a season of pleasure and profit in the great capitals of Europe; another dreams of a happy home, with all the comforts and luxuries of life, beautiful children, a loving wife, radiant with contentment and joy.

These are some of the dreams, these are some of the illusions which rainbow-like appear before the mental vision of the successful Wall Street speculator; elevated into the seventh heaven, when his fortune turns, as turn it will, great and overwhelming is his fall — the bullet hole in the temple, the acid-stained lips, the stiff and lifeless body, lifted from the river, tell the sad tale of disappointment and despair.

Chapter IV

To make money by speculation in stocks, on margin, looks to the uninitiated more easy even than the proverbial inexertion of "rolling off a log."

It is the opinion of the inexperienced that all one has to do is to send an order down to Wall Street in the morning, and along toward evening a van will back up to his front door and unload about a billion dollars in gold bullion. Such is the delusion.

Wall Street, however, is dominated by some of the brainiest and shrewdest men in the country, natural-born sharpers and schemers, and before the average man can get the better of them, except through the merest chance, he will have to eat brain food for a long time.

Stock speculation, as I say, looks easy; the stocks can go only two ways, either up or down — you do not have to spend any time looking out for their dodging sideways — all that you have to do is to buy when they are low, and sell when they are high. But after the novice has tried it awhile, for some mysterious reason he changes his mind completely about its being easy and telegraphs for money to get home. He is forced to conclude that there is no more difficult way to make money, and no easier or surer way to lose it. He finds, although he cannot explain it or account for it, that somehow every time he buys stocks they go down, and every time he sells them short for a decline, they go up.

Occasionally, perhaps, he really gets his mind on the right side of the market, but at these times he never has the courage of his convictions to invest; he most likely is dissuaded by some one's opinion or casual remark, and so he stands by and looks on, torn and exasperated with always losing his opportunity, which is almost as harrowing as losing his money. If perchance he would have the courage of his convictions, he is then not in a position to trade, his capital being tied up in bad ventures, or by this time entirely lost.

If you have ever talked with old Wall Street speculators (the majority of them, by the way, rather seedy looking fellows) you may have noticed that their conversation is almost entirely upon what they might have made, but didn't. There is always an "if" that stood in the way of their making millions; they glow with the great opportunities and wonderful possibilities of Wall Street speculation, but theirs is a tale of great opportunities lost and a direful dirge of harrowing regrets.

It is a peculiar feature of Wall Street speculation that the novice never gets his courage worked up to buy stocks until the market is right on the top, and he never concludes to sell until the market is clear on the bottom.

It is truly remarkable what accuracy a greenhorn is capable of in this direction. If you could watch one of them trade and then do just the opposite yourself, in a short time, you ought to be in a position, financially, where you would require the services of private detectives to accompany you about and protect your person from cranks and the curious.

Now what is the reason for this? Why is it that a greenhorn executes such peculiar antics, and in his efforts to make money at the game, relieves himself of his last dollar? Well, the novice and all outsiders, old-timers for that matter, are dancing to the music of the so-called "insiders", who, I can assure you, never fiddle for nothing. Who these insiders are and how the game is run, I will endeavor to explain.

No one is in a position to know anything about the future course of the stock market, except those connected with the large banking interests, the officers and directors of the corporations, whose stocks and bonds are traded in, on the New York Stock Exchange, the pool managers or operators and the largest brokerage houses. This constitutes the faction known as the "insiders" or as "underground Wall Street" and while the market is of course governed, considerably, by general conditions, these people, through their vast interests, are large factors in creating and forcing conditions, and they virtually control and manipulate the game and direct the course of the market's fluctuations, as they please; or if, in any event, the market is beyond control, they are in a position to turn quickly with it, in advance of the public.

Since the insiders really control the market, to forecast the course of its stock fluctuations is like trying to guess what another man is going to do, who after you have made your guess comes around and quietly finds out just what it is, and then to fool you, goes and does the contrary. Now, do you think that you are a sharp enough guesser to make money under such conditions? Those of you who have tried the shell game, sometime, know how difficult it is to beat another man at his own delusive tricks; and so you will find it in Wall Street.

The position of the insiders, you will see, is peculiarly advantageous. The large New York banking interests, for example, know the true and not the reported condition of the money market, which is a great factor in stock manipulation, and they, consequently, know about what the bank statement will be each week, before it is sent out to the public.

If for the purpose of making money appear scarce and high, cash has been withdrawn from the clearing house banks and deposited in trust companies or locked up temporarily in safe deposit vaults, or sent to the interior uncalled for, or carried over to Jersey City, as is sometimes done during a "bear raid" upon the market, these people know it. If there is news of any nature, which will affect the market, they know it in advance, even before it is sent out on the news tickers, and they, of course, take advantage of their position, accordingly.

After the officers and directors of a corporation have quietly plundered it into bankruptcy, their next effort is to unload as much of its stock as possible upon the unsuspecting public, and at the very highest prices; then if for example the sworn financial statements of such a company are being padded and doctored, by skillful bookkeeping and perjury, so as to make its business appear in a prosperous condition, the insiders know it, but mind you the outside public do not; they are fed with the most glowing and optimistic reports on this company's condition and prospects, so that they will be induced to buy the stock.

The large brokerage houses may not be in quite so advantageous a position, as the other insiders, yet they know from their books and the general trend of Wall Street affairs which side of the market the public are on, who of course are to be made to lose anyway, and they know about what the position of the insiders is — both very valuable information.

The great advantage of the insiders in this game is, therefore, perfectly manifest and accounts for the reason why the "dear public," as the "lambs" or outsiders are affectionately called, are always kept on the wrong side of the market and the reason why they cut up such surprising antics. Can you wonder at it? What chance have they, but to lose, lose, always lose.

In this connection, a scheme resorted to by the president of one of the large industrial trusts, for the purpose of unloading his stock upon the public, is both interesting and illustrative. The president, from his intimate knowledge of the trust's affairs, knew that its stock must soon rapidly depreciate in market value; he, therefore, called in his brother-in-law and said to him, confidentially, "Now if you want to make some money just buy our stock, it is going to have a big advance."

So the brother-in-law bought eagerly; he not only bought but he quietly passed the word to his friends and they in turn passed it on to their friends, among whom were widows and young women school teachers. They all rushed in and bought to hold for large profits, The stock made a trifling advance, at first, after which it began to decline and kept on declining, until it had dropped about 25 percent.

The brother-in-law then came around to the trust magnate and said, "What are you trying to do, are you trying to ruin me? I have lost $18,000 on that fine tip of yours." "Oh well," said the trust president, "that's all right, don't worry about such a little matter; here is a check for your $18,000, and it is mighty cheap at that, for I unloaded nearly $5,000,000 of my stock on the little tip and at top prices. I guess the news of that big advance must have leaked out somehow."

Chapter V

But why cannot one trade in stocks on the advice of his broker, you may ask. The brokers ought to be experts in the game; they have the advantage of long experience and close proximity to the market and the large brokerage houses have the benefit of intimate business relations with the insiders. Well, notwithstanding what the brokers may know about the market situation, do not believe for a moment, that they are going to give any valuable information to their small fry customers or to the outside public, as some might be led to suppose. That wouldn't do; if the brokers gave out such information, they, for instance, could not market the stocks of the large inside interests, which might be in their hands for sale, or could not buy stocks for them, on the bottom, and would thus lose their valuable patronage.

If an insider or a manipulator of the market holds stocks that he is anxious to dispose of, because he knows that they will depreciate in market price, and he accordingly puts them into the hands of a broker to sell, the broker is expected to call attention to these stocks in his market letters, recommending them to his customers and the public as just what they should buy for an immediate advance and for large profits. The lambs at such times rush in and buy, and the insiders sell.

The business of the New York broker, you will see, is to keep the public, who confidingly pursue their advices, misled and on the wrong side of the market. The public, that good thing (to borrow an expression) must be made to continually pour into this great hopper, the glittering gold, to feed the greedy mill of Wall Street speculation, that it may grind out colossal fortunes for a few rich insiders.

Let me give you an illustration of the effect it would have upon a broker's business and upon the market generally, if he told all that he might know and gave out correct information, in his letters of advice. Suppose, for instance, some big market manipulator has run a stock, say Southern Pacific, up twenty or thirty points and has concluded that it is now about time for him to commence unloading on the "lambs." This manipulator has an immense line of stock and must begin to unload early and feed it out gradually, so as not to break the price, or he is going to "get left." While doing this, he must pretend to be buying; while buying 2,000 shares he will perhaps sell 5,000 shares at the game time; every scheme must be exploited, to make a market for the stock and so induce the public to come in and kindly take it off his hands before the bottom drops out.

At such times he calls in the reporters or gladly welcomes them, when, they come round on their quest for news, and sets forth his alleged views on the market situation. With reasons wise and plausible, he enlarges upon the great prosperity of the country and the sound condition of business, and affirms his honest belief in the further improvement of the stock market, and especially predicts a sharp advance in the stocks which he is now ready to unload. These views are then written up by the reporters for the public to read. Suppose, at this juncture, the manipulator gives some broker an order to sell 25,000 shares of his Southern Pacific at certain figures or for what they will bring, and the broker should tell the public, through his market letters, or should whisper around to his customers, that this heavy operator was selling Southern Pacific and that he had an order from him to dispose of 25,000 shares. If the broker did that, every one who held the stock would at once conclude that the boom was over and would rush to sell his own holdings; the crowd would fairly fall over one another to sell out first and obtain the highest price, and before the large manipulator could unload much of anything, Southern Pacific would go down like a thousand of brick. Very likely too the rest of the market would be carried down with it.

Should the market manipulator be thwarted in this manner by his broker, he would be very apt to look upon him as a "chump," and forever afterward, that broker would not be rushed much with business from this operator nor from any of the other heavy interests in the "Street."

It will be readily seen that it is the broker's mission under such circumstances to deceive and bewilder the public. It makes a market for the stocks and insures more profitable business from his rich customers, and moreover he considers it his religious duty to keep the game running "right." It is quite evident then that one will not acquire wealth beyond the dreams of avarice, by following a broker's advice.

Chapter VI

Perhaps you say, "It seems to me that the public would come to realize, after a while, what dangers beset them in Wall Street and consequently keep out of speculation; that the withdrawal of the public would cut off Wall Street's source of revenue and thus spoil this fine sport, such fun for the boys, but such death to the frogs.'" —No, this does not seem to be the conclusion drawn by the inexperienced. Wall Street is. an institution that has been running *a long* time now and there are plenty of victims, coming on all the while, who seeing others go to ruin there, on every hand, yet think that *they* can beat the game — such is its peculiarly delusive and dangerous nature.

Wall Street insiders do not worry themselves over a scarcity of "lambs;" they go on the old theory, somewhat inelegantly expressed, that a "sucker," as they say, is born every minute, on a general average, and, consequently, there will always be an inexhaustible supply. This, however, seems to me a rather high average; the people universally are becoming more and more enlightened and not so gullible as they once were, and I would not be surprised if this general average has been reduced now to something like a "sucker" born every other minute. This average, nevertheless, makes a good liberal supply and a thriving business for Wall Street.

As for the Wall Street crowd, generally, the Wall Street brokers and the insiders, who run the game, let me say, right here, by way of warning, that a ring of more consummate rascals never get together — never; and these people are the more dangerous, for the reason that they present the polished appearance of eminent respectability and fair dealing.

If a broker is engaged in carrying speculative accounts on margin, he is running what, in reality, is a gambling institution, in which one man gets another man's money for nothing. Furthermore, this is the very worst form of gambling — simply ruinous to most people who engage in it. To make in the game is worse than to lose, because it finally lures men on to lose their all, not only money, but hope, courage and capacity for honest work.

Such an occupation, from its very nature, certainly has no remarkably high moral uplift in it; but on the contrary a tendency to develop men without a conscience, and consequently you will find New York brokers, and especially Wall Street manipulators, hard and heartless, with no more con-science than a stone. Wouldn't it be foolish to expect anything else, in an open game of "dog eat dog and the Devil take the hindmost?"

If then one is going into Wall Street, as a speculator, he has to look out for Wall Street, and if he goes into the "Street" understanding conditions and methods as they are, that is, if he goes in to steal and should then get "stole," what is he going to say of do about it anyway? But when people are first drawn into Wall Street speculation, they do not understand these matters; in fact, they generally know less than nothing about the game, because what ideas they have on the subject are all wrong, their knowledge constituting, we might say, a minus quantity; they are what is called in the "Street" "swift losers" and are certainly most innocent, easy and pitiful victims.

When we come to consider the position of the insiders in the stock market, relative to that of the outsiders, it is very evident that with the insiders, as I have said, the element of chance is practically eliminated. The insiders are so powerful and so much feared that if, for instance, one of the big "bears" wishes to depress the market, about all that he has to do is to say "boo" and down it goes — at the word everybody rushes to sell.

By making market conditions appear precisely the opposite of what they really are, the insiders keep the public on the losing side and put themselves on the winning side. This is the principal part of what is known as stock market manipulation and is accomplished in a hundred skillful and mysterious ways, too dark and devious to investigate here, in detail.

In this connection, it will be understood, that you cannot have a market where every one is of the same opinion — sentiment must be divided — when, for instance, one wishes to sell stocks, there must be another on hand who thinks it for his advantage to buy, and vice versa; that makes the necessary two sides to the market.

This sentiment in Wall Street is made to order for the "lambs" by the insiders and fashioned to suit their own purposes. The newspapers are very potent factors in accomplishing this end and are always used by the manipulators to steer the public upon the wrong side. Very little financial news gets into the papers, which will not further the interests of the insiders. What the newspaper reporter must have, of course, is "copy" and his pay for it; he must hand it in, at just such a time; he has no means or opportunity of investigating the truth of what he hears and writes; he does not have much time even to write it; so the inside manipulators lie to the reporters, the reporters, innocently, let us hope, mislead the newspapers and the press, though doing the best it can, misleads the people.

The speculative public feed upon these lies, form their opinions upon them, and then plunge into the stock market, with their money, to double it, and come out paupers.

In the end, it is true, the press arrives at the facts; but it is too late then for the speculator; he reads with empty pockets. The market has long since discounted the facts. Hence it follows that if one would get a correct idea of the stock market situation from the newspapers, he must read it from between the lines, or spell it for himself, from figures, which are often given out incorrect or in such form as to deceive. Do you wonder that the public always lose, when the newspapers are about their only source of information upon which to forecast the course of the market.

This may not be the fault of the press, because it is generally impossible to obtain the facts immediately affecting the market, so carefully are such matters kept guarded; but on this point we will refrain from mentioning certain subsidized financial sheets, published in the Wall Street district, and we will pass over those financial writers for the daily press, who are bribed by the manipulators to give such a coloring to their articles as their employers may dictate.

By the time the insiders are ready to sell their stocks, you see it is comparatively easy, through these methods, to have the public all deceived into believing that it is now just the time for them to buy if they would become rich. And on the other hand, when the insiders are ready once more to buy stocks, it is as easy to have the public again misled into thinking that now is the time for them to sell, if they would get out before the crash comes.

Wall Street speculation might be likened to a crooked game of cards. Suppose in crossing the Atlantic, on one of the great ocean liners, you fall in with some "poker sharps," who have been lying in wait for you. They have the cards all plainly marked, but in such a manner that the marks cannot be seen by you, even if suspected. Now, what chance do you think there would be for you to win, no matter how well you understand the game? As with the insiders in the stock market, these sharpers take no chances. In addition to the marked cards, suppose that you are at the disadvantage of being a greenhorn at the game, and dependent upon the other players to tell you how to play, while they are old "card sharps" and make gambling a steady occupation. Don't you think that your chances would be slimmer still, if possible? In case you won anything at all, it would be a voluntary contribution, on their part, for the purpose of inveigling you in deeper; and thus cleaning you to a finish. What folly to put up your money under such conditions.

So it is with the Wall Street game, you, inexperienced, are playing with marked cards, as it were, and are in the hands of old sharpers, who, through the press and brokers' and tipsters' letters, are actually telling you how to play into their hands. In appearance, these sharpers are very kind, dignified and respectable gentlemen, well calculated to disarm suspicion; but your chances of winning are just as propitious in Wall Street as in the poker game on the ocean steamer — the game just as respectable and the methods employed against you analogous. Consequently it is a foregone conclusion that, when a novice hands his money into a broker's office for margin, it is goodbye money and when he writes out an order for a trade in stocks, he is sending a written invitation to disaster.

Such is the nature of the Wall Street game and such are the methods of those who operate it. Is there anything more heartless or despicable? "Al" Adams, the notorious policy king, was duly exposed, properly railed at by the press and finally lauded where he belongs; but infamous and pitiless as his game may have been, it was a mere bagatelle compared with the great game of the multi-millionaires in Wall Street.

Chapter VII

Most of you, doubtless, have heard of "bucket shops," and perhaps some of you may have wondered to what branch of the hardware trade or to what department of the cooperage business they belong. This, however, is a kind of shop which pertains to Wall Street alone, rather than to any line of legitimate business; and what sort of an institution this is permit me to explain.

A regular broker, when he receives an order to buy or sell stock, has it executed on the floor of the Stock Exchange, that is, he buys the stock; and has it delivered to him to hold for his customer or in case of a short sale, he sells the stock, then borrows and delivers it to another broker, for the purchaser, these deliveries being made through the Stock Exchange Clearing House.

The proprietor of a "bucket-shop" on the contrary does not do this; he merely enters the transaction on his books the same as though he had really bought or sold the stock, and he, therefore, holds no stock for his customer.

For example, suppose you give a bucket-shop proprietor an order to buy 200 shares of a certain stock at par, that is, for $100 a share. As the purchase price of the 200 shares would be $20,000, you deposit $2,000 with your so-called broker, as a ten point, or, in other words, a 10 percent margin, on the purchase price of the stock. Then suppose the stock declines from 100 to 90, at which figure 90, the stock is sold at the 10 percent or $2,000 market decline. Since the proprietor has not bought the stock, but merely carried the trans-action on his books, he has had nothing in his possession to depreciate in value and no money has really been lost in the deal by any one.

Nevertheless, the bucket-shop proprietor seizes your $2,000 deposited with him as margin; and he also charges you with interest on $18,000, money which you are supposed to have borrowed, as the balance over your $2,000 required to buy the $20,000 worth of stock, but which money in fact was never loaned; and he also charges you commissions for both buying and selling the stock, which he has neither bought nor sold for you.

The bucket-shop business virtually consists in transferring, the customer's deposits to the credit of the bucket shop and in charging the customer commissions and interest for doing it.

It is the policy of Wall Street, that when a man is relieved of his money, he must be charged high for having it done, otherwise he might suspect that he had been robbed. After paying high for the service, the victim goes away much better satisfied and thinks that all has been done for him that could be.

This business, it will be seen, is profitable to the proprietor, when the market goes against the customer, which is generally the case. The customer does not lose any more than he would, with a regular broker, in the execution of the same orders; but the customer is placed at the disadvantage of having his so-called "broker" working against him, all the time, and watching to seize the money, which he has deposited as margin. In fact it is said that bucket-shop firms generally divide up the money, deposited with them, as soon as received, they feel so sure of it. When the market goes in favor of the customer, of course the proprietor loses; but on the whole, it makes a very profitable business, if large enough, and about a sure thing.

As these institutions all pose before the world as bankers and have the supreme assurance to style themselves, "Bankers and Brokers," in dazzling gilt letters, few of their customers ever know the difference or suspect that their orders are "bucketed" — they merely know in the end that they have been cleaned out.

Considering the manner in which the bucket-shop business is managed, one of the most pathetic situations that I know of is to see a trader, in one of these institutions, when the market runs against him, go around to the proprietor or manager of the place and ask his advice as to what he shall do, in order that he may get out of his trouble.

When the trader loses, the proprietor makes, and when the trader makes, the proprietor loses. After you are once good and safe in Hades, why not approach his Supreme Majesty and tremblingly ask him, if he will please show you a crack or a rathole, somewhere, to crawl out of — it would be as diplomatic and you would as likely escape.

Some of the regular brokers, on the New York Stock Exchange, "bucket" their small orders, such as they think are on the wrong side of the market, the same as would be done in a regular bucket-shop; that is, they bucket the orders of the lambs and their small-fry traders, who are generally wrong, and thus the broker cleans up the whole thing, margin, interest and commissions.

The broker reasons about as follows: "Here is a 'lamb,' who wants to speculate; he is going to lose, anyhow; 'a fool and his money are soon parted,' and I may as well have his money as some trader or the bucket-shop next door. Why shouldn't I work this game for all there is in it? Business is business. Since the lamb is about to be slaughtered, I may as well slaughter him and get what he will render, as my competitor across the way."

This Wall Street moralizing would not seem so harsh, perhaps, if, under the circumstances, the broker did not quietly throw all the dust possible in his customer's eyes, to bewilder and mislead him and thus keep him on the wrong side of the market, make him lose and then say to him afterward, "I am very sorry but you did it yourself."

If I were not going to trade very heavily, and assuming that a bucket-shop firm is financially responsible, as some are, notwithstanding all that may be said against such an institution, I would much prefer it to a so-called regular brokerage house, where they "bucket" part of their orders. It is about the same old confidence game, in either place, for that matter; but as the advice of a bucket-shop proprietor would naturally be looked upon with suspicion, he keeps more quiet and does not try to confound his customers so much; he lets them work out their own destruction.

This, of course, may take a little longer than where the customer is led straight up to the precipice and pushed off; but the bucket-shop proprietor relies upon the old and very true theory, that "if you give a calf enough rope it is sure to hang itself sooner or later," and that there is no need of being in such a hurry about it.

If, however, the bucket-shop is not financially responsible, as many small ones are not, when you lose you don't get it, and then when you make you don't get it; this constitutes a kind of double twister which holds out faint hope of vast wealth; but on the contrary the prospect of a rapid depletion of your exchequer.

A New York Stock Exchange brokerage firm, doing business in the Wall Street district for many years, reaps a rich harvest in the "bucketing" business from the lambs throughout the country. The advertisements of this firm and the market letters of one of its members are published widely, in the country papers, for the purpose of attracting the attention of the unsophisticated. There can be no more lucrative and easy business than that of luring in the green-horns, gaining their confidence and taking the first crack at them. When the lambs come into the "Street," this firm receives the lion's share of their business and after their money is once put into the hands of these sharpers for margin account, they do not intend that their customers shall ever get away with a dollar of it.

No identification is required when the newcomer arrives to deposit his money, but later, if he wishes to withdraw his account and is fortunate enough to have anything on the books to withdraw, every barrier possible is put in his way. He must be identified first, now that they know him, and no one brought for the purpose is satisfactory. If the brokers can keep him a little longer they know that they are sure of his whole account.

For the purpose of getting the customer interested in the market again, possibly his attention is drawn with much skill to some market "tip," through which he is led to believe that he can make "big money." If he bites on the right side, that is on the losing side for him, his order is "executed" with remarkable celerity, and reported as quickly as it can be set down on a book, lest he might change his mind and cancel it; but should he bite on the winning side, his order is not "executed," very likely more margin is demanded or some other effectual obstruction is raised. Needless to say, they make short work of him; and his money is very soon all transferred to the credit of the firm.

Chapter VIII

A word might be said regarding the two Stock Exchanges in New York City, the New York Stock Exchange and the Consolidated Exchange. It is generally considered more safe to do business with the New York Stock Exchange firms than with those on the "consolidated," because by dealing with New York Stock Exchange firms you enjoy the protection of the older and stronger institution and the protection of its rules.

There may be a certain guaranty of security, from the fact that the largest brokerage firms are on the older exchange (although the largest firms are often the first to fail); but whatever there may be in this supposition, you will find that the New York Stock Exchange is an association organized for the protection of the brokers against the public; it is not even incorporated, so as to become that much amenable to the law; one broker very naturally can be expected to lie for another, as they must stand together in times of trouble, consequently, the public can expect little protection from such an institution. Although the brokers may be perfectly square among themselves, as a matter of absolute necessity, in the execution of business on the floor of the Stock Exchange, yet if they get a chance to "do" you, you are done, and you may as well throw up both hands, and as Mark Twain said to the outlaws who "held him up in the western wilds," Go through me, please, as quickly as possible, and I will do as much for you some time."

Chapter IX

I have tried thus far to explain in a measure how the "dear public" are handled by the insiders, and relieved of their cash, or, in other words, bow they "shear the lambs;" although I must confess that in giving an account of Wall Street methods I find it necessary to tone down the facts considerably, in order to gain credence for what is said. Those, who have always lived in an atmosphere removed from Wall Street and have had no personal experience here simply could not believe the whole truth if told; it would be impossible for them to conceive that any such men or methods exist.

At long intervals, however, occasions arise, when the public are really given a little rest. On the bottom of a "bear market," the public are so thoroughly cleaned out and scared out that only a few remain, holding on to their stocks; the "lambs" are about all dead now, and those who survive are likely to soon pass away.

As the insiders and investors hold nearly all the stocks, picked up at panic prices, they have nothing else to do but to turn and eat each other, and a battle of the giants is sometimes inaugurated. Certain large and powerful interests wish to dislodge large blocks of stock held on margin by other large speculative interests. Jealousy exists among the big men in Wall Street the same as elsewhere in the world of strife.

Since the market is about ready to be advanced twenty or thirty points, one large interest cannot bear to see another get the benefit of the advance; each wishes to gobble up the other's stock, if possible — or perhaps some corporation desires to acquire control of a certain property at rock bottom figures. So they go to work to run prices down still farther, clear below the bottom, and depress the market to such an extent that holders of these large blocks of stock will be forced out of them through exhausted margins.

This is called "gunning" for stocks, and is accomplished in various ways; for instance, by "selling the market," curtailing the money supply, calling loans, and by the large interests putting in orders to buy on a scale down when there are scarcely any other buying orders in the market. These are dangerous times for the small fellows, in case there should be any of them left carrying stocks; for if they get in the way when the "battle royal" is on, they are sure to be hurt.

Did you ever see two big bull dogs fighting furiously over a bone? Well, they remind me of the insiders fighting, or "gunning," for one another's stocks, The bull dogs growl and snarl and snap and bite at each other, and perhaps some little poodle becoming mixed in the fray gets snapped clear in two, and the big dogs in their ferocity never know it at all. They, of course, are after the bone, but it is the last of the little poodle just the same.

We take occasion to observe here that it is easy to avoid the fate of this little fellow by keeping entirely out of the *melee*. Fascinating as the game of chance may be to some natures, it can scarcely be considered wise to put your head into a lion's mouth just to see whether or not it gets snapped off.

Chapter X

Perhaps the Wall Street "tipsters" would feel slighted, if I passed them by, and not wishing to have any hardness over the matter, I will introduce them for a few moments.

There are certain people in Wall Street known as "tipsters" who advertise that they can tell you how to speculate and that they will advise you every day, for a consideration, whether the market is going up or going down. This may look like a great boon, but you will find that if you take their advice and follow it very long, instead of playing the Wall Street game in New York City, you will be playing croquet at the poorhouse.

These "tipsters" issue daily letters through the mails to their customers, who pay in advance anywhere from five to twenty dollars per month for being told how to acquire fabulous wealth. As a rule, these fellows are dangerous frauds and sometimes unscrupulous scoundrels, who are in the employ of pools to unload stocks upon outside speculators and investors. The lambs send in their money to the tipsters, and pay as usual, to be led on to ruin.

Once in a while, however, some passably honest fellow will set up in Wall Street as a "tipster," and will try to do the best he can. Of course, he is not an insider — far from it — nor a medium, nor a veiled prophet, and he does not know any more about what the insiders are doing or which way the market will go than you do. You may be just as good a guesser as he. If the tipster could successfully predict the market movements, it is evident that he would not have to bother with writing market letters every day; he could soon sail around the Mediterranean in his own yacht, having nothing to worry him.

The letters of some tipsters, let me say here by way of parentheses, are comparatively harmless, as they give you the priceless inside information, the gist of which is, that if the market doesn't go up, it will go down, and if it doesn't rain, there will probably be a long dry time; but the shrewdest tipsters pursue this course; they make their letters of advice both "bullish" and "bearish," that is, part of the same letter predicting an advance, and part of it predicting a decline. This leaves the speculator somewhat in doubt, to be sure, and more or less bewildered; but the tipster is safe anyhow. No matter which way the market goes he can pick out an isolated sentence somewhere in his letters that will be all right. Afterward he can harp on this one sentence and direct the attention of his clients to it, for the purpose of showing how correct his forecasts of the market are, and then tell his customers, if they would only follow his advice they would make money.

A certain Wall Street broker writes two market letters each week; one appears in the financial column of a popular New York daily, and the other reaches the public through the mails in the form of a broker's letter, each letter being published over a different name. This broker having an eye to business and mindful of the necessity of two sides to the market, although the two letters are published at the same time, usually predicts in one that the market will advance, and in the other that the market will decline.

But, occasionally, a passably honest fellow, as I was saying, sets up as a tipster; since he guesses the best that he can he may sometimes strike it right;

223

his customers increase and he becomes quite a little power in the "Street," on account of his following. Assuming that the tipster has any such good luck as this, when the insiders learn that he is putting his customers on the right side of the market, how they do go for him — surreptitiously, of course. If the tipster cannot be bribed, which he generally can be, with "puts" and "calls" on stocks, they employ every means in a way that he would not suspect, to "stuff him," give him points, lie to him, and thus get his clients on the wrong side of the market, and make a tool out of him for themselves. He then becomes very valuable to the insiders, for the purpose of unloading stocks upon the public at the top, and for frightening the "lambs" out at the bottom.

To use the simplest kind of an illustration, an outsider might as well contract to predict which way a toad will always jump, as to agree to tell which way the stock market will fluctuate. After the toad jumps the prophet can tell, but not before — just as what is called "hindsight," in Wall Street, is always good, so much better than foresight. The prophesaier may think that he knows from the looks of the toad, from the direction of its nose, for instance, which way it will jump; he finds, nevertheless, that its looks are deceptive, and that just before leaping it is apt to turn suddenly and spring in the opposite direction,

It goes without saying that if the tipster were an insider his honest advice would be invaluable; but the insiders, I can assure you, have nothing to give away; you will not find them advertising to predict market movements for the "lambs," in consideration of $5 a month, correct advice on which would be worth millions. Furthermore, if they published such information, it would utterly ruin the game. Knowing the unfailing source of the advice, everybody would be of one opinion and all on the same aide of the market. It is the difference of opinion, as I have explained, which makes the game possible; there must be one side to furnish the profits and the other side to rake them in.

These are some of the methods — these are some of the hidden forces — which are working constantly and insidiously toward relieving the public of that $100,000,000, and much more, year after year. Have you ever contributed anything toward that fund? If so, instead of handing the money over to these sharpers, would it not be better if you had given it to your orphan asylum or to your hospital or to your old ladies' home, or to your wife even — for wives, as you know, are more or less objects of charity! But I must not ask such aggravating questions.

Many of the public, however, have been somewhat fortunate, we might say, in their Wall Street losses, for the reason that they may now pose as philanthropists, and as generous contributors to a certain worthy charity — an unexpected distinction, to be sure, since they made their contributions without knowing it at the time, and I may add without any very generous impulses.

Who was it, if I may ask, by way of illustration, that paid for the libraries, which have been donated so liberally to various cities and towns in the United States and Great Britain. Who, in reality, earned and contributed the money for their establishment? Was it the "Laird of Skibo Castle," or he deluded investors in every city, village and hamlet, who bought the common stock of the

U.S. Steel Corporation, and got nothing for their money? Were not they the real contributors after all? Let us see, for, if this is the case, it will be a consolation to many.

When the U.S. Steel Corporation was formed, the larger steel properties in this country were sold to the big trust for twice and three times their actual value. The Carnegie Steel Company, for instance, was turned over to the trust for $100,000,000 more than the property bad been offered for one year before. In reality it was being sold to the public this time, and the public were buying at the seller's own price — no questions asked, no objections raised. The public is always so "easy"—why shouldn't prices be doubled and trebled? What a temptation!

In the end the vast profits of these great iron masters, on the sale of their properties, were to be taken from the pockets of the victims who would buy the common stock of the U.S. Steel Corporation on the New York Stock Exchange. This, needless to say, was to be so adroitly managed that those, who went from being victimized in this way, would never suspect what was going on until it was too late.

The steel trust was to issue over half a billion dollars par value of common stock, without a dollar of assets behind it, and recommend it to the confiding as a sound investment security — more than $500,000,000 of stock, in its intrinsic value absolutely worthless, to be foisted upon the public for the purpose of catching the unwary!

This is what in Wall Street is called "High Finance," or to use a more modern term, "Morganeering."

When it comes to the last analysis, therefore, it will be found that the purchasers of this worthless stock were the real contributors of the money which, founded the libraries in question, since from their pockets came the enormous profits of the donor, which grew out of this great stock-juggling swindle, enriching him and impoverishing thousands. Let us, at least, give the real contributors the satisfaction of regarding the ostensible donor as their trustee.

Who bought this stock? The small capitalist, the small tradesman, farmers, mechanics, clerks, and old women even, with a few hundred dollars laid aside to bury themselves with; this is the class of people who were "worked" through falsehood and large dividends (while the stock was being sold) to unload "Steel Common" upon. They got the pretty pictures called stock certificates, the great iron masters and financiers got their money.

Now, don't you think that these unfortunates ought to have a few library buildings, especially if they contain any books on Wall Street's financial methods? But I presume it is safe to say that many of those, who were "fleeced" on Steel Common, have been cramped worse since for the necessities of life than they have been for fine library buildings, and that many of them could use their money, if they had it, to better advantage at home, for the purpose of keeping the wolf from the door.

Yet who shall say that the establishment of these libraries does not constitute a wise and enduring charity, and who shall say that therein the giver is not a munificent benefactor of the present and of coming generations, for whose charities the recipients should be truly thankful? No matter how vast the donor's wealth, and no matter what its sources, he might have kept it all for himself, being under no legal obligation to contribute any part of his millions to charity.

An acquaintance of mine went down to Coney Island one afternoon with a roll of bills in his pocket. Some "bunco steerers" got hold of him, and it was not over twenty minutes before he did not have a cent. But after the "bunco steerers" had appropriated all of his money, one of them said that he felt sorry to see him in such a predicament, and gave him a dollar with which to get back to the city. Upon his return he was telling me what gentlemen they were, how kind they appeared to be, and that he did not know what would have become of him if it had not been for their generosity.

What I have said thus far will give you some idea of the perils that await the adventurer in Wall Street. But the public never learn how to keep out of danger in stock speculation, and never can, for as soon as they have one trick well mastered a new one is sprung upon them, which no one outside the shrewd sharpers of Wall Street's inner circle would have the assurance or the ingenuity to invent.

To the inexperienced Wall Street is ever an alluring light, toward which men seem drawn by some peculiar power. Continually the moths keep flying into the flame, until their wings are scorched off and their charred carcasses fall at the foot of the caudle with swarms of the other dead.

Part II - It's Tragedies - Chapter XI

Now let me give you one little instance, showing how people are drawn unawares into stock speculation and financially ruined. A particular case will perhaps give a clearer understanding of Wall Street methods and present a more vivid picture of the speculator's life than any generalizations that I could make.

In a small town, situated in the State of Connecticut, a country merchant had been doing business for forty years. He was sixty years old now, and as the result of a lifetime of patient toil and careful economy he had accumulated what in those parts was a considerable fortune. As his income was sufficient for himself and his wife to live upon very comfortably, and as his health had partially failed he concluded to dispose of his business and retire.

A wealthy farmer in the neighborhood, having a son not in love with agriculture, wished to establish him in the mercantile trade, and when he heard that old man Brown wanted to sell his business he bought him out, store, stock, good will and all; he took the property at a fair price and paid for it in full. The old merchant always kept a large bank account, as he bought his goods for cash, and when he looked at his bankbook, after depositing the farmer's check, he had good reason to feel quite satisfied and happy. All his assets were reduced to money now, and, of course, he was looking for trouble, and trouble had all eyes peeled looking for him. In cases of this kind the parties generally meet before long and arrange for an interview.

When a man, who has devoted his life to one kind of business, finally sells out and converts his property into cash he is always an easy prey for swindling schemers. He thoroughly understands the business in which he spent his life, and, therefore, made money at it, but when he comes to handling his slippery cash in other lines, especially in those of a speculative nature, my observation has been that be nearly always gets cleaned out; and if he goes into Wall Street it seems that the more careful and conservative a business man he has always been the more he will lose his head here.

But let us watch this old merchant and see him double his money. For years he has had his eye on the market for dry goods and groceries and for produce; he tried to buy his goods when the market was low, and sell his produce taken in barter when the market was high. This he generally did, and he thought he was a pretty sharp old duck at it, as in fact he really was. In watching the other markets his attention had now and then been drawn to the Wall Street stock market, and the thought that, if you ever had a good chance, he would like to take a crack at it sometime.

He always had understood that what one required to make money in Wall Street was capital — that money makes money there, and he had the capital now. Then it would be such an easy and such a pleasant occupation; he couldn't stand on his feet the way he used to all day in the store; but he could sit in the easy chairs of a broker's office and watch the stock market quotations all right. He knew that he would like the business, and he thought it just about exciting enough to be interesting.

His wife, from what little she had heard concerning stock speculation, was somewhat wary at first, when her husband began to talk of going into Wall Street; but the old man said that he didn't see any great difference between buying 100 shares of stock at 90 and selling them at 110, and buying so many sacks of flour at wholesale and selling them out for a profit at retail, except that it was a mighty sight less work to buy and sell the stock than it was the flour and ton times more money in it — anyway, "nothing ventured nothing gained."

The old man did not realize it, but he imbibed these ideas from reading certain books and pamphlets, which brokers are continually sending out through the mails for the purpose of inveigling the public into Wall Street; and in this kind of literature, brokers, very naturally, make a special effort to veneer their gambling game with the appearance of a respectable business. If they can get people to reading these little books, they know from experience that, sooner or later, the readers will become interested in Wall Street, and come to be offered up, as it were a burnt offering, upon its altar of avarice and greed.

This reasoning of the old gentleman did look rather plausible, and as he was not going in very heavy, anyhow, his wife said that if he thought money could be made so easily down there in Wall Street, he better go along and make some.

It was as wise to say this as anything else, for when a man once gets the speculative Wall Street fever, and is smitten with the mad desire to lose his money in the quickest way possible, it is useless to advise him against it, nothing will stop him — you might as well advise a person stricken with the typhoid to reduce his temperature from one hundred and four degrees Fahrenheit down to ninety-eight and one-half — it would have the same effect.

So the old man takes a good-sized New York draft from his account at the bank, sets out for the Metropolis and deposits his money with a responsible Wall Street broker for margin account. Of course, at the time this old merchant is attracted by the stock market it is toward the end of a "bull campaign," when stocks are selling near the top and are about ready to turn downward. In fact, it is exceedingly seldom that a novice is drawn into Wall Street when the market is around the bottom. In any event, if he should come in and want to buy stocks at such a time, the brokers would scare him out of his wits. It is always during the loud bull chorus and the grand hurrah, on the last end of a boom, that the "lambs" are called in to be fleeced.

As we have seen, when the market is around the top, every lie and every wile of which the human mind could be capable is employed by the insiders, for the purpose of inducing the public to buy their stocks; but after a quick manipulated decline and the market begins to touch bottom the insiders quietly pick up the stocks again.

At these times the lambs and the small fry, if they want to buy on margin, are told by the brokers that the market looks like going lower, and on account of the condition of the money market, or for some other plausible reason, they can only buy stocks for cash, that is, outright and not on margin. This course serves to keep the public out of the market just when they should buy. When stocks were selling 20 or 30 percent higher, brokers were perfectly willing to carry all one could hold on a five or ten point margin, and they thought it perfectly safe at that, but now when stocks are down say thirty points and about to advance, they do not think it safe for the lambs to buy on a margin.

The fact is, the brokers, on these occasions of unusual opportunity, very likely when money is scarce and high, want their cash and credit to buy stocks for themselves and for a few of their favored customers and friends. They are not employing their money and credit now for the benefit of the small traders — the chances are too good; but wait a while until the market makes a good sharp advance, and the same brokers will be ready again on the top to carry on margin all the stocks that the public wish to buy. They know that it is only a short interval before the money put into their hands for margin account will be confiscated into their own pockets, or appropriated in the interests of the insiders. This is the policy pursued by most of the New York Stock Exchange brokers.

After a quick manipulated decline, to which we have just referred, the conditions, of course, are different from those prevailing after a period of prolonged and steady liquidation, like that of 1902-1903. In the latter case, when such thorough liquidation has been forced, it is necessary for a long wait before the insiders manipulate the market anew, in order to give the general public ample time to recuperate from their overwhelming losses, bury the suicides, console the broken-hearted, and accumulate more money in the channels of honest industry; meanwhile the Wall Street magnates are enjoying the proceeds of their last coup from the stock market, basking in the sunshine of the Riviera, cruising along the Mediterranean, reposing beneath Italian skies, and hobnobbing with princes in the castles of Europe. But after due time, when the common people become worth the game, some new scheme is devised by Wall Street to lure the public into the stock market once more and clean them out again. And so the good work goes on.

But we will return now to our rural merchant. His broker had no more than caught sight of him, when he was recognized as one of the "lambs," and as he has deposited quite a large sum for margin account, his kind friend and adviser, the broker, tries to make an estimate of how much more money the old man has hack to be relieved of, and then advises him to buy, buy, Buy.

The broker knows that his customer, being inexperienced, would not sell stocks short for a decline, as he should at this time, even if he urged him to — he would not understand the transaction. Moreover, since prices appear to be near the top, the broker has stocks himself for sale, as well as orders from old customers to sell their holdings at top-notch figures, and he is interested in making a market for them.

More than likely, however, his broker advises him to buy, then "buckets" his orders and takes the chances; but the chances are very few in such n case if the broker can get his customer to give purchasing orders at inflated prices, when the market is at a dizzy height.

Our rural friend, having now become a little more accustomed to the turmoil down in Wall Street, and having got his sand up on good advice and encouragement from his broker, sails in and buys for a starter 200 shares of St. Paul, that is 200 shares of the Chicago, Milwaukee & St. Paul R. E., a speculative favorite in Wall Street. Everything is more or less lively along toward the end of a "bull campaign," especially St. Paul stock, which made an advance of nearly three points the same day that he bought it, and netted a profit on the 200 shares of over $500.

This set the old man nearly crazy. When he compared such a method of making money to selling salt mackerel and drawing thick molasses in cold weather, and then waiting for the pay until his customers sold their steers or butchered their hogs — when he made these comparisons be could not help reflecting upon what a fool he had been during all his past life. He determined now to get immensely rich; he had the capital to do it and he was not going to be very long about it either.

As St. Paul seemed to be a good jumper, the next day he bought 500 shares more. After he bought the stock it sagged a little, and he wondered what was the matter, but between 2 and 3 p. m. the market rallied and St. Paul closed about a point and a half higher than where he bought it, and he stood, on the books of the brokers, something like $1,200 ahead for the two days.

He was crazier than ever now. All the tipsters in Wall Street said that the market was going a great deal higher, and stated the prices to which the more active stocks would advance. Accordingly, he began to figure out how heavy a burden his margin account, including profits, would carry, and the next day he loaded up with all the stocks that his funds would hold on a safe ten-point margin.

Along in the afternoon of the same day the market began to drop off easily, money was loaning at 10 percent on call, and it was reported that the National City Bank had been calling loans, which was the case. The Standard Oil crowd, who control the National City Bank and various other Wall Street banks, and who, by the way, virtually run the stock market to suit themselves, having completed the sale of their speculative holdings, and, moreover, having sold stocks short (that is without having them), were now anxious to put the market down as far as possible, buy in their short sales at low prices, and accumulate stocks for another advance.

Aided by the inflated condition of the market, which they had previously fostered and encouraged to sell out on, they proceed to force prices down, among other methods by making money scarce and high and by setting afloat direful and alarming rumors.

The allied Standard Oil banks and their correspondents throughout the country are said to control nearly one-half of the money in the U.S., and in times of inflation, the National City Bank alone (to say nothing of the others) has anywhere from one hundred and forty to one hundred and fifty million dollars out in loans, a considerable part of this amount, loaned in Wall Street "on call," and upon securities, as collateral, which are dealt in by speculators on the New York Stock Exchange.

You can readily see what a power these banks are to the Standard Oil people in manipulating the market either up or down. Since they hold so many loans in their various banks, upon stocks carried on margin, the business of brokers and the large operators and their speculative position is an open hook to these great manipulators, and they consequently know just when, where and how to strike a blow of death to the market. The National City Bank accordingly begins to call loans, right and left, which precipitates upon the market thousands of shares of stock, held by this bank as collateral. Since borrowers are unable to obtain accommodations elsewhere, their certificates of stock, put up as collateral security for loans, are sold at the market. Other banks are soon compelled to pursue the same course in order to protect their loans upon rapidly depreciating collateral, which brokers and other borrowers are unable to keep margined up to bank requirements. Frightened holders of stocks begin to unload and "old-timers" to sell short; and the market is soon deluged with securities, nearly every one wild to sell and few wishing to buy.

The Standard Oil crowd thus ultimately succeed in precipitating a panic, Wall Street failures and general demoralization and disaster, shaking the financial world of both hemispheres to its remotest corners. In this way they confiscate the money of the public into their own capacious pockets, already so generously ailed.

Chapter XII

This was a phase of the speculative situation which the old merchant little understood; he thought that the market must soon recover, and as general business was still in a flourishing condition, he looked for an advance in stocks to prices still higher than they had yet reached. He did not know that Wall Street anticipates and discounts long in advance all the prosperity in sight, even through the most powerful lenses. He did not know that a burst of glory in the business world is a signal for the insiders in the stock market to unload upon an eager public, and then start the manipulation of decline and panic.

The fifth day after being launched upon this, at first smooth sea of speculation, the old man found the waters becoming exceedingly rough and dangerous. The market kept on sagging; it had a good start now and by night his profits were all wiped out and he had lost about $5,000 besides.

As a merchant, be had not been accustomed to losing money that fast and it began to start the cold sweat upon his brow; he stood around dazed and looked on, while his hard-earned money was melting away by the thousands. His kind friend the broker did not seem to be much in evidence at this juncture; he did not see him around anywhere to advise what he should do. The old man concluded, however, to hang on to his stocks until the market would turn in his favor, and in that way not lose anything after all.

The situation in Wall Street was now beginning to look exceedingly dismal, where only a few days before everything appeared so roseate. All the bad news seemed to have been dammed back for months and let out at this time systematically. The next day he was out about $10,000 more, and was called by his broker for additional margin at once; so in order to save what money he had in, and see the thing through, he gave the broker a cheek for all that he had left in his bank up in Connecticut. Down, down, down, the stocks tumbled; with dark, haggard faces speculators pace the floor of brokers' offices, in all the anxieties of hell, with trembling hands they hold the ticker tape, which tells the sad story, and see the savings of a lifetime swept from their grasp — yonder sits a man glaring at the floor, half-crazed, contemplating suicide — men see themselves irretrievably ruined, and drop dead at the ticker! But how the Standard Oil people and other insiders are now making money out of these unfortunates on their short sales; and what bargains they are picking up in cheap stocks, forced from the hands of weak holders, and that of course is enough — no gold mine on earth ever turned out profits with such rapidity.

Presently the old merchant was almost paralyzed by another call for additional margin. If he failed to comply at once his stocks would be closed out, and he would lose everything. His own resources had become entirely exhausted; but obtaining the endorsement of a friend, he borrowed some money at his country bank, and poured that also into the howling vortex. Then came a little rally; the market was getting near the bottom, but at last it took another slide down and plunged the old man to his financial ruin.

After this the market rallied and started on its course upward. Although the old merchant had a small margin on his account, at the lowest quotations reached on the decline, nevertheless his broker closed him out, right on the bottom and just as the market was turning for a prolonged advance. At these opportune times, when stocks are depressed far below their intrinsic value, the insiders are particularly anxious to take over the cheap stocks of the "lambs," especially after the latter have brought their last dollar into Wall Street for the purpose of carrying their accounts through a decline. It keeps this money in the "Street" and likewise leaves the "come-ons" without any stocks and without any hope of recovering their money. More greenhorns and more margins are now in order — and thus thrives Wall Street.

The way the old fellow took on in the broker's office when he learned that he had been sold out and hopelessly ruined was the source of considerable sport with the broker and his clerks for several days afterward. At first, when he complained about his misfortune, the broker and his office manager gave him the "hoarse laugh," or what is sometimes called the "grand haha;" but when they saw how agitated he was, they thought that perhaps it would be better policy to handle him differently; so they changed their tactics a little and slapped him on the back and said, "Awfully sorry, old man, awfully sorry; but we just had to close you out, you know; if you had put up more margin, we would have carried you through." The facts of the case are, most likely, that they had "bucketed" his orders or disposed of his stocks soon after the decline began; but, notwithstanding this, had kept him handing in money to "margin down his account," and they were now alarmed, when the market was apparently near the bottom, lest he might put up a large margin and thus give them no good chance to scoop him.

Needless to say, now that the victim had been plundered of his last dollar and more (for he was in debt to his bank), he was of no further use to the broker, in fact, like the ruined player at Monte Carlo, a bad advertisement.

At Monte Carlo, however, when a player loses his all, it is the humane custom of the establishment to provide him with sufficient money for his expenses home; but not so in Wall Street — the victim can walk home or blow his brains out or jump from the top of a twenty-story building, nobody cares. Accordingly, the chief concern of the broker, in this case, was to get rid of the old man, as quietly and gracefully as possible. But this little matter was skillfully and successfully managed, since the broker had become a trained expert in this line through long practice.

That night, away from the noise of the street, in the quiet of his little room at the hotel, the old man sits, with his face in his hands, and thinks it all over again. The full realization of his disaster now begins to settle down upon him. Ruined! ruined! worse than ruined, and sixty years old! For forty years, he and his faithful wife had toiled and saved; he never took a vacation, he never had any time or thought that he could afford to attend a theater or a lecture. His wife did her own work and helped in the store. He not only worked all day, but posted books half the night. Competition was keen and profits were small, which, with the loss of a few had accounts every year, made the process of accumulating a fortune somewhat slow, but he was industrious, careful and close; he had allowed himself few pleasures and little recreation; he never thought that lie had time to rest, and in acting as proprietor, general manager, buyer, salesman and book-keeper in his store, he was too tired even for pleasure when his work was over.

Most everything for which life is worth living, except work, he had crowded out of his existence. He had always been getting ready to enjoy himself when he had saved so much money. He had always entertained the laudable ambition of making his old age and that of his wife comfortable and free from care and worry. This ambition he had fully realized when he was drawn into Wall Street. Could he go through it all again and begin over where lie started, forty years ago? could he go home now and tell his wife? could he go back and face the community and his debt at the bank, without a dollar? No! No! sick, disheartened, half insane, he clutches his revolver and blows his brains out.

Now who murdered that man. The scoundrels who manipulated the Wall Street game drew him into it and got his money. They are really the ones who murdered him, as well as thousands of others, who have suffered the same deplorable fate; these scoundrels are morally, if not legally, responsible. That is the way to become immensely rich and do it quick — kill people for their money! But do it systematically and within the law, mind that you do it indirectly and within the law. This please recognize as the severest irony, on my part; but I want to give you a little idea of the methods employed in Wall Street.

The suicides which follow in the wake of stock market manipulation are something appalling, and notwithstanding the efforts of certain pious Wall Street magnates to throw an odor of sanctity over Wall Street and lead the public to believe that it is a divine institution, few I think are as yet convinced that driving men to suicide can be regarded as a highly moral occupation, no matter how indirect the methods employed, no matter how religious those engaged in it, or how profitable the business.

Chapter XIII

The next morning the newspapers made slight mention of the old merchant's death, something as follows: "Suicide of wealthy country merchant, while temporarily insane, no other cause known for the deed, as he had no family or financial troubles." He was not of much account anyway in a great city like New York; and since the brokers hushed the little matter up as much as possible lest it might hurt business, this is the last that the public ever heard about the incident — and Wall Street goes on, luring in more victims, ruining more lives, wrecking more homes, spreading more misery and driving more men to insanity and death.

Although the financial kings of Wall Street already possess hundreds of millions of dollars, although among their number are men, whose individual wealth is greater than the assessed valuation of some whole States, yet so great is their sordid greed that none of them hesitate at methods of this kind for a single instant — provided they can clutch more money! more money!

Now don't you think that Wall Street speculation is a wicked game, a gigantic robbery, rather than a legitimate business, and don't you think that such a game ought to be stopped I say that speculation in stocks on a margin should be constituted a crime under the law, as it is in reality. It fosters a ring of idle gamblers, parasites upon society, who prey upon the fortunes of the honest and industrious; since people are a menace to the legitimate business interests of the country and an element of danger to the republic.

Petit larceny is promptly punished, as it should be; but why indorse grand larceny and let the big thieves go free? We must confess that the man who commits petit larceny generally has neither influence nor money, and that when this fact comes to light the vigor with which he is pounced upon is truly pitiful; we must likewise acknowledge that the big thieves have such fabulous wealth as would make Croesus feel poor; but, notwithstanding this, under what code of morals or under what true system of jurisprudence should the petty pilferers be punished, and the wholesale robbers allowed to fatten and flourish, immune from restraint and punishment tinder the law.

If robbery is only committed on a scale sufficiently grand and colossal, the majesty of the law is appalled; if a few smooth Wall Street gentlemen defraud the public out of their honestly acquired wealth and take it by the scores of millions. Justice stands by paralyzed and helpless, in the presence of a crime of such stupendous proportions, as to be outside the scope and contemplation of the law — but with what heavy hands she lays hold of the man who steals a chicken! For these absurdities and inconsistencies in our jurisprudence, let us hope that the slow growth of the law will ultimately evolve effectual remedies.

Members of Congress and of other legislative bodies, as well as Presidents of the United States, if in league with market manipulators and speculating in Wall Street, should be compelled by law to forfeit the office, which they thus prostitute to private gain. The speculating legislator or other government official employs his power, not for the welfare of his constituency or the country at large, but merely for his own private pocket and without the slightest regard for the peoples' interests, which he is employed to protect. Such are Wall Street's statesmen and patriots, of which we have had an example in at least one President.

Furthermore, should not the amount of wealth which one man shall be allowed to roll up, under some unusual advantage, be regulated by law, and the dangerous and disturbing billionaire rendered impossible? There is of course a difference of opinion on this question, some political economists maintaining that if an individual were limited in his acquisitions, to say fifty million dollars, instead of to a possible billion, it would work complete stagnation and paralysis to personal ambition and personal enterprise. I would not assume to be an authority on this point; but I think that the consensus of opinion is, that it can scarcely be safe for one man, like our greatest millionaire, to bold so ranch money power in this Republic, that all the rest of the financial world simply does not dare to oppose him, no matter how predatory or piratical his ambitions; to oppose whom means absolute ruin and annihilation; that it can scarcely be consistent with the general welfare for one man to become so powerful that he may own Legislatures and benches of judges, and even presume to dictate to the Senate of the United States.

What other influence is there, in this country, let me ask, that is breeding with so great rapidity, the lamentable spirit of socialism and anarchy?

Chapter XIV

Let us return, now for a moment to the old lady, the merchant's wife. It is a deplorable fact, that, when the head of a household is ruined financially, his family, through no fault of theirs, must often suffer more than he. I will not attempt to depict the old lady's feelings when she learned the true situation -- a widow and nearly destitute in her old age.

After the funeral is over, she tries to think what she can do. Her home even was sold, for that was a part of the store property and went with it. Years ago, in the distribution of her father's estate, the farm which he had left was sold and the proceeds divided among seven or eight children, and she had received from that source a small sum of money. This she had kept on interest, always adding the increase to the principal until it had amounted to five or six hundred dollars. This money, heretofore almost forgotten, is now her only resource. Out of it she paid the funeral expenses and then took what remained and turned it over to an old ladies' home. It at least might buy her a place to die.

Upon receiving notice of her admission to the home, she sots out for the place where she is to pass her last sad and lonely years. Feebly and tearfully she climbs the long steps and presents herself at the office of the institution. The authorities are sorry that they can give her no better accommodations; but it is the best that they can do. She will be satisfied with anything, she says; then she follows an attendant down a long oil-cloth covered hall, up two flights of stairs, down another long narrow hall to room 67, a little cell-like apartment, with one north window. The door is unlocked for her, she steps slowly in and closes it. The room is furnished with two chairs, a dresser and a white cot bed. She takes off her cloak and lays it on a chair, puts her long crepe veil thoughtfully on the dresser, contemplates the bare walls, so suggestive of her desolation, then falls upon her knees beside her little cot and sobs the hot tears of loneliness and despair.

But what became of the money of these old people and that of others who lost in the same way? Where is it? This money has not been destroyed; it has merely changed hands, without an equivalent being given. But who got it? I will tell you. Through the intricacies of the game, this money has passed into the hands of the great capitalists of Wall Street, never to return to those who, with a life-time of toil, honestly earned it. What will become of it? The greater portion of it, doubtless, will remain in the strong boxes of those whose iron grasp now holds it. But let us throw the most favorable light possible upon the situation. As it is easy to be generous with other people's money, part of this old merchant's fortune, together with a tithe from much more made in the same way, may sometime constitute a gift, which one of these great capitalists turns over, with a loud report, to a university or a theological seminary or to some other charity. He hands it over, as a sort of conscience fund, to give him a fresh start in more Wall Street enterprise of the same kind, and the world looks on and says, "This is indeed true charity, God bless the philanthropist!"

Perhaps, that very night, while the old lady was sobbing beside her little cot, the fortune which she and her husband had toiled so long and hard to earn, flashed in a tiara of diamonds from the head of a rich broker's wife at the opening night of the Metropolitan Grand Opera — diamonds, wondrously beautiful, dazzlingly brilliant, crystalized human tears. If you could go around that row of parterre boxes and write the history of all those pearls and all those rubies and all those diamonds, it would compose a tragedy that would make your heart bleed.

What an enchanting scene is the opening night of the Metropolitan Grand Opera! The rarest gems on earth dance in ten thousand lights; beautiful women, the soft perfume of exotic flowers and the voluptuous swell of grand music thrill the soul — verily, "the cup runeth over," and all hearts seem filled with every joy. But how can we help reflecting upon what a contrast is this brilliant scene to that in the little room at the old ladies' home — yet what do these people care about this desolate widow and their thousands of other victims? Absolutely nothing—in fact their victims, if thought of at all, are the subject of sarcasm and jest; they are the "lambs that got fleeced."

There must not be any sentiment in business, is their doctrine — it interferes. If you would make millions, business must be utterly heartless, utterly heartless! Those terse aphorisms, "Business is business" and "Do others or they will do you" receive much admiration here, as maxims both of high moral worth and of great practical utility; but such sentiments as "A good name is rather to be chosen than great riches, and loving favor rather than silver and gold," have been crossed out and labeled "back numbers" and "no good in Wall Street"

If there is any doctrine which this class of people dotes on, it is that of "the survival of the fittest." Applicable as this doctrine is, in the world of strife, its application here seems somewhat perverted and paradoxical since, in Wall Street, the most consummate trickster and the most heartless scoundrel with the biggest pile of dollars is the fittest and he is the one who does the surviving. And then the following is much relied on in justification of Wall Street methods: "For whosoever hath, to him shall be given, and he shall have more abundance: but whosoever hath not, from him shall be taken away, even that he hath." This passage, of course, refers to the acquisition of more knowledge of the truth, as the theologians tell us, but the money kings of Wall Street like to give its interpretation a little twist in their favor, and say that it refers to the acquisition of more greenbacks, by the big fellows from the little ones. In fact, this class of people appear to hold the opinion that if they would succeed in anything questionable or crooked, there is nothing like misinterpreting the Scriptures their own way, so as to apparently justify them in their rascality before the public.

This is a little of Wall Street theology and Wall Street business ethics. Do you wonder that such theologians could insert about eight hundred million dollars of wind into the U.S. Steel Trust and something like forty million dollars more into the United States Shipbuilding Trust, and then sell it to the public without a twinge?

Coming from Wall Street, I hope that I shall not be misunderstood as proselyting for this kind of a creed — far from it — nor for any particular creed, being engaged in legal instead of evangelistic work, I thought, nevertheless, that I should merely touch upon the convenient theology and ethics of Wall Street, as well as upon its other phases, especially since those, who have made the most conspicuous successes here have been particular to pose before the public as eminent churchmen. The connection of such men with churches, however, has done more to spread infidelity and cast reflection and ridicule upon the good cause of the church than almost anything else.

The success of this class of gamblers has an influence for evil upon the business world that is little realized, success through their methods being a contradiction to the good old business maxim that "Honesty is the best policy" and a travesty upon it. The moral law seems perverted here. Wrong appears right and right wrong. Young men look down from the galleries and far off corners of that great Opera House and say, "If you would make millions, that is the way, speculation, gambling, rascality, anything but honest work. The rascal is exalted and his victim disgraced."

Since these great Wall Street magnates are continually kept before the public, as shining examples of success for the youth to emulate, is it any wonder that the business world is becoming more and more shrewd, dishonest and unscrupulous! The young man says to himself, when imitating the great financiers and capitalists of our day, "Can I be sufficiently dishonest and at the same time sufficiently pious to succeed in life; can I be just dishonest enough to graze State prison, hut at the same time keep out through bribery, perjury and hypocrisy!"

The effect of this influence crops out in all kinds of so-called "hot air" and "get rich quick" swindles, 520 percent. Miller games, discretionary pool frauds, turf investment companies, etc., etc., which relieve the confiding public of anywhere from ten to twenty millions of cold cash at one sweep.

Chapter XV

The experience of this Connecticut merchant, which I have given you, is only one little case among thousands. Think of the misery, think of the tears, think of the disgrace and remorse which the tremendous losses of the public to these Wall Street sharpers, year after year, certainly entails. Who can realize it? The massive iron doors of State prison clank behind a man, from some responsible and trusted position of business life; in an hour of temptation, he was drawn into Wall Street speculation, with trust funds. He lost. The court and jury say he is guilty of grand larceny. He has lost the money bequeathed into his charge by a father, for the support and education of several young children. They are now left destitute. When he reflects upon what he has done, through this alone as punishment, he suffers all the torments of the damned; but in addition to this, he must go to prison and wear the stripes, for ten long weary years. Dazed, they lead him from the courtroom, all he hears is the heart breaks of his wife and innocent children, disgraced by him forever. Into a solitude worse than death they lead him and clank behind the doors of his eternal doom.

Such is his fate; but what about the Wall Street sharpers who drew him into, this trouble and who now have the money of these children, safely deposited, to their already stupendous bank accounts — what about them? Oh, they are all right; they pose as financiers, great "captains of industry," and as men of remarkable genius in the business world. The general public do not understand and the people who acquire their wealth in this manner take every precaution possible that the public shall not understand; sometimes they endow churches and teach Bible classes, as a blind, or pass the Sacrament of the Lord's Supper at the celebration of Holy Communion.

This renders their course of crime easy and profitable and enables them at the same time to be looked upon by those who do not know them and their methods as highly respected citizens and Christian gentlemen; but notwithstanding what their appearance may be before the public, I have often wondered, when they are teaching Sunday school and passing the Sacrament, what kind of an appearance they are making before God, the God of love for all mankind, the God of the fatherless.

The church is a strong fortress behind which such high up rascals like to entrench themselves, in whom the church is deceived and for whose membership, therefore, it is not responsible, unless the church knowingly fosters such people and contends for them, as is sometimes the case, because they always pay heavily for their protection. They can afford to; there is money in it.

Chapter XVI

So much for Wall Street and its woes, its tricks and its tragedies, its heartlessness and its hypocrisy; and now will you permit me to give a word of advice:

If you are inexperienced in Wall Street methods and contemplate going into that maelstrom of speculation, take your money, five, ten, twenty, or thirty thousand dollars or whatever you may anticipate venturing with, have it all stacked up in nice now bills, put it into your grip and go right direct with it to some of the great Wall Street financiers, and say "Here, Mister, is my $30,000, in good money; it is a large share of what I possess, but it is yours now, take it quick. I thought of using it as margin in Wall Street speculation, but I have concluded that you will get it anyway in the end, and you can have it now; you might just as well take it first as last, and a great deal better; it, will save me much time and worry, many a wrinkle and many, a gray hair and I will go right back home and give my attention to my business, before it is ruined, for I can't keep my mind on Wall Street and on my business too."

To hand over money in that prodigal manner may seem, on first consideration, manifestly rash and foolish; but if you must do either the one or the other, go into Wall Street speculation or hand the money over, the latter is altogether the better course. It will save burning out your soul in the protracted fires of suspense, anxiety and worry; it will save your health; it will save you from shattered nerves and from shattered bruin; it will save you from a physical and mental condition incapacitated for honest business or professional life; it will save losing faith in your fellow man, and in your God.

There is, of course, a glamour about the possibility of making a hundred dollars in a minute, but that possibility is the siren's silver voice, that will likely lure you on to the rocks of ruin.

One would almost think that King Solomon must have had some experience in Wall Street speculation and then sat down and wrote in his proverbs as follows: "He that hasteneth to be rich hath an evil eye, and considereth not that poverty shall come upon him." If young men will take that advice, keep out of Wall Street that "hasteneth to be rich," and go to work at something honest and useful and stick to it, they will be successful and happy and "poverty shall not come upon them."

He who aspires to go through this life the easiest is almost sure to go through the hardest and finally come to a wretched and abandoned old age. What a contrast between the old age of the man who brings to the evening of life the fruits of honest industry and the satisfaction of lifelong usefulness to his fellow men, and the old age of the insane gambler who brings in his bony, trembling hands nothing but the semblance of a wasted life.

Will you picture to yourself a deep and dark canyon; below are jagged rocks and a great river; 1,000 feet above, the brow of the canyon projects over the rocks and the river. Not far from the edge of this precipice a man stands; he is blindfolded and groping in the darkness. He does not realize his danger — the river is so far below that he cannot hear it. He may wander away from this yawning chasm, but not likely; and even if he would, an enemy in whose power he is stands close by, watching to turn him in the opposite direction. Moreover, the slippery rock beneath his feet slopes toward the edge of the precipice, and blindfolded, he naturally will drift in the course of the least resistance. Nearer and nearer, he gropes toward the edge. Now we see him stand on the very brink. One more step, whispers his enemy, and you are safe. He takes it — when down, down, down to death and destruction he plunges upon the sharp and jagged rocks, below.

This is the position of the speculator in Wall Street. Can you afford to take the chances of that perilous position? If so, then to Wall Street, with money, mind, body and soul, and there take your chance on life and death, your chance on Heaven and Hell.

THE PITFALLS OF SPECULATION
Thomas Gibson - 1906

Contents

Chapter I – Introduction - The Public Attitude Toward Speculation

The public attitude toward speculation is generally hostile. Even those who venture frequently are prone to speak discouragingly of speculative possibilities, and to point warningly to the fact that an overwhelming majority of speculative commitments result in loss, while those who venture not at all, and consequently are incompetent to judge, dismiss the subject with the statement that marginal trading is gambling, pure and simple, and is therefore pernicious.

Those who enter into the subject a little farther, and attempt to adduce more specific argument against speculative possibilities, lay stress upon the statement that manipulation, trickery and wholesale deception render it impossible for the outsider to enter the field safely or intelligently. These statements, usually unsupported, and frequently insupportable, are accepted by the prejudiced multitude as gospel truth, without any attempt being made to examine their foundation or correctness.

So far as the question of gambling is concerned, it would be entering a very large field to attempt to define just what is and what is not gambling.

The idea that the man who buys a certain stock outright invests, while he who buys on margin gambles is a popular fallacy. The speculator purchases in the hope of an advance, and if two purchases are made for parallel reasons, one for cash, and one on margins, both purchases are speculative.

That speculative fluctuations are largely used as a basis for gambling operations, is unquestionably true, and possibly an acceptable dividing line may be drawn on the following hypothesis: gambling, in the general acceptance of the term, is founded upon blind chance, the equal possibility of certain events occurring or not occurring; this is modified in some cases by the exercise of superior skill in such games as admit of skill; but fundamentally, gambling is wholly dependent upon the equal chances of two or more opposed individuals.

The trader who takes "flyers" with no knowledge of his subject, or the properties in which he deals, merely gambles on the ultimate rise and fall of the market; but the trader, who, after careful investigation and study, purchases a property, either outright or on margins, because he has reasons for believing it to be cheap, and that it will enhance in value, is a speculator.

Those composing the gambling element are in the majority, and it is needless to say, are the greatest losers; in fact their losses foot up almost the sum total of speculative deficiency, and consequently the sum total of the gains reaped by the real speculator.

The statement that most public commitments are made on no better foundation than a mere guess, may seem a trifle bold, and the counter statement may be made that few people purchase a stock without some reason for so doing. This is admitted on the same basis that the man who bets on a certain number at roulette because it has not recently appeared, or in hope of an immediate repetition, considers that he has a reason for his action. Thus a great number of amateur, or semi-professional traders, buy a certain commodity for no better reason than that the stock has declined, or, more frequently, from a participation in a period of speculative intoxication. They can give reasons for their ventures, but they are without foundation, and are no more worthy of consideration than the reasons given by the roulette player for "staking" upon a certain number.

On the other hand, the speculator, with a carefully acquired knowledge of the normal value of certain properties, fully posted on conditions in general, and those affecting, or liable to affect his favorite property in particular, patiently waits the opportunity to buy, not at a normal price, but at a price far below the actual value of his property. He knows that speculative prices move in cycles, more or less pronounced and prolonged, and in the revolution of this cycle he will be given an opportunity not only to purchase at a price far below a normal valuation, but to sell at a price far above it.

This looks simple enough in the telling, and is merely the operation of Anselm Rothschild's famous advice, "buy cheap and sell dear." But when the statement is made that over 80% of public purchases are made at the approximate high tide of a market and about the same percentage of sales at the approximate low tide, in short, that the most simple and reasonable methods of making money are not only disregarded, but actually reversed, a great field for analysis and discussion presents itself.

Manipulation and trickery are vastly overestimated: popular prejudice continually accords to such causes events which were brought about almost wholly by the composite folly of public participators in speculative affairs, and which could not possibly have been effected by any individual interests.

That these stages of undue depression and inflation are to some extent assisted by the shrewd minority, is true; but the great work is that of the public itself.

That the money-making minority foresee, and take advantage of these extremes, is unquestionable. They are the cause of all speculative movements of importance, and through the errors and losses of the lambs the accumulations of successful operators are made possible.

After a careful examination, covering a period of ten years, and a study of the methods of successful and unsuccessful traders as shown in some thousands of speculative accounts, the following facts are adduced:

1st—The greatest causes of loss in speculation are ignorance, over-speculation, and carelessness, of importance in the order named.

2nd—The popular fallacy that business methods are not applicable to speculation is wholly erroneous.

3rd—Not one speculator in a thousand applies ordinary business precautions to his trades, nor founds his ventures upon knowledge of any value.

4th—The correct trader has little to fear, and much to gain from manipulative tactics.

5th—While extremes of prices move in irregular cycles, no "system" for judging changes is possible, or tenable, as such mechanical attempts to forecast price changes do not contemplate changed conditions, or provide for accident. The advocates of the "Chart System" are legion, and yet it is impossible to find a single permanent and substantial gain made by this method.

6th—The general idea that the actual value, and probable future of a property cannot be intelligently based, is erroneous.

7th—The greatest speculative profits are made in stocks, and the greatest speculative losses, in staples: wheat, corn, cotton, etc.

8th—There are certain technical stages, or conditions of markets which are followed by certain invariable results, the study and recognition of which is valuable, and not difficult. These "ear-marks" are in some cases very plain, and do not in any way smack of the "systems" deprecated above, but are more or less visible signs of effects following certain causes.

9th—Almost every general idea of speculation is the exact reverse of the truth. Sometimes this is caused by false reasoning, but most frequently by the innate false appearance of the market quotations. For example, greatest activity and interest in a market occurs around top prices; while dullness and stagnation are invariable when properties are unreasonably low in price.

10th—Persistent short selling of stocks is fashionable in a certain class of semi-professional traders, and almost invariably results in loss.

11th—Tips are illogical. Any widespread dissemination of advance information as to a projected movement would defeat its own object. The so-called "tip"' is usually mere guess work. The general consensus of public opinion on this subject is correct, i.e., tips are valueless; and yet the public continues to use them largely as a basis of trading.

12th—Too great facilities for obtaining information and executing orders, is, to the ordinary trader, of no advantage, and is frequently a source of loss. (The accounts mentioned above show the most intelligent trading to have been done by traders who were without facilities to interfere with their own original plans through fright or confusion.)

13th—Speculation is a safe business when business methods are applied to it. The changes in prices of standard properties offer yearly greater opportunities for profit than any other field. That is to say, for reasonable profits, not for the amassing of fortunes on small capital, in a brief period, but for steady accumulation of money and valuable knowledge. So great are the opportunities offered by speculative changes, that with proper methods and self-control, the poor man cannot afford to overlook them.

To make these rather radical statements in a general way is wholly insufficient; each statement must be supported by the presentation of convincing precedent and clear reasoning, and it is the purpose of these articles to point out the reasons for the failure of the majority, as well as the methods by which the minority succeed. This done, the knowledge so gained must be insulated into useful channels, and combined into flexible rules, and inflexible laws.

It is not claimed that it is possible to set down in print a formula for speculative success: much depends upon the individual. A man is not a machine, and will be frequently swerved into paths which he, himself, knows to be dangerous, and an individual incapable of clear thinking and correct application of accrued knowledge, would not succeed at this, or any other business.

The most that may be hoped for, consequently, is to point out certain facts which will lead to a correct line of thinking, or open the way to profitable discussion. To this end, the various causes of loss mentioned will be discussed in turn.

Chapter II - Ignorance, Over-Speculation, Etc.

Ignorance, over-speculation, and the innate false appearance of market stages are the principal causes of speculative loss, and are the principal causes of the great cycles of speculative extremes. These extremes are variously attributed to specific causes, affecting certain securities, to good or bad business conditions, or to accident or manipulation; but the fact of the matter is that the wide swings of the market are brought about almost wholly by the errors and ignorance of the great body of traders known as the public. Conditions change, accidents occur, and manipulation exists, and all have their effect; but unless these factors were supplemented by alternate waves of general over-confidence, and subsequent undue depression, the fluctuations in market quotations for standard properties would be confined to such narrow limits that the repeated opportunities to purchase such properties at prices far below, and to sell them at prices far above a normal value, would be eliminated.

Almost all the commitments made by public traders are made on faith, or on misleading surface appearances. The advice of people absolutely incapable of passing intelligent opinions, is eagerly listened to and frequently acted upon; large dividends on low-priced stocks are made the basis of optimistic views and shallow arguments; the fact that a certain stock has dragged back in a generally strong market,—usually the best evidence in the world of something radically wrong with that particular stock,—incites what may be very undesirable purchases. The development of certain long-heralded events, such as the payment, or increase of a dividend, is considered a good reason for the purchase of the security affected, when in fact it is no reason at all, as Wall Street always anticipates and discounts probable good news. These and a hundred and one other reasons, mostly ill-founded, are the groundwork of the great bulk of public ventures, and the individuals who operate on these unreliable signs, with full knowledge of the fact that the public has been misled by them time and again, seldom attempt to investigate the intrinsic value of the property in which they have assumed and paid cash for a proprietary interest. Such an investigation is usually considered useless or impossible. If this were true any participation whatever in speculative affairs would be folly, but fortunately this common opinion is itself the result of ignorance.

Over-speculation, the composite result of ignorance, greed, and false appearances, may be classed as the primary cause of wide variations in prices, for as much too high as a market is carried by rash participation at high prices, just as much too low will it sink in the ensuing decline. The ill-advised traders who rush in at high prices with inadequate capital are the first to suffer; their overthrow topples over other weak accounts, and so on down the line, until the last of the wobbly row of bricks has fallen.

It might be contended that when this process of elimination had brought prices of good properties to a fair valuation, purchasers would be easily found, and such might be the case, were it not for the fact that the great lights of speculative finance know full well that the technical position of the market is still bad; that many venturers, already financially weakened by the decline from abnormal to normal prices, are in a position which they can be forced to abandon; that the pendulum of prices will swing to the other extreme, and they refrain from buying at normal prices for the good and simple reason that they know they can eventually buy at prices that are very low. Perhaps these low prices will come about unaided, through the internal rottenness of the technical situation; perhaps the desirable consummation will require a little assistance, such as the passing of a dividend or two, the closing of a few mills or the laying off of a few men, all of which actions can in the future be pointed out as good and conservative business moves, but which will be received by the public with anger and disgust; for so dense is general ignorance on this one subject that the payment of a dividend is always considered good, and the reduction or passing of a dividend is always considered bad; a bond issue, for whatever purpose, is an unmixed evil, and so following.

The professional bear element also assists in the final downfall of prices. They will be well aware of the assailable condition of the weakened long interest, and will attack the market for the purpose of reaching stop-loss orders or forcing crippled speculators to sell. These same bears may later be hoist with their own petard, for a chronic bear is a chronic loser, but meanwhile they assist the successful campaigners materially by forcing a temporarily lower level of prices and supplanting weak long accounts with a short interest, which is in itself a great advantage to the bull element.

So familiar is the experienced speculator with public weakness that he is usually found operating in direct reversion to prevailing sentiment. He knows by careful and clearheaded investigation the normal value of the property or properties in which he trades, and at such time as he finds the current quotations far below this fixed point and the public inveighing bitterly against his favorite issues, he begins his purchases. It does not require much shrewdness to deduce the fact that if a certain standard security has passed out of public, or weak hands, it has of necessity been concentrated in the strong hands of the giants of finance, and that the purchaser at such periods is at least in good company. He has no fear of any abnormal shrinkage in the value of his holdings, as such sudden shrinkages are the result of panic or financial necessity, to which the present holders are not subject. He also knows that any manipulation must now be for the purpose of creating higher prices, as the next great speculative move will be to resell the cheaply purchased properties at high prices, and the public being absent, there is no one to manipulate against. He is certain that unless all precedents fail, he will, at some future time, see high prices and general good feeling supplant the present depression.

As has been stated, the innate false appearance of speculative surroundings does much to influence public participation at the wrong period. When stocks are low in price the brokerage offices are deserted, the newspapers say little of speculative affairs, transactions are limited, and those who have been worsted in the preceding decline speak in pessimistic terms of the future. A long period of dullness almost invariably follows a severe decline, new lambs must be born and the old ones suffered to grow a new fleece, and dullness is always unattractive. But at the crest of a great movement all is activity. Excited groups gather about the tickers and predict future events founded principally on illusions or hope, and stories of quickly acquired gains are heard on every hand. A fever of speculation fills the air and men who had no thought of venturing during the time of depression and low prices now purchase anything and everything at prices that are very high.

The mistakes discussed above—ignorance; the belief that speculative riches are the result of luck rather than of judgment, over-speculation and misleading surface appearances, combine to make it possible for the shrewd and successful minority to buy and sell periodically to great advantage by an almost exact reversal of public methods and beliefs. Their operations are not founded on such reversion, but on study and knowledge of past precedent, present conditions and future probabilities. The fact that public opinion is diametrically opposed to their views may be cheerfully considered as excellent proof of the correctness of their deductions, as the public is usually wrong.

If the statements made above are admitted to be correct the lesson they teach is obvious. To result successfully, speculative ventures must be based on sound reasoning and a knowledge of correct normal values; on a willingness to confine operations to reasonable limits and upon emancipation from the moving influences of general exhiliration or depression. The individual who begins or pursues his operations on these great fundamental principles has taken a great step toward the goal of success.

Chapter III - Manipulation

There are two classes of manipulative tactics indulged in by the inside workers of Wall Street; the long range tactics of the great but silent workers who lay a plan contemplating a complete speculative cycle from high to low prices, and the more frequent and drastic operations of room traders who find a market in a bad technical position and operate for known effects, either as a matter of immediate profit or to rid themselves of a dangerous following. The success of both is dependent upon public folly.

In the first class lies the hidden and carefully calculated work of haute finance. It consists of creating, or helping to create, false impressions as to the value of a certain property, of lending encouragement to buy at high prices, or to sell (or at least to refrain from buying), at low prices. The motives are obvious: to create a demand for the goods for sale, and to create a supply of the goods whose purchase is contemplated.

This high form of financiering is always helped by shrewd choosing of propitious periods and surroundings, and its moving factors, though potent with result, are so veiled and untraceable as to render supportable criticism impossible.

The recent price movements of the properties of the U.S. Steel Corporation furnish a pointed example of this method of financiering. The stocks were offered to the public at prices which were really fair, statements were issued which were unquestionably correct, and dividends were paid which were doubtless earned. The periodical reports were rosy, but they were true. The great earnings were made, and called attention to the high tide of a period of unusual activity and prices, but the public did not take the trouble to ascertain this important fact. They saw only one thing, that large dividends were being paid, and still larger earnings being carried to surplus, by a company whose stocks were selling at low prices. They looked neither backward nor forward, but glued their eyes upon the insufficient facts of the present. A little knowledge would have proven that not only were the recent and present earnings unusually large, but that all such abnormal periods are followed by a reaction.

These simple facts, known and recognized in the abstract as being true of all businesses, were lost in the greed and fever of speculation. Knowledge and study played no part in the affair; the present was all-sufficient, and the public bought largely, both for investment and on margins; and by the same token, the promoter sold. Later the earnings fell off, which was perfectly natural, money was lavishly disbursed, their holdings increased by the purchase of new properties; the surplus dwindled, and dividends on the common stock were reduced and eventually suspended altogether.

A public change of heart took place, and views of the company's future changed from extreme rosiness to cross-grained cynicism. Again the present was made the only standard; the stock was watered; the common shares were absolutely worthless; future dividends were impossible, etc.

The fact that a great deal of money had been intelligently diverted into channels which could not but enhance the future value of the corporation was not considered, and so, during a natural period of reaction, the disgusted public gradually relinquished their holdings, and they passed back, little by little, into the hands of their original owners at prices ridiculously low.

From the standpoint of the great manipulators, it was beautifully done. Not one argument could be brought against them which could not be amply defended. "We paid dividends because we earned them, and you, our stock-holders, clamored for them and approved of them; we gave to the world state-ments of every dollar received and disbursed; nothing was misrepresented, nothing was concealed. When the iron and steel business suffered a relapse, and our surplus had been lowered by excellent and necessary expenditures, we did what every business man does—decreased our expenses and our dividends until an improvement was apparent. We are not responsible for the actions of Wall Street, and if you, as an individual, made ill-advised purchases and sales, or over-speculated, that is no fault of ours. Yes, we did, as individuals, sell some stocks at prices which we considered fair, and likewise repurchased at prices which are considered low. That was a matter of business, and was our privilege. We have absolute confidence in our properties and their future and always have had. You cannot blame us for your mistakes; you beat yourselves; get out!"

This is unanswerable, but the fact remains that these men knew what the effect of their actions would be and acted accordingly. No one who has a personal acquaintance with Mr. Morgan and his principal lieutenants would harbor any thought of their having participated in the general enthusiasm, and making the error of themselves believing there would be no reaction in the large earnings and good condition of the affairs of the Steel Corporation. Never.

That they had faith in their properties is literally true, and it is doubtful if the largest holders would have parted so freely with their stocks but that they knew absolutely what would happen, and that the stocks would perforce be returned to them at low prices. Neither did they find it necessary to cripple or permanently injure their great consolidation to bring about their grand coup. The shares had the same inherent value at the lowest range, as at the highest.

It is unquestionably true that if the magnates "who never speculate" had not foreseen and acted upon public folly, no dividends would have been paid which could not have been maintained, and instead of the wild pyrotechnics and wide-price range of steel stocks, the properties would have steadily increased in value from the birth of the concern.

There is nothing new in all this—it is a time-honored method of speculative financiering, from the repetition of which the public seems to learn nothing, and from which the most powerful interests make their largest returns.

The second class of manipulation, more recognizable as such, is more brief as to period and more restricted as to results, but is potent enough at times to bring about changes and appearances which either force or frighten holders out of a good position, or mislead them into a bad one.

The cry is frequently heard that the public is not in the market, and this state of affairs is usually pointed out as a reason for stocks not advancing. This view is another evidence of the reversed reasoning so prevalent in speculative matters.

The very last thing the great speculators want in the market is such an interest at low prices, or even at midway points in an advance. So undesirable, in fact, is such an element that its presence means defeat for the sponsors of the deal themselves, and a projected movement is sometimes abandoned temporarily on account of too large a following. The most approved method, however, is to "shake out" and discourage this following. The process is simple; the great inside element finding themselves in company of numerous "tailers," whose weakness and liability to panic on the slightest pretext may ruin their own devices, take advantage of just such known weakness, and with the assistance of the professional bears, proceed to drive their undesirable friends away. To accomplish this, support is withdrawn and a portion of the accumulated holdings sold ostentatiously. The bear element, fully aware of the assailable state of the market, assists the manipulators by heavy sales and vicious drives. The enthusiastic public, crippled, discouraged and disgusted, drop their holdings, and a considerable number of half-baked bears join in the same game of "follow the leader," until a short interest is created. Meanwhile, the original projectors replace their holdings at opportune times, perhaps at a lower average than that at which their spectacular sales were made, perhaps not—but the physicking has been accomplished, the atmosphere is cleared, and the "deal" which they had never for a moment contemplated abandoning, goes merrily on until such time as another purging may be necessary.

These two forms of speculative tactics, with their various off-shoots, constitute the fundamental basis of manipulation. They are widely different; the one, the long distance work of the great "financier" who pays no heed to ordinary movements, but works toward a great end; the other, the tactics of purely speculative interests. The first is responsible for the long swing of the market; the second for many of its sharp intermediate changes; but both are united in one thing, they work together for the undoing of the general public.

The man who invests, or speculates for the long swing may, like the first class, disregard all ordinary hippodroming, and await certain results.

The man who indulges more freely in speculative ventures must bring to his aid clear thinking, study and vigilance. Above all things he must provide for sharp changes financially, and if he is caught in a flurry, his embarrassment will be only temporary.

In both cases everything depends upon an intelligent basis of normal valuation, for to that basis, if correctly estimated, the price of his holdings will eventually revert. All the manipulation, accident and trickery in the world can not keep prices too low nor too high for long. The needle of the compass may be disturbed and swing nervously from side to side, but it must point to the true north at last.

Chapter IV - Accidents

Accidents or unexpected events frequently mark the beginning of sharp or extended declines. It is generally considered that anything in the nature of an accident must be in favor of the bear element.

This theory in the abstract is sound enough, as accident and disaster are nearly synonymous, but careful consideration of the subject will develop the fact that in the speculative world accidents are more frequently the excuse for, than the cause of, any severe or extended decline, and their effects are to be measured by the stage and condition of the market, rather than by their actual capacity for evil.

Nothing in the nature of the unforeseen can be conceived as happening which could permanently injure or retard the growth and value of good properties.

The U.S. has such recuperative power that the naturally increasing value of her properties can easily overcome the temporary effects of unforeseen occurrences. It is reasonable to believe that if all the accidents which have occurred and have been pointed out as the cause of great market changes in the last ten years had never happened, stocks would still be at the same approximate level as they are today.

It is admitted that accidents frequently administer the little shove to an already bad state of affairs which hastens a decline that must have eventually and inevitably occurred, accident or no accident. This is not wholly an unintended evil, as it may be the means of checking excesses, which, if allowed to continue, might result in even more severe consequences.

On the other hand, an accident may sometimes mark the very beginning of a great upward movement by frightening from the market at low prices weak and foolish speculators whose very presence spells danger, and attracting to it farseeing men who gauge prices by values.

The danger of adverse litigation, (which may be classed among unforeseen events), against good properties is slight. Annually, numerous tirades are begun against combinations and individual corporations in the legislative halls, or in the columns of the public press, supplemented by the railing of the notoriety-seeking charlatans who find it popular to inveigh against capital in general, but the fact remains that no measures will be taken, or at least no measures can endure, that will prevent the builders of railroads, or the capitalizers of great industries from making good returns on their money, or from seeing their investments grow in value through the advance of demand and population. Such measures, expounded by dreamers, or socialistic tin-horn tooters, strike at the very foundation of business extension, and per contra, any individual or coterie of individuals, who seek to overdo the extension of capital, or make it bring exorbitant and unnatural returns, will, like the toad in the fable, burst by self-inflation.

Stripped of these two extremes, business conditions are sound and solid, and gradual growth and prosperity are assured.

The unexpected calling of loans, the exportation of gold, the killing of crops, sharp changes in the attitude of foreign markets, etc., are matters which are to be expected annually, either as natural or manipulated events under any and all conditions, and are almost wholly impotent to change the course of a long swing to high or low prices. Like the boy who cried "Wolf, Wolf," on every occasion, they lose their importance by repetition.

True, these minor signs may to the close student sometimes appear as straws indicating the course of the financial wind, but generally speaking, nothing short of a widespread and severe disaster can change the course of the great cycles of speculation, the repeated and unchecked revolutions of the wheel of fortune. A good illustration of the statement that accidents frequently prove merely the puff of wind which topples over an already rotten structure, is found in the death of the late R.P. Flower. This unexpected occurrence was followed by a radical and extended decline in the properties known as the "Flower Stocks." It cannot be reasonably claimed that the cancellation of Mr. Flower's personality affected the securities in question, as the number of stocks in the group, and the fact that he had no voice in the affairs of some of his favorites, combined to render any personal direction of the internal workings of the properties involved, impossible. His personal efforts, for instance, could not have sustained Brooklyn Rapid Transit above par; the stock was not, and never has been worth the prices at which it sold. It may, probably will, at some future day be cheap at that figure, but at the time in question, the price was premature, if not ridiculous. What followed Mr. Flower's demise must have occurred from its own inherent weakness, sooner or later; the event simply hastened the inevitable.

It is not the intention in the above illustration to cast any aspersions upon the methods or memory of the financier; he was sincere, but an enthusiast. He told his friends certain things would happen, and believed they would. His speculative campaign attracted to him a large and dangerous following, and his views of values were based more upon optimism than reason. He was honest, but he was mistaken.

The death of a great financier is always considered for its probable market effect, which must, of course, be measured by the actual result. The probability of such an event acting as a fillip to an already over-strained condition may be eliminated on the theory that in such cases they become excuses, not causes. It is not reasonable to believe that the removal of any one man from the financial map will be followed by any sustained depression. The affairs of such men almost invariably revert to good hands by direct succession, and the popular fallacy about rich men's sons is being continually disproved by such men as the Vanderbilts, George Could, and Ogden Armour.

Mr. Gould's death was, if anything, a boon to the speculative world; he was a trickster and a wrecker; his son is a "builder-up." Even in the improbable event of a great financier dying intestate his holdings would quickly find a resting place in strong hands at their true value.

The danger of widespread epidemic has always been regarded as a bear point, and were it not for the fact that the advance of science and the improvement in sanitary conditions now invariably confines even the most contagious and virulent diseases to limited areas, the devastations of a plague might be seriously regarded. As it is, the probability of any material damage from such a source is remote, and the bears, wont to welcome with open arms, ruin, devastation and death, have almost discarded them as weapons.[*]

The most serious of all events classed as accidents, is war, with its heavy entail and general disruption of affairs. That our country will not be plunged into a disastrous or prolonged war must be taken on faith, and the struggles of other nations, in which we are not involved, is productive of more good than evil; as, while it may bring about the forced selling of some of our securities held abroad, it also places the U.S. in the position of a huckster, and makes a market for our products at materially higher prices, which prosperous condition must be reflected in all lines of business. No better example of this could be given than the recent struggle between Russia and Japan.

The contention is therefore made that while accident is frequently made the excuse for speculative declines, it is seldom the cause, and that if conditions are sound and prices low, any sharp decline brought about by unforeseen happenings creates opportunities which would otherwise not have existed. On the occasion of public fright at such stages, it is frequently the case that great men come to the "assistance" of the market, and buy stocks heavily, (when they are low enough), and are hailed as public benefactors. That such purchases are made from purely philanthropic motives is, to say the least, doubtful. The speculator, therefore, who has mapped out a well-formed plan of operation, can afford to ignore the probability, or possibility of accident, except to provide for any sudden flurry occasioned by such causes; or, if an active operator, may sometimes take advantage of unreasonable fright and apprehension to replace, or increase his holdings.

There is no gainsaying the fact that a serious accident or event is possible; but to be effective it must be in the nature of a far-reaching disaster, and may be viewed by the trader with about the same degree of apprehension as he views the danger of being struck by lightning in his daily walks.

---

[*] In the cholera scare of 1892, when the "yellow flag," indicating cholera on board, was shown outside the New York harbor, an excited bear rushed upon the floor of the exchange, shouting, "Hurrah, hurrah, the cholera is here." He was suspended.

Chapter V - Business Methods In Speculation

Few men embark in a business pursuit of any kind without a careful examination of the prospects and environments of their ventures. If a business, or an interest in a business; is to be purchased, the past, present and probable future of that business are carefully examined. The assets and liabilities are compared, the record of past sales and profits are considered, and the probable future of the community, or territory from which the business draws its revenue, is given particular attention, and also, the danger of a decimation of profits through competition is considered. The character of the individuals concerned as partners or managers is weighed, and if found wanting, the proposition is discarded, as confidence between men is the foundation of all successful combinations.

Neither does the prospective purchaser enter his field without some special education for the business in hand, or at least not without a determination to watch and learn daily something of the technicalities of his enterprise.

These simple facts are recognized the world over as merely plain, sensible precautions adopted for all business men in all businesses— all except one— the widely patronized business of speculation.

This disregard of recognized business rules and laws is caused largely by the fact that the multiplicity of speculative properties with their large capitalizations stagger the ordinary mind, and lead a man into the error of considering himself incapable of grappling with so great a problem, and partly by a misplaced confidence in the expressed belief of others.

The opinions of brokers are given a degree of credence to which they are seldom entitled, for, sad to relate, the lack of study and method is almost as prevalent behind the office railing as outside of it, in addition to which the desire to make commissions frequently leads the broker to an expression of encouraging views running parallel with the ideas of the client, whether such views are sincere or not.

The emphatic opinions of friends and acquaintances are also greatly overrated at times, especially if the advisor has been fortunate in his recent ventures, which fact alone is a dangerous and insufficient guide. This willingness to accept the alleged thinking and knowledge of others frequently results in almost total elimination of thought and knowledge as a basis of operation. It is doubtful if a single case of sustained success in speculative ventures can be pointed out that was not founded upon individual study and investigation.

The idea that large properties cannot be investigated intelligently is a mistake. Every standard listed security must, under the rules of a well conducted exchange, offer to the public every facility for such investigation. The size of a property is only a matter of degree, a multiplication of what represents and belongs to a single share of stock; or, per contra, the value of one share of stock is a division of the whole.

Facts and figures as to assets, earning capacity, territory and past history are easily obtainable,[1] and the value of the deductions resulting from the

---

[1] See the Art of Wall Street Investing.

thorough and painstaking scrutiny of a property is to be gauged only by individual capacity for clear thinking, stripped of foolish credulity and pigheaded prejudice.

The advantages of choosing for operations the standard properties listed upon the New York Stock Exchange are manifold. There is always a market for these properties, which is not true of wild-cat securities; they are admitted to the benefits of the exchange on demonstrated merits, and under inflexible rules. True, a few bad properties have made their way into the exchange, but they have been the exception, not the rule.

The governors of the exchange are men of unquestioned business integrity and honor, and exercise every precaution to exclude undesirable stocks.

It may be contended that the public has been dumped, time and again by the fluctuations of listed stocks, which is exactly true; but that has been the fault of public error, and not of the rules of the stock exchange, nor lack of merit in the properties themselves.

The man who begins his investigations as to the actual value of a listed property, therefore begins with one which holds a high place in the business world, and which certainly has some value. It is his business, therefore, to estimate carefully this value, and upon the result to base his operations.[2] This knowledge of an approximate valuation will prove of great importance, and will materially aid the possessor, and prevent him from undue exhilaration or depression.

He may reasonably argue that all general depression will be followed by improvement, and that every bubble of inflation will be pricked. U.S. will take care of itself and all of its good properties.

Matters of moment bearing upon his particular property will, of course, be weighed carefully, and, if of sufficient importance, may necessitate the changing of his basis of valuation, either to a higher or a lower level, but this will be done carefully and slowly.

One thing the investigator may safely consider in his favor, and that one thing is of high importance: that the good properties of a new country are certain to gradually advance in value, with a tendency to restricted fluctuations until final absorption takes place.

This fact is easily explained: a new country offers in the sudden development of its virgin resources opportunities which render fair percentage returns unattractive, and speculative, or even investment capital seeks these channels. But as these opportunities are gradually restricted by development, money seeks the dividend paying properties which will yield perpetual returns.

The man who speculates in a business-like manner will at once see the necessity of entirely eliminating abnormal possibilities and rashness from his plan of operation. The difference between expecting from the market what is reasonable and expecting too much; and between buying what can be reason-

---

[2] The writer's views as to be the best method of making such an investigation will appear in a succeeding chapter.

ably protected, and even increased, and plunging, is exactly the difference between success and failure.

He who buys one thousand shares of stock on a total capital of ten thousand dollars is ruined before he begins trading. He may succeed once, twice, or twenty times, but his ultimate failure is as certain as death.

Many men with sound ideas, and whose ventures have proved ultimately the correctness of their views, have, by the one fault of over-trading, become paupers, when, with business methods, they might have become millionaires.

It is one of the many strange facts about the great field of opportunity called speculation, that men who consider ten percent a good return on capital in ordinary business are wholly dissatisfied with one hundred percent in a speculative venture.

The business man in speculation will find it expedient to divorce himself from the alluring attractions of the ticker itself. Many traders whose long range views of values and approaching conditions are good, get their noses so close to the ticker as to shut out the true perspective. They deceive themselves into the belief that they are keeping well posted by haunting the brokerage offices and following the mass of good, bad and indifferent gossip, conflicting opinions, canards, and predictions, as well as being swayed by the innumerable flurries which occur almost daily, and are always accompanied by an excuse. For a man is human, and no matter how phlegmatic by nature or cultivation, is more or less moved by these pernicious influences.

Anything worthy of consideration may better be considered in cold blood, than in the active time and place of speculation, and if commitments have been intelligently made and provided for, propinquity to the ticker will far oftener prove a detriment than an aid to profits. There are no doubt many professional scalpers, whose business is the chasing of fractions, who watch the slightest variation in quotations, and by so doing make some money—a great deal less, by the way, than is popularly supposed—and who find their constant presence at the ticker a necessity to their particular scheme of operation, but these articles are not written for their benefit.

The time spent in gathering a bewildering mass of false impressions, so untrustworthy as to be ridiculous, and so numerous as to be confusing, can be much more profitably spent as every really successful operator spends his time, in study and sound reasoning.

The choosing of a broker is important, financial responsibility and personal integrity being the first considerations. Brokers who offer reductions from the fixed standard of interest and commissions should be regarded with suspicion; such advantages are usually dearly purchased. Standard charges are not unreasonably high, and are not to be considered a drawback if general methods are correct.

A good broker may also frequently aid in the forming of opinions, or in the confirmation of opinions already formed; but as every trader, to succeed, must do his own thinking, this is not of so much importance as is the assurance of stability and probity. It is cold comfort to see one's carefully figured deductions confirmed, and then see the results vanish in the failure of an unreliable house, and yet this same event occurs again and again.

Summing up, the man who speculates in a business-like way trades only in standard properties with whose history, physical condition, earnings and prospects he has thoroughly familiarized himself; forms for himself a careful estimate of normal value and uses this value as a gauge by which to decide when prices are too low and too high; takes into consideration also the technical condition of the market, and does not embark with bad company, even at low prices; is not misled by the thrills of inflation, or the chills of depression; operates, not for the purpose of gathering a small profit from many transactions, but to gather a large profit from a few; trades with responsible middle-men, and, above all things, is patient. In short, he maps out for himself an intelligent and well-founded plan of operation, contemplating all that may occur, and having mapped it out, follows it. Very few speculate in this manner, and— very few succeed.

Chapter VI - Market Technicalities

The study of technicalities, of which little is generally known, and about which nothing has been written, is of great importance to the speculator, and particularly to the active trader.

The two most glaring, as well as the most important technical appearances which mark the top and bottom of a speculative cycle, have been commented on in a previous chapter; they consist of dullness and stagnation at the bottom of a movement, and crazy recklessness and universal participation at the other extreme.

In addition to the facts that have already been presented in regard to these two extremes, the following rule may be set down:

It is practically impossible for an overbought market to advance materially, or for an over-sold market to decline materially.

This seemingly radical statement is so well based as to be operative regardless of actual values. That is to say, if a certain stock is selling at sixty and is intrinsically worth par, it is very unlikely that it will reach par while there exists a general marginal participation for the long account; and on the other hand, a stock which is selling at par and is worth only sixty, will not decline if there is a heavy short interest in it.

These statements may at first blush seem opposed to the previous contention that any security must eventually seek its correct level; not so, for the fact is that correct levels will finally be reached, but not until the preponderance of participating opinion has been equalized; or, what is more common, exactly reversed.

There have been many cases where the better class of traders have made a strong favorite of a certain security, and have been wholly unable to account for its dullness or depression. Frequently their original deductions have been correct, but after long and patient waiting for the price of the stock to readjust itself to what they correctly considered its true valuation, they have withdrawn in disgust, or have even allowed themselves to believe that there must be some concealed rottenness about the affairs of the corporation which they are unable to ferret out.

The analysis of this state of affairs is neither profound nor difficult. First, and most important, is the fact that the buying power which is necessary to any marked advance is absent. The public having made a favorite of the stock has loaded up and is waiting for an advance. The public buying is completed, and no matter how inviting the proposition may be, so far as intrinsic merit goes, the big men will not buy while this public interest exists. They will not participate in a deal which contemplates a hoi polloi partnership, and aside from this, they are aware of the fact that they can certainly purchase cheaper in time if the present holders are left to their own devices.

In order to pursue any deal looking to an advance in the security in question, the professionals realize that should they enter the lists now they would be working for public benefit. They must not only buy in a restricted market at advancing prices, but must be prepared to take over at higher prices the present holdings of the public.

This is not the method used by great speculators; they do not bid for and assist the public in its speculative affairs, but accept at low prices what the public is throwing away. The professional element therefore cannot be counted on to forward prices. They will wait.

Meanwhile the numerous friends of the stock sit and twiddle their thumbs and wonder what in the world is the matter.

This state of affairs, it is evident, would cure itself in time through the certain and unstoppable assertion of intrinsic merit, but the required time will not be granted by the impatient holders. Something entirely different (and more rapid) will occur. The impatient public will throw over its stocks in disgust one by one, and each decline will confirm others in the belief that there is "something rotten" in the stock. It being impossible to uncover or point out anything detrimental, something is invented, and the well-meant plans of the holders end in a general decline, and after a time, in the hands of people who know both values and methods, the stock is first absorbed, then galvanized into activity, and finally hippodromed back into public hands at prices higher than they had first figured as its value.

The statements made above are not calculated to encourage the public trader. It certainly looks as if he had a hard row to hoe when even intrinsic valuation, correctly estimated, will not always produce satisfactory results; but the knowledge of this important technical condition and its cause and effect will prove of the highest value to the trader. He may reason as follows: I have figured and estimated the value of this security and find it to be too low, but unfortunately it is a public favorite. Its cheapness is so apparent as to attract to it a large following incapable of either patient waiting or sustained action. The widespread nature of these holdings, and the character of the holders render any concerted action for a more or less manipulated advance out of the question. On the other hand, the holders who now believe in the stock will daily grow more impatient at its torpidity, and will eventually begin to liquidate. This will be followed by numerous canards inimical to its price, and the stock will, at the bottom prices, be friendless so far as the public is concerned. When this consummation is reached, the stock will rest in the hands of men who possess all the qualifications of speculative success—patience, money and a full knowledge of how to start the machinery of an advance at the right time.

In following this reasoning the trader is doing exactly what the great inside interests do, and if he refrains from purchasing, even at low prices, when a security is too popular, he may rest assured that he will be able to purchase more cheaply in time. The chances are a hundred to one that no safe or material advance will occur under such conditions. The amateurs and the professionals cannot win on the same side in a speculative deal. It is the survival of the fittest, and the trader can soon decide with which side he wishes to identify himself. On the one hand are narrow margins, over-speculation, absolute lack of method; on the other, wealth, knowledge, concentration, and organization.

These are cold, hard facts and require only the directed exercise of good reasoning to be taken advantage of.

The same rule in inverse ratio applies to an oversold market, except that the danger to the seller is even greater. The professionals, a purely speculative party with whom the greater lights of speculation do not hesitate to ally themselves occasionally, are always on the lookout for an over-sold market, and the squeeze they sometimes administer to a widespread short interest is very severe.

There is nothing in the speculative world more hazardous than short-selling in a numerous company. In digesting the above statements, the question naturally arises: "How may a bad technical condition be recognized?" This is not so difficult as it might appear.

It is first necessary to lay aside any preconceived personal opinions and prejudices bearing on the stock in question, and conduct inquiries unhampered by "the wish that is father to the thought."

The published opinions and interviews in the newspapers, the expression of opinions among the speculators generally, and if possible, a frank inquiry from a friend at court, viz.: a broker who has means of knowing whether or not a widely scattered and considerable long or short interest exists—will usually prove sufficient

A successful Western trader for many years gained this information from the books of a single large private wire house in Chicago, and claimed that he found the method an infallible barometer, and that he would frequently find every office of the company's system on one side of a stock, with scarcely a single trade on the other side. This man, whose word there is no reason to doubt, made the interesting statement that at the approximate high prices of Steel Preferred and Amalgamated Copper he found that the long account in these two stocks, representing the operations of a large and indiscriminate public trade, exceeded those of all other stocks combined, without a single short trade, and that later when Steel Preferred had sold below fifty and started on its upward road, there was not one of the hundred offices in the system whose customers were not short of the stock, while the long account was limited to a few scattered trades.

Such a state of affairs is astonishing, and were it not for a realization of the loss and suffering brought about by such widespread folly, it would be laughable.

The wide general swing of a stock market from high to low prices is marked by an almost unvarying set of extraneous appearances which may be used to advantage by the observant trader.

The bottom of the cycle is marked by dullness and a sawing back and forth in narrow limits, with general sympathizing in the entire list. The successful large interests are accumulating stocks by their time honored method of picking up offerings and bidding for nothing. When this extended period of torpidity has left the public sufficiently bare of stocks, and has also created distrust and pessimism, the advance begins.

The beginning of a bull period is almost always marked by the bidding up of a single stock, and is followed by the picking up of one stock after another until the entire list of values has been materially advanced. There is a hazy public idea that a bull movement is accompanied by a general advance which extends to all active securities. This is not shown by any precedent, but on the other hand the culmination of a bull market is marked by just such a general advance. This may be explained by the statement that the genuine and intermediate advance from low prices to the approximate top is more or less assisted and engineered by the inside factors, who, however well fortified in organization and funds, would not be guilty of endangering themselves, (a la public), by attempting too much at once. These interests, therefore, concentrate efforts and capital, and lift their stocks one at a time, probably returning to the first security in time, and again furthering their favorites in rotation. This is the one and only stage of a market in which a considerable number of public traders make money, for the appearance of one stock after another advancing sharply is so glaring that the more or less sophisticated trader learns to recognize the appearance, and to buy a stock the minute he sees it "start," or develop sudden activity. This period is the brief and golden time for the trading element, but alas, they either over-speculate so rashly that the first natural reaction or engineered shake-out lands them bottom side up, or they absolutely refuse to recognize that there is a top to a movement, and are caught with a large line at the highest prices.

As has been stated, the actual culmination is usually marked by a general advance, which means that the public has entered the lists in force, and are buying any thing at any price. This is the exact condition for which the insiders have worked and waited—a broad and general market for their holdings.

Another public idea is that in the course of a bull market from one extreme to the other there are numerous setbacks and shake-outs. There is nothing in history to show that this view is correct; such declines are limited to one or two breaks of importance during the progress of the entire cycle. This mistake of looking for repeated reactions of importance is another factor which works against the public, for, having seen one or two shake-outs followed by a continuation of the advance, they look for an indefinite repetition of such action, and do not recognize the fact that there will eventually be a decline with no subsequent advance.

The question at once asks itself: "How may the tap of the market be discerned, and the dangers of the eleventh hour be avoided?" The answer is more or less complex.

It is, of course, necessary above all things to revert to the estimated and fixed value of the stocks traded in and to find out how much above this normal point the securities are selling. This done, common sense, plus prudence, and minus piggishness, may determine the question and dictate the time for liquidation. This action, however, once decided upon must be adhered to with great rigidity, for thousands of traders who thus take time by the forelock have been dissatisfied afterwards by seeing a still greater advance in which they had no interests, and through greed and impatience have re-entered the lists at a most inopportune time.

The trader who realizes his profits, and sees a further advance follow his own withdrawal from the market, may console himself with the fact that he has made and secured a profit; that trying to guess the exact extreme of a cycle is hazardous, and that the advance which followed his withdrawal is unsound, being founded on speculation rather than valuation.

But this is a digression from the technical phase of the matter. So far as it is possible to judge the culmination of a speculative campaign by extraneous appearances, it may be said that a long period of backing and filling, a swinging back and forth of prices at the approximate high level marks the beginning of the end. This is occasioned by the following facts:

The definition of the "top" of a market is that point at which the great traders have almost in unison decided to unload, and per contra, the public has reached its highest degree of enthusiasm. At the beginning of this period the insiders possess an enormous aggregate of stocks which must be sold in such a manner as not to break the market. This operation will take weeks, or even months to accomplish, as any precipitate selling would be disastrous. The wise element, therefore, sells all the market will absorb without any severe decline, and ceases selling, or even takes the buying side at the first appearance of "softness." In short they do all they can to maintain a good feeling and high prices, at the same time parting with securities as rapidly as possible.

This statement may convey the impression that the shrewd speculators act in unison. This is true, but not necessarily in the sense that there is any preconceived arrangement between them. The unison is more or less unconscious, and is founded on the fact that there are only two sides to the market—the right side and the wrong side, and that those of the speculative world who have sufficient wisdom and experience to know what is right are working to the same end, while all the inexperienced or unthinking horde are working on theories diametrically opposed to reason or even probability.

A careful perusal of the above statements will bring out the following stages as the appearance of a speculative cycle:

First, a long period of dullness, then the rocketing of one stock after another until the entire list has been greatly advanced, one or two shake-outs (always accompanied by specious excuses), a renewal of the advance, and finally general participation and a long period of "seesawing." These, so far as precedent goes, are the earmarks of a bull period, and may be exactly reversed in a long decline, except that in declines the general list is more greatly affected; that is to say, the whole list crumbles at once.

Aside from the fundamental principles considered above there are numerous minor technicalities which are of value to active traders, but are dangerous and not wholly dependable. For instance, the appearance of strength and heavy buying in a certain security in a low and weak market is almost invariably followed by a decided advance in that particular stock. The analogy of this feature is that this unnatural moving against the current shows heavy accumulation for some reason which will probably be developed later. But such an appearance in a high market might mean exactly the reverse, as one stock may be bid up sharply to permit of liquidation in a dozen others under cover of the sympathetic good feeling engendered by the isolated advance.

The minor technicalities are of use only to experienced traders who have every facility for acting upon them, and to enlarge upon them in a work of this character would be to run the risk of being misunderstood, or even of making statements which might be misleading. In view of this fact, and also as they are not of primary importance, any discussion of them is omitted.

If the idea has been conveyed in the above statements that technical conditions or appearances may be made the sole groundwork of speculative operations, let the impression be at once corrected. That these appearances and conditions exist, and that they can be made valuable by correct application there is no doubt. Every affair of life is preceded by certain signs, and "coming events cast their shadows before" in the stock market as well as in other affairs. But these appearances should be made use of as valuable adjuncts to more solidly formed opinions; as a confirmation of judgment more tangibly adduced, or as warnings of possible danger.

Care has been taken to present nothing in these pages which cannot be analyzed and explained, and while the statements made are confirmed by both logic and precedent, they may be easily contorted or abused.

Chapter VII - Tips

The tip may be briefly described as illogical. In considering this statement the dividing line between tips and information must be clearly drawn, for one is frequently found masquerading in the habit of the other.

The difference may be acceptably defined by saying that a tip is a statement that certain market movements will occur, with no accompanying reason for such movement, and that information points to the expectation of movements, founded on demonstrable probabilities.

"Smith says to buy steel," is a tip; "Smith says that the price of steel is low and that earnings are increasing," is more or less informative. In one case

Smith is taken on faith and in the other his statement is open to investigation and confirmation.

The illogical character of tips will at once be apparent to the student of technical conditions. The large operator who contemplates a manipulated movement of any importance, even if such movement be based on sound reasoning, jeopardizes his own chances of success by creating a public following. This fact is so well recognized by large operators, that where a projected deal is discovered by too many people or where inside intentions have leaked in the form of a tip, they frequently abandon their plans entirely or temporarily. This point has already been discussed under the head of Technicalities, but is here reiterated as being pertinent to the subject.

The promoter of a certain speculative movement who takes the public into his confidence, is therefore either foolhardy or insincere, and the ordinary man who receives a tip may be sure his knowledge is public property. If he has good reasons for believing to the contrary and that he is the recipient of valuable and circumscribed information, his action of course depends largely on his confidence in his patron's ability to perform what is promised. He simply acts on the principle that the capacity of his informant is superior to his own, and that his integrity is unquestioned.

There are no doubt cases where manipulators have put into circulation a whispered word which they were confident would travel and be made the basis of considerable buying at a period when they wished to sell. It is related of the late Jay Gould that when approached by the pastor of a rich and fashionable New York Tabernacle, he whispered to him that purchases of Pacific Mail were very advisable, and that he, Gould, would reimburse him from his private purse if operations in that stock resulted in loss. When the pastor came to him later, deeply distressed by his large personal loss, Mr. Gould was as good as his word and promptly handed him a check to cover the deficit. "But how about my parishioners?" inquired the reverend gentleman, "you placed no ban of secrecy upon me, and their losses are enormous." To which Mr. Gould replied calmly, "They were the people I was after." Whether or not the story is true, it points a moral.

It may be said that it would be possible for a manipulator to create public buying in a stock of sufficient volume to advance prices materially, and to thus assist or accomplish his object. This has been done, but aside from the hazard to the manipulator himself through being in the company of an easily frightened herd, which he could not control, it must be admitted that the advance created by a certain amount of buying must be offset by the ensuing liquidation, and some one must suffer.

The individual who imagines himself astute enough to evade this danger, simply flatters himself that he is wiser than his fellows, and even if he is justified in this belief, the composite result is unchanged.

The great majority of so-called tips are, however, founded on nothing better than guesswork or pure invention. Although valueless, openly distributed and untraceable to any reliable source, they are always clothed in a garb of mystery and importance and are capable of much mischief, for there is a considerable speculative element who possess no individual ideas of importance and who will act rashly on the most ill-founded advice.

If the distribution of such advice were limited to charlatans and mountebanks the effects would be greatly reduced, but many of the recognized brokerage concerns load their private wires with just such matter for the purpose of creating business, usually beginning their messages with the statement that "we have it from a good source" and ending with a ridiculous injunction to keep it dark. This statement is not lightly made, but is founded upon proven and provable fact. The statement does not in any way reflect upon houses which give out such current gossip for what it is worth and allow the patrons to decide for themselves what is wheat and what is chaff. Even under such circumstances the dissemination of such news is capable of harm, but the distributors cannot be considered culpable. They are merely the purveyors of news unaccompanied by comment or recommendation. The brokerage offices of the country are daily visited by people who have had their imagination inflamed, or their cupidity aroused by personal ideas or exaggerated stories of speculative possibilities. As they possess no special knowledge of speculative affairs they are soon lost in a maze of intricate figures, which not being understood, are productive of nothing but indecision and mental confusion. To this numerous class the tip at once appeals. Out of the mass of conflicting reports, technicalities and evasions, comes the terse advice, "Buy Southern Pacific." Here, at last, is something definite, and its air of being confidentially imparted, its transmission by telegraph from a distant city by a great brokerage concern, and its decided tone combine to lend it an importance which it in no way possesses. The man who wants to do something, but does not know what to do, acts upon it at once, and even the more seasoned traders who will cheerfully admit that tips are worthless, are moved by advice so unimportant.

And right here a word in regard to following the advice of so-called "leaders" in speculative shares or commodities. Of late this game of follow my leader has been more or less popular, especially in the cereals and in cotton. Sometimes the outspoken views of these self-constituted mentors are made public by published interviews or even by means of paid advertisements, in which emphatic opinions and advice are set forth.

This form of public invitation, fathered by names of more or less importance or notoriety in speculative circles, is frequently effective in creating a considerable following. A little analytical thought will adduce the fact that the individual who invokes such a following must do so for one of two reasons: either because he is ignorant of the necessary ingredient of a successful campaign or because he wishes to sell what he is inviting the public to buy. Take your choice.

Follow mentally the operation of such advice and the danger is most apparent. At the first sign of this public touting the men of weight and importance who are interested in the stock or commodity involved, far from welcoming such assistance, liquidate their holdings quietly and step aside. They may be convinced of the merits of their original venture, and may even admit that the arguments set forth by the public prophet are correct, but they also know that his advice will invariably result in the commodity recommended passing from strong into weak hands, a fact which reduces the chances of profit, and increases the danger of decline, or even panic.

The trader who believes in his speculative Daniel may see the most favorable signs for a time, but he may ponder on this fact: that however honest his prophet may be in his advice he will not publicly express himself as to a consummation or reversal of his ideas and hopes until he, himself, has liquidated.

In other words, after the amiable instructor of the people has sold to his own followers all he possesses he may bluffly and candidly state that he has sold out, and advise his friends to do likewise in a market which will not now absorb their composite holdings.

The danger in such a campaign as that illustrated above is increased just in proportion to the chief promoter's influence. Each new public follower means a worse condition of affairs, and all such campaigns have finally terminated in disaster. The leader of these "come-on-boys" affairs is always a tremendous gambler, and usually an unscrupulous one.

It goes without saying that tips are frequently more or less correct. If founded on mere guesswork, the chances of success or failure are equal. If the tip failed always or even in a large majority of cases, the evil would cure itself, but the percentage of satisfactory results is great enough to encourage its deluded followers.

So prevalent is this practice of trading on flimsy advice that a large number of concerns dignified with the title of "Information Bureaus" have recently been formed. As these concerns continue to increase in number and scope, it is the natural presumption that they find followers. These "Bureaus" make extravagant claims of inside information and advance knowledge of certain future market movements in the face of the fact that no man, great or small, knows positively the result of even one day's movement. The greatest speculator or manipulator in Wall Street may enter the arena in the morning confident of certain results, and leave it at night a ruined man.

Nevertheless, claims of accurate foreknowledge by these mountebanks find a resting place in the minds of people otherwise intelligent. It is needless to add that the tipping bureau exploits its correct guesses in glowing colors, and maintains a dignified silence on the subject of its errors.

The man who invests in such so-called "information" may save his money and obtain just as good results by basing his operations on the flipping of a coin.

The concerns criticized above are in no way to be confounded with the reliable bureaus of information, of which a few are in existence. These latter are exactly what their names suggest. They gather, compile and distribute general news on speculative matters, and are useful to the active trader in presenting to him statistical results involving considerable labor, and general news which might have been overlooked. Such bureaus do not issue tips; they may allude to the existence of a certain tip, but only as a matter of current gossip. In this regard they are no more to be criticized than the editor of a newspaper who prints the record of a murder.

So far as the efficiency of the tip is concerned as shown by precedent, it may be dismissed by again falling back on the statement that no sustained speculative successes are traceable to its use.

The tip holds no dangers for the man who knows because he has taken the trouble to find out. If it conflicts with his well-grounded opinions it is discarded as being merely an unsupported statement, and opposed to more dependable deductions. If it accords with his opinions it is of no value as it is merely a belated expression of what he already knows. To such individuals the only tangible effect of which the tip is capable is its possible stimulation to investigation.

Chapter VIII - Mechanical Speculation

Any system or method of speculation which is founded on repetition, or which contemplates ventures founded entirely on certain prices being reached regardless of conditions or values, may best be described as mechanical.

The use of such methods is extensive, and even where no set figures or forms are employed we find the average trader continually harping on last month's or last year's low points and forming for himself a mental chart by which he is frequently induced to make commitments.

Of these numerous mechanical methods of speculation only two possess sufficient merit to warrant serious consideration. These two exceptions are the scale order and the stop loss order, both of which may be made useful under certain conditions. That these methods are frequently abused goes without saying. They are often made the sole basis of operations instead of adjuncts, in which case they fail of their purpose.

Either method is useful only as an auxiliary to sound judgments already formed. So employed they possess certain merit in that they permit of a fixed mechanical arrangement for accumulation or protection.

The contention is here submitted that the scale order should be used only for the purpose of acquiring a line of stocks at low prices, and the stop loss order for the protection of profits after an advance. Otherwise employed they become useless, and in some cases even assist in producing loss.

The intelligent use of the scale order contemplates the purchase of a certain stock or commodity at fixed intervals below the first purchase price until the total proposed purchase is completed, the mechanical principle being that an advance of one-half the decline on which the purchases are made leaves the trader without loss, and the broader general principle being that the votary of the method at all times allows for declines due to accidents or errors of judgment. If such declines occur, he gradually acquires his line at a lower average price for the whole.

As an example, embodying both these principles, suppose that a purchase of one thousand shares of Union Pacific common is contemplated. The sealer begins his purchases at, say 100, taking one hundred shares at that price and entering an order to buy one hundred shares at fixed points below the first price, say for instance, at 99, 98, 97, 96, 95, 94, 93, 92 and 91, at which last named price his purchase would be completed at an average price of 95.

The amount to be purchased on each decline, the width of the gap between declines, and the point to which purchases are to be continued are of course matters of individual determination. The principal drawback to this method, which is at once apparent, is the danger of the original, or some intermediate purchase, being made at such a low point as to prevent the accumulation of the proposed line. In the extreme case of only the initial purchase having been possible, the trader finds himself with a profit on only one hundred shares of stock where he had intended to carry one thousand. But this argument against the merits of the method may be answered as follows:

The average speculator may safely assume that a decline from the point he considers low is probable. If he happens to catch the low price it is an accident and not because of his method, whose virtues must be reserved for future usefulness. He may congratulate himself on an unusually fortunate purchase and be satisfied with his comparatively small but quickly acquired gains. A profit is a profit, and the market is always with him. On the other hand, if he is so good a judge of the market that his purchase was a result of judgment rather than accident, he has no use for the scale order or any other such assistance.

The scale order is frequently misused by depending too much upon inherent virtues which it does not possess. That is to say, it is made the basis of operations which are indulged in more on a belief in the merits of the method than on any intelligently formed opinion of the probable action of the stock, or a sufficient consideration of actual value, technical conditions, etc. The probabilities of an advance equal to half the preceding decline is upheld by precedent and makes the method alluring, but granting such an advance, and no more, nothing has been gained when it materializes.

In short, it may be said that the scale order used as a basis for poor purchases is generally useless. So employed it differs from ordinary methods only in the fact that it will take the trader a little longer to lose his money.

But he who admits that natural market action, manipulation or accident render it improbable that even a careful study of his intended venture will find for him the lowest price and who wishes to adopt a methodical plan of operation—for him the scale order presents some very favorable features, and is recommended for serious consideration.

The study of precedent will show that the scaling method could have been successfully employed in almost every standard listed security. In fact precedent will show entirely too much, in that it presents the fact that the method carried out indefinitely would seldom have resulted in loss from any point, high or low. Even taking the worst possible example, a stock so greatly inflated and so widely discredited as Amalgamated Copper, scaling from its extreme high price of 130 in 1901 to the extreme low price of 33 in 1903 would give an average price of 82, a point recently exceeded in market prices. But such figuring as this is useless. An extended campaign of this kind contemplates the use of a vast sum of money, always available in cash.

The danger of pursuing statistics so alluring as those presented by a study of past market movements as applied to the scaling process lies in pointing to what money can do rather than what it should do, and in indulging in mental and statistical proofs, the actual operations of which are past the possibilities of the purse. Even if the financial equation is granted, few men possess the stability, patience and courage to adhere to the rules of such an extended and unsatisfying campaign, and without such adherence the whole structure falls to the ground.

The best use that can be made of the scale order is, therefore, to use it only for the methodical making of purchases already deemed advisable. If the first purchase by this method is made at the point at which prior investigation and judgment has pointed out as the time to buy, irrespective of any inherent virtues which may lie in the scaling process, it can seldom result in injury, and will generally prove beneficial. If the method is adopted it must be adhered to rigidly, unless for some good reason the deal is abandoned entirely. In the majority of cases this is not done, the operator for some reason, impatience, greed, or fright, changing his plans, in which case the usefulness of the method is impaired or eliminated.

The stop loss order is one of the most abused of the methods employed by traders, for, like the scale order, it is frequently used at the wrong periods, or given credit for too much inherent virtue.

In speaking of this method, no reference is made to the stop order as employed by brokers for self-protection, in which case it is a matter of necessity. The point to be considered is its value when used voluntarily by the trader for his own benefit.

There is an axiom among traders that the best principle in speculation is to take small losses and large profits. So popular is this axiom that many speculators consider it the great secret of success, and in following it employ the stop loss order continually in a most haphazard manner.

The expressed theory of small losses and large gains sounds good and is all very well in itself, but it may be relegated entirely to a class who wish to gamble on quotations on a reversal of ordinary public methods, which is to take large losses and small profits. The small loss trader pins his faith wholly to the belief that a market will swing not to, but past the point where he placed his stop loss.

On this theory all intelligent figuring as to the probable future movements is eliminated, and the success is based wholly on mechanical chance, in which case the probability of loss and gain is exactly the same; that is to say, the probability of ten losses of one point each, or one gain of ten points, is the same. Those who combat the truth of this statement at once array themselves as opposed to the expressed and accepted consensus of opinion of the world's greatest students of the doctrine of mathematical chance.

To contend that any element of intelligent forecast of market movement could be combined with the use of the small loss theory as outlined above, is untenable, for if a purchase is made because research has shown such purchase warranted by conditions and the price of the stock, we find the stop loss trader

in the ridiculous position of selling his holdings below a price he first considered should be cheap, at which point he should in reality be contemplating
further purchases.

So rooted in some minds is the principle of small loss and large gain, that
an attack on the virtues of such a proceeding will no doubt be bitterly
contested. The argument against it however, is sound; it is purely mechanical,
cannot be combined with intelligent operations, has no marked success to its
credit, and is not adopted by successful traders, i.e. those who buy because
they consider a thing too low, and sell because they consider it too high.

But there are certain periods when the use of a fixed limitation of decline
is entitled to consideration. The trader may find himself in possession of
certain profits in a market which is high, but which his judgment tells him
may, for technical or other reasons, still advance materially. At such a period
he may wish to provide against accident, or a vicious raid by placing stop loss
orders below his holdings at a point which will insure him the bulk of his
profit, advancing the point at which loss shall be stopped as the market
advances.

Taken the year round, the chance of loss or profit from such a course is, as
has been stated, demonstrably equal; but in the case of high prices, the
extraneous dangers of accident or manipulation, and the advisability of protecting profits by systematic orders contemplating such dangers, the placing of
stop orders is frequently useful. Even at such periods its principal virtue lies in
the pre-arrangement of a desirable course which might be disturbed by mental
confusion or personal absence.

It is a debatable question whether it would not be better to buy when
conditions and prices show that purchases are warranted, and, per contra, to
liquidate when danger threatens or when prices look high enough. But to most
traders systematic arrangement is desirable, and to some minds absolutely
necessary.

As recommended above, the scale order and stop loss order in no way
interfere with the workings of study and judgment, and are frequently employed by traders whose opinions are entitled to respect. Let the fact be taken
to heart however, that employed as a means of speculation, rather than as an
aid to it, neither method possesses any merit whatever.

"Chart System"

There is an incredibly large number of traders who pin their faith to the
so-called "chart system" of speculation, which recommends the study of past
movements and prices, and bases operations thereon. So popular is this plan
that concerns which make a business of preparing and issuing such charts do a
thriving business.

The theory propounded is that history repeats itself, and that because a
property sold at a certain low price on some previous occasion and then
advanced, the same thing will occur again! There are various offshoots and
modifications of the system, but the basic plan is founded wholly on repetition,
regardless of actual conditions. The idea is absolutely fatuous, entirely untrust-

worthy, and highly dangerous. The study of the past is interesting and instruct-ive in showing what may be expected in the way of general movements, but when we are asked to throw reason and research to one side in favor of only half-demonstrated repetitions, the theory becomes untenable.

The chart traders would have us pore over musty records of past move-ments, and have us buy a stock at a certain price because it sold there before, without stopping even to investigate the fact that conditions in that particular stock have changed materially. The votary of this plan might find himself cheerfully buying the shares of a bankrupt and ruined corporation in its very process of financial disintegration, or on the other hand might refrain from purchases at very low prices because it sold at still lower prices on some previous occasion. Another class of retrospective speculators base their operations on seasons, or even corresponding weeks and months, forming their opinions on insufficient research, or on nothing at all. If there were in truth any certain period of the year or month from which movements would occur, the whole world would know it, and such knowledge would reverse expectations by the rotten technical conditions it would create.

It is useless to enlarge upon the various methods employed by the mechanical traders, for they are all alike in that they resolve the whole specu-lative structure into a gambling machine, with a large percentage against the player. To the large number of people who risk their money in this manner, and who contend that there is no use in trying to accurately forecast probable movements by actual investigation, let the following statement be made:

The man who buys a stock at fifty dollars a share because he has good reasons for believing that it is worth one hundred dollars, or who sells at one hundred dollars on account of having good reasons for believing it worth only fifty dollars, is the only man in the speculative world who succeeds.

When the study and thought necessary to forming such conclusions intel-ligently are eliminated in favor of any or all other methods, the colossal error is made of expunging from the plan of operations the only possible chance of sustained success, the great basic principle to which all other knowledge, technical or statistical, is purely subsidiary.

Chapter IX - Short Selling

The practice of short selling, which was formerly largely confined to the professional element, has of late years become quite fashionable among those members of the trading public who speculate regularly, and has been even more disastrous than have ventures for the long accounts.

The basis for this action, and the growing popularity of the short side is founded on natural pig-headed pessimism which will listen to no argument, and is incapable of clear reasoning; or what is more common, on contentions so shallow and silly that it seems superfluous to record them on a printed page.

Everywhere one hears the belief expressed that the "big money" is made on the short side, and that the greatest inside speculators are Bears. This view is entirely erroneous.

One of the favorite arguments of the public bear element is as follows: the public generally buys, and the public generally loses money. Therefore the buying side is the losing side and the short side is the winning side. By this absurd and wholly unfounded deduction many bears are created.

Now, the fact of the matter is that the fortunes made on the short side of stocks are few and far between, while those accumulated by judicious operations on the long side are legion. The public loses its money, not because it purchases, but because its purchases are made at the wrong periods and its methods of operation are bad.

The accumulated wealth of the Vanderbilts, Rockefellers, Astors and Goulds has accrued from the continued increase in the valuation of properties in which they were interested. True, all these lights of finance have been justly accused at times of operating for lower prices. This is particularly true of the late Jay Gould, who was widely known as a wrecker. But the wrecking operations were solely for the purpose of driving other holders out of a certain corporation and creating a sentiment and condition which would permit of the purchase of a controlling interest in the corporation in question at low prices.

So few have been the individuals who operated on the short side habitually and successfully that the names of Travers and Cammack stand out in bold relief among the horde of great traders, and the operations of the successful minority were carefully calculated as to periods and safety. Their skillful work and clear foresight would probably have made more money for them if their operations had been reversely conducted.

"It took me ten years, and cost me two fortunes to become an optimist, but it was worth all it cost," said a successful speculator of today, and in that terse sentence is much food for thought. It is possible to make money on the short side of the market, but it is very difficult, and the man who is capable of acting with enough judgment and decision to accumulate gains working against the current is doubly capable of succeeding by swimming with it.

The semi-professional traders who trade on the short side, as a rule, exercise no more judgment or study of actual valuation than do the army who purchase. They are moved by blue talk and general pessimism, and sell at the bottom and are frightened out at the top. Their operations are simply bad in inverse ratio. There is one difference: the purchaser who has the means and patience to stand by an ill-timed purchase will eventually see daylight, while there is no certainty of this desirable consummation for the bear. On the other hand, he may see his venture grow more and more disastrous as time and the advance of the country increases the value of the stock he has sold. The cycles of speculation will of course bring him occasional hope, but these cycles occurring from a gradually ascending pivotal point carry him further from his original price at each revolution.

The short seller of stocks has against him at all times the natural future enhancement of values, and more specifically, the earnings and dividends of the securities in which he trades.

To make this more clear let us say that one hundred shares of a certain stock, paying 6%, are sold short at par, its normal price, and the commitment endures for one year. For the sake of argument all speculative movements will be eliminated, and the assumption made that at the end of the year the selling price of the stock is still par. It will be seen that the seller has had his account charged with six hundred dollars in dividends, and thus while there has been no advance in the posted value of his stock, he has lost six hundred dollars.

This does not hold good in the case of a purchase, for even if the high rate of 6% is paid on the unmargined balance, these charges are covered by the dividends credited to the stock, and the normal gain of 6% has been made on the actual money deposited as margin.

For example: one hundred shares of a 6% stock purchased at par on ten points margin, and sold at the same price one year later, shows as follows:

Total purchase price of stock...$10,000
Marginal deposit...1,000
Unpaid balance..$9,000

Int. for 1 yr at 6% on unpaid balance................................$540
Credit account dividends..600
Credit balance...60

Or 6% on the thousand dollars actually involved. And on the other hand: One hundred shares of the same stock sold at par repurchased at the same price one year later:

Total credit from sale of stock...$10,000
Total debit from purchase...$10,000
Debit for one year's dividends..600

A loss of $600. If it is presumed that one thousand dollars has been deposited as margins, on which amount an allowance of 6% has been made by the broker, there is still a net deficit of $540, with no adverse market action.

In the above examples no account is taken of commission charges, but the exhibit is in no wise affected by this omission, as the commission charges on the short side would increase the loss on that commitment exactly as much as it decreases the gain on the purchase.

It will be seen, therefore, that the short seller has working against him at all times a tangible effect capable of exact demonstration. The contention is sometimes made that short commitments are seldom carried for any considerable period, and that the man who sells short today and repurchases tomorrow, escapes this onus. This view is so shallow that it is unnecessary to state to thinking men that the difference is wholly a matter of degree, and that the Bear in dividend paying shares swims constantly against the current.

What is true of one year is equally true of one day, and repeated short time operations multiply the infinitesimal drawback until it is as great as when lumped on one longer contract.

And the seller of non-dividend paying stocks is no better off, for he combats either the earnings which are accruing, or the gradual enhancement of the stock through a wise distribution of these earnings. In short, whether a habitual short seller sells dividend or non-dividend paying shares he tampers continually with progress. He makes his venture on the side of disaster, accident, dishonesty, mismanagement, and pessimism, rather than on the side of gradual improvement in the business affairs and conditions of the country.

Another pitfall which besets the short seller is the danger of deliberate cornering, or of a fight for control in his stock. Tremendous advances are possible in either case, and even if his sales have been made at high prices he faces this hazard. The plea that such great twists are infrequent will not do, for to be overtaken by one such squeeze in a decade is sufficient to wipe out a great portion, or all, of the accumulated gains of that period.

Concentration of wealth and power make such upward manipulation more possible from day to day, and this latter statement develops another argument, and another important fact in answer to that argument.

The argument is simply that history shows that severe breaks, and drives against certain stocks have been made more frequently than corners or squeezes. Drives have been made against a certain stock which in a few days carried that stock to ridiculously low figures, and later it was repurchased by the same interest which wrought the havoc in values.

This is admitted—as a record of the past. Such action is out of the question today. The method is pursued to some extent, but great declines in a brief period no longer come from savage individual attacks on certain securities. The reason for this is simple; the concentration of capital mentioned above, makes such action too hazardous. There was a time when Mr. Keene would, for a single great interest, pound the price of Sugar off twenty, thirty, or forty points in a day or two, and then repurchase it at low figures. Mr. Keene will never do it again, for the enormous sales necessary to accomplish this coup would place him and his sponsors in danger of losing control of the stock. There are now other powerful interests well enough aware of the value of Sugar stock which would welcome any opportunity of wresting the control from present hands, and if the well-named manipulator were to do today what he did even a decade ago, he would wake up some morning not only minus the control of the property, but opposed, in a market sense, to interests even more powerful than those he represented.

This places the moneyed speculative interests in the position of allowing public folly, rather than individual efforts, to bring about great declines and low prices, under which condition the danger of losing control is a matter of vigilance and a matching of wits, or possibly a community of interests against this same public.

There is no gainsaying the fact that it is possible to so accurately judge of values and periods as to make money on both sides of a market cycle, but those who have been successful in so doing may be numbered on the fingers.

The frequently quoted aphorism of a great latter day speculator: "If it's a good sale at all it's a good short sale," meaning that if one is justified in selling holdings to realize profits, he is also justified in selling short, will not bear the light of calm analysis.

There is a vast difference between accepting accumulated profits, and being absolutely free from further risk with an acquired gain in bank, and being in a position to lose heavily through market action.

In view of the above facts it would appear that for the speculator in the ordinary walks of life, the safest course is to confine operations to purchases of stocks when they are cheap, and to limit sales to the realizing of profits. This course necessitates periods of non-participation which are decidedly beneficial. It permits the operator to look with an unprejudiced eye upon market actions, frees him of a direct percentage working against him in dividends and earnings, and best of all, maps out for him a fixed and settled plan of operations, conducted with the current of irresistible improvement and certain accretion.

Chapter X - What 500 Speculative Accounts Showed

An examination of almost four thousand speculative accounts, extending over a period of ten years, developed results interesting and instructive in many ways. The examination was of an exhaustive character, and covered operations of every conceivable nature in both stocks and cereals.

In these accounts all the errors of speculation were distinctly illustrated.

The three principal points developed by the investigation were that 80% of the accounts showed a final loss; that the tendency to buy at the top and sell at the bottom was most prevalent; and that most of the operations appeared to be of a purely gambling character. The further fact was established that success almost invariably led to excesses.

The mass of figures derived from so extensive an examination being voluminous and complicated, it was considered advisable to simplify the matter for presentation in this work, pursuant to which decision, the following plan was hit upon.

It was decided to use for illustration a single stock, trading in which predominated in the operations covering a certain period. In order that the illustration should be perfectly fair it was decided to make the period begin and end with the stock considered, selling at the same approximate price.

As U.S. Steel Common offered the best illustration, 500 accounts, either confined to operations in this stock, or showing a large percentage of deals in that security, were selected. The period originally contemplated was from January to December of the year 1901, but was discarded on the theory that the results shown would be abnormal, owing to the panic of May ninth of that year. It might be contended that the tremendous losses sustained in this panic were offset by the unusual opportunities for purchases at low prices, but as few purchases were shown it was thought best to seek a period during which nothing abnormal occurred, but which presented numerous advances and declines of an ordinary character.

Such a condition existed from July, 1901, to March, 1903, during which time there were numerous advances and declines in Steel Common ranging between 29 and 46. In July, 1901, the stock sold at 37, and in March, 1903, it touched the same price, and as the price at the beginning and ending of the period is the same, and furthermore is nearly midway between highest and lowest prices, it would appear that about equal chances had been presented for profit or loss if the element of knowledge and mental acumen were canceled.

In other words, viewed wholly as a gambling proposition the chances, not considering the percentage of commissions, were about equal. The reason for making this comparison will be apparent later.

The books of the different firms showed a marked unanimity of public action at all times, reflecting a general consensus of opinion. This applied not only to the 500 accounts chosen for this illustration, but to all which were originally examined.

In selecting these 500 accounts every precaution was taken to exercise absolute fairness. No picking over was indulged in, as it is obvious that the balance of gain or loss might be thrown materially to one side or the other by such a process. In order to prove the total result as compared with the whole, the loss on the entire number of shares handled in the 500 accounts was compared with the loss on the total number of shares in the entire four thousand accounts, (operations in grain and other commodities not being considered), and the result was found to be harmonious.

No preconceived ideas nor prejudices were permitted to enter the investigation, the object sought being to establish figures which might be considered fairly indicative of what usually occurred in public speculative affairs under normal conditions.

It will be understood that the facts and figures hereafter presented were based wholly upon total results, the entire number of accounts being finally viewed in a composite light. On this theory the following results were discovered:

Three hundred and forty-three accounts resulted in a net loss at their termination; 88 accounts resulted in a net profit; 52 accounts were even or showed inconsiderable differences. The result of 17 accounts is unknown, as the Steel stocks represented were taken up by the purchasers, in all cases at a considerable paper loss.

Total deficit on all losing accounts...............................**$1,245,000**
Total gain on all profitable accounts...............................**288,000**
Leaving a net deficit of..**$957,000**

The total number of shares handled was 1,112,000, of which 820,000 shares were originally purchases, and 292,000 originally short sales.

The total brokerage charges, commissions, interest, etc., were $275,000, which amount is included in the total loss.

The comparative losses on short sales, share for share, were about 20% greater than the losses on purchases.

The favorite method of operation was to purchase or sell on slight reactions from high or low prices.

The average price of all purchases for long account was 42 and the average price of all short sales was 35.

The scale order was employed in 53 accounts, (42 long and 11 short), but was either abandoned or interfered with in all but eight instances.

There were numerous evidences of systems being used; this is not susceptible of proof, but the uniform character of the trading as shown by constant repetitions was considered good evidence of a fixed method. Over 80% of the accounts of this description resulted in loss.

In 23 instances an inverted scale order was employed, purchases being made at fixed intervals as the stock advanced. This is the principle called "going with the market." It failed in every instance.

In considering the above figures, the first and most vital point is the predominance of loss over profit under conditions as nearly equal as possible to present. The reason for considering the matter in the light of a gambling transaction was to develop the fact that the total loss was distinctly greater than the percentage against the trader as represented by commissions, the loss being $957,000, and the commission charges only $275,000.

As the price of the stock at the beginning and end of the period considered was the same, and as nothing of an abnormal character occurred, this additional loss must be attributed to other causes, and here the mechanical drawback ends and the personal equation enters.

Everything being equal, the surplus loss of $682,000 must be attributed to erroneous mental operations, and when the further fact is considered that the average price paid for stocks was 42, and the average price at which stocks were sold was 35, the theory that the public reverses the methods dictated by reason is confirmed. It is apparent that if this proclivity had not been indulged in the result would have been a net profit; that is to say, if 37 had been taken as a pivotal point, and purchases made below, or sales above it, numerous gains could have been made on either side, especially on purchases, as the short seller would have had about 6 points in dividends against him during the period, which has not been considered in the figures given, but which is reflected with considerable accuracy in the composite result. An examination of financial columns and current gossip at corresponding periods of high and low prices showed no well founded reasons for the consensus of opinion at such times.

The gossip rather reflected than incited the prevailing cheerful or pessimistic feeling, and no particular mischief can be attributed to this source.

Next in importance to the suicidal tendency to sell cheap and buy dear was the widespread evidence of greed. In almost every case where an account was successfully begun, the operations were immediately extended in volume until, even after a large number of successful results, a single reverse wiped out the entire credit. Even those operators who showed apparent good judgment in buying and selling were subject to this fault to so marked a degree that after being right nine times and wrong once, they were on the debit side of the ledger.

The inability of the average trader to map out a plan and follow it was also distinctly exemplified. Methods and systems begun and pursued for a time with mathematical precision almost invariably ended in a mass of indiscriminate operations caused apparently by fright or confusion in case of loss, and exhilaration and enthusiasm if successful.

Another interesting development was that the accounts of those speculators who operated from a distance, or from points where no brokerage office was located, made a better showing than those of local traders. The losses were smaller and the gains larger. The contrast was so marked that it would appear that isolation has its advantages. The marginal provision made by these distant traders was more ample, and the operations were fewer in number. These two points alone were a decided advantage. They also escaped the ill-advised action frequently induced by flurries and canards, and altogether seemed to operate more intelligently, possibly because the opportunities to make fools of themselves were restricted.

In considering the above figures and deductions, it must be constantly borne in mind that the market covered a comparatively narrow range for an active stock; that no unusual opportunities for profit or loss existed, and that the end of the period showed the stock unchanged in price.

In comparing it with a great cycle of speculative prices the results would be greatly magnified. The object in view was to submit results entirely of a normal nature. It is doubtful whether operations in U.S. Steel stock were particularly desirable at any time during the period mentioned, as it presented no great immediate promise, and numerous dangers at all times. There were many surface indications of a warning character, The stock was untried; the earnings were comparatively so large as to suggest inflation, and the fact of it being a public favorite was proof of a bad technical condition.

The student of the technical position of shares would have reasoned that the enormous floating supply of the stock in public speculative hands would make any marked or sustained advance impossible, as any considerable appreciation in the market price would meet with enough selling to stop the upward trend, while the danger of panic or severe decline would be increased for exactly the same reasons.

It is therefore probable that the better class of traders shunned the stock entirely, especially when the fact is considered that numerous other active stocks presented better opportunities during the period considered.

For instance, Louisville & Nashville made and maintained an advance of $25 per share from July, 1901, to March, 1903, the advance being justified by improved conditions in the South.

Nevertheless U.S. Steel was the public favorite, and was obviously the best example of public speculation.

Viewed in the light of comparative results, the loss of $682,000 on total transactions of 1,112,000 shares may at first blush be considered small, only a little over fifty cents per share, but it must be remembered that this was a total deficit on all operations, and that the numerous profits made at various times were used as an offset to losses. The question is, why should any loss have occurred when there was no decline in market valuation?

If the barometrical character of the examination outlined above is admitted, the fact is established that a loss was sustained which can be attributed to nothing but mistaken methods and impulses. In other words, the actual percentage against the trader was more than trebled by personal actions, a thing which would not have been possible with any mechanical gambling device.

The matter presented in this chapter offers much food for thought. It is not in line with the alluring view of speculative opportunities frequently presented to the public eye. The statements already made that speculation could be made profitable, are in no way modified, but the disease must be diagnosed before it can be treated, and some of the medicine necessary to financial health has a bitter taste.

Written large between the lines of every disastrous speculative account are the reasons for failure. True, this is cold comfort, for the losses represented cannot be recovered by analysis, but the lesson may be of great value danger-ous rocks by a process of shipwrecking is an unpleasant method of acquiring knowledge, but a most forcible one.

Chapter XI - Grain Speculation

As a confirmation of the preconceived theory that the percentage of loss in grain speculation was much greater than in stocks, an examination of accounts was undertaken based on the same general lines outlined in stocks.

The commodity chosen for investigation was No. 2 Wheat, and the transactions considered were made on prices established on the Chicago Board of Trade.

The period covered was from January, 1901, at which time the price was 76 to December, 1903, when the price was 77.

During this period of three years the lowest price touched was 63 in July, 1901, and the highest price, 95 in September, 1902.

These figures are presented as evidence of numerous wide speculative movements occurring between the same comparative basic prices at the beginning and ending of the three years.

Five hundred accounts were found available for dissection, and the same appearance of unanimity of operations as that apparent in stocks was shown.

The principal seeming difference between stock and grain trading was that the public indulged more freely in operations for the short account in grain than in stocks. Several instances were discovered where for a time the preponderance of operations were for short account, invariably at low prices and on the eve of an advance.

All the errors illustrated in stocks were found to exist in grain on a magnified scale. The tendency to buy at the top, and sell at the bottom, was particularly marked, and while the average buying price of 79 may look low, it may be said in explanation that the prices of 95 in 1902, and in 1903, were of a manipulated nature, and of very brief duration, and that comparatively few transactions were possible at very high prices. If these two abnormal periods are eliminated, the average price was high. The investigation resulted as follows: 412 accounts showed a final loss, 74 accounts showed a final profit, 14 accounts were neutral, the total deficit on all losing accounts was $923,000.

The total gain on all profitable accounts, $52,000, leaving a net deficit of $871,000.

The total amount of grain handled was 90,000,000 bushels (the speculative equivalent of 900,000 shares of stock), of which 62,000,000 bushels were originally purchases, and 28,000,000 originally short sales.

The total brokerage charges were $112,500. The comparative losses on short sales were 16% less than on purchases.

The scale order was employed in 140 accounts, (92 long and 48 short), but was pursued to an uninterrupted conclusion in only 21 instances.

The average buying price was 79, and the average selling price 70.

The principal facts illustrated as compared with stock operations are a net loss of $757,000 over and above an actual mechanical percentage of only $112,500, and the small total of gross profits as compared with the total of gross losses.

It has been stated that the grain investigation was begun with the preconceived opinion that losses in grain would be proportionately larger than those in stocks, and the result, as far as it goes, is confirmatory. It is only fair to state in this respect that losses shown in corn were comparatively larger than in stocks, but much smaller than in wheat. This is probably explained by the fact that corn has undergone a readjustment of valuation through its increased uses, and enormous increase of exportation, both of the cereal itself and its byproducts, and also the fact that we raise 80% of the world's corn, and that available acreage is about exhausted.

These facts were so patent as to be of assistance to even the obtuse mind of the ordinary speculator, and as purchases predominated, and the price has gradually advanced, comparative losses were smaller.

The preconceived opinion as to losses in grain operations was based upon the irrefutable fact that study and judgment must in such operations be largely superseded by purely gambling principles. In other words, the probable price of grain cannot be intelligently forecasted by the ordinary speculator, as no reliable figures are obtainable, and no prophecies as to future conditions can be reliably adduced. The annual crop scares are not dependable, and actual conditions which bear upon future prices are available only to the chosen few who can afford to make their own expensive investigations!

It is needless to say that possessors of valuable knowledge do not diffuse their information, nor expose their operations to public view until the psychological moment arrives at which they wish to sell.

It is possible to obtain figures as to the earnings of corporations, and such figures being at hand, the rest is a matter of judgment and study, but no figures which may be considered a safe basis of operations are obtainable for cereals.

In addition to the gambling elements which this lack of knowledge injects into operations in cereals, they are much more subject to manipulation. The record of a single individual "dumping" the entire speculative public in wheat, is not rare in the history of grain speculation, and the capital employed in the operation would not make a hearty meal for Wall Street.

There is another drawback to grain speculation as compared with stocks, and while it is apparently overlooked or ignored by the average trader, it is important, and is as follows:

The possessor of 100 shares of stock bought at a normal price, is the recipient of dividends, or may naturally expect ultimate improvement in his security if it is a good one.

The possessor of 10,000 bushels of grain at a normal price is subject to storage charges and insurance, and has equal chances of profit or loss in future prices.

To illustrate this: The man who invests $10,000 in a 6% stock, at par, receives $600 per year on his investment, while he who invests the same amount in 10,000 bushels of wheat at $1.00 per bushel, pays about $1,200 a year to carry his property. This is looking at the matter as a cash proposition, but the comparative drawback cannot be escaped by any form of operations for the long account, whether the transaction be for one day or one year.

The optional nature of grain presents another drawback in that an unfortunate operation cannot be continued indefinitely, except by the process of transferring to more deferred options with a multiplication of commission charges. Even by this process the transferred trade may be regarded in the light of a new transaction, as the buyer's original reasons for believing that the present, or coming crop, would be salable at a certain price before the maturity of the option purchased, have been entirely obliterated by the lapse of time, and he now finds himself depending upon the chances of recovering in the new transaction the losses sustained in the old.

If he accepts and pays for the commodity, and a year later finds that the price has advanced 12 cents, his position is in no way improved, as the expense of carrying his product for that period has offset the higher market value.

The trader who purchases wheat has against him, therefore, all the ordinary drawbacks of misleading appearances, manipulation, etc., but in addition, the element of purely gambling chance is greatly increased, and a tremendous submerged percentage added.

The foregoing statements at once suggest the question, "If successful operations for the long account are so difficult, why should not operations on the other side present advantages in direct inverse ratio?"

The point is well taken, and the answer is simply, "they do present such opportunities." This advantage is illustrated to some extent by the fact that operations for the short account, in grain, showed a larger ratio of profit, or rather, a smaller ratio of loss, than was found in purchases.

But in public short selling we find that a too general recognition of its advantages would lead to the undoing of the trader by creating a technical position which would be very inviting to the moneyed manipulators. This danger must be considered, as well as the fact that the theory of accidents being in favor of the short seller of stocks, is exactly reversed in grain. For instance, war, classed as the greatest of all calamities under certain conditions, is an invariable reason for higher prices in food products. The tendency to sell at low prices also prevails and must be overcome if operations for the short account are to prove profitable; but brushing aside all these elements of accident or error, it may be stated that the short seller of cereals possesses a distinct advantage.

The fact will no doubt be pointed out that short operations have proved uniformly disastrous in the past few years. While this is granted, it in no way interferes with the arguments but rather supports them in its demonstration of the possibilities of manipulation by one or two individuals. But there is another reason for this reversal of form which was apparently recognized by a few men and stubbornly overlooked by the majority. The fact is that all staples have recently undergone a process of revaluation to a higher basis and that the seller of every product has worked against the current of this readjustment.

That the public is slow to recognize changed conditions is demonstrated by the fact that the period of high prices from the latter part of 1888 to early in 1892 finally educated them to consider one dollar the normal price of wheat at just the time when a readjustment to lower valuation took place and enormous losses were sustained by a tenacious adherence to this theory of dollar wheat until the expensive lesson had been ground into them that a change had occurred. The more recent readjustment to high prices was likewise unrecognized and vigorously combated.

This is a very marked evidence of the fact that speculators generally move more on a mental chart of recent market action than upon any broad lines of thought.

It would be really amusing to review the opportunities set forth by the advocates of the so-called chart system as applied to grain trading for the last fifteen years. We find them in the position of purchasing wheat through a period of depression and later selling it persistently through a period of advancing prices, for it must be admitted that changed conditions cannot be contemplated in a fixed system founded on past, not future events. The votaries of the charts will no doubt attempt to evade this statement by demonstrations covering an insufficient period or by claiming that changed conditions were recognized and their little machines readjusted to meet them. The first refutation is simply unfair, and if the second is true, correct recognition would have been sufficient without any auxiliary machinery.

The difficulty of successful operations in cereals by ordinary traders is very pertinently shown by the remarks made by the most successful bucket shop man in the United States.

"I can better afford to trade flat in grain than to trade in stocks at one quarter commission; they have nothing to go on."

This is the statement of a man who looked upon the matter in a purely gambling light and admitted that he could eliminate the actual percentage in grain transactions and depend wholly upon the speculator beating himself.

Even the greater lights of speculation, fortified by large capital, have found the hazards of grain speculation so great, and the most careful forecasts so unreliable, that in many instances, and after disastrous experiments, they have transferred their operations wholly to stocks. Mr. James R. Keene twice retired from the Chicago arena a badly whipped man, and it is related of him that he refused an intimate friend financial assistance in a grain deal with the terse remark that he would be doing him no kindness, as it was impossible to win.

This is, of course, an extreme view, for money lost by one man must necessarily be gained by another; but this fact does not interfere with the broad general principle that stocks of good corporations are productive, and that the possession of staples is an expense. One is for perpetual existence and natural enhancement, the other for consumption.

The contention of Mr. Keene that it is impossible to make money in cereal speculation cannot be wholly concurred with. The man who is astute enough to foresee a final readjustment of values or who purchases staples at an extremely low price in periods of depression, and vice versa, will succeed; but the average grain trader will find his opportunities and possibilities reduced, and his obstacles multiplied by comparison with operations in stocks.

Chapter XII - Suggestions as to Intelligent Methods

In deciding what to buy and when to buy it, the speculator faces the most formidable of his problems, for upon his decision upon these two points rests success or failure.

It will be necessary for him to concentrate upon this task research, labor and clear thinking with technical knowledge and sustained by precedent.

In approaching the first phase of the question—What to buy?—it may be well to employ the time-honored method of elimination, and to consider primarily what not to buy.

It seems incredible that the numerous oil, mining, and other companies which advertise large returns on low priced stocks, or immense values for small investments, should find a market, but the fact remains that the money annually invested in this class of stocks is so considerable an amount as to demand some comment, and warrant a note of warning. This class of so-called securities may be said, by and large, to have no value at all. Securities which have an actual dividend earning power of any probable duration do not go begging long in this day and age, and are seldom advertised for sale in the newspapers.

Let this fact be remembered: a mine, an oil well, or any other producing company with a demonstrable value can command a market price at all times. That is to say, if the owner, or owners of a mine can show a certain amount of ore in sight, or can prove that such ore exists, they can command a fair price for that ore as surely as if the commodity were flour in a storehouse instead of gold, silver, or copper in a mine. Any man who has a knowledge of mining affairs, (and who has no mining stock for sale), will confirm this statement.

If, therefore, the sellers of stock in such companies have a property, capable of producing a certain commodity which may be sold at a profit, they must, in order to reap any substantial benefit from the "stocking" operation, sell as much of the stock at high prices as to cover the great expense of time, a costly advertising campaign, officers' salaries, a large commission to fiscal agents, (usually 20%), and leave a margin of profit for themselves. They must, in short, sell to the public at about double the value placed on the property by men of wisdom and experience.

There are no doubt cases where the promoters of such securities believe that the value of their own property is greater than any appraised market, in which case we find their judgment opposed to that of shrewd men seeking to invest capital. In such opposition of judgment the owners may be right—the chances are a hundred to one that they are wrong.

But even the above examples are too broad, for the great majority of these concerns have no property of any demonstrable value whatever. Their stocks are made, like Hodge's razors, to sell. The promoters depend upon golden promises, statements misleading, and public gullibility to create a market for their stocks. That they are able to sell them at all is remarkable.

These companies use every means for deceiving the public. They employ the best of writers to get up glowing prospectuses, and not infrequently the names of prominent men are found among their officials or directors. These latter individuals participate sometimes through ignorance and enthusiasm, sometimes through actual dishonesty. In either case it may be justly stated that a prominent name added to the roster of an advertising company is not sufficient proof of the property's merit.

In addition to these facts there is no recognized market for this class of stocks, and they cannot be disposed of like listed securities, at a moment's notice. This is in itself a great drawback.

In making these statements there is no prejudice nor desire to be unfair. There are no doubt exceptions to the rule, but these exceptions are so rare that the best plan possible is to eschew all such properties entirely no matter how alluring the promises, or how apparently well founded the venture. There are plenty of good listed securities, the prices of which periodically reach high and low points, the value of which is founded upon recognized business principles and necessities.

The listed securities of Wall Street are divided into two distinct classes: Industrial and Railroad; and viewed from a speculative standpoint the former class is the most hazardous, in that they are generally more subject to manipulation, competition, or harmful legislation. Those who possess a sufficiently tenacious speculative memory will recall the affairs of the Whiskey trust and the Cordage trust and their sad demise; and while great declines, and even assessments, have occurred in railroad stocks, they have always eventually proved their real value. Good Industrials may occasionally be purchased safely and profitably, but the rails present the same opportunities, and are safer and more open to comprehensive investigation and correct judgment.

At the rails, therefore, we stop. It may be argued that the process detailed above is a matter of degree, and that it might be continued until only government, or other gilt edged bonds, remained; but the question here discussed is speculation, and it is taken for granted that what is sought is the golden mean between certain loss and certain gain percent; i.e. properties which combine a fair amount of stability and future promise with periodical opportunities for advantageous purchases and sales.

Viewing the future of railroad securities in a broad general light, their gradually increasing value appears certain. The continued increase of population produces for them present returns from travel and shipping, and the demands of the settled districts ensure more permanent returns. So far as probable competition is concerned, it grows daily less with the concentration of capital. It is likely that even today the projectors of a railroad which would come into harmful competition with present lines would find it impossible to raise the money for the furtherance of their plan.

A brief perusal of statistics will show that the oldest and best railroad securities, representing the properties traversing a densely populated territory, are subject to the smallest comparative range of fluctuation. These stocks are gradually undergoing a process of absorption which will in time reach to the newer roads of less developed country.

The West, with its enormous undeveloped territory and resources, presents great promise to the prophetic mind. The problem of extensive irrigation is yet to be solved, but aside from agricultural pursuits, the West possesses a wealth of mineral and lumbering industries, and possibilities which independently guarantee its future.

"The Atchison Railroad is a streak of rust running through a desert," said the elder Woerishoffer thirty years ago, as he industriously sold the stock short at prices which would seem ridiculously low today. Possibly Atchison bore that aspect at that time, but today it is a modern, well equipped, dividend paying property, traversing a rich and constantly improving territory. The improvement of that brief period is significant.

The South also presents promise of great future improvement. The readjustment of cotton prices to a higher general level, and the development of important mineral resources are combining to dispel the long lethargy of this section, and the growing competitive importance of its gulf ports is too glaring to be misunderstood.

The believer in the continued growth and prosperity of the U.S., the progress of the largely undeveloped West, and the awakening South may safely assume a gradual and rapid growth in the value of railroad securities of these sections. The consensus of intelligent opinion points to their long-continued improvement and advance.

The contention is therefore made and offered for consideration that the railroad properties of the West and South offer the best speculative opportunities, combined with the greatest degree of safety.

The foregoing will, possibly, appeal to the reader as looking rather to the long future of properties than to immediate speculative opportunities, but the fairness of the following statement must be admitted: The hazards of speculation are so great that it is expedient to primarily consider a solid groundwork for ventures. The trader who deals in stocks, the future of which he considers secure, can operate more actively and courageously than under other circumstances. It does not follow that because he has faith in the long future of his chosen properties, he shall at once jump in and buy and await the accretion of time. The proposed plan of operation—to await low prices—is in no way changed by the cheerful view of the future.

Having formed a definite idea as to the outlook of a certain group of properties, the investigator has narrowed his research to individual stocks. In this he will be guided by three periods—the past, present, and probable future.

In examining the history of a stock it will be found that in almost all cases the security has undergone, in early stages, a radical advance and decline. This is largely occasioned by the fact that the public always makes a favorite of a new security, and will participate freely in the affairs of an untried corporation, while standard issues go begging. This brings about a state of affairs already explained both technically and theoretically, and offers to the moneyed interests an opportunity to sell their holdings to the public at high prices, and recover them later at their own figures. Thereafter, the stock will probably take its place among the standards of the Street, and follows the general swing to high and low extremes with a gradual trend toward increased valuation.

Eliminating this abnormal period of initiation, the investigator will find a careful study of the past to be of great value. In all cases it will be found that earnings have gradually increased, allowing, of course, for abnormal periods of depression and inflation. The fixed charges and expenses have also increased, and by an examination of both these factors, as well as an allowance for the diversion of funds for purposes of purchase and improvement, which expenditures if intelligently made must add to the value of the property, the net result of the past may be considered a reasonable guide to future expectations.

The mere payment of dividends cannot be accepted as a safe basis of value, for dividends are often paid to the great detriment of the property, and on the other hand are frequently withheld when they might be safely paid. Earnings are the all important point, and when the investigator has answered to his satisfaction the questions, "What have they earned, and what have they done with the money?" he may consider himself well on the way to his goal.

With this record of the past formed, the present earnings may be scrutinized. They may recently have undergone a sudden advance out of proportion to normal growth, or vice versa. In either case a reversal of present conditions may be confidently expected.

This simple form of reasoning applied to the affairs of the U.S. Steel Company in 1901-1903 would have sounded a most distinct note of warning, the correctness of which has been amply demonstrated.

The probable future is based upon a gradual improvement from the normal value of the present as indicated by the past.

The consideration of assets, so far as a railroad is concerned, must be founded principally on its ability to earn, and continue earning perpetually.

Minus its usefulness, the total assets of the greatest railway system in existence would be little better than a mass of old junk; but if a million dollars has been so expended as to bring a continued fair return, that amount may be considered an asset. The investigator therefore finds that his calculations must be based almost wholly upon the ability of a property to increase its earning power until territorial development reaches high tide, and thenceforth to maintain such earnings indefinitely.

It will not be necessary for the trader, personally, to compute the various and voluminous figures which show the net earnings—that is to say, the amount applicable to distribution to the various bond and stock holders. A comprehensive statement of income and expenditure may be obtained from different published statistical works, or by application to the secretary of the corporation in question. With these figures before him, the task of the student is one of examination rather than of compilation, and with such information at hand, the matter may be viewed in the same light as any other ordinary business transactions. The total income, less the fixed charges, is the amount applicable to dividends and surplus.

The man who undertakes such an investigation will be surprised at the ease with which he may arrive at interesting results.

The legal provisions of the company, the rights of holders of preferences, and of holders of common stock, etc., are all matters which should be examined, as they frequently have an important bearing on values.

If the plan mapped out has been intelligently followed, the investigator should, by comparing his result with the value of money, be able to judge of the normal value of any standard security. If his figures vary materially from the market price, and no important error nor omission has been made, the stock is selling either below or above a fair valuation, and the information which was the object of all his research has been gained. Possessed of this valuable knowledge, the speculator now turns his attention to the second phase of the question—the time to buy. It may be that the price of his favorite security is very low, but that a bad technical position exists which will warrant a belief in lower prices, or an extended period of dullness. This situation has already been sufficiently enlarged upon.

Recapitulating the matter offered above for consideration, the course recommended would appear as follows:

First, decision as to the securities to be dealt in, eliminating all wildcat and untried stocks, and choosing for operations standard listed securities.

Second, determining what stocks offer the greatest promise of continued increase in value, as determined by territory and its probable development.

Third, an examination of the physical and financial condition of the individual property, or properties, chosen, and a forecast of the probable future, based upon the demonstrated past.

Fourth, the fixing of a present normal value to be used as a pivotal point in actual operation.

Fifth, a consideration of the manipulative and technical conditions of the machine speculative in order to be able to judge of the more immediate action of the market. In other words, to locate the position of the stocks, whether in weak hands or strong.

This form of reasoning should not appear complicated; it is the same process which any business man would pursue in following a determination to enter the grocery business, and yet it may be emphatically stated that not one speculator in a hundred enters his field equipped with even the most desultory knowledge of what he is doing. Out of ten traders in U.S. Steel Preferred who were experimentally questioned two years ago, only half the number knew what the issue of preferred stock amounted to; only two were aware of the important fact that the dividend on the preferred stock was cumulative, and not one was reasonably well posted as to its properties and earnings.

And yet every one of these individuals could adduce specious reasons why the stock should advance or decline, reasons which at best were incomplete, and at their worst, silly or false. The outcome of their individual efforts has not been followed, but it is safe to surmise that all made mistakes which research, coupled with intelligent judgment, would have prevented.

In the plan of study submitted in this chapter, there will, no doubt, be a sense of incompleteness, but the object has been rather to guide the reader into a correct line of reasoning and investigating than to adduce specific cases or pile up statistical proof.

Everything is left to individual effort and judgment, and the man who begins the process of research suggested will make rapid progress. One developed fact will suggest another point to be investigated, and the process will become interesting and profitable.

The man who studies and knows, is the only man who makes permanent gains in speculation.

To those who refute the possibility of obtaining the necessary information for the forming of such opinions, or who consider the task too great or too complex for the ordinary mind, let the fair reply be made, "Try it." It is this hazy idea of mystery where none exists which deters the ordinary speculator from even attempting to use his own brains, and which leads him to base his operations upon hearsay or guesswork. Cases will occur where concealment, either partial or total, will be found. For such the remedy is simple: let these properties alone.

If the first step toward the investigation of the affairs of Amalgamated Copper had been taken, it would have appeared at once that the corporation was a mere shell, a holding company, and furthermore, a blind pool of the most pronounced type. The value of such knowledge employed in a negative sense, that is, in preventing operations in such hippodromed stocks, is a matter of history. The enormous public losses sustained in Amalgamated Copper would have been impossible in any business on earth except speculation, for in any other business affair examination would have been the first thought, and negotiations under parallel conditions would have been abruptly dropped.

It is not meant to say that a mere examination of figures and periods is by any means sufficient, but it is believed that once started in the correct path of examination and judgment, as opposed to the prevalent methods of guesswork and gambling, the trader will find ample opportunities and incentive for pursuing his researches to a logical conclusion. After this has been accomplished, success will be measured by his own capabilities and business acumen.

The chapter headed, "Analyzing Railroad Securities," in Mr. John Moody's book, "The Art of Wall Street Investing," will be of great assistance to the student who attempts to follow out the suggestions made above.

Chapter XIII - Conclusion

The three stages necessary to the development of the theories advanced in this work were, first, a recognition of the fact that public ventures were, considered as a unit, generally disastrous; second, an analysis of the causes which were responsible for this unsatisfactory fact; and finally, a confirmation of such analysis by statistical exhibits.

Relative to the latter feature, the necessarily condensed and restricted nature of the figures submitted may be considered insufficient evidence, but as it is certain that there is never a material division of public speculative opinion at any time, the books of even one house with a public clientele may be considered a fair indication of all others.

If the four thousand accounts, with their tens of thousands of operations, could be presented in detail, this unanimity of action would be more apparent, and their barometrical value greatly magnified. The figures submitted, however, are confirmatory and not basic, and while they are important, in that they dovetail with preconceived opinions, the logical conclusions presented must stand on their own bottom.

That the public loses money in speculation is a notorious fact; that such losses take place in an arena which presents equal opportunities for profit or loss is indisputable, and it must follow, as the night the day, that the losses sustained are the result of mistaken judgment, erroneous methods, or misleading appearances.

In presenting the pitfalls which beset the path of the speculator, and suggesting a means of avoiding them, it is felt that a thorough understanding of such dangers was necessary to safety and maximum good results.

Fortified with a knowledge of the machinery of the speculative world, and its workings, the trader may indulge much more actively in his ventures than if he depended wholly upon even the most excellent judgment of intrinsic value. Thus the trader who is justified in believing general or individual current prices to be at low ebb, may act boldly and frequently with good results. He enters his campaign satisfied that material decline is improbable, that public liquidation is complete, and that the next important move will be upward. He brings to bear upon his operations his knowledge of technical conditions and natural market actions, and his foundation being secure, makes repeated successes. He bears constantly in mind the fact that a limit will eventually be reached, a fact which is easily submerged by undue enthusiasm, and he knows that it is far better to quit too soon than too late.

All these things are a distinct advantage in increasing profits and preventing loss, but they are of secondary importance. They are the branches, without which it is possible for the trunk to thrive, but which, themselves, will die if removed from the parent stem.

The great basic principle of speculation, the foundation upon which the entire structure rests, is the recognition of value. No sustained success is possible without this knowledge, and most failures are traceable to the lack of it. Yet so generally is this important element disregarded, or refuted, that we find it playing only a small part, or no part at all, in the operations of the average speculator.

In the speculative world we find many men capable of clear thinking, correct analysis, and sound business judgment falling over each other in the rush to make purchases of properties of which they know nothing. The incentive to such purchase may be a whispered tip, or contagious enthusiasm, and the ridiculous equation of luck plays no inconsiderable part. The result is always the same.

To those who contend that all the obtainable knowledge of speculative anatomy is limited and unreliable, let this fair question be put:

Was there ever to your personal knowledge a period of speculative extremes where all, or most of the appearances and conditions herein detailed did not exist in recognizable form? To be more specific, when the public favorite, U.S. Steel, was selling at its lowest prices were not the technical appearances of dullness, pessimism, and public disgust as distinct as the activity and optimism had been at high prices? And furthermore, were not the figures by which an intelligent estimate of real values and probabilities could have been demonstrated in the face of claims of watered stock, lack of demand, and general decay, always obtainable?

It was stated in the first chapter of this work that the maximum result obtainable in such a treatise would be the direction of thought into proper channels. The theories, and even the established facts advanced will no doubt meet with opposition from that class of persons who allow a general denial to take the place of answering arguments, and who sniff at theoretical deductions. Such shallow reasoners may at once be relegated to the ranks of the numerous whist players who maintain and express an opinion that there is nothing in the "book game," and who, in the face of overwhelming evidence that they are wrong, go on losing games, and actually take pride in proclaiming to the world their benighted condition.

Theories, if correct, are embryotic facts, the value of which lies wholly in their proper application, and no refutation, of even a faulty theory, is worthy of consideration unless accompanied by answering argument.

There is, however, a large class of men capable of clear thought and sound judgment who speculate unsuccessfully through allowing these faculties to be contorted, or lie dormant before the apparent mystery enveloping the affairs of the bourse. The properly directed exercise of the capabilities of these men would soon rob the speculative arena of both its mystery and its bugbears, and resolve it into a place of business where extraordinary opportunities were annually presented.

To this latter class, the statements and deductions made herein are respectfully submitted.

STUDIES IN TAPE READING
Richard D. Wyckoff (Rollo Tape) - 1910

Contents

Introductory

There is a widespread demand for more light on the subject of Tape Reading. Thousands of those who operate in the stock market now recognize the fact that the market momentarily indicates its own immediate future; that these indications are accurately recorded on the tape; therefore those who can interpret what is imprinted on the narrow paper ribbon have a distinct advantage over the general public.

Such an opinion is warranted, for it is well known that many of the most successful traders of the present day began operations as Tape Readers, trading in fractional lots of stock with a capital of only a few hundred dollars.

Speaking of Joe Manning, one of the shrewdest and most successful of all the traders on the floor of the New York Stock Exchange, a friend of mine once said: "Joe and I used to trade in ten share lots together. He was an ordinary trader, just as I am. We used to hang over the same ticker."

The speaker was, at the time he made the remark, still trading in ten-share lots, while I happened to know that Joe's bank balance—his active working capital— amounted to $100,000, and that this represented but a part of the fortune built on his ability to interpret the language of the tape.

Why was one of these men able to amass a fortune, while the other never acquired more than a few thousand dollars at the same pursuit? Their chances were equal at the start so far as capital and opportunity go. The profits were there, waiting to be won by either or both.

The answer seems to be in the peculiar mental qualifications, highly potent in the successful trader, but unpossessed by the other. There is, of course, an element of luck in every case, but pure luck could not be so sustained in Manning's case as to carry him through operations covering a term of years.

Livermore used to trade solely on what the tape told him, closing out everything before three o'clock. He traded from an office and paid the regular commissions, yet three trades out of five showed profits. Having made a fortune, he invested it in bonds and gave them all to his wife. Anticipating the 1907 panic, he put his $13,000 automobile up for a loan of $5,000, and with this capital started to play the bear side, using his profits as additional margin. At one time he was short 70,000 shares of Union Pacific. His whole line was covered on one of the panic days, and his net profits were a million dollars!

By proper mental equipment we do not mean the mere ability to take a loss, define the trend, or to execute some other move characteristic of the professional trader. We refer to the active or dormant qualities in his make-up; viz., the power to drill himself into the right mental attitude; to stifle his emotions, such as fear, anxiety, elation, recklessness; to train his mind into obedience so that it recognizes but one master—the tape. These qualities are as vital as natural ability, or what is called the sixth sense in trading.

Some people are born musicians, others seemingly void of musical taste, develop themselves until they become virtuosos. It is the I WILL in a man which makes him mediocre or pre-eminent—in Wall Street parlance, "a dub" or "a big trader."

Jacob Field is another exponent of Tape Reading. Those who knew "Jakey" when he began his Wall Street career, noted his ability to read the tape and follow the trend. His talent for this work was doubtless born in him; time and experience have intensified it.

Whatever laurels James R. Keene won as operator or syndicate manager, do not detract from his reputation as a Tape Reader. His scrutiny of the tape was so intense that he appeared to be in a trance while his mental processes were being worked out. He seemed to analyze prices, volumes and fluctuations down to the finest imaginable point. It was then his practice to telephone to the floor of the Stock Exchange, ascertain the character of the buying or selling, and with this auxiliary information complete his judgment and make his commitments.

At his death Mr. Keene stood on the pinnacle of fame as a Tape Reader, his daily presence at the ticker bearing testimony that the work paid and paid well.

One might say: "These are rare examples. The average man never makes a success of Tape Reading." Right you are! The *average* man seldom makes a success of anything.

Success in this field usually results from years of painstaking effort and absolute concentration upon the subject. It requires the devotion of one's whole time and attention to the tape. He should have no other business or profession. "A man cannot serve two masters," and the tape is a tyrant.

One cannot become a Tape Reader by giving the ticker absent treatment; nor by running into his broker's office after lunch, or seeing "how the market closed" from his evening newspaper. He cannot study this art from the far end of a telegraph or telephone wire. He should spend twenty-seven hours a week at the ticker, and many more hours away from it studying his mistakes and finding the "why" of his losses.

If Tape Reading were an exact science, one would simply have to assemble the factors, carry out the operations indicated, and trade accordingly. But the factors influencing the market are infinite in their number and character, as well as in their effect upon the market, and to attempt the construction of a Tape Reading formula would seem to be futile. However, something of the kind (in the rough) may develop as we progress in this investigation, so let us preserve open minds.

What is Tape Reading?

This question may be best answered by first deciding what it is not.

Tape Reading is not merely looking at the tape to ascertain how prices are running.

It is not reading the news and then buying or selling "if the stock acts right."

It is not trading on tips, opinions, or information.

It is not buying "because they are going up," or selling "because they look weak."

It is not trading on chart indications or by other mechanical methods.

It is not "buying on dips and selling on bulges."

Nor is it any of the hundred other foolish things practised by the millions of people without method, forethought or calculation.

Tape Reading seems to us: The science of determining from the tape the immediate trend of prices.

It is a method of forecasting, from what appears on the tape *now,* what is likely to appear in the future.

Tape Reading is rapid-fire horse sense. Its object is to determine whether stocks are being accumulated or distributed, marked up or down, or whether they are neglected by the large interests. The Tape Reader aims to make deductions from each succeeding transaction—every shift of the market kaleidoscope; to grasp a new situation, force it, lightning-like, through the weighing machine of the brain, and to reach a decision which can be acted upon with coolness and precision.

It is gauging the momentary supply and demand in particular stocks and in the whole market, comparing the forces behind each and their relationship, each to the other and to all.

A Tape Reader is like the manager of a department store; into his office are poured hundreds of reports of sales made by the various departments. He notes the general trend of business— whether demand is heavy or light throughout the store—but lends special attention to the lines in which demand is abnormally strong or weak. When he finds difficulty in keeping his shelves full in a certain department, he instructs his buyers, and they increase their buying orders; when certain goods do not move he knows there is little demand (market) for them, therefore, he lowers his prices as an inducement to possible purchasers.

A floor trader who stands in one crowd all day is like the buyer for one department—he sees more quickly than anyone else the demand for that class of goods, hut has no way of comparing it to that prevailing in other parts of the store.

He may be trading on the long side of Union Pacific, which has a strong upward trend, when suddenly a break in another stock will demoralize the market in Union Pacific, and he will be forced to compete with others who have stocks to sell.

The Tape Reader, on the other hand, from his perch at the ticker, enjoys a bird's eye view of the whole field. When serious weakness develops in any quarter, he is quick to note, weigh and act.

Another advantage in favor of the Tape Reader: The tape tells the news minutes, hours and days before the news tickers, or newspapers, and before it can become current gossip. Everything from a foreign war to the passing of a dividend; from a Supreme Court decision to the ravages of the boll-weevil is reflected primarily upon the tape.

The insider who knows a dividend is to be jumped from 6 percent to 10 percent shows his hand on the tape when he starts to accumulate the stock, and the investor with 100 shares to sell makes his fractional impress upon its market price.

The market is like a slowly revolving wheel: Whether the wheel will continue to revolve in the same direction, stand still or reverse depends entirely upon the forces which come in contact with its hub and tread. Even when the contact is broken, and nothing remains to affect its course, the wheel retains a certain impulse from the most recent dominating force, and revolves until it comes to a standstill or is subjected to other influences.

The element of manipulation need not discourage any one. Manipulators are giant traders, wearing seven-leagued boots. The trained ear can detect the steady "clump, clump," as they progress, and the footprints are recognized in the fluctuations and the quantities of stock appearing on the tape. Little fellows are at liberty to tiptoe wherever the footprints lead, but they must be careful that the giants do not turn quickly.

The Tape Reader has many advantages over the long swing operator. He never ventures far from shore; that is, he plays with a close stop, never laying himself open to a large loss. Accidents or catastrophes cannot seriously injure him because he can reverse his position in an instant, and follow the newly-formed stream from source to mouth. As his position on either the long or short side is confirmed and emphasized, he increases his line, thus following up the advantage gained.

A simon-pure Tape Reader does not care to carry stocks over night. The tape is then silent, and he only knows what to do when it tells him. Something may occur at midnight which may crumple up his diagram of the next day's market. He leaves nothing to chance; hence he prefers a clean sheet when the 3 o'clock gong strikes.

By this method interest charges are avoided, reducing the percentage against him to a considerable extent.

The Tape Reader is like a vendor of fruit who, each morning, provides himself with a stock of the choicest and most seasonable products, and for which there is the greatest demand. He pays his cash and disposes of the goods as quickly as possible, at a profit varying from 50 to 100 percent on cost. To carry his stock over night causes a loss on account of spoilage. This corresponds with the interest charge to the trader.

The fruit vendor is successful because he knows what and when to buy, also where and how to sell. But there are stormy days when he cannot go out; when buyers do not appear; when he is arrested, fined, or locked up by a blue-coated despot or his wares are scattered abroad by a careless truckman.

Wall Street will readily apply these situations to the various attitudes in which the Tape Reader finds himself. He ventures $100 to make $200, and as the market goes in his favor his risk is reduced, but there are times when he finds himself at sea, with his stock deteriorating. Or the market is so unsettled that he does not know how to act; he is caught on stop or held motionless in a dead market; he takes a series of losses, or is obliged to be away from the tape when opportunities occur. His calculations are completely upset by some unforeseen event or his capital is impaired by overtrading or poor judgment.

The vendor does not hope to buy a barrel of apples for $3 and sell them the same day for $300. He expects to make from nothing to $3 a day. He depends upon a small but certain profit, which will average enough over a week or a month to pay him for his time and labor.

This is the objective point of the Tape Reader—to make an average profit. In a month's operations he may make $4,000 and lose $3,000—a net profit of $1,000 to show for his work. If he can keep this average up, trading in 100-share lots, throughout a year, he has only to increase his unit to 200, 300, and 500 shares or more, and the results will be tremendous. The amount of capital or the size of the order is of secondary importance to this question: Can you trade in and out of all kinds of markets and show an average profit over losses, commissions, etc.? If so, you are proficient in the art. If you can trade with only a small average loss per day, or come out even, you are rapidly getting there.

A Tape Reader abhors information and follows a definite and thoroughly tested plan, which, after months and years of practice, becomes second nature to him. His mind forms habits which operate automatically in guiding his market ventures.

Long practice will make the Tape Reader just as proficient in forecasting stock market events, but his intuition will be reinforced by logic, reason and analysis.

Here we find the characteristics which distinguish the Tape Reader from the Scalper. The latter is essentially one who tries to grab a point or two profit "without rhyme or reason"—he don't care how, so long as he gets it.

A Scalper will trade on a tip, a look, a guess, a hearsay, on what he thinks or what a friend of a friend of Morgan's says.

The Tape Reader evolves himself into an automaton which takes note of a situation, weighs it, decides upon a course and gives an order. There is no quickening of the pulse, no nerves, no hopes or fears. The result produces neither elation nor depression. There is equanimity before, during and after the trade.

The Scalper is a bob-tailed car with rattling windows, a jouncing motion and a strong tendency to jump the track.

The Tape Reader is like a Pullman coach, which travels smoothly and steadily along the roadbed of the tape, acquiring direction and speed from the market engine, and being influenced by nothing else whatever.

Having thus described our ideal Tape Reader in a general way, let us inquire into some of the requisite qualifications. First, he must be absolutely self-reliant. A dependent person, whose judgment hangs upon that of others, will find himself swayed by a thousand outside influences. At critical points his judgment will be useless. He must be able to say: "The facts are these; the resulting indications are these; therefore I will do thus and so."

Next he must be familiar with the technicalities of the market, so that every little incident affecting prices will be given due weight. He should know the history, earnings and financial condition of the companies in whose stock he is trading; the ways of the manipulators; the different kinds of markets; be able to measure the effect of news and rumors; know when and in what stocks it is best to trade; measure the forces behind them; know when to cut a loss and take a profit.

He must study the various swings and know where the market and the various stocks stand; must recognize the inherent weakness or strength in prices; understand the basis or logic of movements. He should recognize the turning points of the market; see in his mind's eye what is happening on the floor.

He must have the nerve to stand a series of losses; persistence to keep him at the work during adverse periods; self-control to avoid overtrading; a phlegmatic disposition to ballast and balance him at all times.

For perfect concentration as a protection from the tips, gossip and other influences which abound in a broker's office, he should, if possible, seclude himself. A small room with a ticker, a desk and private telephone connection with his broker's office are all the facilities required. The work requires such delicate balance of the faculties that the slightest influence either way may throw the result against the trader. He may say: "Nothing influences me," but unconsciously it does affect his judgment to know that another man is bearish at a point where he thinks stocks should be bought. The mere thought, "He may be right," has a deterrent influence upon him; he hesitates; the opportunity is lost. No matter how the market goes from that point, he has missed a cog and his mental machinery is thrown out of gear.

Silence, therefore, is a much needed lubricant to the Tape Reader's mind.

The advisability of having even a news ticker in the room, is a subject for discussion. The tape tells the present and future of the market. On the other hand, the news ticker records what *has* happened. It announces the cause for the effect which has already been more or less felt in the market.

Money is made in Tape Reading by anticipating what is coming—not by waiting till it happens and going with the crowd.

The *effect* of news is an entirely different proposition. Considerable light is thrown on the technical strength or weakness of the market and special stocks by their action in the face of important news. For the moment it seems to us that a news ticker might be admitted to the sanctum, provided its whisperings are given only the weight to which they are entitled.

To evolve a practical method — one which *any* trader may use in his daily operations and which those with varying proficiency in the art of Tape Reading will find of value and assistance— such is the task we have set before us in this series.

We shall consider all the market factors of vital importance in Tape Reading, as well as methods used by experts. These will be illustrated by reproductions from the tape. Every effort will be made to produce something of definite, tangible value to those who are now operating in a hit-or-miss sort of way.

Chapter II - Preliminary Suggestions

When embarking on any new enterprise, the first thing to consider is the amount of capital required. To study Tape Reading "on paper" is one thing, but to practice and become proficient in the art is quite another. Almost anyone can make money on imaginary trades, for these require no risk of any kind— the mind is free from the strain which accompanies an actual venture; fear does not enter into the situation; patience is unlimited.

All this is changed when even a small commitment is made. The trader of slight experience suffers mental anguish if the stock does not go his way; he fears a loss, hence his judgment becomes warped, and he closes the trade in order to secure mental relief.

As these are all symptoms of inexperience, they cannot be overcome by avoiding the issue. The business-like thing to do is to wade right into the game and learn to play it under conditions which are to be met and conquered before success can be attained.

After a complete absorption of every available piece of educational writing bearing upon Tape Reading, it is best to commence trading in ten share lots, so as to acquire genuine trading experience. This may not suit some people with a propensity for gambling, and who look upon the ten-share trader as a piker. The average lamb with $10,000 wants to commence with 100 to 500-share lots —he wishes to start at the top and work down. It is only a question of time when he will have to trade in ten-share lots.

To us it seems better to start at the bottom with ten shares. There is plenty of time in which to increase the unit if you are successful. If success is not eventually realized you will be many dollars better off for having risked a minimum quantity.

It has already been shown the *The Magazine of Wall Street* that the market for odd lots on the New York Stock Exchange is most satisfactory, so there is no other excuse for the novice who desires to trade in round lots than greed-of-gain, or get-rich-quick. Think of a baby, just learning to walk, being entered in a race with professional sprinters!

In the previous chapter we suggested that success in Tape Reading should be measured by the number of *points* profit over *points* lost. For all practical purposes, therefore, we might trade in one-share lots, were there no objection on the part of our broker and if this quantity were not so absurdly small as to invite careless execution. Ten shares is really the smallest quantity that should be considered, but we mention one share simply to impress upon our readers that in studying Tape Reading, better keep in mind that you are playing for *points,* not dollars. The dollars will come along fast enough if you can make more points *net* than you lose. The professional billiardist playing for a stake aims to *out-point* his antagonist. After trading for a few months do not consider the dollars you are ahead or behind, but analyze the record in points. In this way your progress may be studied.

As the initial losses in trading are likely to be heavy, and as the estimated capital must be a more or less arbitrary amount, we should say that units of $1,000 would be necessary for each ten-share lot traded in at the beginning. This allows for more losses than profits, and leaves a margin with which to proceed. Some people will secure a footing with less capital; others may be obliged to put up several units of $1,000 each before they begin to show profits; still others will spend a fortune (large or small) without making it pay, or meeting with any encouragement.

Look over R. G. Dun & Co.'s Causes of Commercial Failures, and you will find the chief causes to be: (1) Lack of capital, and (2) Incompetence.

Lack of capital in Wall Street operations can usually be traced to over-trading. This bears out the epigram, "Over-trading is financial suicide." It may mean too large a quantity of stock in the initial operations, or if the trader loses money, he may not reduce the size of his trade to correspond with the shrinkage in his capital.

To make our point clear: A man starts trading in 100-share lots on 20 points margin. After a series of losses he finds that he has only $200 remaining. This is still 20 points on ten shares, but does he reduce his orders? No. He risks the $200 on a 50 or 100-share trade in a last desperate effort to recoup. After being wiped out he tells his friends how he "could have made money if he had had more capital."

Incompetence really deserves first place in the list. Supreme ignorance is the predominant feature of both Wall Street lamb and seasoned speculator. It is surprising how many people stay in the Street year after year, acquiring nothing more, apparently, than a keen scent for tips and gossip. Ask them a technical question that smacks of scientific knowledge of trading and they are unable to reply.

Such folks remain on the Street for one of two reasons: They have either been "lucky" or their margins are replenished from some source outside of Wall Street.

The proportion of commercial failures due to Lack of Capital or Incompetence is about 60 percent. Call the former by its Wall Street cognomen—

Overtrading—and the percentage of stock market disasters traceable thereto would be about 90.

Success is only for the few, and the problem is to ascertain, with the minimum expenditure of time and money, whether you are fitted for the work.

These, in a nutshell, are the vital questions up to this point:

Have you technical knowledge of the market and the factors which move it? Have you $1,000 or more which you can afford to lose in an effort to demonstrate your ability at Tape Reading?

Can you devote your entire time and attention to the study and the practice of this science?

Are you so fixed financially that you are not dependent upon your possible profits, and so that you will not suffer if none are forthcoming now or later? There is no sense in mincing words over this matter, nor in holding out false encouragement to people who are looking for an easy, drop-a-penny-in-the-slot way of making money. Tape Reading is hard work, hence those who are mentally lazy need not apply.

Nor should anyone to whom it will mean worry as to where his bread and butter is coming from. Money-worry is not conducive to clearheadedness. Over-anxiety upsets the equilibrium of a trader more than anything else. So, if you cannot afford the time and money, and have not the other necessary qualifications, do not begin. Start right or not at all.

Having decided to proceed, the trader who is equal to the foregoing circumstances finds himself asking, "Where shall I trade?"

The choice of a broker is an important matter to the Tape Reader. He should find one especially equipped for the work who can give close attention to his orders, furnish quick bid and asked prices, and other technical information, such as the quantities wanted and offered at different levels, etc. The broker most to be desired should never have so much business on hand that he cannot furnish the trader with a verbal flash of what "the crowd" in this or that stock is doing. This is important, for at times it will be money in the pocket to know just in what momentary position a stock or the whole market stands. The broker who is not overburdened with business can give this service; he can also devote time and care to the execution of orders.

Let me give an instance of how this works out in practice: You are long 100 Union, with a stop-order just under the market price; a dip comes and 100 shares sells at your stop price—say 164. Your careful, and not too busy broker stands in the crowd. He observes that several thousand shares are bid for at 164 and only a few hundred are offered at the price. He does not sell the stock, but waits to see if it won't rally. It does rally. You are given a new lease of life. This handling of the order may benefit you $50, $100 or several hundred dollars in each instance, and is an advantage to be sought when choosing a broker.

The house which transacts an active commission business for a large clientele is unable to give this service. Its stop-orders and other orders not "close to the market," must be given to Specialists, and the press of business is such that it cannot devote marked attention to the orders of any one client.

Hence, it would seem that our Tape Reader had better search for a small commission house which has one New York Stock Exchange member, an office partner and only one or two employees.

The number of clerks is a good index to the amount of business done. Their fewness is not a reflection on the strength, standing, or brokerage ability of the house. Some people are good brokers and have ample capital, but they do not understand the science of business getting.

In a small house, such as we have described, the Tape Reader is less likely to be bothered by a gallery of traders, with their diverse and loud-spoken opinions. In other words, he will be left more or less to himself and be free to concentrate upon his task.

The ticker should be within calling distance of the telephone to the Stock Exchange. Some brokers have a way of making you or a clerk walk a mile to give an order. Every step means delay. The elapse of a few seconds may result in a lost market or opportunity. If you are in a small private room away from the order desk, there should be a private telephone connecting you with the order clerk. Ponderous, ice-wagon methods won't go in Tape Reading.

Orders should generally be given "at the market." We make this statement as a result of long experience and observation, and believe we can demonstrate the advisability of it.

The process of reporting transactions on the tape, consumes from five seconds to five minutes, depending upon the activity of the market. For argument's sake, let us consider that the *average* interval between the time a sale takes place on the floor and the report appears on the tape is half a minute.

A market order in an active stock is usually executed and reported to the customer in about two minutes. Half this time is consumed in putting your broker into the crowd with the order in hand; the other half in writing out and transmitting the report. Hence, when Union Pacific comes 164 on the tape and you instantly decide to buy it, the period of time between your decision and the execution of your order is as follows:

Minutes.
The tape is behind the market......1/2....Time elapsed before broker can execute the order is 1.......for a total of 1 1/2 minutes.

It will therefore be seen that your decision is based on a price which prevailed half a minute ago, and that you must purchase if you will, at the price at which the stock stands one minute hence.

This might happen between your decision and the execution of your order:

UP 164   1/8 . 1/4 . 3/8 . 1/2 . 1/4 . 1/8 . 164

and yours might be the last hundred. When the report arrives you may not be able to swear that it was bought at 164 before or after it touched 164 1/4. Or you might get it at 164 1/2, even though it was 164 when you gave the order, and when the report was handed to you.

Just as often, the opposite will take place — the stock will go in your favor. In fact, the thing averages up in the long run, so that traders who do not give market orders are hurting their own chances.

An infinite number of traders, seeing Union Pacific at 164, will say: "Buy me a hundred at 164."

The broker who is not too busy will go into the crowd, and, finding the stock at 164 1/8 at 1/4 will report back to the office that "Union is 1/8 bid."

The trader gives his broker no credit for this service; instead he considers it a sign that his broker, the floor traders and the insiders have all conspired to make him pay 1/4 percent higher for his 100 shares, so he replies:

"Let it stand at 164. If they don't give it to me at that, I won't buy it at all."

How foolish! Yet it is characteristic of the style of reasoning used by the public. His argument is that the stock, for good and sufficient reasons, is a purchase at 164. At 164 1/8 or 1/4 these reasons are completely nullified; the stock becomes dear, or he cares more to foil the plans of this "band of robbers" than for a possible profit.

If a stock is cheap at 164 it's cheap at 164 1/4.

If you can't trust your broker, get another.

If you think the law of supply and demand is altered to catch your $25, better reorganize your thinking.

Were you on the floor you could probably buy at 164 the minute it touched that figure, but of this there is no certainty. You would, however, be 1 1/2 minutes nearer to the market. Your commission charges would also be practically eliminated. Therefore, if you have seventy or eighty thousand dollars which you do not especially need, buy a seat on the Stock Exchange.

A Tape Reader who deserves the name, makes money in spite of commissions, taxes and delays.

If you don't get aboard your train, you'll never arrive.

Giving limited orders loses more good dollars than it saves. We refer, of course, to orders in the big, active stocks, wherein the bid and asked prices are usually 1/8 apart. Especially is this true in closing out a trade. Many foolish people are interminably hung up because they try to save eighths by giving limited orders in a market that is running away from them.

For the Tape Reader there is a psychological moment when he must open or close his trade. His orders must therefore be "at the market." Haggling over fractions will make him lose the thread of the tape, upset his poise and interrupt the workings of his mental machinery.

In scale buying or selling it is obvious that limited orders must be used. There are certain other times when they are of advantage, but as the Tape Reader generally goes with the trend, it is a case of "get on or get left." By all means "get on."

The selection of stocks is an important matter, and should be decided in a general way before one starts to trade. Let us see what we can reason out.

If you are trading in 100-share lots, your stock must move your way one point to make $100 profit.

Which class of stocks are most likely to move a point? Answer: The high-priced issues.

Looking over the records we find that a stock selling around 150 will average 2 1/2 points fluctuations a day, while one selling at 50 will average only one point. Consequently, you have 2 1/2 times more action in the higher priced stock.

The commission and tax charges are the same in both. Interest charges are three times as large, but this is an insignificant item to the Tape Reader who closes out his trades each day.

The higher priced stocks also cover a greater number of points during the year or cycle than those of lower price. Stocks like Great Northern, although enjoying a much wider range, are not desirable for trading purposes when up to 300 or more, because fluctuations and bid and asked prices are too far apart to permit rapid in-and-out trading.

The trend of the general market is largely made by the following stocks, in the order named:

Union Pacific
Reading
Steel Common
St. Paul
Anaconda
Smelters

Union Pacific is a leader because there is a large floating supply, a broad market and wide swings; it is popular with floor traders, big and little. Southern Pacific is its running mate, but owing to the smaller number of shares of the latter afloat, it seldom disputes for the leadership.

Reading's daily swings are on about the same scale as Union Pacific. There is only $70,000,000 of it outstanding. The floating supply is small, owing to the large blocks held by other roads, or by permanent investors. Hence, it is easy to manipulate. The comparative scarcity of the stock is shown in the frequency of fluctuations between sales. It is a very satisfactory stock for Tape Reading operations.

Steel common reflects the five million shares outstanding and the consequent widespread public interest. It is useful as a barometer of the market and of public sentiment, but its swings are rarely wide enough for the Tape Reader, as they average only about a point a day.

St. Paul is one of the truest stocks for trading purposes. It is manipulated at times, but generally it responds automatically to the slightest change in market temper. Its daily movements are not as wide as Union Pacific or Reading.

Anaconda is the leading copper stock, has some satisfactory moves and offers good opportunity for trading.

Smelters is one of the most highly manipulated issues on the list, erratic, often difficult to follow, at other times easy. Its daily range is usually equal to the others. One gets plenty of action in Smelters, but not nearly the steadiness, nor the clearly defined trend prevailing in the other big stocks.

As a result of observation and years of trading experience, we prefer Union Pacific and Reading. These two issues are often the chief hinges on which the door of the market turns—Union the upper, Reading the lower hinge. It is unnecessary for anyone to go beyond these except in times when the industrials dominate the market; in this case, Anaconda, Smelters or Steel will replace them.

It is better for a Tape Reader to trade in one stock than two or more. Stocks have habits and characteristics which are as distinct as those of human beings or animals. By a close study the trader becomes intimately acquainted with these habits and is able to anticipate the stock's action under given circumstances. A stock may be stubborn, sensitive, irresponsive, complaisant, aggressive; it may dominate the tape or trail along behind the rest; it is whimsical and coquettish. Its moods must be studied if you would know it and bend it to your will.

Study implies concentration. A person who trades in a dozen stocks at a time cannot concentrate on one.

The popular method of trading (which means the unsuccessful way) is to say: "I think the market's a sale. Smelters, Copper and St. Paul have had the biggest rise lately; they ought to have a good reaction; sell a hundred of each for me."

Trades based on "thinks" seldom pan out well. The selection of two or three stocks by guesswork, instead of one by reason and analysis, explains many of the public's losses. If a trader wishes to trade in three hundred shares, let him sell that quantity of the stock which he knows most about, or which is entitled to the greatest decline. Unless he is playing the long swing he injures his chances by trading in a lot of stocks at once. It's like chasing a drove of pigs—while you're watching this one the others get away.

Better to concentrate on one or two stocks and study them exhaustively. You will find that what applies to one does not always fit the other: each must be judged on its own merits. The varying price levels, volumes, percentage of floating supply, investment values, the manipulation and other factors, all tend to produce a different combination in each particular case.

Chapter III - The Stock List Analyzed

In the last chapter we referred to Union Pacific as the most desirable stock for active trading. A friend of mine once made a composite chart of the principal active stocks, for the purpose of ascertaining which, in its daily fluctuations, followed the course of the general market most accurately. He found Union Pacific was what might be called the market backbone, while the others, especially Reading, frequently showed erratic tendencies, running up or down, more or less contrary to the general trend. Of all the issues under inspection, none possessed the all-around steadiness and general desirability for trading purposes displayed by Union Pacific.

But the Tape Reader, even if he decides to operate exclusively in one stock, cannot close his eyes to what is going on in others. Frequent opportunities occur elsewhere. In proof of this, take the market in the early fall of

1907: Union Pacific was the leader throughout the rise from below 150 to 167. For three or four days before this advance culminated, heavy selling occurred in Reading, St. Paul, Copper, Steel and Smelters, under cover of the strength in Union. This made the turning point of the market as clear as daylight. One had only to go short of Reading and await the break, or he could have played Union with a close stop, knowing that the whole market would collapse as soon as Union turned downward. When the liquidation in other stocks was completed, Union stopped advancing, the supporting orders were withdrawn, and the "pre-election break" took place. This amounted to over 20 points in Union, with proportionate declines in the rest of the list.

The operator who was watching only Union would have been surprised at this; but had he viewed the whole market he must have seen what was coming. Knowing the point of distribution, he would be on the lookout for the accumulation which must follow, or at least the level where support would be forthcoming. Had he been expert enough to detect this, quick money could have been made on the subsequent rally.

While Union Pacific constitutes the backbone, this important member is only one part of the market body, which after all is very like the physical structure of a human being.

Suppose Union is strong and advancing; suddenly New York Central develops an attack of weakness; Consolidated Gas goes off; American Ice becomes nauseatingly weak; Southern Railway and Great Western follow suit. There may be nothing the matter with the "backbone," but its strength will be affected by weakness among the others.

A bad break may come in Brooklyn Rapid Transit, occasioned by a political attack, or other purely local influence. This cannot possibly affect the business of the grangers, transcontinentals, or coalers, yet St. Paul, Union, and Reading decline as much as B. R. T. A person whose finger is crushed will sometimes faint from the shock to his nervous system, although the injured member will in no wise affect the other members or functions of the body.

The time-worn illustration of the chain which is as strong as its weakest link, will not serve. When the weak link breaks the chain is in two parts, each part being as strong as its weakest link. The market does not break in two, even when it receives a severe blow. If something occurs in the nature of disaster, whereby the money situation, investment demand, public sentiment, or corporate earning power, are deeply affected, a tremendous break may occur, but there is always a level, even in a panic, where buying power becomes strong enough to produce a rally or a permanent upturn.

The Tape Reader must endeavor to operate in that stock which combines the widest swings with the broadest market; he may therefore frequently find it to his advantage to switch temporarily into other issues which seem to offer the quickest and surest profits. Hence it is necessary for us to become familiar with the characteristics of the principal speculative mediums that we may judge their advantages in this respect, as well as their weight and bearing upon a given market situation.

The market is made by the minds of many men. The state of these minds is reflected in the prices of securities in which their owners operate. Let us examine some of the individuals, as well as the influences behind certain stocks and groups of stocks in their various relationships. This will, in a sense, enable us to measure their respective power to affect the whole list or the specific issue in which we decide to operate.

The market leaders are, as already stated, Union, Reading, Steel, St. Paul, Anaconda and Smelters. Manipulators, professionals and the public derive their inspiration largely from the action of these six issues, in which, except during the "war" markets of 1914-16, from forty to eighty percent of the total daily transactions are concentrated. We will therefore designate these as the "Big Six."

Three stocks out of the Big Six are chiefly influenced by the operations of what is known as the Kuhn-Loeb-Standard Oil party. Their four stocks are Union, St. Paul, and Anaconda. Of the other two, Smelters is handled by the Guggenheims, while Steel, controlled by Morgan, is unquestionably swung up and down more by the influence of public sentiment than anything else. Of course the condition of the steel trade forms the basis of important movements in this issue, and occasionally Morgan or some other large interest may take a hand by buying or selling a few hundred thousand shares, but, generally speaking, it is the attitude of the public which chiefly affects the price of Steel common. This should be borne strictly in mind, as it is a valuable guide to the technical position of the market, which turns on the over-bought or oversold condition of the market.

Next in importance come what we will term the Secondary Leaders; viz., those which at times burst into great activity, accompanied by large volume. These are termed Secondary Leaders, because while they seldom influence the Big Six to a marked extent, the less important issues usually fall into line at their initiative.

The principal Secondary Leaders are:
Atchison
Baltimore & Ohio
Brooklyn Rapid Transit
Colorado Fuel
Consolidated Gas
Erie
Great Northern
Northern Pacific
Illinois Central
Louisville & Nashville
Missouri Pacific
Norfolk & Western
New York Central
Pennsylvania
Republic Iron & Steel
Southern Pacific
American Sugar

Another group which we will call the Minor Stocks is comprised of less important issues, mostly low-priced, and embracing many public favorites, such as:

American Car & Foundry
Chesapeake & Ohio
Chicago Great Western
Colorado Southern
Denver & Rio Grande
Interborousjh
Missouri, Kansas & Texas
Ontario & Western
Rock Island
Southern Railway
Wabash

Some people, when they see an advance inaugurated in some of the Minor Stocks, such as Chesapeake & Ohio, Ontario & Western, or Rock Island, are led to buy Pennsylvania, Reading and other Primary or Secondary Leaders, on the ground that the latter will be bullishly affected. This sometimes occurs; more often it does not. It is just as fallacious to expect a 5,000-share operator to follow a 100-share trader, or a 100-share man to be influenced by the 10-share trader.

The various stocks in the market are like a gigantic fleet of boats, all hitched together and being towed by the tugs "Money Situation," and "Business Conditions." In the first row are the Big Six; behind them, the Secondary Leaders, the Minors, and the Miscellaneous issues in the order named. It takes time to generate steam and to get the fleet under way. The leaders are first to feel the impulse; the others follow in turn. Should the tugs halt, the fleet will run along for awhile under its own momentum, and there will be a certain amount of bumping, backing and filling. In case the direction of the tugs is changed abruptly, the bumping is apt to be severe. Obviously, those in the rear cannot gain and hold the leadership without an all-around readjustment.

The Big Six are representative of America's greatest industries—railroading, steel making, and mining. It is but natural that these stocks should form the principal outlet for the country's speculative tendencies. The Union Pacific and St. Paul systems cover the entire West. Reading, of itself a large railroad property, dominates the coal mining industry; it is so interlaced with other railroads as to typify the Eastern situation. Steel is closely bound up with the state of general business throughout the states, while Anaconda and Smelters are the controlling factors in copper mining and the smelting industry.

By classifying the principal active stocks we can recognize more clearly the forces behind their movements. For instance, if Consolidated Gas suddenly becomes strong and active, we know it will probably affect Brooklyn Union Gas, but there is no reason why the other Standard Oil stocks should advance more than slightly and out of sympathy. If all the stocks in the Standard Oil group advance in a steady and sustained fashion, we know that these capitalists are engaged in a bull campaign. As these people do not enter deals for a few points it is safe to go along with them for awhile, or until distribution becomes apparent.

An outbreak of speculation in Colorado Fuel is not necessarily a bull argument on the other Steel stocks. If it were based on trade conditions, U. S. Steel would be the first to feel the impetus, which would radiate to the others.

In selecting the most desirable stock out of the Kuhn-Loeb-Standard Oil group, for instance, the Tape Reader must consider whether conditions favor the greatest activity and volumes in the railroad or industrial field. In the former case, his choice would be Union Pacific or St. Paul; in the latter, Anaconda.

Erie may come out of its rut (as it did during the summer of 1907, when it was selling around 24), and attain leadership among the low-priced stocks. This indicates some important development in Erie; it does not foreshadow a rise in all the low-priced stocks. But if a strong rise starts in Union Pacific, and Southern Pacific and the others in the group follow consistently, the Tape Reader will get into the leader and stay with it. He will not waste time on Erie, for while it is moving up 5 points, Union Pacific may advance 10 or 15 points, provided it is a genuine move. Many valuable deductions may be made by studying these groups.

Experience has shown that when a rise commences in Atchison (a Secondary Leader), the Big Six is about done and distribution is taking place, under protection of the strength in Atchison and others in its class. Sugar acts in a similar capacity for the Standard Oil group. Professional traders used to call these stocks "Indicators."

The absence of inside manipulation in a stock leaves the way open for pools to operate, and many of the moves that are observed in these groups are produced by a handful of floor or office operators, who, by joining hands and swinging large quantities, are able to force their stock in the desired direction.

U. S. Steel is swayed by conditions in the steel trade, and the speculative temper of the general public, assisted occasionally by some of the insiders. No other stock on the list is such a true index of the attitude of the public, or the technical position of the market. Including those who own the stock outright, and those who carry it on margin, probably a quarter of a million people here and abroad closely follow its movements. Reports of the steel trade are most carefully scrutinized, and the corporation's earnings and orders on hand minutely studied by thousands.

This great public rarely sells its favorite short, but carries it "paid for," or on margin until a profit is secured, or until it is shaken or scared out in a violent decline. Hence, if the stock is strong under adverse news, we may infer that public holdings are strongly fortified, and that confidence abounds. If Steel displays more than its share of weakness, an untenable position of the public is indicated.

The other steel stocks are dominated by the giant corporation, and do not often furnish indications of value to Tape Readers, except at the end of a long rise.

At this point public sentiment becomes intensely bullish and spreads itself in the low-priced speculative shares. Insiders in the junior steel stocks take advantage of this and are able to advance and find a good market for their holdings.

The Equipment Stocks find their chief inspiration in the orders for cars, locomotives, etc., placed by the railroads. These orders are dependent upon general business conditions. Consequently the equipment issues can seldom be expected to do more than follow the trend of prosperity or depression.

We should thus introduce ourselves to the principal speculative mediums and their families, each of which, upon closer acquaintance, seems to have a sort of personality. If we stand in a room with fifty or a hundred people, all of whom we know, as regards their chief motives and characteristics, we can form definite ideas as to their probable actions under a given set of circumstances.

So it becomes the Tape Reader to acquaint himself with the most minute details pertaining to these market identities, also with the habits, motives and methods of the men who make the principal moves on the Stock Exchange chess-board.

Chapter IV - Stop Orders, Trading Rules, &c.

When a person contemplates an extensive trip, one of the first things taken into account is the expense involved. In planning our excursion into the realms of Tape Reading we must, therefore, carefully weigh the expenses, or fixed charges in trading.

Were there no expenses, profit-making would be far easier—profits would merely have to exceed losses. But no matter whether you are a member of the New York Stock Exchange or not, in actual trading profits must exceed losses *and expenses.* These are incurred in every trade, whether it shows a gain or a loss. They consist of:

Commission on 100 shares...... ....…....$25.00
"Invisible eighth" 12.50
(Difference between bid and asked price, assuming that you buy and sell at the market price.)
Tax on sale 2.00
$39.50

in addition to interest if the trade is carried over night.

By purchasing a New York Stock Exchange seat, the commission can be reduced to $1 per hundred shares, if bought and sold the same day, or $3.12 if carried over night. This advantage is partly offset by interest on the cost of the seat, dues, assessments, etc., which amount to nearly $5,000 per annum on a seat costing $75,000.

The "invisible eighth" is a factor which no one—not even a member—can overcome. The bid and asked price is never less than an eighth apart. If the market be 45 1/4 @ 3/8 when you buy, you will as a rule, pay 3/8. Were you to sell it would be at 1/4. This hypothetical difference follows you all through the trade and has been designated by the writer as the "invisible eighth."

The Tape Reader who is a non-member must, therefore, realize that *the instant he gives an order* to go long or short 100 shares, *he has lost* $39.50. In order that he may not fool himself, he should add his commissions (1/4) to his purchase price, or deduct them from his selling price *immediately.* People who boast of their profits usually forget to deduct expenses. Yet it is this insidious item which frequently throws the net result over to the debit side.

The expression is frequently heard, "I got out even, except the commissions," the speaker evidently scorning such a trifling consideration. This sort of self-deception is ruinous, as will be seen by computing the fixed charges on 10 trades —$395—or on 20 trades—$790. Bear in mind that a loss of $39.50 on the first trade leaves double that amount—$79— to be made on the second trade before a dollar of profit is secured.

It therefore appears that the Tape Reader's problem is not only to eliminate losses, but to cover his expenses as quickly as may be. If he has a couple of points profit in a long trade, there is no reason why he should let the stock run back below his net buying price. Here circumstances seem to call for a stop order, so that no matter what happens, he will not be compelled to pay out money. This stop should not be thrust in when net cost is too close to the market price. Reactions must be allowed for.

A Tape Reader is essentially one who follows the immediate trend. An expert can readily distinguish between a change of trend and a reaction. When his mental barometer indicates a change he does not wait for a stop order to be caught, but cleans house or reverses his position in a twinkling. The stop order at net cost is, therefore, of advantage only in case of a reversal which is sudden and pronounced.

A stop should also be placed if the operator is obliged to leave the tape for more than a moment, or if the ticker gets out of order. While he has his eye on the tape the market will tell him what to do. The moment this condition does not exist he must act as he would if temporarily stricken blind—he must protect himself from forces which may assail him in the dark.

I know a trader who once bought 500 shares of Sugar and then went out to lunch. He paid 25 cents for what he ate, but on returning to the tape he found that the total cost of that lunch was $5,000.25. He had left no stop order, Sugar went down ten points, and his broker wore a MM (more margin button) in his lapel.

The ticker has a habit of becoming incoherent at the most critical points. Curse it as we may, it will resume printing intelligibly when the trouble is overcome—not before. As the loss of even a few inches of quotations may be important, a stop should be placed at once and left in until the flow of prices is resumed.

If a trade is carried over night, a stop should be entered against the possibility of accident to the market or the trader. An important event may develop before the next day's opening by which the stock will be violently affected. The trader may be taken ill, be delayed in arrival, or in some way be incapacitated. A certain allowance must be made for accidents of every kind.

As to where the stop should be placed under such conditions, this depends upon circumstances. The consensus of shrewd and experienced traders is in favor of two points maximum gross loss on any one trade. This is purely arbitrary, however. The Tape Reader knows, as a rule, what to do when he is at the tape, but if he is separated from the market by any contingency, he will be obliged to fall back upon the arbitrary stop.

A closer stop may be obtained by noting the "points of resistance"—the levels at which the market turns after a reaction. For example, if you are short at 130 and the stock breaks to 128, rallies to 129, and then turns down again, the point of resistance is 129. In case of temporary absence or interruption to the service, a good stop would be 129 1/8 or 129 1/4. These "points of resistance" will be more fully discussed later.

If the operator wishes to use an automatic stop, a very good method is this: Suppose the initial trade is made with a one-point stop. For every 1/8 the stock moves in your favor, change the stop to correspond, so that the stop is never more nor less than one point away from the extreme market price. This gradually and automatically reduces the risk, and if the Tape Reader be at all skilful, his profits must exceed losses. As soon as the stop is thus raised to cover commissions, it would seem best not to make it automatic thereafter, but let the market develop its own stop or "signal" to get out.

One trouble with this kind of a stop is that it interferes with the free play of judgment. A homely illustration will explain why: A tall woman and a short man attempt to cross the street. An automobile approaches. The woman sees that there is ample time in which to cross, but he has her by the arm and being undecided himself backs and fills, first pushing, then pulling her by the arm until they finally return to the curb, after a hairbreadth escape. Left to herself, she would have known exactly what to do.

It is the same with the Tape Reader. He is hampered by an automatic stop. It is best that he be free to act as his judgment dictates, without feeling compelled by a prior resolution to act according to hard and fast rule.

There is another time when the stop order is of value to the Tape Reader, viz., when his indications are not clearly defined. The original commitment should, of course, be made only when the trend is positively indicated, but situations will develop when he will be uncertain whether to stand pat, close out, or reverse his position. At such a time it seems better to push the stop up to a point as close as possible to the market price, without choking off the trade. By this we mean a reasonable area should be allowed for temporary fluctuations. If the stock emerges from its uncertainty by going in the desired direction, the stop can be changed or cancelled. If its trend becomes adverse, the trade is automatically closed.

Fear, hesitation and uncertainty are deadly enemies of the Tape Reader. The chief cause of fear is over-trading. Therefore commitments should be no greater than can be borne by one's susceptibility thereto.

Hesitation must be overcome by self training. To observe a positive indication and not act upon it is fatal—more so in closing than in opening a trade. The appearance of a definite indication should be immediately followed by an order. Seconds are often more valuable than minutes. The Tape Reader is not the captain—he is but the engineer who controls the machinery. The Tape is the pilot and the engineer must obey orders with promptness and precision.

We have defined a Tape Reader as one who follows the immediate trend. This means that he pursues the line of least resistance. He goes with the market—he does not buck it. The operator who opposes the immediate trend pits his judgment and his hundred or more shares against the world's supply or demand and the weight of its millions of shares. Armed with a broom, he is trying to stay the incoming tide.

When he goes *with* the trend, the forces of supply, demand and manipulation are working for and with him.

A market which swings within a radius of a couple of points cannot be said to have a trend, and is a good one for the Tape Reader to avoid. The reason is: Unless he catches the extremes of the little swings, he cannot pay commissions, take occasional losses and come out ahead. No yacht can win in a dead calm. As it costs him nearly half a point to trade, each risk should contain a probable two to five points profit, or it is not justified.

A mechanical engineer, given the weight of an object, the force of the blow which strikes it, and the element through which it must pass, can figure approximately how far the object will be driven. So the Tape Reader, by gauging the impetus or the energy with which a stock starts and sustains a movement, decides whether it is likely to travel far enough to warrant his going with it—whether it will pay its expenses and remunerate him for his boldness.

The ordinary tip-trading speculator gulps a point or two profit and disdains a loss, unless it is big enough to strangle him. The Tape Reader must do the opposite—he must cut out every possible eighth loss and search for chances to make three, five and ten points. He does not have to grasp everything that looks like an opportunity. It is not necessary for him to be in the market continuously. He chooses only the best of what the tape offers.

His original risks can be gradually effaced by clever arrangement of stop orders when a stock goes his way. He may keep these in his head or put them on the "floor." For my own part I prefer, having decided upon a danger point, to maintain a mental stop and when the price is reached close the trade "at the market." Reason: There may be ground for a change of plan or opinion at the last moment; if a stop is on the floor it takes time to cancel or change it, hence there is a period of a few minutes when the operator does not know where he stands. By using mental stops and market orders he always knows where he stands, except as regards the prices at which his orders are executed. The main consideration is, he knows whether he is in or out.

The placing of stops is most effectual and scientific when indicated by the market itself. An example of this is as follows:

Stop Orders, Trading, Rules, etc.

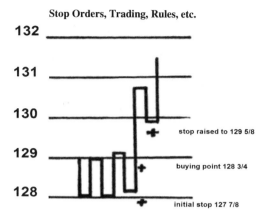

Here a stock gives a buying indication at 128 3/4. Obviously, if the indication be true, the price will not again break 128, having met buying sufficiently strong to turn it up twice from that figure and a third time from 128 1/8. The fact that it did not touch 128 on the last down swing forecasts a higher up swing; it shows that the downward pressure was not so strong and the demand slightly more urgent. In other words, the point of resistance was raised 1/8. Having bought at 128 3/4, the stop is placed at 127 7/8, which is 1/4 below the last point of resistance.

The stock goes above its previous top (129 1/8) and continues to 130 3/4. At any time after it has crossed 130 the operator may raise his stop to cost plus commission (129). The stock reacts at 129 7/8, then continues the advance to above 131. As soon as a new high point is reached the stop is raised to 129 5/8, as 129 7/8 was the point of resistance on the dip.

In such a case the initial risk was 7/8 plus commissions, etc., the market giving a well deemed stop point, making an arbitrary stop not only unnecessary but expensive. The illustration is given in chart form, but the experienced Tape Reader generally carries these swings in his head. A series of higher tops and bottoms are made in a pronounced up swing and the reverse in a down swing.

Arbitrary stops may be used at any time, especially if one wishes to clinch a substantial profit, but until a stock gets away from the price at which it was entered, it seems best to use the stops it develops for itself.

If the operator is shaken out of his holdings immediately after entering the trade, it does not prove his judgment in error. Some accident may have happened, some untoward development in a particular issue, of sufficient weight to affect the rest of the list. It is these unknown quantities that make the limitation of losses most important. In such a case it would be folly to change the stop so that the risk is increased. This, while customary with the public, is something a Tape Reader seldom does. Each trade is made on its own basis, and for certain definite reasons. At the outset the amount of risk should be decided upon, and, except in very rare instances, should not be changed, except on the side of profit. The Tape Reader must eliminate, not increase his risk.

Averaging does not come within the province of the Tape Reader. Averaging is groping for the top or bottom. The Tape Reader must not grope. He must see and know, or he should not act.

It is impossible to fix a rule governing the amount of profit the operator should accept. In a general way, there should be no limit set as to the profits. A deal, when entered, may look as though it would yield three or four points, but if the strength increases with the advance it may run ten points before there is any sign of a halt.

We wish our readers to bear fully in mind that these recommendations and suggestions are not to be considered final or inflexible. It is not our aim to assume the role of an oracle. Rather, we are reasoning things out on paper, and as we progress in these studies and apply these tentative rules to the tape, in actual or paper trading, we shall probably have occasion to modify some of our conclusions.

A Tape Reader must close a trade

(1) when the tape tells him to close;

(2) when his stop is caught;

(3) when his position is not clear;

(4) when he has a large or satisfactory profit.

The first and most important reason for closing a trade is: The tape says so. This indication may appear in various forms. Assuming that one is trading in a leader like Union Pacific or Reading, the warning may come in the stock itself. Within the ribbon of sales recorded on the tape, there runs the fine silken thread of the trend. It is clearly distinguishable to one sufficiently versed in the art of Tape Reading, and, for reasons previously explained, is most readily observed in the leaders. Hence, when one is short of Union Pacific and this thread suddenly indicates that the market has turned upward, it is folly to remain short. Not only must one cover quickly, but if the power of the movement is sufficient to warrant the risk, the operator must go long. In a market of sufficient breadth and swing, the Tape Reader will find that when it is time to close a trade, it is usually time to reverse his position. One must have the flexibility of whalebone, and entertain no rigid opinion. He must obey the tape implicitly.

The indication to close a trade may come from another stock, several stocks or the general market. For example, on the day of the Supreme Court decision in Consolidated Gas, suppose the operator was long of Union Pacific at 11 o'clock, having paid therefore 182 3/4.

Between 11 and 12 o'clock Union rallied to 183 1/2, and Reading, which was more active, to 144. Just before, and immediately after, the noon hour, tremendous transactions took place in Reading, over 50,000 shares changing hands within three-quarters of a point. These may have been largely wash sales, accompanied by inside selling; it is impossible to tell. If they were not, the inference is that considerable buying power developed in Reading at this level and was met by selling heavy enough to supply all bidders and prevent the stock advancing above 144 3/8. Large quantities coming within a small range indicated either one of two things: (1) That considerable buying power suddenly developed at this point, and the insiders chose to check it or to take advantage of the opportunity to unload. (2) The demonstration in Reading may have been intended to distract attention from other stocks in which large operators were unloading. (There was no special evidence of this, except in New York Central.)

If the selling was not sufficient to check the upward move, the market for Reading would have absorbed all that was offered and advance to a higher level, but in this case the selling was more effectual than the buying, and Reading fell back, warning the operator that the temporary leader on the bull side of the market had met with defeat.

If a stock or the whole market cannot be advanced, the assumption is that it will decline—a market seldom stands still. At this point the operator was, therefore, on the lookout for a slump.

Reading subsided, in small lots, back to 143 7/8. Union Pacific, after selling at 183 5/8, declined to 183 1/4. Both stocks developed dullness, and the whole market became more or less without feature.

Suddenly Union Pacific came 183 1/8 500.183,200.182 7/8,500.3/4, indicating not only a lack of demand, but remarkably poor support. Immediately following this, New York Central, which sold only a few minutes before 400.131 1/2 came 131,1700.130 1/4.500.130. This demonstrated that the market was remarkably hollow and in a position to develop great weak-ness. The large quantities of New York Central at the low figure, after a running decline of a point and one-half, showed that there was not only an absence of supporting orders, but that sellers were obliged to make great concessions in order to dispose of their holdings. The quantities, especially in view of the narrowness of the market, proved that the sellers were not small fry.

Coupled with the wet blanket put on Reading and the poor support in Union Pacific, this weakness in New York Central was another advance notice of a decline. On any indication of this kind, the operator must be ready to jump out of his long stock and get short of the market.

While waiting for his cue, the Tape Reader has time to consider which stock among the leaders is the most desirable for selling. He quickly chooses Reading, on the ground that the large lots which have apparently been distributed around 144 will probably come into the market as soon as weakness develops. Reason: The outside public generally buys on just such bulges as the one which has taken place in Reading. A large volume, even if accompanied by only a fractional advance, has the effect of making the ordinary trader intensely bullish, the result being that he bites off a lot of long stock at the top of the bulge. This is exactly what the manipulator wishes him to do. We have all heard people boast that their purchase was at the top eighth and that it had the effect of turning the stock down Those who make their purchases after this fashion are quickest to become scared at the first appearance of weakness, and throw overboard what they have bought. In choosing Reading, therefore, the

Tape Reader is picking out the stock in which he is likely to have the most help on the bear side.

At 12.30 the market is standing still, the majority of transactions being in small lots and at only fractional changes. Reading shows the effect of the recent unloading. It is coming out 500.143 3/4,500.5/8,400.1/2,3/4. The operator realizes that Reading is probably a short sale right here, with a stop order at 144 1/2 or 5/8 on the ground that the bulls must have an extraordinary amount of buying power to push the stock above its former top, where, at every eighth advance over 144 3/8, they will encounter a considerable portion of 50,000 shares. This reasoning, however, is all aside from our main argument, which is to show how the cue to get out will be given by stocks other than that in which the operator is working.

Union Pacific shows on the tape in small lots at 182 3/4; New York Central 1100.130,900.3/8. The rest of the market seems to have all the snap and ginger taken out of it and the operator does not like his position on the long side. He has no definite indication to sell short, however, but feeling that his chances on the long side have been reduced to practically nil by the weak undertone of the market, he therefore gets out of his Union Pacific and waits until the tape tells him to sell Reading short.

Union Pacific weakens to 182 5/8. The others slide off fractionally. The weakness is not positive enough to forecast any big break, so he continues to wait. There are 1800 shares of Union altogether at 182 5/8, followed by 3000 at 182 1/2. Other stocks respond and the market looks more bearish.

Consolidated Gas comes 163 3/4.1/4.163. This is the first sign of activity in the stock, but the move is nothing unusual for Gas, as its fluctuations are generally wide and erratic. The balance of the list rallies a fraction. Gas comes 162 1/2.3/4.500.162 1/4. At this point Gas, which has been very dull heretofore, now forces itself, by its decline and weakness, upon the notice of the operator. He begins to look upon the stock as the possible shears which will cut the thread of the market and let everything down.

12.45— Gas 500.161 1/2. It is very weak. The balance of the list is steady, Union Pacific 182 5/8, Central 130 3/8, Reading 143 3/4. There is a fractional rally — Union Pacific to 182 7/8 and Gas to 162. Plenty of Central for sale around 130; Reading is 143 1/2.

The rally peters out. There is a gradual weakening all around, but the Tape Reader cannot go with the trend until he is sure of a big swing. Central comes 129 3/4, showing that after all the buyers at 130 are filled up considerable stock is still for sale. The others show only in small lots. The market is on the verge of a decline; it is where a jar of any sort will start it down. Union Pacific is heavy at 182 1/2.300.3/8.200.1/2, Reading 143 1/2.3/8.1000 1/2, Central 2000.130.800.1/8.

Here is the thrust he has been looking for! Gas 163 3/4.200.1/2.400.-161.300. 160 1/2.400.160! He waits no longer, but gives an order to sell Reading short at the market. They are all on the run now, Reading 143 1/2.600.3/8. 1300.1/4. Central 130.129 1/2, Gas 500,159 1/2. Something very rotten about Gas and it's a cinch to sell it short if you don't mind trading in a buzzsaw stock.

The market breaks so rapidly that he does not get over 142 3/4 for his Reading, but he is short not far from the top of what looks like a wide open break.

Everything is slumping now—Steel, Smelters, Southern Pacific, St. Paul. Union Pacific is down to 181 5/8, and the rest in proportion.

Gas 158 1/2.158.300.157.156.155.154.153 and the rest "come tumbling after." Reading 141 3/8.500. 1/4.400.141.140 3/4. 500.1/2.200.-140.600.139 3/4.500.5/8. Union 181.180 7/8.3.4.1/2.1/4.600.1/8.500.180.-179 ¾.500.-1/2.300.1/4, Central 127 1/2.

The above illustrates some of the workings of a Tape Reader's mind; also how a break in a stock, entirely foreign to that which is being traded in, will furnish the indication to get out and go short of one stock or another. The indication to close a trade may come from the general market where the trend is clearly developed throughout the list, all stocks working in complete harmony. One of the best indications in this line is the strength or weakness on rallies and reactions.

Of course the break in Gas, which finally touched 138, was due to the Supreme Court decision, announced on the news tickers at 1.10 p. m., but, as is usually the case, the tape told the news many minutes before anything else. This is one of the advantages of getting your news from the first place where it is reflected. Other people who wait for such information to sift through telephone and telegraph wires and reach them by the roundabout way of news tickers or word of mouth, are working under a tremendous handicap.

That not even the insiders knew what the decision was to be is shown in the dullness of the stock all morning. Those who heard the decision in the Supreme Court chamber doubtless did the double-quick to the telephone and sold the stock short. Their sales showed on the tape before the news arrived in New York. Tape Readers were, therefore, first to be notified. They were short before the Street knew what had happened.

Chapter V - Volumes and Their Significance

As the whole object of these studies is to learn to read what the tape says, I will now explain a point which should be known and understood before we proceed, otherwise the explanations cannot be made clear. First of all, we must recognize that the market for any stock—at whatever level it may be—is composed of two sides, represented by the bid and the asked price. Remember that the "last sale" is something entirely different from the "market price." If Steel has just sold at 50, this figure represents what *has* happened. It is history. The *market price* of Steel is either 49 1/8@50 or 50@50 1/8. The bid and asked prices *combined* form the market price.

This market price is like a pair of scales, and the volume of stock thrown out by sellers and reached for by purchasers, shows toward which side the preponderance of weight has momentarily shifted. For example, when the tape shows the market price is 50@1/8. and the large volumes are on the up side.

US   500 . 50 . 1000 . 1/8 . 50 . 1500 . 1/8

In these four transactions there are 700 shares sold at 50 against 2500 taken at 50 1/8, proving that *at the moment* the buying is more effective than the selling. The deduction to be made from this is that Steel will probably sell at 50 1/4 before 49 7/8. There is no certainty, for supply and demand is changing with every second, not only in Steel but in every other stock on the list.

Here is one advantage in trading in the leaders. The influence of demand or pressure is first evidenced in the principal stocks. The hand of the dominant power, whether it be an insider, an outside manipulator or the public, is shown in these volumes. The reason is simple. The big fellows cannot put their stocks up or down without trading in large amounts. In an advancing market they are obliged to reach up for or bid up their stocks, as, for example:

U   182 . 1000 . 1/8 . 1/8 . 200 . 182 . 1500 . 1/8 . 200.1/4
3500 . 3/8 . 2000 . 1/2

Take some opening trades and subsequent transactions like the following:

Volumes and Their Significance

200.....47 1/4	100.....45 7/8	100.....45 7/8
1900...46 3/4	100.....46 1/8	100.....46
100.....46 5/8	100.....46	600.....45 7/8
100.....46 1/2	200.....46 1/4	500.....45 3/4
100.....46 3/8	100.....46 3/8	200.....45 5/8
600.....46 1/4	11 A.M.	100.....45 1/2
100.....46 1/4	300.....46 3/8	100.....45 5/8
600.....46	100.....46 1/8	400.....45 7/8
100.....45 7/8	100.....46	100.....45 3/4
200.....45 3/4	100.....45 7/8	400.....45 5/8
100.....46	100.....46	100.....45 3/4

Here the opening market price was 46 3/4 @ 47 1/4, and the buyers of 200 shares "at the market" paid the high price. All bids at 46 3/4 were then filled. This is proved by the next sale, which is at 46 5/8. The big lots thereafter are mostly on the down side, showing that pressure still existed. The indications were, therefore, that the stock would go lower. A lot of 1900 shares in some stocks would be a large quantity; in others insignificant. These points have a relative value with which traders must familiarize themselves.

Volumes must be considered in proportion to the activity of the market, as well as the relative activity of that particular issue. No set rule can be established. I have seen a Tape Reader make money by following the lead of a 1000-share lot of Northwest which someone took at a fraction above the last sale. Ordinarily Northwest is a sluggish investment stock, and this size lot appeared as the forerunner of an active speculative demand. Now let us see what happens on the floor to produce the above-described effect on the tape.

Let us prove that our theory is correct. A few years ago the control of a certain railroad was being bought on the floor of the New York Stock Exchange. One house was given all the orders, with instructions to distribute them and conceal the buying as much as possible. The original order for the day would read, "Take everything that is offered up to 38." As 38 was about 3 points above the market of the day before, this left considerable leeway for the broker to whom the buying order was entrusted.

He would instruct his floor broker as follows: "The stock closed last night at 35. You take everything offered up to 35 1/2 and then report to me how things stand. Don't bid for the stock; just take it as it is offered and mark it down whenever you can."

In such a case the floor member stands in the crowd awaiting the opening. On the instant of ten o'clock the chairman's gavel strikes and the crowd begins yelling. Someone offers "Two thousand at an eighth." Another broker says "Thirty-five for five hundred." Our broker takes the 2000 at 1/8 then offers one hundred at one-eighth himself, so as to keep the price down. Others also offer one or two hundred shares at 1/8 so he withdraws his offer, as he wishes to accumulate and only offers or sells when it helps him buy more, or puts the price down. The buyer at 35 has 300 shares of his lot cancelled, so he alters his bid to "thirty-five for two hundred." The other sellers supply him and he then bids 7/8 for a hundred." Our broker sells him 100 at 7/8 just to get the price down Someone comes in with "a thousand at five." Our broker says, "I'll take it." Five hundred more is offered at 1/8. This he also takes.

Let us see how the tape records these transactions :

2000 . 35 1/8 . 200 . 35 . 34 7/8 . 1000 . 35 . 500 . 1/8

The Tape Reader interprets this: Opening bid and asked price was 35@ 1/8; someone took the large lot at the high price. The two sales following were in small lots, showing light pressure. The 1000@35 after 34 7/8 shows that on the 7/8@5 market the buyer took the stock at the offered price and followed it up by taking 500 more at the eighth. The demand is dominant and it does not matter whether the buyer is one individual or a dozen, the momentary trend is upward.

To get the opposite side, let us suppose that a manipulator is desirous of depressing a stock. This can be accomplished by offering and selling more than there is a demand for, or by coaxing or frightening other holders into throwing over their shares. It makes no difference whose stock is sold; "The Lord is on the side of the heaviest battalions," as Addison Cammack used to say. When a manipulator puts a broker into a crowd with orders to mark it down, the broker supplies all bids and then offers it down to the objective point or until he meets resistance too strong for him to overcome without the loss of a large block of stock.

The stock in question is selling around 80, we will say, and the broker's orders are to "put it to 77." Going into the crowd, he finds 500 wanted at 79

7/8 and 300 offered at 80. Last sale, 100 at 80. "I'll sell you that five hundred at seven-eighths. A thousand or any part at three-quarters," he shouts.

"I'll take two hundred at three-quarters," says another broker. "A half for five hundred," is heard. "Sold!" is the response. "A half for five hundred more." "Sold!" "That's a thousand I sold you at a half. Five hundred at three-eighths!"

"I'll take a hundred at three-eighths," comes a voice.
"You're on!" is the reply. "Quarter for five hundred." "Sold!" is the quick response. His pounding of the stock would reveal itself on the tape as follows:

---

80 . 500 . 79 7/8 . 200 . 3/4
1000 . 1/2 . 3/8 . 500 . 1/4

If he met strong resistance at 79 it would appear on the tape something like this.

---

79 1/8 . 1000 . 79 . 500 . 79 . 800 . 79 . 300
1/8 . 1000 . 79 . 500 . 1/4 . 3/8 . 200 . 1/2

---

showing that at 79 there was a demand for more than he was willing to supply. (There might have been 10,000 shares wanted at 79.)

Frequently a broker meeting such an obstacle will leave the crowd long enough to phone his principal. His departure opens the way for a rally, as the stock is no longer under pressure, and the large buying order at 79 acts as a back lo for floor traders. So those in the crow bid it up to 1/2 in hopes of scalping fraction on the long side.

Take another case where two broker are put into the crowd — one to depress the stock and the other to accumulate it. They play into each other's hands, and the tape makes the following report of what happens:

---

80 1/8 . 80 . 200 . 79 7/8 . 3/4 . 1000 . 7/8
3/4 . 200 . 5/8 . 500 . 3/4 . 300 . 3/4 . 1/2
3/8 . 1500 . 1/2 . 3/8 . 500 . 1/4 . 1/8

Were we on the floor we should see one broker offering the stock down, while the other grabbed every round lot that appeared. We cannot tell how far down the stock will be put, but when these indications appear it makes us watch closely for the turning point, which is our time to buy.

The Tape Reader does not care whether a move is made by a manipulator, a group of floor traders, the public or a combination of all.

The figures on the tape represent the consensus of opinion, the effect of manipulation and the supply and demand, all combined. That is why tape indications ire more reliable than what *anyone* hears, knows or thinks.

With the illustration of the pair of scales clearly implanted in our minds, we scan the tape, mentally weighing each indication in our effort to learn on which side the tendency is strongest. Not a detail must escape our notice. A sudden demand or a burst of liquidation may enable us to form a new plan, revise an old one or prompt us to assume a neutral attitude.

These volume indications are not always clear. Nor are they infallible. It does not do to rely upon the indications of any one stock to the exclusion of the rest. There are times when certain stocks are rushed up, while volume indications in other active stocks show clearly that they are being distributed as fast as the market will take them. This happens frequently on a large or small scale. Especially is it apparent at the turning point of a big swing, where accumulation or distribution requires some days to complete.

Volumes can be studied from the reports printed in the New York *Evening Sun* or the *Wall Street Journal,* but the real way to study them is from the tape. If one is unable to spend five hours a day at the tape while the ticker is in operation, he can arrange with one of the boys in his broker's office to wind the tape up each day and save it for him. This is done most expeditiously by using an automatic reel, which can be had a any electrical supply store. The tape can then be taken home and studied a leisure. A second reel in the study make it easy to unwind, after which the tape can be made to run across one's desk just as though it were coming from the ticker.

In studying under these conditions do not let yourself be deceived as to your ability to make money on paper. Imaginary trades prove nothing. The way to test your powers is to get into the game. Let it be on as small a scale as you like, but make actual trades with real money.

There are times when the foregoing rule of volumes indicates almost the reverse of what we have explained. On of these instances was described in our last chapter. In this case the transactions

700...143 5/8	2200...144 1/8
500...143 3/4	3500...144 1/4
5000..143 5/8	4000...144 3/8
1700..143 3/4	3000...144 1/4
200....143 5/8	2500...144 1/8
4300..143 3/4	3500...144
3700..143 7/8	400.....144 1/8
100...144	1000...144
12 P.M.	500.....144 1/8
5000..144	1100...144
1300..143 7/8	2000...143 7/8
3000..144	2500...143 3/4
5000..144 1/8	1000...143 5/8
2100..144 1/4	

Turning point in Reading, morning of Jan. 4, 1909 – the day of the Consolidated Gas collapse

in Reading suddenly swelled out of all proportion to the rest of the market and its own previous volume. Not withstanding the predominance of apparent demand, the resistance offered (whether legitimate or artificial) became too great for the stock to overcome, and it fell back from 144 3/8. On the way up these volumes suggested a purchase, shut the tape showed abnormal transactions, accompanied by poor response from the rest of the list. This smacked of manipulation and warned the operator to be cautious on the bull side. The large volume in Reading was sustained even after the stock reacted, but the large lots were evidently thrown over at the bid prices. On the way up the volumes were nearly all on the up side and the small lots on the down side. After 144 3/8 was reached the large lots were on the down side and the small lots on the up.

It is just as important to study the small as the large lots. The smaller quantities are like the feathers on an arrow—they indicate that the business part of the arrow is at the other end. In other words, the smaller lots keep one constantly informed as to what fraction forms the other side of the market. To illustrate: During the first five trades in Reading, recorded above, the market quotation is shown to have been 5/8@3/4; it then changed to 3/4@7/8 and again to 7/8@4. On the way down it got to be 4@1/8, and at this level the small lots were particularly valuable in showing the pressure which existed.

Stocks like Union, Reading and Steel usually make this sort of a turning point on a volume of from 25,000 to 50,000 shares. That is, when they meet with opposition on an advance or a decline it must be in some such quantity in order to stem the tide.

Walk into the hilly country and you will find a small rivulet running quietly on its way. The stream is so tiny that you can place your hand in its course and the water will back up. In five minutes, it overcomes this resistance by going over or around your hand. You fetch a shovel, pile dirt in its path, pack it down hard and say, "There, I've dammed you." But you haven't at all, for the next day you find your pile of dirt washed away. You bring cartloads of dirt and build a substantial dam, and the flow is finally held in check.

It is the same with an individual stock or the market. Prices follow the line of least resistance. If Reading is going up someone may throw 10,000 shares in its path without perceptible effect. Another lot of 20,000 shares follows; the stock halts, but finally overcomes the obstacle. The seller gives another order—this time 30,000 shares more are thrown on the market. If there are 30,100 shares wanted at that level, the buyer will absorb all of the 30,000 and the stock will go higher; if only 29,000 shares are needed to fill all bids, the price will recede because demand has been overcome by supply.

It looks as though something like this happened in Reading on the occasion referred to. Whether or not manipulative orders predominated does not change the aspect of the case. In the final test the weight was on the down side.

The public and the floor traders do not stand aside while the manipulator is at work, nor is the reverse true. Everybody's stock looks alike on the tape.

When a stream breaks through a dam it goes into new territory. Likewise the breaking through of a stock is significant, for it means that the resistance has been overcome. The stronger the resistance the less likelihood of finding further obstacles in the immediate vicinity. Dams are not usually built one behind the other. So when we find a stock emerging into a new field it is best to go with it, especially if, in breaking through it, it carries the rest of the market along.

While much can be learned from the reports printed in the dailies mentioned above, the tape itself is the only real instruction book. A live tape is to be preferred, for the element of speed with which the ticker prints is no small factor.

The comparative activity of the market on bulges and breaks is a guide to the technical condition of the market. For instance, during a decline, if the ticker is very active and the volume of sales large, voluntary or compulsory liquidation is indicated. This is emphasized if, on the subsequent rally, the tape moves sluggishly and only small lots appear. In an active bull market the ticker appears to be choked with the volume of sales poured through it on the advances, but on reactions the quantities and the number of impressions decrease until, like the ocean at ebb tide, the market is almost lifeless.

Another indication of the power of a movement is found in the differences between sales of active stocks, for example:

1000 . 180 . 1/8 . 500 . 3/8 . 1000 . ½

This shows that there was only 100 shares for sale at 180 1/4, none at all at 180 1/4, and only 500 at 180 3/8. The jump from 1/8 to 3/8 emphasizes both the absence of pressure and persistency on the part of the buyers. They are not content to wait patiently until they can secure the stock at 180 1/4; they "reach" for it. On the opposite side this would show lack of support.

Each indication is to be judged not so much by rule as according to the conditions surrounding it. The tape furnishes a continuous series of motion pictures, with their respective explanations written between the printings. These are in a language which is foreign to all but Tape Readers.

Warning

A number of people who have read previous editions of this book have been misled by the apparent ease with which some kinds of markets may be read by means of the volumes. They have erroneously come to the conclusion that all one has to do is sit beside a ticker and observe which side the volumes are on—the buying or the selling side.

This is a great mistake. Owing to changes in the rules of the New York Stock Exchange since the original issue of this book appeared, the value of these volume indications is not as great as before. Under the old rule a buyer who desired to influence the market in an upward direction could bid for 10,000 shares or any other very large quantity, and no one could sell, him any less than the quantity bid for, unless the buyer was willing to take it. Under the present rules, the buyer is obliged to take any part of 10,000 shares, or whatever quantity he bid for.

This revision of the rules, and the other restrictions against matched orders, manipulations, etc., eliminates a very large number of transactions in big quantities at the advanced or the decreased price. It was an old trick of Harriman's and some of the old Standard Oil party, as well as other minor manipulators and floor traders, to make these bids and offers in round lots and have some one else supply or take them for its effect on the market. But the change in the rules has greatly reduced the volume and decreased the value of these indications. Hence, while they are still very suggestive to an observant tape reader, and while the principle is unchanged, it will not do to depend on them entirely.

The volumes which we have been discussing are least liable to mislead when manipulation prevails, for the manipulator is obliged to deal in large blocks of stock, and must continually show his hand. A complete manipulative operation on the long side consists of three parts: (1) Accumulation, (2) marking up, and (3) distribution. In the case of a short operation the distribution comes first, then the mark down and the accumulation. No one of these three sections is complete without the other two. (For full details see my series on Manipulations in Vols. 1 and 2 of *The Magazine of Wall Street.*)

The manipulator must work with a large block of stock or the deal will not be worth his time, the risk and expenses. The Tape Reader must, therefore, be on the lookout for extensive operations on either side of the market. Accumulation will show itself in the quantities and in the way they appear on the tape. Having detected the accumulation, the Tape Reader has only to watch its progress, holding himself in readiness to take on some of the stock the moment the marking-up period begins. He does not buy it at once, because it may take weeks or months for the manipulator to complete his line, and there might be opportunities to buy cheaper. By holding off until the psychological moment he forces someone else to carry the stock for him —to pay his interest. Furthermore, his capital is left free in the meantime.

When the marking up begins he gets in at the commencement of the move, and goes along with it till there are signs of a halt or distribution. Having passed through the first two periods, he is in a position to fully benefit by the third stage of the operation. In this sort of work a figure chart, which I described in another chapter, will help him, especially if the manipulative operation is continued over a considerable period. It will give him a bird's-eye view of the deal, enabling him to drop or resume the thread at any stage.

Chapter VI - Market Technique

On Saturday morning, February 27, 1909, the market opened slightly higher than the previous night's close. Reading was the most active stock. After touching 123 1/2 it slid off to 122 1/2, at which point it invited short sales. This indication was emphasized at 122, at 121 1/2 and again at 121. The downward trend was strongly marked until it struck 119 7/8; then followed a quick rally of 1 1/8 points.

This was a vicious three-point jab into a market which was only just recovering from the February break. What was its effect on the other principal stocks? Union Pacific declined only 3/4, Southern Pacific 5/8 and Steel 5/8. This proved that they were technically strong; that is, they were in hands which could view with equanimity a three-point break in a leading issue. Had this drive occurred when Reading was around 145 and Union 185 the effect upon the others would probably have been very different.

In order to determine the extent of an ore body, miners use a diamond drill. This produces a core, the character of which shows what is beneath the surface. If it had been possible to have drilled into the market at the top of the foregoing rise, we should have found that the bulk of the floating supply in Steel, Reading and some others was held by a class of traders who buy heavily in booms and on bulges. These people operate with comparatively small margins, nerve and experience. They are exceedingly vulnerable, hence the stocks in which they operate suffer the greatest declines when the market receives a jar. The figures are interesting.

	1907-9 Advance.	Points Feb'y, '09 Break.	Percent of break To adv.
U. P....................	84 7/8	12 3/8	14.7
Reading..............	73 7/8	26 3/8	33.6
Steel...................	36 7/8	16 1/2	44.6

The above shows that the public was heavily extended in Steel, somewhat less loaded with Reading, and was carrying very little Union Pacific. In other words, Union showed technical strength by its resistance to pressure, whereas Reading and Steel offered little or no opposition to the decline.

Both the market as a whole and individual stocks are to be judged as much by what they *do* as what they *do not* do at critical points. If the big fellows who accumulated Union below 120 had distributed it above 180, the stock would have broken something like thirty points, owing to its having passed from strong to weak hands. As it did not have any such decline, but only a very small reaction compared to its advance, the Tape Reader infers that Union is destined for much higher prices; that it offers comparative immunity from declines and a possible large advance in the near future.

Even were Union Pacific scheduled for a thirty-point rise in the following two weeks, something might happen to postpone the campaign for a considerable time. But the Tape Reader must work with these broader considerations in full view. He has just so much time and capital, and this must be employed where it will yield the greatest results. If by watching for the most favorable opportunities he can operate with the trend in a stock which will some day or week show him ten points profit more than any other issue he could have chosen, he is increasing his chances to that extent.

A long advance or decline usually culminates in a wide, quick movement in the leaders. Take the break of February 23, 1909: Reading declined from 128 3/4 to 118 and Steel from 46 to 41 1/4 in one day. Southern Pacific, after creeping up from 97 to 112, reached a climax in a seven-point jump during one session. Instances are so numerous that they are hardly worth citing. The same thing happens in the market as a whole —an exceptionally violent movement, after a protracted sag or rise, usually indicates its culmination.

N.Y.STOCK.EXCHANGE.FEB.20.1909

US.OPND	TO
12000.47 5/8	47 7/8

A stock generally shows the Tape Reader what it proposes to do by its action under pressure or stimulation. For example: On Friday, February 19, 1909, the United States Steel Corporation announced an open market in steel products. The news was out. Everybody in the country knew it by the following morning. The Tape Reader, in weighing the situation before the next day's opening, would reason: "As the news is public property, the normal thing for Steel and the market to do is to rally. Steel closed last night at 48 3/8. The market hinges upon this one stock. Let's see how it acts."

The opening price of U. S. Steel, as shown by these reproductions of the original tape, was three-quarters of a point down from the previous closing— a perfectly natural occurrence in view of the announcement. The real test of strength or weakness will follow. For the first ten minutes Steel shows on the tape:

200 . 47 7/8 . 4500 3/4 . 1200 . 7/8 . 1500 . 3/4

without otherwise varying.

Eighteen times the price swings back and forth between the same fractions. Meantime, Union Pacific, which opened at 177 1/2, shows a tendency to rally and pull the rest of the market up behind it.

U						
1200 . 178 . 200 . 1/8 . 400 . 1/4 . 200 . 178 1/4 . 700 . 3/8

Can Union lift Steel? That is the question. Here are two opposing forces, and the Tape Reader watches like a hawk, for he is "going with the market" —in the direction of the trend. Union is up from the opening and Southern Pacific is reinforcing it.

U	AR	SP
500 . 178 3/8	84 5/8	118 3/8 . 500 1/2

But Steel does not respond. Not once does it get out of that 3/4-7/8 rut— not even a single hundred shares sells at 48. This proves that it is freely offered at 47 7/8 and that it possesses no rallying power, in spite of the leadership displayed by the Harriman's.

U	SP	US
500 . 178 3/8	200 3/4 . 118 1/2	1500 . 47 3/4

Union seems to make a final effort to induce a following:

U
2000 . 178 1/8

To which Steel replies by breaking through with a thud.

US
800 . 47 5/8 . 1/2

This is the Tape Reader's cue to go short. In an instant he has put out a line of Steel for which he gets 47 1/2 or 47 3/8, as there are large volumes traded in at those figures.

Union Pacific seems disheartened. The Steel millstone is hanging round its neck. It slides off to 178 3/4.1/4.1/8 and finally to

U	C	CO	US
600 . 178 . 400 . 177 7/8	300 . 73 1/8	66	200 . 47 1/2

The pressure on Steel increases at the low level.

US	NP	US
3500 . 47 1/2	48 . 1 . 103 1/2	47 3/8

Successive sales are made, as follows.

6800 . 47 1/2 . 2600 . 3/8 . 500 . 1/4 . 8800

From this time on there is a steady flow of long stock all through the list. Reading and Pennsylvania are the weakest railroads. Colorado Fuel breaks seven points in a running decline and the other steel stocks follow suit. U. S. Steel is dumped in bunches at the bid prices, and even the dignified preferred is sympathetically affected.

US	PR
500 . 46 5/8 . 3500 1/2	200 . 110 1/4 . 200 1/8 . 1600 . 110

At the end of the two-hour session, the market closes at the bottom, with Steel at 46, leaving thousands of accounts weakened by the decline and a day ahead for holders to worry over.

It looks to the Tape Reader as though the stock would go lower on the following Tuesday. At any rate, no covering indication has appeared, and unless it is his invariable rule to close every trade each day, he puts a stop at 47 on his short Steel and goes his way. (His original stop was 48 1/8.)

Steel opens on the following session at 44 3/4@1/2, and during the day makes a low record of 41 1/4.

A number of lessons may be drawn from this episode: Successful tape reading is a study of Force; it requires ability to judge which side has the greatest pulling power and one must have the courage to go with that side. There are critical points which occur in each swing, just as in the life of a business or of an individual. At these junctures it seems as though a feather's weight on either side would determine the immediate trend. Any one who can spot these points has much to win and little to lose, for he can always play with a stop placed close behind the turning point or "point of resistance."

If Union had continued in its upward course, gaining in power, volume and influence as it progressed, the dire effects of the Steel situation might have been overcome. It was simply a question of power, and Steel pulled Union down.

This study of responses is one of the most valuable in the Tape Reader's education. It is an almost unerring guide to the technical position of the market. Of course, all responses are not clearly defined.

It is a matter of indifference to the Tape Reader as to who or what produces these tests, or critical periods. They constantly appear and disappear: he must make his diagnosis and act accordingly. If a stock is being manipulated higher, the movement will seldom be continued unless other stocks follow and support the advance unless follow and support the advance barring certain specific developments affecting of a stock, the other issues should be watched to see whether large operators are unloading on the strong spots. Should a stock fail to break on bad news, it means that insiders have anticipated the decline and stand ready to buy.

A member of a syndicate once said to me:

"We are going to dissolve tomorrow."

I asked, "Will there not be considerable selling by people who don't want to carry their share of the securities?"

"Oh!" he replied, "we know how every one stands. Probably 10,000 shares will come on the market from a few members who are obliged to sell, and as a few of us have sold that much short in anticipation, we'll be there to buy it when the time comes."

This reminds us that it is well to consider the insider's probable attitude on a stock. The tape usually indicates what this is. One of the muckraking magazines once showed that Rock Island preferred had been driven down to 28 one August, to the accompaniment of receivership rumors. The writer of the article was unable to prove that these rumors originated with the insiders, for he admitted that the transactions at the time were inscrutable. Perhaps they were inscrutable to a person inexperienced in tape reading, but we well remember that the indications were all in favor of buying the stock on the break. The transactions were very large—out of all proportion to the capital stock outstanding and the floating supply. What did this mean to the Tape Reader? Thousands of shares of stock were traded in per day, after a ten-point decline and a small rally. If the volume of sales represented long stock, some one was there to buy it. If there was manipulation it certainly was not for the purpose of distributing the stock at such a low level. So, by casting out the unlikely factors, a tape reader could have arrived at the correct conclusion. The market is being put to the test continually by one element of which little has been said, viz., the floor traders. These shrewd fellows are always on the alert to ferret out a weak spot in the market, for they love the short side. Lack of support, if detected, in an issue generally leads to a raid which, if the technical situation be weak, spreads to other parts of the floor and produces a reaction or a slump all around. Or, if they find a vulnerable short interest, they are quick to bid up a stock and drive the shorts to cover. With these and other operations going on all the time, the Tape Reader who is at all expert is seldom at a loss to know on which side his best chances lie. Other people are doing for him what he would do himself if he were all-powerful.

While it is the smaller swings that interest him most, the Tape Reader must not fail to keep his bearings in relation to the broader movements of the market. When a panic prevails he recognizes it in the birth of a bull market and operates with the certainty that prices will gradually rise until a boom marks the other extreme of the swing. In a bull market he considers reactions of from two to five points normal and reasonable. He looks for occasional drops of 10 to 15 points in the leaders, with a 25-point break at least once a year. When any of these occur, he knows what to look for next.

In a bull market he expects a drop of 10 points to be followed by a recovery of about half the decline, and if the rise is to continue, all of the drop and more will be recovered. If a stock or the market refuses to rally naturally, he knows that the trouble has not been overcome, and therefore looks for a further decline.

Take American Smelters, which made a top at 99 5/8 a few years ago, then slumped off under rumors of competition until it reached 78. Covering indications appeared around 79 1/2. Had the operator also gone long here, he could confidently have expected Smelters to rally to about 89. The decline having been 21 5/8 points, there was a rally of 10 3/4 points due. As a matter of record the stock did recover to 89 3/8.

Of course, these things are mere guide posts, as the Tape Reader's actual trading is done only on the most positive and promising indications; but they are valuable in teaching him what to avoid. For instance, he would be wary about making an initial short sale of Smelters after a 15-point break, even if his indications were clear. There might be several points more on the short side, but he would realize that every point further decline would bring him closer to the turning point, and after such a violent break the safest money was on the long side.

Another instance: Reading sold on January 4, 1909, at 144 3/8. By the end of the month it touched 131 1/2, and on February 23d broke ten points to 118. This was a decline of 24 3/8 points, allowing for the 2 percent dividend. As previously stated, the stock looked like an attractive short sale, not only on the first breakdown, but on the final drive. The conservative trader would have waited for a buying indication, as there I would have been less risk on the long side.

It is seldom that the market runs more than three or four consecutive days in one direction without a reaction, hence the Tape Reader must realize that his chances decrease as the swing is prolonged.

The daily movements offer his best opportunities; but he must keep in stocks which swing wide enough to enable him to secure a profit. As Napoleon said: "The adroit man profits by everything, neglects nothing which may increase his chances."

I once knew a speculator who bought and sold by the clock. He had no idea of the hourly swing, but would buy at 12 o'clock, because it was 12 o'clock, and would sell at 2 o'clock, for the same reason.

The methods employed by the average outside speculator are not so very much of an improvement on this, and that is why so many lose their money.

The expert Tape Reader is diametrically opposed to such people and their methods.

He applies science and skill in his angling for profits.

He studies, figures, analyzes and deduces. He knows exactly where he stands, what he is doing and why.

Few people are willing to go to the very bottom of things. Is it any wonder that success is for the few?

VII - Dull Markets and Their Opportunities

Many people are apt to regard a dull market as a calamity. They claim: "Our hands are tied; we can't get out of what we've got; if we could there'd be no use getting in again, for whatever we do we can't make a dollar."

Such people are not Tape Readers. They are Sitters. They are Billikens ex-grin.

As a matter of fact, dull markets offer innumerable opportunities and we have only to dig beneath the crust of prejudice to find them.

Dullness in the market or in any special stock means that the forces capable off influencing it in either an upward or a downward direction have temporarily come to a balance. The best illustration is that of a clock which is about run down—its pendulum gradually decreases the width of its swings until it comes to a complete standstill, thus:

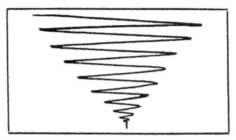

How the market pendulum comes to a standstill

Turn this diagram sideways and you see what the chart of a stock or the market looks like when it reaches the point of dullness.

These dull periods often occur after a season of delirious activity on the bull side. People make money, pyramid on their profits and glut themselves with stocks at the top. As every one is loaded up, there is comparatively no one left to buy, and the break which inevitably follows would happen if there were no bears, no bad news or anything else to force a decline.

Nature has her own remedy for dissipation. She presents the debauche with a thumping head and a moquette tongue. These tend to keep him quiet until the damage can be repaired. So with these intervals of market rest. Traders who have placed themselves in a position to be trimmed are duly trimmed. They lose their money and temporarily, their nerve. The market, therefore, becomes neglected. Extreme dullness sets in.

If the history of the market were to be written, these periods of life-lessness should mark the close of each chapter. The reason is: The factors which were active in producing the main movement, with its start, its climax and its collapse, have spent their force. Prices, therefore, settle into a groove, where they remain sometimes for weeks or until affected by some other powerful influence.

When a market is in the midst of a big move, no one can tell how long or how far it will run. But when prices are stationary, we know that *from this point* there will be a pronounced swing in one direction or another.

There are ways of anticipating the direction of this swing. One is by noting the technical strength or weakness of the market, as described in a previous chapter. The resistance to pressure mentioned as characteristic of the dull period in March, 1909, was followed by a pronounced rise, leading stocks selling many points higher. This was particularly true of Reading, in which the shakeouts around 120 (one of which was described) were frequent and positive. When insiders shake other people out it means that they want the stock themselves. These are good times for us to get in. for then we will enjoy having Mr. Frick and his friends work for *us*.

When a dull market shows its inability to hold rallies, or when it does not respond to bullish news, it is technically weak, and unless something comes along to change the situation, the next swing will be downward.

On the other hand, when there is a gradual hardening in prices; when bear raids fail to dislodge considerable quantities of stock; when stocks do not decline upon unfavorable news, we may look for an advancing market in the near future.

No one can tell when a dull market will merge into a very active one; therefore the Tape Reader must be constantly on the watch. It is foolish for him to say: "The market is dead dull. No use going downtown today. The leaders only swung less than a point yesterday. Nothing in such a market."

Such reasoning is apt to make one miss the very choicest opportunities, viz., those of getting in on the ground floor of a big move. For example: During the aforesaid accumulation in Reading, the stock ranged between 120 and 124 1/2. Without warning, it one day gave indication (around 125) that the absorption was about concluded, and the stock had begun its advance. The Tape Reader having reasoned beforehand that this accumulation was no piker's game, would have grabbed a bunch of Reading as soon as the indication appeared. He might have bought more than he wanted for scalping purposes, with the intention of holding part of his line for a long swing, using the rest for regular trading.

As the stock drew away from his purchase price he could have raised his stop on the lot he intended to hold, putting a mental label on it to the effect that it is to be sold when he detects inside distribution. Thus he stands to benefit to the fullest extent by any manipulative work which may be done. In other words, he says: "I'll get out of this lot when Mr. Frick and his friends get out of theirs."

He feels easy in his mind about this stock, because he has seen the accumulation and knows it has relieved the market of all the floating supply at about this level.

This means a sharp, quick rise sooner or later, as little stock is to be met with on the way up. If he neglected to watch the market continuously and get in at the very start, his chances would be greatly lessened. He might not have the courage to take on the larger quantity.

On Friday, March 26, 1909, Reading and Union were about as dull as two gentlemanly leaders could well be. Reading opened at 132 3/4, high was 133 1/4, low 132 1/4, last 132 5/8. Union's extreme fluctuation was 5/8—from 180 5/8 to 181 1/4. Activity was confined to Beet Sugar, Kansas City Southern, etc.

The following day, Saturday, the opening gave every indication that the previous day's dullness would be repeated, initial sales showing only fractional changes. B. & O., Wabash pfd. and Missouri Pacific were up 3/8 or 1/2. Union was 1/8 higher and Reading 1/8 lower. Beet Sugar was down 5/8, with sales at 32.

Reading showed 1100 . 132 1/2 . 800 . 3/8 , Union 800 . 181 . 400 . 181 . 200 . 1/8 . 400 . 181. A single hundred Steel at 15 1/8. B. & O. 109 7/8 . 3/4. Reading 132 1/2. Beet Sugar 31 3/4 . 400 . 7/8. Union 800 . 180 7/8. Steel 1000 . 45. Beet 800 . 32. Steel 1500 . 45. Reading 132 5/8. Steel 44 7/8. Market dead. Mostly 100-share lots.

Reading 1600 . 132 1/2. Steel 400 . 45. Beet Sugar looks good on the bull side, 300 . 32 1/4 . 700 . 3/8. Union 200 . 180 7/8. Reading 500 . 132 3/8. Union 300 . 180 3/4.

10.15 a. m.—American Sugar now responds slightly to the strength in Beet Sugar. Sugar 200 . 130 7/8 . 600 . 131. Beet 32 1/2 . 600 . 5/8. This stock holds the spotlight. Others inanimate.

Ah! Here's our cue! Reading 2300 . 132 1/2 . 2000 . 1/2. 500 . 5/8. Coming out of a dead market, quantities like these taken at the offered prices can mean only one thing, and without quibbling the Tape Reader takes on a bunch of Reading "at the market."

Whatever is doing in Reading, the rest of the market is slow to respond, although N. Y. Central seems willing to help a little—500 . 127 1/2 (after 1/4). Beets are up to 33 1/4. Steel is 45 1/8, and Copper 71 1/4—a fraction better.

Reading 300. 132 1/4. Steel 1300 . 45 1/8 . 1/4, Union 181. Reading 300 . 132 5/8. Beets 33 1/2. Union 700 . 181 1/8. N. Y. Central 127 5/8 . 600 . 3/4 . 7/8. There's some assistance!

Union 900 . 181 1/8. Reading 132 3/4. Copper 700 . 71 1/2. Reading 800 . 132 7/8 . 133 . 900 . 133 . 1100 . 1/8. Central 300 . 127 3/4. Union 400 . 181 1/8 . 300 . 1/4. Reading 1500 . 133 1/4 . 3500 . 1/2. Not much doubt about the trend now. The whole market is responding to Reading, and there is a steady increase in power, breadth and volume. The rapid advances show that short covering is no small factor. Union 400 . 181 3/8 . 700 . 1/2 . 400. 5/8.

It looks as though a lot of people are throwing their Beet Sugar and getting into the big stocks. St. Paul Copper and Smelters begin to lift a little.

Around 11 a. m. there is a brief period of hesitation, in which the market seems to take a long breath in preparation for another effort. There is scarcely any reaction and no weakness. Reading backs up a fraction to 133 1/4 and Union to 181 3/8. There are no selling indications, so the Tape Reader stands by his guns.

Now they are picking up again— Reading 133 3/8 . 1/2 5/8 . 3/4. Union 181 5/8. N. Y. Central 128 1/8 . 700 . 1/4. Atchison 1000 . 104 1/2 . 600 . 5/8. Northern Pacific 141 1/2 . 5/8. Union 1000 . 181 1/2. 3500 . 5/8 . 2800 . 3/4 . 2800 . 7/8 . 4100 . 182. Steel 45 1/2. Southern Pacific 121. St. Paul 146. Reading 2100 . 133 7/8 . 1100 . 134 . 1700 . 1/8.

From then right up to the close it's nothing but hull, and everything close within a fraction of its highest. Reading makes 134 3/8, Union 183, Steel 46 1/8, Central 128 7/8, and the rest in proportion. The market has gained such headway that it will take dire news to prevent a high, wide opening on Monday, and the Tape Reader has his choice of closing out at the high point or putting in a stop and taking his chances over Sunday.

So we see the advantage of watching a dull market and getting in the moment it starts out of its rut. One could almost draw lines on the chart of a leader like Union or Reading (the upper line being the high point of its monotonous swing and the lower line the low point) and buy or sell whenever the line is crossed. For when a stock shakes itself loose from a narrow radius it is clear that the accumulation or distribution or resting spell has been completed and new forces are at work. These forces are most pronounced and effective at the beginning of the new move — more power is needed to start a thing than to keep it going.

Some of my readers may think I am giving illustrations after these things happen on the tape, and that what a Tape Reader *would have done* at the time is problematical. I therefore wish to state that my tape illustrations are taken from the indications which actually showed themselves when they were freshly printed on the tape, at which time I did not know what was *going* to happen.

There are other ways in which a trader may employ himself during dull periods. One is to keep tab on the points of resistance in the leaders and play on them for fractional profits. This, we admit, is a rather precarious occupation, as the operating expenses constitute an extremely heavy percentage against the player, especially when the leading stocks only swing a point or so per day.

But if one chooses to take these chances rather than be idle, the best way is to keep a chart on which should be recorded every 1/8 fluctuation. This forms a picture of what is occurring and clearly defines the points of resistance, as well as the momentary trend. In the following chart the stock opens at 181 1/4 and the first point of resistance is 181 1/2. The first indication of a downward trend is shown in the dip to 181 1/8, and with these two straws showing the tendency, the Tape Reader goes short "at the market," getting, say, 181 1/8 (we'll give ourselves the worst of it).

After making one more unsuccessful attempt to break through the resistance at 181 1/2, the trend turns unmistakably downward, as shown by an almost unbroken series of lower tops and bottoms.

Dull markets and their opportunities

Chart showing points of resistance in a dull market

These indicate that the pressure is heavy enough to force the price to new low levels, and at the same time it is sufficient to prevent the rally going quite as high as on the previous bulge.

At 180 1/8 a new point of resistance appears. The decline is checked. The Tape Reader must cover and go long. The steps are now upward and as the price approaches the former point of resistance he watches it narrowly for his indication to close out. This time, however, there is but slight opposition to the advance, and the price breaks through. He keeps his long stock.

In making the initial trade he placed a "double" stop at 181 5/8 or 3/4, on the ground that if his stock overcame the resistance at 181 1/2 it would go higher and he would have to go with it. Being short 100 shares, his double stop order would read: "Buy 200 at 181 5/8 stop." Of course the price might just catch his stop and go lower. These things will happen, and anyone who cannot face them without becoming perturbed had better learn self control.

After going long around the low point, he should place another double stop at 180 or 179 7/8, for if the point of resistance is broken through after he has covered and gone long, he must switch his position in an instant. Not to do so would place him in the attitude of a guesser. If he is playing on this plan he must not dilute it with other ideas.

Remember this method is only applicable to a very dull market, and, as we have said, is precarious business. We cannot recommend it. It will not as a rule pay the Tape Reader to attempt scalping fractions out of the leaders in a dull market. Commissions, tax stamps and the invisible eighth, in addition to frequent losses, form too great a handicap. There must be wide swings if profits are to exceed losses, and the thing to do is, wait for good opportunities. "The market is always with us" is an old and true saying. We are not compelled to trade and results do not depend on *how often* we trade, but on *how much money* we make.

There is another way of turning a dull market to good account, and that is by trading in the stocks which are temporarily active, owing to manipulative or other causes. The Tape Reader does not care a picayune what sort of a label they put on the goods. Call a stock "Harlem Goats preferred" if you like, and make it active, preferably by means of manipulation, and the agile Tape Reader will trade in it with profit. It matters not to him whether it's a railroad or a shooting gallery; whether it declares regular or "Irish" dividends; whether the abbreviation is X Y Z or Z Y X—so long as it furnishes indications and a broad market on which to get in and out.

Take Beet Sugar on March 26, 1909, the day on which Union and Reading were so dull. It was easy to beat Beet Sugar. Even an embryo Tape Reader would have gone long at 30 or below, and as it never left him in doubt he could have dumped it at the top just before the close, or held it till next day, when it touched 33 1/2.

American Beet Sugar

Am. Beet Sugar	100.................30	1000.............30 3/4
700.................29 1/4	600.................30 1/2	700.................30 7/8
200.................29 3/8	100.................30 5/8	600.................31
900.................29 1/4	400.................30 1/2	600.................31 1/8
500.................29 3/8	**11 A.M.**	300.................31 1/4
700.................29 1/2	200.................30 1/2	200.................31 3/8
200.................29 5/8	400.................30 5/8	100.................31 1/4
900.................29 3/4	900.................30 3/4	400.................31 3/8
1100.............29 7/8	100.................30 5/8	400.................31 1/2
1000..............30	200.................30 1/2	100.................31 5/8
500.................30 1/8	200.................30 3/8	200.................31 3/8
100.................30 1/4	100.................30 1/2	200.................31 1/2
100.................30 3/8	100.................30 3/8	300.................31 1/4
100.................30 1/4	600.................30 1/2	200.................31 5/8
600.................30 3/8	500.................30 3/8	200.................31 1/2
1100.............30 1/2	500.................30 1/2	200.................31 5/8
400.................30 3/8	100.................30 3/8	300.................31 1/2
100.................30 1/4	100.................30 1/4	**2 P.M.**
700.................30 3/8	100.................30 3/8	100.................31 5/8
100.................30 1/2	**12 P.M.**	700.................31 3/4
200.................30 3/8	200.................30 3/8	700.................31 7/8
1300.............30 1/4	700.................30 1/8	400.................32
200.................30 3/8	100.................30 5/8	600.................32 1/4
300.................30 1/2	**1 P.M.**	600.................32 1/8
400.................30 5/8	200.................30 3/4	400.................32 1/4
100.................30 3/4	100.................32 5/8	800.................32 1/8
100.................30 5/8	500.................30 1/2	1000.............32 1/4
100.................30 1/2	200.................30 5/8	200.................32 3/8

On March 5, 1909, Kansas City Southern spent the morning drifting between 42 3/4 and 43 1/2. Shortly after the noon hour the stock burst into activity and large volume. Does any sane person suppose that a hundred or more people became convinced that Kansas City Southern was a purchase at that particular moment? What probably started the rise was the placing of manipulative orders, in which purchases predominated. Thus the sudden activity, the volume and the advancing tendency gave notice to the Tape Reader to "get aboard." The manipulator showed his hand and the Tape Reader had only to go along with the current.

Kansas City Southern

500.............43 1/4	200.............43	200.............43
100.............43 3/8	500.............43 1/4	100.............42 7/8
10..............43 1/2	400.............43 1/8	600.............43
200.............43 3/8	100.............43	25..............43 1/4
200.............43 1/2	100.............43 7/8	100.............43 1/4
100.............43 3/8	200.............43 3/4	100.............43 3/8
100.............43 1/2	400.............43	300.............43 1/4
100.............43 1/4	300.............43 7/8	500.............43 1/8
200.............43 1/8	100.............43 3/4	100.............43 1/4
500.............43	**11 A.M.**	400.............43 3/8
200.............43 1/8	800.............44 1/4	900.............44 3/4
12 P.M.	400.............44	500.............45
100.............43 3/8	**1 P.M.**	1800............44 7/8
500.............43 1/2	200.............44 1/4	300.............44 5/8
100.............43 5/8	800.............44 3/8	**2 P.M.**
400.............43 3/4	100.............44 1/4	200.............44 1/2
200.............43 7/8	300.............44 3/8	100.............44 3/8
1200............43 3/4	600.............44 1/2	1000............45 1/2
400.............43 7/8	100.............44 3/8	300.............45 5/8
2300............44	700.............44 1/2	600.............45 1/2
1300............44 1/8	600.............44 5/8	100.............45 3/8
1400............44 1/4	800.............44 3/4	500.............45 1/2
400.............44 3/8	200.............44 5/8	1200............46 5/8
1500............44 1/4	300.............44 3/4	200.............46 3/4
400.............44 1/8	200.............44 5/8	100.............46 5/8
1800............44	300.............44 3/4	700.............46 3/4
200.............44 1/8	700.............44 7/8	400.............46 3/4

The advance was not only sustained, but emphasized at certain points. Here the Tape Reader could have pyramided, using a stop close behind his average cost and raising it so as to conserve profits. If he bought his first lot at 44, his second at 45, and his third at 46, he could have thrown the whole at 46 5/8 and netted $406.50 for the day if he were trading in 100-share units, or $2,032.50 if trading in 500-share units.

Chapter VIII - The Use of Chart as Guides and Indicators

Many interesting queries have been received by THE MAGAZINE OF WALL STREET relating to the use of charts. The following is a representative communication:

Referring to your figure chart explained in Volume 1 of the Magazine of Wall Street, I have found it a most valuable aid to detecting accumulation or distribution in market movements. I have been in Wall Street a number of years, and like many others have always shown a skeptical attitude toward charts and other mechanical methods of forecasting trends; but after a thorough trial of the chart on Union Pacific, I find that I could have made a very considerable sum if I had followed the indications shown. I note your suggestions to operators to study earnings, etc., and not to rely on charts, as they are very often likely to mislead. I regret that I cannot agree with you. You have often stated that the tape tells the story; since this is true, and a chart is but a copy of the tape, with indications of accumulation or distribution, as the case may be, why not follow the chart entirely, and eliminate all unnecessary time devoted to study of earning, etc?

Let us consider those portions of the above which relate to Tape Reading, first clearly defining the difference between chart operations and tape reading.

The genuine chart player usually operates in one stock at a time, using as a basis the past movements of that stock and following a more or less definite code of rules. He treats the market and his stock as a machine. He uses no judgment as to market conditions, and does not consider the movements of other stocks; but he exercises great discretion as to whether he shall "play" an indication or not.

The Tape Reader operates on what the tape shows *now*. He is not wedded to any particular issue, and, if he chooses, can work without pencil, paper or memoranda of any sort. He also has his code of rules—less clearly defined than those of the chart player. So many different situations present themselves that his rules gradually become intuitive—a sort of second nature evolved by self-training and experience.

A friend to whom I have given some points in Tape Reading once asked if I had my rules all down so fine that I knew just which to use at certain moments. I answered him thus: When you cross a street where the traffic is heavy, do you stop to consult a set of rules showing when to run ahead of a trolley car or when not to dodge a wagon? No. You take a look both ways and at the proper moment you walk across. Your mind may be on something else but your judgment tells you when to start and how fast to walk. That is the position of the trained Tape Reader.

The difference between the Chart Player and the Tape Reader is therefore about as wide as between day and night. But there are ways in which the Tape Reader may utilize charts as guides and indicators and for the purpose of reinforcing his memory.

The Figure Chart is one of the best mechanical means of detecting accumulation and distribution. It is also valuable in showing the main points of resistance on the big swings.

A figure chart cannot be made from the open, high, low and last prices, such as are printed in the average newspaper. There are but three publications from which such charts may be constructed; viz., the official N. Y. Stock Exchange list, published by F. E. Fitch, 47 Broad St., N. Y., the N. Y. *Evening Sun,* and the *Wall Street Journal.* For general accuracy, reliability and economy, we prefer the *Evening Sun,* which costs, postpaid, only 20 cents a month, or $2 a year.

```
                        52
                        51 51
                    50 50    50 50
                    49 49 49 49 49 49
                    48        48
                    47        47                              47
46                  46        46 46 46                        46
45                  45        45 45 45 45 45                  45
44                  44        44    44 44                     44
43        43  43    43        43                              43
42        42 42 42 42 42      42                              42
41 41        41 41      41    41     41 41 41                 41
40 40 40 40   40      40 40   40     40                       40
39 39 39 39 39        39 39 39        39    39      39 39 39
38 38    38          38 38            38    38 38 38  38 38 38
37 37                                 37 37 37   37 37 37
36                                    36    36
                                            35
                                            34
```

Figure chart of Amalgamated Copper During the 1903 Panic

We produce a Figure Chart of Amalgamated Copper showing movements during the 1903 panic and up to the following March (1904). It makes an interesting study. The stock sold early in the year at 75 5/8 and the low point reached during the above period was 33 5/8. The movements prior to those recorded here show a series of downward steps, but when 36 is reached, the formation changes, and the supporting points are raised. A seven-point rally, a reaction to almost the low figure, and another sixteen-point rally follow.

On this rally the lines 48-49 gradually form the axis and long rows of these figures seem to indicate that plenty of stock is for sale at this level. In case we are not sure as to whether this is further accumulation or distribution we wait until the price shows signs of breaking out of this narrow range. After the second run up to 51 the gradually lowering tops warn us that pressure is resumed. We therefore look for lower prices.

The downward steps continue till 35 is touched, where a 3G-7 line begins to form. There is a dip to 33 5/8, which gives us the full figure 34, after which the bottoms are higher and lines commence forming at 38-9. Here are all the earmarks of manipulative depression and accumulation—the stock is not allowed to rally over 39 until liquidation is complete. Then the gradually raised bottoms notify us in advance that the stock is about to push through to higher levels.

If the Figure Chart were an infallible guide no one would have to learn anything more than its correct interpretation in order to make big money. Our correspondent says, "after a thorough trial of the chart on U. P. I find that I could have made a very considerable sum if I had followed the indications shown." But he would not have followed the indications shown. He is fooling himself. It is easy to look over the chart afterwards and see where he could have made correct plays, but I venture to say he never tested the plan under proper conditions.

Let anyone who thinks he can make money following a Figure Chart or any other kind of a chart have a friend prepare it, keeping secret the name of the stock and the period covered. Then put down on paper a positive set of rules which are to be strictly adhered to, so that there can be no guesswork. Each situation will then call for a certain play and no deviation is to be allowed. Cover up with a sheet of paper all but the beginning of the chart, gradually sliding the paper to the right as you progress. Record each order and execution just as if actually trading. Put Rollo Tape down as coppering every trade and when done send him a check for what you have lost.

I have yet to meet the man who has made money trading on a Figure Chart over an extended period.

Any kind of a chart will show some profits at times, but the test is: How much money will it make during a year's operations?

The Figure Chart can be used in other ways. Some people construct figure charts showing each fractional change instead of full points. The idea may also be used in connection with the Dow, Jones & Co. averages or *N. Y. Times* average prices. But for the practical Tape Reader the full figure chart first described is about the only one we can recommend.

Its value to the Tape Reader lies chiefly in its warnings of important moves thus putting him on the watch for the moment when either process is completed and the marking up or down begins.

The chart gives the direction of coming moves; the tape says "when."

The ordinary single line chart which is so widely used, is valuable chiefly as a compact history of a stock's movements. If the stock which is charted were the only one in the market, its gyrations would be less erratic and its chart, therefore, a more reliable indicator of its trend and destination. But we must keep before us the incontrovertible fact that the movements of every stock are to a greater or lesser extent affected by those of every other stock.

This in a large measure accounts for the instability of stock movements as recorded in single line charts.

Then, too, as shown in foregoing studies in this series, one stock may be the lever with which the whole market is being held up, or the club with which the general list is being pounded. A chart of the pivotal stock might give a strong buying indication, whereupon the blind chart devotee would go long to his ultimate regret; for when the concealed distribution was completed his stock would probably break quickly and badly.

This shows clearly the advantage of Tape Reading over chart playing. The Tape Reader sees everything that is going on: chart player's vision is limited. Both aim to get in right and go with the trend, but the eve that comprehends the market as a whole is the one which can read this trend most accurately.

If one wishes a mechanical trend indicator as a supplement and a guide to his Tape Reading, he had best keen a chart composed of the average daily high and low of ten leading stocks, say Union, Reading, St. Paul, N. Y. Central and Erie among the railroads, and Anaconda. Smelters, U. S. Steel, Car Foundry and Westinghouse among the industrials. First find the average high and average low for the day and make a chart showing which was touched first. This will be found a more reliable guide than the Dow, Jones averages, which only consider the closing bid of each day, and which, as strongly illustrated in the

May, 1901, panic, frequently do not fairly represent the day's actual fluctuations.

Such a composite chart is of no value to the Tape Reader who scalps and closes out everything daily. But it should benefit those who read the tape for the purpose of catching the important five or ten point moves. Such a trader will make no commitments not in accordance with the trend, as shown by this chart. His reason is that even a well planned bull campaign in a stock will not usually be pushed to completion in the face of a down trend in the general market. Therefore he waits until the trend conforms to his indication.

It seems hardly necessary to say that an up trend in any chart is indicated by consecutive higher tops and bottoms, like stairs going up, and the reverse by repeated steps toward a lower level. A series of tops or bottoms at the same level shows resistance. A protracted zigzag within a short radius accompanied by very small volume means lifelessness, but with normal or abnormally large volume, accumulation or distribution is more or less evidenced.

Here is a style of chart especially adapted to the study of volumes. The following rough sketch will give an idea of it:

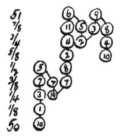

Volume Figure Chart

When made to cover a day's movements in a stock, this chart is particularly valuable in showing the quantity of stock at various levels. Figures represent the total 100 share lots at the respective fractions. Comparisons are readily made by adding the quantities horizontally. Many other suggestions may be derived from the study of this chart.

An important point in connection with the making of charts is the treatment of a stock which sells ex-dividend. Many people consider a dividend as equal to a corresponding decline in market price, in fact, a prominent publisher of charts follows this method. We do not agree. In our opinion when a stock sells ex-dividend the scale should be changed so that the stock will show the same relative position as before the dividend. For instance, if a stock is 138 before a dividend amounting to 2 percent and sells at 136 ex-dividend, the 138 line becomes the 136 line, etc.

The proficient Tape Reader will doubtless prefer to discard all mechanical helps, because they interfere with his sensing the trend. Besides, if he keeps

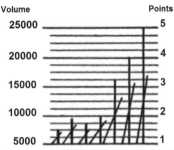

Chart Showing Daily Volume and Width of Swing

the charts himself the very act of running them distracts his attention from the tape on which his eye should be constantly riveted. This can of course be overcome by employing an assistant; but taking everything into consideration—the division of attention, the contradictions and the confusing situations which will frequently result—we advise students to stand free of mechanical helps so far as it is possible.

Our correspondent in saying "a chart is but a copy of the tape" doubtless refers to the chart of one stock. The full tape cannot possibly be charted. The tape does tell the story, but charting one or two stocks is like recording the actions of one individual as exemplifying the actions of a very large family.

Chapter IX - Daily Trades vs. Long Pull Operations

Just now I took a small triangular piece of blotting paper three-eighths of an inch at its widest, and stuck it on the end of a pin. I then threw a blot of ink on a paper and put the blotter into contact. The ink fairly jumped up into the blotter, leaving the paper comparatively dry.

This is exactly how the market acts on the tape when its absorptive powers are greater than the supply—large quantities are taken at the offered prices and at the higher levels. Prices leap forward. The demand seems insatiable.

After two or three blots had thus been absorbed, the blotter would take no more. It was thoroughly saturated. Its demands were satisfied. Just in this way the market comes to a standstill at the top of a rise and hangs there. Supply and demand are equalized at the new price level.

Then I filled my pen with ink, and let the fluid run off the point and onto the blotter. (This illustrated the distribution of stocks in the market.) Beyond a certain point the blotter would take no more. A drop formed and fell to the paper. (Supply exceeded demand.) The more I put on the blotter the faster fell the drops. (Liquidation—market seeking a lower level.)

This is a simple way of fixing in our minds the principal opposing forces that are constantly operating in the market— absorption and distribution, demand and supply, support and pressure. The more adept a Tape Reader becomes in weighing and measuring these elements, the more successful he will be.

But he must remember that even his most accurate readings will often be nullified by events which are transpiring every moment of the day. His stock may start upward with a rush—apparently with power enough to carry it several points; but after advancing a couple of points it may run up against a larger quantity of stock than can be absorbed or some unforeseen incident may change the whole complexion of the market. The Tape Reader must be quick to detect such changes, switch his position and go with this newly formed trend.

To show how an operator may be caught twice on the wrong side in one day and still come out ahead, let us look at the tape of December 21, 1908.

Union Pacific opened below the previous night's close: 500 . 179 . 6000 . 178 3/4 and for the first few moments looked as though there was some inside support. Supposing the Tape Reader had **BOUGHT 100 UNION PACIFIC AT 178 7/8,** he would have soon noticed fresh selling orders in sufficient volume to produce weakness. Upon this he would have immediately **SOLD 200 UNION PACIFIC AT 178 1/4**, putting him short one hundred at the latter price. The weakness increased and after a drive to 176 1/2, two or three warnings were given that the pressure was temporarily off. A comparatively strong undertone developed in Southern Pacific as well as other stocks and short covering began in Union Pacific, which came 600 . 176 5/8 . 1000 . 3/4, then 177 1/4. Assuming that the operator considered this the turn, he would have **BOUGHT 200 UNION PACIFIC AT 176 7/8**, which was the next quotation. This would have put him long. Thereafter the market showed more resiliency, but only small lots appeared on the tape.

A little later the market quiets down. The rally does not hold well. He expects the stock to react again to the low point. This it does, but it fails to halt there; it goes driving through to 176, accompanied by considerable weakness in the other active stocks. This is his indication that fresh liquidation has started. So he **SELLS 200 UNION PACIFIC AT 176.**
That is, he dumps over his long stock and goes short at 176.

The weakness continues and there is no sign of a rally until after the stock has struck 174 1/2. This being a break of 6 1/4 points since yesterday, the Tape Reader is now wide awake for signs of a turn, realizing that every additional fraction brings him nearer to that point, wherever it may be.

After touching 174 1/2 the trend of the market changes completely. Larger lots are in demand at the offered prices. There is a final drive but very little stock comes out on it. During this drive he **BUYS 100 UNION PACIFIC AT 174 7/8** and as signs of a rally multiply he **BUYS 100 UNION PACIFIC AT 175 1/4.**

From that moment it is easy sailing. There is ample opportunity for him to unload his last purchase just before the close.

Sells 100 Union Pacific at 176 5/8

Bought	Sold	Loss	Profit
178 7/8	178 1/4	$62.50	....
176 7/8	178 1/4	....	$137.50
176 7/8	176	87.50	....
174 7/8	176	....	112.50
175 1/4	176 5/8	....	137.50
Commissions and taxes........		135.00	....
		$285.00	$387.00
			285.00
Net profit for the day...$102.50			

This is doing very well considering he was caught twice on the wrong side and in his wigglings paid $135 in commissions and taxes.

Success in trading being chiefly a question of reducing and eliminating losses, commissions, interest and revenue stamps, let us see whether he might have used better judgment. His first trade seems to have been made on what appeared to be inside buying. No trend had developed. He saw round lots being taken at 178 3/4 and over and reasoned that a rally should naturally follow pronounced support. His mistake was in not waiting for a clearly defined trend. If the buying was strong enough to absorb all offerings and turn the market, he would have done better to have waited till this was certain. When a stock holds steady within a half point radius it does not signify a reversal of trend, but rather a halting place from which a new move in either direction may begin.

Had he followed the first sharp move, his original trade would have been on the short—not the long side. This would have saved him his first loss with its attendant expenses, aggregating $89.50, and would have nearly doubled the day's profits.

His second loss was made on a trade which involved one of the finest points in the art of Tape Reading, viz., that of distinguishing a rally from a change in trend. A good way to do this successfully is to figure where a stock is due to come after it makes an upturn, allowing that a normal rally is from one-half to two-thirds of the decline. That is, when a stock declines two and a half points we can look for at least a point and a quarter rally unless the pressure is still on. In case the decline is not over, the rally will fall short.

What did Union do after it touched 176 1/2? It sold at 176 5/8 . 3/4 . 177 1/4. Having declined from 179 1/8 to 176 1/2, 2 5/8 points, it was due to rally at least 1 1/4 points, or to 177 3/4. Its failing to make this figure indicated that the decline was not over and that his short position should be maintained.

Furthermore, that last jump of half a point between sales showed an unhealthy condition of the market. For a few moments there was evidently a cessation of selling, then somebody reached for a hundred shares offered at 177 1/4. As the next sale was 176 7/8 the hollowness of the rise became apparent.

While this rally lasted, the lots were small. This of itself was reason for not covering. Had a genuine demand sprung from either longs or shorts a steady rise, on increasing volumes, would have taken place. The absence of such indications seems to us now a reason for not covering and going long at 176 7/8.

It is very difficult for anyone to say what he would actually have done under the circumstances, but had both these trades been avoided for the reasons mentioned, the profit for the day would have been $421, as the 100 sold at 178 1/4 would have been covered at 174 7/8, and the long at 175 1/4 sold out at 176 5/8. So we can see the advantage of studying our losses and mistakes, with a view to benefiting in future transactions.

As previously explained, the number of dollars profit is subordinate to whether the trader can make profits at all and whether the points made exceed the points lost. With success from this standpoint it is only a question of increased capital enabling one to enlarge his trading unit.

A good way to watch the progress of an account is to keep a book showing dates, quantities, prices, profits and losses, also commission, tax and interest charges. Beside each trade should be entered the number of points net profit or loss, together with a running total showing just how many points the account is ahead or behind. A chart of these latter figures will prevent anyone fooling himself as to his progress. People are too apt to remember their profits and forget their losses.

The losses taken by an expert Tape Reader are so small that he can trade in much larger units than one who is away from the tape or who is trading with an arbitrary stop. The Tape Reader will seldom take over half a point to a point loss for the reason that he will generally buy or sell at, or close to, the pivotal point or the line of resistance. Therefore, should the trend of his stock suddenly reverse, he is with it in a moment. The losses in the above mentioned Union Pacific transactions (5/8 and 7/8 respectively) are perhaps a fair average, but frequently he will be able to trade with a risk of only 1/4, 3/8, 1/2.

The fact that this possible loss is confined to a fraction should not lead him to trade too frequently. It is better to look on part of the time; to rest the mind and allow the judgment to clarify. Dull days will often constrain one for a time and are therefore beneficial.

The big money in Tape Reading is made during very active markets. Big swings and large volumes produce unmistakable indications and a harvest for the experienced operator. He welcomes twenty, thirty and fifty-point moves in stocks like Reading, Union or Consolidated Gas—powerful plays by financial giants.

And this fact reminds us of one of the things we have heretofore intended to reason out: Is it better to close trades each day, or hold through reactions, and if necessary, for several days or week in order to secure a large profit?

The answer to this question depends somewhat upon the temperament of the Tape Reader. If his make-up be such that he can closely follow the small swings with profit, gradually becoming more expert and steadily increasing his commitments, he will shortly "arrive" by that route. If his disposition is such that he cannot trade in and out actively, but is content to wait for big opportunities and patient enough to hold on for large profits, he will also "get there."

It is impossible to say which style of trading would produce the best average results, because it depends altogether upon individual qualifications.

Looking at the question broadly, we should say that the Tape Reader who understood the lines thus far suggested in this series, might find it both difficult and less profitable to operate solely for the long swings. In the first place, he would be obliged to let twenty or thirty opportunities pass by to every one that he would accept. The small swings of one to three points greatly outnumber the five and ten-point movements, and there would be a considerable percentage of losing trades no matter how he operated.

Many of the indications, such as the extent of reactions, lines of resistance, etc., will be found equally operative in the broader swings, just as an enlargement of a photograph retains the lines of its original.

Tape Reading seems essentially a profession for the man who is mentally active and flexible, capable of making quick and accurate decisions and keenly sensitive to the most minute indications. On the other hand, trading for the larger swings requires one to ignore the minor indications and to put some stress upon the influential news of the day, and its effect upon sentiment; he must stand ready to take larger losses and in many ways handle himself in a manner altogether different from that of the small swing trader.

The more closely we look at the proposition, the more the two methods of operating seem to disunite, the broad swing plan appearing best adapted to those who are not in continuous touch with the ticker and who therefore have the advantage of distance and perspective.

There is no reason why the Tape Reader should not make long swing trading an auxiliary profit producer if he can keep such trades from influencing his daily operations.

For example, in the previously mentioned shake-down in Reading from 144 3/8 to 118, on his first buying indication he could have taken on an extra lot for the long swing, knowing that if the turn had really been made, a rally to over 130 was due. A stop order would have limited his risk and conserved his profits as they rolled up and there is no telling how much of the subsequent forty point rise he might have secured.

Another case was when Steel broke from 58 3/4 (November, 1908) to 41 1/4 in February. The market at the time was hinging on Steel and it was likely that the Tape Reader would be operating in it. His first long trade under this plan would be for at least a hundred shares more than his usual amount, with a stop on the long pull lot at say 40 3/4. He would naturally expect a rally of at least 8 3/4 points (to 50), but would, in a sense, forget this hundred shares, so long as the market showed no signs of another important decline. When it reached 60 he might still be holding it.

The above are merely a couple of opportunities. Dozens of such show themselves every year and should form no small part of the Tape Reader's income. But he must separate such trades from his regular daily trading; to allow them to conflict would destroy the effectiveness of both. If he finds the long pull trade interfering with the accuracy of his judgment, he should close it out at once. He must play on one side of the fence if he cannot operate on both.

One can readily foresee how a trader with one hundred shares of Steel at 43 for the long pull, and two hundred for the day, would be tempted to close out all three hundred on indications of a decline. This is where he can test his ability to act in a dual capacity. He must ask himself: Have I good reason for thinking Steel will sell down five points before up five? Is this a small reaction or a big shake-down? Are we still in a bull swing? Has the stock had its normal rally from the last decline? These and many other questions will enable him to decide whether he should hold this hundred shares or "clean house."

It takes an exceptionally strong will and clear head to act in this way without interfering with one's regular trading. Anyone can sell two hundred and hold one hundred; but will his judgment be biased because he is simultaneously long and short—bullish and bearish? There's the rub!

The real Tape Reader is apt to prefer a clean slate at 3 p. m. every day, so that he can sit down to his ticker at the next morning's opening and say, "I have no commitments and no opinion. I will follow the first strong indication." He would rather average $100 a day for ten days than make $1,000 on one trade in the same length of time. The risk is generally limited to a fraction and having arrived at a point where he is showing even small average daily profits, his required capital per 100 shares need not be over $1,500 to $2,000.

Suppose for sixty days on 100-share operations his average profits over losses were only a quarter of a point—$25 a day. At the end of that time his capital would have been increased by $1,500, enabling him to trade in 200 share lots. Another thirty days with similar results and he could trade in 300-share lots, and so on. I do not mention these figures for any other purpose than to again emphasize that the objective point in Tape Reading is not large individual profits, but a continuous chipping in of small average not profits per day.

About two months ago, I am told, a man from the West came into the office of THE MAGAZINE OF WALL STREET, and said that he had been impressed by this series on Tape Reading, and had come to New York for the sole purpose of trying his hand at it. He had $1,000 which he was willing to lose in demonstrating whether he was fitted for the work.

He was advised not to trade in over ten-share lots, and was especially warned against operating at all until after he had actually studied the tape for two or three months.

Recently, I am informed, he called again and related some of his experiences. It seems that he could not abstain from trading, but started within two or three days after he decided on a brokerage house. He stated that during the two months he had made forty-two trades of ten shares each and had never had on hand over twenty full shares at any one time. He admitted that he had frequently mixed guesswork and tips with his Tape Reading but as a rule he had followed the tape.

His losses were seldom over a point and his greatest loss was one and a half points. His maximum profit was three points. He had at times traded in other stocks beside the leaders. In spite of his inexperience, and his attempt to mix tips and guess with shrewd judgment, he was ahead of the game, after paying commissions, etc.

This was especially surprising in view of the trader's market through which he had passed. While the amount of his net profit was small, the fact that he had shown any profit during this study period was reason enough for congratulation.

Another handicap which he did not perhaps realize was his environment. He had been trading in an office where he could hear and see what everyone else was doing, and where news, gossip and opinions were freely and openly expressed by many people. All these things tended to influence him, and to switch him from his Tape Reading.

I have no doubt that having mastered the art of cutting losses and keeping commitments down, he will soon overcome his other deficiencies. Given a broad, active market, he should show increasing average daily profits.

Speculation is a business. It must be *learned.*

Chapter X - Various Examples and Suggestions

Recent trading observations and experiments have convinced me that it is impracticable and almost impossible to gauge the extent of a movement by its initial fluctuations. Many important swings begin in the most modest way. The top of an important decline may present nothing more than a light volume and a drifting tendency toward lower prices, subsequently developing into a heavy, slumpy market, and ending in a violent downward plunge.

In a previous number I suggested that the Tape Reader select only those moves which seem to offer opportunities for wide swings. My opinion now is that the operator should aim to catch every important swing in the leading active stock. To do this he must act promptly when a stock goes into a new field or otherwise gives an indication, and he must be ready to follow wherever it leads. If it has been moving within a three-point radius and suddenly takes on new life and activity, bursting through its former bounds, he must go with it.

I do not mean that he should try to catch every wriggle. If the stock rises three points and then reverses one or one and a half points on light volume, he must look upon it as a perfectly natural reaction and not a change of trend. The expert operator will not ordinarily let all of three points get away from him. He will keep pushing his stop up behind until the first good reaction puts him out at close to the high figure. This leaves him in a position to repurchase on the reaction, provided no better opportunity presents itself. Having purchased at such a time, he will sell out again as the price once more approaches the high figure, unless indications point to its forging through to a new high level.

Every movement of the market and of each stock passes through stages corresponding to those in the life of an individual, aptly described by my old college chum, Bill Shakespeare, as "The Seven Ages." The Tape Reader aims to get in during Infancy and out at Old Age.

Usually a movement gives signs when it begins to totter. An example was given in the rise in Union Pacific about June 21st to 23d (1909), when the stock rose from 187 7/8 to 194 5/8, accompanied by an abnormal advance in the preferred. Each morning the London price for both issues came higher and there was persistent buying all day in the New York market. After touching 194 5/8 the movement completely fizzled out. Buying demand ceased. The preferred reacted sharply, and the common came back to 193 7/8. Thereafter its rallies were feeble, the pressure was all on the down side, and on June 26th, it was still heavy at 191 7/8. A new bull movement may have its birth during great weakness or pressure. Just prior to the above time, Reading was pounded down to 147 5/8, then to 147 1/4, and the resistance which it offered at this level gave notice that a new swing was about to be inaugurated. These were signs that the Tape Reader had better get bullish. Purchases could have been made with only a fractional risk, and subsequent profits were chiefly on the bull side. Two or three days later the price touched 155 1/2, then it went above 158.

The more we study volumes, the better we appreciate their value in Tape Reading. It frequently occurs that a stock will work within a three-point range for days at a time without giving one a chance for a respectable-sized "scalp." Without going out of these boundaries, it suddenly begins coming out on the tape in thousands instead of hundreds. This is evidence that a new movement has started, but not necessarily in the direction which is first indicated. The Tape Reader must immediately go with the trend, but until it is clearly defined and the stock breaks its former limits with large and increasing volumes, he must exercise great caution. The reason is this: If the stock has been suddenly advanced, it may be for the purpose of facilitating sales by a large operator.

The best way to distinguish the genuine from the fictitious move is to watch out for abnormally large volumes within a small radius. This is usually evidence of manipulation. The large volume is simply a means of attracting buyers and disguising the hand of the operator.

A play of this kind took place when Reading struck 159 1/4 on June, 1909. I counted some 80,000 shares within about half a point of 159— unmistakable notice of a coming decline. This was a case where the stock was put up before being put down, and the Tape Reader who interpreted the move correctly and played for a good down swing would have made considerable money.

We frequently hear people complaining that "the public is not in this market," as though that were a reason why stocks should not go up or the market should be avoided. The speaker is usually one of those who constitute "the public," but he regards the expression as signifying "every outsider except myself." In the judgment of many the market is better off without the public. To be sure, brokers do not enjoy so large a business, the fluctuations are not so riotous, but the market moves in an orderly way and responds more accurately to prevailing conditions.

A market in which the public predominates represents a sort of speculative "jag" indulged in by those whose stock market knowledge should be rated at 1/8. Everyone recognizes the fact that when the smoke clears away, the Street is full of victims who didn't know how and couldn't wait to learn. Their plungings produce violent fluctuations, however, and in this respect are of advantage to the Tape Reader who would much rather see ten-point than three-point swings.

To offset this, there are some disadvantages. First, in a market where there is "rioting of accumulated margins," the tape is so far behind that it is seldom one can secure an execution at anywhere near his price. This is especially true when activity breaks out in a stock which has been comparatively dull. So many people with money, watching the tape, are attracted by these apparent opportunities, that the scramble to get in results in every one paying more than he figured; thus the Tape Reader finds it impossible to know where he is at until he gets his report. His tape prices are five minutes stale and his broker is so busy it takes four or five minutes for an execution instead of one or two minutes.

In the next place, stop orders are often filled at from small fractions to points away from his stop price—there is no telling what figure he will get, while in ordinary markets he can place his stops within 1/4 of a resistance point and frequently have the price come within 1/8 of his stop without catching it.

So it is a question whether, all things considered, the presence of the public is a help or a detriment to successful Tape Reading.

Speaking of stop orders: The ways in which one may manipulate his stops for protection and advantage, become more numerous as experience is acquired. If the Tape Reader is operating for a fractional average profit per trade, or per day, he cannot afford to let a point profit run into a loss, or fail to "plug" a larger profit at a point where at least a portion of it will be preserved.

One of my recent day's trading will illustrate this idea. I had just closed out a couple of trades, in which there had been losses totaling slightly over a point. Both were on the long side. The market began to show signs of a break, and singling out Reading as the most vulnerable, I got short of it at 150 1/4. In a few moments it sold below 150. My stop was moved down so there couldn't be a loss, and soon a slight rally and another break gave me a new stop which insured a profit. A third drive started, and I pushed the stop down to within 1/4 of the tape price at the time, as it was late in the day and I considered this the final plunge. By the time my order reached the floor the price was well away from this latest stop and when the selling became most violent I told my broker to cover "at the market." The price paid was within 1/4 of the bottom for the day, and netted 2 5/8 after commissions were paid.

I strongly advocate this method of profit insuring. The scientific elimination of loss is one of the most important factors in the art, and the operator who fails to properly protect his paper profits will find that many a point which he thought he had cinched has slipped away from him.

It is also a question whether, in such a case, the trade had better not be stopped out than closed out. When you push a stop close behind a rise or a decline, you leave the way open for a further profit; but when you close the trade of your own volition, you shut off all such chances. If it is your habit to close out everything before three o'clock daily, the stop may be placed closer than ordinarily during the last fifteen minutes of the session, and when a sharp move in the desired direction occurs, the closing out may be done by a stop only a fraction away from the extreme price. This plan of using stops is a sort of squeezing out the last drop of profit from each trade and never losing any part that can possibly be retained.

Suppose the operator sells a stock short at 53 and it breaks to 51. He is foolish not to bring his stop down to 51 1/4 unless the market is ripe for a heavy decline. With his stop at this point he has two chances out of three that the result will be satisfactory: (1) The price may go lower and yield a further profit; (2) The normal rally to 52 will catch his stop and enable him to put the stock out again at that price; (3) The stock will rally to about 51 1/4, catch his stop and then go lower. But he can scarcely mourn over the loss of a further profit.

If the stock refuses to rally the full point to which it is entitled, that is, if it comes up to 51 1/2 or 5/8 and still acts heavy, it may be expected to break lower, and there usually is ample time to get short again at a price that will at least cover commissions.

There is nothing more confusing than to attempt scalping on both sides of the market at once. You may go long of a stock which is being put up or is going up for some special reason, and short of another stock which is persistently weak. Both trades may pan out successfully, but meantime the judgment will be interfered with and some foolish mistake will be made in four cases out of five. As Dickson G. Watts said, "Act so as to keep the mind clear, the judgment trustworthy." The mind is not clear when the trader is working actively on two opposing sides of the market. A bearish indication is favorable to one trade, and unfavorable to the other. He finds himself interpreting every development as being to his advantage and forgetting the important fact that he is also on the opposite side.

If you are short of one stock and see another that looks like a purchase, it is much better to wait until you have covered your short trade (on a dip if possible), and then take the long side of the other issue. The best time for both covering and going long is on a recession which in such a case serves a double purpose. The mind should be made up in advance as to which deal offers the best chance for profit, so that when the moment for action arrives there will be nothing to do but act.

This is one great advantage the Tape Reader has over other operators who do not employ market science. By a process of elimination he decides which side of the market and which stock affords the best opportunity. He either gets in at the inception of a movement or waits for first reaction after the move has started. He knows just about where his stock should come on the reaction and judges by the way it then acts whether his first impression is confirmed or contradicted. After he gets in it must come up to expectations or he should abandon the trade. If it is a bull move, the volume must increase and the rest of the market offer some support or at least not oppose it. The reactions must show a smaller volume than the advances, indicating light pressure, and each upward swing must be of longer duration and reach a new high level, or it will mean that the rise has spent its force either temporarily or finally.

Tape Reading is the only known method of trading which gets you in at the beginning, keeps you posted throughout the move, and gets you out when it has culminated.

Has anyone ever heard of a man, method, system, or anything else that will do this for you in Wall Street?

It has made fortunes for the comparatively few who have followed it.

It is an art in which one can become highly expert and more and more successful as experience sandpapers his work and shows him what to avoid.

Chapter XI – Obstacles to be Overcome — Possible Profits

Mental poise is an indispensable factor in Tape Reading. The mind should be absolutely free to concentrate upon the work; there should be no feeling that certain things are to be accomplished within a given time; no fear, anxiety, or greed.

When a Tape Reader has his emotions well in hand, he will play as though the game were dominoes. When anything interferes with this attitude it should be eliminated. If, for example, there be an unusual series of losses, the trader had better suspend operations until he discovers the cause.

Following are some of the obstacles which are likely to be encountered:

1. One may be trading too often. Many opportunities for profit develop from each day's movements; only the very choicest should be acted upon. There should be no haste. The market will be there tomorrow in case today's opportunities do not meet requirements.

2. Anxiety to make a record, to avoid losses, to secure a certain profit for the day or period will greatly warp the judgment, and lead to a low percentage of profits. Tape Reading is a good deal like laying eggs. If the hen is not left to pick up the necessary food and retire in peace to her nest, she will not produce properly. If she is worried by dogs and small boys, or tries to lay seven eggs out of material for six, the net proceeds may be an omelet.

The Tape Reader's profits should develop naturally. He should buy or sell because it is the thing to do—not because he wants to make a profit or fears to make a loss.

3. The market may be unsuited to Tape Reading operations. When prices drift up and down without trend, like a ship without a rudder, and few positive indications develop, the percentage of losing trades is apt to be high. When this condition continues it is well to hold off until the character of the market changes.

4. One's broker may be giving poor service. In a game as fine as this, every fraction counts. Executions of market orders should average not over two minutes. Stop orders should be reported in less time as such orders are on the floor and at the proper post when they become operative. By close attention to details in the handling of my orders, I have been able to reduce the

average time of my executions to less than one minute. The quickest report obtained thus far required but twenty-five seconds. To the best of my knowledge this is a record for New York Stock Exchange executions of orders given from an office.

A considerable portion of my orders are executed in from thirty to forty seconds, varying according to whether my broker is near the 'phone or in a distant crowd when the orders reach the floor and how far the identical "crowd" is from his phone.

I have arranged a special order slip which distinguishes my orders from others. It reads:

The selling slips read, *"Sell at the bid price and report instantly."* Such orders leave nothing to the discretion of the broker. He cannot "try to do better" than the momentary bid or offered price. Like Paddy at the wake, his business is to "hit the first head that opens its mouth."

Ordinarily it is expected and is really an advantage to the general run of speculators to have the broker use some discretion; that is, try to do better, providing there is no chance of losing his market. But I do not wish my broker to act thus for me. My indications usually show me the exact moment when a stock should be bought or sold under this method, and a few moments delay often means a good many dollars lost.

With the execution of orders reduced to a matter of seconds, I can also hold stop orders in my own hands and when the stop price is reached, phone the order to buy or sell at the market. Results are very satisfactory as my own broker handles the orders and not the specialist or some other floor broker.

To return to the question of mental equilibrium: The Tape Reader should be careful to trade only in such amounts as will not interfere with his judgment. If he finds that a series of losses upsets him it is an easy matter to reduce the number of shares to one-half or one-quarter of the regular amount, or even to ten shares, so that the dollars involved are no longer a factor. This gives him a chance for a little self-examination.

If a person is in poor physical condition or his mental alertness below par for any reason, he may be unable to stand the excitement attending the work. Dissipation, for example, may render one unfit to carry all the quotations in his head, or to plan and execute his moves quickly and accurately. When anything of this kind occurs which prevents the free play of all the faculties it is best to bring the day's work to a close.

Some of my readers may think it futile to aim for a fractional average profit per trade when there are many full points per day to be made by holding on through days and weeks and getting full benefit of the big moves. Admitting that it is possible to make many more points at times there is a risk of losses corresponding to the profits and the question is not how much we can *make,* but how much we can make *net.*

Tape Reading reduces profit-making to a manufacturing basis.

To show how the nimble eighths pile up when their cumulative power is fully employed, I have prepared a table representing the results of 250 trading days, starting with a capital of $1,000. It is assumed that the Tape Reader has reached that stage of expertness where he can average one trade a day and a profit of $12.50 per trade, and that as fast as $1,000 is accumulated he adds 100 shares to his trading unit.

These results depend solely upon the Tape Reader's ability to make 1/8 more than he loses per day. There is no limit to the number of shares he can trade in, provided he has the margin. If he is at all proficient his margin will not be depleted more than a few points before he makes up his losses and more. He is not pyramiding in the ordinary sense of the word; he is simply doing an increasing volume of shares as his capital expands. All progressive business men increase commitments as fast as warranted by their capital and opportunities.

What a profit 1/8 per day would amount to in 250 days if profits were used as additional margin.

100 shares	$12.50 a day	$1,000.00 in	80 days
200 "	25.00 "	1,000.00 "	40 "
300 "	37.50 "	1,012.50 "	27 "
400 "	50.00 "	1,000.00 "	20 "
500 "	62.50 "	1,000.00 "	16 "
600 "	75.00 "	1,050.00 "	14 "
700 "	87.50 "	1,050.00 "	12 "
800 "	100.00 "	1,000.00 "	10 "
900 "	112.50 "	1,012.50 "	9 "
1000 "	125.00 "	1,000.00 "	8 "
1100 "	137.50 "	962.50 "	7 "
1200 "	150.00 "	1,050.00 "	7 "
		$12,137.50 "	250 "

Less tax.....................1,942.00

Net profit..............$10,195.50

Assuming that there are about three hundred Stock Exchange sessions in the year, the two hundred and fifty days figured represent five-sixths of a year or ten months. From that time on, having struck his gait, the Tape Reader can, without increasing his unit to over 1200 shares, make $900 a week or $46,800 a year.

One trader who for years has been trying to scalp the market and who could never quite overcome the "kitty," reports this his first attempts at applying these rules resulted in a loss of about $20 per trade. This he gradually reduced to $12, then to $8, finally succeeding in throwing the balance over to the credit side and is now able to make a daily profit of from $12 to $30 per 100 shares. This is doing very well indeed. I have no doubt that his profits will continue to increase.

Some people seem to hold the opinion that as the profits desired are only 1/8 average per trade one should limit himself in taking profits. Perhaps I have not made myself clear in this respect.

I buy and sell when I get my indications. In going into a trade I do not know whether it will show a profit or a loss, or how much. I try to trade at a point where I can secure protection with a stop from 1/4 to 1/2 point away, so that my risk is limited to this fraction plus commission and tax. If the trade goes in my favor I push the stop up as soon as possible, to a point where there can be no loss.

I do not let profits run blindly but only so long as there appears no indication on which to close. No matter where my stop order stands, I am always on the watch for danger signals. Sometimes I get them way in advance of the time a trade should be closed; in other instances my "get out" will flash onto the tape as suddenly and as clearly defined as a streak of lightning against a black sky.

When the tape says "get out" I never stop to reckon how much profit or loss I have or whether I am ahead or behind on the day. I strive for an increasing average profit but I do not keep my eye so much on the fraction or points made or lost, so much as on myself.

I endeavor to perfect myself in clearheadedness, quickness of thought, accuracy of judgment, promptness in planning and executing my trades, foresight, intuition, courage and initiative. Masterful control of myself in these respects will produce a winning average—it is merely a question of practice.

To show how accurately the method works out in practice, I will describe one recent day's trading in which there were three transactions, involving six orders (three buying and three selling). *The market did not go one-eighth against me in five orders out of the six.* In the sixth, the stock went above the selling price at which my order was given. Details follow:

I had no open trades. Kansas City Southern, which had been intensely dull, came on the tape 2600 at 46 3/4. I gave a buying order and before it could reach the "post" the Tape said 46 7/8 and 47. The stock rose steadily and after selling at 48 5/8 and coming back to 48 1/2 I gave the selling order. It did not touch 48 5/8 again.

The next trade was in Reading. I saw that it was being held in check in spite of its great strength. The stock had opened at 158. After a certain bulge I saw the reaction coming. When it arrived, and the stock was selling at 157 1/2, I gave the buying order, got mine at 157 5/8. It immediately rose to 158 3/4. I noted selling indications and gave the order while the stock was at that price on the tape. It did not react sufficiently to warrant my picking it up again and later went to 159 3/8, which was 5/8 above my selling indication.

Southern Pacific suddenly loomed up as a winner and I bought it at 135. It promptly went to 135 1/2. The rest of the market began to look temporarily over-bulled, so I gave my order to sell when the stock was 135 1/2, which proved to be the highest for the day, making the fifth time out of six orders when my stock moved almost instantly in my favor.

This illustration is given as an example of the high percentage of accuracy possible under this method of trading. I do not pretend to be able to accomplish these results except occasionally, but I am constantly striving to do so in a large percentage of my trades.

If one makes 2 3/8 points one day and loses 2 points in the next two days, he is 3/8 ahead for the three days, or an average of 1/8 per day. He may have losing and winning streaks, get discouraged and lose his nerve at times, but if he is made of the right stuff he will in time overcome all obstacles and land at the desired goal.

Chapter XII – Closing the Trades—Suggestions for Students

The student of Tape Reading, especially he who puts his knowledge into actual practice, is constantly evolving new ideas and making discoveries which modify his former methods. From each new elevation he enjoys a broader view; what were obstacles disappear; his problems gradually simplify.

We have previously defined Tape Reading as the art of determining the *immediate* trend of prices. If one can do this successfully in the majority of his trades, his profits should roll up. But scenting the trend and getting in right is only one-half of the business. Knowing when to close a trade is just as important if not the most important part of a complete transaction.

At a certain point in my trading, I became aware that a large percentage of my losing trades resulted from failure to close at the culmination of what I have termed the immediate trend. An example will make this clear: New York Central was on a certain day the strongest stock in a bull market which showed a tendency to react. The pressure was on Reading and Steel. My indications were all bullish, so I couldn't consistently sell either of the latter short. I was looking for an opportunity to buy. The market began to slide off, Reading and Steel being the principal clubs with which the pounding was done. I watched them closely and the moment I saw that the selling of these two stocks had ceased, gave my order to buy New York Central, getting it at 137 1/4. It never touched there again, and in ten minutes was 139 bid for 5,000 shares.

Here I should have sold, as my buying indication was for that particular advance. Especially should I have sold when I saw the rise culminate in a spectacular bid which looked like bait for outside buyers. Of course the stock might have gone higher. The main trend for the day was upward. But for the time being 139 was the high point. I knew the stock was due to react from this figure, and it did, but at the bottom of the normal reaction selling broke out in fresh quarters and the whole market came down heavily. The result was that my profit was only a fraction of what it ought to have been.

This is the way the trade might have been made: I should have sold when 139 was noisily bid, and when the reaction had run its course, picked it up again, provided indications were still bullish. If they were not I would have been in the position of looking to get short instead of waiting for a chance to get out of my long.

Having reserved in the early part of this book the right to revise my views, I will here record the claim that the best results in active Tape Reading lie in scenting the moves as they occur, getting in when they start and out when they culminate. This will in most cases cause failure to get *all* of the moves in the one most active stock for the day, but should result in many small profits, and I believe the final results will exceed those realized by sitting through reactions with any one stock.

Objections to the latter method are many. One is, the change in leadership which frequently occurs several times during the same session. It being the purpose of the Tape Reader to keep in the leading stock, he must aim to shift from one issue to another as they come to the front.

It is exasperating to see your stock lose its prominence and "turn dead" on your hands, especially if it occurs at a point where part of the profit has disappeared. And there is little comfort in a half-point profit when some other issue would have shown three times as much. Each day's session should be made to yield the highest possible amount of revenue, just as though it were the last day on which trading could be done, and there seems no better way of obtaining these results than by the method mentioned above.

The decks are thus kept clear for whatever offers; there is no dead wood about.

There is a very wide difference in mental attitude between the man who feels compelled to get out of something and one who is long of money and looking for a chance to make a fresh trade.

The start and finish of one of the small swings is best illustrated by a triangle, the narrow end representing the commencement, and the wide end the culmination. The width, an upward/downward move would appear thus:

These figures denote the widening character of a move as it progresses and are intended to show how volume, activity and number of transactions expand until, at the end, comparatively active conditions prevail. The principle works the same in the larger swings; witness the spectacular rise in Union Pacific within a few sessions marking the end of the August, 1909, boom.

After closing out a trade the tape will tell on the following reaction whether you are justified in taking the same stock on again or whether some other issue will pay better. Frequently a stock will be seen preparing for a move two or three swings ahead of the one in which it becomes the leader. This is a fine point, but with study and practice the most complicated indications clarify.

And now a word about the many who are endeavoring to turn this series to practical account. The results which are attainable depend solely upon the individual. Each must work out his own method of trading, based on suggestions derived from these studies or from other sources. It will doubtless be found that what is one man's meat is another's poison, and that no amount of "book larn-in" will avail if the student does not put his knowledge to an actual test in the market.

It is surprising how an acquaintance with subjects relative to the stock market, but seemingly having no bearing upon Tape Reading, will lead to opportunities or aid in making deductions. And so when asked what books will best supplement these Studies, I should say: Read everything you can get hold of. If you find but a single idea in a publication it is well worth the time and money spent in procuring and studying it.

Wall Street is crowded with men who are there in the hope of making money, but who cannot be persuaded to look at the proposition from a practical business standpoint. Least of all will they study it, for this means long hours of hard work, and Mr. Speculator is laziness personified. Frequently I have met those who pin their faith to some one point, such as the volumes up or down, and call it Tape Reading. Others, unconsciously trading on mechanical indications, pretend to be reading the tape. Then there is a class of people who read the tape with their tongues, calling off each transaction, a certain accent on the higher or lower quotations indicating whether they are bullish or bearish. These and others in their class are merely operating on the superficial. If they would spend the same five or six hours a day (which they now practically waste) in close study of the *business* of speculation, the result in dollars would be more gratifying at the end of the year. As it is, the majority of them are now losing money.

It is a source of satisfaction, however, that these Studies which, I believe, are the first practical articles ever written on the subject of Tape Reading, have stirred the minds of many people to the possibilities in the line of scientific speculation. This is shown in the numerous communications received by THE MAGAZINE OF WALL STREET, many of them from traders situated in remote localities. In the main, the writers, who are now carrying on long distance operations for the big swings are desirous of testing their ability as Tape Readers. No doubt those who have written represent but a small percentage of the number who are thus inclined.

To all such persons I would say: Before you can make a success of Tape Reading you must acquire a broad fundamental knowledge of the market. A professional singer who was recently called upon to advise a young aspirant said: "One must become a 'personality' —that is, an intelligence developed by the study of many things besides music." It is not enough to know a few of the underlying principles; one must have a *deep* understanding.

To be sure it is possible for a person to take a number of the "tricks of the trade" herein mentioned and trade successfully on these alone. Even one idea which forms part of the whole subject may be worked and elaborated upon until it becomes a method in itself. There are endless possibilities in this direction, and after all it matters little *how* the money is extracted from the market, so long as it is done legitimately.

But real Tape Reading takes everything into account—every little character which appears on the tape plays its part in forming one of the endless series of "moving pictures." In many years' study of the tape, I do not remember having seen two of these "pictures" which were duplicates. One can realize from this how impossible it would be to formulate a simple set of rules to fit every case or even the majority of them, as each day's session produces hundreds of situations, which, so far as memory serves, are never repeated.

The subject of Tape Reading is therefore practically inexhaustible, which makes it all the more interesting to the man who has acquired the "study habit."

Having fortified himself with the necessary fundamental knowledge, the student of Tape Reading should thoroughly digest these Studies and any others which may be obtainable in future. It is not enough to go over and over a lesson as a school boy does, driving the facts into his head by monotonous repetition; tapes must be procured and the various indications matched up with what has been studied. And even after one believes he understands, he will presently learn that, to quote the words of a certain song, "You don't know how much you know until you know how little you know." One of my instructors in another line of study used to make me go over a thing three or four times after I *thought* I knew it, just to make sure that I did.

I should say that it is almost impossible for one who has never before traded from the tape to go into a broker's office, start right in and operate successfully. In the first place, there are the abbreviations and all the little characters and their meanings to know the abbreviations of the principal stocks; it is necessary to know *everything* that appears on the tape, so that nothing will be overlooked. Otherwise the operator will be like a person who attempts to read classic literature without knowing words of more than four letters.

It is a common impression in the Street that anyone who has the price can buy a seat on the Stock Exchange and at once begin making money as a floor trader. But floor trading is also a business that one has to learn, and it usually takes months and years to become accustomed to the physical and nervous strain and learn the ropes.

Frequent requests are made for the name of someone who will teach the Art of Tape Reading. I do not know of anyone able to read the tape with profit who is willing to become an instructor. The reason is very simple. Profits from the tape far exceed anything that might be earned in tuition fees.

In addition to the large operators and floor traders who use Tape Reading in their daily work, there are a number of New York Stock Exchange members who never go on the floor, but spend the session at the ticker in their respective offices. Experience has taught them that they can produce larger profits by this method, else they would not follow it. The majority of them trade in 500-share lots and up and their business forms an important share of the daily volume.

A number of so-called semi-professionals operate on what may be termed intuitive tape reading. They have no well-defined code of rules and probably could not explain clearly just how they do it, but they "get the money" and that is the best proof of the pudding.

The existence of even a comparatively small body of successful Tape Readers is evidence that money making by this means is an accomplished fact and should encourage others.

One of the greatest difficulties which the novice has to overcome is known by the slangy but expressive term, "cold feet." Too many people start and dabble a little without going far enough to determine whether or not they can make a go of it. And even those who get pretty well along in the subject will be scared to death at a string of losses and quit just when they should dig in harder. For in addition to learning the art they must form a sort of trading character, which no amount of reverses can discourage nor turn back and which constantly strives to eliminate its own weak points such as fear, greed, anxiety, nervousness and the many other mental factors which go to make or unmake the profit column.

Perhaps I have painted a difficult proposition. If so, the greater will be the reward of those who master it. As stated at the beginning, Tape Reading is hard work. There seems no good reason for altering that opinion.

Chapter XIII – Two Days' Trading

Below is a record of transactions made by me, results having been obtained by following the methods suggested in the within series on Tape Reading. The object is to show the possibilities along this line and to encourage the many who are now endeavoring to master the art.

It will be observed that out of fifteen transactions, figuring on the buying and selling prices alone, there were thirteen profits and only one loss. One transaction showed neither profit nor loss.

Seven trades were on the long side and eight on the short. The stock fluctuated between 166 3/4 and 170 3/8 (3 5/8 points) during these two sessions, and gave numerous trading opportunities.

All transactions were protected by a close stop, in some cases not more than 1/8 or 1/4 from the original buying or selling price. These stop orders were not always put on the floor for the reason that in such active trading, stops could be changed or cancelled more quickly when they were carried in the head and executed "at the market" when the price hit the required figure.

Two Day's Trades

		Bought	Sold	Loss	Profit
200	Reading	long..............167 1/2	168 1/4		3/4
200	"	short.............167 1/4	168 3/8		1 1/8
200	"	long..............167 1/4	168 3/4		1 1/2
200	"	short.............169 5/8	169 3/4		1/8
200	"	short.............169	169 1/2		1/2
200	"	short.............169 1/8	170		7/8
200	"	short.............169 5/8	170		3/8
200	"	short.............168 1/8	169 7/8		1 3/4
200	"	long..............168	168		even
200	"	long..............168 1/4	168 3/4		1/2
200	"	short.............168	169 1/4		1 1/4
200	"	short.............168 1/8	169 1/4		1 1/8
200	"	long..............168 1/8	168 1/2		3/8
200	"	long..............168 1/4	169		3/4
200	"	short.............169 1/4	168 3/8	7/8	.....
2700				7/8	11

Commission...3 3/8		
Tax (about)..1/4		
		4 1/2
Net profit, in points..........................		6 1/2

Chapter XIV – The Principles Applied to Wider Savings

The first edition of this book having been exhausted, it has been my privilege to edit the foregoing chapters in preparation for the second edition. This has required a consideration of the principles therein set forth, and has enabled me to test and compare these principles in their adaptation to the stock market of 1916.

I find that in no important degree is it necessary to modify what has been written. While the character of the trading has altered since the outbreak of the European War, this change represents more a shifting of the leadership and a widening of the swings, due to extraordinary conditions.

Proof that these rules and methods are correct is also found in their adaptation to other forms of trading, chief among which is the detection of accumulation and distribution at certain important turning points in the market.

I have used this method successfully in forecasting the market for these principal swings and find it to be a much more comfortable way of following the market, because it is not so confining.

Preparation for a long upswing or downswing, as well as for the intermediate movements which are numerous, is clearly apparent to those who understand the art of Tape Reading.

In judging the market by its own action, it is unimportant whether you are endeavoring to forecast the next small half hourly swing or the trend for the next two or three weeks. The same indications as to price, volume, activity, support and pressure, are exhibited in the preparation for both. The same elements will be found in a drop of water as in the ocean, and vice versa.

A study of the stock market means a study in the forces above and below the present level of prices. Each movement has its period of preparation, execution and culmination, and the most substantial of movements are those which make long preparation. Without this preparation and gathering of force, a movement is not likely to be sustained. On the other hand, the greater the preparation, the greater the probable extent of the swing.

Preparation for the principal movements in the market will very often occupy several months. This may be preceded by a decline, in which large operators accumulate their stocks. They may even precipitate this decline in order to pave the way for such accumulation.

Large operators differ from small ones in their ability to foresee important changes in stock market values from six months to a year in advance, and to prepare themselves therefor. A study of these preparatory periods discloses to these who understand the anatomy of market movements the direction and possible extent of the next big swing. Thus, a study of these important turning points, principal among which are booms and panics, is the most essential.

Small operators should take a leaf from the book of those who buy and sell enormous quantities of securities. It is their foresight which enables them to profit. To cultivate foresight means to study technical and other conditions.

In a lecture at the Finance Forum, New York, the writer showed how all influences of every sort affecting the stock market are shown on the tape, and in the changes in prices. A copy of this lecture accompanies each copy of this book, and is sent gratis in order that the reader may thoroughly understand the advantage of studying the fluctuations instead of the fundamental factors such as crops, money, politics, railroad earnings, etc., all of which are finally interpreted into the prices which appear on the tape.

While I would not for a moment discourage the student from acquiring a knowledge, and giving some consideration to the Fundamental Statistics, the advantages of studying the action of the market, as a guide to future prices, are productive of too great results to warrant their dilution with factors which are really of secondary importance. I make this claim because of my conviction that the position of large operators is more important than the so-called basic factors.

For several years past I have applied the principles in this book to the forecasting of the swings of from 5 to 20 points. Results have been highly satisfactory.

For this reason I can recommend that the subject be studied with a view to the formation of a method of trading, especially adapted to the individual requirements of those who wish to follow this intensely interesting and highly profitable pursuit.

PSYCHOLOGY OF THE STOCK MARKET
G. C. Selden - 1912

Contents
I – The speculative cycle
II – Inverted reasoning and its consequences
III – "They"
IV – Confusing the present with the future - discounting
V – Confusing the personal with the general
VI – The panic and the boom
VII – The impulsive vs. phlegmatic operator
VIII – The mental attitude of the individual

Chapter I - The Speculative Cycle

Most experienced professional traders in the stock market will readily admit that the minor fluctuations, amounting to perhaps five or ten dollars a share in the active speculative issues, are chiefly psychological. They result from varying attitudes of the public mind, or, more strictly, from the mental attitudes of those persons who are interested in the market at the time.

Such fluctuations may be, and often are, based on "fundamental" conditions—that is, on real changes in the dividend prospects of the stocks affected or on variations in the earning power of the corporations represented—and again they may not. The broad movements of the market, covering periods of months or even years, are always the result of general financial conditions; but the smaller intermediate fluctuations represent changes in the state of the public mind, which may or may not coincide with alterations in basic factors.

To bring out clearly the degree to which psychology enters into the stock market problem from day to day, it is only necessary to reproduce a conversation between professional traders, such as may be heard almost any day in New street or in the neighboring cafes.

"Well, what do you know?" says one trader to the other. "Just covered my Steel," is the reply. "Too much company. Everybody seems to be short."

"Everybody I've seen thinks just as you do. Each one has covered because he thinks everybody else is short—still the market doesn't rally much. I don't believe there's much short interest left, and if that's the case we shall get another break."

"Yes, that's what they all say—and they've all sold short again because they think everybody else has covered. I believe there's just as much short interest now as there was before."

It is evident that this series of inversions might be continued indefinitely. These alert mental acrobats are doing a succession of flip-flops, each one of which leads up logically to the next, without ever arriving at a final stopping-place.

The main point of their argument is that the state of mind of a man short of the market is radically different from the state of mind of one who is long. Their whole study, in such a conversation, is the mental attitude of those interested in the market. If a majority of the volatile class of in-and-out traders are long, many of them will hasten to sell on any sign of weakness and a decline will result. If the majority are short, they will buy on any development of strength and an advance may be expected.

The psychological aspects of speculation may be considered from two points of view, equally important. One question is, What effect do varying mental attitudes of the public have upon the course of prices? How is the character of the market influenced by psychological conditions?

A second consideration is, how does the mental attitude of the individual trader affect his chances of success? To what extent, and how, can he overcome the obstacles placed in his pathway by his own hopes and fears, his timidities and his obstinacies?

These two points of view are so closely involved and intermingled that it is almost impossible to consider either one alone. It will be necessary to take up first the subject of speculative psychology as a whole and later to attempt to draw conclusions both as to its effect upon the market and its influence upon the fortunes of the individual trader. As a convenient starting point it may be well to trace briefly the history of the typical speculative cycle, which runs its course over and over, year after year, with infinite variations but with substantial similarity, on every stock exchange and in every speculative market of the world— and presumably will continue to do so as long as prices are fixed by the competition of buyers and sellers, and as long as human beings seek a profit and fear a loss.[3]

Beginning with a condition of dullness and interest in the market, mostly, at this time, of the activity, with small fluctuations and very slight public interest, prices begin to rise, at first almost imperceptibly. No special reason appears for the advance, and it is generally thought to be merely temporary, due to small professional operations. There is of course, some short interest. An active speculative stock is never entirely free from shorts.

As there is so little public speculation at this period in the cycle, there are but few who are willing to sell out on so small an advance, hence prices are not met by any large volume of profit taking. The smaller professionals take the short side for a turn, with the idea that trifling fluctuations are the best that can be hoped for at the moment and must be taken advantage of if any profits are to be secured.

Soon another unostentatious upward movement begins, carrying prices a trifle higher than the first. A few shrewd traders take the long side, but the public is still unmoved and the sleeping short interest—most of it originally put out at much higher figures—still refuses to waken.

Gradually prices harden further and finally advance somewhat sharply. A few of the more timid shorts cover, perhaps to save a part of their profits or to prevent their trades from running into a loss. The fact that a bull turn is coming now penetrates through another layer of intellectual density and another wave

---

[3] To be "short of stocks" means, essentially, that the operator has sold stocks for future delivery.

of traders take the long side. The public notes the advance and begins to think some further upturn is possible, but that there will be plenty of opportunities to buy on substantial reactions.

Strangely enough, these reactions, except of the most trifling character, do not appear. Waiting buyers do not get a satisfactory chance to take hold. Prices begin to move up faster. There is a halt from time to time, but when a real reaction finally comes the market looks "too weak to buy," and when it starts up again it often does so with a sudden leap that leaves would-be purchasers far in the rear.

At length the more stubborn bears become alarmed and begin, to cover in large volume. The market "boils," and to the short who is watching the tape, seems likely to shoot through the ceiling at almost any moment. However firm may be his bearish convictions, his nervous system eventually gives out under this continual pounding, and he covers everything "at the market" with a sigh of relief that his losses are no greater.

About this time the outside public begins to reach the conclusion that the market is "too strong to react much," and that the only thing to do is to "buy 'em everywhere." From this source comes another wave of buying, which soon carries prices to new high levels, and purchasers congratulate themselves on their quick and easy profits.

For every buyer there must be a seller—or, more accurately, for every one hundred shares bought one hundred shares must be sold, as the actual number of *persons* buying at this stage is likely to be much greater than the number of persons selling. Early in the advance the supply of stocks is small and comes from scattered sources, but as prices rise, more and more holders become satisfied with their profits and are willing to sell. The bears, also, begin to fight the advance by selling short on every quick rise. A stubborn bear will often be forced to cover again and again, with a small loss each time, before he finally locates the top and secures a liberal profit on the ensuing decline.

Those selling at this stage are not, as a rule, the largest holders. The largest holders are usually those whose judgment is sound enough, or whose connections are good enough, so that they have made a good deal of money; and neither a sound judgment nor the best advisers are likely to favor selling so early in the advance, when much larger profits can be secured by simply holding on.

The height to which prices can now be carried depends on the underlying conditions. If money is easy and general business prosperous a prolonged bull movement may result, while strained banking resources or depressed trade will set a definite limit to the possible advance. If conditions are bearish, the driving of the biggest shorts to cover will practically end the rise; but in a genuine bull market the advance will continue until checked by sales of stocks held for investment, which come upon the market only when prices are believed to be unduly high.

In a sense, the market is always a contest between investors and speculators. The real investor, looking chiefly to interest return, but by no means unwilling to make a profit by buying low and selling high, is ready, perhaps, to buy his favorite stock at a price which will yield him six percent on his investment, or to sell at a price yielding only four percent. The speculator cares nothing about interest return. He wants to buy before prices go up and to sell short before they go down. He would as soon buy at the top of a big rise as at any other time, provided prices are going still higher.

As the market advances, therefore, one investor after another sees his limit reached and his stock sold. Thus the volume of stocks to be carried or tossed from hand to hand by bullish speculators is constantly rolling up like a snowball. On the ordinary intermediate fluctuations, covering five to twenty dollars a share, these sales by investors are small compared with the speculative business. In one hundred shares of a stock selling at 150, the investor has $15.000; but with this sum the speculator can carry ten times that number of shares.

The reason why sales by investors are so effective is not because of the actual amount of stock thrown on the market, but because this stock is a permanent load, which will not be got rid of again until prices have suffered a severe decline. What the speculative sells he or some other trader may buy back tomorrow.

The time comes when everybody seems to be buying. Prices become confused. One stock leaps upward in a way to strike terror to the heart of the last surviving short. Another appears almost equally strong, but slips back unobtrusively when nobody is looking, like the frog jumping out of the well in the arithmetic of our boyhood. Still another churns violently in one place, like a side-wheeler stuck on a sandbar.

Then the market gives a sudden lurch downward, as though in danger of spilling out its unwieldy contents. This is hailed as a "healthy reaction," though it is a mystery whom it can be healthy for, unless it is the shorts. Prices recover again, with everybody happy except a few disgruntled bears, who are regarded with contemptuous amusement.

Curiously, however, there seems to be stock enough for all comers, and the few cranks who have time to bother with such things notice that the general average of prices is now rising very slowly, if at all. The largest speculative holders of stocks, finding a market big enough to absorb their sales, are letting go. And there are always stocks enough to go around. Our big capitalists are seldom entirely out of stocks. They merely have more stocks when prices are low and fewer when prices are high. Moreover, long before there is any danger of the supply running out, plenty of new issues are created.

When there is a general public interest in the stock market, an immense amount of realizing will often be absorbed within three or four days or a week, after which the deluge; but if speculation is narrow, prices may remain around top figures for weeks or months, while big holdings are fed out, a few hundred shares here and a few hundred there, and even then a balance may be left to be thrown over on the ensuing decline at whatever prices can be obtained. Great speculative leaders are far from infallible. They have often sold out too soon and later have seen the market run way to unexpected heights, or have held on too long and have suffered severe losses before they could get out.

In this selling the bull leaders get a good deal of undesirable help from the bears. However wary the bulls may be in concealing their sales, their machinations will be discovered by watchful professionals and shrewd students, and a considerable sprinkling of short sales will be put out within a few points of the top. This is one of the reasons why the long swings in active speculative stocks are smaller in proportion to price than in inactive specialties of a similar character—contrary to the generally received impression. It is rare that any considerable short interest exists in the inactive stocks.

Once the top-heavy load is overturned, the decline is usually more rapid than the previous advance. The floating supply, now greatly increased, is tossed about from one speculator to another at lower and lower prices. From time to time stocks become temporarily lodged in stubborn hands, so that part of these shorts take fright and cover, causing a sharp upturn; but so long as the load of stocks is still on the market the general course of prices must be downward. Until inventors or big speculative capitalists again come into the market, the load of stocks to be carried by ordinary speculative bulls increases almost continually. There is no lessening of the floating supply of stock certificates in the Street, and there is a gradual increase in the short interest; and of course the bulls have to carry these short sales as well as the actual certificates, since for every seller there must be a buyer, whether the sale be made by a short or a long. Shorts cover again and again on the sharp breaks, but in most cases they put out their lines again, either higher or lower, as opportunity offers. On the average, the short interest is largest at low prices, though there are likely to be periods during the decline when it will be larger than at the final bottom, where buying by shorts often helps to avert panicky conditions.

The length of this decline, like the extent of the preceding advance, depends on fundamental conditions; for both investors and speculative capitalists will come into the market sooner if all conditions are favorable than they will in a stringent money market or when the future prospects of business are unsatisfactory. As a rule, buyers do not appear in force until a "bargain day" appears. This is when, in its downward course, the heavy load of stocks strikes an area honeycombed with stop loss orders.* Floor traders seize the opportunity to put out short lines and a general collapse results.

Here are plenty of stocks to be had cheap, and shrewd operators—large and small, but mostly large or on the way to become so—are busy picking them up. The fixed limits of many investors are also reached by the sharp

---

* A stop loss order, or more briefly "stop order," is an order to sell as soon as a certain specified price is reached below the current price at the time the order is placed. For example, is Steel common is selling at 90, a holder who wishes to limit his possible loss may direct his broker to sell it if the price declines to 88. Or if the trader is "short" of Steel common, the current market being 90, he may place an order to buy the necessary stock to "cover" – or to deliver to the purchaser – if the price advances to 92, thus limiting his loss to about two "points," or dollars per share.

break, and the stocks they buy disappear, to be seen in the Street no more until the next bull turn.

Many shorts cover on such a break, but not all. The sequel to the "bargain day" is a big short interest which has overstayed its market, and a quick rally follows; but when the more urgent shorts get relief, prices sag again and fall into that condition of lethargy from which this consideration of the speculative cycle started.

The movements described are substantially uniform, whether the cycle be one covering a week, a month, or a year. The big cycle includes many intermediate movements, and these movements in turn contain smaller swings. Investors do not participate to any extent in the small swings, but otherwise the forces involved in a three-point turn up and down are substantially the same as those which appear in a thirty-point cycle, though not so easy to identify.

The fact will at once be recognized that the above description is, in essence, a story of human hopes and fears; of mental attitude, on the part of those interested, resulting from their own position in the market, rather than from any deliberate judgment of conditions; of an unwarranted projection by the public imagination of a perceived present into an unknown though not wholly unknowable future.

Laying aside for the present the influence of fundamental conditions on prices, it is our task to trace out both the causes and the effects of these psychological elements in speculation.

Chapter II - Inverted Reasoning And Its Consequences

It is hard for the average man to oppose what appears to be the general drift of public opinion. In the stock market this is perhaps harder than elsewhere; for we all realize that the prices of stocks must, in the long run, be controlled by public opinion. The point we fail to remember is that public opinion in a speculative market is measured in dollars, not in population. One man controlling one million dollars has double the weight of five hundred men with one thousand dollars each. Dollars are the horsepower of the markets— the mere number of men does not signify.

This is why the great body of opinion appears to be bullish at the top and bearish at the bottom. The multitude of small traders must be, as a plain necessity, long when prices are at the top, and short or out of the market at the bottom. The very fact that they are long at the top shows that they have been supplied with stocks from some source.

Again, the man with one million dollars is a silent individual. The time when it was necessary for him to talk is past—his money now does the talking. But the one thousand men who have one thousand dollars each are conversational, fluent, verbose to the last degree.

It will be observed that the above course of reasoning leads up to the conclusion that most of those who talk about the market are more likely to be wrong than right, at least so far as speculative fluctuations are concerned. This is not complimentary to the "moulders of public opinion," but most seasoned newspaper readers will agree that is it true. The daily press reflects, in a general way, the thoughts of the multitude, and in the stock market the multitude is necessarily, as a logical deduction from the facts of the case, likely to be bullish at high prices and bearish at low.

It has often been remarked that the average man is an optimist regarding his own enterprises and a pessimist regarding those of others. Certainly this is true of the professional trader in stocks. As a result of the reasoning outlined above, he comes habitually to expect that nearly every one else will be wrong, but is, as a rule, confident that his own analysis of the situation will prove correct. He values the opinion of a few persons whom he believes to be generally successful; but aside from these few, the greater the number of the bullish opinions he hears, the more doubtful he becomes about the wisdom of following the bull side.

This apparent contrariness of the market, although easily understood when its causes are analyzed, breeds in professional traders a peculiar sort of skepticism—leads them always to distrust the obvious and to apply a kind of inverted reasoning to almost all stock market problems. Often, in the minds of traders who are not naturally logical, this inverted reasoning assumes the most erratic and grotesque forms, and it accounts for many apparently absurd fluctuations in prices which are commonly charged to manipulation.

For example, a trader starts with this assumption: The market has had a good advance; all the small traders are bullish; somebody must have sold them stock which they are carrying; hence the big capitalists are probably sold out or short and ready for a reaction or perhaps for a bear market. Then if a strong item of bullish news comes out—one, let us say, that really makes an important change in the situation—he says, "Ah, so this is what they have been hulling the market on! It has been discounted by the previous rise." Or he may say, "They are putting out this bull news to sell stocks on." He proceeds to sell out any long stocks he may have or perhaps to sell short. His reasoning may be correct or it may not; but at any rate his selling and that of others who reason in a similar way, is likely to produce at least a temporary decline on the announcement of the good news. This decline looks absurd to the outsider and he falls back on the old explanation "All manipulation."

The same principle is often carried further. You will find professional traders reasoning that favorable figures on the steel industry, for example, have been concocted to enable insiders to sell their Steel; or that gloomy reports are put in circulation to facilitate accumulation. Hence they may act in direct opposition to the news and carry the market with them, for the time at least.

The less the trader knows about the fundamentals of the financial situation the more likely he is to be led astray in conclusions of this character. If he has confidence in the general strength of conditions he may be ready to accept as genuine and natural, a piece of news which he would otherwise receive with cynical skepticism and use as a basis for short sales. If he knows that fundamental conditions are unsound, he will not be so likely to interpret bad news as issued to assist in accumulation of stocks.

The same reasoning is applied to large purchases through brokers known to be associated with capitalists. In fact, in this case we often hear a double inversion, as it were. Such buying may impress the observer in three ways:

1. The "rank outsider" takes it at face value, as bullish.
2. A more experienced trader may say, "If they really wished to get the stocks they would not buy through their own brokers, but would endeavor to conceal their buying by scattering it among other houses."
3. A stilt more suspicious professional may turn another mental somersault and say, "They are buying through their own brokers so as to throw us off the scent and make us think someone else is using their brokers as a blind." By this double somersault such a trader arrives at the same conclusion as the outsider.

The reasoning of traders becomes even more complicated when large buying or selling is done openly by a big professional who is known to trade in and out for small profits. If he buys 50,000 shares, other traders are quite willing to sell to him and their opinion of the market is little influenced, simply because they know he may sell 50,000 the next day or even the next hour. For this reason great capitalists sometimes buy or sell through such big professional traders in order to execute their orders easily and without arousing suspicion. Hence the play of subtle intellects around big trading of this kind often becomes very elaborate.

It is to be noticed that this inverted reasoning is useful chiefly at the top or bottom of a movement, when distribution or accumulation is taking place on a large scale. A market which repeatedly refuses to respond to good news after a considerable advance is likely to be "full of stocks." Likewise a market which will not go down on bad news is usually "bare of stock."

Between the extremes will be found long stretches in which capitalists have very little cause to conceal their position. Having accumulated their lines as low as possible, they are then willing to be known as the leaders of the upward movement and have every reason to be perfectly open in their buying. This condition continues until they are ready to sell. Likewise, having sold as much as they desire, they have no reason to conceal their position further, even though a subsequent decline may run for months or a year.

It is during a long upward movement that the "lamb" makes money, because he accepts facts as facts, while the professional trader is often found fighting the advance and losing heavily because of the over-development of cynicism and suspicion.

The successful trader eventually learns when to invert his natural mental processes and when to leave them in their usual position. Often he develops a sort of instinct which could scarcely be reduced to cold print. But in the hands of the tyro this form of reasoning is exceedingly dangerous, because it permits of putting an alternate construction on any event. Bull news either (1) is significant of a rising trend of prices, or (2) indicates that "they" are trying to make a market to sell on. Bad news may indicate either a genuinely bearish situation or a desire to accumulate stocks at low prices.

The inexperienced operator is therefore left very much at sea. He is playing with the professional's edged tools and is likely to cut himself. Of what use is it for him to try to apply his reason to stock market conditions when every event may be doubly interpreted?

Indeed, it is doubtful if the professional's distrust of the obvious is of much benefit to him in the long run. Most of us have met those deplorable mental wrecks, often found among the "chair-warmers" in brokers' offices, whose thinking machinery seems to have become permanently demoralized as a result of continued aerobatics. They are always seeking an "ulterior motive" in everything. They credit—or debit— Morgan and Rockefeller with the smallest and meanest trickery and ascribe to them the most awful duplicity in matters which those "high financiers" would not stoop to notice. The continual reversal of the mental engine sometimes deranges its mechanism.

Probably no better general rule can be laid down than the brief one, "Stick to common sense." Maintain a balanced, receptive mind and avoid abstruse deductions. A few further suggestions may, however, be offered:

If you already have a position in the market, do not attempt to bolster up your failing faith by resorting to intellectual subtleties in the interpretation of obvious facts. If you are long or short of the market, you are not an unprejudiced judge, and you will be greatly tempted to put such an interpretation upon current events as will coincide with your preconceived opinion. It is hardly too much to say that this is the greatest obstacle to success. The least you can do is to avoid inverted reasoning in support of your own position.

After a prolonged advance, do not call inverted reasoning to your aid in order to prove that prices are going still higher; likewise after a big break do not let your bearish deductions become too complicated. Be suspicious of bull news at high prices, and of bear news at low prices.

Bear in mind that an item of news usually causes but one considerable movement of prices. If the movement takes place before the news comes out, as a result of rumors and expectations, then it is not likely to be repeated after the announcement is made; but if the movement of prices has not preceded, then the news contributes to the general strength or weakness of the situation and a movement of prices may follow.

Chapter III - "They"

If a man entirely unfamiliar with the stock market should spend several days around the Exchange listening to the conversation of all sorts of traders and investors, in order to pick up information about the causes of price movements, the probability is that the most pressing question in his mind at the end of that time would be "Who are 'They'?"

Everywhere he went he would hear about "Them." In the customers' rooms of the fractional lot houses he would find young men trading in ten shares and arguing learnedly as to what They were to do next. Tape readers— experts and tyros alike—would tell him that They were accumulating Steel, or distributing Reading. Floor traders and members of the Exchange would whisper that they were told They were going to put the market up or down, as the case might be. Even sedate investors might inform him that, although the situation was bearish, undoubtedly They would have to put the market temporarily high in order to unload Their stocks. This "They" theory of the market is quite as prevalent among successful traders as among beginners—probably more so. There may be room for argument as to why this is so, but as to the fact itself there is no doubt. Whether They are a myth or a definite reality, many persons are making money by studying the market from this point of view.

If you were to go around Wall street and ask various classes of traders who They are, you would get nearly as many different answers as the number of people interviewed. One would say, "The house of Morgan," another, "Standard Oil and associated interests"—which is pretty broad, when you stop to think of it; another, "The big banking interests;" still another, "Professional traders on the floor;" a fifth, "Pools in the various favorite stocks, which act more or less in concert;" a sixth might say, "Shrewd and successful speculators, whoever and wherever they are;" while to the seventh, They may typify merely active traders as a whole, whom he conceives to make prices by falling over each other to buy or to sell.

Indeed, one writer of no small attainments as a student of market conditions believes that the entire phenomena of the New York stock market are under the control of some one individual, who is presumably, in some way or other, the representative of great associated interests.

It is obviously impossible to trace to its source, tag and identify any sort of permanent controlling power. The security markets of the world move pretty much together in the broad cyclical swings, so that such a power would have to consist of a worldwide association of great financial interests, controlling all of the principal security markets. The average observer will find it difficult to masticate and swallow this proposition.

The effort to reduce the science of speculation and investment to an impossible definiteness or an ideal simplicity is, I believe, responsible for many failures. A.S. Hardy, the diplomat, who was formerly a professor of mathematics and wrote books on quotations, differential calculus, etc., once remarked that the study of mathematics is very poor mental discipline, because it does not cultivate the judgment. Given fixed and certain premises, your mathematician will follow them out to a correct conclusion; but in practical affairs the whole difficulty is in selecting your premises.

So the market student of mathematical turn of mind is always seeking a rule or a set of rules "sure thing" as traders put it. He would not seek such rules for succeeding in the grocery business or the lumber business; he would, on the contrary, analyze each situation as it arose and act accordingly. The stock market presents itself to my mind as a purely practical proposition. Scientific methods may be applied to any line of business, from stocks to chickens, but this is a very different thing from trying to reduce the fluctuations of the stock market to a basis of mathematical certainty.

In discussing the identity of Them, therefore, we must be content to take obvious facts as we find them without attempting to spin fine theories.

There are three senses in which this idea of "Them" has some foundation in fact. First, "They" may be and often are roughly conceived of as the floor traders on the Stock Exchange who are directly concerned in making quotations, pools formed to control certain stocks, or individual manipulators.

Floor traders exercise an important influence on the immediate movement of prices. Suppose, for example, they observe that offerings of Reading are very light. Declines do not induce liquidation and only small offerings of stock are met on advances. They begin to feel that, in the absence of unexpected cataclysms, Reading will not decline much. The natural thing for them to do is to begin buying Reading on all soft spots. Whenever a few hundred shares are offered at a bargain, floor traders snap up the stock.

As a result of this "bailing out" of the market, Reading becomes scarcer still, and traders, being now long, become more bullish. They begin to "mark up prices." This is not difficult, since they are for the time being, practically unanimous in a desire for higher prices. Suppose the market is 81 1/8 bid, offered at 81 1/4. They find that only 100 shares are for sale at 1/4, and 200 are offered at 3/8. As to how much stock may be awaiting bids at 1/2 or higher, they cannot be sure, but can generally make a shrewd guess. One or more traders take these offerings of perhaps 500 shares, and make the market 1/2 bid. The other floor traders are not willing to sell at this trifling profit, and a wait ensues to see whether any outside orders are attracted by the movement of the price, and if so, whether they are buying or selling orders. If a few buying orders come in, they are filled, perhaps at 5/8 and 3/4. If selling appears, the floor traders retire in good order, take the offerings at lower prices, and try it again the next day or perhaps the next hour. Eventually, by seizing every favorable opportunity, they engineer an upward move of perhaps two or three points without taking any more stock than they want.

If such a movement attracts a following, it may easily run ten points without any real change in the prospects of the Reading road— though the prospects of the road may have had something to do with making the stock scarce before the movement started. On the other hand, if large offerings of stock are encountered at the advance, the boomlet is ignominiously squelched and the floor traders make trifling profits or losses.

Pools are not so common as most outsiders believe. There are many difficulties and complications to be overcome before a pool can be formed, held together, and operated successfully, as we had opportunity to observe some time ago in the case of Hocking Coal & Iron. But if a definite pool exists in any stock, its operations are practically a reproduction, on a larger scale and under a binding agreement, of the methods employed by floor traders over a smaller range and in a mere loose and voluntary association resulting from their common interests. And the individual manipulator is only a pool consisting of one person.

Second, many conceive "Them" as an association of powerful capitalists who are running a campaign in many important speculative stocks simultaneously. It is safe to say that no such permanent and united association exists, though it would be hard to prove such a statement. But there have been many times when a single great interest was practically in control of the market for a time, other interests being content to look on, or to participate in a small way, or to await a favorable chance to take the other side.

The "Standard Oil crowd," the "Morgan interests," etc. will at once occur to the reader as having been, at various times in the past, in sole control of an important general campaign. At present the great interests are generally classified into three divisions—Morgan, Standard Oil, and Kuhn-Loeb.

A definite agreement among such interests as these would be possible, for limited and temporary purposes. Each so-called interest consists of a loosely bound aggregation of followers, having only one thing in common—control of capital. Such an "interest" is not an army, where the traitor can be court-martialed and shot; it has to be led, not driven. True, the known traitor might be put to death, financially speaking, but in stock market operations the traitor cannot, as a rule, be known. Unless his operations are of unusual size, he can successfully cover his tracks.

From this second point of view, "They" are not always active in the market. Great campaigns can only be undertaken with safety in periods when the future is to a certain extent assured. When the future is in doubt, when various confusing elements enter into the financial and political situation, leading financiers may be quite content to confine their stock market operations to individual deals, and to postpone the inauguration of a broad campaign until a more solid foundation exists for it.

Third, "They" may be conceived simply as speculators and investors in general—all that miscellaneous and heterogeneous troop of persons, scattered over the whole world, each of whom contributes his mite to the fluctuations of prices on the Stock Exchange. In this sense there is no doubt about the existence of Them, and They are the court of last resort in the establishment of prices. To put it another way, these are the "They" who are the ultimate consumers of securities. It is to Them that everybody else is planning, sooner or later, directly or indirectly, to sell his stocks.

You can lead the horse to water, but you can't make him drink. You or I or any other great millionaire can put up prices, but you can't make Them buy the stocks from you unless They have the purchasing power and the purchasing disposition. So there is no doubt that here, at any rate, we have a conception of Them which will stand analysis without exploding.

In cases where a general campaign is being conducted, the "They" theory of values is of considerable help in the accumulation or distribution of stocks. In fact, in the late stages of a bull campaign the argument most frequently heard is likely to be something as follows: "Yes, prices are high and I can't see that future prospects are especially bullish—but stocks are in strong hands and They will have to put them higher to make a market to sell on." (Some investors make a point of dumping over all their stocks as soon as this veteran warhorse of the news brigade is groomed and trotted out.) Likewise, after a prolonged bear campaign, we hear that somebody is "in trouble" and that They are going to break the market until certain concentrated holdings are brought out.

As this is very likely to be nothing but dust thrown in the eyes of that most gullible of all created beings—the haphazard speculator. When prices are so high in comparison with conditions that no sound reason can be advanced why they should go higher, a certain number of people are still induced to buy because of what "They" are going to do. Or, at least, if the public can no longer be induced to buy in any large volume, it is prevented from selling short for fear of what They may do.

The close student of the technical condition of the market—by which is meant the character of the long and short interests from day to day—is pretty sure to base his operations to a considerable extent on what he thinks They will do next. He has in mind Them as described in the first classification above—floor traders, pools and manipulators. He gets a good deal of help from this conception, crude as it may appear to be— largely, no doubt, because it serves to distract his mind from current news and gossip, and to prevent him from being too greatly influenced by the momentary appearance of the market.

When the market looks weakest, when the news is at the worst, when bearish prognostications are most general, is the time to buy, as every school-boy knows; but if a man has in mind a picture of a flood of stocks pouring out from the four quarters of the globe, with no buyers, because of some desperately bad news which is just coming over the ticker, it is almost a mental impossibility for him to get up the courage to plunge in and buy. If, on the other hand, he conceives that They are just giving the market a final smash to facilitate covering a gigantic line of short stocks, he has courage to buy. His view may be right or wrong, but at least he avoids buying at the top and selling at the bottom, and he has nerve to buy in a weak market and sell in a strong one.

The reason for the haziness of the "They" conception in the average trader's mind is that he is only concerned with Them as They manifest Themselves through the stock market. As to who They are he feels a mild and detached curiosity; but as to Their manifestations in the market he is vitally and financially interested. It is on the latter point, therefore, that he concentrates his thoughts.

But inasmuch as definite, painstaking analysis of a situation is always better than a hazy general notion of it, the trader or investor would do much better to rid his mind of Them. The word "They" means nothing until it has an antecedent; and to use it continually without having any antecedent in mind is slipshod language, which stands for slipshod thinking. They, in the sense of the big banking interests, may be working directly against Them in the sense of individual manipulators; the manipulator, again, may be trying to trap Them in the sense of floor traders.

A genuine knowledge of the technical condition of the market cannot be summed up in any offhand declaration about what They are going to do. You cannot determine the attitude toward the market of every individual who is interested in it, but you can roughly classify the sources from which buying and selling are likely to come, the motives which are likely to actuate the various classes, and the character of the long interest and short interest. In brief, after enough study and observation, you can always have in mind some kind of an antecedent for Them, and must have it, if you base your operations on technical conditions.

Chapter IV - Confusing the Present with the Future— Discounting

It is axiomatic that inexperienced traders and investors, and indeed a majority of the more experienced as well, are continually trying to speculate on past events. Suppose, for example, railroad earnings as published are show- ing constant large increases in net. The novice reasons, "Increased earnings mean increased amounts applicable to the payment of dividends. Prices should rise. I will buy." Not at all. He should say, "Prices have risen to the extent represented by these increased earnings, unless this effect has been counter- balanced by other considerations. Now what next?"

It is a sort of automatic assumption of the human mind that present conditions will continue, and our whole scheme of life is necessarily based to a great degree on this assumption. When the price of wheat is high farmers increase their acreage because wheat-growing pays better; when it is low they plant less. I remember talking with a potato-raiser who claimed that he had made a good deal of money by simply reversing the above custom. When potatoes were low he had planted liberally; when high he had cut down his acreage—because he reasoned that other farmers would do just the opposite.

The average man is not blessed—or cursed, however you may look at it— with an analytical mind. We see "as through a glass darkly." Our ideas are always enveloped in a haze and our reasoning powers work in a rut from which we find it painful if not impossible to escape. Many of our emotions and some of our acts are merely automatic responses to external stimuli. Wonder- ful as is the development of the human brain, it originated as an enlarged ganglion, and its first response is still practically that of the ganglion.

A simple illustration of this is found in the enmity we all feel toward the alarm clock which arouses us in the morning. We have carefully set and wound that alarm and if it failed to go off it would perhaps put us to serious inconvenience; yet we reward the faithful clock with anathemas.

When a subway train is delayed nine-tenths of the people waiting on the platform are anxiously craning their necks to see if it is coming, while many persons on it who are in danger of missing an engagement are holding themselves tense, apparently in the effort to help the train along. As a rule we apply more well-meant, but to a great extent ineffective, energy, physical or nervous, to the accomplishment of an object, than analysis or calculation.

When it comes to so complicated a matter as the price of stocks, our hazi- ness increases in proportion to the difficulty of the subject and our ignorance of it. From reading, observation and conversation we imbibe a miscellaneous assortment of ideas from which we conclude that the situation is bullish or bearish. The very form of the expression "the situation is bullish"—not "the situation will soon become bullish"—shows the extent to which we allow the present to obscure the future in the formation of our judgment.

Catch any trader and pin him down to it and he will readily admit that the logical moment for the highest prices is when the news is most bullish; yet you will find him buying stocks on this news after it comes out—if not at the moment, at any rate "on a reaction."

Most coming events cast their shadows before, and it is on this that intelligent speculation must be based. The movement of prices in anticipation of such an event is called "discounting," and this process of discounting is worthy of a little careful examination.

The first point to be borne in mind is that some events cannot be discounted, even by the supposed omniscience of the great banking interests — which is, in point of fact, more than half imaginary. The San Francisco earthquake is the standard example of an event which could not be foreseen and therefore could not be discounted; but an event does not have to be purely an "act of God" to be undiscountable. There can be no question that our great bankers have been as much in the dark in regard to some recent Supreme Court decisions as the smallest "piker" in the customer's room of an odd-lot brokerage house.

If the effect of an event does not make itself felt before the event takes place, it must come after. In our discussion of discounting we must bear this fact in mind in order that our subject may not run away with us.

On the other hand an event may sometimes be over discounted. If the dividend rate on a stock is to be raised from four to five percent, earnest bulls, with an eye to their own commitments, may spread rumors of six or seven percent so that the actual declaration of five percent may be received as disappointing and cause a decline.

Generally speaking, every event which is under the control of capitalists associated with the property, or any financial condition which is subject to the management of combined banking interests, is likely to be pretty thoroughly discounted before it occurs. There is rarely any lack of capital to take advantage of a sure thing, even though it may be known in advance to only a few persons.

The extent to which future business conditions are known to "insiders" is, however, usually overestimated. So much depends, especially in America, upon the size of the crops, the temper of the people, and the policies adopted by leading politicians, that the future of business becomes a very complicated problem. No power can drive the American people. Any control over their action has to be exercised by cajolery or by devious and circuitous methods.

Moreover, public opinion is becoming more volatile and changeable year by year, owing to the quicker spread of information and the rapid multiplication of the reading public. One can easily imagine that some of our older financiers must be saying to themselves, "If I only had my present capital in 1870, or else had the conditions of 1870 to work on today!"

A fair idea of when the discounting process will be completed may usually be formed by studying conditions from every angle. The great question is, when will the buying or selling become most general and urgent? In 1907, for example, the safest and best time to buy the sound dividend-paying stocks was on the Monday following the bank statement which showed the greatest decrease in reserves. The market opened down several points under pressure of liquidation, and many standard issues never sold so low afterward. The simple explanation was that conditions had become so bad that they could not get any worse without utter ruin, which all parties must and did unite to prevent.

Likewise in the Presidential campaign of 1900, the lowest prices were made on Bryan's nomination. Investors said at once, "He can't be elected." Therefore his nomination was the worst that could happen—the point of time where the political news became most intensely bearish. As the campaign developed his defeat became more and more certain, and prices continued to rise in accordance with the general economic and financial conditions of the period.

It is not the discounting of an event thus known in advance to capitalists, that presents the greatest difficulties, but ceases where considerable uncertainty exists, so that even the clearest mind and the most accurate information can result only in a balancing of probabilities, with the scale perhaps inclined to a greater or less degree in one direction or the other.

In some cases the uncertainty which precedes such an event is more depressing than the worst that can happen afterward. An example is a Supreme Court decision upon a previously undetermined public policy which has kept business men so much in the dark that they feared to go ahead with any important plans. This was the case at the time of the Northern Securities decision in 1904. "Big business" could easily enough adjust itself to either result. It was the uncertainty that was bearish. Hence the decision was practically discounted in advance, no matter what it might prove to be.

This was not true to the same extent of the Standard Oil and American Tobacco decisions of 1911, because those decisions were an earnest of more trouble to come. The decisions were greeted by a temporary spurt of activity, based on the theory that the removal of uncertainty was the important thing; but a sensational decline started soon after and was not checked until the announcement that the Government would prosecute the U.S. Steel Corporation. This was deemed the worst that could happen for some time lo come, and was followed by a considerable advance.

More commonly, when an event is uncertain the market estimates the chances with considerable nicety. Each trader backs his own opinion, strongly if he feels confident, moderately if he still has a few doubts which he cannot down. The result of these opposing views may be stationary prices, or a market fluctuating nervously within a narrow range, or a movement in either direction, greater or smaller in proportion to the more or less emphatic preponderance of the buying or selling.

Of course it must always be remembered that it is the dollars that count, not the number of buyers or sellers. A few great capitalists having advance information which they regard as accurate, may more than counterbalance thousands of small traders who hold an opposite opinion. In fact, this is a condition very frequently seen, as explained in a previous chapter.

Even the operations of an individual investor usually have an effect on prices pretty accurately adjusted to his opinions. When he believes prices are low and everything favors an upward movement, he will strain his resources in order to accumulate as heavy a hand of securities as he can carry. After a fair advance, if he sees the development of some factor which might cause a decline—though he doesn't really believe it will —he thinks it wise to lighten his load somewhat and make sure of some of his accumulated profits. Later when he feels that prices are "high enough," he is a liberal seller; and if some danger appears while the level of quoted values continues high, he "cleans house," to be ready for whatever may come. Then if what he considers an unwarranted speculation carries prices still higher, he is very likely to sell a few hundred shares short by way of occupying his capital and his mind.

It is, however, the variation of opinion among different men that has the largest influence in making the market responsive to changing conditions. A development which causes one trailer to lighten his line of Stocks may be regarded as harmless or even beneficial by another, so that he maintains his position or perhaps buys more. Out of a worldwide mixture of varying ideas, personalities and information emerges the average level of prices—the true index number of investment conditions.

The necessary result of the above line of reasoning is that not only probabilities but even rather remote possibilities are reflected in the market. Hardly any event can happen of sufficient importance to attract general attention which some process of reasoning cannot construe as bullish and some other process interpret as bearish. Doubtless even our old friend of the news columns to the effect that "the necessary activities of a nation of one hundred million souls create and maintain a large volume of business," may influence some red-blooded optimist to buy 100 Union; but the grouchy pessimist who has eaten too many doughnuts for breakfast will accept the statement as an evidence of the scarcity of real bull news and will likely enough sell 100 Union short on the strength of it.

It is the overextended speculator who causes most of the fluctuations that look absurd to the sober observer. It does not take much to make a man buy when he is short of stocks "up to his neck." A bit of news which he would regard as insignificant at any other time will then assume an exaggerated importance in his eyes. His fears increase in geometrical proportion to the size of his line of stocks. Likewise the overloaded bull may begin to "throw his stocks" on some absurd story of a war between Honduras and Romania, without even stopping to look up the geographical location of the countries involved.

Fluctuations based on absurdities are always relatively small. They are due to an exaggerated fear of what "the other fellow" may do. Personally, you do not fear a war between Honduras and Romania; but may not the rumor be seized upon by the bears as an excuse for a raid? And you have too many stocks to be comfortable if such a break should occur. Moreover, even if the bears do not raid the market, will there not be a considerable number of persons who, like yourself, will fear such a raid, and will therefore lighten their load of stocks, thus causing some decline?

The professional trader, following this line of reasoning to the limit, eventually comes to base all his operations for short turns in the market not on the facts but on what he believes the facts will cause others to do—or more accurately, perhaps, on what he sees that the news is causing others to do; for such a trader is likely to keep his fingers constantly on the pulse of buying and selling as it throbs on the floor of the Exchange or as recorded on the tape.

The non-professional, however, will do well not to let his mind stray too far into the unknown territory of what others may do. Like the "They" theory of values, it is dangerous ground in that it leads toward the abdication of common sense; and after all, others may not prove to be such fools as we think they are. White the market is likely to discount even a possibility, that chances are very much against our being able to discount the possibility profitably.

In this matter of discounting, as in connection with most other stock market phenomena, the most useful hint that can be given is to avoid all efforts to reduce the movement of prices to rules, measures, or similarities and to analyze each case by itself. Historical parallels are likely to be misleading. Every situation is new, though usually composed of familiar elements. Each element must be weighed by itself and the probable result of the combination estimated. In most cases the problem is by no means impossible, but the student must learn to look into the future and to consider the present only as a guide to the future. Extreme prices will come at the time when the news is most emphatic and most widely disseminated. When that point is passed the question must always be, "What next?"

Chapter V - Confusing the Personal with the General

In a previous chapter the fact has been mentioned that one of the greatest difficulties encountered by the active trader is that of keeping his mind in a balanced and unprejudiced condition when he is heavily committed to either the long or short side of the market. Unconsciously to himself, he permits his judgment to be swayed by his hopes.

A former large speculator on the Chicago Board of Trade, after being short of the market and very bearish on wheat for a long time, one day surprised all his friends by covering everything, going long a moderate amount, and arguing violently on the bull side. For two days he maintained this position, but the market failed to go up. He then turned back to the short side, and had even more bear arguments at his tongue's end than before.

To a certain extent he did this to test the market, but still more to test himself—to see whether, by changing front and taking the other side, he could persuade himself out of his bearish opinions. When even this failed to make any real change in his views, he was reassured and was ready for a new and more aggressive campaign on the short side.

There is nothing peculiar about this condition. While it is especially difficult to maintain a balanced mind in regard to commitments in the markets, it is not easy to do so about anything that closely touches our personal interests. As a rule we can find plenty of reasons for doing what we very much want to do, and we are still more prolific with excuses for not doing what we don't want to do. Most of us change the old sophism "Whatever is, is right" to the more directly useful form "Whatever I want is right." To many readers will occur at once the name of a man prominent in public life who seems very frequently to act on this motto.

If Smith and Jones have a verbal agreement, which afterward turns out to be greatly to Jones' advantage, Smith's recollection is that it was merely a loose understanding which could be canceled at any time, while Jones remembers it to have been a definite legal contract, perfectly enforceable if it had only been written. Talleyrand said that language was given us for the purpose of concealing thought. Likewise many seem to think that logic was given us for (the purpose of backing up our desires.

Few persons are so introspective as to be able to tell where this bias in favor of their own interests begins and where it leaves off. Still fewer bother to make the effort to tell. To a great extent we train our judgment to lend itself to our selfish interests. The question with us is not so much whether we have the facts of a situation correctly in mind, as whether we can "put it over."

When it comes to buying and selling stocks, there is no such thing as "putting it over." The market is relentless. It cannot be budged by our sophistries. It will respond exactly to the forces and personalities which are working upon it with no more regard for our opinions than if we couldn't vote. We cannot work for our own interests as in other lines of business—we can only fit our interests to the facts.

To make the greatest success it is necessary for the trader to forget entirely his own position in the market, his profits or losses, the relation of present prices to the point where he bought or sold, and to fix his thoughts upon the position of the market. If the market is going down the trader must sell, no matter whether he has a profit or a loss, whether he bought a year ago or two minutes ago.

How far the average trader is from attaining this point of view is quickly seen from his conversation, and it is also true that a great deal of the literature of speculation absolutely fails to react this conception.

"You have five points profit—you had better take it," advises the broker. Perhaps so, if you know nothing about the market; but if you understand the market the time to take your profit is when the upward movement shows signs of culminating, regardless of your own deal.

"Stop your losses; let your profits run" is a saying which appeals to the novice as the essence of wisdom. But the whole question is where to stop the losses and *how far* to let the profits run. In other words, what is the *market* going to do? If you can tell this your personal losses and profits will take care of themselves.

Here is a man who has done a great deal of figuring and has proved to his own satisfaction that seven points is the correct profit to take in Union Pacific, while losses should be limited to two and one-half points. Nothing could be more foolish than these arbitrary figures. He is trying to make the market fit itself around his own trades, instead of adapting his trades to the market.

In any broker's office you will notice that a large part of the talk concerns the profits and losses of the traders. Brown had a profit of ten points and then let it get away from him. "Great Scott!" says his wise friend. "What do you want? Aren't you satisfied with ten points profit?" The reply should be, though it rarely is, "Certainly not, if I think the market is going higher."

The fact is that the more a trader allows his mind to dwell upon his own position in the market the more likely it is that his judgment will become warped so that his mind is blind to those considerations which do not fall in with his preconceived opinion,

"Get them out with a small profit," I once heard one broker say to another. "If you don't they will hang on and take a loss. They never get profit enough to satisfy them." A good policy, probably, if neither the broker nor his customer had any real knowledge of the market; but mere nonsense for the trader who aims to be in the slightest degree scientific.

Until you try it, you have almost no idea of the extent to which you may be rendered unreasonable by the mere fact that you are committed to one side of the market. "In the market, to be consistent is to be stubborn," some one has said; and it is true that the mart of strong will and logical intellect is often less successful than the more shallow and volatile observer, who is ready to whiffle about like the weathercock at any suspicion of a change in the wind. This is because the strong man has in this instance embarked upon an enterprise where he cannot use his natural force and determination—he can employ only his faculties of observation and interpretation. Yet in the end the man of character will be the more permanently successful, because he will eventually master his subject more thoroughly and attain a more judicial attitude.

The more simple-minded, after once committing themselves to a position, are thereafter chiefly influenced and supported by the illusions of hope. They bought, probably, as a result of some bullish development. If prices have advanced, they find that the market "looks strong," a good deal of encouraging news comes out on the tickers, and they hope for large profits. After five points in their favor, they hope for ten, and after ten they look for fifteen or twenty.

On the other hand, if prices decline they charge it to "manipulation," "bear raids," etc., and expect an early recovery. Much of the bear news appears to them to be put out maliciously, in order to cause prices to decline further. It is not until the decline begins to cause a painful encroachment upon their capital that they reach the point of saying, If "They" can depress prices like this in the face of a bullish situation, what is the use of fighting them? By a flood of short sales, they can put prices down as much as they like"— or something of the sort.

Such traders are suffering merely from youth, or lack of sound business sense, or both. They have a considerable period of study before them, if they persist until they get permanently profitable results. Most of them, of course, do not persist.

A much more intelligent class, many of whom are properly to be considered as investors, do not allow their position in the market to blind them so far as current news or statistical developments are concerned, but do permit themselves to become biased in regard to the most important factor of all—the effect of a change in the price level.

They bought stocks in the expectations of an improved situation. The improved situation comes and prices rise. Nothing serious in the way of bear news appears. On the contrary, bull news continues plentiful. Under the conditions they see no reason for selling.

Yet there may be a most important reason for selling—namely, that prices have risen sufficiently to counterbalance the improved situation—and they would see and appreciate this fact if they were in the position of an uninterested observer.

One of the principal reasons why investors of this class allow themselves to become confused as to the influence of the price level is because a bull market nearly always goes unreasonably high before it culminates. The investor has perhaps, in several previous instances, sold out at what he thought was a fair price level, only to see the public run away with the market to a point where his profits would have been doubled if he had held on.

It is in such cases that an expert knowledge of speculation is essential. If the investor has not this knowledge, and cannot obtain the dependable advice of one who has it, then he must content himself with more moderate profits and forego the expectation of getting the full benefit of the advance. But with a fair knowledge of speculative influences, he can fix his mind on the development of the campaign, regardless of his own holdings, and can usually secure a larger profit than if he depended merely upon ordinary business "common sense."

The mistake is made when, without any expert knowledge of speculation, he permits himself to hold on in the hope of higher prices after a level has been reached which has fairly discounted improved conditions.

Not one trader in a thousand ever becomes so expert or so seasoned as to entirely overcome the influence his position in the market exerts upon his judgment. That influence appears in the most insidious and elusive ways. One of the principal difficulties of the expert is in preventing his active imagination from causing him to see what he is looking for just because he is looking for it.

An example will make this dear. The expert has learned from experience, let us say, that the appearance of "holes" in the market is a sign of weakness. By a "hole" is meant a condition of the market where it suddenly and un-accountably refuses to take stock. A few hundred shares of an active stock are offered for sale. Sentiment is generally bullish, but there is no buyer for that stock. Prices slip quickly down half a point or a point before buyers are found. This, in an active stock, is unusual; and although the price may recover, the professional does not forget this treacherous failure of the market to accept moderate offerings. He considers it a sign of an "over-bought" market.

Now suppose the trader has calculated that an advance is about to culmin-ate and has taken the short side in anticipation of that event. He suspects that the market is over-bought, but is not yet sure of it. Under these circumstances any little dip in the price will perhaps look to him like a "hole," even though under other conditions he would not notice it or would think nothing about it. He is looking for the development of weakness and there is danger that his imagination may show him what he is looking for even though it isn't there!

The same remarks would apply to the detection of accumulation or distribution. If you want to see distribution after a sharp advance, you are very likely to see it. If you have sold out and want to get a reaction on which to repurchase, you will see plenty of indications of a reaction. Indeed; it is a sort of proverb in Wall Street that there is no sort so bearish as a sold-out bull who wants a chance to repurchase.

In the study of so-called "technical" conditions of the market, a situation often appears which permits a double construction. Indications of various kinds are almost evenly balanced; some things might be interpreted in two different ways; and a trader not already interested in the market would be likely to think it wise to stay out until he could see his way more clearly.

Under such circumstances you will find it an almost invariable rule that the man who was long before this condition arose will interpret technical condition as bullish, while the man who was and remains short, sees plain indications of technical weakness. Somewhat amusing, but true.

In this matter of allowing the judgment to be influenced by personal commitments, very little of a constructive or practically helpful nature can be written, except the one word "Don't." Yet when the investor or trader has come to realize that he is a prejudiced observer, he has made progress; for this knowledge keeps him from trusting too blindly to something which, at the moment, he calls judgment, hut which may turn out to be simply an unusually strong impulse of greed.

It has often been noted by stock market writers that since the great public is bearish at the bottom and bullish at the top, it could make its fortune and beat the multi-millionaires at their own game by simply reversing itself—buying when it feels like selling and selling when it feels like buying. Tom Lawson, in the heyday of his publicity, seems to have had some sort of dream of the public selling back to Standard Oil capitalists the stocks which it had bought from them and thus bringing everything to smash in a heap—the philanthropic Thomas, doubtless, being first properly short of the market.

This wrongheadedness of the public is perhaps not so great as formerly. A great number of small investors buy and sell intelligently and there has been some falling off in the gambling class of trade on the New York Stock Exchange— much to the satisfaction of every one, except, perhaps, the brokers who formerly handled such business.

It remains true, nevertheless, that the very moment when the market looks strongest, is likely to be near the top, and just when prices appear to have started on a straight drop to the zero point is usually near the bottom. The practical way for the investor to use this principle is to be ready to sell at the moment when bull sentiment seems to be most widely distributed, and to buy when the public in general seem most discouraged. It is especially important for him to bear this principle in mind in taking profits on previous commitments, as his own interests are then identified with the current trend of prices.

In a word, the trader or investor who has studied the subject enough to be reading this book, probably could not make profits by reversing himself, even if such a thing were possible; but he can endeavor to hold himself in a detached, unprejudiced frame of mind, and to study the psychology of the crowd, especially as it manifests itself in the movement of prices.

Chapter VI - The Panic and the Boom

Both the panic and the boom are eminently psychological phenomena. This is not saying that fundamental conditions do not at times warrant sharp declines in prices and at other times equally sharp advances. But the panic, properly so-called, represents a decline greater than is warranted by conditions, usually because of an excited state of the public mind, accompanied by exhaustion of resources; while the term "boom" is used to mean an excessive and largely speculative advance.

There are some special features connected with the panic and the boom which are worthy of separate consideration.

It is really astonishing what a hold the fear of a possible panic has upon the minds of many investors. The memory of the events of 1907 undoubtedly operated greatly to lessen the volume of speculative trade from that time to the present. Panics of equal severity have occurred only a few times in the entire history of the country, and the possibility of such an outbreak in any one month is smaller than the chance of loss on the average investment through the failure of the company. Yet the specter of such a panic rises in the minds of the inexperienced whenever they think of buying stocks.

"Yes," the investor may say, "Reading seems to be in a very strong position, but look where it sold in 1907—at 70![4]

It is sometimes assumed that the low prices in a panic are due to a sudden spasm of fear, which comes quickly and passes away quickly. This is not the case. In a way, the operation of the element of fear begins when prices are near the top. Some cautious investors begin to fear that the boom is being overdone and that a disastrous decline must follow the excessive speculation for the rise. They sell under the influence of this feeling.

During the ensuing decline, which may run for a year or more, more and more people begin to feel uneasy over business or financial conditions, and they liquidate their holdings. This caution or fearfulness gradually spreads, increasing and decreasing in waves, but growing a little greater at each successive swell. The panic is not a sudden development, but is the result of causes long accumulated.

The actual bottom prices of the panic are more likely to result from necessity than from fear. Those investors who could be frightened out of their holdings are likely to give up before the bottom is reached. The lowest prices are usually made by sales for those whose immediate resources are exhausted.

---

[4] Equal to $35 per share of $50 par, as now quoted.

Most of them are taken by surprise and could raise the money necessary to carry their stocks if they had a little time; but in the stock market, "time is the essence of the contract," and is the very thing that they cannot have.

The great cause of loss in times of panic is the failure of the investor to keep enough of his capital in liquid form. He becomes "tied up" in various undertakings so that he cannot realize quickly. He may have abundant property, but no ready money. The condition, in turn, results from trying to do too much—greed, haste, excessive ambition, an oversupply of easy confidence as to the future.

It is noticeable in panic times that a period arrives when nearly every one thinks that stocks are low enough, yet prices continue downward to a still lower level. The result is that many investors, after thinking that they have "loaded up" near the bottom, find that it is a false bottom, and are finally forced to throw over their holdings on a further decline. This is due to the fact mentioned above, that final low prices are the result of necessities, not of opinions. In 1907, for example, every one of good sense knew perfectly well that stocks were selling below their value—the trouble was that investors could not get hold of the money with which to buy.

The moral is that low prices, after a prolonged bear period, are not in themselves a sufficient reason for buying stocks. The key to the situation lies in the accumulation of liquid capital, which is most quickly evidenced by the condition of the banks. This subject, however, takes us outside our present field.

It is to a great extent because the last part of the decline in a panic has been caused not by public opinion, or even by public fear, but by necessity, arising from absolute exhaustion of available funds, that the first part of the ensuing recovery takes place without any apparent reason.

Traders say, "The panic is over, but stocks cannot go up much under such bearish conditions as now exist." Yet stocks can and do go up, because they are merely regaining the natural level from which they were depressed by "bankrupt sales," as we would say in discussing dry goods.

Perhaps the Word "fear" has been overworked in the discussion of stock market psychology. It is only the very few who actually sell their stocks under the direct influence of the emotion of fear. But a feeling of caution strong enough to induce sales, or even a fixed belief that prices must decline, constitutes in itself a sort of modification of fear, and has the same result so far as prices are concerned.

The effect of this fear or caution in a panic is not limited to the selling of stocks, but is even more important in preventing purchases. It takes far less uneasiness to cause the intending investor to delay purchases than to precipitate actual sales by holders. For this reason, a small quantity of stock pressed for sale in a panicky market may cause a decline out of all proportion to its importance. The offerings may be small, but nobody wants them.

It is this factor which accounts for the rapid recoveries which frequently follow panics. Waiting investors are afraid to step in front of a demoralised market, but once the turn appears, they fall over each other to buy.

The boom is in many ways the reverse of the panic. Just as fear keeps growing and spreading until the final crash, so confidence and enthusiasm keep reproducing each other on a wider and wider scale until the result is a sort of hilarity on the part of thousands of men, many of them comparatively young and inexperienced, who have made "big money" during the long advance in prices.

These imaginary millionaires appear in a small swarm during every prolonged bull market, only to fall with their wings singed as soon as prices decline. Such speculators are, to all practical intents and purposes, irresponsible. It is their very irresponsibility which has enabled them to make money so rapidly on advancing prices. The prudent man gets only moderate profits in a bull market—it is the man who trades on "shoestring margin" who gets the biggest benefit out of the rise.

When such mushroom fortunes have accumulated, the market may fall temporarily into the hands of these daredevil spirits, so that almost any recklessness is possible for the time. It is this kind of buying which causes prices to go higher after they are already high enough—just as they go lower in a panic after they are plainly seen to be low enough.

When prices get above the natural level, a well-judged short interest begins to appear. These shorts are right, but right too soon. In a genuine bull market they are nearly always driven to cover by a further rise, which is, from any common sense standpoint, unreasonable. A riot of pyramided margins drives the sane and calculating short seller temporarily to shelter.

A psychological influence of a much wider scope also operates to help a bull market along to unreasonable heights. Such a market is usually accompanied by rising prices in all lines of business and these rising prices always create, in the minds of business men, the impression that their various enterprises are more profitable than is really the case.

One reason for this false impression is found in stocks of goods on hand. Take the wholesale grocer, for example, carrying a stock of goods which inventories $10,000 in January, 1909. On that date Bradstreet's index of commodity prices stood at 8.26. In January, 1910, Bradstreet's index was 9.23. If the prices of the various articles included in this stock of groceries increased in the same ratio as Bradstreet's list, and if the grocer had on hand exactly the same things, he would inventory them at about $11,168 in January, 1910.

He made an additional profit of $1,168 during the year without any effort, and probably without any calculation on his part. But this profit was only apparent, not real; for he could not buy any more with the $11,168 in January, 1910, than he could have bought with the $10,000 in January, 1909. He is deceived into supposing himself richer than he really is, and this fallacy leads to a gradual growth of extravagance and speculation in every line of business and every walk of life.

The secondary results of this delusion of increased wealth because of rising prices are even more important than the primary results. Our grocer, for example, decides to spend this $1,168 for an automobile. This helps the automobile business. Hundreds of similar orders induce the automobile company to enlarge its plant. This means extensive purchases of material and employ-ment of labor. The increased demand resulting from a similar condition of things in all departments of industry produces, if other conditions are favor-able, a still further rise in prices; hence at the end of another year the grocer perhaps has another imaginary profit, which he spends in enlarging his residence or buying new furniture, etc.

The stock market feels the reflection of all this increased business and higher prices. Yet the whole thing is psychological, and sooner or later our grocer must earn and save, by hard work, economical living and shrewd calcu-lation the amount he has paid for his automobile or furniture.

Again, rising stock prices and rising commodity prices react on each other. If the grocer, in addition to his imaginary profit of $1,168 sees a ten percent advance in the prices of various securities which he holds for invest-ment, he is encouraged to still larger expenditures, and likewise if the capitalist notes a ten percent advance in the stock market, he perhaps employs additional servants and enlarges his household expenditures so that he buys more groceries. Thus the feeling of confidence and enthusiasm spreads wider and wider like ripples from a stone dropped into a pond. And all of these develop-ments are faithfully reflected by the stock market barometer.

The result is that, in a year like 1902 or 1906, the high prices for stocks and the feverish activity of general trade are based, to an entirely unsuspected extent, on a sort of pyramid of mistaken impressions, most of which may be traced, directly or indirectly, to the fact that we measure everything in money and always think of this money-measure as fixed and unchangeable while in reality our money fluctuates in value just like iron or potatoes. We are accustomed to figuring the money-value of wheat, but we get a headache when we try to reckon the wheat-value of money.

When a fictitious situation like this begins to go to pieces, the stock market, fulfilling its function of barometer, declines first, while general busi-ness continues active. Then the "money sharks of Wall Street" get themselves roundly cursed by the public and there is a widespread desire to wipe them off the earth in summary fashion. The stock market never finds itself popular unless it is going up; yet its going down undoubtedly does far more to promote the country's welfare in the long run, for it serves to temper the crash which must eventually come in general business circles and to forewarn us of trouble ahead so that we may prepare for it.

It is generally more difficult to distinguish the end of a stock market boom than to decide when a panic is definitely over. The principle of the thing is simple enough, however. It was a good supply of liquid capital that started the market upward after the panic was over. Similarly it is exhaustion of liquid capital which brings the bull movement to an end. This exhaustion is shown by higher call and time money rates and a steady rise in commercial paper rates.

Chapter VII - The Impulsive versus the Phlegmatic Operator

The observer of market conditions soon comes to know that there are two general classes of minds whose operations are reflected in prices. These classes might be named the "impulsive" and the "phlegmatic."

The "impulsive" operator says, for example, "Conditions, both fundamental and technical, warrant higher prices. Stocks are a purchase." Having formed this conclusion, he proceeds to buy. He does not try or expect to buy at the bottom. On the contrary he is perfectly willing to buy at the top so far, provided he sees prospects of a further advance. When he concludes that conditions have turned bearish, or that the advance in prices has over-discounted previous conditions, he sells out.

The "phlegmatic" type of investor, on the other hand, can hardly ever be persuaded to buy on an advance. He reasons, "Prices frequently move several points against conditions, or at least against what the conditions seem to me to be. The sensible thing for me to do is to take advantage of these contrary movements."

Hence when he believes stocks should be bought he places an order to buy on a scale. His thought is:

"It seems to me stocks should advance from these prices, but I am not a soothsayer, and prices have often declined three points when I felt just as bullish as I do now. So I will place orders to buy every half point down for three points. These speculators are a crazy lot and there is no knowing what passing breeze might strike them that would cause a temporary decline of a few points."

Among large capitals, and especially in the banking community, the "phlegmatic" type naturally predominates. Such men have neither the time nor the disposition to watch the ticker closely and they nearly always disclaim any ability to predict the smaller movements of prices. They are entirely ready, nevertheless, to take advantage of these small fluctuations when they occur, and having plenty of capital, they can easily accomplish this by buying or selling on a scale.

As a matter of fact, the market is usually full of scale orders, and the knowledge of this and of the way in which such orders are handled is decidedly helpful in judging the tone and technical position of the market from day to day.

The two types of operators above described are always working against each other. The buying or selling of the "impulsive" trader tends to force prices up or down, while the scale orders of the "phlegmatic" class tend to oppose any movement.

For example, let us suppose that banking interests believe conditions to be fundamentally sound and that the general trend of the market will be upward for some time to come. Orders are therefore placed by various persons to buy stocks every point down, or every half, quarter, or even eighth point down.

On the other hand, the active floor traders find that, owing to some temporary unfavorable development, a following can be obtained on the bear side.

They perceive the presence of scale orders, but they think stocks enough will come out on the decline to fill the scale orders and leave a balance over.

To put it another way, the floating supply of stocks has become, at the moment, larger than can comfortably be tossed about from hand to hand by the in-and-out class of traders. The market must decline until a part of this floating supply is absorbed by the scale orders which underlie current prices.

These conditions produce what is commonly called a "reaction." Once this surplus floating supply of stocks is absorbed by standing orders, the market is ready to start upward again. If the general trend is upward, far less resistance will be encountered on the advance than was met on the reaction; hence prices rise to a new high level. Then profit-taking sales will be met on limited or scale orders at various prices, and as the market advances the floating supply will gradually increase until it again becomes unwieldy and another reaction is necessary.

Eventually a level is reached, or some change in condition appears, which causes these scale buying orders to be partially or entirely withdrawn, and selling orders to be substituted on a scale up. The bull market will not go much further after this change takes place. It has now become easier to produce declines than advances. The situation is the reverse of that described above, and a bear market follows.

Commonly there is a considerable period around top prices when scale buying orders are still found on declines, but profit-taking sales are also met on advances, so that the market is kept fluctuating within comparatively narrow limits for a month or more. In fact, it is likely to be kept on this level so long as public buying continues greater than public selling. This is some-times called "distribution." A similar period of "accumulation" often occurs after a bear market has run its course, and before any important advance appears.

A close watch of transactions, or a study of continuous quotations as pub-lished in certain newspapers, often enables the experienced trader to discover when the most important of these scale orders are withdrawn or reversed.

A bull market which is full of scale buying orders encounters "support," so-called, on declines. Bears are timid about driving down prices, because they are continually "losing their stocks." They say that "very little stock comes out on declines;" hence there is a certain appearance of caution in the way the market goes down, and the activity of trade shows, in a broad way, a falling off at lower prices. On the advances, however, a following is obtained and activity increases.

Toward the end of the bull market a change is noticeable. Prices go down easily and on larger transactions, while advances are sluggish and opposition is met at higher levels where profit-taking orders have been placed. The very day when scale buying orders in a stock are withdrawn can oftentimes be disting-uished.

In a bear market, "pressure" appears in place of "support." The scale orders are mostly to sell as the market rises. Only a small following of pur-chasers is obtainable on advances, hence the activity of business, in a general way, falls off as prices go up. The end of the bear market is marked by the reappearance of "support" and the removal of "pressure," so that prices rebound quickly and sharply from declines.

The common assumption is that this "support" or "pressure" is supplied by "manipulators." But it is quite as likely to result from the scale operations of hundreds of different persons, whose mental make-up prevents them from buying or selling in the "impulsive" way.

Chapter VIII - The Mental Attitude of the Individual

In previous chapters we have seen that many, if not most of the eccentricities of speculative markets, commonly charged to manipulation, are in fact due to the peculiar psychological conditions which surround such markets. Especially, and more than all else together, these erratic fluctuations are the result of the efforts of traders to operate, not on the basis of facts, nor on their own judgment as to the effect of facts on prices, but on what they believe will be the probable effect of facts or rumors on the minds of other traders. This mental attitude opens up a broad field of conjecture, which is not limited by any definite boundaries of fact or commonsense.

Yet it would be foolish to assert that assuming a position in the market based on what others will do is a wrong attitude. It is confusing to the uninitiated, and first efforts to work on such a plan are almost certain to be disastrous; but for the experienced it becomes a successful, though of course never a certain method. A child's first efforts to use a sharp tool are likely to result in bloodshed, but the same tool may trace an exquisite carving in the hands of an expert.

What, then, should be the mental attitude of the intelligent buyer and seller of securities?

The "long pull" investor, buying outright for cash and holding for a liberal profit, need only consider this matter enough to guard against becoming confused by the vagaries of public sentiment or by his own inverted reasoning processes. He will get the best results by keeping his eye single to two things: Facts and Prices. The current rate of interest, the earning power of the corporations whose stocks he buys, the development of political conditions as affecting invested capital, and the relation of current prices to the situation as shown by these three factors—these constitute the most important food for his mind to work upon.

When he finds himself wandering off into a consideration of what "They" will do next, or what effect such and such events may have on the sentiment of speculators, he cannot do better than to bring himself up with a short turn and sternly bid himself "Back to common sense."

For the more active trader the situation is different. He need not be entirely unregardful of values or fundamental conditions, but his prime object is to "go with the tide." That means basing his operations to a great extent on what others will think and do. His own mental attitude, then, is a most important part of his equipment for success.

First, the trader must be a reasoning optimist. A more horrible fate can scarcely be imagined than the shallow pessimism of many market habitues, whose minds, incapable of grasping the larger forces beneath the movements of prices, take refuge in a cynical disbelief in pretty much everything that makes life worth living.

Owing to the nature of the business, however, this optimism must be of a somewhat different character from that which brings success in other lines. As a general thing optimism includes the persistent nourishing of hope, an aggressive confidence, the certainty that you are right, a firm determination to accomplish your end. But you cannot make the stock market move your way by believing that it will do so. Here is one case, at any rate, where New Thought methods cannot be directly applied.

In the market you are nothing but a chip on the tide of events. Optimism, then, must consist in believing not that the tide will continually flow your way, but that you will succeed in floating with the tide. Your optimism must be, in a sense, of the intellect, not of the will. An optimism based on determination would, in this case, amount to stubbornness.

Another quality that makes for success in nearly every line of business is enthusiasm. For this you have absolutely no use in the stock market. The moment you permit yourself to become enthusiastic, you are subordinating your reasoning powers to your beliefs or desires.

Enthusiasm helps you influence other men's cannot make the stock market move your way by this (unless you happen to be a big bull leader). You wish to keep your mind as clear, cool and unruffled as the surface of a mountain lake on a calm day. Any emotion—enthusiasm, fear, anger, depression—will only cloud the intellect.

Doubtless it would be axiomatic to warn the trader against stubbornness. It cannot be assumed that any operator would consciously permit himself to become stubborn. The trouble arises in drawing the line between, on the one hand, persistence, consistence, pursuit of a definite plan until conditions change; and, on the other, stubborn adherence to a course of action which subsequent events have proved to be erroneous.

A day in the country, with the market forgotten, or if necessary forcibly ejected from the thoughts, will often enable the trader to return with a clarified mind, so that he can then intelligently convict or acquit himself of the vice of stubbornness. Sometimes it may become necessary to close all commitments and remain out of the market for a few days.

One of the most common errors might be described as "getting a notion." This is due to the failure or inability of the trader to take a broad view of the entire situation. Some particular point in the complex conditions which usually control prices, appeals to him strongly and impresses him as certain to have its effect on the market. He acts on this single idea. The idea may be all right, but other counter-balancing factors may prevent it from having its natural effect,

You encounter these "notions" every day in the Street. You meet a highly conservative individual and ask him what he thinks of the situation. "I am alarmed at the rapid spread of radical sentiment," he replies. "How can we expect capital to branch out into new enterprises when the profits may be swept away at any moment by socialistic legislation?"

You say mildly that the crops are good, the banking situation sound, business active, etc. But all this produces no impression upon him. He has sold all his stocks and has his money in the banks. (He is also short a considerable line, but he doesn't tell you this.) He will not buy again until the public becomes "sane."

The next man you talk with says: "We cannot have much decline with the present good crop prospect. Crops lie at the basis of everything. With billions of new wealth coming out of the ground and flowing into the channels of trade, we are bound to have prosperous conditions for some time to come."

You speak of radicalism, adverse legislation, high cost of living, etc.; but he thinks these are relatively unimportant compared with that new wealth. Of course, he is long of stocks.

"To make the worse appear the better reason," said Mr. Socrates, some little time ago. It is too bad we can't have Socrates' comments on Wall Street. The Socratic method applied to the average speculator would produce amusing results.

Beware of saying, "This is the most important factor in the situation," unless the action of the market shows that others agree with you. Every human mind has its own peculiarities, so presumably yours has, though you can't see them plainly; but the stock market is the meeting of many minds, having every imaginable peculiarity. However important some single factor in the situation may appear to you, it is not going to control the movement of prices regardless of everything else.

An exaggerated example of "getting a notion" is seen in the so-called "hunch." This term appears to mean, when it means anything, a sort of sudden welling up of instinct so strong as to induce the trader to follow it regardless of reason. In many cases the "hunch" is nothing more than a strong impulse.

Almost any business man will say at times, "I have a feeling that we ought not to do this," or "Somehow I don't like that proposition," without being able to explain dearly the grounds for his opposition. Likewise the "hunch" of a man who has watched the stock market for half a lifetime may not be without value. In such a case it doubtless represents an accumulation of small indications, each so trifling or so evasive that the trader cannot clearly marshal and review them even in his own mind.

Only the experienced trader is entitled to a "hunch." The novice, or the man who is not closely in touch with technical conditions, is merely making an unusual ass of himself when he talks about a "hunch."

The successful trader gradually learns to study his own psychological characteristics and allow to some extent for his customary errors of judgment. If he finds that he is generally too hasty in reaching a conclusion, he learns to wait and reflect further. After making his decision, he withdraws it and lays it up on a shelf to ripen. He makes only a part of his full commitment at the moment when he feels most confident, holding the remainder in reserve.

If he finds that he is usually overcautious, he eventually learns to be a little more daring, to buy a part of his line while his mind is still partially enveloped in the midst of doubt.

Most of the practical suggestions which can be offered are necessarily of a somewhat negative character. We can point out the errors to be avoided much more successfully than we can lay out a course of positive action. But the following summary may be useful to the active trader:

(1) Your main purpose must be to keep the mind clear and well balanced. Hence, do not act hastily on apparently sensational information; do not trade so heavily as to become anxious; and do not permit yourself to be influenced by your position in the market.

(2) Act on your own judgment, or else act absolutely and entirely on the judgment of another, regardless of your own opinion, "Too many cooks spoil the broth."

(3) When in doubt, keep out of the market. Delays cost less than losses.

(4) Endeavor to catch the trend of sentiment. Even if this should be temporarily against fundamental conditions, it is nevertheless unprofitable to oppose it.

(5) The greatest fault of ninety-nine out of one hundred active traders is being bullish at high prices and bearish at low prices. Therefore, refuse to follow the market beyond what you consider a reasonable climax, no matter how large the possible profits that you may appear to be losing by inaction.

The author hopes that his comments and suggestions may be of some service in helping readers to avoid unwise risks and to apply sound principles of analysis to the investment or speculative situation.

ONE-WAY POCKETS
Don Guyon – 1917

The Ninety-five Percent

At the fag-end of the never-to-be-forgotten "war brides" market, or, to be more exact, in December, 1915, I began in a casual sort of way to analyze the accounts of half a dozen of the firm's most active traders. Like the great majority of our customers, these traders had been bullish on the munition and standard industrial stocks during the great speculative boom of that year, and now, with the stocks in which they had been operating up from 15 to 100 points each, their profits were relatively small and their commitments larger than at any preceding stage of the movement.

This in itself was not a Wall Street phenomenon. The same condition prevailed in most of our active accounts and, in fact, had prevailed at the top of every bull market throughout my experience in the brokerage business. It was obvious that the precepts so sagely laid down by writers of market letters and authors of works on speculation had been disregarded or forgotten by the public. The latter had been told time and again to buy securities "when they are low" and to sell them "when they are high"; to take "small losses" and "large profits"; to avoid "over-trading," and to do many other equally indefinite things which seem so easy to do when one embarks on a speculative venture that all thought of actually doing them is soon forgotten.

These venerable Wall Street "do's" and "don'ts" have always reminded me of the "Stop! Look! Listen!" signs encountered on a day's motor trip, whose number and sameness cause them to be disregarded. If, instead of carrying the hackneyed warning, one sign should announce "Trains average a mile a minute here," and another, "Two auto parties killed at this crossing last year," the rate of mortality among motorists might show a falling off.

In the same way, speculative advice and trading rules, to be given proper consideration, ought to be definite and based on specific data. This was one of the things that I had in mind when I started upon an analysis of these particular accounts. Another was that *the only speculative method that would prove profitable in the long run must be the reverse of that followed by the consistently unsuccessful public.*

Of course, the public has no fixed method of trading, but its collective operations must be wrong in principle or else more than five percent of the average brokerage firm's customers would be able to survive a complete market cycle. The reader who thinks that five percent is a low estimate of survivors should ask his broker how many, if any, active accounts showed net profits made during the period in which Steel moved from par to above 136 and back again. Even the liberal extra dividends paid on this greatest and most popular of securities failed to offset the speculative blunders committed by those who traded in it.

A Speculative Delusion

It is far more important, to my way of thinking, to know when a poor quality of buying or selling goes into the market than to be apprised of the operations of the large financial interests; yet one has only to whisper the magic words "good buying" or "good selling" to gain the immediate attention of any Wall Street speculator. The circulation of a mere rumor that the Morgan interests are accumulating Steel or that the Standard Oil crowd is getting out of St. Paul is sure at any time to create a market following. Most of the tips that are hawked about the Street are based on the supposition that somebody-or-other of consequence is buying or selling certain stocks.

I do not know of a single case where anyone has been able to make money consistently by following information of this character, even when the information comes to him first Hand.

There are two fundamental and a dozen incidental reasons why it can not be done. One of the fundamental reasons is that even a broker who is executing orders for a large pool or individual operator can not tell whether his client is actually buying or selling on balance. A dozen other brokers may have been given buying or selling orders in the same stocks by the same interests and these orders are placed in so circuitous a manner that only the operator himself knows what has happened at the close of the day.

An equally important objection to following "good buying" or "good selling" is that; while it may eventually prove profitable in the case of the principal, it is likely to prove highly unprofitable to anyone who attempts to turn it to his own speculative advantage. For example, in the summer of 1917 certain capitalists bought Union Pacific heavily around 130 because they considered it intrinsically cheap there or desired to support the market. They were able to carry it without inconvenience through the subsequent decline and to buy more at lower levels. Eventually they will sell this stock at a profit, but speculators, playing for a turn rather than a long pull, who followed this "good buying," were, of course, compelled to take substantial losses. One of the big pools in Steel began to get rid of its holdings when the stock was selling at about 120, but this did not prevent Steel from rising to 136, nor did it save several large traders, who were cognizant of the character of the selling which had gone into the stock, from taking a severe drubbing on the short side.

The war stocks and many of the rails were well sold during the 1915-1916 bull market long before their top prices were reached, and in the great bear market of 1917 securities of all classes were well bought ten, twenty and thirty points above the figures which they eventually touched.

Looking at the matter from a somewhat different angle, it is well to bear in mind that even the best business and financial minds are not infallible in Wall Street, as witness the recent undoing of the New England statesman and multi-millionaire who had so many unfortunate investments in public utility securities, and, going back ten years, the evaporation of one of the great Standard Oil fortunes, possessed by as keen a financier as the history of the Street has known. Even the king of manipulators, the late James R. Keene, went broke three times, while John W. Gates, in spite of his early successes, quit the game a loser. Yet any speculator would have mortgaged his home to follow the market operations of these men.

Detecting "Bad" Buying and Selling

How, then, can the speculator who possesses only limited means hope to beat the Wall Street game by following buying and selling operations which he may consider to be "good"? The answer is that although he does hope to do so, he seldom succeeds.

"Bad" buying and "bad" selling, however, can be detected with a fair degree of certainty, and *it is the purpose of this book to show when buying and selling of such character have occurred in the past, and, therefore, under what market conditions they are likely to occur in the future.*

Certain large operators now recognize the importance of ascertaining what stocks are bought or sold for weak accounts and govern their own market operations accordingly. This information is sometimes obtained by an inside scrutiny of bank loans and a study of the demand for stocks in the loan crowd on the Exchange, or it may be furnished regularly to important customers by members or employees of brokerage firms. If the operator discovers that there is an extensive outside following in General Motors and a scattered short interest in Bethlehem Steel B, he will sell the former and buy the latter stock on the supposition that in each case the public, following long-established tradition, is wrong.

Losses in War Brides

To return to the analysis of the six customers' accounts: Before this was completed, some ten weeks after I began my investigation, the market had worked to a lower level and the profits originally shown in the six accounts under survey had been transformed into actual losses—and this in spite of the fact that stocks had lost, on an average, less than 40 percent of their previous advance!

Anyone who is familiar with Wall Street bookkeeping will realize what a laborious task it was to go over six active accounts for eight months back and to post to separate sheets the various prices at which stocks were bought and sold during that period. In order to simplify the work I selected for analysis the trades made in five active issues which at some time or other during the period under review—from July 1, 1915, to February 29, 1916—had been dealt in actively for each of the six accounts. The stocks selected were United States Steel, Crucible, Baldwin, Westinghouse and Studebaker.

Taking each stock individually and considering the six accounts collectively, as though they represented the operations of one man, the following figures were produced:

UNITED STATES STEEL

Opening Price, July 1, 1915..................................	59 3/4
Low Price for period...	58 1/8
High Price for Period..	89 1/2
Closing Price, Feb. 29 1916.................................	82 3/4
Net Advance...	23
Customers' Average Buying Price.........................	81 1/2
Customers' Average Selling Price.........................	80 5/8
Average Loss, less commissions...........................	7/8

CRUCIBLE STEEL

Opening Price, July 1, 1915..................................	31 7/8
Low Price for period...	29
High Price for Period..	109 7/8
Closing Price, Feb. 29 1916.................................	73 1/4
Net Advance...	41 3/8
Customers' Average Buying Price.........................	85 3/8
Customers' Average Selling Price.........................	79 3/4
Average Loss, less commissions...........................	5 5/8

BALDWIN LOCOMOTIVE

Opening Price, July 1, 1915..................................	64 1/2
Low Price for period...	64
High Price for Period..	154 1/2
Closing Price, Feb. 29 1916.................................	102
Net Advance...	104
Customers' Average Buying Price.........................	38
Customers' Average Selling Price.........................	111 1/2
Average Loss, less commissions...........................	7 1/8

STUDEBAKER CORPORATION

Opening Price, July 1, 1915..................................	59 3/4
Low Price for period...	58 1/8
High Price for Period..	89 1/2
Closing Price, Feb. 29 1916.................................	82 3/4
Net Advance...	23
Customers' Average Buying Price.........................	81 1 /2
Customers' Average Selling Price.........................	80 5/8
Average Loss, less commissions...........................	7/8

WESTINGHOUSE ELECTRIC

Opening Price, July 1, 1915..................................	48 7/8
Low Price for period...	47 3/4
High Price for Period..	74 7/8
Closing Price, Feb. 29 1916.................................	63 1/4
Net Advance...	14 3/8
Customers' Average Buying Price.........................	62 5/8
Customers' Average Selling Price.........................	61 1/4
Average Loss, less commissions...........................	1 3/8

It will be noted that in spite of the large net gains scored by these stocks during the period, *the average price at which each stock was bought for the six accounts was higher than the average price at which it was sold.*

The transactions represented completed trades in approximately 46,600 shares. Fortunately for the customers, 22,200 shares were Steel stock, in which the average loss sustained was relatively small.

What the Order Book Showed

When the sensational advances that had occurred during the preceding summer and fall were recalled it was difficult to understand how anyone who was long of stocks at that time, as these speculators usually were, could have had all of their profits wiped out in such a brief period, and it was not until their individual trades were examined that any light was shed on the subject. At the risk of boring the reader I shall review in a general way the operations of the six customers.

The fact that impressed me most forcibly was that *the trading methods of each had undergone a pronounced and obviously unintentional change with the progress of the bull market from one stage to another.* As later investigation showed this tendency to be general, it may be classed with a number of psychological phenomena that cause the great majority of speculators to do the direct opposite of what they ought to do.

When the bull market was in its infancy each of the accounts referred to showed purchases of industrial stocks at prices which a few months later appeared ridiculously cheap. The purchases were made because of the belief that securities were then selling much below their intrinsic value and future prospects, yet advances of from one to three points brought these stocks, bought for a "pull" rather than for day-to-day trading purposes, back upon the market. When Steel was in the sixties and Baldwin was nearly 100 points below the figure it finally reached, the accounts showed scores of completed transactions yielding profits of less than two points, liberally interspersed with losses.

Then, as a gradually higher level was established, these stocks were repurchased, usually at prices considerably higher than those at which they had previously been sold. At this stage larger profits were the rule; three, five, seven and even ten points were taken. The advance had become so extensive that several attempts were made by the office trading element to find the top of the market with short sales, and as Baldwin, Crucible and similar fast movers were selected as the medium for these attempts, the experiments were almost invariably disastrous.

Short selling, however, was merely an incidental feature of the operations shown in the accounts under analysis. As one "war bride" after another soared to unheard of heights, stocks were bought freely, and they were not for sale even when the purchaser had ten or fifteen points profit. What was fifteen points? Hadn't Bethlehem advanced over 500?

Stop loss orders were not in general use at this level. They had been freely placed— and caught—during the secondary stage of the movement, and now that the stocks thus stopped had been repurchased at higher prices, the customers were evidently determined not to be shaken out again.

At that period each of the accounts showed huge profits, and, thanks to the vigilance displayed at the margin desk, were fairly well protected against a sudden break, but the tendency to over-trade was unmistakable. The customer who three months ago had been eager to take a point profit on 100 shares of stock, would not take ten points on 1,000 shares of the same stock now that it had doubled in price.

Buying on the Way Down

Another tendency shown was to look for bargains in stocks which apparently were selling out of line with the rest of the list, or which, having had an earlier advance, were not moving now. Baldwin Locomotive furnished a striking example of this belated bargain-hunting. Having advanced from 26 to 154 in less than nine months, it looked cheap to a good many people when it later sold between 110 and 120, especially as at that time other war stocks were making new high records. Each of the fix accounts showed purchases of Baldwin in this lower range, and it is probable that it was there that the grand distribution took place. The wild rise above 150 was made largely at the expense of the short account, but the public bought it "to have and to hold" after this high figure had been reached.

In fact, my analysis indicated that *it was on reactions from the extreme high figures that most stocks were handed out.* Purchases made at or near the top were, as a rule, not carried so far as those made at a lower level. In the latter case the purchasers seemed to retain their confidence longer because of the recollection of the higher prices and the hope that sooner or later those prices would be seen again.

War stocks reached the top in October, 1915, but there was an uprush, led by Steel and other seasoned issues, during the last week of the year. Had it not been for the torpedoing of an American boat during the New Year interim, it is likely that the advance, at least so far as the old-line securities were concerned, would have been carried somewhat farther. As it was, however, the submarine issue with Germany became the controlling factor for the next two months, with the result that prices had a very severe tumble, especially in the case of the war shares.

Logically, these stocks should not have suffered at all on the prospect of our entrance into the war, but they had been so completely distributed and were now so weakly held that, it will be recalled, they broke wide open; Steel, on the other hand, declined only ten points from its top, with a dividend off, and other standard issues held equally well.

By the end of February, 1916, the six accounts had been pretty thoroughly liquidated. Some of the liquidation was forced by marginal requirements, but most of it was voluntary. In comparing the selling orders which had gone into the accounts during the decline with the price movements for that period, I noted that once more there had been a marked change in trading methods. Stop orders, disdained at the higher level, were again placed a few points below the market; the tendency to buy on declines, observed after the first sharp reaction from the top, was no longer in evidence; instead, the accounts showed sales, first on all rallies, and later during the breaks that occurred as pessimism and rumor caused wave after wave of public selling.

Waves of Public Buying and Selling

The analysis of the six accounts had exposed several glaring defects in trading methods which, as every student of the stock market knows, are common with the speculative public. However, it is one thing to show how past losses could have been transformed into profits if different methods had been followed, and something else again to lay down hard and fast rules to govern future operations.

I did not feel justified in even attempting this latter feat without pursuing the investigation on a broader scale and along somewhat different lines; so, commencing March 1, 1916, I kept for the period of a year a daily record of *the total number of shares which our house bought and sold, later selecting for special analysis the periods during which there was a marked preponderance on either side of the account.* These periods, during which our customers were either buying heavily or selling heavily on balance, might last only a day or continue for four or five weeks, when there would be either a general shift to the other account or the volume of purchases and sales would again run fairly even.

I kept in conjunction with this record of shares bought and sold a record of *The New York Times'* average prices for industrial stocks, it being an industrial market. Thus the range within which public buying or selling took place was always ascertainable; and I therefore had a sort of statistical history of what happened in the market before, during and after each wave of public bullishness or bearishness. It will be noted by reference to the accompanying table that *each buying period was followed by a lower range of stock prices and, with one exception, each selling period was followed by a higher range.* This table covers the year from March 1, 1916, to March 1, 1917; it shows the duration of each buying and selling period, the range of price averages during that period, and the total number of shares bought and sold for our customers at such time.

Period -	Range Of avgs.	Shares Bought	Shares Sold
Mar. 13-20	100-103	36,700	22,600
Mar. 20-22	88-90	7,300	16,500
Mar. 23-April 12	96-99	101,200	61,300
Apr. 22-24	87-90	7,100	15,500
May 13-June 17	94-96	129,100	99,100
June 26-Aug. 10	88-92	78,000	114,200
Aug. 15-Sept. 2	94-98	83,100	117,700
Sept 23-Oct 7	106-109	120,800	81,500
Oct. 9-16	102-105	40,900	61,400
Nov. 2-27	113-117	274,700	131,000

Nov. 28-Dec. 11..................	111-113	162,500	91,400
Dec. 12-18..................	102-106	49,900	90,500
Dec. 21..................................	90-93	6,900	21,800
Dec. 23-Jan. 29.................	94-96	138,000	100,100
Feb. 1-3..........................	83-86	14,300	25,700

In this compilation I omitted the transactions shown in several of our large accounts, first, because they represented the dealings of operators who are too important and frequently too successful to be classed with the general public; secondly, because when these operators were active in the market their dealings were of such magnitude as to offset the buying or selling of our other customers; and, thirdly, because to give the exact total of purchases and sales might disclose the identity of the firm.

It must not be assumed that all of the transactions embodied in the table represented speculative dealings; many of them were of a so-called investment character, but their volume was small in comparison with the total, so I have not attempted to differentiate between investment and speculative transactions. In fact, I have never been able to determine satisfactorily where investment ends and speculation begins, and am rather inclined to regard the terms as merely relative.

The Same Speculative Errors

This analysis of transactions affords corroborative evidence of the same general trading faults that were revealed in the six accounts previously reviewed. Once again the public sold too soon, repurchased at higher figures, bought more after the market had turned and finally liquidated on the breaks. What was true of this one house was undoubtedly true of other houses having a scattered public clientele, and what was true of the period under review I believe to have been true in a general way of all similar periods in the history of Wall Street.

The foregoing analysis does not tell the full story of the speculative blunders that were committed. This could be done only by presenting a vast and complex array of figures, which would confuse rather than enlighten the average reader. I have determined, therefore, merely to refer briefly to a few of these blunders, utilizing the information gleaned from a day-to-day study of the books to outline a plan of operations and a set of trading rules, which are submitted in another chapter.

Even Steel, which runs more nearly true to speculative form than any other stock, finally proved a disastrous medium of speculation to most of our customers. They sold it for both the short and the long account within a week after it had moved above the trading area—79-89—where it had rested for ten months. Then they bought it above 125, despite the extent of its previous advance and the large turnover, and they bought it again five points further down because it looked cheap. They sold Steel heavily in the peace panic of December, 1916, and the break that culminated in the following February.

They purchased the coppers on a grand scale on the strength of tips and merger rumors in November and later when the market had given unmistakable evidence of having turned. It should be mentioned parenthetically that most of the copper shares bought at that time were carried until the fall of 1917, when everything went overboard.

Remembering the high prices at which Studebaker had previously sold, they absorbed it eagerly when the Maxwell stocks were being run up, although the backwardness of Studebaker was a subject of comment among careful observers of market signs.

Central Leather, Lackawanna Steel and other favorites of the period were frequently sold short when their moves were "on" and later bought for the same customers when they began to tire.

Many a pool operating in a 1915 favorite had been unable to complete its liquidation during the original war share market, but was able to do so a year later under cover of the strength displayed in the other parts of the list.

The public's memory for former high prices usually proves to be more of a liability than an asset. The expectation that these high prices will again be reached causes them to buy many a dead speculative dog which is stuffed and mounted for the occasion. When the long-suffering rails again come into their own, which will be sooner than most people expect if one may judge from their absence from speculative accounts and bank loans at the time this book is being written, many long-memoried speculators will probably find in a rail market an excuse for loading up with Crucible Steel, Industrial Alcohol and other "war brides" that may seem to them to be selling "out of line" with the rest of the list.

"Coppering" the Public

Selecting the wrong time to buy and the wrong time to sell and the wrong stocks to be bought and sold, plus the drain of commissions, cause the speculative losses of the outside public. Just why the public should almost invariably do the wrong thing in Wall Street can be explained only on psychological grounds. To attempt the explanation here might prove of some academic interest, but would serve no practical purpose.

The main point to bear in mind is that the public's speculative play is wrong. If an opposite plan of operations can be adhered to, or, in gambling parlance, if the public can be "coppered," there would seem to be a reasonable chance to beat the Wall Street game. It is not enough to know merely that the public is buying or selling. Under certain conditions, notably when they follow the trend, outside speculators frequently have large paper profits, although as a class they never buy near the bottom or sell near the top. The important thing is to detect when public buying or selling is what Wall Street terms "bad." The foregoing analysis, having done this with reference to speculative movements of the past, can be used to advantage, I believe, in outlining a method of doing so in future operations.

In the following chapters I present a speculative plan covering a complete market cycle, using as its basis the information derived from the analysis of customers' accounts. The plan ignores money market conditions, earnings, crops, steel production and other so-called fundamentals, taking into account only the inside or technical market conditions.

To tell a speculator to base his operations on his interpretation of fundamental factors is to leave him just where he started. Most speculators at present try to interpret these factors and fail to do so successfully because they place too much importance on certain factors and not enough on others. *The market itself determines the relative importance of all factors more accurately than any speculator can hope to interpret them.*

On the other hand, the operating plan is not akin to any of the arbitrary systems of chart play which have been in vogue during recent years. There was a time in Wall Street when chart students could and frequently did make money by playing their various systems, but that was before the Street was surfeited with literature treating of market technique. Now the followers of charts are legion; two out of every three active traders keep either a written or a mental record of tops, bottoms and accumulating and distributing areas, and consequently are fooled persistently by the large operators, who "work" the chart readers and their following at every available opportunity.

Determining the Trend

No speculative program can be carried out successfully unless it conforms to the market's trend; therefore, the characteristics of the market when the trend is up, when it is down and when it is undefined must be understood.

When a market fluctuates for several weeks or months within a narrow range one of these three things is happening: Pools and large operators are accumulating securities by absorbing the offerings of tired holders; or they are distributing certain stocks under cover of artificial strength in others; or the market is actually in a state of uncertainty and awaiting a fresh impulse.

The exact status of the market under such conditions can not be determined definitely at the time. The condition of brokers' loans and the direction of the last big swing may afford valuable indications, but even these are by no means conclusive. The market may come to a temporary halt after a contraction of loans and a decline in prices; then, after a brief period of quiet, fall to a still lower level. On the other hand, stocks may rest after a rise and an expansion of loans, and when profit-taking sales have been absorbed, resume the forward movement.

None but the most cautious trader can hope to beat such a market, and he can do so only by buying near the bottom of each swing and selling near the top, accepting small profits and never allowing a commitment to run into a loss beyond the range within which the stock in which he is operating has been fluctuating. Except for the floor trader, who can jump quickly and escapes the payment of commissions, it is a market to let alone.

How a Bull Market Starts

Before applying rules for operating in a bull market it is necessary, of course, first to determine when stocks are actually in a bull swing. Most traders seem to become convinced of the genuineness of a movement in either direction only when it approaches a culmination. This was indicated strikingly in the analysis of accounts. *The start* of practically every bull market *is indicated in one of two ways.*

The orthodox indication is afforded when the market, after a protracted period of dullness and narrow fluctuations, *breaks through the trading area,* with increased activity on the advances. Sometimes all classes of stocks join in the movement, while at other times one stock or group is taken up at a time. To avoid mistaking a false move in a few easily manipulated stocks for a genuine bull market, this indication should not be accepted until the recognized leaders have entered new territory. The other reliable indication of the start of an upward swing is afforded when, after a period of declining prices or, less frequently, dullness, *the market advances or refuses to go down following the receipt of bad news.* It is not enough that there should be temporary strength in these circumstances; the test of the market position should be applied for an entire day, and *stocks should be bought only when,* after thorough dissemination of the unfavorable news, *the market finally advances above the point where it was before the news was received.*

A striking case in point was afforded by the action of stocks on May 9, 1917. The market had been going down steadily for nearly two months. On that date the front pages of the daily newspapers carried bad news from every quarter: The Russian Provisional Government had apparently collapsed, troops were deserting, anarchy reigned; submarine sinkings were on the increase and British statesmen were in the last throes of pessimism; the Anglo-French offensive on the western battle front had petered out; Congress was going to enact tax measures of a more drastic nature than had been expected; profits were to be restricted, prices fixed, huge bond issues were pending, and it seemed certain that thereafter the U.S. would have to carry the financial and much of the military burden of the war. The worst that Wall Street had feared since our entrance into the conflict apparently had come to pass.

The market greeted this array of unfavorable developments with a fairly steady opening; stocks then broke to lower levels, but late in the day rallied vigorously under the leadership of Steel, which had opened at 114. Its extreme low for the day was 112. but it finally got above the opening figure, and, followed by the munition, equipment and other steel stocks, kept right on going up for three weeks, until it made a new high record at 136.

It is on occasions such as that referred to, when every impulse seems to urge the average trader to sell stocks, both for the long and the short account that the market should be bought, just as it should be bought when it affords definite indications of having moved out of a trading area.

In either case buying orders—at the market—should be placed in the stocks selected as soon as the genuineness of the movement is established. Prompt action is essential at such a time, for professional Wall Street is quick to detect a change in the character of the speculation, and the trader who requires more than twenty-four hours to make up his mind to buy is frequently scared out of doing so by the extent of the advance that has occurred by that time.

The "Bell Cow"

It is just as important to determine *what* to buy as it is to determine when. A selection of two or three active stocks is recommended, provided that you do *not commit the error of picking the ones that have shown the greatest weakness, on the supposition that they should have the best recovery.*

The issues to select are *the active ones that have declined the least* in ratio to the prices at which they are quoted. Every bull market has a "bell cow," which usually turns out to be a stock that has held well when the rest of the list was weak. Bethlehem, U.S. Steel, General Motors, Baldwin, Crucible and Industrial Alcohol all served as "bell cows" in the various major and minor bull movements of the past two or three years, just as St. Paul, Union Pacific and other standard rails did in markets of earlier days, always to the great profit of those who had faith in the persistent strength which they had displayed in the face of weakness elsewhere.

Order Cancellations

Before making your commitment determine approximately what you will do if your stocks advance and *determine definitely what you will do if they decline— and then do it.* The important thing to remember is that you are better qualified to map out your plan of action before taking a position in the market than you are afterward. The judgment of the best trader is bound to be warped by his commitments.

If you are operating on stop orders, which is recommended when purchases are made at this stage of the market place them at the time your order is executed, and *do not raise, lower or cancel them* unless your plan of trading, determined upon at the time of making your original commitment, contemplates doing so. In other words, do not change your mind because of your later interpretation of the news or the action of the market. Our order clerk tells me that in the case of fully ninety percent of order cancellations the stock is either eventually sold at a lower price or bought at a higher price than it would have been had the original order been allowed to stand, and this estimate is confirmed by my own observations.

From a speculative standpoint it is better to be deaf and blind than to permit your market operations to be influenced by what you hear or read. Wall Street rumors, always plausible, are seldom confirmed. They are disseminated by news tickers, brokers, information bureaus, financial editors, publicity agents, professional tipsters and ordinary gossips. These disseminators of news are generally wrong even when they are not subsidized, and subsidy reaches the most unexpected places.

The Menace of News

During the recent great era of speculation interviews were granted by pro-minent bankers, mergers which never materialized were announced, national and state legislation was proposed, misleading reports were compiled by certain copper, automobile and munition companies, statements were issued by public officials and there is reason to believe, speeches were delivered in the British Parliament—all for the purpose of inducing the public to buy or sell certain stocks at a certain time. These incidents were apart from routine developments of similar character that occur daily in Wall Street even during less eventful times.

I do not wish it to be inferred from this that the large Wall Street interests are in league to swindle the speculative public. The truth of the matter is that news deception is practiced by individuals and pools of high and low degree, but each works separately for his or its own interests. News may be inspired by a group of lightweight curb brokers and hungry mining men from Arizona, operating in Western Pete, pfd., or by a pool manager representing members of our very best families.

It might be just as well to take this opportunity to point out that camouflage of a similar sort is resorted to by merchants who advertise bargain sales, manufacturers of proprietary articles who obtain (for a consideration) testimonials from doctors, actresses and laymen; Oregon apple growers; life insurance agents; real estate dealers; the corner saloonkeeper; candidates for public office and all women who use pads, powder, paint or puffs. The practice is national, not local to Wall Street.

News can seldom be utilized by the public for market purposes, even when its authenticity is beyond question. For instance, if tomorrow morning's newspapers should announce the death of the President or the failure of the great "corner house," or the complete destruction of Gary, Indiana, it is more than likely that stocks sold on the news would bring the lowest prices of the day, for the very good reason that each seller would be competing with thousands of other sellers who would have learned the news at the same time.

The Correct Use of Stop Orders

When buying in either of the circumstances described heretofore place your stop order *a point below the low figure* which was reached by the stock selected on the day when the market indicated that it had turned upward, thus protecting yourself in the event of a false move or the selection of a stock possessing individual points of weakness. If the move is really "on" and your stock is to participate in it, it is not likely that an opportunity will be afforded the public to get aboard at the former low figure, especially as at the beginning of an advance there is no weak following in the market to afford the pools the incentive to play for a further dip and consequent shake-out.

The purpose of placing a stop order is to guard against one's interpretation of the market being absolutely wrong. If the trend seems to be up when it really is down or if a stock appears to be in process of distribution when in fact it is being accumulated, a stop order will prevent a poor guess from resulting in a serious and perhaps disastrous loss. When it develops that market conditions are the reverse of what they seemed to be when the original commitment was made, there surely is no longer any reason to retain a position taken on these false premises.

The soundness of the principle upon which the use of stop orders is based is obvious; however, a stop order should not be placed for the purpose of restricting a loss to a certain number of points or fractions thereof, but only to close out arbitrarily a commitment when the price movement indicates that this should be done.

In order to make my point clear, let us assume that Steel had been fluctuating between 90 and 95 for several weeks. If you were long of Steel the proper place to put your "stop" would be at 89, whether the stock had been purchased at 90 or 94. If you were short of it the "stop" should be placed at 96, regardless of the price at which you had put it out.

In brief, a stop *order ought to be placed without reference to the figure at which 46 your comment was made, but solely with regard to the price movement itself.* The failure of most traders to observe this distinction is the reason why such a large proportion of "stops" - probably seven or eight out of every ten—are caught.

Seeing the First Reaction Through

Assuming that you are now long of stocks and that the market has had a vigorous advance for, say, two days, do not make the mistake of trying either to find the top or to play for a temporary reaction, no matter how firmly convinced you may be that the advance has been "too fast" or has gone "too far." By referring to the analysis of customers' accounts you will observe that it is at this stage of a bull market that most of those who have guessed right as to the trend commit the error of playing against it. I advise not only against short selling at this stage of the advance, but also (because of what the cold figures show) *against the sale of long stock.* I realize that this is opposed to the old Wall Street theory that "no one ever goes broke by taking a profit"; nevertheless I have observed quite a number start to go broke by taking small profits when they should have taken big ones.

Such an advance invariably carries farther than the traders who fight it expect, and the reaction, long overdue, finally comes when the "shorts" have been thoroughly cowed and the sold-out bulls, their patience exhausted, are scrambling to repurchase securities which they disposed of ten points lower.

Stocks are inclined to look much weaker than they really are when a bull market suffers its first reaction, which, while sharp and severe, is not likely to wipe out more than half of the previous advances. Having retained your original line of stocks throughout this reaction, your position is still strong enough to enable you to *increase your commitments when the market shows' the first sign of resistance.* Before it does so the trading public will probably have become pretty well convinced that the bull movement is over.

The reaction may drag through a week or it may fulfill its mission in a day, but in either event it may be depended upon to catch the stop loss orders placed by traders a few points under the top. Having done this, it usually rallies so quickly that the traders have no opportunity to get back their stock except at higher prices. The same principles should govern your selection of securities here as at the lower level, and stop loss orders should be placed in a manner similar to that previously outlined. Do not, however, "stop" your original line of stock here or otherwise disturb the stop loss orders affecting it.

A major bull market has several sharp reactions before it finally culminates, and even in a minor movement most stocks, barring some extremely adverse happening, may be depended upon to return to their previous high figures or thereabouts. That is why it is advisable to *see the first reaction through* and wait for the resultant recovery before selling out any long stock, rather than to guess how high the market will go on the original advance.

The Great Distributive Stage

Whether it be after the first severe break or the fourth or fifth, the time will came when, instead of resuming the advance, stocks will merely mark time in the vicinity of their previous tops. The old leaders will be supplanted by new ones, which, by running into higher territory, will give the unwary speculator the impression that the forward movement has been resumed. Stocks that are being distributed will have *sharp but short-lived advances,* followed by *gradual declines,* and the entire market will bear a highly irregular appearance.

Before this stage is reached the market usually has several successive days in which the volume of sales is very large and speculative excitement is intense.

As suggested in an early chapter, I do not believe that as much genuine distribution takes place then as later, at the somewhat lower trading level which is almost invariably established under the top prices.

My theory, formed from the study of customers' accounts, is that while the volume days witness a great deal of "washing," such stock as the pools and large operators are able to sell on balance is taken by the "shorts" and by traders who hope to make a quick turn; that these highly speculative buyers are quick to run when it appears that offerings are in the ascendancy; that their stock, coming on the market, causes the sharp break that usually marks the culmination of the movement; that on this break pool support is encountered and as a consequence the market rallies.

So far its action has been similar to that displayed on several similar occasions, and the outside public, remembering this, again become buyers. Their orders are placed in all of the active stocks from one to several points below the tops and while the demand from this source is being satisfied the market moves back and forth within a trading range. *This is the great distributing stage.* Its duration depends upon the extent of the previous advance, the volume of the pool offerings and the buying capacity of the public.

When the symptoms already noted are observed and the market fails to advance to new ground, *get out of all stocks and stay out,* regardless of the strength displayed by certain issues or the bargains seemingly presented by others. Not only is this the time to sell long stock, but If you are so constituted it is also the time to put out a line of "shorts." The many sharp rallies that occur at this level afford ample opportunity to do so at advantageous prices.

When and What to Sell Short

Just as you were advised when the upward movement started to buy those stocks which had displayed the greatest evidence of accumulation, so you are now advised to sell the issues in which the distribution at this level has apparently been completed.

If Steel, after an extended advance and large volume near the top, is now fluctuating within a range, say, from two to six points under its high figure, while Crucible, after an equally important advance, can be sold within a half point or so of its top, the average outside speculator will prefer to sell Crucible; yet the probabilities under such circumstances favor Steel as the safer short sale. If Steel has been losing ground while Crucible has displayed strength, the indications are that it has been well sold; on the other hand, the Crucible pool must have taken stock in order to hold the issue strong in the face of profit-taking sales of Steel, and the stock so taken may not come into the market until a materially higher figure has been reached. Limit your losses on the short side just as you did on the long by the use of "stops," placing them a point or two above the high prices touched by the stock in which you are trading. There are certain Wall Street authorities who oppose the use of stop orders because of their abuse by many traders; they favor instead a system of "averaging." But what would have happened to the speculator who averaged his short sales of Bethlehem, General Motors, or any one of a dozen similar stocks in the war share market, or his purchases of Studebaker, St. Paul, Bethlehem, or any one of fifty other stocks in the bear market of 1917? An investor with an unlimited bank account may beat the stock market by averaging, but the speculator who attempts to do so must sooner or later meet with disaster.

Covering "Shorts" Too Soon

When the public demand has been satisfied at the higher level the market works into a lower range. Having put out "shorts" on the rallies in the distributing area, you can well afford to increase your line when the market breaks through the previous trading level, once more seeking out the stocks in which the distribution seems the farthest advanced.

Lines of short stock that are put out early in a bear market are almost invariably covered too soon, only to be resold at lower prices, just as long stock, bought at the start of a rising market, is quickly disposed of and later repurchased at higher figures. In each case the extent of the movement is at first underestimated. "Stand pat" on your "shorts," therefore, and disregard the sharp rallies which now and then interrupt the decline, *covering your complete line only when the market no longer goes down on bad news or when it moves upward through a trading area,* as described in referring to the start of a bull movement.

The Effect of Short Sales

There has been so much thoughtless comment of late regarding the effect of short sales upon the stock market that I want to emphasize the fact that a large short interest, even when aggressive, is not an element of weakness, but of strength. In time of panic it provides a potential buying power which otherwise would not exist. Every short contract eventually must be retired, and the sharp rallies that occur from time to time in a bear market are due primarily to buying of this character.

In order to check the great fall in security values during the bear market of 1917, the Stock Exchange authorities attempted to curb short selling by requiring members to furnish daily a list of the stocks which they were borrowing, i.e., short of, and also a list of the customers for whose accounts the borrowing occurred. This action came as an overnight surprise on November 2 and sufficed to force the retreat of a large part of the floating short interest at the opening that morning. The net result was an advance of from three to five points in the leading stocks, and the sustaining influence of covering operations having been eliminated, the market proceeded on its downward course, only in a faster and less orderly fashion. It is true that several weeks later the Exchange authorities took similar steps to discourage short selling among floor traders and that shortly thereafter the market rallied, but when this second action was taken the market had already appeared to many astute students of technical conditions to be thoroughly sold out, no longer going down on bad news and showing more vigorous rallying powers than had been in evidence for several months past.

Short selling never checked a bull market; on the contrary, the market usually turns when the last remaining buyer power has been removed by the "running in" of the short interest. The bear market of 1917, like the one of ten years previous, was wrongly attributed to short selling! In each period some of the severest losses were sustained by high-grade investment securities, including gilt-edged railroad and public utility bonds, which even the wildest stretch of imagination can hardly picture as mediums for short selling.

As every Wall Street observer knows, there is practically no market for specialties and investment issues in times of panic, and it is not uncommon for securities of this class to break five and ten points between sales, while Steel, the favorite short sale of the professional and semi-professional element, seldom "skips a heart-beat," which is to say that buying orders are encountered every eighth down.

Playing for a Pull

I have endeavored to trace the course of a speculative cycle, to designate as definitely as possible the points at which securities should be bought and sold, and to outline the factors to be taken into account in their selection. In doing so I have not attempted to distinguish between a major and a minor cycle for the reason that the same trading principles and methods apply to each. In fact, even the most minute daily fluctuations are merely a reproduction on a reduced scale of what takes place during the course of a major movement.

Board room traders and semi-professionals might, I suppose, apply these principles to their day-to-day trading operations, though in the case of any but floor traders I strongly advise against doing so, or, for that matter, against daily trading of any kind. For the average man to attempt to beat Wall Street by guessing fluctuations is to commit financial hari-kari. There are a half dozen good reasons why it can not be done, the best being that too close application to the ticker causes the loss of one's perspective.

The few who make money in the stock market await what they consider exceptional opportunities and then play for profits that are worth while. They look ahead a week or a month or a year, as the case may be, and disregard the changes that occur in the price movement in each daily session, which to the daily trader assume exaggerated proportions.

The Method and the Man

The operating method I have outlined is not fool-proof or otherwise infallible; it will not enable a ten-share trader operating on a five-point margin to buy a Stock Exchange seat next month; neither will it reduce speculation to a mere formula. *But the speculator who adheres closely to its rules may at least rest assured that his trading methods are diametrically opposed to the trading methods of the great majority of speculators—and the great majority of speculators are, as we know, consistent losers in Wall Street.*

I have no illusions regarding the average speculator or his ability to confine his operations to any one method, no matter how clearly deemed it may be. Several recent attempts to induce friends and customers to restrict their dealings to the plan outlined have been only partly successful, except in the case of one trader who is doing so through a separate and modest account, while he continues to buy and sell at random on a large scale on his regular account.

The man who applies this or any other speculative method successfully must be able to exercise patience and self-control, to withstand all forms of mental temptation, to ignore the dictates of fear and greed and to disregard everything he hears, sees or reads that may cause the slightest deviation from his course. There are many men who can do this part of the time, some who can do it most of the time, but those who can do it continuously are either supermen or automatons. So I shall not hazard a guess as to the proportion of readers who will be able to take full advantage in a speculative way of the method outlined in this book; but it is my confident belief that those who fail to do so will fail, not because of any fundamental weakness in the plan itself, but solely because of their own inability to carry it through.

TIDAL SWINGS OF THE STOCK MARKET
Scribner Browne - 1918

Contents

Chapter I - What Is Meant by Tidal Swings

I do not know whether the term "tidal swings" has been used before in connection with stock market fluctuations, and that does not especially matter. I use it because it expresses fairly well an idea which can, I believe, be more fully and clearly explained than has been done heretofore.

As everybody knows—and many of us have had the fact forced home to us at times by rather painful experiences—stock prices are constantly changing, and even bond prices, supposed to be more stable, pass through certain long cycles of change extending over several years or even a decade.

For example, an average of ten high-grade bonds sold at 109 in 1902, at 100 in 1903, at 107 in 1905, at 88 in 1907, near 103 in 1909, and near 78 in 1918. In the thirteen years from 1905 to 1918, the value of the average high-grade bond, $1,000 par, fell over $300.

Such bonds represent the greatest possible safety for an investment, outside the bonds of the United States Government and our principal municipalities. They are found in the strong boxes of the most conservative investors, trust estates, and savings banks. When we see that they fell an amount equal to 30 percent of their par value in thirteen years, it is, useless to pretend that the investor can afford to neglect the fluctuations of prices. It is a subject of vital interest to everybody, and most of all, in many cases, to those who pay least attention to it and imagine themselves to be almost unaffected by it.

Naturally, the prices of stocks have wider changes than those of bonds—since a bond represents a definite amount of money to be paid at maturity, while a share of stock represents merely a certain fraction of participation in the profits of a company after the bond interest has been paid. The profits of nearly all companies vary greatly from year to year and the prices of these companies' stocks naturally vary with their profits, in addition to being subject to many other influences.

These fluctuations in the prices of stocks may be roughly classified as follows:

(1) Small changes due to the variations of demand and supply from hour to hour. These are for the most part dependent on the views of those persons who happen to be buying or selling any stock at the time.

(2) Price movements lasting from one to several days, due in part to the news which comes out during the period, or to the speculative condition of the market, or to the operations of big traders or investors.

(3) The "minor swings," which may last anywhere from a week to a month or even several months. By this term is meant general movements of the market for many stocks together. Some of these stocks will move widely, some only a little, with all degrees between. Other stocks may at the same time remain almost motionless and some may even be moving counter to the general market.

The more important of these minor swings are shown on the graph of stock prices which appears on the insert at end of this book.

(4) The "tidal swings," lasting from one to five years, and carrying the market as a whole over a wide range of price changes.

Some will deny the "tidal" character of these swings. That is, no one can deny that these long swings of prices do as a matter of fact take place, but some will assert that they have no regularity and are due merely to the changes in business and investment conditions which happen to be occurring at the time.

It is quite true, certainly, that these swings of the market show no such exact mathematical regularity as the tides. They are based on laws of economics, not of mathematics or of astronomy. The tides are in conditions, not in time.

I think the existence of the tidal swings, as well as some of the conditions which contribute to cause them, will become evident as we proceed. In the meantime, a glance at the graph herewith will serve to show what is meant by the term and what has been the general character of these swings for the last fifteen years.

What the Graph Shows

The graph shows the principal movements of a daily average of the prices of twenty and fifty stocks. Owing to the constant changes in corporations, it is impossible to select any representative group of stocks which can be fairly used throughout the entire period.

The average of twenty railroad stocks, which has been faithfully kept up by the Dow-Jones Bureau for many years, fairly indicates the swings of the market down to the beginning of the war; but since then it has ceased to be representative. Therefore, an average of fifty stocks, twenty-five rails and twenty-five industrials, which has been compiled daily by the New York *Times* since 1912, is used in the last six years of the graph.

The diagram shows nine of these swings in full, with a part of another— the upward swing which ended in September, 1902. The extreme points which may be taken as separating the swings occurred in the following months:

410

September, 1902.
October, 1903.
January, 1906.
November, 1907.
August, 1909.
July, 1910.
October, 1912.
September, 1914.
November, 1916.
December, 1917.

The lowest point of 1914 is taken as September, while the Stock Exchange was closed. It is, of course, impossible to say just when the lowest prices would have been made if the exchange had remained open. They would probably have been as low as those of 1907, and would very likely have been made in August, when the first crash came. The lowest curb prices for most stocks were made in September and October.

I doubt if any one can look over this graph and reach the conclusion that these broad swings of the market were purely the result of chance. The operation of some sort of law or laws is almost self-evident.

Even in the matter of duration there is more regularity than would be expected. It might be supposed that economic forces would have little to do with time. In some periods they might naturally be expected to work rapidly and powerfully and at other times slowly and gently. But we find the duration of these swings of the market to have been as follows:
Bull markets:

2 years, 3 months.
1 year, 9 months.
2 years, 3 months. 2 years, 2 months. Bear markets: 1 year.
1 year, 11 months.
11 months.
1 year, 11 months.
1 year, 1 month.

In connection with the bear markets it should be noted that the principal part of a bear market, during which prices fall rapidly, usually lasts not over one year—for example, December, 1906, to November 1907; August, 1909, to July, 1910; October, 1912, to July, 1913.

Where We May Look for Causes

Where may we reasonably look for the causes of these great tidal movements of prices?

The market itself, in the sense of the records of transactions, gives us four kinds of data— and four only:

(1) Prices!

411

(2) The number of shares sold at each price, or within any period.

(3) Time; that is, the approximate time at which each transaction takes place, or the number of hours, days, or weeks which elapse between a low price and a high price, between two high prices, etc.

(4) The relations among the above data for different securities, or for different classes of securities.

The thousands of newspaper columns which are written every year in regard to the "character" or "condition" of the stock market—as distinguished from news announcements or the effect of rumors—are all based upon the conclusions of the writers drawn from the above four factors. As is well known, such conclusions are apt to vary widely.

Every permanent holder of a share of stock has in view the return on his investment in the form of the dividends he is getting or hopes to get; that is, the percent his money earns or will earn. But the "money rate" represents the same thing on money loaned, and the yield on a bond represents the same thing again on money invested in that bond. Evidently we may find some interesting relationships here.

As to business conditions, the earnings on any stock—and through the earnings, eventually, the dividends—depend very largely on the activity of business; so there is manifestly a connection between that and the return that the investor will get on the money he has in stocks.

It will be observed that none of the above factors go to the bottom of the matter. That is, I have mentioned a number of factors which are interdependent—each one may reasonably be supposed to influence the others—but I have not mentioned any primary cause for the whole series of phenomena. Of this, more later.

Chapter II - How Prices Are Made—What Is Meant by Demand and Supply

All prices are, under normal conditions, regulated by the relation between demand and supply, is a truism that has been impressed upon us from our earliest childhood.

Most economic maxims, however, are found to contain some kind of a "joker" which greatly modifies their definiteness.

The joker in the supply-and-demand truism lies in the words "under normal conditions." The war, especially, has shown us the importance of this qualification.

We have all had the opportunity during the war to see that a broad and general demand on the one hand and a broad and general supply on the other will result in the establishment of prices fairly approximating conditions— prices such as the law would call "reasonable"—but that any variation from these "normal conditions" of supply and demand affords opportunities for the exercise of some degree of personal control over prices by individuals or by groups acting in harmony.

This fact is of special importance in considering stock prices. There are many stocks for which both demand and supply are broad and general. Of these U.S. Steel common is the best example. So many different people own it, either for investment or speculation, and there is such a large trade in it from day to day, that its price is adjusted to changed conditions with reasonable promptness.

The same is often true of a stock in which the actual daily trade is small, but of which the ownership is widely distributed among intelligent investors— such as Union Pacific, for example. For several years there has been little motive for active speculation in this stock and daily transfers of it have been comparatively small. Nevertheless, so many investors are watching it that its price closely approximates the investment conditions which might be expected to control it under economic laws.

There are a considerable number of high-grade investment stocks which are closely watched by investors, in spite of their inactivity.

On the other hand, there are many other stocks of which the "floating supply" is small and for the most part concentrated in the hands of a few persons. It is quite obvious that those persons can if they wish, or if they find it profitable, or if they imagine it will be profitable, establish for such a stock a price higher or lower than would naturally be warranted by the investment conditions affecting it.

This would do no harm if the public would refuse to buy such a stock at artificially high prices or to sell it at artificially low prices; but the public does not possess that degree of wisdom. Hence the establishment of artificial prices for any stock—usually called "manipulation"— does do harm to the outside speculators who try to follow the manipulation, and would long ago have been suppressed if anybody could find a way to suppress it without interfering with the right of freedom of contract and thus doing more damage than good.

Moreover, who shall say when the price of a stock is legitimate and when it is artificial? Evidently, this would require some sort of superman, not yet developed on the earthly plane. It very often happens that a price which is regarded as artificial afterward proves to have been entirely warranted by conditions, those conditions having been at the time known to only a few persons.

It is evident, therefore, that we cannot dispose of the question, "How are stock prices made?" by an easy generality or ready-made formula.

Urgency vs. Quantity

So far as actual sales of any stock are concerned, demand and supply are always exactly equal. For every share bought there must necessarily be a share sold, and vice versa.

This perfectly obvious fact is by no means generally recognized in current stock market comment. "There was heavy buying of Reading today," writes the reporter. Manifestly there must have been equally heavy selling, since no one could buy unless some one else would sell to him.

What is meant is that there was urgent buying of Reading. The size of the buying order in the market would amount to nothing unless the buyer were ready to bid up the price in order to get the stock. There might be buying orders for 10,000 shares of Reading at 90 and selling orders for only 1,000, but this would not have any effect on the price unless some buyer was willing to pay 90 1/8.

Clear thinking in this matter is essential. Many investors seem to be hopelessly confused about it. If, for example, 10,000 shares of Steel common are recorded as bought—and sold—at 125, then 25,000 at 125 1/8, 15,000 at 1/4, 30,000 at 1/8, 40,000 at 1/4, etc., one observer will be saying, "Big demand for Steel," and at the same moment another will remark, "Somebody is feeding out a lot of Steel." The simple fact is that these figures show only two things:

(1) An active market for Steel.
(2) That buyers have been willing to raise their bids from 120 to 120 1/4.

Any conclusions in regard to the character of the market *derived from these figures* must be based on those two premises and on them alone.

I shall later show that certain broad conclusions may be drawn from the activity of the market, in the sense of the number of shares bought and sold in a day or week. And I do not deny that some "tape-readers" of many years' experience may get help in "sensing" the immediate movement of a stock from the volumes shown on the tape. But the most important point to be steadily kept in mind by the ordinary observer of stock market phenomena is the urgency of the demand or supply.

Who Makes Stock Prices?

Closely connected with the question how stock prices are made is the question who makes them, or what are the sources of demand and supply? For example, "Good buying in Steel today" is a telegram that often goes out over brokers' private wires. It means that some of the people who are believed to be buying Steel have usually proved good judges of the market, or that the buyers are people who have abundant funds to hold their stock in case the price should decline.

The persons who buy and sell stocks may be roughly classified as follows:

(1) *Investors,* who buy chiefly for dividends, but naturally do not despise an additional profit when obtainable.

(2) *Long pull speculators,* who often carry stocks for several years. They are chiefly interested in getting a profit—selling higher than they buy—but often they are also influenced by the dividends they may obtain while they own their stocks. They usually consider themselves, and are commonly called, investors, in order to distinguish them from more active speculators.

In the long run—although it is usually difficult to predict how long the run may be—these two classes really "make the market," because their commitments are reasonably permanent.

The man who buys a stock because he believes it to be low—whether he has in mind the dividends or the prospects of profit—and who will not sell *simply because the stock goes still lower,* gives the market for that stock permanent support. His influence continues just so long as he holds his shares. Likewise if he sells at what he believes to be a high price and refuses to repurchase at a higher price, he has added just so much to the permanent load the market for that stock must carry.

Of course I do not mean that investors and long pull speculators always sell higher than they buy, although generally speaking it is true that a majority of active traders are likely to lose and the conservative class of long pull investors are likely to add profits to their dividends.

Investors are necessarily influenced by their own financial condition as well as by the condition of the market.

(3) *Big operators,* who endeavor to exercise some degree of control over the price of a stock or a group of stocks. They are, of course, speculators, and they are often wrong, but in most cases the fact that they have obtained, or have kept, money enough to be classed as big operators shows that they have expert knowledge of conditions. The term "pool" is often applied to a group of such operators acting together in one stock.

The general method of these operators is to select a time when a stock is believed to have unusually good prospects; then to depress the price by offering large blocks of the stock until they find that they can no longer buy back these sales any lower than the sales were made; next to "accumulate" as much of the stock as possible at low prices; then to bid the stock up steadily by continued purchases; and finally to sell (or "distribute") all their holdings to "the public"— that is, to speculators attracted into the market by the rapid rise of prices.

The same method is followed on the bear side by simply reversing purchases and sales.

This scheme is not so easy as it sounds. It sometimes goes wrong and the force liquidation of the pool causes a very weak market, since the pool gets no sympathy but "plenty of help" in its selling. Operators of this class', to be successful, have to be very shrewd judges not only of investment conditions but of the psychology of other speculators.

One difficulty encountered by such a pool is that a considerable number of followers generally get wind of what is going on, either by the information which leaks out in devious ways or by watching the behavior of the market, and "ride" on the pool's back for part of the movement. This is particularly annoying to the pool's managers.

Floor Traders

(4) *Floors traders;* that is, members of the Stock Exchange operating for their own account. Their principal income is usually derived from taking advantage of fractional fluctuations. Having no commissions to pay, they can make a greater number of trades with small profits or losses, with the subject of having a net profit at the end of the day or the week.

Most floor traders "work on the bull side" or on the bear side, according to their judgment of the technical condition of the market at the moment; that is, although in and out of the market frequently, they have a net balance of commitments on one side or the other. In this respect most of them are likely to be aligned on the same side, not through definite collusion, but through following some leader or because they see the same things and logically reach the same conclusions.

Sometimes they discover that they have been "filled up" by larger operators and sell out hastily, causing a quick break; or that they are "oversold" on the short side, so that their urgency to repurchase results in a sharp rally in the price. In this way the operations of floor traders sometimes causes a narrow, swaying movement of prices up and down over a range of a few points.

(5) *Active traders through commission houses* or miscellaneous speculators. Of these there is the greatest possible variety—as many kinds of them as there are kinds of people in the world. Probably they have only one trait in common, the desire to make money rapidly.

Chapter III - Relation Between Money and Stocks

In the first chapter I explained the meaning of the term "tidal swings," showed that they do, as a matter of fact, occur with a certain rough regularity, and briefly indicated the directions in which we may reasonably look for the causes of these broad movements. And since all price changes must necessarily be a result of demand and supply, I discussed in the second chapter the nature and special characteristics of demand and supply as we see them in the stock market.

In examining into the causes of tidal swings, it must be understood that we are dealing for the most part with what might be called "secondary" causes—that is, with factors which are interdependent, in the sense that each one influences all the others. If we try to get down to the primary or fundamental cause of the tidal swing in stock prices, we enter the realm of psychology, where it is impossible to apply any definite standards of measurement. Ultimately, stock prices are made by the minds of men, and most minds are superficial—liable to be influenced by appearances rather than fundamentals, or to "make the worse appear the better reason," as one Socrates remarked some years ago. Incidentally, this accounts for the fact, often noticed by members of the exchanges, that the most successful stock speculator is not the deep man but the ready man —the man who is skillful at perceiving, from whatever source, the drift of speculative sentiment, right or wrong.

The word psychology has been overworked of late and for that reason may bring a smile from "practical men," but there is no doubt of its importance as an element in speculation, and fundamentally the tidal waves in prices and business conditions are due to certain mental limitations or misconceptions of people in general which can hardly be described in any other way than as "psychological." This phase of the subject will be taken up in a later chapter. In the meantime let us begin with some of the factors which are logically related to stock prices and which are capable of being recorded in figures and may therefore be spread out and examined over a series of years.

Money and Stocks

An investor puts his money into stocks with a view to interest return (present or prospective). His real object is to get the highest interest rate compatible with safety. Instead of buying stocks he could of course lend the money out at interest, and the money rate represents the rate of interest he would get in that way. Evidently, therefore, there is a logical connection between the money rate and the level of stock prices.

The longest-term investment for idle money outside the security markets is found in commercial paper. For that reason the rate for commercial paper in New York is used to represent the money market in general. An easy comparison is made between the monthly average commercial paper rate and the general course of the stock market.

It is true that, broadly speaking, stocks rise when the money rate is low and fall when it is high, which is what would naturally be expected.

The result is that we have tidal swings in money rates similar to those in stocks.

In the sixteen period from 1902 - 1918 there have been two cases of panic which have carried money rates out of their natural course. The first was the money panic in the fall of 1907 when commercial paper rose to 8 percent—a rate which, under modern business conditions, could be due only to fear. (It must be borne in mind that we are dealing with the rate on strictly prime paper at New York. Rates on inferior paper or in some of the more distant sections of the country would naturally be higher.)

The second instance of abnormal rate was in the War Panic of 1914 when 7 percent was touched.

These panic rates for money represented a sort of temporary aberration from the course of the tidal swing.

The smaller fluctuations in the commercial paper rate are mostly due to seasonal conditions. Money is naturally higher in the fall when the crops are being moved than it is in the winter and spring, when business is less active. These seasonal changes can be eliminated, or compensated, by a method of averaging, if desired, but that is unnecessary for our purpose.

Money as a Guide

Making a closer comparison, the highest point of the money rate corresponds pretty closely with the lowest level of stock prices, but that the lowest point of the money rate does not coincide with the highest stock prices.

This difference is due to speculation. When stocks are falling public speculation is at a low ebb and prices are made by investors, who have an eye chiefly to interest return. But a bull market is accompanied by growing speculation, so that when stocks are high, prices are made largely by speculators, with whom interest return is only a minor factor. Hence the money rate has its most direct influence at the end of a bear market, and only an indirect and partial influence when stocks are high.

Nevertheless, a rising money rate will eventually check speculation. In 1902 the 6 percent rate for commercial paper marked the end of the bull market, and in 1906 the highest average of stock prices was in January after money first touched 6 percent in December, 1905. In December, 1909, the 6 percent rate was touched, although the monthly average was 5 percent and the same rate marked the culmination of the bull market of 1912.

In each of these cases, it will be noted, speculation was able to keep stock prices rising at the same time with the advance in the money rate, but it was not able to maintain the rise after the 6 percent rate was reached, Business requirements began to draw money away from the stock market, leaving the speculators suspended in air. Then relatively high money rates continued to prevail until the stock market was thoroughly liquidated.

Since 1914 the war and the new Federal Reserve Bank system have disturbed the natural swing of the money market. The flood of gold which flowed to our shores during 1915 and 1916, coming at the same time with the great reduction in the legal requirements for bank reserves, caused unprecedentedly low rates for money throughout the bull stock market which culminated in November, 1916.

In a word, during the war we had a war market because the war was a more powerful influence than the money rate. Now that the war is over I see no reason to doubt that the relations between money and stocks will be similar to those that preceded the war. In fact, I should say that the money rate would be an even better guide than before the adoption of the Federal Bank system, for money panics will either be entirely obviated or greatly reduced in severity by the provisions of the new Jaw.

Difference between Money and Capital

It is important to remember that a scarcity of capital for permanent investment is not the same thing as scarcity of money, although there is usually a close connection between the two. The term money, as we use it in discussing money rates, means *that fund of capital which is temporarily idle or available for short-term purposes.* It may or may not be available for permanent investment also.

For example, investors might be unwilling to invest their capital on less than a 6 percent basis; but that very fact might lead them to leave their money in the banks and the banks might lend it on call at 3 percent or in time loans at 4 or 5 percent. It has frequently been the case that high interest returns on permanent investments have been temporarily accompanied by very low money rates. Such a disparity is always followed by a readjustment of both security prices and money rates. Under normal conditions, such a readjustment is nearly always accomplished in less than a year.

Briefly, then, stock prices are near the bottom when the commercial paper rate is highest; and a bull stock market cannot climb much further after the paper rate rises to 6 percent.

A sharp fall in the money rate from a high level is usually followed by rising stock prices.

It is probably safe to say that a wide bull swing cannot be carried through without the aid of a low money rate; but under exceptional conditions, a bull market may culminate before any considerable rise in the money rate occurs.

Chapter IV - Relation Between Bonds and Stocks

Since both bonds and stocks are essentially nothing but convenient ways of investing money so as to make it earn more money, or investments intended to yield an income— either now or in the future—it is evident that there should be some sort of relationship or similarity in the broader fluctuations of these two classes of securities.

One the other hand the important differences between bonds and stocks must be borne in mind. The value of high grade bonds depends primarily upon the supply of capital available for investment as compared with the quantity of investment securities offered in the markets.

In fact, in the case of good Government or municipal bonds this is practically the sole price-making factor, since the security behind such bonds is so ample as to eliminate almost entirely all possible doubts about the payment of interest and principal when due. So far as those bonds are themselves concerned, there is no reason why there should be any change worth mentioning in the rate of interest yield to the investor from one year to another. The reason for change is found, not in the bonds, but in general investment conditions— that is, in the relation between the supply of capital and the demand for it.

Nearly all corporation bonds are influenced to some extent by the current earnings of their companies—a trifle in the case of the strongest, a great deal in case of the weakest. But any average of the prices of a number of high grade bonds will be found to reflect the changes in the conditions affecting capital much more closely than it reflects changes in earnings.

Stocks, however, are far more directly dependent for their dividends upon the earnings of their companies, and they are also greatly influenced by the attitude of the public toward speculation. Hence while prices of high-grade bonds depend chiefly upon a single factor, prices of stocks depend upon at least three general factors.

Bonds and Stocks

There has been a general downward drift in bond prices for 15 years, while there has been no such general declining tendency in stock prices. This is due to the effect of the "Major Cycle" or "20-Year Cycle," and since 1914 to the effect of the war, which has modified the Major Cycle.

It is a historical fact that the United States (we will not extend the inquiry to foreign nations at this time) tends to accumulate capital for about ten years and thereafter to dissipate its capital for about the same period. Thus in a broad way we were accumulating capital from 1873 to about 1883 and dissipating capital from 1883 to 1893, accumulating from 1893 to 1902 and dissipating since then.

The period of accumulation generally begins after a panic of greater or less severity, such as 1857, 1873, 1893, or 1914; since such a panic shocks the public into saving money, and the memory of the shock instills caution into everybody for years afterward.

It is a matter of course that the ten year period is only a rough approximation and that events lengthen or shorten it. Thus the panic of 1914 would naturally have ended the period of dissipation of capital, but the war developed to such gigantic dimensions as to compel the further dissipation of capital on a scale never before known.

Stocks also have felt the force of this longtime capital factor, but in 1915 and 1916 its influence was more than counterbalanced by the phenomenal earnings of industrial companies.

The Logic of Fluctuations

The lowest prices for bonds have coincided pretty closely with the low of stocks but the high of bonds has preceded the high of stocks; also that the war has upset the regularity of these movements.

There is a sound philosophy underlying these facts. When stocks are at the bottom, speculative holdings of the public have been pretty much squeezed out. Investors are making the prices and they are most strongly influenced by the income return afforded them. This, as we have seen, is the principal factor influencing bonds. Hence it is natural that, at the low point of the swing, bonds and stocks should be moving nearly in harmony.

At high prices, however, stocks are strongly influenced by big earnings and by public speculation. These factors carry stocks upward for a time after bonds have become stationary or have begun to decline.

It is notable that the first good rally in the monthly average of high grade bond prices after a panic (accompanied, as we saw in the last article, by high money rates) has heretofore indicated that an upward tidal swing in stocks would follow.

Bonds have usually shown a declining tendency for about six months by the time stocks are at the top. This is noted in 1902, 1905, 1909 and 1912. The general reasons for this fact have already been explained.

After a declining tendency in bonds which has now lasted 16 years, a broad upward swing of the Major Cycle during a period of years is naturally to be expected, when once the end of the present rapid dissipation of capital is reached.

Chapter V - Relation Between the Market and Business Conditions

The statement that there must be a connection between the broad changes in business conditions and the tidal swings of the stock market is so obvious as hardly to require demonstration. Stock dividends are based on the earnings of the corporations issuing the stocks, and those earnings change with changes in the activity of business. Hence it is clear that the prices of stocks are in part dependent on business property or depression.

The important question is, What is the nature of this relationship between stocks and business? Which factor precedes the other, or do they move in unison? If, as we may reasonably expect, we find some degree of regularity in their fluctuations, is the degree of regularity great enough to afford us any practical assistance in judging the future of the stock market or the outlook for business?

Measuring Business Activity

Any reliable record of the quantity of business handled, either in all lines or in any great, fundamental branch of activity, will of course show to some extent changes in business conditions.

The only record that would reflect business activity exactly would be a record of all goods produced and all goods exchanged, expressed in quantities—that is, in tons, bushels, dozens, and so on. No such statistical record is to be had, and it is not at all probable that anything of that kind will ever be available. The labor of keeping track of such statistics and of collecting and compiling the figures would be prohibitive.

It follows that we cannot have a complete and accurate record of business conditions. What we have to do is to look over the various figures available and select those which come the nearest to expressing general business activity. There are at least four classes of figures which may be used for this purpose. All have their defects and their advantages. I will discuss them as briefly as possible.

I. BANK CLEARINGS.—For many years a fairly complete record has been kept of the total money value of checks passing through the bank clearing houses. There have been minor variations in the figures included, but not sufficiently to interfere seriously with the broad changes to be observed.

This is the record most commonly used in discussing business activity. It has, however, two serious defects. First, the large sales of securities, on the stock exchanges and outside of them, are all paid for by checks and therefore appear in the bank clearings. Many of these sales are speculative and therefore may not closely correspond with changes in the actual production and sales of goods intended for consumption.

This difficulty is often remedied in part by taking the bank clearings outside of New York City —since in that city somewhat more than half of the bank clearings usually represent sales of securities. But there is still a considerable speculative element left in the bank clearings outside New York. The second great defect in bank clearings as a business record lies in the fact that they show, not the quantity of goods manufactured and exchanged, but the money value of those goods. Hence if the price of any article rises, the bank clearings based on that article will rise also, even without any change in the actual quantity of that article that is being made or sold. So in a time of generally rising prices the bank clearings may show a great gain without any gain at all in the quantity of goods being handled. At the time this is written, the general level of prices has risen almost 100 percent in a little over three years. Under such conditions it is evident that bank clearings will afford a very poor measure of business activity.

It might be though that this difficulty could be avoided by dividing the bank clearings by an index figure representing the general price level, but actual experiment shows that this plan is not a success. The trouble is that we have no way of knowing what part of the bank clearings is based on things which have risen or fallen in price.

II. RAILROAD GROSS EARNINGS.—In a rough way, the gross earnings of all the railroads in the country change with changes in business. Variations in mileage operated are not enough to vitiate the results. Changes in rates, however, do interfere seriously. A 10 percent increase in rates would, of course, cause a 10 percent gain in gross earnings without any change in the tonnage hauled. If we had figures showing the number of tons of freight transported monthly, that trouble would be eliminated, but such figures are not now available.

There is also a very wide "seasonal variation" in gross earnings, since the roads haul much more business in the fall than in the winter and spring. This variation can be allowed for by computations based on past years, but the results are rather unsatisfactory.

A still greater difficulty is that a complete tabulation of gross earnings is not available until two months or more after the business was actually hauled. This keeps the statistician constantly behind time.

III. COMMODITY PRICES.—Rising prices stimulate business and falling prices depress it. Depending on that principle, we could, before the war, get a very good idea of business activity by keeping a record of the average level of commodity prices. Several index numbers of these prices are made up monthly, Bradstreet's and Dun's being perhaps as good as any and promptly available.

But this principle holds good only under reasonably normal conditions. When, as at present, the rise in prices is in part due to a great inflation of credit, resulting largely from changes in our bank laws, or when it is due to actual famine in various lines, so that a further rise in price fails to cause any perceptible increase in production, then we can no longer conclude that higher prices mean more active business. They may in fact check business by causing widespread apprehension.

IV. UNFILLED ORDERS.—If we had a complete record of the unfilled orders (measured in quantities) of all the business concerns in the country, that would give us a better and earlier index to commercial activity than anything else. The orders come first. Production follows. Next comes transportation. Still later, payment for the goods. Hence orders precede all such figures as iron production, railroad gross earnings (even if those were obtainable as soon as earned, instead of long afterward), or bank clearings.

Unfortunately, most companies are very shy about giving out their unfilled orders. The only current record we have that would be available for this purpose is the unfilled tonnage statement of the U. S. Steel Corporation, which is given out regularly on the 10th of each month for the last day of the preceding month.

True, this is the statement of a single corporation, which may be affected by special conditions; but the Steel company is such a predominating factor in the steel and iron business of the United States, and the steel business is such an important index to activity in all lines of construction, that its statement of unfilled orders is entitled to more weight than might at first be imagined.

A large part of the steel manufactured is always used for new construction, and new construction is the best index of changes in business conditions. Consumption of goods in other ways, outside of new construction, varies somewhat, but varies far less than the quantities of material used in new construction. In fact, in the United States at any rate, large new construction is necessary in order to create and maintain what we call "prosperity."

Chapter VI - Influence of Psychology on the Broad Movements of Prices

Perhaps "psychology" is not just the right word to express the idea, but it is difficult to find a better one. Prices, as has often been said, are made by the minds of men. Hence there is always involved a certain mental factor which we may call psychology without severely wrenching the English language. There is no doubt about the influence of this mental factor on the immediate speculative movements of prices. So far as the first effect is concerned, what people think about some piece of news is much more important than its actual influence on earnings or on financial conditions, for it is what they think that causes them to put in orders to buy and sell and the real effects do not come until later—sometimes very much later.

Psychology as a "Long Pull" Factor

When, however, we come to the consideration of the tidal swings of the market, the influence of people's mental attitudes is not so easily discerned. It is plain that "fundamental" factors are closely connected with the tidal swings. Where then does "psychology" come in?

It comes in two ways: First, it is one influence along with other influences, in causing the broad movements of prices. Second, it participates as one cause of some of the so-called fundamental factors themselves.

An illustration or two will make this clear. During a speculative boom in the market, when stocks "look strong" and one issue after another is jumping to new high prices day by day, a great many people feel that they are really losing money by not participating in the advance. The whole atomsphere of the Street becomes permeated with optimism. Making money seems easy—in fact, it is easy, for the moment. And this general feeling of cheerfulness and confidence leads many people to buy stocks, thus putting prices higher than they would otherwise have gone.

When the market begins to decline these buyers first look upon the fall as a "natural reaction." After the decline goes still further, they recognize the fact that they have been wrong but think prices will recover later on. At still lower prices, they conclude that they should have sold, and promise themselves that they will do so on the next good rally. When the market has fallen still further they reason that stocks are then too low to sell—that they are "cheap."'

But conditions keep getting worse, losses keep getting bigger and bigger. At length the same persons who bought under the influence of optimism at or near the top fall into a mood of excessive depression and sell out. One tells himself that he sells because the market is low and will be for a long time to come under a net set of conditions which entirely change the situation. Another sells because although prices are low, he believes he can reinstate his holdings still lower. Still another sells because he has become disgusted with the stock market and has made up his mind to get out of it and let it alone in future.

But underlying all the varied reasons which losing speculators give themselves for selling at low prices, is the central "psychological" factor of general depression, discouragement and gloom.

And this feeling of gloom is not confined to stock market circles. It extends throughout many industries. In that way it influences the "fundamental" conditions which affect the earnings of corporations, and thus comes back to the stock market by a roundabout route.

For example, in the last article I showed that the unfilled orders of the U.S. Steel Corporation afford a fair index to the general activity of business. But those orders are all placed by human beings, whose minds are often subject to the same influences that affect the minds of investors. The buyer of steel holds back his orders as long as he thinks prices are likely to go lower. But when he thinks steel prices are on the up grade he orders ahead as far as possible. Hence there is a psychological factor in the Steel orders, and to a greater or less extent in every form of business activity.

One Cause of Extreme Prices

It is easy enough to see how all these things react on one another, with the result that prices go too high in boom times and too low in times of depression. In other words, here is one of the important causes of the tidal swing.

At the top, stock prices are high because trade is booming and, to some extent at least, trade is booming because stock prices are high. At the bottom, people are selling their stocks because industrial conditions are dull, and business men hesitate to place their orders for goods partly because the depression of the stock market has spread into business circles.

The novice may ask, "If that is so, why do prices ever stop going up or down when once they get started?"

It is because a lot of investors, and especially a lot of wealthy men and big financial interests, are too hard-headed and have too much actual knowledge of what securities are really worth in the long run, to allow themselves to be carried away by "psychology." We all know men who seem to be incapable of enthusiasm. Such men are likely to be selling when everybody else seems to want to buy. We know others whose spirits seem to rise in the face of difficulty and whose courage is the strongest when others are ready to give up. Those men are buyers at times of acute depression.

While speculators are merrily buying stocks at inflated prices, bankers, big financiers, managers of trust estates, the investment departments of insurance companies, are coldly applying to those prices the yardstick of interest return on the money.

In a word, there are two classes: (1) Those who buy because they think prices are going up and sell because they think prices are going lower; and (2) those who buy because they believe prices are low and sell because they think prices are high. The difference between the two is as wide as the poles. Class (1) has the greatest immediate effect on prices—often runs away with them, in fact. Class (2) eventually checks a boom and supports the market in a panic.

Measuring the Effects of Psychology

I have been able to illustrate by graphs, the relation of the stock market to money rates, to bonds, and to business conditions. There is no way to show the effects of psychology except by the study of the market itself.

A culminating boom in stocks is characterized by an active market, feverish price movements and big transactions, without much change in the general level of prices. This condition follows a major bull market. Such a period of activity at a high level, is often called a period of distribution. I don't think it is a very happy or accurate term, but it answers the purpose.

A depression is characterized by sharp declines at very low prices, with great activity, followed by a period of dullness, narrow price changes and comparatively stationary prices, still at a low level, but usually somewhat above the lowest point touched in the first decline. This is usually called a period of accumulation, by which is meant that shrewd investors, large and small, are picking up the stocks that speculators are throwing over at a sacrifice.

Both in the boom and in the panic or depression, the public's state of mind is a factor of considerable importance, but one which we have no direct way of studying or measuring. Its effects can be estimated only by closely watching the character of the market and the nature of the buying and selling.

These are best observed by keeping a daily record of average prices and volume of transactions. They are also reflected to some extent in newspaper comment.

Chapter VII - Price Movements in Bull and Bear Markets

In the first chapter of this series I mentioned the fact that bear markets are usually shorter than bull markets. The subject is of sufficient importance to warrant a more thorough examination.

It is understood, of course, that the tidal swings are not limited by time. They are created by conditions, which may work themselves out slowly or quickly, in a great variety of ways. At the same time, as we have already seen, the combined upward and downward swing involved in a "Minor Cycle" usually does, as a matter of fact and history, occupy a period of three or four years.

This is because about that length of time is necessary for the conditions which cause the swing to work themselves out. Economic forces always work slowly.

Analysis of Fifteen Years

If we examine the broad market movements of the past fifteen years, we arrive at substantially the following time schedule:

Months Bear, Sept., 1902 to July, 1903.............	10
Accumulation, July, 1903 to April, 1904...........	9
Bull, March, 1904 to Jan., 1906.......................	22
Distribution, Jan. to Dec., 1906........................	11
Bear, Dec., 1906 to Nov., 1907.........................	11
Accumulation, Nov., 1907 to Feb., 1908............	3
Bull, Feb., 1908 to Aug., 1909............................	17
Distribution, Aug. to Dec.,1909.........................	4
Bear, Dec., 1909 to July, 1910............................	6
Accumulation, July to Oct., 1910.......................	3
Bull, Oct., 1910 to Sept.,1912............................	23
Bear, Oct., 1912 to June, 1913...........................	8
(July, 1913, to Oct., '14, deranged by war.)	
Bull, Oct., 1914 to Nov., 1916............................	23
Bear, Nov., 1916 to Dec., 1917..........................	13

Some of these periods need a little comment. I have classified the period from October, 1910, to September, 1912, as a bull market in spite of the fact that it embraced a sort of minor bear market for two months in August and September, 1911. This exceedingly sharp reaction was due for the most part to foreign selling. Europe really feared war then, and we have since learned that its fears were justified, although the war did not break out until nearly three years later. The result was a big setback in prices, but I believe the entire period should be classified as a long, slow bull market.

At the top of the upward swing which culminated in 1912 there was no long period of distribution, and the same was true in the fall of 1916. In the latter instance there had already been a good deal of distribution throughout the year, and a good deal more was done on rapidly falling prices during December and January.

As to the period from June, 1913, to the War Panic of 1914, we can hardly say that it was a part of a normal bear market. It practically defines classifl-cation. General investment conditions were favorable to an advance but prices refused to rise. We can see now that the reason lay in apprehension of the war which finally came in July. The war had cast its shadow before, like most coming events.

In the above list we have five complete bear markets, lasting 10, 11, 6, 8 and 13 months respectively, or an average of about 9 1/2 months.

On the other hand, the four bull markets lasted 22, 17, 23 and 23 months, an average of about 21 months, or a little more than twice the average length of the bear markets.

About the same relation will be found in smaller movements. For example, the distribution period of 1906 included a quick fall and a rise lasting about twice as long; the decline in the middle of 1911, already mentioned, was very sharp; and of course the war break of 1914 was unprecedentedly precipitous.

The Reason

It is easy to see the reason for this difference. The stock market is always carrying a load of "undigested" securities. When a new issue of stock is brought out it usually goes first into the hands of speculators or speculative investors, since it is not "seasoned" enough for the sort of investor who expects to hold his stocks indefinitely for their dividends. In some instances practically the whole issue may eventually drift into the strong boxes of investors who will not sell it, and the load is then off the market. But in other cases this never happens. U.S. Steel common is a notable example. The company was formed in 1901, but about half of the common stock is still in the hands of people who are more interested in market profits than they are in its dividends.

During a bull swing a considerable part of the market's load of undigested stocks is frequently passing from one owner to another. Nine-tenths of the public work entirely on the bull side. It is only the semi-professional who takes the short side. Hence on reactions in a bull market, there are plenty of new buyers to come in and carry the load. But once a bear market is fairly started, nobody really wants to carry stocks except the investor who pays no attention to prices and merely looks at the dividends. Speculators and speculative investors who have stocks have them because they are waiting for a chance to "get out," either with a profit or with a smaller loss than they have at the moment. When they give up and sell out, or as frequently happens in the case of holders on margin, are forced out, there are few buyers. Hence prices decline more rapidly than they advanced in the bull market.

To draw a metaphor from the force of gravitation, since the market carries a load it has to be pushed up but falls down of itself. Therefore it naturally falls faster.

Influence of Commodity Prices

The attempt has several times been made to show that bear markets are normally longer in periods when the tendency of commodity prices is downward than when commodity prices are rising. Thus it has been calculated that from 1871 to 1896, when the broad tendency of commodity prices was downward, bear markets averaged nearly as long as bull markets, while since 1896, with a general upward drift of commodity prices, bull markets have been about twice as long as bear markets.

I was at first inclined to think that some connection might be traced here, but on further reflection I doubt it. I do not see on what reasoning it could be soundly based. I believe it is far more likely that the difference since 1896 is due to the great change in the character of the stock market.

A big, widespread public speculation in this country really had its birth in the great bull market which started in 1897. The market of earlier years was a much narrower affair, pretty much confined to genuine investors and to a small number of professional speculators and their followers. This is probably the reason for the change in the relative length of the up and down swings.

It is, in fact, very little use to study the markets of a quarter of a century ago. We are living now in a new world, financial, economic, business and investment, as compared with that earlier period.

How This Affects the Investor

This discussion of the relative length of bull and bear markets may seem at first glance a little bit technical, but it has a very real application to practical investing.

In the first place, since no bull market for twenty years has lasted less than a year and a half, the investor who holds stocks when the market starts or who buys them early in the bull movement does not need to be in a hurry about taking his profits. And that is something which the average speculative investor is very likely to do. In fact, the principal reason why he loses money is that he takes a small profit and a big loss.

If he has stocks when the bull market begins— having very possibly carried them over from the previous bull movement—he argues that since conditions are very bearish no great advance is likely, and that he should therefore sell his stocks on the first fair advance and await an opportunity to repurchase at a lower price. He does this, and perhaps the market reacts, but not so much as he expects and the final result is that prices go up without him. He dislikes to buy his stocks back at a higher price than where he sold, so he keeps waiting for a break, until at last the market becomes very strong and conditions appear to him so bullish that he concludes the only thing to do is to buy at the market— but by that time prices are relatively high. If he had judged the market by a broad consideration of the tidal swings, remembering that a bull market lasts one and a half or two years, he would have been much better off.

The same thing is true of the bear market. The investor who buys after a year or so of falling prices is in a comparatively safe position, even regardless of all other considerations. He will not buy at the bottom, but it is doubtful whether anybody ever does that, except by accident.

Another point is that, in view of the length of the average bull market, the holder of dividend-paying stocks has a material advantage over the owner of non-dividend payers. Carrying a non-dividend stock for a couple of years means quite a bit of interest money. The dividend-paying stock usually carries itself, since the dividends on the average will about pay for the use of the money.

A non-dividend paying stock may of course be such a bargain that it pays to buy it even with the handicap of loss of interest, but it takes a good deal more skill and knowledge of the markets to pick out such a stock than to select a good dividend-payer.

Bearing these points in mind, the investor who never takes the short side should be able to get dividends on his money about two-thirds of the time. And when a bull market has continued that his best policy is to turn his stocks into money and buy one-year notes or commercial paper, or plan in some way to use his money outside the market for about a year.

As for the investor who is not prejudiced against the short side—and to me operations on the short side appear just as legitimate and just as useful to the community as on the long side— it is evident that he should, as a rule, get nearly double the profits in the same time as on the long side.

But it is dangerous, from the long pull point of view, to take the short side after six months or more of bear market—and that is just when the average speculator is most tempted to take it. Short sales, if made at all, should be put out early in the bear market. Then the seller will be in a position to afford support to the market by buying back when stocks are at their weakest.

Chapter VIII - What the Volume of Transactions Shows

Almost every one who watches the behavior of the stock market, even in a casual way, has noticed that a sharp rise in prices is nearly always accompanied by a large volume of transactions, and that the volume of trade is also heavy in times of panic. This is a very natural condition. A wide swing in prices reaches a larger number of standing orders to buy or sell, so that more orders are executed, and it also attracts a greater number of those day-to-day speculators who try to "go with the tide."

An illustration will make clearer the working of this principle. Suppose the price of a stock after a prolonged decline reaches 80, rallies to 85, and again reacts to 81. The fall to 80 is caused by liquidation. Holders of the stock have become discouraged and are throwing it over. Also, since the price is breaking down into new territory, "stop orders" are constantly reached—that is, a certain number of holders of the stock have decided that they will not risk any more money, but will sell out if the price falls to a figure they have set in advance, as 83, 81, etc. Again, brokers are sometimes forced to sell some stock they are carrying for speculators because margins are getting too low for the safety of the broker.

The natural result is that the price falls rapidly and a great number of orders are executed— in other words, large transactions.

But after the stock rallies to 85 and starts to return toward 80 again the situation is different. The price is not now dropping into new territory, but is merely retracing a decline previously recorded. Fewer "stop orders" are reached and holders on margins are better protected, since the weak accounts were closed out on the first break.

The situation then depends on who bought the stocks which were sold on the first break. If they were bought by speculators "for a turn" and are sold out on the rally to 85, the burden on the market will not be reduced and there will be renewed activity and wide price movements as soon as the market gets fairly started down again. But if the stocks liquidated were bought by investors, who intend to hold them for some time or for a greater advance in prices, transactions on the second decline will be considerably lighter than on the first.

Connection between Prices and Volumes

We may lay down the general principle, then, that the volume of transactions in the market depends on two factors:

(1) Extent of price changes.
(2) Extent of public participation in the market.

Wide price changes bring larger transactions than narrow ones, when the extent of public participation is the same. And a large public participation in the market will bring greater volumes for the same price changes than a small public participation.

In each "minor cycle" of the stock market— usually covering, as we have seen, three or four years—there is one point which may be identified as the *period of rest.* This comes after the bear market has ended and before the next bull market begins. The volume of trade for all stocks month by month in connection with the price movement, these periods of rest may be easily identified in the following months:

May and June, 1904. February, 1908. September, 1910.
January and February, 1915.

As soon as a bull market starts, after such a period of rest, transactions normally begin to increase. In a broad way, they continue to increase as long as prices rise and remain heavy *during the first liquidating period which begins the ensuing bear market.* These first liquidating periods are as follows:

Last quarter of 1902. First quarter of 1907. January, 1910. Last quarter of 1912. December, 1916.

During the remainder of the bear market transaction show a disposition to fall off, but there are usually a few days of big transactions when the bear market ends. These do not show up clearly in the monthly volumes because they are likely to be preceded and followed by dullness. Then comes the period of rest from which we started. Those who want to sell, or are compelled to sell by lack of funds to carry their stocks, are for the most part out of the market, while those who want to buy have not yet made up their minds to take hold.

Apparent Exceptions

Readers who have referred to the graph have already noticed a few exceptions to the general program above explained. The only important exceptions, however, occur in the period which covers the last half of 1910, the whole of 1911, and the first three quarters of 1912, which I have previously characterized as a bull market carried on in the face of great difficulties. Transactions during this period did not show the normal increase characteristic of a bull market, because of the influence of the second main factor mentioned above—a great falling off in public participation. And the heavy transactions during the very sharp reaction of August and September, 1911, were due chiefly to foreign liquidation in fear of war, which, as we have since learned, came within a hair's breadth of breaking out then.

Even in this case, however, the normal increase in transactions appeared when the upward movement was renewed in 1912; but a new high point in volume of trade was not reached during the brief and somewhat artificial rise with which the whole movement culminated in October, 1912.

Smaller Movements

It is notable that these same principles apply to smaller movement of the market. For example, after the considerable reaction in the second quarter of 1905 we note a sort of intermediate period of rest, and we see the same thing again in August, 1906; February, 1912, and July, 1916. Likewise the top of a considerable rally in a bear market is usually accompanies by increased transactions.

Those who wish to note these smaller movements would do well to construct a weekly graph on the same plan as this monthly graph. A weekly graph will show more exceptions to the working of the principles than a monthly graph, because public participation may vary greatly at times from week to week, and weekly transactions may be interfered with by holidays, wire troubles in heavy storms, etc.

Even a daily graph will show substantially the same conditions, but with still more exceptions due to the fact that it does not show what part of a day was characterized by a general upward price movement and what part by a downward movement.

The thought may occur to the reader, Why not make an hourly graph and catch the small turns in the market? But still more difficulties are encountered here because the normal volume of trade varies in different hours. The first hour is usually the most active as a result of overnight orders. The last hour is relatively active because of the fact that many floor traders close all their trades at the end of the day. The hour from 12 to 1 is normally inactive, since many traders are at luncheon, and this influence also has some effect on the hour from 1 to 2. Again, the receipt of special items of news may affect transactions during certain hours. The fact must be emphasized that *the operation of all stock market principles is approximate only.* The factors affecting the market are not mathematical, and the man of a mathematical turn of mind rarely makes a good speculator. From the investment or "long pull" standpoint, the stock market is a business proposition. From the speculative standpoint it is a study of the psychology of the speculator. (Incidentally, that is why the business man usually fails as an active speculator—he is not a psychologist.)

Reactions and Rallies

The behavior of volumes on reactions in a bull market is worthy of some comment. Such reactions usually occur in one of two forms. They may present the appearance of a small bear market, with a day or two of active liquidation at the bottom of the reaction, followed by a brief period of rest; or they may be characterized by a gradual falling off in volume as prices sag slowly lower and by a renewal of activity when the upward swing is resumed.

Which one of these two forms of reaction occurs in any particular case depends partly on the news and partly on the "vulnerability" of the bull accounts outstanding. The sinking of the *Lusitania,* for example, precipitated violent liquidation on a reaction in a bull market, followed by a brief pause. But when holders of stocks cling persistently to their position on a reaction and no bear news of special importance comes to it, transactions will become smaller at the decline.

Rallies in a bear market differ from reactions in a bull market for two reasons; because the public works almost entirely on the long side, and because the professional short interest is easily driven to cover.

If the rally does not go far enough to cause any general covering of shorts, activity will fall off on the advance and will soon increase when the downward swing is resumed. In other cases the shorts are driven to cover by a violent rise, and that is all there is to the rally. In still other instances a certain amount of public buying may come in after the shorts have covered, so that an active rise is followed by a gradual "petering out" of the volume of transactions while the price level still remains near the top of the rally.

In estimating the probable character of a rally before it takes place, it is necessary to bear two points in mind: the extent of the short interest, and the amount of public buying which may reasonably be expected to come in at an advance.

Day-to-day news has less influence on a rally than it has on a reaction. This is because news is not so likely to induce the public to buy on a rally in a bear market as it is to scare them into selling on a reaction in a bull market.

Chapter IX - The Selections of Securities—Bonds or Stocks?

The eight preceding chapters have been devoted to the general principles underlying the tidal swings of the market—the fundamental cause and the manner in which they work themselves out. An understanding of these principles is necessary to the investor who wishes to take advantage in a practical way of these broad "cyclical" movements.

The remaining articles of the series will deal more directly with the investor's actual operations. That is, having in mind the general principles and the various details in regard to their manifestation which have already been brought out, what shall the investor do about it?

Evidently he will try to buy securities as near as may be to the beginning of the upward swing and to sell them as near as may be to the end of it, and if he is so minded he will endeavor to sell short near the beginning of the downward swing and to cover his sales near the end of it. That much is obvious. He may also try to buy, under some conditions, on a considerable reaction in the upward swing, or to sell short on an important rally during the course of the downward swing. That will depend upon his temperament and *should,* at any rate, depend on his financial and personal condition—the degree of risk he is warranted in taking.

Selections of Securities

An important question in this connection is: What securities shall be selected? What classes and what companies?

For this purpose stocks are almost always better than bonds. By turning to the graph at the end of this volume, you will notice that in the bull market of 1904 and 1905 the bond average advanced about 6 points while stocks gained 50 points. In the bull market of 1908 and 1909, bonds rose 14 points, but stocks advanced nearly 50 points, and in 1915 and 1916 the difference was still more pronounced.

The bond averages there shown are based on high-grade bonds. The fluctuations of speculative bonds—or those not so strongly secured— are wider, but usually not equal to the price changes in stocks. Some of the so-called "income" bonds are practically equivalent to stocks, and fluctuate just about as much as stocks.

This does not mean, however, that the investor in bonds can afford to ignore the tidal, swings. I have already shown that these movements are very important to him. It means that the investor whose main object is to make a profit in addition to income can usually get better results in stocks than in bonds.

Next, to what general class of stocks shall the investor turn in planning to take advantage of the tidal swings?

The Question of Dividends

In the matter of dividends, he will prefer, when operating on the long side, to buy stocks paying dividends which give a liberal interest return on the money invested, so that his profits may be in addition to dividends and not instead of dividends. He will naturally avoid stocks on the one hand having earnings so small that no dividends are paid, and on the other hand stocks so strongly protected by big earnings that they fluctuate but little and give but a small interest return on the money required to carry them.

He will select stocks which pay dividends, but which are nevertheless regarded as in the speculative class. Stocks of this kind have the double advantage, for his purpose, of relatively wide fluctuations and dividends which show a good interest return on the price.

For the short side, if he wishes to follow that side, he will select non-dividend paying stocks. He should not be prevented from this by the fact that such stocks naturally sell on a lower plane of values than dividend-payers, for he cares nothing about whether the stock is high or low in comparison with others — he is interested solely in its relative fluctuations. It is better for him to sell short a non-dividend-payer at 40 and buy it back at 25 than to sell one-third as much of a dividend-payer at 120 and buy it back at 75, after having been charged with whatever dividends were paid during the time he was short of the stock. (Since the holder of a stock gets the dividends, the short who has sold to him must pay those dividends out of his own pocket.)

The short must, however, avoid those non-dividend-paying stocks which represent rapidly growing companies and are therefore just about to emerge into the dividend-paying class. If a stock of this class begins to pay dividends or even if the prospects for dividends improve greatly during a downward tidal swing, it may fail to decline or may even advance against the general current of the market.

As between railroad and industrial stocks, the industrials are now decidedly the better for the tidal-swing investor. The rails has narrower fluctuations, the dividend return on them is smaller in proportion to price, and the nature of the railroad business is more stable than that of industrial companies.

Yielding Over 10 Percent

For example, turning to the last table of "Industrial Earnings, Dividends and Income Yields" in *The Magazine of Wall Street* I find that there were 19 stocks in the list for which the income yield on the price was over 10 percent. It is a great help to the tidal-swing investor to be getting over 10 percent on his money all the time it is invested in a stock; even though his primary purpose is to take advantage of the swing in the price.

I also find in that table six non-dividend-paying stocks which are selling near or above 40—and this at a time when stock values in general were relatively low. Just after a bull market culminates there is always a considerably wider choice than this in the matter of non-dividend-payers.

Other things being equal, the investor who wishes to take advantage of the swings will prefer an active, listed stock, so that he is always assured of a good market whenever he wishes to buy or sell. And since there are plenty of those stocks there is very little object in his going into an unlisted or inactive issue.

Choosing Special Issues

In the matter of the particular stock or stocks to be selected, the tidal-swing investor has great opportunity for the exercise of judgment and sound business sense.

The best stock to select for a purchase is naturally one which has been showing a steady increase in the annual percent earned year by year and which appears to have good prospects for a continuation of this same tendency.

For example, turning back to the bargain days of 1914, we note certain industrial stocks for which earnings had been showing a decidedly progressive tendency:

	1911	1912	1913
Gen. Motors	15.7%	17.3%	38.8%
Kresge......................	....	8.7	14.7
Woolworth.................	....	8.9	11.0
Sears, Roebuck............	17.0	19.3	21.2
Tenn. Copper	8.1	21.9	19.3
Utah Copper	39.7	53.5	50.7
Pittsburgh Coal pfd..........	5.1	7.5	10.1
Bethlehem Steel	6.7	6.9	27.4
Rep. Iron & Steel............	0.7	1.7	5.0
U. S. Steel	5.9	5.7	11.1

All these issues did well in the ensuing bull market, but the largest returns were reaped by those investors who had imagination enough to conceive what the war meant to Bethlehem Steel, General Motors, and the more speculative issues among the steels and coppers.

In this case the special conditions created by the war were the controlling element. Under more normal conditions the important point is to select the stocks of companies which are in the growing stage, which are just beginning to get results from the foundation which has been laid in recent years—not companies which have already "arrived," or which are not likely to arrive. I have said that the best stocks to sell short after a bull swing culminates are the non-dividend-payers. There is one exception to this— stocks on which the dividends are about to be passed. It is more difficult to select these, of course, and it is perhaps unwise for the novice to attempt it unless he has competent assistance. Yet it really required no very high degree of statistical knowledge or judgment in the fall of 1912, for example, to see that New Haven was on the down grade; or to see in the latter part of 1913 that M., K. & T. was getting into trouble.

Diversification of Holdings

The investor for income generally prefers to diversify his holdings among different industries, different classes of stocks, or between stocks and bonds, so that if something unexpected happens to one industry or one company he will not be so heavily affected by it as he would have been if his holdings had happened to be all in that line or that stock.

The tidal-swing investor may well employ this principle in a modified form by distributing his holdings among several of those issues which seem to him the most desirable. In 1914, for example, a distribution among one motor stock, one steel, one copper, and one chain store issue would have given excellent average results.

An important aid in selecting stocks for the swing is to observe the relative strength of various issues during the minor movements which take place around the turning point of the main swing. For example, after the investor believes a bear market has ended, suppose he finds that the prices of two stocks, which we will call A and B, have fluctuated as follows during a period of, let us say two months:

	Stock A	Stock B
High	79	52
Low	72	48
High	75	51
Low	69	47
High	74	53
Low	70	50

It is clear that Stock B has shown considerably better resistance to the selling pressure than Stock A. On the small downward moves B's declines have been less in proportion than A's, while B's advances have been relatively better than A's.

The principle is so obvious as to require no elaboration. It has much less value during the progress of the upswing or the downswing. It is most useful around the turning points, when a bull market is culminating, or when a bear market is drawing to a close and the upward movement is beginning.

Chapter X - Following the Trend

We have seen that the upward or downward "leg" of a tidal swing usually lasts from one to two years—the entire period, from the low point of one swing to the low point of the next, or from the high point of one to the high point of the next, being usually three or four years.

Therefore, the investor who endeavors to buy after the down swing has ended and to sell after the upward movement has culminated will change his position only once in about one and three quarter years on the average. This requires a good deal more patience than the ordinary investor has. So nearly everybody who is interested in the market tries to "follow the trend" while the swing is in progress—buying on reactions during the upward move or selling on rallies during the down swing.

It is a question whether the average investor, whose business in life lasts perhaps thirty years, would not get better results in the end by waiting patiently for what he believes to be the end of the swing before changing his position. But since, as a matter of fact, very few are willing to do that, it is essential to discuss the best methods of following the trend while a swing is in progress.

It may be mentioned in passing that the word "trend" is a more or less comparative term. For example, notice the year 1906 on the graph herewith. The downward tidal swing began with January of that year, so that the downward trend, as I am using the word, prevailed throughout the year. But an operator who was trying to follow the more immediate speculative fluctuations would identify an upward trend from July to October, 1906.

Extent of Reactions and Rallies

Taking the term trend to mean the direction of the tidal swing, we note from the diagram that out of four complete bull markets shown three were interrupted, at about the middle of their course, by a reaction extending to more than ten points for the average used. The fourth, that from November, 1907, to August, 1909, did not show a single reaction of ten points. The exact extent of the four principal reactions in this last movement, as measured by twenty rails, was as follows:

	Points
Jan. 18 to Feb. 17, 1908......................	9.71
May 18 to June 22, 1908.....................	6.49
Sept. 29 to Sept. 22, 1908...................	6.90
Jan. 2 to Feb. 23, 1909.......................	7.03

In the five bear markets shown there is only one instance of a rally extending to ten points— that in the last half of 1906. But every bear market has been interrupted by one or more rallies of about five points. This corresponds with our previous observation that bear markets are usually shorter and sharper than bull markets. The reasons for this have been explained.

One important point to be noted is that *a reaction of five points or more occurred near the beginning of every bull market.* It is on this customary reaction that the investor generally has his best and safest buying opportunity.

On the other hand, it is evidently not safe for the investor to wait for an important rally after he believes a bull market has culminated. This is a very common mistake.

The average investor will not be able to estimate the probable extent of any reaction or rally which may occur in the course of a main swing. His attempts to do so are likely to be little better than guess work.

It will be noted, also, that during these sixteen years *no extended reaction occurred in any bull market until the movement had been in progress for at least a year.*

Conclusion

It would be useless to attempt to lay down any hard and fast rules for the investor who endeavors to join in the trend after a swing is well under way. He can see for himself, by examining the graph, what his chances are - and it may be added that he would not be materially helped by extending the examination to years previous to those shown. The last decade is a better guide than any previous decade because there is always a gradual change in the general conditions surrounding the market.

The following suggestions, however, may be useful:

(1) During the first year of a bull market, or at any time in a bear market, probabilities do not favor a reaction or rally of more than five points in the averages.

(2) In the second year of a bull market, probabilities favor a reaction of ten points or more, followed by an advance to a new high point. This is due to increased public participation in the market, so that a greater proportion of the supply of stocks is in "weak hands."

In connection with the graph of stock prices shown at the end of this book, the question has doubtless occurred to many readers whether the change from 20 railroad stocks to 50 railroad and industrial stocks, with the necessary shifting of the scale, does not seriously interfere with the continuity of the graph and perhaps give a misleading impression of the general course of the market. From time to time, also, some one writes us that we ought to use the "logarithmic scale" for these graphs. The practical effect of this would be to widen the fluctuations of the 50 stocks as compared with those of the 20 stocks, so that the new point of 1914 (while the stock exchange was open—we have no means of knowing how low the market would have gone if the exchange had remained open throughout the war panic) would have been the same as the low of 1903, while the high point of 1916 would have been considerably above the highs of 1906 and 1909.

This is a somewhat technical point and has no important bearing on the principles discussed in these articles, but for the benefit of those interested I add a letter received from a prominent civil engineer and my reply thereto.

Chapter XI - Some Practical Suggestions
The preceding articles have covered, in condensed form, those factors which I believe to be of the greatest value to the investor in forming his judgment as to the broad tidal movements of stock prices. It remains to add some practical suggestions which may aid in summarizing the whole and in putting it into actual use.

Only a part of that collection of facts and conclusions upon which the investor's judgment will be based can be reduced to graphic form, but those factors which can be represented in that way should be. There is no reason why the student should burden his memory with relationships which can be committed to a graph.

Statistics in Graphic Form
A graphic record of the following is highly desirable: The weekly range of some standard average of stock prices.

Weekly volume of shares traded in on the New York Stock Exchange.

Weekly range of a standard average of bond prices.
The interest rate on prime commercial paper of about six months' maturity, at New York City. This may be recorded at the end of each week, as changes are usually gradual.

Unfilled tonnage of U.S. Steel Corporation monthly, as given out by the company.

All these may easily be combined on one large graph, which will then cover money, bonds, stocks and business conditions. As we have seen in previous articles, it is the interrelations among these four which shed perhaps the clearest light on the tidal swing of stocks.

The necessary figures are easily obtained from various publications. The New York Sunday *Times* contains satisfactory averages and quotes commercial paper rates. Total sales of stocks for the week appear in the Monday edition. U.S. Steel orders are published as soon as given out by the company. The weeks should be plotted as close together as possible on the graph, so that a view of the movements over a year or more can easily be obtained.

The graphs used with these articles have all been constructed on the monthly basis because weekly graphs covering so many years would be too unwieldy to print. The principles brought out appear even more clearly on the weekly graphs than on the monthly.

In regard to the selection of individual stocks, an almost unlimited amount of work can be done if desired. The investor who keeps no special records on these will get the most direct help, when the time comes, from the several "Bargain Indicators" and condensed statements of industrial earnings and dividends over a period of years which appear regularly in *The Magazine of Wall Street*. These show fairly well the trend of earnings for each stock.

But the more the investor knows about the earnings and prospects of various companies the better, when it comes to selecting issues which are most likely to advance or decline, and it is not a bad idea to keep weekly graphs of the price range of some of the more attractive, issues in which the investor thinks it probable that he might wish to make a commitment. This is especially desirable in connection with the principle touched upon at the end of Chapter IX.

Averaging

A question of considerable importance is whether the investor, when he believes the time has come to buy, should purchase his full line at once or should buy a part of it and wait to see whether he can buy the rest cheaper. This is known as "averaging." It may be done "on a scale"—for example, buying at 30, 28, 26, and so on down—or by buying half one's requirements and then waiting until the time seems ripe to buy the other half.

When the investor confines his efforts to trying to buy as near to the bottom of the tidal swing as he can and sell as near the top, I see no advantage in averaging. He has only one man's judgment to use and all he can do is use it. There is inevitably a certain point where he believes that the market has just turned. He might as well buy or sell at that point, since that represents his best judgment. If he has caught the turning point closely, he is more or less of a "wizard." But whether he has or not, he has done his best and can do no otherwise. If he buys only half his intended line and waits to buy the other half later that means that he is using his best judgment on only half.

In nine cases out of ten, probably, the market will go against him somewhat after he makes the purchase. He will then say, "I could have done better by averaging." True enough, but would he? Or would he have waited until the golden opportunity slipped away entirely? For, as we have seen, that it just what the great mass of the public does.

The case is somewhat different, however, when he endeavors to follow the trend by buying or selling in the course of a movement which is already in progress. The average investor's guess as to the bottom of a reaction in a bull market or the top of a rally in a bear market is worth very little, and it is important for him to avoid getting heavily loaded up near the beginning of a reaction only to see prices fall far below his purchase price.

In this case he is no longer buying at bargain levels. He is buying after a considerable advance in the belief that the market will advance still further. He must therefore be more cautious, and may well follow the principle of buying "on a scale," or of buying at first only a part of what he is able carry.

Use of Stop Orders

Another question is, Should stop orders be used? (The stop order is an order to sell when the price touches a stated figure below the current market, or to buy when the price reaches a fixed figure above the market.)

For example, suppose that the investor concludes in February, 1904, that the market has turned for a long upward swing and buys at a price represented by 93 on the scale of average prices. Should he then place an order to sell in case the market goes lower than it sold in September, 1903, on the theory that such a movement would prove him wrong and he would then better get out and wait for the next opportunity? Or should he patiently hold his position and wait for prices to recover?

This depends on the man—on how much money he has in proportion to his commitment, and whether he is of the speculative or the investment temperament. It is impossible to lay down a rule as to which method is the better, because that depends on how often or to what extent the investor is going to be wrong.

We may say this, however, that whichever method the investor decides upon, he must follow it consistently. He must not buy with the intention of holding on until he has a satisfactory profit, and then when the market turns weak change his plan and decide to sell out and try again, or buy with the intention of using a stop order and then cancel the stop order, through unwillingness to take a loss, when the price begins to approach his order. Such changes of plan always result in confusion.

Another common use of the stop order is to prevent a profit from running into a loss. For example, if a stock bought at 80 advances to 85, the buyer then puts in an order to close his deal in case the price again falls to say 80 1/2. He can then forget the trade and proceed to use his funds in other stocks if an opportunity presents itself. Evidently the higher the general scale of prices rises, the more important it is to prevent a profit from running into a loss. When the prices are low it is not usually desirable for the tidal swing investor to use this plan, since it may result in his being closed out on a reaction just before the market is ready to start on a prolonged advance. If he has bought after due consideration and has exercised ordinarily good judgment, he will usually do better to hold his position during early reactions in the market—which are, of course, highly probable—without being alarmed if his first paper profit runs into a temporary loss.

But when a purchase has been made on a reaction in the middle of a bull market, so that the buyer has paid considerably more for his stocks than he would have had to pay if he had bought near the bottom, it is desirable to apply this principle of preventing a profit from running into a loss; because if it turns out that he has misjudged the situation, so that a bear market has caught him unawares, his loss may eventually become large.

It will be seen that there is a greater possibility of this after such a trade, made in the middle of the bull market, has shown a fair paper profit than there was when the investor made his purchase, because the bull market will then be just that much farther advanced in its course.

To make this a little clearer, suppose during the summer reaction in the bull market of 1916, a purchase had been made at the level represented by the price of 85 for the 50 stock average. Prices then advanced above 100 and by the end of the year had again declined to about 90. Assuming that the investor had up to that time failed to recognize the beginning of the bear market, if he once allowed his purchase at 85 to begin to run into a loss he would be likely— following the theory that merely another reaction in the bull market was taking place—to allow prices to fall to perhaps 75 before becoming discouraged and selling out. He would have been considerably better off if he had "stopped" his trade at 85 on the assumption that he might be wrong, and that even if he was right he still had the chance of repurchasing as low or lower than he had sold.

On the other hand, if he had bought at the level of 60, when the stock exchange reopened in 1914, he would have been wrong in placing a stop at 60 1/4 after the first advance to 65, as he would then have been closed out near the bottom of the first reaction and at a very low range of prices.

The stop order is a very helpful device, but judgment and discrimination must be employed in making use of it.

Conclusion

Throughout these articles I have endeavored to avoid giving the impression that the application of the principles explained will enable any one to buy at the bottom and sell at the top, or that sudden wealth can be acquired by following the tidal swings.

The investor's greatest danger is *getting in too much of a hurry.* Having started with the determination to act conservatively, he is liable to be gradually led astray into the field of active speculation, which is a profession in itself and something entirely different from endeavoring to follow the tidal swings.

The fact can hardly be emphasized too strongly that the study of the tidal swings is merely *an aid to the investor proper*—a means of enabling him to increase his average yearly returns on his capital.

It would be easy to figure out with pencil and pad just how great the investor's profits would be if he bought within five points of the bottom and sold within five points of the top of each broad swing of the market, and the result would be impressive—but unimportant. The optimism generated by such hindsight calculations has often caused heavy losses by those who overestimated their ability to do in the future what they saw might have been done in the past.

It has been estimated by G.C. Selden, in his book "Investing for Profit," that an experienced investor of sound judgment may not unreasonably hope for an average return of 20 percent annually, including both interest and profits. I see no reason to disagree with that statement, but of course every-thing depends upon that one word "judgment." It is to the cultivation of judgment and the avoidance of impulsive action that the investor's efforts must be constantly directed.

If such efforts are somewhat facilitated by what I have had to say in these chapters, my hopes will have been fully realized.

HOW I TRADE AND INVEST IN STOCKS AND BONDS
Richard D. Wyckoff - 1922

Contents

FOREWORD

During the last thirty-three years I have been a persistent student of the security markets. As a member of several Stock Exchange firms, as a bond dealer, trader and investor, I have come into active contact with many thousands of those who are executing orders and handling markets, as well as those who deal in such markets, namely traders and investors.

For the past fifteen years I have edited and published *The Magazine of Wall Street,* which at this writing has the largest circulation of any financial publication in the world.

These experiences have given me an opportunity to study not only the stock and bond markets, but all those related thereto, and have enabled me to observe the forces which influence these markets and the human elements which contribute so largely to their activity and wide fluctuations.

Out of this experience I have evolved or adopted or formulated certain methods of trading and investing, and some of these I have collected and presented in the pages which follow.

My purpose in preparing this book has been two-fold. Primarily, I have in mind the thousands of new investors who find the securities market a vast, technical machine, too complex to be understood by many. It has been my effort to do away with this impression—to emphasize the fact that, in Wall Street as anywhere else, the chief essential is common sense, coupled with study and practical experience. I have attempted to outline the requirements for success in this field in a way that will be understandable to all.

Furthermore, as I learned in preparing my first book, "Studies in Tape Reading," it is of great personal advantage for me to write out and thus clarify and crystallize in my own mind the principles upon which I endeavor to operate. And so, from both standpoints it seemed to me well worthwhile to arrange my impressions in methodical and coherent order.

RICHARD D. WYCKOFF - Great Neck, L. I. March, 1922.

I hold that a man who is longheaded, who foresees and judges accurately, has an advantage over his neighbor, and it is not accounted immoral for him to use that advantage because he is individually better fitted for the business; and it inheres in him by a law of nature, that he has a right to the whole of himself legitimately applied. If one man, or twenty men, looking at the state of the nation here, at the crops, at the possible contingencies and risks of climate, at the conditions of Europe; in other words, taking all the elements that belong to the world into consideration, be sagacious enough to prophesy the best course of action. I don't see why it is not legitimate. - Henry Ward Beecher.

Chapter I – First Lessons

At the suggestion of my first employer in Wall Street, I began the study of railroad and other corporation statistics about the time my trousers were being lengthened from knee to ankle and I was receiving the munificent sum of $20 per month. This was in 1888.

With numerous interruptions my studies continued until 1897, when I began to put them into practice by purchasing one share of St. Louis & San Francisco common at $4 per share. At that time some of the other leading stocks were selling at the following prices: Union Pacific 4, Southern Pacific 14, Norfolk & Western 9, Atchison 9, Northern Pacific 11. Reading 17. To put it mildly, prices were very low. Many roads were just emerging from, or were still in, receivership, and Irish dividends were the rule.

As I saved a little money I began to buy more one share lots and finally I became such a pest in this respect that the Stock Exchange firm which I "favored" with my orders said they didn't care for the business, whereupon I decided to buy more shares, of fewer varieties.

This is the way most people begin their operations—by purchasing outright, believing that they are safe. It is true they are safe in the possession of their certificates once they have them in their safe deposit boxes, but in no other respect. They are not safe against fluctuations or shrinkages in value or earning power. Nevertheless, if their securities are well selected, and bought at the right time, the chances are strongly in favor of their making money.

It was my practice about that time to sit up nights, read the financial papers, and study probably future values of securities, and when I didn't have money enough to buy, I would make my selections just the same and write my imaginary purchases in a book with reasons alongside why they should ultimately be worth more money. Two of these I still retain in my memory, viz., Chicago, Burlington & Quincy at 57, and Edison Electric Illuminating of New York, at 101.

I mention these incidents because they illustrate a very good way for anyone to begin to learn the business of trading and investing in securities. Just as in any other line it is practice that makes perfect, and most of the fatalities in

Wall Street can be traced to lack of practice. You don't have to risk real money when you are learning, and I always advocate two or three years—not two or three months, mind you—of this kind of study and paper practice when one is seriously considering participation in this greatest of all games. But study and practice are the two things farthest removed from the minds of the majority. Everyone knows that people who engage in speculation for the first time do not want to bother with such details. The average man who comes to Wall Street comes to speculate, although he may pay in full for his purchases. All he asks is to be told "something good." That is not speculation, it is gambling; for speculation, to quote Thomas F. Woodlock, "involves the use of intelligent foresight." Most people use neither foresight nor intelligence.

It might seem to the reader a long while to wait, but in my case I did not begin to invest until eight years after I started to study, and I did not commence trading for six years after that, so it may be admitted that I went to school and got a foundation knowledge which has been of inestimable value.

In connection with my one-share purchases I found that although I had correctly figured financial conditions and earning power of the companies whose securities I held, their prices would often fluctuate widely as a result of general market conditions. In other words, a stock might go down, although everything in the way of intrinsic value and future possibilities pointed upward; so I made up my mind that there were other factors to be considered and found that these were principally three, viz., manipulation, technical conditions and trend of the market.

In order to study the market closely I identified myself with a leading N.Y. Stock Exchange house which did a big business for some prominent operators, and there I learned how necessary it is to observe the proposition, not from the standpoint of the outsider who is endeavoring to anticipate the fluctuations from what he sees on the surface, but from the standpoint of the insider who is a factor in influencing prices.

Investigation proved that many of those who were thus able to affect prices often made the same mistakes as small traders, only their errors ran into big money, which, however, was not out of the proportion to their profits. Years before, in my clerical capacity in the brokerage business, I had noticed tendencies among small traders which I now found magnified many diameters in the case of large operators.

In the study of technical conditions, which was my next step, I found that the most important factor was the trend of the market and that the overbought or oversold condition of the market had the most to do with the immediate direction of the next swing.

No doubt the principles which will be found in my book, *"Studies in Tape Reading,"* were rattling around in my head for a long time before I wrote them out, and as I did this they clarified and crystallized. When I realized this, I began to put them into practice by trading in ten share lots, although I had operated in a much larger way some years before. It seemed to me that, with the right principles and a sufficient amount of practice, I could gradually build up my trading on a strong foundation that would not lead to flash-in-the-pan results but to a steady increase in speculative ability and consequent profits.

Being in the brokerage business, my immediate object was to make more money for my clients, because I realized that this was the only way in which they would become permanent and successful clients. My ultimate object, however, was to get out of the brokerage business and devote my time to the security markets, and it is a satisfaction to say that I arrived at that point some years ago.

Unlike many who operate in order that they may make money with which to enlarge their market operations, I am more interested in realizing profits so that I may have more money to invest. Just as its staff writers, through the columns of *The Magazine of Wall Street,* advocate that the business man take his surplus and invest it in sound securities, so I make a business of trading and invest the profits which result. In a word, I trade so that I may invest.

But let us go back a little and note some of the points which came to me while I was studying the subject in an objective way.

The market operations which were carried on in the office of my first employers were not significant because it was a small firm and did not have many customers. The head of the firm traded a little and made some money, because he seemed to understand what he was doing. Most of the customers, on the other hand, neither understood nor made money. Once in a while some one would come in and plunge around, pay a lot of commissions, and then go away disgusted with the business. Traders of this sort should have been disgusted with themselves. The majority seemed to look upon it as a sport or an adventure in which they hoped to prove that their judgment and ability were better than those of all who they knew had failed.

Nearly everyone seemed to be just guessing. One man certainly carried off the palm at the business of buying at the top and selling at the bottom. Another told me how he had taken one little Reading 3rd Income Bond, worth about $300, and by pyramiding on the rise in Reading during former years had run up an equity of something over $250,000. But at this particular time he was down to a shoestring again.

"We had one old fellow who bought nothing but the very highest grade railroad bonds, and only when they were very low. Collecting these and clipping coupons was a mania with him and in order to indulge his mania he economized to the point of using a piece of plain manila twine to hold his eye glasses. He and other out-and-out investors were the most satisfactory clients because they kept coming around year after year, while those who speculated disappeared one after the other. As for the latter, I noticed a very marked tendency to accept a small profit and stand for a big loss.

About that time I heard of a prominent Brooklyn man who after several attempts at speculation said to himself, "I know the secret of this game—these traders are all taking small profits and big losses. I will open a bucket shop and when they do this they will force me to take small losses and big profits." He did. And in a short while he bought a couple of hotels and was rated as a millionaire. No doubt he mistrusted his own ability to trade as the others were doing and followed strictly this profitable principle (the bucket shop proprietor may have two different kinds of principles although they are spelled the same way), but he knew if he got into the business he would be obliged by the very ignorance of his clients, to make more money than he lost.

Turning again to my brokerage office, I must say that impressions derived there were not conducive to speculation, but showed the marked advantages of shrewd investing.

The next firm with which I became identified was one which had private wires, branch offices and a considerable number of clients, large and small. Some of them were big traders and a few were very successful. Here I really began to learn something from observation of their methods. The one who impressed me most strongly was a high official of the telegraph company from which we leased some of our wires. He stuck out from the rest because of his fixed policy of cutting his losses short (here was that same principle bobbing up again). He never gave an order unless it was accompanied by a two-point stop. He dealt in the most active and widely fluctuating issues on both sides of the market. Unlike many of the customers who were "fluent losers" he was the only man whom I remember as being persistently successful. He would usually trade in two hundred share lots at a time and generally managed to get a little larger profit than the two points and commission which he risked.

While I was with that firm the panic of 1893 occurred. G.E. declined from 114 to 20, and American Cordage crashed down from 140 to reorganization levels. This experience showed me what risks people ran who made speculative commitments without limiting their possible losses or watching them closely and getting out when they found they were wrong. The market for these and other stocks simply melted away, there being few buyers and many compulsory sellers. I had seen these things before in the Baring panic of 1890 but they did not make the same impression on me because I had not come into such close contact with those who were making speculative commitments of considerable size.

A few years later I secured a position with a large, ambitious and growing N.Y. Stock Exchange house which had private wires, branch offices and correspondents all over the country. Its long list of customers and its important connections made it develop rapidly into one of the biggest houses in the Street. Here I was able to obtain a still broader view of the markets, for the concern did a big cotton and grain, as well as stock and bond, business. Many of their people made considerable money. A few made spectacular profits in a short while, but I observed that their sudden wealth led to over-extension and big losses because they evidently did not have the same judgment where larger amounts were involved. This was another point in favor of the slowly building up process.

The big wire houses in Boston, Philadelphia and Chicago poured their business over our wires, but not knowing the operations of their individual customers, I could only judge by the composite that was presented to me through having everything come in the name of the house. Two kinds of operations were evidently going on. One was a large inflow of buying and selling orders, evidently arising from those who were endeavoring to antici-pate the immediate fluctuations. The result of these was indicated in a corresponding inflow of money to margin such transactions and take care of the losses which resulted in the net, proving that the traders in other cities were no different from those I had met here; that is, that they were more or loss unpracticed and inefficient at the business.

The other kind of dealings impressed me the most. They consisted of a steady line of orders to purchase securities like Atchison General Mortgage 4's, and Incomes, Norfolk & Western preferred, Union Pacific preferred, and the better grade of stocks and bonds in companies just emerging from receiver-ship. These were bought in very large quantities and shipped away, principally to the West. Evidently there were some people in that great railroad center, Chicago, and in its tributaries, who were familiar with the railroad business, and who saw possibilities in the future for such stocks and bonds in spite of a disastrous past.

In the bull market which began with McKinley's first election in 1896, and ran for several years, these Union Pacifies, Readings, Atchisons and others which had been through receivership, reorganization and assessment, multi-plied many times in value and furnished the most striking lesson I had received so far.

It was plain that the most successful class of our clients was the farsighted investors who held, or were often able to pick up, stocks like Reading and others at less than the amount of the cash assessment that had been paid in. For these assessments they were usually given preferred stocks, and when the mar-ket prices of the latter eventually rose to around par, they had their assessment money back and either a recovery of their former losses or a big profit on the common stocks which they had acquired at the low figures.

I had a good many lessons in speculation during my four years with that firm. It being a bull period there were numerous instances of the development of small accounts into big ones. Governor Flower was the bull leader at the time and some of his stocks went from small to big figures. He had a large following, was perfectly honest with it and made a great deal of money for the public until the day he ate too many radishes at his fishing club in Riverhead, Long Island, and passed away. Next morning most of those who had made money on the bull side and had loaded up with many times what they started with lost the bulk of it at the opening.

One of my fellow clerks gave an illustration of what could be done with a little money. Starting with a small quantity of stock he pyramided until he realized the sum of $3,000, which looked very large to a thirty-dollar-a-week clerk. I found that he was not basing his judgment on the news, but on a study of the fluctuations. His specialties were American Sugar and Brooklyn Rapid Transit. Out of his profits he bought a home for himself, paying his three thousand dollars down, "so they couldn't get it away from him." He kept charts of the market and studied them intelligently, just as many other people then known as "chart fiends," were doing.

To keep charts in those days was looked upon as making one fit for the squirrels. In and out of many brokerage offices there hustled wild-eyed individuals with charts under their arms, who would hold forth at length on double tops and bottoms and show you just where and how and why the "big fellows" were doing this or that with their favorite stocks. Yet none of them seemed to have much money. Possibly it was because they followed a strict set of rules and did not use much intelligence. It seems that the charts told them exactly what to do!

Successful students of the market were few but there were some; and I began to get a line on their methods of reasoning. I was surprised to find that the market itself did give frequent evidence of its future course and began to investigate along those lines. It did not interfere with my study of intrinsic value and earning power but rather supplemented it, for I often found that statistics and the action of the market would all point in the same direction. So far as manipulation was concerned, it appeared to have one of three objects: Making the public buy, sell or keep out. And I judged that the manipulators were endeavoring to do the opposite. The market at that time consisted of a comparatively few stocks, although they were increasing. The dominant trading factor was James R. Keene. The Rockefeller party was active in some of its stocks. Morgan had not yet "sprung" the Steel Trust, Gates and Harriman were just coming over the horizon, and the Gould sun was about setting. It was a market which could be easily stung by a group of new powerful interests working in harmony, but while public participation and volume of trading was large, it was not to be compared with the markets of today in the number of participants or the large number of stocks dealt in.

Having secured a new angle on the market I began myself to try to judge it from its own action, principally with regard to the general trend. Dow's theory of price movement made a considerable impression on me. I understood clearly his theory that there were three distinct market movements going on simultaneously—(1) the long trend extending over a period of years; (2) the thirty to sixty day swings; (3) the small swings running from one to several days. The value of these suggestions appeared to be great when properly applied.

I thirsted for stock market and investment knowledge but much to my regret there were very few people who could assist me and very little printed matter which was of any value whatever. So I had to dig it out for myself, the best I could. It was a slow process or else I was not bright enough to absorb it quickly, but I made progress, as I will show in succeeding chapters.

Chapter II - Profitable Experiences

Having accumulated enough money to go into business for myself, I resigned from the big wire house and began to deal in unlisted securities. Later on, with some associates, I formed a New York Stock Exchange firm, became the managing partner and for a number of years continued in the stock brokerage business. This put me in intimate touch with the operations of customers, and a number of other large operators.

I had not watched these traders for long before I reached three definite conclusions as to trading methods. They were as follows:

(1) The majority of those who were buying and selling securities were almost totally ignorant of the business.
(2) They were mentally lazy. They showed no desire to increase their knowledge of the subject, but anybody who gave them tips or so-called "information" held the greatest attraction for them.
(3) Very little educational literature was obtainable, even if the trading element had been inclined to devote thought and study to self-preparation.

It was astounding to see how men, shrewd, careful and successful in their own business, would come down to the Street and throw caution to the winds when they undertook to deal in stocks or bonds.

I had reached a point where I was a fair judge of the market; and I did my level best to aid them. As time went on, I did manage to help many people make considerable money; but I found that most of them wanted to lean —not to learn. They just drifted along, guided by hope of profit and pursued by fear of loss.

The clientele with which I came into contact during those years gave me a clear idea of the psychology of the average trader and investor, and I found that as a rule his viewpoint of the market was very much warped; that he did, most of the time, the opposite of what the large and experienced operator would do, because he judged by the surface conditions of the market and not by the highly important technical conditions. A clear understanding of these technical conditions, I saw, was most vital to anyone who expected to operate successfully. And so it came about that for a considerable time I devoted most of my thought and attention to the investment side of securities rather than the speculative.

After founding, during the panic of 1907, *The Magazine of Wall Street,* then known as *The Ticker,* I began to receive numerous inquiries from people who were anxious to learn more about the swings of the market, and I also received contributions of articles from those who had studied these subjects. Another kind of communication contained a description of methods more or less mechanical on which the writers desired opinions. At that time there was a wide interest in the search for a method of operating which would do away with fallible human judgment. And while this seemed to be a species of rainbow-chasing, there is no doubt that I was able to learn much from a study of the different kinds of recorded market actions. Some of the points which I had acquired through the examination of numerous ideas submitted and some other points which I studied out for myself greatly aided me in judging the market.

The reason for this is that all graphs, charts, diagrams, etc., which form pictures of the movements of individual stocks or groups of securities, are but the concrete history of the impression of many minds upon the market. And my object in studying along this line was not to follow these indications blindly, but to see what kind of mental operations caused them. By thus reasoning out the good and bad points in the psychology of the public I hoped to get at the true method of operating.

So right here I would like to say a good word for all forms of graphs which are apt to be greatly abused and misused by people who have never taken the trouble to investigate their value. There is scarcely a business or profession today that does not employ graphs as indicators of conditions, operations, etc., in thousands of different forms. What, therefore, could be more logical than to adopt graphs as a means of seeing and clarifying such a complex proposition as the security market?

As time went on, my publication office became the center of interest to a great number of people who had tackled this problem from various angles, and in the examination of their ideas and by the adoption of good and the elimination of the bad points, I gradually formed a fairly clear idea as to how a permanent success might be established by one willing to devote his time and attention to the matter, making all else secondary. As demand arose from many quarters for information on the subject of judging the market from its own action, I decided to make a specialty of this subject, study it out and write about it as I went along. The outcome of this was the book, *"Studies in Tape Reading,"* which has since been reprinted in many editions. And the principles therein stated have not changed through all the vicissitudes of the market during the dozen years which have elapsed since the book first appeared in serial form in *The Magazine of Wall Street.* Many people will say it is one thing to write about a difficult proposition like the security market, and quite another to put your ideas into practical operation, that is, to make money out of them. Suffice it to say that, since I wrote that book, I have made a very considerable amount of money for myself and in the aggregate millions of dollars for my subscribers by applying the methods therein set forth, viz., judging from the future course of the market and of individual securities by their own action. And I expect to keep on making, each year, much more money than I spend, because the principles in that book are absolutely sound and practicable, as proven by the dollars derived from the market thereby.

In *"Studies in Tape Reading"* I suggested trading for daily profits with the object of making a fractional profit over losses, expenses, commissions, etc., on the average, per day. But eventually I found that I could get much better results by operating for the five, ten and twenty point swings. Furthermore, I learned that to operate in the latter way was to lessen the nervous strain occasioned by watching the tape every minute of the day and carrying all the quotations of the leading active stocks and their previous action in my head.

I found that the real money was to be made in the important swings running thirty to sixty days on the average, in which accumulation or distribution was clearly marked while the movement was in its preparatory stages. Experience showed that every well planned and well executed campaign in the market had three stages:

First, in the case of an upward movement, the accumulation would appear and this might run several weeks or months.

Next, would be the marking up stage, where the stock was forced upward by either bullish news or aggressive buying until it reached the level where distribution could take place.

The third stage was that of distribution.

Operations for the decline would be the opposite of this cycle.

Very often I found a stock that was being marked up would be driven far beyond the point where a substantial and satisfactory profit could be realized, but as large operators work on an average buying and selling price rather than on a definite figure, in such cases their distribution would take them on the way down. For instance, if a stock was accumulated within a range of from 50 to 60 and the objective average selling point was 80, the issue might be driven up to par and then sold on the way back to 70, so that 80 or better would be the average price received for what was sold.

These points are explained so that the reader may get an idea of how I worked out my problems, my object being to find out or reason out what the large operator did and how he did it; then I could operate in the same way, and probably with greater success. *I saw the great advantage that lay in operating with the mental attitude of the professional trader instead of the attitude of the unsophisticated outsider.*

As previously stated, I first tested out my theory by dealing in fractional lots of stocks. My progress was often halted by unexpected changes in the market, my own tendency to get away from my principles, new developments which caused me to revise many details, and lastly, the necessity for a long series of transactions which would give me a background of experience in this particular way of dealing.

Before I was really successful, I had to practically rebuild my own trading character. One of my greatest difficulties was impatience. Being of an active disposition I could not sit still long enough to allow a big profit to accumulate. In certain periods the brokers made more in commissions than I made in profits. At other times I allowed myself to be influenced by other considerations rather than the action of the market. But finally I overcame most of these faults and began to reap a real benefit from all the thought and self-training I had put into my work.

Without going into all the many details connected with judging the market, which with long practice resolved themselves into a sort of intuition, as explained in *"Studies in Tape Reading,"* it is enough to say that I have since been successful in anticipating what were apparently the turning points in the ten to twenty point swings in the market. And as every one with a knowledge of the market will understand, success in this line consists in having a greater aggregate profit over the year than the total amount of losses, including commissions, tax and interest charges.

I realize that people in general hold to the illusion that any man who can make money in the stock market should make it by the million. The public seems to think that once you know how to tap the money reservoir all you have to do is let it ran. No fallacy could be more misleading. It is true that a few large traders make spectacular profits at times. But their losses are usually in proportion, and these you never hear of. Those who make millions risk millions— often all they have on a single operation. And they frequently go broke—a condition which I never have experienced in the stock market, simply because I have never allowed myself to get into a vulnerable position. I have withstood several panics without serious losses.

Making a whole lot of money all at once is not my trading objective. I use a comparatively small amount of money in trading—not over five or ten percent of my loose capital—because I have no desire to spread myself out too thin, or operate in such a way that any unexpected event will cripple me. I know that there are a number of people who look upon profits as a means of enlarging their operations. My method is to pull down the profits and invest them in safe income-paying securities, preferably those which have an opportunity to enhance in value.

There is a much greater satisfaction in operating with a small amount of money for various reasons: It makes you more careful, because, having set yourself to the task of realizing a large profit on a limited amount of operating capital, you plan your moves shrewdly and do not take risks such as you would if operating with more money. In the next place you feel that you are risking very little to make considerable. There is vastly more satisfaction in making $10,000 on a $5,000 capital than in making the same amount where $25,000 is employed. The operations which have been the most gratifying to me are those in which I have taken, at various times, $3,000 and put it into an account in a broker's office where I could get the right kind of service at a time I expected a move of twelve or fifteen points in a certain security. One of my favorite stocks in this respect has always been U.S. Steel with which I have probably had greater success than any other issue. A few years ago, when I was very busily engaged and could not watch the market all day, I used to wait for U.S. Steel to get into position where I expected such a sharp upward or downward move and then I would buy (or sell) 300 shares, placing a three point stop order for protection. Every two points up I would buy another hundred shares, protecting each additional lot with a three-point stop. After the stock had risen about ten points I would discontinue buying. By that time I would have 800 shares. I would take my profit on a further advance or raise the stop order so that I was sure to have at least several thousand dollars profit.

In the particular year that I mentioned above, I did very little trading except for three such campaigns in U.S. Steel, where not more than $3,000 original margin was used in each campaign, but from which my net profit was about $20,000. This is what I call "good trading" because it was done with very limited risk and the profits were large in proportion to the original amount. After the first campaign, the profits were sufficient to supply the capital for the second and third operations.

Now this is not intended to convey that I, or anyone else, can continue to trade indefinitely with uninterrupted success. It merely illustrates one method of operating which has the advantages described. It always reminds me of a warship which, instead of turning its broadside to the enemy, shows only its bow and thus makes much less of a target. Quite a number of men in Wall Street operate in this way.

You don't hear about them, because they don't happen to be publishing magazines or writing books. As an old friend of mine told me a few days ago, speaking of a former member of a New York Stock Exchange firm:

"He is the most successful speculator I ever met. He will watch a stock carefully and when he judges by its action that it is ready for an important move, he will buy perhaps 500 shares. If it goes in his direction he will buy additional lots every point up, but if it should decline two or three points after he has bought it, he will throw it out immediately on the ground that his first judgment was wrong. He has made so much money now that he takes up, and pays for, ten-thousand-share lots of stock, which in itself is evidence of what he has accomplished." Before I go any further, let me say that not every man is adapted to trading in stocks. In fact, very few are fitted for the work if it is undertaken as an art, a business, a profession, or whatever else you wish to call it. One reason is that most men have a commercial training, and this unfits them for dealing actively in securities. One of the worst traders I ever knew was a man who was highly successful, in fact, had made a fortune in real estate. His method was to buy lots on the fringe of the city and sell them out whenever he secured a substantial profit. He applied this method to the stock market. The result was that he bought in all kinds of markets, and very often had to carry securities for months or years before he could get out. He did not realize that the tendency might change its course several times a year, and there are cross currents and counter currents which must be allowed for, which are not present in real estate.

The merchant who buys his goods wholesale, knowing that there is an established market which will yield him perhaps a ten percent profit after overhead and selling expenses, is also handicapped when he comes to Wall Street. One reason is that he is accustomed to buying before he sells, *whereas a man who is trading in securities should be able, ready and willing to sell short with as great facility as if buying for long account.* The merchant is familiar with the market in his own field. He judges that market by the supply and demand, and his purchases are made accordingly; but in Wall Street he does not study supply and demand because it is a very technical subject and requires close attention for a number of years before one can master it. Even then, the best and most experienced traders have their bad times and their unfortunate seasons when the character of the market becomes too puzzling or for some reason their judgment is not up to par.

The manufacturer sells short when he takes orders for goods he has not yet manufactured. He sees orders for these goods piling up and thereupon covers his short transactions by purchasing the raw material and eventually manufacturing and delivering the finished goods; but when he enters the business of buying and selling securities, selling short is the last thing he wants to do.

From this it will be seen that special training is necessary if one is to avoid joining the ranks of those who have met the enemy and have been defeated.

Bear in mind that I am referring to the business of active trading and not to the business of investing successfully, which is an entirely different proposition, as will be described later.

Some of the principles which I have found to be advantageous in trading are as follows: The Main Factor is the Trend. If you work in harmony with the trend of the market, your chances for success are three or four times what they would be if you buck the trend. That is, if you buy in a bull market, the trend will, under ordinary circumstances, give you a profit; but if the trend of the market is downward, and you take a long position, the only way you can get out is on the incidental rally. This brief statement covers the point about as well as could be done in many chapters.

Risk should almost invariably be limited. Not only the experience of those whose trading I have observed but my own experience proves that whenever one departs from this general principle he is inviting serious losses. The best way to limit your risk is to form a habit of placing two or three point stops behind any trade which is made for the purpose of deriving a profit from the fluctuations. Harriman contended three-eights of a point, or one point, was enough; but of course he was originally a trader on the floor of the Stock Exchange. The most successful traders have followed this rule and its importance cannot be overestimated.

Anticipated profits should be at least three or four times the amount of risk. It must be expected that a percentage of your transactions will show a loss. The trader should aim to have such large profits on his successful trades that the losses and other expenses will still leave him something to the good. Profits can often be protected by moving stop orders up or by selling one-half of the commitment in order to mark down the cost of the remaining half. Many articles on this subject have appeared in past volumes of *The Magazine of Wall Street*.

One should be able to deal freely on both sides of the market. Any one who is unable to do this had better become an investor instead of a trader, buying in panics or on big declines such securities as appear to be selling below their intrinsic value.

Dealings should be in the active stocks. In order to make a profit, a stock must move. A great deal of money and many opportunities are lost by traders who keep themselves tied up in stocks which are sluggish in their action. In a commercial line you would not carry goods on your shelves indefinitely—you would keep your stock moving. In trading, keep on moving stocks!

You should either make a business of trading or else not try to be a trader. You cannot be successful at trading any more than you can be at mining, manufacturing, doctoring or anything else, unless you are trained for it. And by "training" I do not mean an occasional dab. Incidentally, unless you are peculiarly adapted to the business you had better become an intelligent investor instead of an unintelligent trader.

Chapter III - Why I Buy Certain Stocks and Bonds

There is an old adage, "It is easier to make money than to keep it." I not only aim to make money, but to keep it and make it grow.

The latter is often the biggest problem of all. It involves something like defensive trench warfare. There is your back line of solid investments, bought principally for income and whatever increase in principal may result. In front of these is your second line of defense against poverty and old age, consisting of securities bought for income and profit. Out in front is your line of speculative securities which you handle so as to gain further ground, without losing your hold on your second and third line of defenses.

In choosing the better grade of securities I give serious consideration to such especially advantageous issues as equipment notes. These are known as a "pawn broker's security" because they are generally issued to secure a purchase of locomotives and cars on which a payment of ten or twenty percent is made by a railroad company. The balance of the obligation is paid off in annual installments covering ten, fifteen or twenty years. As the obligation is thus annually reduced, the security for the remaining equipment grows larger and larger each year, in proportion to the indebtedness, so that toward the end of the equipment trust period the amount of the security in the shape of rolling stock increases to many hundred percent of the amount remaining to be paid. Equipment trusts are, therefore, to be regarded as prime investment mediums.

In spite of the many difficulties surrounding the construction and development of American railroads, I believe there is scarcely an instance where equipment bonds have been defaulted upon. Such issues are therefore well adapted to the final protection of one's investment stronghold.

Another line of income-bearing securities which I frequently favor may be found in the numerous issues of short term notes, which are excellent mediums for funds that are being put aside for specific purposes, and which will be required on a definite date. I find that their yield is often more liberal than one would expect, considering the character of the companies issuing these notes and the yield of their other securities. Due to the vagaries of the investment market, I have often picked up bargains in notes, especially those which were convertible into other securities. But one must be very careful in the selection of these, as any question as to a company being able to meet its obligations will come to the surface as the time approaches for the maturity of its short term notes.

When it comes to safe bond investments, I generally favor properties whose promise to pay is absolutely sound, but whose security is beyond question, and if possible I like, in addition, large equities such as treasury assets, as in the case of Union Pacific, oil lands, and other subsidiaries as in the case of

Southern Pacific, holdings in affiliated railroad systems, as in the Pennsylvania Railroad treasury, etc.

My object in making money in securities is to have more money to invest. When I make money in the market, I don't look upon it is a means of trading in a larger way, but I consider the income that money will produce—not only the immediate income, but what in addition might be yielded from the increase in the principal if the original money is properly invested.

Long ago, for the most part, I adopted Harriman's principle which was: "I am not interested in 10 percent. I want something that will grow." And so, in selecting securities, I try in the main to pick out those which have not small but great possibilities.

There are various kinds of investors. Some want the highest grade bonds even though the income return is small. Others want preferred stocks which yield from 6 to 8 percent and which, unlike bonds, never come due, and pay their dividends indefinitely, if properly selected. Next come those investors who are willing to buy the best class of common stocks in an endeavor not only to secure dividends but to see their principal enhance in value, and are satisfied with a moderate profit.

With the major part of my available funds, I invest in a somewhat different way, realizing that the number of years in which a man may operate successfully is limited. I want to put as much money as I can into investment channels where it will grow rapidly so that I can put the increment to work again on the same basis.

Being close to the seat of operations in the financial district I see too many opportunities for profitable investment and increase in principal to allow any substantial amount of money to remain idle. While I always have a certain amount of money in high grade investments, I have not reached the age or the stage where I think more of income than of increase in principal value. As I grow older, no doubt the proportion of securities bought for income will increase, but at age 46, as the insurance companies say, I consider that, in my particular case, it is too early for me to develop into a chronic coupon clipper.

High-grade securities and coupons are, however, the proper medium for the majority of those who read this book—emphatically for those who are not experts in distinguishing real investments and real opportunities. They should remain in the income-only stage, so far as most of their funds are concerned.

While there are seasons particularly advantageous for certain operations in the security market, and while these seasons may often seem a long time in coming, one has only to look up the record of the fluctuations in high grade bonds to know that once in a great while they are on the bargain counter. December, 1919 was one of those times, and I was not blind to the fact. It is seldom, indeed, that one can secure the old line, railway bonds, safe beyond question, at such prices as were obtainable then, and with such a long term of years to maturity. In the belief that my investor readers may be interested in knowing what factors convinced me that bonds were "too low" at that time, I append an analysis of the financial situation as I then wrote it, and which was published in the columns of *The Magazine of Wall Street.*

"While it is always time to buy securities for income only, when they can be had at a rate satisfactory to the buyer, this appears to be a time of times, and unless another world cataclysm should occur, a duplicate of this situation may not be seen for another ten or twenty years.

"In former years the railroads were about the only mediums for safe bond investments; but we today have a large variety of industrial and other kinds of mortgages which afford equal if not greater safety, and in many cases a larger net return.

"These are times when a man is justified in loading up with these high grade securities, that is, buying twice as many as he wants to keep permanently. This he can readily do by purchasing and paying for only half of the quantity he buys, carrying the securities in his bank, and gradually paying off the balance out of income. It matters not whether this income arises from these investments or from his business or other outside sources. Any bank with which you have dealt with will be glad to extend this accommodation; in fact, it will increase the bank's respect for your judgment.

"The present time (December, 1919) affords a rare opportunity. Such an operation should yield not only a substantial profit on the extra quantity which you now purchase, but this profit applied to the reduction of the cost of the balance of the bonds which you now acquire will so enhance the net income from the entire operation that the opportunity should by no means be overlooked.

"Never before have high grade bonds, legal for savings banks in New York State, sold so low as late in 1919. A glance over the list shows that many leading issues are selling at from ten to twenty-five points below their high figures of two years ago. Take old line investments like Union Pacific 1st 4's, having twenty-seven years to run, netting about 5.25%; Southern Pacific Ref. 4's of 1955, netting 5.45%; Norfolk & Western consolidated 4's, 1996, 5.23%; Louisville & Nashville gold 5's of 1937, 5.09%; Chicago & Northwestern general 3's of 1987 netting 5.26%; Burlington general 4's of 1958, netting 5.43%. These are all bonds which will recover sharply in price as soon as the money situation definitely changes, and the limit of foreign government emissions has been seen.

"The Union Pacific 4% bonds of 1947, selling at about 82, are around 18 points under their market price of two years ago, and one only has to await changed conditions to see a bond of this type rise to its natural level. If this should occur in three years, the average increase in value would be 6% per annum, which, added to the nearly 5% current return on the investment should mean an annual return of about 11%. If such an advance should occupy five years, the return would be 8%. These figures spell *opportunity.*"

One field which has attracted me has been bank stocks, and the reasons were very clearly set forth in a series of articles on this subject appearing in *The Magazine of Wall Street.*

In selecting securities of banks and other financial institutions, one is in the same position as the person who is driving an automobile. He has usually three speeds in his gear case. He can travel slowly on the first set of gears, or a little faster on the second set, or very fast on "high." The institution which does an old style banking business may be likened to the first set of gears. It makes progress within a certain radius, but when a bank takes on a trust department, or a close affiliation with a trust company, making the two parts of one institution, it may be regarded as traveling on second speed. But there is still another type of institution which includes both the above and embraces an additional function which in the financial district is a very advantageous one to the stockholder. I refer to a bank which owns or is affiliated with a "Security Company" for the purpose of underwriting and conducting syndicate and investment security operations, which are, of course, very profitable.

I have been buying stocks in a dozen or more New York financial institutions. I put these in the custody of a trust company, separate from any other securities, so that dividends, rights, and stock distributions would all be paid in to this one account and reinvested in the same class of securities. My observation has shown that to secure the greatest benefit from bank stock investments, one should not spend the income derived therefrom, nor sell his rights, nor sell any stock distributions that are given, because these in time generate other melons of the same sort, and this second generation gives birth to successive series of children and grandchildren, which eventually roll up a very substantial amount of both income and principal.

In placing these securities with the trust company for safekeeping and reinvestment, I told the trust officer of the institution that this account would be in debt most of the time, because

I would buy ahead of the income and I would expect the trust company to loan whatever moneys were required for that purpose.

During the latter part of 1919 two of these opportunities developed: The Bankers Trust Co. directors recommended an increase in the capital stock from $15,000,000 to $20,000,000, the new stock to be offered to shareholders at a price of $100 per share. This is on the basis of one share of new stock for every three shares of old. Holding shares of Bankers Trust, which cost in the neighborhood of $485 per share, I was entitled to subscribe to new stock at $100, which brought the average cost down to about $389 per share.

In time these new shares will be producing other stock dividends, rights, or cash dividends, so that eventually I may have a considerable amount of Bankers Trust Co. stock. By reinvestment of income in whatever form it is distributed, the cost of this Bankers Trust Co. stock will be reduced to a very low figure.

Another case of this kind appeared not long ago in the form of a notice sent to stockholders of the Chase National Bank, which I purchased at about $675 per share. Stockholders were asked to vote on an increase in the capital stock of the bank from $10,000,000 to $15,000,000, with a proportionate increase in the shares of the Chase Securities Co., which is affiliated with the bank. Holders were to be allowed to subscribe to one new share of the Bank stock and one new share of the Securities Company, for each two old shares thereof held prior to December 26, 1919. The subscription price was $250 for one share of stock of the Bank and one share of stock of the Securities Co. I have no doubt that in time the value of all these shares, viz., the new, which I have bought, and the old which will sell ex-rights, will recover to the price which I paid for the old stock, which was $675 per share. This means that I have faith not only in these and the other banking institutions in which I have become a stockholder, but in the men behind them, and in the future of New York City as the world's banking center.

I estimate that the average return over a period of years, allowing for rights, melons, regular and extra cash distributions, etc., in the leading issues is something over 12% per annum. At this rate, my investment should double itself in a period of something between six and seven years, allowing for the reinvestment of all dividends of every sort in the same class of securities.

The small percentage of failures among banking institutions, now that they are under such rigid control by the Federal authorities, makes their securities adapted to the conservative investor who is looking toward income enhancement and safety. My own selection included a larger proportion of shares in those institutions which have security companies attached, because these combine two companies in one, and in all cases they are being conducted with highly profitable results to the shareholders.

This taking a sum of money and planting it in a certain field without drawing down the income, but with intent to profit by its growth, may be followed out to whatever degree the investor desires. It may be begun with one share of one bank stock, or any other kind of stock or bond. It is an investment operation, but it is undertaken for income and profit, not with the idea of deriving or withdrawing that profit, but to make it yield additional sums for investment. It is a great deal like a savings bank account for the man with a small amount of cash. I remember how, with a great deal of pride, I started my first savings account with a five dollar bill (because the bank would not open an account for less), and how much satisfaction I derived from being able to add a few more fives and tens.

The man or woman who is obliged to withdraw his or her interest or, in case of a rainy day, pull down part of the principal, will be handicapped in an operation of this sort, but the object should be to make these deficiencies up when the skies again clear and to keep expenses within bounds so that the additions made annually will rapidly increase the earning power of the principal.

Chapter IV – Unearthing Profit Opportunities

When I buy bonds and other high-grade securities for income and profit, I favor those which for special reasons are well adapted to my purpose.

First, I consider those which are selling below their intrinsic value, based on character of security. In such a case I do not lay too much stress on the interest return, although in some cases it is large. The question of marketability is important with me, however, because I prefer issues that can be instantly turned into cash. The reason for this is that always I desire always to be in a position to take advantage of a threatened panic or bargain opportunity, and as

I watch the market and the general situation very closely, I frequently detect signs of trouble way in the distance and prepare for it.

In the case of certain 5% bonds which I hold, these are well secured, earning a big surplus, which for some reason or another is concealed. Selling around 60, the income is very large if figured to maturity, but in selecting this bond I had my eye more on the probability that the investment public will wake up to its real value and mark its price up twenty or twenty-five points within the next two or three years. In case of an advance to 85 within three years, there would be about 8% profit per annum, to be added to the flat yield of the bond. Such a 5% bond at 60, would net about 8%, disregarding any reinvestment of income. If, on top of this, I realize another 8% in three years, the income plus profit would be 16% per annum.

A class of bond which I hold and always favor, is the convertible. The advantages of convertible bonds have been too often described in past issues of *The Magazine of Wall Street* to necessitate repetition here, but if one would make a persistent study of these convertible issues, he would find every year new opportunities for making growing investments. Whatever is a little complicated for the average investor is apt to be overlooked and neglected. To get the best results one should be familiar with the technicalities of many kinds of convertible bonds and the stipulations under which they are issued. In some cases it does require some figuring to find out just what can be done with these issues.

For my own investment I am seldom attracted to convertible bonds solely from the standpoint of income, but only when I see possibilities in the securities into which they are convertible. In 1918 I bought $100,000 of a certain convertible bond because I saw great future possibilities in the stock into which they were convertible at par. At that time the stock was selling close to the price of the bonds, viz., around 90. Observation of the action of the bonds during the period of weakness in the stock convinced me that the bonds would not decline very much even if the stock were to break ten or fifteen points, because the investment value of the bonds kept them up at a level where the interest return to the investor brought in buying enough to sustain the market price. By purchasing the convertible bonds I would have something that I need not be concerned about, and I was sure that, if the investment public realized the intrinsic value in the stock, my convertible bonds would follow the stock along up.

This is exactly what happened. Sometime later the stock rose twenty-five points and the bonds kept a little above it, until one day the bonds were selling so much higher than the stock that I sold the bonds and bought the stock instead, thus marking down the cost of my bonds by an amount representing the difference between the price of the two securities.

This marking down the cost, by the way, is a very important factor in making investments. I keep it constantly in mind. Every investor should remember that by selling a portion of his holdings at a profit he is reducing the cost of the balance. It is good practice. I will elaborate later.

Naturally, in dealing, as I do, in all kinds of securities, there are quite a number of reasons for my going into a stock.

In 1913 or 1914 I wrote a series on "Which Kind of a Stock Is Best?" This was done as much for my own information as for my subscribers, and while I am on this subject I should like to say that I take my own medicine. In searching the security market I have a twin purpose, viz., to find investment opportunities for my own money and to tell my subscribers about them. I figure that what is good enough for my subscribers is good enough for me. At the same time I wish to say that I make mistakes at times; so does everybody, no matter how long he has been in the field.

My constant aim is to show my readers, directly or between the lines, how they may be able to judge for themselves. As was written by an author unknown to me: "There are men who will take no initiative on their own responsibility, who will undertake nothing without consulting others as to the feasibility of the schemes and plans they have in view. When a man puts more confidence in another than in himself he is bound to lose all will power and become a mere dependent, awaiting orders as to the course of action. It is impossible for such a man to get along in the world and make a success of his own life. When opportunity comes along he is afraid to seize it without asking his neighbor's opinion."

So what I and my staff try to do is to make our readers think and plan and carry out their campaign in the investment field just as they do in their own business. This was one of my purposes in writing the series, "Which Kind of a Stock is Best?" As those articles progressed they indicated that the chain store and mail order stocks were, in many respects, better than the other leading groups such as steel, copper, railroad, telephone, etc., the principal reason being that these companies were putting more of their earnings back into their business than any other single group.

And so I bought Sears, Roebuck & Co., because its history shows that every three or four years a stock dividend is declared. This has been the practice of the company for many years. By this method Sears, Roebuck & Co. keep the cash in their business and use it for healthy and profitable expansion. The stockholder who owns a hundred shares is given twenty-five or thirty-three shares of new stock, which adds to his income without cutting down the working capital of his company. This twenty-five or thirty-three shares additional will, in ensuing years, probably yield another six or eleven shares and these, in turn, will eventually breed other little stock dividends, all of which, added to the original shares, should in time double the quantity of an investor's holdings, without any further investment of cash by him.

The purchase of a stock like Delaware, Lackawanna & Western Railroad is one which I made for an entirely different reason. Its dividend yield did not attract me, but having been over the property I realized what an enormous amount had been expended on improvements of far-reaching importance. One official is quoted as saying that they have invested, in road and equipment, money for expenditures that could easily have been put off for twenty or twenty-five years. You may say, "That is a strange reason for investing in a railroad stock when the railroad situation is so unfavorable." But let me tell you that when you buy into a company like that, with enormous equities buried as a result of successful operations in the past, you will eventually see a still greater return, because one of these days the railroads, including Lackawanna, will again come into their own.

Lackawanna, at the end of 1918, had a profit and loss surplus of $57,247,984 against a total outstanding stock of $42,277,000. In June, 1909, it declared a cash dividend of 50% out of its surplus, and a stock dividend of 15%. In November, 1911, it declared a stock dividend of 35%, payable in stock of the Lackawanna railroad of New Jersey. The system is only 980 miles long, but it is the Croesus among railroads. From 1906 to the present time, 160 is the lowest it has sold. In May, 1919 it touched 217. Hence, when in October, 1919, I saw it decline to around 180 on a threatened coal strike, I considered it cheap, and if it should decline further I would regard it as a greater bargain.

Wall Street history shows that securities more often reach their low point when some danger or disaster is threatened, than upon the actual occurrence of these incidents, and the reason the low point is made just prior to, or at the time the event actually occurs, is: By that time every one who is subject to fear-of-what-will-happen, has sold out. When the thing does happen or is prevented, there is no more liquidation, and the price rallies on the short interest, or else on the investment demand created by the improved situation.

It was for these reasons that I bought Delaware, Lackawanna & Western railroad Company's stock.

Speaking of high priced stocks like Sears, Roebuck, Lackawanna and others, there is a very important reason why these are cheaper than the very low-priced stocks. Many of the shares selling in the 10's, 20's and 30's represent very little earning power. In many cases only one or two percent is being earned on the latter issues, with little or no prospect of dividends. Stocks paying 5 to 8% range from $60 to $100 per share. On this basis a stock paying 1% could be worth from $12 to $20. This would indicate that a non-dividend payer is worth somewhere between nothing and $12. Everything above that is hope capitalized.

Yet we have seen many non-dividend payers sell at all sorts of prices before their initial declaration. American Can, for example, sold not long ago at 68 without ever having paid a dividend. Brooklyn Rapid Transit, in 1899, sold, as a non-dividend payer, at 137; it did not make its first dividend disbursement for ten years after that.

But take the stocks selling at $200 to $400 per share and upward, and in normal times you generally find intrinsic values, future prospects, or earning power, or all combined, which justify these prices and more. Most of the very high priced stocks have hidden equities which may not benefit the stockholders right away, but which are working for them just the same. These factors may not interest the man who is long today and short tomorrow, but they do interest the permanent investor who has his eye on the development of the corporation and the future growth of the various industries and the country in general. That is why I favor high-priced stocks rather than very low-priced speculative issues.

Chapter V – Some Experiences in Mining Stocks

The investor who always chooses securities of companies who constantly put money back into their properties, will scarcely ever go wrong, but he must be constantly on the alert to notice any change in policy due to altered conditions, or to control of the property getting into other hands. The New York, New Haven & Hartford Railroad was formerly an example of progressive and conservative management and for many decades was considered a high grade investment. But the time came when a policy of expansion brought the New Haven to grief. Of this there were many signs, especially when the persistent character of the liquidation indicated that something was wrong.

Carnegie said, "Put all your eggs in one basket and watch the basket." I would distribute my eggs and watch all of the baskets.

Never get married to a security. You may have it salted down, but there is no reason why you shouldn't freshen up your list every once in a while by going over and carefully considering what you hold and whether something else wouldn't work to better advantage for you. I find I get best results by considering each investment a separate little business enterprise. When I buy a security I figure that while as a bondholder I am a creditor and my money is secured this is not true when I become a stockholder. That makes me a partner in the enterprise and as such I want to be a live partner, not a dead one; for if I don't look after my own interests nobody else will.

That explains one reason why I like to be associated in partnership with people who are high class in every respect—because I know that they are not lying awake nights planning ways to do me or the other stockholders out of our money. Possibly no corporation head is beyond criticism, but anyone who puts his dollars into corporations like U.S. Steel, Bethlehem Steel, General Motors, General Electric and other leaders in industry and finance may rest assured that these companies are being run by the highest type of industrial captains who are intent upon making their enterprises profitable to the hundreds of thousands of big and little stockholders.

"Choose your company" is therefore a good precept for the investor.

There used to be a gang of highwaymen operating here in the Street and using the leading railroad and industrial shares as the scissors by which they parted the public from its money, but that day is rapidly passing. Leaders in finance learned long ago that they could make more money by the square deal than in any other manner. Nevertheless, I find that it pays to be sceptical until you are convinced by the past record of those in the management that they are working in your interest and not in their own.

For my own benefit, as well as that of every reader of *The Magazine of Wall Street,* I am investigating these essential factors more than ever before. It is not enough for one to know that a certain development is indicated by the surface facts and conditions—I want to get down into the root of things and find out why. For this reason I employ investigators, lawyers, mining and oil engineers. I send people to different parts of the country to get the local color and all the angles on a proposition.

After employing one engineer I sometimes send another to check him up. It might cost a few thousand dollars, but when you are putting real money into an enterprise you cannot be too sure, nor investigate too thoroughly. Not long ago I had two mining enterprises put up to me, which on a cursory examination looked good. It cost me two thousand dollars to have these properties examined, and on the engineer's reports I turned them down. In one case the mine has turned out better than was first represented to me. Either or both of these properties might develop into big mining enterprises, but taking all the facts into consideration I concluded they were not good enough for me to invest in.

While an engineer's report is by no means the last word on a property, it is a hundred times better to have an expert opinion than to take your own or some other layman's view; yet the peculiar part of mining is that even though the most eminent engineers may give an adverse report on a property, it may eventually fool them.

Mining has a great fascination for me. In fact, what came out of the ground was always of peculiar interest to numerous members of the Wyckoff family. The original Wyckoff, after landing in New York in the early sixteen hundreds, had charge of Peter Stuyvesant's estate, which was located in downtown New York, where the Hudson Terminal Building now stands. His descendant, my grandfather, who organized the Hanover Fire Insurance Co., and was one of the original interests in the Hanover National Bank, was also deeply interested in mining. He invented a separation process back in the fifties and successfully mined gold in the State of Virginia before and during the Civil War near where the Battle of the Wilderness was fought.

If I had my business career to plan over again, I would be inclined to favor mining engineering, for it is an interesting profession; but in visiting numerous mining properties and watching the methods of engineers and the difficult conditions which often prevail in the different mines, I can readily see how Old Mother Earth can fool the best of them. For that reason I never go into a mining enterprise unless I am prepared to lose every cent I put into it.

But there are many ways in which even a layman can check up such an imposing person as the mining engineer. I have made considerable money in mining stocks, and I expect to make a great deal more because I have learned a lot thus far and will use what knowledge I have to better advantage in the future.

First of all, I want to know who are the interests behind the mine—whose dollars are alongside of mine. Have they a record for successfully developing other mining enterprises? What mistakes have they made? Were they fooled themselves or did they fool the stockholders—which or both? Along what line is the development work now proceeding? Is the company properly financed? What is the character and reputation of the engineer who is guiding the development work? Is the metal or mineral which they are producing such that an advantageous market is afforded now and at all times? If it is a gold, silver or copper mine, what is the outlook for those metals? Are future conditions so shaping themselves that the mine can be regarded as more or less of a manufacturing and therefore an investment proposition? Is the nature of the ore such that it will peter out within a few years or is there a certain deposit of ascertainable value which can be diamond-drilled and its value estimated? Under these conditions, what is the probable life of the mine and the estimated profit per share during that period? These and dozens of other questions are what I ask myself and others before putting my money into a property.

Some mines are highly speculative; some are at or approaching the invest-ment stage. My problem is to get aboard the best of them before they get to a stage where the cream is all off. In other words, I want some of the cream, and in order to get it I frequently have to go in early and sit in for a long time before the skimming process can be accomplished.

Sometimes I go into a mining, stock in order to derive a profit from the fluctuations in the market price, and other times to get my profit out of the ground. In order to illustrate this point I will explain an operation in Magma Copper, which stock I have held in substantial quantity for over four years. I was coming downtown one day when a friend whom I met told me there was "something doing" in Magma, and suggested that I watch it. I did watch it, and saw that careful buying was proceeding. (I always lay more stress on the action of the market than on what anybody says.) As I remember, the stock originally came out at about $12 per share, rose to $18, then sold off to around $15. When he told me this it was up to $20, indicating that new influences were at work.

I decided to buy 200 shares and await further developments. The price hung around the same figure for a day or two, when suddenly my broker called me up and said Magma was 21 bid, whereupon I immediately gave him an order to buy 500 shares at the market. He had to pay 22 for some of it. I then bought another 500 shares, which cost me a point or so higher. As I always like to buy something that is "hard to purchase," the action of this stock pleased me very much, especially as it closed that night around 28 or 29.

Then I set out to find what it was all about, and I learned that the character of the ore in Magma had been discovered to be such that if it was present in any great quantity the mine would be one of the most important in this country, for insiders would then consider it worth $200 per share. So I told my friends about it.

No doubt the bucket shops were heavily short of this stock, because when the urgent buying continued, the price rose rapidly, until in about three weeks it sold at 69, and I had about $55,000 profit on my 1,200 shares.

Did I take this profit? I did not. I did not go into it for that amount of money. Have I been joshed about not taking it during the time the stock has wiggled back and forth between 25 and 55 for the last four years? I have. Why did I not take it? I'll tell you: Because when I bought that stock I resolved that more money was to be made out of the mine than out of the fluctuations—unless someone was lying. And following my usual resolution to be prepared

465

for the loss of whatever I put into any mine, I made up my mind to sit with my $23,000 investment in Magma until it proved to be either a fake or a bonanza.

It has proved to be a bonanza, and although the stock is today selling for only one-half of its high price of 69, I not only have the same opinion of its future as was indicated in 1915, but I have many, many more reasons, for believing in the soundness of the enterprise.

Magma Copper Company is capitalized at $1,500,000 authorized, and $1,200,000 outstanding stock of $5 par value. There being only 240,000 shares, a price of 35 represents a market value of $8,400,000. The leading interest is Col. William B. Thompson, who, in the last twelve or fifteen years, has made more millions in mining securities than any other man in Wall Street.

Ever since the real value of the property was discovered Mr. Thompson and his friends have been steadily accumulating Magma, until now, out of the 240,000 shares, there are not more than 20,000 shares in the hands of the public. How do I know this? Because I have gone to very great trouble and expense to check it up from various angles. I am not taking anybody's word; I have got at the facts, not only from a Wall Street point of view. A few months ago I visited the property, and with my mining engineer went down to the 1,400-foot level. I saw 40% to 60% bornite on all sides of me in some of the tunnels and cross-cuts.

The property is being developed on a tremendous scale, and now that its new shaft has been completed, it is ready for quantity production. Its silver and gold values so reduce the cost of its copper that it is one of the lowest priced producers in this country today. And down below there is a world of ore.

Those who know Colonel Thompson best say he will never sell his Magma. For my part, I intend to wait until I see him start to distribute, and then they can have mine.

Carping critics will say, "He's trying to boost Magma, so he can sell it." Let them carp. I don't care whether anyone who reads this buys Magma or not. It makes no difference either to Colonel Thompson, to me, or to my friends and subscribers who have bought the stock on the strength of what they have read in *The Magazine,* and who hold most of the 20,000 shares to which I have referred. All I wish to say to them is: Hold it, and you won't be sorry. As for professional parasites and self-appointed critics, let me call their attention to the fact that I talk, write, investigate, trade and invest in nearly all securities on the New York Stock Exchange and outside at one time or another. Hence, criticisms may as well be prepared in advance and arranged alphabetically for easy and prompt access when required.

This experience in Magma illustrates the advantage of thoroughly investigating and then sticking to your holdings like grim death, or until something occurs which, for a definite reason, causes you to change your position. I do not claim that the paper profit in Magma thus far is any criterion, but I wish to emphasize the importance of making a resolution in connection with investment or speculative transactions and basing that resolution on sound premises—making of them a sort of statistical rock upon which you may place your feet and stand there indefinitely.

Lots of people have said, "Why didn't you sell out and buy back cheaper?" Personally, I have never made any money by trading backward, by which I refer to the hindsight which is so frequently flourished in Wall Street as an indication that the flourisher is blessed with an acute foresight.

Had I sold at the high price, I could of course have bought back on a scale down, or a lower figure, then resold and re-bought, but as I have said, I was not in that kind of an operation, although it took considerable strength of purpose to resist at times. Ore in the ground, when combined with first-class management, ample capital and big personal commitments on the part of those who are running the property, is about as safe as money in the bank; but it must be the right kind of ore and in such quantity that it will yield a very large return in proportion to the original investment.

Elsewhere the reader will find reference to the difficulty in waiting for a big profit, but in the main people have less trouble with their patience when they face a large loss. There is one way in which most of this difficulty can be overcome, and that is by carefully assembling the facts when you enter a commitment and continually checking up all along the line for the entire time that you hold it. There is no need for guesswork, if one will take the trouble. It is merely a question of how much labor and expense you are willing to go to in order to make your investment successful.

We succeed in proportion to the amount of energy and enterprise we use in going after results. Success is not for the man who is willing to sit down and wait for something to fall into his lap.

It is poor policy, I find, to wait for Opportunity to knock at your door. I train my ear so that I can hear Opportunity coming down the street long before it reaches my door. When Opportunity knocks, I try to reach out, grab Opportunity by the collar and yank it in.

Chapter VI - The Fundamentals of Successful Investing

One of the most important considerations when making an investment is to understand the nature and condition of the industry which that security represents. Look over the mediums which John D. Rockefeller and others of his family select, and you will find that they are mostly in the necessities of life—oil, gas, food or other near necessities, such as iron, steel, harvesting machinery, etc. These are branches of endeavor in which there is an already created and continual demand—human need of fuel, light, eatables, or materials necessary to produce them. It is a good point to bear in mind.

As I get deeper and deeper into this problem of making money in securities, and then making the securities make more money, new avenues for thought, research and investigation are constantly developing. Of late I have been more than ever impressed with the importance of understanding the present condition and future tendency of the industries represented by the multitudinous corporations whose shares are listed or unlisted in New York and elsewhere. It was for this reason that I established in *The Magazine of*

Wall Street a department known as Trade Tendencies. This feature is worthy of careful study.

While in former years I usually began with a consideration of the trend of the market, and then passed to the choice of security, I now line the factor's up in the following order:

(1) Long trend of the market.

(2) Nature and tendency of the industry.

(3) Trend of the selected company's affairs (toward improvement or contrary).

(4) Character and reputation of the management.

(5) Financial position and earning power.

(6) Position in relation to the intermediate, i.e., the thirty to sixty-day swings.

When all of the above prove up to my satisfaction I feel safe in making an investment.

Of course, there are other considerations, but these are the most important.

Practically everyone agrees, and I have proved in another series of articles, how vitally important it is to know the long trend of the market. This is the compass by which all courses should be steered. It is so fundamental that there is little ground for discussion, but I may say that it is one of the main points in successful investment. The reason is that even when a purchase is not well-timed, it is likely to show a profit at sometime or other if the broad general tendency of prices be upward. Even poor weak stocks advance to some extent in a bull market. On the contrary, if a person buys a stock in a bear market, he is likely to have to carry it a very long while. If it be in a weak financial position, he may have to see it through a receivership, or he may decide to sell out at a big loss in order to save what little remains. From this it will be seen how important is knowledge of the long trend.

Suppose I have decided that the automobile industry is in a very sound, prosperous and promising condition, and I am considering an investment in one of the best of the automobile companies' shares. I would not feel justified in making this investment unless satisfied that the long trend of the market is upward. The action of the market discounts the business situation six months to a year in advance; prices of stocks point farther ahead than any individual can see, and because these prices represent the combined or composite opinion of the millions of people who are dealing in securities. They express themselves by their purchases and sales; hence a study of the tendency of the general market and of individual stocks is a study of the minds of men.

Therefore, when I decide that the automobile industry is in a favorable position, and that the long trend of the market is upward, I set about to select the company engaged in that industry; then I determine (a) whether the tendency of its business is toward improvement or to the contrary; (b) character and reputation of the management; (c) financial position and earning power; (d) position of the stock or bond in relation to the general market and its position in the intermediate swings (if it be a stock) represented by the thirty to sixty-day movements in prices.

It is not claimed that I go through any set formulas, but this is the general plan of reasoning which I follow, and which, through long association with the various kinds of market securities, financial statements and periodical swings in prices has become almost instinctive, so that it takes me only a short time to make up my mind that a proposition measures up to my requirements.

At the beginning, of course, I had to sit down like anybody else and pore over a mass of data and statistics and look up records just as a lawyer, doctor, or anyone else has to do when he first begins to practice. But trading and investing is like any other pursuit—the longer you stay at it the more technique you acquire, and anybody who thinks he knows of a short-cut that will not involve "sweat of the brow" is sadly mistaken.

Pertaining to the matter of condition and outlook for the industry in which I might be considering a venture, I want to show how it should take precedence over many other factors which are included in the examination of a contemplated investment. When I first came down to Wall Street, there was practically only one industry represented on the New York Stock Exchange—that of railroading. Everything revolved around the state of the crops, because wheat, corn, oats and other crops were the country's mainstay, and most of the speculative campaigns by large operators like Gould, Keene, Philip Armour, Deacon White and others, started with the crop outlook as the base.

That condition has changed. We have many hundreds of industries represented by the listed and unlisted securities that are now freely dealt in by investors, and this list is being added to every week. So, while the railroad stocks are still a factor, there are more oils than rails and a great many more motors than there used to be. All these groups are subject to various influences which affect their respective industries, and in many cases their industries are so intertwined that prosperity or depression in some is bound to bring about a similar condition in others.

The automobile industry is a striking example of this. If, as one high official has stated, there is a latent demand for two million automobiles, it means that there exists a like possibility of expansion in the rubber tire, steel and oil industries. Another instance is found in the rails. The roads having been handed back to their owners, once their financial position and earning power is assured, there will immediately spring up an unprecedented demand for railway equipment. This in turn would favorably affect the steel industry, because the railroads are such very large consumers of rails and other equipment requiring the use of steel.

Then comes the secondary consideration of the effect of prosperity in these lines upon other industries. Included in automobile manufacture must be literally hundreds of allied lines such as concerns making bodies, tops, radiators, motors, wheels, etc., now that the indirect effect of a prosperous condition in the automobile trade is disseminated through thousands of different channels.

The two factors above named have a still greater influence upon the spending power of the millions whose earnings are kept at a high level by reason of the demand for labor and materials, and what is known as the spending power of the public runs into thousands of trade avenues, resulting in a great stimulation of all lines of industry.

Perhaps I have got away from my subject a little, but it is interesting to follow a thought towards its logical conclusion.

The above condition therefore brings about, directly and indirectly, a stimulation of various lines, while in other industries, working under adverse conditions, the effect is contrary; hence we must conclude that there are numerous tendencies going on in the market all the time, some being reflected by higher prices for these groups of securities, while prices of other groups are declining. This will make clear why it is so important to study the various lines of business in order to choose, by a process of elimination, those which are likely to show the best results, even if conditions in other lines are somewhat unfavorable. I have seen cases where the progress of a certain industry more than offset the declining tendency of the general market, resulting in certain stocks going up while most others were going steadily downward. When I can make an investment in which the condition of that trade is ideal, and when the long trend of the market is strongly upward, with all the above-named factors satisfactory, I feel rather certain that the outcome will be profitable.

These points being settled, the next step is to decide what stock in that industry is in the best position as regards earning power and financial strength, character and reputation of management, etc. From an investment standpoint the above factors should dominate, but from a speculative standpoint, the matter of technical position would have almost equal weight.

In selecting a stock for income and profit, or choosing one which I buy primarily for profit, I always like to choose the one which will make the greatest amount of money for me in the shortest length of time. This is where a study of technical position comes in. A certain stock may look good to me because it has risen from 100 to 150 and then reacted under an assault by the bears (but without any especial change in its fundamental position, outlook or earning power) to a price of 110. If it shows at that level strong resistance to pressure, I would much rather buy it than some stock which was still in the range of distribution after being marked up 40 or 50 points and made very active around the top. These are but simple examples of a study of the action of different stocks and some of my reasons for choosing one rather than the other after giving due weight to all the other factors in the case.

It is strange how people will continue to ignore the important elements just referred to. Probably it is because they do not understand the operations that underlie the fluctuations in securities and which are responsible for many of their movements. I refer to the campaigns mapped out and carried out by pools consisting of groups of a few or many men who look far ahead and observe the approach of a situation which will enable them to buy or sell to advantage.

As Dow used to say: "The public rarely sees values until they are pointed out,"—which means that the public does not lead, but is led in speculation. It rarely acts until it is told to act, or until action of some sort is suggested by a bit of verbal information, a market letter, etc.

But there is another kind of suggestion which is the most potent in its influence on the public, and that is the action of the market itself. A rising price for a stock suggests still higher prices and declining quotations bear the inference that prices are going lower. Pools work on this weakness, which is due to ignorance on the part of the public. They accumulate a stock without advancing its price; then, when market conditions are favorable, they bid the stock up. This excites public buying, because people always want to get in on something that is "going up." Vice versa, groups will often try to depress a stock, counting on the public's support when the issue begins to decline.

It long ago occurred to me that success in the security market demanded an understanding of the operations of those who were most influential, because these interests had been studying the business and operating in the market for many years and were therefore experts. It was sound reasoning to suppose that a knowledge of the principles which they used in their market operations would enable one to detect their thumb-prints on the tape and to follow with pleasure and profit.

Large interests are practically always in the market. They usually have their scale orders in on both sides so that they buy on declines and sell on rallies. They always have money with which to buy on declines, because they sell on the rallies. They thus realize a profit as well as supply funds for the next decline. If the public would learn to do this, there would be fewer stock market fatalities.

It is difficult to over-emphasize the importance of studying the technical position, particularly when making a speculative commitment. Many people may say, "What is a weak or a strong technical position?" My reply is, in brief, that a stock is in a weak technical position on the bull side when it has been purchased and is held by a large number of outside speculators; when most of these are looking for a profit; when the price of the stock has advanced to a point where no further buying can be stimulated for the time being. It stands to reason that when buying power is exhausted a stock mast decline, no matter how strong its finances, management or earning power.

On the other hand, a stock is in a weak technical position on the short side when the bears have exhausted their ammunition by selling all they can afford and when the buying power of investment and speculative purchasers is such that it resists the pressure of the bears; in other words, when demand over-comes supply. The weakness in such a position is found in the fact that all those who are short are potential bulls; they must, sooner or later, cover their commitments in order to close their trades. They do not wish to remain short indefinitely. It is a well-known fact that bears have less courage than bulls, and they are often obliged to buy at higher prices because the technical position becomes so strong that they cannot force the price lower. Bears, after they have sold short, are an element of strength, not of weakness.

Much could he written on this subject, which, while far from being an exact science because of the numerous and changing influences that are being thrown into the market at almost every moment, is a study which well warrants the attention of every investor and trader. The old adage "well bought is half sold" should always be borne in mind, and while this study of the technical position is a point which people get around to last, one's security market education is not complete without it, nor can it be mastered without patient study, long experience and practice.

There are many men in Wall Street and throughout the country who make a practice of taking profits in accordance with their ideas of proportion, something like this: They say, "Fifty points is a big profit, even if it is on a small lot of stock; therefore, I will take it" Others say to themselves, "I have a profit of a hundred percent on my investment and that's good enough. I will let someone else have the rest." In the case of American Graphophone, I followed a different rule. The number of points, or the percentage of profit, did not influence me. The fluctuations were interesting, but whether the stock went op or down, I decided to wait for it to reach a certain point before I would take profits. This meant the point where the insiders began to sell.

Chapter VII - The Story of a Little Odd Lot

In previous articles I have referred to the importance of a thorough understanding of the industry represented by the security in which you have decided to invest. One cannot place too much emphasis on this point. Some people, when they look at the list of securities quoted in the dailies, do not know whether the abbreviated titles refer to railroads, industrials, or billy-goats. But they ought to know and especially should they be acquainted with the history, finances and character of management of their chosen enterprises.

For a long time I have been familiar with the history and development of the phonograph industry, and have made calculations as to its future trend. For many years it was largely monopolized through the protection of patents which some people disputed but which were at any rate effective. And so when in February, 1919, I was having lunch with a friend, and he told me something important was likely to come out of the approaching meeting of the American (now Columbia) Graphophone Company, I knew that back of any immediate development in that company's affairs there was a solid foundation for what might occur.

We were discussing how the millions of soldiers who went to the war were coming back music-crazy, and how their experiences abroad and in American camps proved to them the value of the phonograph in the home; how people who never before could afford such luxuries were now able to buy, resulting in an unprecedented demand for both machines and records.

"I understand," said my friend, "that the announcement to follow the Columbia meeting is likely to put the stock to 150."

As the issue was then selling around 135. I did not pay much attention to it, and had almost forgotten the incident when one morning, coming down to the office, I noticed in my newspaper a small announcement to the effect that the Columbia directors had declared a dividend of $2.50 per share in cash and one-twentieth of a share in stock. Elsewhere in the paper, among the obscure news items, it was suggested that it would be the policy of the Graphophone Company in future to disburse a certain amount of cash every quarter and a small stock dividend as well. Both the official announcement and the small news item were couched in such modest terms that the significance thereof did not appear on the surface.

But a little mental calculation worked out like this: $2.50 per share per quarter meant $10 a year. One-twentieth of a share per quarter was four-twentieths, or one-fifth of a share per annum. At the market price of the stock, 135, this one-fifth of a share equals $27 per share per annum, or a total of $37 per share—counting cash and value of stock—dividend. Conclusion: The price should advance from $200 to $300 per share, dependent upon how certain the regularity of the stock dividends intended to be paid.

Upon reaching the office I phoned the company's headquarters and found that the management planned to declare these quarterly stock dividends at the one-twentieth rate indefinitely, so I started to invest at least $15,000 in American Graphophone common at the market price. Evidently other people were awake to what that little announcement meant, for there were lots of buyers and few, if any, sellers. I finally succeeded in buying two twenty share lots, averaging 164, and the next that was offered to me was around 179. As this was a long way from the price at which I started to buy, and I didn't like to bid up against so much competition, I decided to give the forty shares to my wife and to see what I could do for her with the little odd lot. Soon the price was 180, then 200 bid, with hardly any transaction in the meantime.

These forty shares of stock cost $6,575, which, while not much of an investment, had great possibilities, considering its size, as I will show. It was not my first transaction in Graphophone, for I had made considerable money in it on previous occasions, buying it around 70, selling at 135, re-buying around 110, and carrying it up to 160. Considering these transactions, the forty shares cost me much less than nothing.

About five years ago *The Magazine of Wall Street* published an article on the phonograph industry, which showed it to be in a very prosperous condition with an outlook that was exceptionally promising. A certain New York stock broker, knowing that the stock of the old American Graphophone Company had been well distributed many years before, and that control was to be had in the open market, went to Wilmington, Del., and succeeded in obtaining a fifteen-minute interview with the du Pont interests. The upshot of this was that the du Ponts acquired control, buying the stock from below par up to nearly $200 per share for the last of their stock.

Then began a period of development and expansion under the new and more progressive management. In consequence, the company had made very great strides in the last few years. During this time the stock, which had reached 196 or thereabouts, gradually declined, until in the summer of 1918 it was selling around $50 per share. Somewhere between that level and the 135 figure which prevailed when my attention was again called to it, those in control evidently saw an opportunity to "put it over big," just as they had in G.M. and other large corporations in which they were interested, with a resulting scarcity of stock when the news came out.

I knew that the new corporation which had recently taken over the old was supplied with an issue of common stock far in excess of what was to be used in the exchange for the old shares, and in this dividend announcement I read between the lines and was able to forecast more accurately than if I had not been familiar with the past history of the Columbia, and had not studied du Pont methods of financing and development.

In the previous chapter you will find a reference to the technical position. It would be difficult to imagine one stronger than that prevailing in this stock after the news came out, because, in simple Wall Street parlance, "there was none of it for sale." And it was not long before the stock sold at over $300 per share.

During the summer, while I was on a long trip to Alaska and the Coast, I used to get the New York papers from seven to fifteen days late, but I knew that anything big or important would take several weeks to consummate, so I would have ample notice.

With frequent resting spells and reactions the stock climbed steadily to $400, and then to $500 per share, and with each fresh advance the stock dividends which were being distributed quarterly became more valuable; that is, the one-fifth of a share per annum (consisting of four quarterly payments of one-twentieth of a share) had a value of $40 per share when the stock sold at $200; $60 per share at $300; $80 per share at $400; and $100 per share when the price advanced to $500. It was the closest thing to "lifting itself by its boot-straps" that I had ever seen.

On the 40 shares the first dividend amounted to 2 shares; the second to 2.1 shares, making 44.1 shares. By that time the shadows of coming events began to show, for the company announced that it would shortly exchange the old stock of $100 par, for new stock of no par value, and that each holder of one share of old would receive ten shares of new stock. Occasional transactions on the Curb had been in the neighborhood of $500 per share, and now the new stock began to be traded in "when issued" between 43 and 50, and during the month of August, 1919, ran up as high as 59. At the level of 43 to 46 during August and September the stock showed excellent resistance, while the rest of the market remained weak, and from its action I came to the conclusion that we were approaching the "fireworks" stage.

Along in October the stock was listed on the New York Stock Exchange and began to be very active, advancing rapidly several points per day until it reached 75. The volume of trading greatly increased. In some sessions there were from 50,000 to 75,000 shares dealt in, to say nothing of the odd lots which were not recorded. Numerous newspaper articles called attention to the company's development. I watched it work back and forth between 70 and 75, and when I saw certain indications appear, made up my mind that if it again declined to 70 I would sell part of what once was an odd lot.

The 44.1 shares were by that time exchanged for 441 shares of new stock, and soon afterward a dividend of a fraction over 22 shares was received, making 463 shares,

worth $70 per share..$32,410.00
Plus 3 dividends at 2.50/share..315.25
                                                                $32,725.25

Less cost of original 40 shares.........................$6,575.00
Paper profit at $70/share...............................$26,150.25

The stock dividends which were coming along quarterly amounted to 23 shares or $1,610 worth per quarter, or $6,440 per annum if the stock remained at $70. Add to this the cash dividends, which, on the new stock amounted to one-tenth of the old, and were being paid at the rate of 25 cents per share, or $1 per annum, the income amounted to about $6,900 on an original investment of less than $6,600.

That was a big percentage, provided the stock stayed at $70 per share, but the action of the stock indicated that insiders were selling at least a part of their line, perhaps enough to get back their original investment. Deciding that when insiders sell it is time for outsiders to sell, I disposed of 263 shares at 70, which gave back the original $6,575, besides $12,080.25 in cash, in addition to 200 shares paid for in full.

In fact, allowing for the profit and cash dividends, these 200 shares cost about $60 a share less than nothing. So I didn't see how my wife could lose on that transaction.

Selling part of the lot put me in a good position for another reason. If the insiders were to support the stock on a decline, then lift the price to a new high level, I could take advantage of it with the remainder of my holdings. But if, as was more likely, they allowed the stock to sag off, I could replace what I had sold at a lower level and then take advantage of any secondary advances and distribution that might occur.

The points to bear in mind in regard to this little deal in odd lots are these: I knew the industry, its present over-sold condition and its future trend. Also the position of the Columbia Company with relation thereto. Inside inform-ation said the stock would advance 15 points. It was wrong; the price rose hundreds of points. The information on which I really acted was open to everyone. I confirmed the facts at the company's office.

By putting myself in the place of the insiders I was able to follow their reasoning and see the purpose behind their campaign. I took profits when they did, thus placing the account in a strong cash position, beyond the possibility of loss.

Surface or present conditions were not considered, but only the facts which indicated what the future would be. Technical conditions were closely watched for signs of moves by the insiders. Selling around the top provided the cash with which to replace at a lower figure.

I did not get a full hundred percent of the possibilities in this little deal, but came mighty close to it.

My experience with American Graphophone shares show what can occasionally be done with odd lots, and disputes those who believe that fractional lots of stock are too small to bother with and should be ignored. I have described the matter in detail so that the reasons for every move are clearly set forth, and trust that the suggestions herein will be found of suggestive value to my readers.

Chapter VIII - Rules I Follow in Trading and Investing

Some people may form an impression, based on my previous articles, that when one acquires the proper amount of training and experience, making money by trading and investing in securities is an easy proposition. I hasten to correct either this impression or another which might also have been formed: that it is easy sailing for me personally.

I have yet to find the man, in or out of Wall Street, who is able to make money in securities, continuously or uninterruptedly. My experience is no different from that of many individuals who are known as successful Wall Street men. Like every one else, I have my good and bad periods. Sometimes it appears as though everything I touch pans out well, and at other times everything seems to go wrong. It is much like any other line of business. Success in trading means an excess of profits over losses. Success in the investment field means more good than bad investments. If any one tells you he can be almost invariably successful, put him down as trying to impose on your credulity. One hundred percent accuracy was a height not even attained by the late J. P. Morgan. James E. Keene often said he was doing well if he could be right six times out of ten. I often used to call on him and watch him trading over his ticker on the fifth floor of the Johnson Building, 30 Broad Street, and there was many a time when I could plainly see from the nervous way in which he worked back and forth from his ticker to his telephone, and paced up and down the floor like a caged lion, that things were not going well. In his thirty or forty years, Wall Street career he went broke more than once.

I went into Harriman's office one day and found him a veritable bull in a china shop, because the market had been going contrary to his expectations.

In the present generation Jesse Livermore's operations are the most spectacular, but he is not by any means always right. Like all other traders, big or little, he makes serious mistakes at times. He has personally described to me his methods in detail. They provide for mistakes, accidents, errors in judgment and those unexpected happenings which every big or little operator must allow for.

One of the cleverest and most experienced traders on the floor of the New York Stock Exchange—a man who usually makes $300,000 a year out of his floor trading—said to me, "Whenever I take a position in a stock and find that it is running into a sufficient loss to amount to $20,000 or $25,000, and it begins to bother me in my day-to-day trading, I close it out."

Now go into the investment field and take the published annual list of investment securities owned by any of the big life insurance companies such as the Equitable, Mutual, New York Life, or others who have the very best connections in the financial district, and whose investments are made under the advice and guidance of eminent financiers, attorneys, experts and actuaries. You find the same thing—frequent investments which turn out badly and which have to be written down and charged off.

Success in either field, therefore, depends upon whether your profits exceed your losses and income—how close you can come to one hundred percent accuracy. So no matter how long or how hard you study, nor how careful, conservative and experienced your guide, your counsel or your bankers, you must anticipate a certain portion of unfortunate investments and operations.

It is for this reason that many (but not all) of my investments are made with intent not only to realize large profits but to offset these occasional and unavoidable losses. I have found some men who claim that they never take a loss. This may be true, but I would rather take losses than take an inventory of the final result of such operations, because it is bound to show a number of securities that are miles away from their cost and which should be listed merely either as "Hopes" or "Faint Hopes."

This reminds me of a very clever trading rule followed by Jesse Livermore. Unless a stock shows him a profit within two or three days after he buys or sells it short, he closes the trade, on the ground that his judgment was wrong as to the immediate action of the stock, and he cannot afford to be tied up. He says, "Whenever I find myself *hoping* that a trade will come out all right, I get out of it."

Livermore's purpose in this rule is to keep his trading capital in circulation; never allowing it to become congested. It is a good rule. Think it over, and you will recall that you have often not only lost money by sticking to a hopeless proposition, but you have lost many, many opportunities.

Another Livermore principle is the cutting of losses, Of course, in his 10,000, 20,000 or 50,000 share campaigns he cannot place stop orders like a 100, 200 or 500 share trader, but he usually has a mental stop and when it is reached he closes out the trade.

It will be observed that Livermore, by the use of these two rules, has both a time and a price stop. He will not devote his margin (capital) to a transaction for more than a few days, and he will not let the trade run against him for more than a few points. While he, so far as I know, originated the first rule, the second, viz., the use of stop orders, has been one of the first principles of successful operators for many years. Harriman, Keene, and a host of others have advocated the absolute limitation of risk.

While I have made it a practice to limit my risk in most cases, I can trace most of my principal losses to my failure to place stop orders when the trades were made. And while I have always studied the limitation of risk and generally endeavored to trade in a way that will keep the risk down to a minimum, I have very often delayed placing a stop order until the opportunity was lost, and in some cases these losses have run into five or ten points when they might just as well been limited to two or three. These incidents are of value because they show what should be avoided.

In trading I get the best results by watching carefully for an important turning point, limiting my risk, and trading for the ten or twenty point swings. But very often when I have the time to devote to it, and I feel myself in harmony with the market, I like to trade actively. Jumping in and out of stocks to the extent of 5,000 or 10,000 shares a day in the aggregate is a lot of fun, but is usually more profitable for the broker than for the trader, because of the immense handicap he is under in trying to pay commissions, taxes, and losses out of the small daily swings and get a profit besides. A trader on the floor of the New York Stock Exchange has an advantage over a non-member, whose total expenses on such business under the increased commission rates run from $1,000 to $2,000 a day.

The worthwhile changes in security prices do not generally occur within the same session. The market movement or the situation which produces it must have time in which to develop. As Charles Hayden once said to me, "The day to buy is not the day to sell."

Subscribers to *The Magazine* frequently write me and explain that they are far removed from the market and ask whether they had not better come to New York or go to Chicago so as to be in "close touch with things." Very often this "closeness" is a handicap. One's real studying is done away from the market, not in a broker's office.

The best work I ever did in judging the market was when I devoted one hour a day in the middle of each session. I did not come to Wall Street. I had no news ticker. I seldom read the news items but judged solely from the action of the market itself; hence I was not influenced by any of the rumors, gossip, information or misinformation with which the Street is deluged day after day.

The out-of-town investor is therefore not under as much of a handicap as he might suppose. If he is trading and can get the result of the day's operation in time to give his orders next morning, he is better off than the majority of the people who come down here and hang over the ticker. His opinions are formed from the facts. He must know how to assemble these and draw the proper conclusions. But all he needs is the highest, lowest and last prices of the stocks which he is watching. Without being at all egotistical I believe I could go around the world and having arranged to have these few details of a stock like U.S. Steel or any other active issue cabled to me daily, I could cable my orders and come back with a profit. It would not be necessary for me to be advised of the volume of trading in that, stock or the general market, although in some instances this might help. Certainly I would not care to have any news of any kind included in the cables.

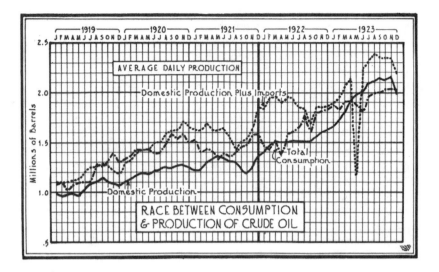

Chapter IX - Forecasting Future Developments

In previous chapters I have referred to the value of foresight in the field of investment, and the advantages of keeping your money working where it will produce the best results in the shortest time. I like to go cross-lots toward an objective point. One way to do this is to keep a constant eye on the relative position of the different industries in order to see where the greatest advantage lies.

One hardly needs to do more than read the papers nowadays to form the opinion that certain industries are in an excellent position. But which of these is best?

The steel industry is apparently prosperous. The industry seems likely to go through in a belated way the filling of a vast commercial and industrial vacuum which resulted from the war's absorption of steel.

The resumption of building operations will be a big factor in the steel business for the nest several years. We all know that the country is underbuilt, and a revival of building activity which has of late become apparent, means very big things for the steel trade.

Now that the railroads are back in the hands of their owners we may expect increased orders for rails, cars and locomotives, all of which will absorb quantities of steel. This should also produce a highly prosperous condition in the railway equipment business for some years to come.

I have been turning these matters over in my mind recently because I am very confident of the future of the market and I want to know which stocks in the most favored industry are likely to produce the most for me both from the standpoint of income and profit. Market movements, when correctly forecasted, pay more dollars than dividends.

While there are many of the minor industries in a very favorable position at present, I have concluded that one in particular stands head and shoulders above all the rest and that is the petroleum industry. The accompanying graph indicates that consumption has run ahead of production for the past two years and there is no sign of any change in this trend. This, in conjunction with the forecast by Walter C. Teagle, president of the Standard Oil Co. of N.J., gives us the backbone of the statistical position of oil. Mr. Teagle estimates that by 1925 the world will require 675,000,000 bbls. of crude oil against 376,000,000 produced in 1920 —an increase of 78 percent. He asks where such an enormous quantity of oil is coming from. If he cannot tell, you and I need not guess.

Should any further assurance be required, we can refer to a report filed by the British Board of Trade in London whose Central Committee reported that demand was tending to outstrip the world's present supply.

It is plain, therefore, that there is a threatened world shortage of oil and that this situation cannot be cured for a long time to come. I am therefore putting money into the best class of oil stocks, for while there are many promising opportunities in other fields I regard this, for the time being, as the best industry in which to take a substantial position on the long side. My reason is that the margin of profit in the producing and refining of oil, especially the former, will be a very substantial one—probably much larger, figuring on a per share basis, than in the steel, equipment, automobile, or other of the leading industries whose output may be expanded by the building of more plants and hiring more men. It is different with the oil business. Oil must be sought; and it is not always to be found where you expect to find it. Many of the old fields are playing out. Many of the 10,000 and 15,000 barrel gushers of a year ago are now running in the dozens or hundreds and in not a few cases have to be pumped at that.

The Banger Field on July 1, 1919, was producing 160,000 bbls. a day. By February 1, 1920, this had dropped to 80,000 barrels daily. The Burk-burnett Field has shown a very marked falling off, due to close drilling. Many of the biggest wells in Mexico have declined, owing to economic conditions, salt water invasion, or possible change of formation, due to volcanic eruptions.

There is a scarcity of new fields. We hear about discoveries in various sections of this and other countries, but it will require a good many prolific fields to keep pace with the ravenous consumptive demand. It is apparent that in the oil industry there is no point of saturation, because the trade is continually working to make up a shortage which practically every year pulls down the visible supply.

The increase in the amount of machinery of all kinds and the elimination of hand labor is an important point in the demand, as each bit of machinery requires more lubrication and the lubricating material always has its base in crude oil. Automobiles are not only consumers of gasoline, but of great quantities of lubricating oil as well.

Tractors are developing another big new avenue of consumption and must in time supplant the horse on the farm, as the motorcar has done in the cities. In Seattle there is not today a single horse, so far as I have been able to ascertain.

The year 1894 does not seem so long ago, yet when at that time I told some one that one of these days we would be traveling in horseless carriages, I was laughed at as being a dreamer.

Now I wish to record another similar dream. It is that the streets of New York and all other great centers will, before many years, be underlaid with pipes which will carry fuel oil for use instead of coal in heating, manufacturing and other purposes. And here is a suggestion to any of my readers who are in a position to secure charters from their respective communities, for some day these charters will be worth a lot of money.

The day will soon pass when men shall be sent down into mines to haul up coal, put it on railroad trains, transport it hundreds of miles, unload it into coal carts, truck it through city streets, dump it into cellars and shovel it into furnaces.

Enormous oil tanks, similar to gas tanks now in use, should contain the liquid fuel which can be controlled by the mere turning of a valve or the operation of a thermostat.

No shoveling coal, or taking out ashes! This should make life in city or country more attractive, especially to those who have to hustle for the 5:15. But to the manufacturer, the owner of office buildings, or apartments, this development will have a much broader application, for it will mean the elimination of a number of factors that now contribute to the raising of rent, operating and manufacturing costs.

You may not follow this suggestion but somebody will, and a lot of somebodies will make a lot of millions in this way.

Practically every industry, from the peanut stand to the railroad loco-motive and the enormous industrial plant, consumes oil in many ways. The world of machinery could not exist without oil. The use of machinery and particularly internal combustion motive power is spreading throughout the world. There are vast areas which are merely in the kerosene stage which will eventually be developed to the automobile and tractor stage. Carry the thought further and we see the likelihood that before many years we shall be shipping not only passengers but freight through the air, all of which means a still greater demand for crude oil to be converted into gasoline and lubricating oils.

These are some of the reasons why I have bought oil stocks during recent months. And why, in our Investment Letter, we have recommended these securities to our subscribers. By reason of the crying demand for crude, many of the refineries which have contracted to supply refined products are bidding against each other, so the companies which really hold the winning cards are the producers.

I anticipate a period of enormous profit-making in leading oil companies, particularly where they are entrenched in the field of production.

Most people make their mistake when averaging by starting too soon; or, if they are buying on a close scale, say one point down, they do not provide sufficient capital to see them through in case the decline runs two or three times as many points as they anticipate. I recall a friend who, after seeing Union Pacific sell at 219 in August, 1909, thought it very cheap at 185 and much cheaper at 160. That made it a tremendous bargain at 135. He bought at all those figures. But at 116, his capital was exhausted, and, as they put it in Wall Street, "he went out with the tide."

Chapter X - Truth About "Averaging Down"

A great deal of money is lost or tied up by people who make a practice of averaging. Their theory is that if they buy a security at 100 and it goes to 90, it is that much cheaper, and the lower it goes the cheaper it grows. Like all Wall Street rules and theories, this is sometimes true; but there are a great many times when a security will decline in market price while its intrinsic value and earning power are shrinking even more swiftly.

While a decline in price is often due to a slump in the general market for bonds or stocks, or both, owing to some circumstance affecting a certain group of stocks, it also frequently occurs that the price is going down because of an inherent weakness in the company's affairs or a diminution of its prospects. Knowledge of such an influence is often confined to the few who are in close touch with the company's affairs. Sometimes there is a gradual development toward the unfavorable side; then again there may be an overnight happening which causes a radical change in former estimates or value.

Whatever the cause of a decline, the question of averaging is one that puzzles people who have bought at higher prices and are wondering whether averaging is not a good way out. Very often it proves to be the way to get in deeper. Hence, in order intelligently to judge whether to average, it is necessary to know what caused the decline.

I remember, a few years ago, buying a certain stock at around 45. Sometime after I bought it the price declined to about 30, at which point I afterward learned the stock was underwritten; so that to the insiders everything above 30 represented profit.

The company was doing a splendid business but the stock had been badly handled, and those who were responsible for its market action ran away and left the new baby on the public's doorstep. Knowing that the stock was in the hands of the public, I did not average at 30, but waited until it was down to around 15. Then I bought an equal amount. This I sold at ten points profit which marked my original cost down to $35. The stock then declined to 12 and I bought again, reselling at 16, reducing my cost to about 31. Some months later it advanced to 38, where I sold. This let me out about even, allowing for interest.

These transactions ran over two or three years and serve to illustrate a good way of averaging out on a bond or stock which has been disappointing in its action. It is a method employed by large interests who, as previously described, often work on a much closer scale and take advantage of all the small variations in the market.

Why did I buy the stock when it was down? And why didn't I sell at a loss? Because I made investigations through the company's officials, and found that the corporation was in a very prosperous condition, having reduced its obligations and increased its earning power during the time when the stock was declining from 45 to a fraction of that figure. It was a case where intrinsic values were on the increase while the market price was decreasing.

Thus I kept myself always in a position where I could buy more in case it went still lower and by selling on the rallies I provided the funds for repurchasing. Having bought the first lot (to average around 15) I was then in a position to sell it on a rally and re-buy it on a decline, so that whichever way the market went I would benefit. Had the price declined to 10 and then 5, I would probably have bought an equal amount or perhaps double the quantity at the low level—always with my eye on the compass, which was the company's physical, financial and commercial condition.

Stocks like this sometimes decline of their own technical weight, that is, the amount of shares that are pressing in liquidation, combined with an absence of support; or they may be put down—that is, artificially depressed by those who are desirous of accumulating at the low levels. In this case I believe there was a combination of both influences.

Most people make their mistake when averaging, by starting too soon; or, if they are buying on a close scale, say one point down, they do not provide sufficient capital to see them through in case the decline runs two or three times as many points as they anticipate.

I recall a friend who, after seeing Union Pacific sell at 219 in August, 1909, thought it very cheap at 185 and much cheaper at 160. That made it a tremendous bargain at 135. He bought at all those figures. But at 116, his capital was exhausted and, as they put it in Wall Street, "He went out with the tide."

Eighty-five or ninety percent of the business, investment and speculative mortalities are due either to over-trading or lack of capital, which when boiled down are one and the same thing. And those who average their investment or speculative purchases supply in a great many instances, glaring examples of the causes of failure.

Years ago, when Weber & Fields formed one of the star theatrical attractions in New York, they used to have a scene in a bank where one of the team was the banker and the other the customer of the institution.

The "official" observing his "customer" at the wicket, made the very pertinent inquiry, "Put in or take out?" I was reminded of this recently when thinking of the number of people who come down to the Street year after year, and with varying results (mostly bad, I must agree), keep on putting in and taking out until they either make a success or a failure of it. And I am continually asking myself, as a sort of test question, whether in putting in or taking out I am making progress or going backward. Like the frog who was trying to jump out of the well, I sometimes slip, but every year I can see that I am making progress.

There are seasons when it pays me to stick very close to shore, because, by reason of other influences, my judgment is not up to par. Sometimes, however, I am stubborn enough to keep on fighting through these periods, because no one can stay in the security market for a great many years without growing used to punishment. It has already been explained that success means more good than bad investments or ventures, so the readers of previous chapters will understand just what I mean.

Everyone should occasionally sit down and take account of stock—not securities, but his own ability, judgment, and what is most important, results thus far obtained. If he finds that the past few months or years have been unsatisfactory and unprofitable, judging from the amount of time, thought, study, and capital employed, he should suspend operations until he ascertains the cause; then he should set about to cure it. This can be done by study and practice (on paper or with ten share lots or single thousand dollar bonds if necessary) until he is confident that he has overcome the difficulty.

It may be that he is a chronic bull and finds himself in a bear market. I have frequently discovered that I was out of tune with the market, although I am never a chronic bull or bear, but always the kind of an animal the situation seems to call for.

It has been a great advantage to me, however, to have gone off by myself at times and figured out just where I stood, and, if things were going wrong, why? I find that it is more important to study my misfortunes than my triumphs.

Chapter XI - Conclusions as to Foresight and Judgment

It must be apparent from the foregoing chapters, that during the years I have spent in Wall Street I have not only kept my eyes and ears open, but have gained much as a result of study, practice and experience. It is logical to suppose that I have formed certain definite conclusions with regard to the business of trading and investing, and that these, if frankly and clearly stated and fully appreciated by those who read, should be of considerable value to the many who have not devoted so much time or effort in the same line of work.

No one can stay at it for even a short time without acquiring a certain knowledge, and it is for each to decide whether he is content to plod along in a desultory way, or go in for an intensive study of the subject. My recommendation to readers is that they take it up seriously even if they have not a single dollar to invest at present. The time will come when they will have funds for investment and the greater their store of information on the subject, the greater the incentive for saving or acquiring money in any legitimate way and the more profitable the outcome.

In an atmosphere of deceptive surface indications and false news, reports, gossip, methods, etc., such as one encounters in Wall Street, it is sometimes difficult to know just what one is trying to do and how well or how badly he is doing it. It is not easy to size yourself up and to see just what are your basic principles, and how well you are following them.

Whenever a situation is not entirely clear to me, I find I can clarify it by putting down on paper all the facts, classifying them as favorable and unfavorable. In thus writing it out on paper I not only have time to reason out each point as I go along, but when I get it all down it can be looked over and analyzed to much better advantage.

Following this idea I have written down perhaps fifty different conclusions which I have reached with regard to the business of trading and investing, and these I will take up, one after the other in this and later chapters, for they constitute a partial list of principles which should be recognized and applied, according to individual requirements.

These points are about equally divided between investment and speculation, but it is also difficult to determine where one begins and the other ends that in many cases I shall be obliged to treat them in combination. The thing we are trying to accomplish is an increase in our personal wealth, and whether this is done by the careful investment and slow accretion of money, the income of which is reinvested in order to enhance the principal sum, or whether we endeavor to increase our principal by attempting to forecast movements of security prices and to profit thereby—all that is something which each person must decide for himself.

Both my primary and my ultimate object is the safe and profitable investment of my funds. I say primary because that is my first and principal object and I use the term ultimate because eventually I expect to become an investor for income only. Provision for himself and family during the later years of his life is what every red-blooded man is working for. Some men—James E. Keene was one—continue to trade in stocks until they are very old. But most people want to feel that from at least sixty on they will be free from the necessity of making money on which to live during their declining years.

Trading profits should therefore be used to increase the principal sum which is invested in income-bearing securities, preferably those which will grow in market value. Income from such investments should be made to compound itself by re-investing it as received.

If one is not adapted to trading he should prove it to his own satisfaction and then abandon the business. He should then attempt to become an intelligent and successful investor. Failing of this, he should turn to savings banks and mortgages or other non-fluctuating mediums for the investment of his funds. A friend of mine once had something over $100,000 worth of bonds, a few of which he deposited with a broker as margin. The bonds were his backlog; they represented the result of his savings from the time he first entered business, and were bringing in a good income, besides having possibilities. As he traded back and forth, he found that he was gradually taking some of the bonds which he had in his box, and putting them up with the broker, until finally he reached a point where nearly half of the bonds were gone. This, he decided, was conclusive evidence of the fact that he was not adapted to the business of trading. He therefore discontinued trading and resumed the saving tactics by which he had accumulated the first hundred bonds.

That was some years ago. He has now over $200,000 worth, and when at rare intervals he ventures into the speculative arena, he does it very timidly and with only trifling sums.

I recommend this man's course to those who have had similar experiences, but with this exception: If they are willing to devote themselves to the task, they will doubtless overcome their difficulties and be more successful with the added study and experience. But to go right on putting good money after bad, not only reflects on a man's business judgment but indicates a weakness in his character which he had best conquer in short order. The experiences of our earlier years are well and cheaply bought if we really profit by them.

No one can avoid having his capital tied up at times in mediums which are not satisfactory. But there should be no hesitation about switching, even though it necessitates the taking of a loss in your present holdings. A good security will make up this loss much faster than one which is mediocre. So the question which one should ask himself with relation to all of the securities which he holds, is this: "Are there any other issues which will work for me more profitably and in a shorter time than these? I cannot afford to let money sleep, nor have it work slowly. I am like a merchant: I must turn my money over as often as I can, so that the average yearly return will be at its maximum."

One's capital should be made to do the greatest service in the shortest length of time. This applies both to trading capital and investment capital. I have found that it is best to use only a small part of the total available capital for trading. To employ all or most of it is a fatal mistake, for in case of an unforeseen situation, ensuing a large loss, one is obliged to begin over again; whereas if the bulk of the capital is invested where it is safe, returns an income, and will probably enhance in value, then in case of a calamity a part of it can be turned into cash in order to renew trading operations.

But this should occur in only rare instances. When a man finds that he has a certain sum invested and that this sum is diminishing on account of his pulling it down for trading purposes, he is on the wrong track and had better stop short and take account of himself before he travels further. A person who cannot be successful in trading with a small amount of capital, will unquestionably lose a large amount if he employs it.

In making one's capital do the greatest amount of work in the shortest length of time, it is necessary to be forever on the lookout for better opportunities than those which you now have. If you hold bonds which are selling between 90 and 95, and which may, in a good bond market, advance to 110, you would not be justified in retaining them if you can buy another bond which is just as well secured, just as marketable, and has all the other good points of your present security, besides being convertible into a security which has excellent prospects of an advance to a very much higher figure.

Should you own a preferred stock which is paying its 7 percent and showing on the average only one and a half times its dividends, whereas you can buy, at the same price, another preferred stock which is earning three or four times its dividend, taking the average of a number of years, it is by all means best to make the exchange. It is highly important to find out just what we can and cannot do, but we should not be discouraged too soon. I have met thousands and thousands of people who were endeavoring to make money in speculation and regret to say that very few are really qualified to become successful traders of any importance.

But there are hundreds of thousands of successful investors, and it is toward this avenue of success and independence that I hope to turn the attention of most of my readers. By studying "the public" and its ways, I have learned what kind of operations the majority are best fitted for; while it is a peculiar fact that very few people delude themselves into thinking that they are good physicians, surgeons, lawyers or dentists, they do try to fool themselves into believing that they are good investors and speculators.

Look around you—do you find that among your acquaintances 100% are well-to-do and successful business men? Are not the majority just plodding along, neither getting rich nor poor? Well, that is just as true in Wall Street as it is in business. You can generally pick the brilliant successes and count them on the fingers of one or both hands, depending on the size of your circle of acquaintances.

People are successful in business because, while they make mistakes at first, they study these mistakes and avoid them in future. Then by gradually acquiring a knowledge of the basic principles of success, they develop into good business men. But how many apply this rule to their investing and trading? Very few do any studying at all. Very few take the subject seriously. They drift into the security market, very often "get nipped," as the saying is, avoid it for a while, return from time to time with similar results, then gradually drift away from it, without ever having given themselves a chance to develop into what might be good traders or intelligent investors.

This is all wrong. People go seriously into the study of medicine, the law, dentistry, or they take up with strong purpose the business of manufacturing of merchandising, but very few ever go deeply into this vital subject which should be seriously undertaken by all.

Now we all admit that the average man is mentally lazy. He hates work, mental or physical, doesn't want to spend an hour every evening, or even once a week, except at bridge, poker, or something else equally diverting and interesting. Those who do employ their time profitably are headed toward wealth and independence; but in many cases the poker players will later be supported by their children.

But to return to our subject, it should not take more than a few years for a person to find out whether he is qualified for trading or whether he should devote himself to the investment side of the proposition.

The cultivation of foresight is most essential. In the main it is the man with the greatest amount of foresight who is most successful in the security market. Foresight is the very essence of speculation. Without the use of it a person is not speculating at all— he is merely taking chances—gambling.

One of the late J. P. Morgan's strong points was his ability to foresee and therefore to anticipate the vast changes in financial conditions and security prices. It was marvelous how he frequently predicted, months in advance, the outcome of certain involved business and financial situations which were not understood or anticipated by anyone else. This was one of the qualities that made him great. It enabled him to engage in vast undertakings, of which the U.S. Steel Corporation is a conspicuous example, but there are many other industrial monuments to his financial genius which was, after all, built around his marvelous foresight.

It was foresight which made E. H. Harriman a great man. It enabled him to anticipate the development of the Union Pacific and Southern Pacific Railroads and nerved him to undertake the stupendous task of creating a railroad empire.

Harriman once held an ordinary job—just like you and I once did, or do now—and if he, through the cultivation of foresight, and the other qualities which made him pre-eminent, could accomplish such splendid results, then you and I can, by the exercise of the talents with which we are blessed, advance our personal fortunes by concentrating on the development of our own foresight. It will prove of value, not only in our investments, but in every undertaking which we enter—financial, business or personal—during our whole lives. So let us give close attention to the subject. A large part of such success as I have already attained is due to my having formed the habit of looking ahead to see in what direction future events are likely to run.

It is better to depend on your own judgment than on that of any other person. If you have not reached a point where you can do this, better continue your studies and practice until you can form a sound, independent judgment on which you can base your commitments.

We hear a great deal in Wall Street about "inside information" and the value of big connections. But I have found that the man who depends the most on his own judgment is headed for success if he has not already attained it. It is very easy to be swayed by the multitudinous opinions that are bandied around the Street and which may be had for nothing because they are generally worth it.

Suppose you are a most intimate personal friend of a man who is putting through a big deal in a security which is listed on the New York Stock Exchange. He tells you all the facts and puts you in a position to buy, with a thorough knowledge of what is going on. You do buy, and perhaps you make money, but more often than not it will turn out when you come to realize, you will be so enthused by your inside knowledge that you will not sell at the right time, or a hitch will occur which turns your profit into a loss, or your big man is out of town, or something is happening to the market which he cannot explain.

But suppose you do get away with a profit— you are apt to be so carried off your feet that at your very next opportunity you will think you have Wall Street by the tail and will plunge with all you have made and all you have besides, and eventually end up with a loss. The kind of money which does you the most good is that which you make through your own efforts. All Wall

Street is trying to get something for nothing. Don't join the crowd. Rather, "buck it"—the crowd is generally wrong. Become one of the successful few who build stone upon stone until they have a solid foundation of knowledge and experience which will last them all their lives.

If I believed that the people who are now reading and studying the numerous articles which appear in *The Magazine* would, five or ten years from now, still be looking to it for easy ways to make money, I should be very much discouraged. But if, as I believe, a great many will, through its teachings, be induced to become students and ultimately intelligent and successful investors, then I will feel that the many years of hard work which I have put into the publication have been well rewarded.

Down in New Street, on the block between Wall Street and Exchange Place, you will find, on any pleasant day, a lot of Wall Street "Ghosts" sunning themselves. And by way of explanation let me say that a Wall Street Ghost is one who has tried to make money in the market and failed. He is the saddest sight in all the financial district. Once a prosperous and perhaps wealthy businessman, he is now reduced to mere driftwood among the eddies which surround the Stock Exchange. In and out of the brokerage offices you find him rambling in a hopeless fashion, always on the lookout for "tips." The red-headed bootblack and Jim, the shoelace man, are types of his confidants. He always know where everything is going, but never gets anywhere himself.

I don't know what becomes of these old "Ghosts" who drift about the old stamping ground, but it is instructive to know that their ranks are recruited from the people who never tried to cultivate a judgment of their own, but always depended on that of others.

The longer your experience, the better background you have for comparison, and the greater your ability to judge and forecast correctly. As conditions are constantly changing, no two markets are alike and no two daily sessions are similar; but markets and sessions and panics and booms all have certain characteristics which should be carefully studied and intimately understood.

The man who has never been through a panic would be apt to find himself badly rattled. Under a pressure of excitement and nervous strain he would probably do the wrong thing. But anyone who has experienced a number of panics, knows how to conduct his operations so as to take the utmost advantage of such a rare opportunity, provided he has previously put himself in a position to buy at the low prices.

To some people it may be discouraging to say that you must keep at this business for many years in order to become highly successful; but is not this what you must do in your own line of business? Are not the best business and professional men those who have had the longest practice?

You cannot go into any phase of endeavor and make money or become prominent "just like that"—you must serve your apprenticeship. Of course, if you want to join the ranks of the large percentage of people who spend their declining years in the care or custody of their children or relatives, or in institutions, then you can afford to ignore my suggestion that work and study and long experience are essential. But if you have imagination and can picture yourself as possessing wealth and contentment in your old age, you will immediately admit that it is well worth your while to devote serious attention to this subject.

You have to live anyhow, so why not live well? It all depends on you, for you can generally take out in as great a measure as you put in.

By long experience I do not mean merely reading the financial columns for thirty or forty years; one does not gain experience in that way. I refer to the practical experience of investing in stocks and bonds; making mistakes; finding out why and profiting thereby in future.

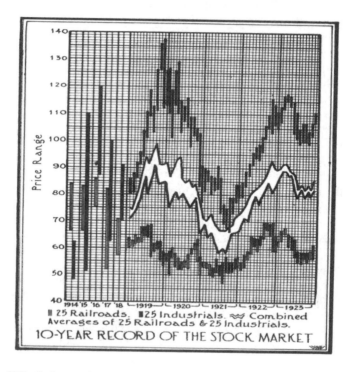

10-YEAR RECORD OF THE STOCK MARKET

Chapter XII - Safeguarding Your Capital

The question is not whether you can make money with your original capital but whether you will cease because of the loss of this initial money at the very outset.

There is everything in getting a good start. In a preceding chapter it was shown that I did not begin to invest until eight years after my studies had commenced, and that I did not begin trading until six years after that. Just how long the average investor should pursue his studies without putting his ideas into practical operation is a matter for each individual to decide, but there should be a thorough understanding of the theoretical side before the first ventures or investments are actually made.

A person becomes competent in other fields because he has generally gone through a long period of practice and preparation. A physician for example, goes to college, attends clinics, rides in an ambulance, serves in hospitals, and, after some years of preparatory work, hangs out a sign. In Wall Street the same M.D. would hang out his sign first; then proceed to practice. In one way the doctor's work, in and out of Wall Street, bears resemblance, inasmuch as when he begins to practice his profession he has to acquire patients. In Wall Street it is spelled "patience." Both are absolutely necessary to his success.

The Magazine of Wall Street has often repeated warnings against beginning to operate before you know how; but the truth will bear many repetitions, and as our circle of readers is constantly widening we are again emphasizing this point.

If Wall Street could only retain the same clientele year after year and add to it the many who for the first time find themselves with investment or trading capital, we should have four million and five million share days instead of one and two million. It is strange that in the financial district, which is the very heart of the nation's commercial and industrial structure, there is such a woeful lack of understanding of what the public requires in the way of assistance.

My organization has devoted a great deal of effort to showing the brokerage houses that in order to permanently retain their clients, steps should be taken to educate them. We have offered to sell the banking, brokerage and investment houses quantities of literature at cost and have tried to show the brokerage fraternity how important it is to disseminate educational books and pamphlets on this subject, in order that their clients, through genuine knowledge, might become permanent instead of transient, patrons of their respective houses. But with rare exceptions, our appeals have fallen upon ears that were deaf. Brokers would rather go on securing, at great expense, new clients to take the place of those who become discouraged and fall by the wayside. Some day a brokerage house will be evolved which has, as a permanent part of its organization, an educational department whose business it will be to see that its clients are properly informed as to just what they should do and how they should do it. Meantime, the individual investor is deprived of assistance from the logical source whence it should come.

The people who really stay at the business and continue year after year to buy and sell securities can generally be classified into two divisions. First, those who have outside sources of income and are continually bringing money into the street, and, second, those who are successful in their operations and thereby increase their capital, or to a greater or lesser extent maintain themselves out of what they thus realize. It is unfortunate that the percentage of those who bring money to Wall Street is so large and that many do not realize that it is their lack of knowledge and their inefficient methods in the financial field which bring such unsatisfactory results.

491

Lawyers, doctors, surgeons and other professional men are obliged, under state laws, to pass certain examinations and receive certificates showing that they are competent to practice. This is for the protection of the public, but no way has been provided whereby the public can be protected against its own operations in the security market. It would be a good thing if the financial lives of more customers of brokerage houses could be sustained by making them pass an examination as to knowledge of the subject and ability to take care of themselves. Many states require applicants to pass an examination before they are given permission to drive an automobile on the public highways. In one case it is a physical and in the other a financial risk.

A certain amount of mistakes and a percentage of unfortunate investments are to be expected, no matter how well you start or how expert you become. But you should always preserve your trading or investment capital by never putting yourself in a position to have this wiped out. As the Irishman said, "It is better to be hurted than kilt." Lack of capital and over-trading, being the cause of most misfortunes, are the result of being too heavily committed in one direction or another.

Investors who begin with even a single one hundred dollar capital have the choice of being conservative or of over-trading, but through ignorance many do not realize just when they are over-reaching and when their operations may be designated as conservative. In order to avoid a danger, they must know where it lies. It would be foolish for a corporal to lead an army into a strange country; and just as foolish for any novice to marshal his capital and launch into one or another phase of buying or selling stocks or bonds, without previous study.

A cross-section of the public's operations would show lack of interest when prices are low and the market is dragging along. When prices begin to advance the public begins to buy and this buying increases in proportion to the extent and rapidity of the advance until, at the top of an important movement, the public is 95% bullish and, as a rule, loaded up. The more uninterrupted the advance, the greater and more rapid the increase in public commitments.

Examining the cross-section in a panic we would find that those who went heavily long on the way up and at the top are selling out or being sold out. The buying is by new recruits, consisting of bargain-hunting people who have never before bought securities, combined with the comparatively few who sold while prices were high, and who therefore have money to invest.

Prices may have advanced steadily for a couple of years prior to the panic and those who began with a small amount of capital may have accumulated good round sums when figured at the high prices—mostly paper profits. But as bear markets are generally both swift and severe, these profits are quickly swept away, so that often those who have been piling them up for two years often lose them in thirty or sixty days.

You may say to yourself: "Oh, well, the public may do that, but I'm not one of the public." But the fact is, unless you are a trained and experienced trader or investor, or have, to some extent, a claim to being an insider, a professional or semi-professional, then you are one of that vast majority which constitutes the great American speculative and investing public. The sooner you realize this fact the more quickly you can adjust yourself to your proper position in the financial scale.

The point of difference between the public and those who are not of this class is found in the fact that the public is not sophisticated; in other words, not trained in the business. If you are trained, you are not a member of that body.

Having thus classified yourself it is your business to ascertain how you can proceed without danger to the point where you can safely and profitably depend upon your own judgment. My personal opinion is that this can best be done by a course of study before beginning operations, because a satisfactory outcome is the result of knowledge plus capital. If you lack either the knowledge or the capital or both you cannot succeed, so the logical course is to get the knowledge first, meanwhile saving or setting aside the capital.

It is stupidity which makes people "rush in where angels fear to tread." And there is something about the Wall Street atmosphere which makes people think that whatever is to be done must be done at once, otherwise the opportunity will get away from them. I find that opportunities are coming along all the time, and that the majority are not as good as they look. So the best ones are worth waiting for.

The young man with his first money might very well spend his spare time for five years in study, investigation, self-training, in order to find out whether he is an investor, a trader, or a speculator, and the more he learns about it the greater he will realize how very ignorant he was at the beginning. If, at the age of thirty, he sees the necessity for study, and at thirty-five he has accumulated some capital which in the meantime has been reposing in the savings banks or in high grade bonds or mortgages, he should not even then go in with the idea of cleaning up a fortune, but with intent to cautiously and conservatively proceed, so that during the entire balance of his life he will steadily build up his fund of investment knowledge and capital on a constantly broadening base.

This matter is not anything that has to be hustled—you can pursue your regular business with this as a sideline or hobby, if you like. You can't learn everything in a minute, but of course the more time you can devote to it the more rapidly you can proceed to practice.

The main point, as I have said, is to so preserve your initial capital that you will never be deprived of it, and the way to do this is to learn what you are about before you go about it.

It is well to study the methods of other large and successful operators and investors.

Much can be learned from this source. There is great value in imitation, but of course we must select the individuals whose methods have been scientific and whose results speak for themselves.

When I was a small boy I became interested in the study of music. Some of my teachers were better qualified than others, but the one under whom I made the most progress was the one who interested me in the broad aspect of the art by inducing me not merely to practice hard but to attend the best of concerts and operas; to study the theory of music, the history of great composers, the characteristics of great compositions, the principles of harmony, etc. This teacher would, when I was learning a particularly difficult passage on the piano or organ, sit down and play it for me so that I could imitate. The result was that I became so interested in my lessons that I devoted to them practically all of my spare time and money.

That is the way to go into this subject. While you cannot expect big financiers or large and successful traders to sit down and tell you just how they do it, there is, in these enlightened days, a world of literature bearing on the subject. Past volumes of *The Magazine* contain many articles of this nature. Your public libraries are all supplied with helpful material. Many hints are to be derived from a study of the methods of successful men.

"There is no place in the modern world for the unskilled; no one can hope for any genuine success who fails to give himself the most complete special education. Good intentions go for nothing, and industry is thrown away if one cannot infuse a high degree of skill into his work. The trained man has all the advantages on his side; the untrained man invites all the tragic possibilities of failure."

Chapter XIII - How Millions Are Lost in Wall Street

Many years ago there was a stock dealt in on the New York Curb called Arlington Copper. The "mine" was said to be over a hundred years old and, with the modern methods which could be applied to the low-grade ore in the property, the promoters claimed they would be able to make a very big profit.

The seat of this operation was at Arlington, N.J., a small residential town just across the meadows from Jersey City. One could step on an Erie train and be there in twenty minutes. He could have seen a lot of old workings, and a lot of rock that was pointed out as ore. The round trip might have cost a dollar and occupied three hours.

Did any of the people who eagerly purchased the stock on the Curb take a trip over to Arlington to see what they were buying? They did not. They were "too busy," or they had to be home at 6:30, as they had a "dinner engagement." Possibly their meal time or their evening's social affair was more important than the many thousands of dollars which they put into this stock, but in any event Arlington Copper passed away as many "good things" are apt to do.

One does not have to look far to find many illustrations of this point. The public does not investigate, but buys and sells on somebody's say-so, and without using the precautions that would surely be applied in its own particular line of business.

For many years I have been impressed with the necessity of having investigation precede investments, instead of succeeding them. Take the field of patents and calculate, if you can, how many hundreds of millions are sunk each year in somebody's newfangled idea as to how this or that should be done. In discussing this matter with an expert mechanical engineer the other day, it developed that 97% of the patents that are taken out are either of no commercial value or are never developed to a point where they realize a profit. Yet, as he said, "There are many big men in this town whose ear you can get quicker with a new patented appliance than in any other way. They will lay aside their own line of business and take up your new mechanism, if it is something that tickles their fancy." But that is only one field.

It is impossible to estimate how many hundreds of millions are lost because of improper preliminary investigation of the commercial, financial and technical aspects of the enterprises which absorb such a large proportion of the public wealth. Yet there is no other way in which money may be so intelligently spent as in safeguarding capital.

Most people do not know how to investigate an enterprise. Some one comes along with a newly patented washing machine. He needs $25,000 to "develop it." He would like to get you and some of your friends to put up $5,000 each. He will give you 51% interest in the business. He invites investigation. But you and your friends do not really investigate - you get hold of somebody who is already in the washing machine business and ask what he thinks of it. He is not an expert; he doesn't know the patent situation - all he knows is whether he can sell the machine he is now handling and whether he thinks this is better than his, but he has no broad understanding of the business because all he is handling is one little machine in one little corner of the U.S.A. A few hundred or a few thousand dollars spent in a thorough investigation would save a lot of trouble, time and money.

The same principle applies to an oil, mining, railroad, industrial, or any other kind of enterprise. Money spent in careful investigation is insurance against loss. It is also productive of information which will be valuable in case you desire to go into the business or buy shares.

An enterprise in which I have an interest has recently decided to put a new product on the market. The demand had been established and greatly exceeded the supply. There was no question as to the company's ability to make the goods and sell them, but there was a question as to just what grade of goods would best please the public and just how they should be sold. So a very broad survey of the whole industry was ordered, with the result that the company is now in a position to go forward with its new goods in an intelligent way, along the line of least resistance. It is this sort of prevision which makes for success.

It is a remarkable and confirmatory fact that the officials of this company frequently take speculative fliers and make investments in securities, but their investigations seldom go beyond the stage of a surface inquiry as to the opinion of one or two parties, including the broker who is at the other end of the telephone listening for an order.

That reminds me of a point I have often made as to the ethics involved, in the client asking and the broker giving an opinion as to a contemplated investment or speculation. Personally, I believe that the client should know what he wants to do before he approaches the broker and that the latter's function is to execute the order and finance the operation. Many people do not agree with me, but it is a matter which we may take up for discussion at another time.

Perhaps you cannot investigate personally, owing to lack of time or knowledge of the subject, but you can always secure the services of those who can.

In one of my previous chapters I stated some of my experiences in mining stocks and showed how I employed mining engineers to examine properties and other engineers to check them up. Mining is only one form of industry which is represented in Wall Street, and I should say that there are many, many more enterprises besides mines that need investigation. Within the past several months a number of propositions have been shown up as representing but a fraction of the value originally claimed for them by the promoters.

What Wall Street needs is some means of "checking up" on the enthusiasm and, in some cases, the deception of those who are engaged in marketing securities. There are two kinds of people in the financial district: those who are trying to help themselves by helping others, and those who are helping themselves to what others possess. It does not take long to find out whether those with whom you are dealing belong to the preferred class.

Investigation of some of the enterprises whose securities are dealt in, is a subject calling for a very wide range of knowledge and ability, and is beyond the reach of the average man. An examination of a property like the Philadelphia Company, for example, or Cities Service or Ohio Cities Gas would require training in a great many different fields, many of which the average investor does not understand. A thorough investigation of such an enterprise would only be justified by a very large investment.

It is for this reason that such a large percentage of people who buy securities are stockholders in U.S. Steel, because the steel business is something they understand, or think they do, and the Steel Corporation is a leader in the frequency and detail of its periodical reports, containing essential statistics of which almost anybody can understand the main features. If some other corporations with complex organizations would make their operations so well understood to the average investor, and by past performances attain such a degree of confidence in the minds of the public, many people might sell their U.S. Steel and buy the other securities. But with the Steel Corporation occupying a position of prominence similar to a mountain surrounded by little hills, it is easy for any one to see just where the mountain stands and its relative breadth and height compared with its neighbor's. The more I study this subject, the greater appears the necessity for "investigation before investing." In the matter of discrimination alone there is such a wide range of conditions and so many angles from which comparisons may be made, that the subject is, except in some instances, highly complicated and calls for a clear and expert judgment before deciding upon a definite course.

Next in importance to knowing what to buy is the question as to when it should be done. I was discussing this matter with an investor today. He referred to the assets and earning power of a big corporation whose securities had recently suffered a very material decline. He could not understand why the stock should go down in the face of such a showing of commercial and financial strength.

My answer was this: "You have an automobile—it consists of a lot of steel, wood, rubber, brass, leather and other material. It requires gasoline, water, air and lubricating oil. Also knowledge as to how to adjust the whole piece of complicated machinery so that all the parts will work harmoniously. The smallest thing about your automobile is the spark. Without it the whole mass becomes junk. With the spark at least you can get the machinery to go, and you might plug along. But: Unless your spark is timed to fire at the exact moment when the piston reaches a certain point of elevation in the cylinder, you might as well get out and walk.

"It is the same way with the stock which you just mentioned. The company has ample working capital, high class management, big earning power, wonderful prospects. It is probably in a better and stronger position than when its stock sold thirty points higher. In this case the 'spark' is represented by the technical position. At 140 the spark was not properly adjusted. At 110 the adjustment has improved, but a study of the technical position of this stock will eventually point out the exact moment when it should be bought; so get all your other factors lined up ready for the time when the technical position shows that it is time to buy."

In the fluctuations of almost every security there comes a time when it may be most advantageously bought or sold, and the training of one's judgment in the making of decisions as to "when," is one of the fine points in the business. It is also one of the least understood.

Certain "authorities" on securities and their markets have very frequently been proven to be badly wrong, principally because they have ignored this important consideration. They may as well ignore the trigger in a gun.

Carnegie's advice: "Put all your eggs in one basket and then watch the basket" might apply to an industrial organization of which he was the head, but it does not apply generally in the field of investment.

One's holdings should be so diversified by commitments in various lines of business, in different localities and subject to dissimilar influences, that no matter what happens, only a small portion of the investment is affected.

Before the Spanish War, our warships used to carry an observation tower which consisted of one solid piece of steel so constructed that a well-directed shot would demolish it, but during the war some bright mind in the navy conceived the idea of a tower consisting of a network of steel strips which took fifteen or more shots in certain spots to knock it down, and thus was the factor of safety vastly increased.

Investors should follow out this plan of protecting themselves by a diversification of investments, just as an insurance company avoids the risking of its capital and surplus on a single building. By spreading its risk over a vast number of buildings in various localities, it is protecting itself against a catastrophe.

Whatever the sum invested, it should be spread among at least ten to twenty different securities, greatly contrasting each other in nature of business, margin of safety, location of the industry, etc. Thus will your funds be hedged about with protection against shrinkage. And in the search for proper mediums you will widen your knowledge by a careful and discriminating study of the subject.

When you stop to think of it, you will see that it is impossible for all securities to have equal value and prospects; therefore some must be better than others. To be able to select the few which are absolutely the best requires a very broad knowledge and great statistical and analytical training and capability. The possession of such qualifications, however, enables one to go cross lots toward his goal of sound investments and money making.

Chapter XIV - Importance of Knowing Who Owns a Stock

It is important to know whether large operators, inside interests, a pool, or the public dominate the market for a certain security or group.

You have often heard the expression, "Stocks are in weak hands." It is a matter of almost decisive importance to know where the stocks making up the leading group of speculative shares or any single security are held.

The reason this is so important is as follows: A combination of bankers will seldom be found on the long side of the market unless they expect a pronounced change in security market conditions in the near future. Their own purchases, therefore, are an indication of probable betterment. When a pool takes hold, it is usually in a certain one or a few issues which are likely to be favorably affected by developments known to a few but not generally known. The same is true of a large individual operator, who takes a position with a big line of stocks because he is confident that the future will cause others to take the securities off his hands at higher levels.

Operations on such a scale are very often the deciding factors in the trend of the market, because of the great quantities of securities which are dealt in. Such purchases exhaust the floating supply and thus lead to a higher level. Large interests and operators also have a way of influencing the market in the desired direction. This we may term manipulation, or advertising, or marking up, or whatever we choose, but it remains a fact, nevertheless, that this is frequently done. Some people claim that there is a "power" which dominates the market, and perhaps this is true to a degree, but not in the sense that many believe. Large interests sometimes work together, or observe each other's attitude by the action of their respective stocks, and thus operate in harmony, but without any actual understanding.

There is, however, another group of people operating in the market almost constantly, and this group is really the largest and most powerful of all. I refer to the investment and speculative public which is, in most cases, untrained, and as a body is unorganized. If the public could get together and operate in harmony so that it would not continually be stepping on its own toes, there would be a different kind of Wall Street; for without the public as a buffer, large interests, pools and operators would be comparatively powerless.

Some may criticize this statement on the ground that it is made off-hand and without any definite proof, but I have had occasion in the past to prove that it is true, and do not consider it necessary to present the facts here. The report of the committee appointed in 1909 by Governor Hughes for the purpose of investigating the workings of the New York Stock Exchange, published in *The Magazine* for August, 1909, refers to the operations of the floor traders, who, "from their familiarity with the technique of dealings on the Exchange and their ability to act in concert with others and thus manipulate values, are supposed to have special advantages over other traders."

I claim that if a few floor traders, properly organized, can get results, the public could, properly organized, control the situation. I merely mention this to illustrate the point that the big thing to know is where the stocks are, because the position of those who control is an indication of their attitude, pose and power.

It will be admitted that some years ago— before the railroads were persecuted and their profits curtailed by innumerable anti-railroad organizations—their securities were largely held by the great banking interests, each controlling its respective groups of securities. The Rockefellers were in St. Paul, New Haven and others, Harriman and Kuhn-Loeb interests in control of the Union Pacific, Southern Pacific, etc., and the Morgans dominated their specialties. But a change has come over the situation, and now I may safely make the statement that the great bulk of shares of the American railroads are in the hands of small investors.

Large interests got out long ago. They saw the handwriting on the wall; they had a right to sell and protect themselves and they did sell. The big ten thousand, fifty thousand and hundred thousand share blocks were split up into small lots and are so held today. The ten shareowner is now more representative of railroad control that at any time in the history of the world and this situation will continue until there is a very radical change in the outlook for the American railroad industry.

Having satisfied myself that this is the situation, I am in a better position to judge the action of the market for these stocks and to decide upon my individual course, so far as I care to trade or invest in the rails. There are exceptions to this rule, but it is safe to say that outside the individual movements in special issues or groups, there is not likely to be any concerted action until large interests see clearly that the future will be brighter and better, otherwise they would not be justified in accumulating.

When this accumulation begins, as it probably will, sooner or later, there will be a very distinct change in the character of the market for railroad stocks. That change will first evince itself in the transactions.

It will be seen from the above how important it is to know who holds the stocks, and how the public, unorganized, is incapable of applying anything but a superficial aid in the dull, dragging, declining markets we have had in this group.

This being the case, the bankers, large operators and pools, are looking elsewhere for their security market profits.

There are some opportunities that are better than any others offering at the moment. One's task is to ferret these out.

It is astonishing how many people in Wall Street work on "hunches." Whenever your friend tells you about the splendid profits he realized in certain transactions, he is almost certain to tell you, "I had a hunch that it was a purchase at that price." But when a loss results from some of his ventures, he does not lay it to a "hunch" but to "hard luck."

People are apt to conduct their investments a good deal as advertising was conducted in former years, when the advertiser's theory was, "put an ad in the paper and see how you come out." To quote from a very interesting address by Mr. M.H. Avram, "Advertising is no longer a hit or miss proposition—it is scientifically conducted and executed along previously determined and experience-proven lines. An advertising campaign may deviate at times as to details, due to circumstances that could not be foreseen, but in its funda- mentals the predetermined line is followed unwaveringly toward success."

In other words, advertising—formerly a very inexact science—has be- come scientific. It is quite within the bounds of possibility that investing may also be put on the same plane. We are making slow but steady progress toward that end.

In writing this book I have endeavored to give examples as to how some of the difficulties in this big subject can be overcome and the last few chapters have been devoted to observations which may help to solve some of these questions. I do not wish to close without saying a word in favor of the careful selection of investment mediums.

As stated at the beginning of this subject, there are some opportunities that are better than any others. When you stop to think of it, you will see that it is impossible for all securities to have equal value and prospects; therefore some must be better than others. To be able to select the few which are absolutely the best requires a very broad knowledge and great statistical and analytical training and capability. The possession of such qualifications, however, enables one to go cross-lots toward his goal of sound investments and money- making.

It is a deeply interesting subject. The more you learn, the more you realize how little you know, and the more anxious you become to acquire proficiency.

While as a nation we are perhaps becoming more studious, we are also more pleasure-loving. And one's desire to study and advance is often hand- icapped by the influences which pull him toward pastimes and recreation. An engineer friend of mine tells me that he never goes to sleep without reading on some educational subject for at least half an hour. This habit, now thoroughly formed, has been of inestimable value to him in his practice. His example may be imitated to very great advantage.

THE STOCK MARKET BAROMETER
William Peter Hamilton - 1922

Contents

Chapter I - Cycles and Stock Market Records

An English economist whose unaffected humanity always made him remarkably readable, the late William Stanley Jevons, propounded the theory of a connection between commercial panics and spots on the sun. He gave a series of dates from the beginning of the seventeenth century, showing an apparent coincidence between the two phenomena. It is entirely human and likable that he belittled a rather ugly commercial squeeze of two centuries ago because there were not then a justifying number of spots on the sun. Writing in the New York Times early in 1905, in comment on the Jevons theory, I said that while Wall Street in its heart believed in a cycle of panic and prosperity, it did not care if there were enough spots on the sun to make a straight flush. Youth is temerarious and irreverent. Perhaps it would have been more polite to say that the accidental periodic association proved nothing, like the exact coincidence of presidential elections with leap years.

Cycles and the Poets

Many teachers of economics, and many businessmen without pretension even to the more modest title of student, have a profound and reasonable faith in a cycle in the affairs of men. It does not need an understanding of the Einstein theory of relativity to see that the world cannot possibly progress in a straight line in its moral development. The movement would be at least more likely to resemble the journey of our satellite around the sun, which, with all its planetary attendants, is moving toward the constellation of Vega. Certainly the poets believe in the cycle theory. There is a wonderful passage in Byron's "Childe Harold" which, to do it justice, should be read from the preceding apostrophe to Metella's Tower. This was Byron's cycle:

"Here is the moral of all human tales, 'Tis but the same rehearsal of the past; First freedom and then glory; when that fails Wealth, vice, corruption, barbarism at last, And history, with all her volumes vast, Hath but one page."

There seems to be a cycle of panics and of times of prosperity. Anyone with a working knowledge of modern history could recite our panic dates— 1837, 1857, 1866 (Overend-Gurney panic in London), 1873, 1884, 1893, 1907, if he might well hesitate to add the deflation year of 1920. Panics, at least, show a variable interval between them, from ten to fourteen years, with the intervals apparently tending to grow longer. In a subsequent chapter we shall analyze this cycle theory, to test its possible usefulness.

Periodicity

But the pragmatic basis for the theory, a working hypothesis if nothing more, lies in human nature itself. Prosperity will drive men to excess, and repentance for the consequence of those excesses will produce a corresponding depression. Following the dark hour of absolute panic, labor will be thankful for what it can get and will save slowly out of smaller wages, while capital will be content with small profits and quick returns. There will be a period of readjustment like that which saw the reorganization of most of the American railroads after the panic of 1893. Presently we wake up to find that our income is in excess of our expenditure, that money is cheap, that the spirit of adventure is in the air. We proceed from dull or quiet business times to real activity. This gradually develops into extended speculation, with high money rates, inflated wages and other familiar symptoms. After a period of years of good times the strain of the chain is on its weakest link. There is a collapse like that of 1907, a depression foreshadowed in the stock market and in the price of commodities, followed by extensive unemployment, often an increase in savings-bank deposits, but a complete absence of money available for adventure.

Need for a Barometer

Read over Byron's lines again and see if the parallel is not suggestive. What would discussion of business be worth if we could not bring at least a little of the poet's imagination into it? But unfortunately crises are brought about by too much imagination. What we need are soulless barometers, price indexes and averages to tell us where we are going and what we may expect. The best, because the most impartial, the most remorseless of these barometers, is the recorded average of prices in the stock exchange. With varying constituents and, in earlier years, with a smaller number of securities, but continuously these have been kept by the Dow Jones news service for thirty years or more.

There is a method of reading them which has been fruitful of results, although the reading has on occasion displeased both the optimist and the pessimist. A barometer predicts bad weather, without a present cloud in the sky. It is useless to take an axe to it merely because a flood of rain will destroy the crop of cabbages in poor Mrs. Brown's backyard. It has been my lot to discuss these averages in print for many years past, on the tested theory of the late Charles H. Dow, the founder of *The Wall Street Journal*. It might not be becoming to say how constantly helpful the analysis of the price movement proved. But one who ventures on that discussion, who reads that barometer, learns to keep in mind the natural indignation against himself for the destruction of Mrs. Brown's cabbages.

Dow's Theory

Dow's theory is fundamentally simple. He showed that there are, simultaneously, three movements in progress in the stock market. The major is the primary movement, like the bull market which set in with the re-election of McKinley in 1900 and culminated in September, 1902, checked but not stopped by the famous stock market panic consequent on the Northern Pacific corner in 1901; or the primary bear market which developed about October, 1919, culminating June-August, 1921.

It will be shown that this primary movement tends to run over a period of at least a year and is generally much longer. Coincident with it, or in the course of it, is Dow's secondary movement, represented by sharp rallies in a primary bear market and sharp reactions in a primary bull market. A striking example of the latter would be the break in stocks on May 9, 1901. In like secondary movements the industrial group (taken separately from the railroads) may recover much more sharply than the railroads, or the railroads may lead, and it need hardly be said that the twenty active railroad stocks and the twenty industrials, moving together, will not advance point for point with each other even in the primary movement. In the long advance which preceded the bear market beginning October, 1919, the railroads worked lower and were comparatively inactive and neglected, obviously because at that time they were, through government ownership and guaranty, practically out of the speculative field and not exercising a normal influence on the speculative barometer. Under the resumption of private ownership they will tend to regain much of their old significance.

The Theory's Implications

Concurrently with the primary and secondary movement of the market, and constant throughout, there obviously was, as Dow pointed out, the underlying fluctuation from day-to-day. It must here be said that the average is deceptive for speculation in individual stocks. What would have happened to a speculator who believed that a secondary reaction was due in May, 1901, as foreshadowed by the averages, if of all the stocks to sell short on that belief he had chosen Northern Pacific? Some traders did, and they were lucky if they covered at sixty-five points loss.

Dow's theory in practice develops many implications. One of the best tested of them is that the two averages corroborate each other, and that there is never a primary movement, rarely a secondary movement, where they do not agree. Scrutiny of the average figures will show that there are periods where the fluctuations for a number of weeks are within a narrow range; as, for instance, where the industrials do not sell below seventy or above seventy-four, and the railroads above seventy-seven or below seventy-three. This is technically called "making a line," and experience shows that it indicates a period either of distribution or of accumulation. When the two averages rise above the high point of the line, the indication is strongly bullish. It may mean a secondary rally in a bear market; it meant, in 1921, the inauguration of a primary bull movement, extending into 1922.

If, however, the two averages break through the lower level, it is obvious that the market for stocks has reached what meteorologists would call "saturation point." Precipitation follows—a secondary bear movement in a bull market, or the inception of a primary downward movement like that which developed in October, 1919. After the closing of the Stock Exchange, in 1914, the number of industrials chosen for comparison was raised from twelve to twenty and it seemed as if the averages would be upset, especially as spectacular movements in stocks such as G.E. made the fluctuations in the industrials far more impressive than those in the railroads. But students of the averages have carried the twenty chosen stocks back and have found that the fluctuations of the twenty in the previous years, almost from day to day, coincided with the recorded fluctuations of the twelve stocks originally chosen.

Dow-Jones Averages the Standard

The Dow Jones average is still standard, although it has been extensively imitated. There have been various ways of reading it; but nothing has stood the test which has been applied to Dow's theory. The weakness of every other method is that extraneous matters are taken in, from their tempting relevance. There have been unnecessary attempts to combine the volume of sales and to read the average with reference to commodity index numbers. But it must be obvious that the averages have already taken those things into account, just as the barometer considers everything which affects the weather. The price movement represents the aggregate knowledge of Wall Street and, above all, its aggregate knowledge of coming events.

Nobody in Wall Street knows everything. I have known what used to be called the "Standard Oil crowd," in the days of Henry H. Rogers, consistently wrong on the stock market for years together. It is one thing to have "inside information" and another thing to know how stocks will act upon it. The market represents everything everybody knows, hopes, believes, anticipates, with all that knowledge sifted down to what Senator Dolliver once called, in quoting a *Wall Street Journal* editorial in the U.S. Senate, the bloodless verdict of the market place.

Chapter II - Wall Street of the Movies

We shall prove, by strict analysis, the fidelity of the stock market barometer, tested over a long period of years. With the aid of Dow's theory of the price movement we shall examine the major swings upwards or downwards, extending from less than a year to three years or more; their secondary interruption in reactions or rallies, as the case may be; and the relatively unimportant but always present daily fluctuation. We shall see that all these movements are based upon the sum of Wall Street's knowledge of the business of the country; that they have no more to do with morality than the precession of the equinoxes, and that manipulation cannot materially deflect the barometer.

Movies and Melodrama

But, to judge from some of my correspondence, the case must not even be argued, because it is alleged that Wall Street does not come into court with clean hands. It has seemed, in the past, at least discouraging to point out how the dispassionate, the almost inhuman, movement of the market has nothing whatever to do with the occasional scandals which disfigure the record of every market for anything anywhere. But the proportion of people who only feel is, to those who think, overwhelming. The former are in such a majority that concession must be made to them, although I still decline to apologize for the stock market. I should as soon think of apologizing for the meridian of Greenwich. To quote one of the best known of Grover Cleveland's useful platitudes, it is a condition and not a theory which confronts us.

In the popular imagination there is a fearful and wonderful picture of Wall Street—something we may call the Wall Street of the movies. What the English call the cinema is our modern substitute for the conventional melodrama of our grandfathers. Its characters are curiously the same. Its villains and vampires are not like anything in real life; but they behave as consistent villains or vampires ought to behave if they are to satisfy critics who never saw a specimen of either. Many years ago Jerome K. Jerome wrote a chapter on stage law. He showed that on the English stage the loss of a three-and-six-penny marriage certificate invalidated the marriage. In the event of death the property of the testator went to the person who could secure possession of the will. If the rich man died without a will the property went to the nearest villain. In those days lawyers looked like lawyers— on the stage. The detective looked like a gimlet-eyed sleuth, and a financier looked so like a financier that it positively seemed to hurt his face.

Financiers of Fiction

Our modern financier on the screen looks like that, especially in the "close-ups." But he is no new creation.

I remember reading a magazine story, a score of years ago, of a stock market coup by a great "manipulator," of the type of James R. Keene. The illustrations were well drawn and even thrilling. In one of them Keene, or his prototype, was depicted bending dramatically over a Consolidated Stock Exchange ticker! It is to be presumed that he was smashing the market with ten-share lots. Only a Keene could do it, and only a Keene of the movies at that. Doubtless the author of the story, Mr. Edwin Lefevre, who was dissipating his talents in hazy financial paragraphs for the New York *Globe* at that time, felt that he had been artistically frustrated. But perhaps he had himself to thank. Here is his own description of such a manipulator. It is in a short story published in 1901, called *The Break in Turpentine:*

"Now, manipulators of stocks are born, not made. The art is most difficult, for stocks should be manipulated in such wise that they will not look manipulated. Anybody can buy stocks or can sell them. But not every one can sell stocks and at the same time convey the impression that he is buying them, and that prices therefore must inevitably go much higher. It requires boldness and consummate judgment, knowledge of technical stock market conditions, infinite ingenuity and mental agility, absolute familiarity with human nature, a careful study of the curious psychological phenomena of gambling and long experience with the Wall Street public and with the wonderful imagination of the American people; to say nothing of knowing thoroughly the various brokers to be employed, their capabilities, limitations and personal temperaments; also, their price."

That is professedly fiction, and, incidentally, more true and respectable as art than the product of the melodrama or the screen. It lays no stress on the deeper knowledge of values and business conditions necessary to assure the existence of the kind of market which alone makes manipulation possible. Truth is stranger than fiction, and perhaps harder to write, although the remark is open to an obvious retort.

Silk Hats and Strained Faces

Not long ago there appeared a letter to a popular newspaper, notorious for what may be called the anti-Wall Street complex. It professed to give, in a series of gasps, the impressions of a Western stranger on visiting Wall Street. One of these "flashlights" was, "silk hats and strained faces." Let me be exact. I have seen a silk hat in Wall Street. It was when Mayor Seth Low opened the new Stock Exchange in 1901. My stenographer, bless her honest heart, said it was real stylish. But financiers of the movies tend to wear silk hats, just as the heroes in melodrama, even when reduced to penury and rags, wore patent-leather shoes. A screen financier without a silk hat would be like an egg without salt. We cannot otherwise infer, as we are required, that he is a bad egg.

"A Long Way Back for Soup"

Only a few years ago there was a severely localized scandal over a "corner" in a stock called Stutz Motor, for which no true market had been established. Nobody was hurt except a few speculators who chose to sell the thing short. They paid up without whining. But it formed an irresistible text for a popular attack upon Wall Street. One of the New York newspapers said that the incident was only in a piece with "the Metropolitan Traction corruptionists, the New Haven wreckers, the Rock Island wreckers," and what it called, with a free rendering of history, "the life insurance corruptionists." This was in a newspaper professing to sell news. It did not tell its readers that the last of the Metropolitan Street Railway financing happened twenty years before. Even the foolish and indefensible capitalization of the surface lines of New York, unloaded on what was then called the Interborough Metropolitan Company, was fifteen years old. The life insurance investigation, which, incidentally, neither charged nor proved "corruption," went back sixteen years. Even the last essay in misjudged New Haven financing, a comparatively minor matter, occurred fully eleven years earlier; that of Rock Island, nineteen years before; while that favorite charge against Wall Street, the recapitalization of the Chicago & Alton, was carried through in 1899 and not a soul saw anything wrong with it until 1907. I suppose I write myself down a hopeless reactionist when I say that, with the fullest knowledge of the facts, I cannot see anything reprehensible in it now.

Widows and Orphans

Even an incident so spectacular as the Northern Pacific corner, with the purely stock market panic which it produced, cannot be pleaded as an example of a kind of manipulation which would disable our barometer. That particular panic occurred in the course of a primary bull market. It produced merely a severe secondary reaction, for the upward movement was resumed and did not culminate until sixteen months afterwards. That incident of 1901, however, is still alive and kicking, so far as the politicians who denounce Wall Street are concerned. It is remarkable that all the stock affected in these bygone incidents is alleged to have been held by widows and orphans. I wish somebody would marry that widow and adopt, or even spank, the orphan. After depriving their trustees of the commonest business sense they have no right to come around in this indelicate way and remind us of our crimes. There is a lucrative engagement waiting for them elsewhere—in the movies.

Dow's Theory True of any Stock Market

Let us be serious, and get back to our text. The law that governs the movement of the stock market, formulated here, would be equally true of the London Stock Exchange, the Paris Bourse or even the Berlin Boerse. But we may go further. The principles underlying that law would be true if those Stock Exchanges and ours were wiped out of existence. They would come into operation again, automatically and inevitably, with the re-establishment of a free market in securities in any great Capital. So far as I know, there has not been a record corresponding to the Dow Jones averages kept by any of the London financial publications. But the stock market there would have the same quality of forecast which the New York market has if similar data were available.

It would be possible to compile from the London Stock Exchange list two or more representative groups of stocks and show their primary, their secondary and their daily movements over the period of years covered by Wetenhall's list and the London Stock Exchange official list. An average made up of the prices of the British railroads might well confirm our own. There is in London a longer and more diversified list of industrial stocks to draw upon. The averages of the South African mining stocks in the Kaffir market, properly compiled from the first Transvaal gold rush in 1889, would have an interest all their own. They would show how gold mining tends to flourish when other industries are stagnant or even prostrated. The comparison of that average with the movement of securities held for fixed income would be highly instructive to the economist. It would demonstrate in the most vivid way the relation of the purchasing power of gold to bonds held for investment. It would prove conclusively the axiom that the price of securities held for fixed income is in inverse ratio to the cost of living, as we shall see for ourselves in a later chapter.

The Fact Without the Truth is False

It is difficult, and with many observers it has proved impossible, to regard Wall Street comprehendingly from the inside. Just as it will be shown that the market is bigger than the manipulator, bigger than all the financiers put together, so it is true that the stock market barometer is in a way bigger than the stock market itself. A modern writer, G.K. Chesterton, has said that the fact without the truth is sterile, that the fact without the truth is even false. It was not until Dow propounded his theory of the price movement that any real attempt had been made to elicit and set forth the truth contained in the fact of the stock market. Can we make it possible for the man whose business brings him into the midst of that whirling machinery to understand the power which moves it, and even something of the way that power is generated? Apparently the only picture which has hitherto reached the popular retina is the distorted image which we have called the Wall Street of the movies.

Homage Vice Pays to Virtue

Why does the swindling oil-stock promoter circularize his victims from some reputable address in the financial district, and use all sorts of inducements to get his stock quoted in the financial columns of reputable metropolitan newspapers? Would he do that if the public he addresses, the investor and the speculator,—the investor in embryo,—really believed that Wall Street was the sink of iniquity which the country politician depicts? If that were truly the case the shady promoter would seek other quarters. But he uses the financial district because he knows that its credit and integrity are the best in the world. Hypocrisy is the tribute which vice pays to virtue. He would have no use for a Wall Street as rotten as himself. Indeed, if the financial district were one tithe as corrupt as the demagogues who abuse it there would be no problem for them to propound. The money center of the U.S. would fall to pieces of its own rottenness. All this is true, and yet if the exact contrary were the case the theory of the stock market movement would still be valid.

Rhodes and Morgan

It will not be charged that the writer is like the dyer's hand, subdued to what he works in, if his illustrations have been chosen mainly from the financial district. There is a Wall Street engaged upon tasks so serious, so exacting, that it has neither time nor inclination to be crooked. If it is true, as we have seen, that nobody can know all the facts which at any one time influence the stock market movement, it is true, as any of us can record from personal experience, that some have far more knowledge than others. The men who really know lift you out of this scuffle of petty criticism and recrimination. When they are rich men their wealth is incidental, the most obvious means to larger ends, but not an end in itself.

When I was following my profession in South Africa, a quarter of a century ago, I was thrown in contact with Cecil John Rhodes. He had definite ideas and large conceptions, far above the mere making of money. Money was necessary to the carrying out of his ideas, to the extension of white civilization from the Cape to Cairo, with a railroad as the outward and visible sign of something of even spiritual significance. In the respect of intuitive intelligence I have met only one man like him—the late J. P. Morgan. It was impossible to follow the rapidity of their mental processes. There was something phenomenal about it, like the performances of mathematically gifted children who can give you the square root of a number in thousands with a few moments of mental calculation. Other well-known men—speaking perhaps from the point of view of a reporter—seemed to have mental processes much like our own. Most of the great captains of industry I have met, like James J. Hill and Edward H. Harriman, had a quality essential to a first-rate thinker. They could eliminate the irrelevant. They could grasp the fundamental fact in a page of verbiage. But Rhodes and Morgan could do more. They could reason to an often startling but sound conclusion before you could state the premises.

Not Indescribable

And these men were rich, almost fortuitously. They had great tasks to accomplish, and it was necessary that they should have the financial means which made achievement possible. In the past few years we have heard a great deal about "ideals," and found that most of them were half-digested opinions. But there is a Wall Street with an ideal. There has usually been, and I hope there always will be, the right man to take the right objective view at the right moment. Not long ago I heard a lecturer setting forth what he called the "indescribable" beauties of the Grand Canyon of the Colorado. In the space of an hour and a quarter he proved conclusively that those beauties were indescribable, at least so far as he was concerned. But Milton could have described them, or the Psalmist. Perhaps any reasonably intelligent man could give you an idea of that natural wonder if he set forth simply the spiritual truth in the physical fact before him.

The Unchangeable

I feel I have said before, perhaps in editorials you read today, and forget tomorrow, what I am saying now. The problems of humanity do not change, because human nature is what it has been as far back as human record tells. "Cycles" are as old as organized humanity. The changes we see are superficial, especially where sincere and intelligent men so legislate that they may the better live together in peace and good will. The human heart is essential to all progress. Reform starts there, and not in the halls of legislation.

The Bells of Trinity

Facing the western end of Wall Street, casting its shadow from the setting sun upon the most criticized and least understood section of a great nation, stands the spire of Trinity. We have often heard its bells ringing the old familiar Christmas hymns. The shepherds will be watching their flocks again, all seated on the ground. It may well be that, hearing those bells, the glory of the Lord shall in some manner shine round about us. There is little that laws can do to make men happier or richer or more contented. There is no form of government today, without its parallel, and warning, in the past. There is none in the past of which it could not be said that only righteousness exalteth a nation. Wall Street knows as well as the most disinterested of its critics that goodness and justice and sacrifice and love are the foundation of all good government, because in that spirit alone a people truly governs itself.

We have said that the laws we are studying are fundamental, axiomatic, self-evident. And in this higher truth surely there is something permanent which would remain if the letter of the Constitution of the United States had become an interesting study for the archeologist, and the surviving writings of our day were classical in a sense their authors never dreamed. Such a foundation is permanent because truth has in it the element of the divine.

Chapter III - Charles H. Dow and His Theory

To judge from a large number of letters received from readers of past discussions on Dow's theory of the averages, and on panic and prosperity cycles generally, that theory is assumed to be something in the nature of a sure way to make money in Wall Street. It may be said at once that it bears no resemblance to any "martingale" or system of beating the bank. Some of the questions show more intelligence and understanding than this, and one of them at least deserves an extended reply.

A Newspaper Man, and More

"Who was Dow, and where can I read his theory?" Charles H. Dow was the founder of the *Dow-Jones* financial news service in New York, and founder and first editor of *The Wall Street Journal*. He died in December, 1902, in his fifty-second year. He was an experienced newspaper reporter, with an early training under Samuel Bowles, the great editor of the Springfield *Republican.* Dow was a New Englander, intelligent, self-repressed, ultra-conservative; and he knew his business. He was almost judicially cold in the consideration of any subject, whatever the fervor of discussion. It would be less than just to say that never saw him angry; I never saw him even excited. His perfect integrity and good sense commanded the confidence of every man in Wall Street, at a time when there were few efficient newspaper men covering the financial section, and of these still fewer with any deep knowledge of finance.

Dow also had the advantage of some years experience on the floor of the Stock Exchange. It came about in a rather curious way. The late Robert Goodbody, an Irishman, a Quaker and an honor to Wall Street, came over from Dublin to America. As the New York Stock Exchange requires that every member shall be an American citizen, Dow became his partner. During the time necessary for Robert Goodbody to naturalize, Dow held a seat in the Stock Exchange and executed orders on the floor. When Goodbody became an American citizen Dow withdrew from the Exchange and returned to his more congenial newspaper work.

Dow's Caution, and His Theory

Knowing and liking Dow, with whom I worked in the last years of his life, I was often, with many of his friends, exasperated by his over-conservatism. It showed itself particularly in his editorials in *The Wall Street Journal,* to which it is now necessary to allude because they are the only written record of Dow's theory of the price movement. He would write a strong, readable and convincing editorial, on a public question affecting finance and business, and in the last paragraph would add safeguards and saving clauses which not merely took the sting out of it but took the "wallop" out of it. In the language of the prize ring, he pulled his punches.

He was almost too cautious to come out with a flat, dogmatic statement of his theory, however sound it was and however close and clear his reasoning might be. He wrote, mostly in 1901 and the first half of 1902, a number of editorials dealing with methods of stock speculation. His theory must be disinterred from those editorials, where it is illustrative and incidental and never the main subject of discussion. It is curious also that in one of his earliest statements of the price movement he makes an indefensible claim. Under the caption "Swings Within Swings," in the Review and Outlook of *The Wall Street Journal* of January 4, 1902, he says:

"Nothing is more certain than that the market has three well defined movements which fit into each other. The first is the daily variation due to local causes and the balance of buying or selling at that particular time. The secondary movement covers a period ranging from ten days to sixty days, averaging probably between thirty and forty days. The third swing is the great move covering from four to six years."

Where Dow Went Wrong

Remember that Dow wrote this twenty years ago, and that he had not the records for analysis of the stock market movement which are now available. The extent of the primary movement, as given in this quotation, is proved to be far too long by subsequent experience; and a careful examination has shown me that the major swing before Dow wrote was never "from four to six years," rarely three years and oftener less than two.

But Dow always had a reason for what he said, and his intellectual honesty assures those who knew him that it was at least an arguable reason. It was based upon his profound belief in the recurrence of financial crises, at periodic intervals (as shown by recorded financial history), of a little more than ten years. Dow assumed for that period one primary bull market and one primary bear market, and therefore split the ten-year period in half. It was rather like the little boy who, being asked to name ten arctic animals, submitted "five seals and five polar bears!"

Panic Dates of Jevons

In the opening chapter we spoke of historic panics, of Professor Stanley Jevons, and of his theory connecting such crises with the recurrence of spots on the sun and their assumed influence upon the weather and crops. I said that the reasoning was about as good as associating presidential elections with leap years. But here are the dates of commercial crises in England as recorded by Jevons, and it is fair to say that they are sufficiently impressive. These years are 1701, 1711, 1712, 1731-32, 1742, 1752, 1763, 1772-3, 1783, 1793, 1804-5, 1815, 1825, 1836, 1847, 1857, 1866, and 1873.

As Dow says in an editorial quoting these dates, published in *The Wall Street Journal* on July 9, 1902:

"This makes a very good showing for the ten-year theory and is supported, to a considerable extent, by what has occurred in this country during the past century."

Dow's account of the successive crises in this country (he had personal experience of three of them—1873, 1884 and 1893) was so good and interesting that it is well worth quoting here. So far as Jevons's dates are concerned, it is curious to note that he omitted one serious crisis near the beginning of his list. That occurred in 1715, and was precipitated by the Scottish invasion of England in that year to restore the Stuarts to the English throne. It is rather human of Jevons to omit it, if, as I suspect, there were not enough spots on the sun in that year to fit the parallel.

Dow on Our Own Crises

Here is Dow's account of our own crises: "The first crisis in the U.S. during the nineteenth century came in 1814, and was precipitated by the capture of Washington by the British on the 24th of August in that year. The Philadelphia and New York banks suspended payments, and for a time the crisis was acute. The difficulties leading up to this period were the great falling off in foreign trade caused by the embargo and non-intercourse acts of 1808, the excess of public expenditures over public receipts, and the creation of a large number of state banks taking the place of the old United States Bank. Many of these state banks lacked capital and issued currency without sufficient security.

1819, 1825, and 1837

"There was a near approach to a crisis in 1819 as the result of a tremendous contraction of bank circulation. The previous increase of bank issues had prompted speculation, the contraction caused a serious fall in the prices of commodities and real estate. This, however, was purely a money panic as far as its causes were concerned.

"The European crisis in 1825 caused a diminished demand for American products and led to lower prices and some money stringency in 1826. The situation, however, did not become very serious and was more in the nature of an interruption to progress than a reversal of conditions.

"The year 1837 brought a great commercial panic, for which there was abundant cause. There had been rapid industrial and commercial growth, with a multitude of enterprises established ahead of the time. Crops were deficient, and breadstuffs were imported. The refusal of the government to extend the charter of the U.S. Bank had caused a radical change in the banking business of the country, while the withdrawal of public deposits and their lodgment with state banks had given the foundation for abnormal speculation.

1847, 1857, and 1866

"The panic in Europe in 1847 exerted but little influence in this country, although there was a serious loss in specie, and the Mexican war had some effect in checking enterprises. These effects, however, were neutralized somewhat by large exports of breadstuffs and later by the discovery of gold in 1848-9.

"There was a panic of the first magnitude in 1857, following the failure of the Ohio Life Insurance and Trust Company in August. This panic came unexpectedly, although prices had been falling for some months. There had been very large railroad building, and the proportion of specie held by banks was very small in proportion to their loans and deposits. One of the features of this period was the great number of failures. The banks generally suspended payments in October.

"The London panic in 1866, precipitated by the failure of Overend, Gurney & Co., was followed by heavy fall in prices in the Stock Exchange here. In April there had been a corner in Michigan Southern and rampant speculation generally, from which the relapse was rather more than normal.

1873, 1884, and 1893

"The panic of September, 1873, was a commercial as well as a Stock Exchange panic. It was the outcome of an enormous conversion of floating into fixed capital. Business had been expanded on an enormous scale, and the supply of money became insufficient for the demands made upon it. Credit collapsed, and the depression was extremely serious.

"The year 1884 brought a Stock Exchange smash but not a commercial crisis. The failure of the Marine Bank, Metropolitan Bank and Grant & Ward in May was accompanied by a large fall in prices and a general check which was felt throughout the year. The Trunk Line war, which had lasted for several years, was one of the factors in this period.

"The panic of 1893 was the outcome of a number of causes— uncertainty in regard to the currency situation, the withdrawal of foreign investments and the fear of radical tariff legislation. The anxiety in regard to the maintenance of the gold standard was undoubtedly the chief factor, as it bore upon many others."

A Weak Prediction

With a caution in prediction which is not merely New England but almost Scottish, Dow, in a typical final paragraph, goes on to say:

"Judging by the past and by the developments of the last six years, it is not unreasonable to suppose that we may get at least a Stock Exchange flurry in the next few years."

So far from being unreasonable, it was not even a daring guess. It was more than a "flurry" in 1907, five years after, when the New York banks resorted to clearinghouse certificates and the stock market grazed a panic by a bare five minutes. But the prediction was made during a primary upward swing which culminated in September of the year 1902, three months before Dow died.

Events soon disproved Dow's five-year primary swings, arrived at by splitting the assumed ten-year cycle in half. There was a primary bear market from September, 1902, lasting nearly a year. A primary bull market originated in September, 1903, becoming definitely marked by June, 1904, and culminating in January, 1907—a period of three years and four months; while the primary bear market which followed it and covered the period of the crisis of 1907 lasted until the following December—a period of eleven months.

Nelson's Book on Speculation

All that Dow ever printed is in *The Wall Street Journal,* and only by search through the precious files of Wall Street's Bible can his theory of the stock market price movement be reconstructed. But at the end of 1902 the late S. A. Nelson wrote and published an unpretentious book called *The ABC of Stock Speculation.* It is long out of print, but may occasionally be picked up from the secondhand booksellers. He tried to persuade Dow to write the book, and, failing that, he incorporated in it all that he could find of what Dow had said on stock speculation in *The Wall Street Journal.* Of the thirty-five chapters in the book, fifteen (Chapters V to XIX inclusive) are editorials, some slightly abridged, from *The Wall Street Journal,* covering such subjects as "Scientific Speculation," "Methods of Reading the Market," "Methods of Trading" and market swings generally—all of them interesting but not suitable for entire reproduction here, although they will be sufficiently quoted in subsequent chapters.

Nelson's is a conscientious and sensible little book. He was a conscientious and sensible little man—one we loved and laughed at, for young reporters could not take him as seriously as he took himself. His autographed copy lies before me as I write, and I can see his pathetic figure and earnest, strained face—he was dying of tuberculosis—as I read his rather conventional discussions on the morality of speculation. He died not long after, far away from his beloved Wall Street, but it was he who evolved the name of "Dow's Theory." It was an honorable ascription, to which Dow is fully entitled; for if many people had recognized meaning in traceable movements in the stock market—the great and useful barometer of trade—it was Dow who first formulated those ideas in a practical way.

Chapter IV - Dow's Theory, Applied to Speculation

We have seen in past discussions of Dow's theory of the stock-market price movement that the essence of it could be summed up in three sentences. In an editorial published December 19, 1900, he says, in *The Wall Street Journal:*

"The market is always to be considered as having three movements, all going on at the same time. The first is the narrow movement from day to day. The second is the short swing, running from two weeks to a month or more; the third is the main movement, covering at least four years in its duration."

It has already been shown that his third and main movement may complete itself in much less than Dow's assumed four years, and also how an attempt to divide the ten-year period of the panic cycle theory into a bear and bull market of approximately five years each led to an unconscious exaggeration. That, however, is immaterial. Dow had successfully formulated a theory of the market movements of the highest value, and had synchronized those movements so that those who came after him could construct a business barometer.

The Truth Beneath Speculation

This is the essence of Dow's theory, and it need hardly be said that he did not see, or live to see, all that it implied. He never wrote a single editorial on the theory alone, but returns to it to illustrate his discussions on stock market speculation, and the underlying facts and truths responsible not only for speculation (using the word in its best and most useful sense) but for the market itself.

It is not surprising that *The Wall Street Journal* received many inquiries as to the assumptions it made on the basis of Dow's major premise. On January 4,

1902, Dow replies to a pertinent question, and any thoughtful reader of these pages should be able to answer it himself. The correspondent asks him, "For some time you have been writing rather bullish on the immediate market, yet a little bearish in a larger sense. How do you make this consistent?" Dow's reply was, of course, that he was bullish after the secondary swing but that he did not think, in view of stock values from earnings of record, that a bull market which had then been operative sixteen months could run much further. It was a curious contraction, incidentally, of his own minimum four-year estimate, but that major upward swing as a matter of fact ran until the following September. It may be said that such a swing always outruns values. In its final stage it is discounting possibilities only.

A Useful Definition

In the same editorial Dow goes on to give a useful definition from which legitimate inferences may drawn. He says:

"It is a bull period as long as the average of one high point exceeds that of previous high points. It is a bear period when the low point becomes lower than the previous low points. It is often difficult to judge whether the end of an advance has come because the movement of prices is that which would occur if the main tendency had changed. Yet, it may only be an unusually pronounced secondary movement."

This passage contains, by implication, both the idea of "double tops" and "double bottoms" (which I frankly confess I have not found essential or greatly useful) and the idea of a "line," as shown in the narrow fluctuation of the averages over a recognized period, necessarily one either of accumulation or distribution. This has been found to be of the greatest service in showing the further persistence of the main movement, or the possible termination of the secondary movement, so apt to be mistaken for the initiation of a new major trend. I shall, in a later chapter, analyze such a "line," made in the stock market in 1914.

Successful Forecast

In subsequent discussions there will be no difficulty in showing, from the various studies in the price movement since 1902, standing for record in the columns of *The Wall Street Journal,* that the method for a forecast of the main market movement and for a correct discrimination between that and the secondary movement had been provided in Dow's theory, and that it has been used with surprising accuracy. A prophet, especially in Wall Street, takes his life in his hands. If his predictions are always of the rosy whatever the facts of the situation may be, he will at worst be merely called a fool for his pains. The charge against him will be far more serious if he sees that a boom has overrun itself, and says so. If he is bearish and right he will be accused of unworthy motives. He will even be held contributory to the decline which he foresaw,

sufficient material here to say that a bear market is normally appreciably shorter than a bull market; perhaps as secondary downward swings in a primary rising average are short and sharp, with a halting recovery consuming a longer time than the decline.

The Market Is Always Right—

It will be shown at a later stage that throughout these great market movements it was possible from the stock market barometer to predict, some valuable distance ahead, the development of the business of the country. These discussions would fail in their purpose if they did not make the subject clear to the unfinancial layman—interesting to the man who never bought a share of speculative stock in his life. A barometer is a necessity for all vessels at sea, from the smallest coasting schooner to the *Aquitania*. It means as much, and even more, to the "Bolivar" of Kipling's ballad, "swamping in the sea," watching, in despair, "Some damned liner's lights go by, like a grand hotel" as it does to the navigating officers on the liner's bridge. There is no business so small that it can afford to disregard the stock market barometer. Certainly there is no business so large that it dare disregard it. Indeed the most serious mistakes in the management of great business have come from a failure of these navigators of the great liners of the sea of commerce to take heed when the passionless, disinterested stock market called their attention to bad weather ahead.

—and Never Thanked

When, in the U.S. Senate, the late Senator Dolliver, reading an editorial of *The Wall Street Journal,* said, "Listen to the bloodless verdict of the market place," he saw the merciless accuracy of that verdict; because it is, and necessarily must be, based upon all the evidence, even when given by unconscious and unwilling witnesses.

No wonder the rural politician can so easily make Wall Street the scapegoat for depressing conditions, affecting his farmer constituents no more than the rest of us. Wall Street is guilty in their eyes, for they are willing enough to hold Wall Street responsible for a condition which it merely foresaw and predicted. It was said in a preceding chapter that the prophet of calamity will make himself hated in any case, and hated all the more if his predictions come true. But Wall Street's predictions do come true. Its predictions of prosperity, duly fulfilled as we have seen, are forgotten. Its predictions of adversity are remembered, and by none more than the man who ignored those predictions and is therefore the more bound to find somebody other than himself to blame.

Wall Street the Farmer's Friend

Wall Street is often called "provincial" by politicians and others actuated by an unreasoning sectional jealousy of the necessary financial center of the country. The country can have only one such center, although the framers of the Federal Reserve Act, overloading it with sectional politics, tried hard to make twelve. The farmers say, or their political spokesman says, "What does

Wall Street know about farming?" Wall Street knows more than all the farmers put together ever knew, with all the farmers have forgotten. It can, moreover, refresh its memory instantly at any moment. It employs the ablest of the farmers, and its experts are better even than those of our admirable, and little appreciated, Department of Agriculture, whose publications Wall Street reads even if the farmer neglects them.

The stock market which began to break at the end of October and the beginning of November, 1919, when the farmer was insanely pooling his wheat for $3 a bushel and his cotton for forty cents a pound, knew more than the farmer about cotton and wheat. And that barometer was telling him then to get out, to sell what he had at the market price and to save himself while there was yet time. He blames Wall Street and the Federal Reserve banking system and everyone but his own deluded and prejudiced self. He thinks he can change it all by getting his Congressman to take an axe to break the barometer. He is trying to break the barometers of the grain trade in Chicago and Minneapolis, the barometers of the cotton trade in New Orleans and New York. Twenty years ago, at the demand of her farmers, Germany broke her grain barometer, with destructive legislation. What was the consequence? She had to construct a new barometer on the old plan, and it was the farmers who paid for it in advance out of their own pockets. The Germans have learned to let free markets alone, a thing the British always knew, and built up the greatest empire, with the widest commerce the world ever saw, on exactly that knowledge.

Chapter VI - A Unique Quality of Forecast

There are two Wall Streets. One of them is the Wall Street of fact, slowly arriving at definition out of a chaos of misconception. The other is the Wall Street of fiction; the Wall Street of sensational newspapers, of popularity-hunting politicians; the Wall Street of false dramatic interpretation, whose characters are no more real than the types of the old-fashioned melodrama of fifty years ago—those caricatures which have had an astonishing and unintelligent revival on the moving-picture screen. It was felt that our second chapter might well be devoted to that popular misconception, Wall Street of the movies.

Major Movements Are Unmanipulated

One of the greatest of misconceptions, that which has militated most against the usefulness of the stock market barometer, is the belief that manipulation can falsify stock market movements otherwise authoritative and instructive. The writer claims no more authority than may come from twenty-six years of stark intimacy with Wall Street, preceded by practical acquaintance with the London Stock Exchange, the Paris Bourse and even that wildly speculative market in gold shares, "Between the Chains," in Johannesburg in 1895. But in all that experience, for what it may be worth, it is impossible to recall a single instance of a major market movement which depended for its impetus, or even for its genesis, upon manipulation. These discussions have been made in vain if they have failed to show that all the primary bull markets and every primary bear market have been vindicated, in the course of their development and before their close, by the facts of general business, however much over-speculation or over-liquidation may have tended to excess, as they always do, in the last stage of the primary swing.

A Financial Impossibility

This is a sweeping statement, but I am convinced of its fundamental truth. When James R. Keene took up the task of marketing two hundred and twenty thousand shares of Amalgamated Copper, for the people who had brought about that amalgamation but had not been able to float the stock, it is estimated that in the course of distribution he must have traded in at least seven hundred thousand shares of that stock. He carried the price to above par to realize a net of ninety to ninety-six for his employers. This was a relatively small stock capitalization; but let us assume that some syndicate, larger than any that the stock market has ever seen, necessarily involving the cooperation of all the great banking institutions, undertook to manufacture the general bull market without which Keene's efforts would have been worse than wasted. Let us concede that this super-syndicate could afford to ignore the large number of active securities outside of the forty active stocks taken in our railroad and industrial averages and defy all trained public opinion. Let us assume that they had accumulated for the rise, against all their previous practice and conviction, without, by some miracle, arousing suspicion, not two hundred and twenty thousand shares of stock, but a hundred times that number.

Anybody who learned in the little red school house that two and two make four must see that we are here leading ourselves into an arithmetical impossibility. This syndicate would presumably not be content with less than a forty-point net profit, and its actual trades, before it had established a broad general market even equivalent to that Keene established for Amalgamated Copper, alone would therefore amount to something like one hundred and twenty million shares, which, taking them at par, would involve financing to the amount of many billions of dollars—so much financing, in fact, that the great banks concerned would presumably relinquish all their other business and confine themselves to the syndicate operations alone. Such a syndicate could not have done this, or a tithe of this, at any time during the existence of our national banking system. Does anybody think it would be possible to undertake such a panic-breeding operation with the assistance of the Federal Reserve system?

Where Manipulation Was Possible

To state the terms of a corresponding bear operation, where every wealthy member of the syndicate is necessarily already a large holder in stocks, bonds, real estate and industrial production, would reduce the whole thing to the wildest absurdity. My mind refuses even to grasp it. Keene, in a broad bull market, to distribute a number of shares amounting to one-twenty-fifth of the common stock alone of the U.S. Steel Corporation, had behind him all the wealth and influence of the powerful Standard Oil group. When he distributed U.S. Steel common and preferred he had behind him not only the great Morgan banking influences but those of every group that came into that steel combination, with the general approval of a public which correctly recognized a wonderful and even unprecedented expansion in production and trade. But even with that backing could he have multiplied his efforts a hundredfold? The merchant, the banker, the manufacturer who studies the stock market barometer with reference to the major swings, can dismiss from his mind altogether the idea that they are falsified by manipulation.

Roger W. Babson's Theory

But the idea is widely held. There is no intention here to arouse or encourage controversy, and if I take an example from Roger W. Babson and his book on *Business Barometers,* he will, I am sure, readily understand that it is not intended in criticism or depreciation of his highly sincere work. It is only fair to Mr. Babson to say, also, that the extract I give here was published in 1909:

"A slowly sagging market usually means that the ablest speculators expect in the near future a period of depression in general business; and a slowly rising market usually means that prosperous business conditions may be expected, *unless the decline or rise is artificial and caused by manipulation.* In fact, if it were not for manipulation, merchants could almost rely on the stock market alone as a barometer, and let these large market operators stand the expense of collecting the data necessary for determining fundamental conditions. Unfortunately, however, it is impossible by studying the stock market alone to distinguish between artificial movements and natural movements; therefore, although bankers and merchants may watch the stock market as *one* of the barometers, yet they should give to it only a fair and proportional amount of weight." —*Business Barometers Used in the Accumulation of Money,* by Roger W. Babson; second edition, 1910.

Mr. Babson's Chart

What sort of barometer should we have if we had to make allowances for a tube of mercury that was too short, or for a general lack of accuracy in the delicate and sensitive mechanism of the aneroid? The stock market barometer is not perfect, or, to put it more correctly, the adolescent science of reading it is far from having attained perfection. But it is not imperfect in the sense Mr. Babson here assumes. It does discharge its function of prediction, when viewed over any reasonable length of time, with almost uncanny accuracy. Let us take a few examples from Mr. Babson's own picture chart, those composite plots above and below a consistently rising line representing the steady increase in a growing country's wealth, and we shall see how the stock market predicted each of them before Mr. Babson had the material to draw them in the squares of his instructive and striking chart. To those who are unfamiliar with a publication so interesting it may be said that he divides his chart with columns for each month of the year vertically, and completes his squares horizontally with numbered lines showing the area covered by all the factors of business, above or below a gradually rising middle line across the chart representing the growing wealth of the country.

How the Stock Market Predicted

It will be observed that where these areas are shallow they tend to become broader in time consumed, and where the time to complete the area is less the depression or expansion is deeper or higher, as the case may be, the black areas above or below being assumed to balance each other, at least approximately. One of these black areas of depression shown in the Babson chart began in 1903, only developing recognizable space in the latter part of that year, and continued throughout 1904, finally emerging above the line of growing wealth in the earlier part of 1905. The stock market anticipated this area of business depression, for a primary bear swing began in September, 1902, and ran until the corresponding month of 1903. Mr. Babson's area of depression was still ruling when the market became mildly bullish, in September, 1903, and strongly bullish before the following June; while the Babson area of depression was not completed till the end of that year—1904. The Babson chart does not show any great degree of expansion until 1906, although it foreshadows it in September, 1905. But the stock market barometer foresaw all Mr. Babson's expansion, and the long bull market continued up to January, 1907, overrunning itself—a tendency of bull markets and bear markets alike.

A True Barometer

Mr. Babson's area of expansion reached its high maximum in 1907, when a bear stock market swing had already set in, continuing for eleven months until early December of that year, predicting that length of time ahead of Mr. Babson's truly calculated area of depression, which was deep, but not long in duration, and lasted till the end of 1908. His subsequent expansion area above the line did not begin to show itself in market strength until the end of July of 1908; but the stock market barometer once again foretold the coming prosperity in a bull market which had its genesis in December, 1907, and its culmination in August, 1909, beginning from that time to predict with equal accuracy, and well in advance, Mr. Babson's next period of depression.

Surely this shows that the stock market is a barometer, and that the Babson chart is more strictly a record, from which, of course, people as intelligent as its industrious compilers can draw valuable guidance for the future. To use a much-abused word, the stock market barometer is unique. You will remember that "unique" is a word which takes no qualifying adjective. Our barometer is not rather unique, or almost unique, or virtually unique. There is just one of it, and it cannot be duplicated. It does predict, as this simple illustration has shown, the condition of business many months ahead, and no other index, or combination of indices, can assume to do that. Our highly scientific and competent Weather Bureau often explodes the fallacy of any assumed radical change in general weather conditions. It does not pretend to go back to the glacial age. It tells us that there have been droughts and hard winters before, coming at uncertain and incalculable intervals. When it attempts specific prophecy—a single particular from its immense collection of generals—it is merely guessing. Does anybody who happened to be in Washington at the time remember the "fair and warmer" weather prophesied over the Taft inauguration? I went over the Pennsylvania Railroad on the following day, when the storm had leveled every telegraph pole between New York and Philadelphia. It was even said that some of the special trains had so far missed the parade that they were not in Washington then. Even the aneroid barometer can only forecast a limited number of hours ahead, according to the atmospheric pressure.

Cycles Overestimated

There are other compilations, and that of Harvard University will be noticed in a more appropriate place. I am inclined to think that all attach too much force to the cycle theory, very much as we have seen that Dow did in splitting the favored ten-year cycle into an assumed but non-existent five-year bear market and a similar five-year bull market. But Mr. Babson would tell you that his areas of expansion and even of inflation, extending not five years but two years or less than three in point of time, do not necessarily blow their tops off in a final explosion and that the bottom does not drop out of his period of depression. A stock market crisis may occur in the middle of a bull market, like the Northern Pacific panic of 1901; or a near-panic, with a development more serious and radical, may occur in the course of a major bear swing in the stock market, as in 1907. Mr. Babson correctly shows that the latter was followed by a business depression that had already been foreshadowed in the downward stock market movement. If all panics and industrial crises arose from the same causes and could be predicted with the suggested rhythmical certainty, they would never happen because they would always be foreseen. This sounds something like an Irish "bull," but it may well stand as a statement of the fact. Was it not an Irishman who said that an Irish bull differed from other bulls in the respect that it was always pregnant? I do not here go deeply into this question of cycles, because it is abundantly clear that the stock market is little moved by any such consideration.

Order Is Heaven's First Law

If Wall Street is the general reservoir for the collection of the country's tiny streams of liquid capital, it is the clearing house for all the tiny contributions to the sum of truth about the facts of business. It cannot be too often repeated that the stock market movement represents the deductions from the accumulation of that truth, including the facts on building and real estate, bank clearings, business failures, money conditions, foreign trade, gold movements, commodity prices, investment markets, crop conditions, railroad earnings, political factors and social conditions, but all of these with an almost limitless number of other things, each having its tiny trickle of stock market effect.

It will be seen from this how true the postulate made in an earlier discussion was when it was said that nobody in Wall Street knows all the facts, to say nothing of the meaning of all the facts. But the impartial, passionless market barometer records them as certainly as the column of mercury records the atmospheric pressure. There is nothing fortuitous about the stock market movement, and I think I have shown that it cannot to any profitable extent be perverted to the ends of deception. There must be laws governing these things, and it is our present purpose to see if we cannot formulate them usefully. Many years ago George W. Cable said: "What we call chance may be the operation of a law so vast that we only touch its orbit once or twice in a lifetime." There is no need to lose ourselves in the mazes of predestination and coordination, or reduce the Westminster Confession to absurdity by saying that We is just one damned thing after another. But we shall all recognize that order is Heaven's first law, and that organized society, in the Stock Exchange or elsewhere will tend to obey that law even if the unaided individual intelligence is not great enough to grasp it.

Chapter VII - Manipulation and Professional Trading

Readers of preceding chapters may well pause here to take count of how much we have been able to infer, and how much of our inference we have been able to prove, starting on the sound basis of Dow's theory of the stock market. We have satisfied ourselves that he was right when he said that there are in progress three definite movements in the market— the major swing, upwards or downwards; its occasional suspension by a secondary rally or reaction, as the case may be; and the incalculable, and for our purposes largely negligible, daily fluctuation. We can satisfy ourselves from examples that a period of trading within a narrow range—what we have called a "line"— gaining significance as the number of trading days increases, can only mean accumulation or distribution, and that the subsequent price movement shows whether the market has become bare of stocks or saturated with an oversupply.

True to Form

But we have been able to go further than this. From the preceding article alone we see that every major swing is justified by the subsequent condition of the country's general business. It has neither needed nor received manipulation. The market consequently has often seemed to run counter to business conditions, but only for the reason which represents its greatest usefulness. It is then fulfilling its true function of prediction. It is telling us not what business is today but what the future course of business will be. News known is news discounted. What everybody knows has ceased to be a market factor, except in the rare instance of a panic, when the stock market is confessedly taken by surprise.

When these articles appeared in serial form in *Barron's,* the national financial weekly, I included the following inference, based upon the reading of our barometer, on September 18, 1921, the date when the quoted paragraph was written. It appeared on November 5, 1921. It was no guess, but a scientific deduction from sound premises, and correctly announced the change in the main direction of the market.

"There is a pertinent instance and test in the action of the current market. I have been challenged to offer proof of the prediction value of the stock market barometer. With the demoralized condition of European finance, the disaster to the cotton crop, the uncertainties produced by deflation, the unprincipled opportunism of our lawmakers and tax-imposers, all the aftermath of war inflation—unemployment, uneconomic wages in coal mining and railroad-ing—with all these things overhanging the business of the country at the present moment, the stock market has acted as if there were better things in sight. It has been saying that the bear market which set in at the end of October and the beginning of November, 1919, saw its low point on June 20, 1921, at 64.90 for the twenty industrials and 65.52 for the twenty railroad stocks."

A Contemporary Example

At the beginning of the last week of August, 1921, it looked as if the bear market might be resumed by the establishment of new low points in both averages. But remembering that the averages must confirm each other, *The Wall Street Journal* said, on August 25th:

"So far as the averages are concerned, they are far from encouraging to the bull, but they do not yet jointly indicate a definite resumption of the main bear movement."

The railroad stocks were forming a "line" at that time, and after a technical break of a fraction of a point through on the lower side it was resumed, and no new low point, indicating a definite resumption of the main bear movement, was given. On September 21st, after a remarkable continu-ance of the line of probable accumulation in the railroad stocks and a confirmatory rally in the industrials, *The Wall Street Journal's* "Study in the Price Movement" said:

"It is beside the point to say that we are facing a hard winter. The stock market is meaningless if it does not look beyond such, contingencies. It seems to be forecasting a solid foundation for better general business in the spring. It may well be that the stage for a primary bull market is being set."

By that time both the industrials and the railroads had well-developed lines of presumed accumulation, and the former had significantly made a higher point than that of the previous rally. *The Wall Street Journal's* analysis of October 4th said:

"By the well-tried methods of reading the stock market averages, only a decline of eight points in the industrial average, and nine points in the rail-roads, or below the low figures of the main bear movement recorded June

20th, would indicate a resumption of that movement. On the other hand, the railroad stocks alone at present figures would need to advance less than a point to record the repeated new high for both averages which would indicate a primary bull market. The industrials have already recorded that point, and both averages have shown a remarkably clear and distinct line of accumulation which is likely at any time to disclose a market bereft of its floating supply of stocks."

In the last paragraph of this closely reasoned analysis it was said:

"Prices are low because all these bearish factors our critics adduce have been discounted in the prices. When the market is taken by surprise there is a panic, and history records how seldom it is taken by surprise. Today all the bear factors are known, serious as they admittedly are. But the stock market is not trading on what is common knowledge today but upon the sum of expert knowledge applied to conditions as they can be foreseen many months ahead."

Henry H. Rogers and His Critics

Here is the application of our theory, and the reader can judge from the subsequent course of the market the value of the stock market barometer. He can even make the same analysis for himself, given the same major premise and carefully tested reasoning from it.

The professional speculator might well encourage the general belief that he is invulnerable and invincible, even if an ignorant public assumes that the cards are stacked against itself and that the professional knows their backs as well as their faces. Many years ago the late Henry H. Rogers, who was not talking for publication, said to me: "The sensational newspapers, which are always attacking John D. Rockefeller and his associates for their wealth, have put millions into the treasury of the Standard Oil Company. You and I know that we are not omniscient or all-powerful. But, by editorial innuendo and suggestion in cartoons, the people who hold us up to popular envy and hate have created exactly that impression. When everybody who may have to do business with us assumes in advance that we can dictate our own terms, we have an invaluable business asset." The same agitation brought about the dissolution of the Standard Oil into its thirty-three constituent companies. That operation trebled the value of Standard Oil shares, and, incidentally, the price of gasoline. Perhaps these newspaper proprietors were holders of the stock. That was before the era of the Ford car, however, and they may have assumed that it was a public service to make the rich owner of a motor car pay more for his gasoline.

A Speculator's Reasoning

Assumption of an unfair advantage for the professional is absolutely baseless. The reasoning of a professional like Jesse Livermore is merely the reasoning presented in this and preceding articles, backed by a study of general conditions. He said on October 3, 1921, that he had been buying, and, giving him the credence of ordinary courtesy for such a voluntary statement, it is clear that he was trying to shape in his own mind what the investing and speculating public would think at a date as far ahead as he could see.

This is not manipulation. These speculators are not creating any false market or deceptive appearance of activity to lure the public into the game, like the "barker" outside a Midway show. On October 3rd Jesse Livermore was quoted in the columns of *Barron's* as saying that "all market movements are based on sound reasoning. Unless a man can anticipate future events his ability to speculate successfully is limited." And he went on to add: "Speculation is a business. It is neither guesswork nor a gamble. It is hard work and plenty of it."

Dow's Clear Definition

Let us compare this with the words of Dow in *The Wall Street Journal* twenty years before. In the editorial of July 20, 1901, he said:

"The market is not like a balloon plunging hither and thither in the wind. As a whole, it represents a serious, well-considered effort on the part of farsighted and well-informed men to adjust prices to such values as exist or which are expected to exist in the not too remote future. The thought with great operators is not whether a price can be advanced, but whether the value of property which they propose to buy will lead investors and speculators six months hence to take stock at figures from ten to twenty points above present prices."

Observe how the none too deftly expressed thought of Livermore parallels the more perfectly shaped definition of the detached and dispassionate Dow. Bernard M. Baruch, after the war, gave evidence before a Congressional committee as to a market operation by which he had largely profited. He showed in the simplest manner that he had merely analyzed a known cause and foreseen clearly its probable market effect. He showed, what nobody who knows him would question, that he had no "inside information," so called, and that no employee in a Washington department had sold the secrets of his office. Wall Street holds such secrets as of little value. They may give an unfair advantage so far as individual stocks are concerned, but they could be entirely neglected with imperceptible loss, even if the secret were not generally as worthless as the seller of it.

A Good Loser—

What is there that was done by James R. Keene or Jay Gould, by Addison Cammack or other great market figure of the past, which could not have been done, in the fairest way, by men of equal brains and intelligence, willing to pay the price of arduous study for the knowledge necessary to success? What is there that Jesse Livermore or Bernard M. Baruch do which is open to criticism? They pay the seller his price, but they do not accept stock sold "with a string to it." The vendor thinks his reasons for selling as good as theirs for buying what he sells. If he were a jobber in the woolen trade, selling his investment in American Woolen stock, or a banker selling U.S. Steel common on the devastating foreign competition which he thinks he foresees, he would consider his own sources of information better than those of the speculators. They take the same risks that he does. They are often wrong, but they do not whimper about it. I have known many operators of this kind, and I never heard them whine when they lost, or boast greatly when they won.

—and a Bad One

But the little gambler who takes the gutter view of Wall Street pits his wits against trained minds, not merely those of the speculators and the professional traders on the floor of the Stock Exchange, but the minds of men whose business requires them to study business conditions. This kind of gambler is a bad loser, and is often highly articulate. He, or those dependent upon him, is lucky if he receives such a lesson at his first venture that he confines his future relation with Wall Street to denouncing it as a gambling hell. It would be all that if the stock market were made by him or people like him. To the everlasting, credit of the country, we may confidently assume that it is not.

Refusing a Partnership With Jay Gould

Dow, who knew Jay Gould well and enjoyed his confidence as much as any newspaper man of the time, largely because of his incorruptible independence, says in one of his editorials that Gould based his position in the stock market primarily on values. He tested that market with purchases of sufficient stock to show whether there was a public response—whether he had correctly foreseen the public appreciation of values which he thought he had recognized. If the response was not what he expected he would not hesitate to take loss after loss of a point or so, in order to reconsider his position from a detached point of view. Some years ago there was a pathetic derelict in New Street, one of the unlovely fringe of any speculative market, who could truthfully say that he had once been offered a partnership by Jay Gould. I have missed his face in recent years, but not a great many years ago he was a promising young member of the Stock Exchange. His execution of orders on the floor was remarkably good. It is a difficult and exacting task. It requires about that combination of instantaneous judgment and action which would mark a star player in big-league baseball.

To this broker a number of Jay Gould's orders were entrusted. No broker, it is needless to say, saw all of them. Gould was so pleased with the way his business was done that he sent for the young man and offered him a limited partnership. To Mr. Gould's surprise, it was refused. The broker actually said: "Mr. Gould, I have executed a great many of your orders and you seem to me to make more losses than profits. That is not a business I want to share." He could not see that his vision was restricted to only one side of Gould's many-sided activities. Opportunity knocked at his door—tried to kick it in—but the young man showed that he could do only one thing well. His administrative judgment would have been worthless, as indeed it afterwards proved, for he drifted out of the Stock Exchange into New Street and from there, I suppose, into oblivion. Truly, many are called but few are chosen.

An Intelligent Trader

Rare talent of any kind commands great rewards for the reason that it is rare. The amateur who regards the market as a gamble starts wrong. He holds on when he is losing and takes small profits, to his continuing regret, when the market is going his way. The speculators he envies, those he charges with cogging the dice and marking the cards, exactly reverse his process. However strong their conviction may be they run quickly when the market does not agree with them or justify the inferences they have drawn. They may be, as Gould often was, too far ahead of the market. One of the most intelligent men I ever met in Wall Street, not long dead, was a former teacher and a fine classical scholar, whose hobby was collecting rare coins but whose business was speculation. He saved no market turns or broker's commissions by partnership in a Stock Exchange house. He was just a speculator, sitting before a customers' board or near a stock ticker. And yet that man, by judgment, study, nerve tempered by caution and, above all, a readiness to see his error quickly, never made less than $30,000 a year; dying at a good age, leaving a comfortable fortune and a collection of rare coins which brought excellent prices.

He would select his stocks on analyzed value and study the market movement. He would buy with confidence but always well within his means. He would take a two-point loss on a thousand shares of stock without hesitation if the market did not move his way. When that discouragement happened he said that he could not form a correct judgment unless he got out and took an objective view. He had originally about the capital which would have been necessary to pay for the education of a doctor or a lawyer, or to start them in business. He gave his undivided but by no means selfish attention to what he had made his business. He was always long of stocks early in a bull market, and in its last stages he generally made a trip to Europe to add to his collection of coins. He was no solitary instance. I could name others like him. But I am not advising any man to speculate, even if he has the moral stamina to comply with the same exacting requirements. If you have a business that you like, one which keeps you comfortably with a margin for the unforeseen, why speculate in stocks? I don't.

The Dial of the Boiler

Some intelligent and many irrelevant questions have been put since these discussions began, and one of them, which has something of both qualities, disputes the economic necessity for the professional speculator. I am not to be drawn into a discussion of academic economics and still less into one of abstract ethical questions. I am describing the stock market barometer as it is and the great and useful service it performs. It is necessary, therefore, to explain its by no means complicated machinery. It is neither as simple as the crude three-foot tube with its column of mercury nor so complex as the highly perfected aneroid instrument. The question whether I would be willing myself to discharge the functions of a professional speculator is beside the point. We do not need to go back to the formal logic of the Greeks twenty-four centuries ago to know that there can be no argument on matters of taste.

Every bit as important as production is distribution, and distribution of capital is the greatest function of Wall Street. The professional speculator is no more superfluous than the pressure gauge of the steam-heating plant in your cellar. Wall Street is the great financial power house of the country, and it is indispensably necessary to know when the steam pressure is becoming more than the boilers can stand. It is important here to avoid getting our metaphors mixed, but the safety valve will occur to anybody. The stock market is all that and more; and the professional speculator, however ignoble or material his motives may be, is a useful and highly dependable part of that machinery. That he may grow rich in the process is neither here nor there, unless we are to adopt the bolshevist doctrine that personal wealth is wicked. There is another doctrine, held by many who would resent the epithet of bolshevism, which is in any country much more dangerous. It holds wealth, with the power it brings, as a thing for envy and not for emulation; that if we cannot legislate everybody rich it is demonstrably possible to legislate everybody poor. One short way to that end would be to eliminate the Stock Exchange altogether. But so long as it exists it is our business to understand it. Perhaps in so doing we may develop useful suggestions for improving the barometer and extending its usefulness.

Chapter VIII - Mechanics of the Market

It has been shown that, for all practical purposes, manipulation has, and can have, no real effect in the main or primary movement of the stock market, as reflected in the averages. In a primary bull or bear market the actuating forces are above and beyond manipulation. But in the other movements of Dow's theory, a secondary reaction in a bull market or the corresponding secondary rally in a bear market, or in the third movement (the daily fluctuation) which goes on all the time, there is room for manipulation, but only in individual stocks, or in small groups, with a well-recognized leading issue. A raid upon the oil group, or upon the bear account in it, with special attention to Mexican Petroleum, may easily have a striking temporary effect. It shakes out some weak holders or it forces a few bears to cover, as the case may be. This sort of professional "scalping" is often in evidence in a secondary swing—for good reasons.

The Trader and the Gambler

Every primary market, bull or bear, tends to overrun itself. As the traders say, there gets to be too much company on the bull side; or conversely, the "loan crowd" shows that too many shorts are borrowing stocks. There is even a premium for lending them, corresponding to what is called a "backwardation" in London. This is the professional's chance. He buys in a market which is oversold or, with testing sales, he tries out the strength of a market which has been bought not wisely but too well. The small speculator, and more particularly the small gambler, suffers at the hands of the professional. He is a follower of "tips" and "hunches." He has made no real study of the things in which he trades. He takes his information without discrimination at second hand, lacking the ability to distinguish good from bad. He has no business in the market, in the first place, and it could get along very well without him. It is a great mistake to suppose that it is he, or people like him, who keep the Stock Exchange houses in business. Every one of these will tell you that their customers are becoming better informed all the time. Of course if ignorant people will sit in a game requiring expert knowledge, against others who understand the game perfectly, they can blame their losses on no one but themselves. They do, in fact, audibly blame Wall Street. A substantial part of the time of most brokers is consumed in protecting people from themselves. It is a thankless job. A fool and his money are soon parted.

Giving a Dog a Bad Name

But it must be obvious that this is no part of the main current of speculation. It bears about the same relation to that current that the daily fluctuation does to the primary market movement. There are, of course, varying degrees of knowledge, but it is a vital mistake to suppose that speculation in stocks (for the rise at least) is a sort of gamble in which no one can win unless there is an equivalent loss by somebody else. There need be no such loss in a bull market. The weak holders who are shaken out in the secondary reactions miss a part of their profits; and, in the culmination of such a movement, a great many people who have lost sight of values and are buying on possibilities only, with the latent hope that they may unload on somebody more covetous than themselves, are apt to get hurt.

So far as blaming Wall Street is concerned, it seems to have become a case of giving a dog a bad name and hanging him. The defaulting bank employee usually pleads something of the kind. All his transactions and contracts are matters of record; but how seldom the court asks him for an exact statement of his speculative account. He says nothing about fast women and slow horses, or the many other devious ways of spending other people's money. He pleads that he was "robbed in Wall Street," and sentimental people take him back to their hearts, registering horror at the temptations of the wicked financial district, whose simplest functions they have not been at the pains to understand.

A small and unsuccessful speculator, chagrined at his inability to make money in the stock market but failing to understand the real reason, picks up a vocabulary of technical phrases which is apt to delude people who know even less of the stock market than himself. He is fond of denouncing the "specialist" and the "floor trader." He classes them with the croupiers of a gambling house, and says that they are not even as respectable as that because their dealer's chance is extortionately larger. To take the floor trader first, it may be pointed out that his small but real advantage only stands him in good stead against the novice who is trying to snatch quick profits in an active market by the merest guessing. No competent broker encourages the outsider to do anything of the kind, and the brokers of my fairly exhaustive acquaintance in Wall Street do their best to get rid of a customer who is apt to be a liability rather than an asset, and is always a nuisance.

The Floor Trader and the Market Turn

There is no intention here to write a textbook on the practice of Wall Street and the Stock Exchange. There are excellent books covering that field. All that is necessary is to make sufficiently clear the mechanics of our barometer, and especially those things which may be assumed, rightly or wrongly, to influence it. It is sufficient to say, therefore, that a "floor trader" is necessarily a member of the Stock Exchange, and is usually a partner in a brokerage house. He unaffectedly operates for himself. He pays himself no commission, and he is at an advantage over the outside speculator in the matter of the market turn, which is, of course, the difference between the bid and asked price in the market. The more active the stock the closer this turn is, but it may be averaged at a quarter of one percent. Assuming that the price of U.S. Steel common is 90 1/4 bid and 90 1/2 asked, the customer who gives an order to sell cannot expect to get better than 90 1/4, while, if he wishes to buy, he must pay 90 1/2. The floor trader can often save this turn or part of it for himself—not, of course, against a customer. He may be able to deal at 90 3/8 or even to sell at the asked price. Whatever he does has its effect in the daily fluctuation. In practice it means that the floor trader can afford to trade for a quick turn where the outsider cannot. In daily custom the trader goes home at the close with his book even, not hesitating to take an occasional loss, or glad to come out even.

"Bucketing"

It is obvious then that the floor trader, snatching a turn of a point or so, has an advantage. If the customer tried to do it he would have the broker's commissions of a legal eighth percent each way against him, with the market turn of a quarter percent; so that, as a mere gamble, he would be betting heavy odds on an even-money chance. A "bucket shop" would encourage him to do that, because the keeper of such an establishment works on the theory of new customers all the time, fleecing them as thoroughly as possible while he has the chance. None of his orders is really executed in the stock market; so that he himself pockets this extortionate dealer's chance. But we are considering the Stock Exchange itself, and its speculative market as a trade barometer. Bucketing is no part of the Stock Exchange's business, and the police can stop it elsewhere—if they choose.

Old and Satisfied Customers

Commission both ways and the market turn do not amount to much if the customer is buying on values, with ample margin, or with the ability to pay for his stock outright, together with the tested belief that the stock he has bought bids fair to look attractive at much higher figures. He is the sort of customer the Stock Exchange houses strive to serve. A house which was in continuous business since 1870 has recently changed its name. It had at least one customer who had been on the books for fifty years, and many for twenty years and longer. This does not look as if the outsider always lost money in Wall Street, or as if the conditions of business made losses inevitable.

A brokerage house, like any other business, works to get new clients all the time, exactly as a paper or magazine works to get new subscribers. But the experienced broker will tell you that while advertising methods will bring the customers, nothing but disinterested service will keep them. I have often noticed that the really successful man in Wall Street is curiously inarticulate. Experience has taught him to keep his tongue between his teeth, and he is not at all communicative. The unsuccessful seem to be unable to keep their losses to themselves, in most cases, and it is usually found that they are thus articulate from a radical defect in character. They habitually do too much talking and too little thinking.

No Apology Offered or Required

This is not an apology for the stock market. Our old friend, our unwilling stepfather, George III, was not renowned for his wit. But when he was offered the dedication of Bishop Watson's celebrated *Apology for the Bible* he asked if the Bible needed an apology? Let us, therefore, content ourselves with merely explaining that part of the mechanism of the stock market which should be understood for a full comprehension of the nature and usefulness of the barometer of the country's business.

"Specialists" in particular stocks, corresponding in a way to the "jobber," or more nearly the "dealer" in the London Stock Exchange, the brokers on the floor who limit their transactions to one or two active issues and are entrusted with orders in those issues by other brokerage houses, are little understood and much vilified. It is falsely assumed that they habitually, or at least occasionally, abuse their confidential position. The specialist has "stop-loss" selling orders in a number of stocks at a point or so below the market price, from brokers instructed to limit their customers' losses in the event of an unexpected decline. It is suggested that the specialist, for his own advantage, brings about that decline. The answer is that even the suspicion of such dealing would cost him his business and his reputation. It recently cost a member his seat on the Exchange, the only instance I recall. Transactions on the floor are by word of mouth, without the passage of a written contract or even the presence of witnesses. The honor of the parties is absolute, and I can hardly recall a case where it was called in question. There must necessarily be occasional misunderstandings, but these are referred for adjustment in the usual way. The specialist could not stay in business if he did not have the interests of the brokers who employ him as much at heart as any other agent in a like position. His very living and standing in business depend upon it.

Professional Trader's Limited Influence

What is the influence of the active bear trader on the averages? It is negligible so far as the major movement is concerned, a small factor in the secondary swings and mainly influential, at times, in particular stocks in the least considerable movement, the daily fluctuation. Such operations do not affect our barometer in any degree worth serious consideration. Remember the character of the twenty railroad stocks and the twenty industrials used in the two averages. Every one of them complies with the stringent listing requirements of the N.Y. Stock Exchange. Each company concerned publishes the fullest possible figures of its operation, at frequent intervals. There are no "inside secrets," of market value, which could by any possibility affect more than a single stock out of forty.

It may be that one of them unexpectedly passes or increases its dividend. The effect upon that particular stock, if there is any real surprise in the matter (which is highly doubtful), is negligible when spread over the other nineteen stocks of the same group. I do not recall any useful illustrative instance; but suppose unexpected dividend action produced a fluctuation of ten points. It would only make a daily difference in the average of half a point, which would be almost instantly recovered if the dividend action presaged no broad general change in business conditions. If there had been any such change we may be entirely sure that it would have already been reflected in the stock market, which would know far more about it than that, or any board of directors.

Short Selling Necessary and Useful

A discussion on the morality of short selling would be utterly out of place here. It is true that the bear cannot profit except where another loses, while the bull at the worst reaps a profit which another man might perhaps have made if he had been attending strictly to his business. But every free market for anything is helped far more than hurt by traders willing to sell short. If, indeed, there were not this liberty the result would be a most dangerous market, liable to an unsupported panic break at any stage of its progress. Voltaire said that if there had not been a God it would have been necessary to invent one. It must have been long ago, in the days when what afterward became the London Stock Exchange did its business in Jordan's Coffee House off Cornhill, that bear selling was invented. It soon became a patent necessity; and it is curious that some of the most serious breaks in the London market have occurred, not in the wildly speculative securities, but in bank stocks, where the English law prohibits short selling. It was unsupported pressure in some bank stocks which helped to make the Baring crisis of 1890 so serious. There is no such valuable support for a falling market as the uncovered bear account. When it is absent, as in this particular instance, nothing but a bankers' combination hastily improvised can check the devastating decline. As the London Stock Exchange was reorganized in 1922 on its old basis, without further government meddling I and regulation, Parliament will repeal this law and substitute as a protection to bank stocks, that complete and constant publicity which is always the public's best safeguard.

Protection of Listing Requirements

When Dow wrote, twenty years ago, of speculation generally, and incidentally of his theory of the market movement, some of the industrial stocks, included in the average and traded in freely on the floor of the Stock Exchange, were in what was then called the unlisted department. It would be difficult to imagine *The Wall Street Journal* speaking today of one of the industrials in the Dow-Jones average as a blind pool. But it did not hesitate to apply that epithet, editorially, to the American Sugar of Henry O. Havemeyer's day. The elimination of the N.Y. Stock Exchange's unlisted department is one of the most creditable instances of reform from within. It was bitterly opposed by some conservative members of the Exchange, mainly those who profited largely by that vicious vested interest. An ex-president of that institution, now dead, took upon himself to berate me loudly, in the presence of his customers, for advocating that eminently necessary reform. He said that such agitators were driving business away from the Wall Street in which they earned their living. He threw out of his office the newspaper and the financial news service with which I was and am connected.

But his own customers made him reinstate both, with humiliating celerity. American Sugar and Amalgamated Copper and the other formerly unlisted securities are still dealt in on the floor of the Exchange. Those companies saw that they laid their management under the gravest suspicion by a refusal to comply with the terms of publicity so wholesomely exacted from reputable companies. Stock Exchange houses are naturally inclined to look askance at reforms advocated from outside. But I have never heard one of them even suggest the restoration of the unlisted department.

Federal Incorporation

It was said in an earlier discussion that something further might be done for the protection of the public, without the enactment of any of these "blue-sky" laws which only embarrass honest enterprise without seriously impeding the operations of the crook. In this discussion I can briefly set forth the sane and successful method which protects the speculator and investor in Great Britain. Under what is there called the Companies (Consolidation) Act of 1908 the London Stock Exchange is enabled to deal in any security the moment it is registered at Somerset House, London. That registration cannot be made until the fullest possible disclosure of purposes, contracts, commissions and everything else has been made. However adventurous the purposes of the company may be, the speculator knows all about them from the start. After that, under this statute, the old common-law rule of *caveat emptor* —let the buyer beware—prevails. It is properly held that the buyer can protect himself, as he should, when he can find out all about the property, its origin and its present conduct, for the fee of a shilling, at Somerset House.

There would doubtless be all sorts of ignorant opposition to Federal incorporation of this kind, with the law enforced and the public protected through limitation in the use of the mails. But I am convinced that it might well be done, and should, of course, be done in a strictly non-partisan spirit.

To the utmost of its ability the N.Y. Stock Exchange protects its members and their customers. But the N.Y. Curb Market Association is simply an unlisted department in itself. I have no reason to believe that its government is not capable and honest, and I have not a word to say against its membership. But sooner or later it is calculated to prove a source of danger an scandal. If any of its members imagine that they have something to lose, in the setting forth of the absolute and original facts about everything in which they deal, they are making exactly the same mistake that ill-advised members of the N.Y. Stock Exchange made when they shirked the disagreeable task of compelling a number of industrial corporations to comply with the listing requirements, on pain of being stricken from the list.

Real Reform from Within

Let me disclaim, however, the intention of crusading, or any bent toward that blatant and ignorant "reform" which has made such costly experiments in recent years. In my experience of it the standards of the Stock Exchange have steadily improved, to the permanent advantage of the investor and of the small speculator, who is, after all, only an investor in embryo. Practices were customary in Dow's day which would not be tolerated now. In any future bull market manipulation on the scale of James R. Keene, when he distributed Amalgamated Copper, would be impracticable, for the reason that the publicity now required by the Stock Exchange, in the accounts of such a company, would make it impossible to persuade the most reckless private speculator that the prospects of the new combination made it worth four times its book value, on any expert test. Even in those days "wash sales" were largely a figment of the public imagination, and "matched orders" were declined by any brokerage house of repute if their nature was suspected. The Stock Exchange rule against fictitious transactions is obeyed in spirit and in word. It was not a mere letter even in those days, whatever it might have been forty years ago, when the infant giant of American industry was only awakening to consciousness of his strength.

Chapter IX - "Water" in the barometer

Every effort has been made to simplify these discussions. They have been offered with the most stringent exclusion of extraneous matter. In serial form they aroused much criticism and comment, some of it illuminating and helpful. But old preconceptions and prejudices still survive. One critic, whose scanty knowledge of the subject appears to have been derived from the reading of perhaps two of these articles, says:

"How can we trust your barometer if we cannot trust the stocks which the Stock Exchange deals in? You have said nothing about overcapitalization. What about water?"

Watered Labor

Water is more unpopular than ever in the U.S. just now. But the financial center of the U.S., with the business of the country in view, is far more concerned about watered labor than watered capital. There is only one way to squeeze the water out of labor—the factory or apartment house which cost a million dollars to build and represents only $500,000 of real value. That way is by bankruptcy. Of the apartment houses that were built in New York, during a period of high wages and "ca' canny" which set in long before the war, very few have not passed through a stage of financial reorganization, due to watered labor in construction, long before rents began to advance. The stock market has a short and simple method of dealing with water in stocks. It exists for the purpose of squeezing that water out. The process does not involve a receivership.

The very word "water" begs the question. You may call the capitalization of an industrial flotation "water" because you do not see the potential values of a great creative organization. But with justice, and better knowledge, the late J. P. Morgan might have called that capitalization intelligently anticipated growth. Whatever it may be—and I shall give an example from the most striking instance, the capitalization of the U.S. Steel Corporation —the stock market is forever adjusting prices to values. The water soon evaporates.

Squeezing Out the Water

To recapitulate, we are studying the stock market barometer, having established the fact of its known and orderly movements—the long primary swing, the secondary reaction or rally, and the daily fluctuation; and to do this we are taking the averages of two groups of stocks—twenty active industrials and twenty active railroads. All adjustments of the prices of these stocks individually must primarily be based upon values. For all practical purposes the Stock Exchange is an open market, and the business of such a market to adjust conflicting estimates to a common basis, which is expressed in the price. By manipulation, James R. Keene advanced the price of Amalgamated Copper twenty years ago to one hundred and thirty, and obviously the group of financiers which offered the stock at par originally, without success, assumed one hundred as value for it. The stock market does not make its adjustments in a day. But, over a period which seems brief in retrospect, it knocked one hundred points off the highest figure Amalgamated Copper attained in a general bull market.

This is the business of the stock market. It has to consider both basic values and prospects. At the close of a major downward movement, a primary bear market, prices will have passed below the line of values. The causes of the liquidation will have been so serious that people have been compelled to realize their holdings at less than their normal worth; less, indeed, than their book value—the worth of the company's assets, that is, irrespective of productive capacity and good will. The prices of the standard stocks will be injuriously affected by the prices of "cats and dogs" dealt in on the Curb market, many of them of such a character that any bank would refuse them as collateral in its loans. When the banks are compelled to call loans made on Stock Exchange securities, the stocks of tested worth, of properties competently and reputably managed, will be the first to suffer because it is those stocks which are pledged in bank loans. The constantly recruited Curb group is highly speculative, but trading there is always limited, and indeed safeguarded, by the large margin which is necessary to carry Curb stocks.

Stock Profits and Income Tax

Conversely, a bull market starts with stocks much below their real value, certain to be helped in anticipation by the general improvement in the country's business which the stock market foresees and discounts. In the long advance values will be gradually overtaken, and toward the close of the advance an uninformed public, incapable of recognizing the bargains which were offering when the movement started, is buying on prospects only. Experienced traders in Wall Street say that when the elevator boy and the shoeblack are asking for bull tips on the market it is time to sell and go fishing. When I sailed for Europe early in October, 1919, to report on financial conditions in Britain and Germany, the market was in the last sanguine stage of a long bull movement. The inflation bull argument then was most curious. It was that the people who had large profits would not sell, and could not sell, because in turning those paper profits into cash they would show such a large earning of income for the year that the tax-gatherer would take a prohibitive share of the profits. We analyzed this fallacy in the smoking saloon of the *Mauretania,* and at least some of the businessmen on board concluded to divide up with Uncle Sam. The argument was preposterous in itself, because it pictured the most vulnerable kind of bull account that it would be possible to conceive. It was glaringly up to be shot at, and the poorest marksman could fill it full of holes. Rough seas stove in five of the *Mauretania's* lifeboats, and put the wireless apparatus out of commission for the last three days of that voyage. When we arrived at Cherbourg we learned that the stock market itself had begun to free the bulls of stocks from the embarrassment of paying excessive income tax. They had not much to worry about in that respect by the end of the year, for the paper profits had been rapidly extinguished.

Well-Distributed Holdings

There is no way of permanently holding up artificial prices created by an overbought market. One great protection to the public is in widely distributed stock ownership. When a single group in Wall Street owns practically all of the stock in a property like Stutz Motor, that group can call the market price anything it chooses. It will not be the "market" price because there will be no real market. Abraham Lincoln pointed out long ago that you could not talk five legs onto a dog by renaming its tail. All the stocks in the average have shared in the wide and healthy distribution of securities. The average holding of Pennsylvania (which has the greatest capitalization of any of the railroads in our average) or of the five and a half million shares of U.S. Steel common is nothing near one hundred shares for each holder. So far as the public is concerned, there is, indeed, safety in numbers.

"Valuation" and Market Prices

To the inquirer quoted at the beginning of this article, who asks, "What about water?" we may answer, well, what about it? He cannot show us any water in the averages. We may go further and tell him that he cannot show us any water, at prices and not at the nominal par, in the whole Stock Exchange list. For the railroads, no valuation which could be instituted by Congress and carried out by a committee of the Interstate Commerce Commission could begin to compare with the market prices of the securities themselves, taken in a normal month of a normal year, with the prices not inflated on overestimated prospects or deflated by forced liquidation, brought about to protect unsalable securities and warehouse receipts not associated with the railroads or the standard industrial companies in any way.

Every scrap of intelligence and knowledge available, uninfluenced in any real degree by manipulation, has been brought to bear in the adjustment of the stock market prices. Reproduction value, real estate value, franchises, right of way, good will—everything else— have been brought into the free-market estimate in a way which no valuation committee appointed by Congress could ever attain. The Interstate Commerce Commission's valuation of a railroad has merely historical worth—if it has any. As a true estimate of the property, if the method of fixing it were commonly just, it is out of date the moment it is printed, or, indeed, months before it is printed. But the Stock Exchange price records the value from day to day, from month to month, from year to year, from bull market to bear market, from one of Jevons's cycle dates to another; and the bankers of America and any other civilized country accept that valuation and advance real money on it, without reference to the arbitrary estimate of the Interstate Commerce Commission.

The Fetish of Watered Stock

It is astonishing to what depths of foolishness the fetish of watered stock has carried this country. The capitalization in stocks and bonds of its railroads, alleged to represent water, is not one-fifth that of the railroads of the British Islands, mile for mile. It is less per mile than that of any European country or of any government or privately owned railroad in Britain's self-governing colonies. I am not afraid to go on record with the statement that the American railroads are uneconomically undercapitalized, on their real value. The charge of watered stock made against the listed industrial corporations is equally absurd. The stock market had far more than squeezed out the water in that capitalization at the Stock Exchange prices current in 1921. It had squeezed blood.

As this is written, U.S. Steel common is selling under $80 a share. But stringent analysis of an industrial corporation offering the most exhaustive figures of any like company in the world gives a book value to the common stock of $261 a share. In the twenty years of its history it has put upwards of a billion dollars into the property in new construction, and so little is this watered in the capital that this new investment out of earnings is represented in property account by only $275,000,000. The quick assets, largely cash, are over $600,000,000 alone, something like $120 a share with the whole concern scrapped. Where is the water? A common stock capital of $550,000,000 looks large, but it is only relatively large. Was not Morgan right if he called this intelligently anticipated growth? If his spirit could revisit the pale glimpses of the moon, surely he would be astonished at his own moderation.

And yet the distribution of the U.S. Steel common and preferred stocks, made in the major swing of a great bull market, was brought about largely by the most stupendous manipulation the market ever saw, under the direction of the late James R. Keene. And what was the end of that manipulation? It was to sell the common stock at fifty and the preferred stock at par. If the people who bought at those prices put the stock away after paying for it, would they have anything to regret even at the low market prices of August, 1921, attained after a major bear swing of unusually long duration?

Buying on Values

Probably some one will charge me with writing a bull argument about Steel common, because I set this simple illustration before the public. There again we have the inveterate prejudice against Wall Street. The facts I have stated are of record, accessible to anybody, perfectly well known to some of the people at least who were selling Steel common in 1921. But they were selling the stock because they needed the money, at a time when most of us needed money. When the Rothschild of the days of Waterloo, a week before the result of that battle was known, was buying British consols at fifty-four, a friend asked him how he could buy with such confidence on an outlook so uncertain. He said that if the outlook were certain consols would not be selling at fifty-four. He knew that with that uncertainty they must necessarily be selling below their value. Everybody needed money at the same time, and he was one of the few people who had any. I suppose no one will ever know how Russell Sage did it, but he could lay his hands upon more real money in a panic than anybody in Wall Street. He believed in quick and liquid assets, short-time paper maturing all the time, call loans and deposits—everything which could be turned into cash, not to hoard but to buy freely when people who had lost sight of values were selling.

A Story of Russell Sage

All sorts of stories are told of Russell Sage and his extraordinary frugality. That is not exactly the word I would use; nor would I call it miserliness, for he was anything but a miser. I remember the last time I ever saw him, when I was a young reporter, or at least a younger reporter. I was trying to find out something about a railroad property in which he was dominant with another financier of nation wide notoriety, or reputation. Lying is a word which is seldom used (or needed) in Wall Street, and it would be better to say that the other financier had given me information calculated to let me deceive myself if I was not exceptionally wide-awake. With the idea, therefore, of seeing if Mr. Sage's terminological inexactitude would differ from his comrade's, with enough significance to enable me to deduce something from the points upon which the two fairy tales did not agree, I went over to see Sage, who was always accessible to the newspaper men.

He greeted me in the most friendly way, as indeed he did anybody whose visit had nothing to do with money. I put my question and he rapidly changed the subject. He said: "Do you know anything about suspenders?" I was exasperated, but I replied modestly that I did not know any more about them than any other wearer. "What do you think of these?" said Uncle Russell, handing me over a pair certainly inferior to those worn by reporters, who are not, or certainly were not at that time, given to undue extravagance in such an article of attire. "What about them?" I asked. "Well, what do you think of them?" said Sage; "I gave thirty-five cents for those." Perhaps I was a little vindictive, having failed to secure even the poor information I had come to seek. I said: "You were robbed. You can get better in Hester Street for a quarter." Sage looked at me doubtfully. "I don't believe it," he said. But he was really troubled. It was not the difference of ten cents, and I would not have sworn to the Hester Street quotation. It was the principle of the thing. His judgment of values had been impugned.

Values and Averages

And there you have it. The things in which Russell Sage dealt had value. He had to know those values, and it was by knowing them when they had ceased to be apparent to other people that he died worth more than $70,000-,000. The stock market barometer shows present and prospective values. It is necessary in reading it to judge whether a long movement has carried the average prices below that line or above it. In looking back over the various analyses of the stock market as a guide to general business, published in *The Wall Street Journal* since Dow died, at the end of 1902, I find a typical instance of the application of the averages which may seem remarkable to the reader, although I regard it as the merest common sense. There is no one so unpopular as the man who is always telling you that he "told you so," but the illustration is impersonal.

A Cautious but Correct Forecast

No severer test could be taken than the interpretation of the averages in what might almost be called the transition period between a bear and a bull market. The bear market which developed from September, 1902, saw its low points in the September of the following year, and it is weeks or even months afterwards before the change in the major swing can be definitely asserted. But on December 5, 1903, *The Wall Street Journal,* after a review of the fundamentally sound tendency of business in then recent years, said:

"Considering the extraordinary advance in wealth of the U.S. during that period, considering that railroad mileage has not increased in anything like the ratio of increase in surplus earnings, and finally considering that the ratio of increase in surplus earnings available for dividends has been at all times in excess of the rise in market prices and at the present time shows a larger percentage on market price than at any time since the former boom started, the question may well be asked whether the decline in stocks has not culminated. There is at least some evidence in favor of an affirmative answer to *that* question."

A Bull Market Confirmed

It would be easy to say that such an opinion could have been given without the help of the averages, but it was given with the price movement clearly in view and at a time when there was an easy possibility that the main bear movement might be resumed. It correctly foresaw the bull market, allowing for the caution necessary in such a prediction and, indeed, for the fact that analysis of the market movement was still in its infancy. The bull market then foreseen ran throughout 1904, and can be said to have terminated only in January, 1907. But some nine months after this editorial analysis of the business situation, judged by the averages, was written, *The Wall Street Journal* tackled the almost equally difficult question of whether the bull market then getting into full swing might be expected to continue. Remember that the advance had been running with moderate but increasing strength for twelve months, which would allow for at least some discounting in values. On September 17, 1904, *The Wall Street Journal* said:

"There is apparently nothing in sight to lead one to believe that railroad values are not on the whole maintaining their high position, and that as time goes on this will bring a further appreciation of prices. Much will depend on the coming winter, which will at all events bring a clear indication of the general trend of values. In the long run values make prices. It is safe to say that if present values are maintained, present prices are not on an average high enough.

"It must further be remembered that the continued increase in the production of gold is a most powerful factor, which cannot fail to be felt in the future as making for higher prices of securities other than those of fixed yield."

A Vindication of the Theory

Note carefully that last line. We have satisfied ourselves that bonds held for fixed income decline when the cost of living rises, and more gold means that the gold dollar will buy less because gold is the world's accepted standard of value. But it stimulates speculation, and the stock market had seen this in 1904, when this was written, even if the houses with bonds to sell thought it rather "unclubby" to say anything which would disturb their business. Of course, these quotations are far from dogmatic, because Dow's Theory was only beginning to be understood. We shall see as the years went on that the theory allowed for much more explicit statements of the market's condition and its prospects. It is sufficient to record how soon the stock market barometer proved its usefulness when Dow's sound method of reading it had been set forth.

Chapter X – "A Little Cloud Out of the Sea – Like a Man's Hand" - 1906

In discussions such as these it is necessary to anticipate objections and explain apparent discrepancies. There is nothing more deceptively fascinating than a hypothesis which holds together too well. Out of that sort of theory much obstinate dogma arises, which seems able to continue its existence after time has proved the theory unsound or inadequate. We have established what is called Dow's theory of the price movement—the major swing, the secondary reaction or rally, and the daily fluctuation—and out of it have been able to evolve a working method of reading the stock market barometer so constituted. But we are to guard ourselves against being too cocksure, and to recognize that while there is no rule without an exception, any exception should prove the rule.

The San Francisco Earthquake

The year 1906 presents an interesting problem in this way. It is the problem of an arrested main bull movement or an accentuated secondary reaction, according to the way you look at it. It has been said that major bull markets and bear markets alike tend to overrun themselves. If the stock market were omniscient it would protect itself against this over-inflation or over-liquidation, as it automatically protects itself against everything which it can possibly foresee. But we must concede that, even when we have allowed for the further established fact that the stock market represents the sum of all available knowledge about the conditions of business and the influences which affect business, it cannot protect itself against what it cannot foresee. It could not foresee the San Francisco earthquake of April 18, 1906, or the subsequent devastating fire.

Tactful to Call it a Fire

If you want to make yourself popular with that somewhat strident individual, the California "native son," you will not even allude to the San Francisco earthquake. In California it is considered bad manners to do anything of the sort. All that is conceded there is the fire. For our purpose the earthquake admits of no argument. Chronic California boosters, however, cannot permit a general impression that there might be, for instance, another earthquake in San Francisco as bad as the last. A fire, on the other hand, might occur to any city, anywhere, without detracting from those natural advantages of climate and other things of which California is so proud. There is nothing more charming than the naivete of the Los Angeles native, who says "It is a fine day, if I say so myself." But earthquakes are different. They put the Pacific coast in a class by itself, and a class not at all to the taste of the inhabitants. As Beau Brummell, the great English dandy of the early years of last century, said: "A hole may be the result of an accident which could happen to any gentleman, but a darn is pre-meditated poverty."

seems to have analyzed his belief in it in any searching way. The general impression is that there is "something in" the idea; that if it is not proved true it should be true; that the world's panic dates themselves indicate a striking degree of periodicity; that, given such periodicity in the past, we may anticipate something like it in the future; that men will always be as stupid in the conduct of their own business as they seem to have been when judged by the records of history.

Basis of the Cycle Theory

Probably this unwillingness to analyze the panic theory arises from the fact that in the eighteenth century, according to Jevons, there were exactly ten noteworthy crises at an average of ten years apart. I am content to waive the one Jevons omitted—that of 1715, when the Scots invaded England—because there were not enough spots on the sun in that year to establish his daring theory of the relation between the two phenomena. We may note that Jevons gave 1793 and 1804-5 as crisis years, while it is of record that our own first panic of the nineteenth century was consequent upon the British capture of the city of Washington in 1814—an event which no cycle could have predicted, unless we are to assume that the cycle theory could have predicted the late war. But, counting 1814, and what Dow calls the "near approach to a crisis" in 1819, there were ten American crises in the nineteenth century.

Let us see how the cyclist—if that is the correct word—approaches the subject. The ten-year interval between the British crisis of 1804-5 and our own of 1814 might stimulate him at first. And the really serious and nation wide crises of 1837 and 1857 would give him a great deal of confidence. He would recall the ten-year intervals of Jevons, and that we had up to 1837 recorded four crises of sorts, in four decades of the new century. We did not greatly share the panic in Europe in 1847, although it was sufficiently serious there to impress itself upon American memory. But when the cycle enthusiast found a real panic in 1857, he cried "Aha! We have now discovered the secret. There is a twenty-year cycle, with a big crisis at each end, and a little crisis in the middle. We may now confidently set about humoring the facts to fit this beautiful theory."

Misfitting Dates

On that showing there should have been another first-class panic, with nation wide consequences, in 1877. But apparently the machinery slipped a cog, for the panic came in 1873. From the devastating folly of overtrading on a greenback basis, it would have come in 1872 but for the accident that we had in that year an enormous wheat crop, which brought splendid prices in the world market because of the almost total crop failure in Russia. Here, then, was a contraction of the interval between great crises. The twenty-year theory was deflated to sixteen, and it is hard to derive much consolation from the fact that the Overend-Gurney failure in London in 1866 had marked a date conveniently between the two great crises. The London panic of 1866 was accompanied by a heavy fall in prices in our Stock Exchange. In April of that year there was a corner in Michigan Southern and rampant speculation. The truthful but cautious Dow says that the relapse from this "was rather more than normal."

But the three panic years 1873, 1884 and 1893 did something to revive the confidence of the ten and twenty-year theorists. The first and the last were crises of almost world wide magnitude and equally far-reaching consequences. Our cyclists said: "That slipup in the reduction to sixteen years for the interval between crises occurring in 1857 and 1873 was merely fortuitous, or at least we shall be able to explain it satisfactorily when we have deduced only a little more about the laws which govern these things." And the twenty-year cyclists prophesied, saying: "There are twenty years between 1873 and 1893. Our barometer is getting into shape. There will be a minor crisis round about 1903 and a major panic in 1913, or not later than 1914."

Lost in Transit

What is the use of the theory, indeed, unless it can be made the basis for at least as much prophecy as that? But between 1893 and 1907 we have an interval of fourteen years. Has the twenty-year period contracted, or the ten-year period expanded, to fourteen years? Is there any dependable periodicity about the thing? We see that there was not the slightest reason for any crisis in the years presumably anticipated by the cycle theorist—1903 or 1913. Indeed, the volume of the world's speculative business was not large enough to make a crisis in those years. It is reasonably certain that a smash cannot be brought about unless an edifice of speculation has been constructed sufficiently high to make a noise when it topples over. What is the value of all this as a forecast for business? I cannot see that it has any. The theory has to make so many concessions—takes so much humoring, in fact—that it ceases to have more than a value for record. We see that the sweeping conclusions based upon the cycle assumption had to be changed again and again. Does much that is really useful remain? I am anything but a sceptic; but this whole method of playing the cycles looks to me absurdly like cheating yourself at solitaire. I can understand stringent rules, arbitrary rules, unreasonable rules, in any game. But my mind fails to grasp a game where you change the rules as you go along.

Are They Equal?

And what becomes of that imposing premise that "action and reaction are equal?" Are they? There is little real evidence to prove the assumption, in recorded human affairs. Of course the holders of that theory may respond, "Well, if they are not equal they ought to be." I cannot even see why they ought to be. Certainly, holding a Christian faith in the perfectibility of human nature, I do not see why crises should not be eliminated altogether. It is easy to see how the periods between them at least seem to have grown longer. The interval between 1893 and 1907 was fourteen years, and 1920 was no panic year.

THE STOCK MARKET BAROMETER - 1922

Unless we are to force the construction of what constitutes a panic until we actually distort it, we can hardly regard the deflation liquidation of 1920 as a typical crisis. It could not begin to compare with the damaging effects of 1893, 1873, 1857, or 1837. It had none of the earmarks of a panic year. I dare say I shall believe, in five years' time that the drastic contraction and deflation were about the best thing that could have happened to us. They should certainly discount all sorts of trouble in the future.

A Business Pathology Needed

There must be some sort of scientific pathology of business affairs, or perhaps it might be better to call it morbid psychology. I have suggested in another chapter how utterly inadequate the records of history are in the vital matter of commerce and all that contributes to it. But we are beginning to acquire a scientific knowledge of the symptoms of the diseases which afflict it. In this respect we have probably made more advance in the past quarter of a century than in all the years since Carthage sold the purple weaves of Tyre to Rome. We may well hope that we are developing a scientific method of diagnosing the symptoms of business disease. There was no such method in 1893, because there were no such records as we have today.

But why need we assume that once every ten years or twenty years, or any other period, the most intelligent part of mankind loses its head and forgets all the lessons of the past? One thing is certain about a panic. It could never occur if it were foreseen. Are we not working toward a sum of knowledge and an accuracy of analysis which will, in a sufficiently safe measure, foresee all but the non-insurable risks—"the act of God and the King's enemies?"

The Federal Reserve Safeguard

I can see a great deal too much politics, and many defects, in the Federal Reserve banking system. But under that system it is hard to imagine a set of conditions which would force the country to resort once more to clearing-house certificates, as it did in 1907 and 1893. It would pass the wit of man to devise a perfect banking system; and what would seem perfect to one would appear utterly inadequate to another. But the progress from the old national banking system to the Federal Reserve system represents the most tremendous stride in business practice which the country has ever seen. Is not the Reserve system itself an entirely new factor for the cycle theorist to consider?

It must not be assumed for a moment that possible crises in the future may be dismissed from consideration. On the contrary, they are certain to come. But may we not hope that, with fuller knowledge, they will be at least in part anticipated and, in their most dangerous effects, radically mitigated?

Teaching the Teacher

If these studies have shown the man who takes an intelligent, even if not a financial interest in Wall Street, that knowledge will protect him there as it will anywhere else, the educational design has been largely accomplished. Certainly one of the desirable educative services of this series has been to show the writer how much there was about the stock market movement which he had never before formulated to himself in any useful fashion. The way to get at the essence of such a proposition is pragmatic—to live with it from day to day. The stock market problem, considered in the light of Dow's Theory, is essentially simple. It can be set forth in a thoroughly useful way, provided only that the teacher is neither a crank nor a quack, a gambler or a crook. Harvard University is performing a greatly needed service in putting out tabulations and index charts on general business conditions which are above suspicion. The compilers have not tied themselves down to dangerous assumptions. They are not lashed to an assumed "medial line" of national wealth with a constant upward tendency at the same rate of speed in good times or bad, which loses its certainty in face of the grim facts of war, and hysterically changes its course.

Does the Physical Law Apply?

Such a system as that of Harvard University is not committed to the proposition that in human affairs action and reaction are equal. That is a fine-sounding phrase, but it should require incalculably more evidence than has yet been adduced to persuade us to adapt a law of physics to something so unstable and elusive as human nature itself. Among the many things which our stock market averages prove, one stands out clearly. It is that so far as the price movement is concerned action and reaction are not equal. We do not have an instance of a bull market offset in the extent of its advance by an exactly corresponding decline in a bear market. And if this is true, as it demonstrably is, about the extent of the price movement in any given major swing, it is still more true about the time consumed. We have seen that bull markets are, as a rule, of materially longer duration than bear markets. There is no automatically balancing equation there. I do not believe there is such an equation in human affairs anywhere. Certainly there is none recorded in history. I am compelled to rely upon others for tabular figure compilations of all kinds, and do not profess to have used my modest razor for the cutting of any of these tables of stone. But in all the study of figures prepared for use in my profession, I have been unable to find a balance of action and reaction.

Duration Incalculable

Certainly the stock market barometer shows nothing of the kind. There is no approximation to the regularity of the pendulum, either in the arc of the swing or its velocity. We see a bear market declining forty points, a bull market advancing fifty points over more than twice the period, a bear market declining nearly sixty points, a bull market recovering forty-five points, a bear market declining less than thirty points, a major swing upward of not much more than twenty points, a bull market advancing nearly sixty points in the industrials with a simultaneous advance of less than thirty in the railroads, and a different period for each successive swing. This, in approximate figures, is the record for a quarter of a century. There is, obviously, a rough periodicity about such movements. But if we begin to twist them into some math-

was able to record a significant rally. Speaking of this preliminary movement, it says that it gives "the impression that it is one of those sharp fluctuations which follow an extreme low point and precede, at greater or less distance, a permanent turn in the tide." That seems fairly courageous and clear as a prediction, and one of exactly the conservative kind business men were being led to expect from the general consideration of the stock market barometer. Let us keep in mind that Dow's theory is not a system devised for beating the speculative game, an infallible method of playing the market. The averages, indeed, must be read with a single heart. They become deceptive if and when the wish is father to the thought. We have all heard that when the neophyte meddles with the magician's wand he is apt to raise the devil.

Reviewing the Collapse

Prediction was anything but a comfortable task in the beginning of a bull market which nobody at that time would concede, much less forecast with any degree of certainty. In an earlier chapter of this series great stress was laid on the suddenness with which business collapsed in 1907. *The Wall Street Journal* recalls the conditions, and the startling change, in its editorial of January 24, 1908: "Consider, for instance, the rapidity with which the pendulum of business has swung in this country from extreme prosperity to great prostration. Almost in a single night the situation changed from one extreme to another. Even after the panic had swept through Wall Street with terrific force a high official of a leading railroad commented upon the fact that the traffic of his line had the day before touched high-water mark. Three weeks later the same official reported that the business of the line had fallen off abruptly. Anecdotes of this kind could be multiplied indefinitely.

"It is only three months since the panic started in Wall Street, and yet that time has been sufficient to produce what amounts to a revolution in the economic conditions of the country. Three months ago there were not cars enough to move the freight. Now there are several tens of thousands of empty freight cars on the sidings and in the terminals. Three months ago the iron and steel trade was at the very height of its activity. It took only five or six weeks to cut off the demand and to close mills. If a chart were drawn to describe the reduction in iron and steel production in the past ten weeks, it would make almost a perpendicular line, so sudden and extreme has been the contraction."

A Bull Market Recognized

These extracts could be supplemented by and contrasted with the uniformly bullish inferences drawn from the stock market barometer during the winter and spring of 1908, when the business of the country was, apparently, in the deepest stage of depression. The depression was recognized; but the fact that the stock market was acting not upon the things of the moment but upon all the facts, as far ahead as it could see them, was never allowed to become obscure. It will be seen that *The Wall Street Journal* set forth the known facts in the paragraphs quoted above. A well-known chart showed its lowest point of depression at that time and did not cross its medial line, to begin its ensuing area of expansion, until the following November. But the stock market anticipated that record by a clear twelve months, and the faithful barometer predicted the recovery when there was apparently not a patch of clear sky on the horizon.

Reprobating the "Frivolous" Recovery

Looking back on those days of early responsibility, it is matter of thankfulness to me to have had Dow's sound theory to back me in the face of unbelievably virulent criticism. In the mind of the demagogue Wall Street can never be forgiven for being right when he is wrong. The country at that time was full of all kinds of agitation for the curbing, controlling, regulating and general bedeviling of business. Discontent was general, and it was a winter of unemployment. Some of the letters received, in which this bullish attitude of the stock market was denounced in the most unmeasured terms, would sound funny now, although they were anything but funny then. We seemed to be in the position of the "coon" at the country fair who puts his head through a hole in a sheet as a target for those willing to pay their nickels for the privilege of a shot at him. The lightest accusation was that Wall Street was "fiddling while Rome was burning." The general charge took the form that guilty manipulation by gamblers was in progress. If you will refer back to the twenty-five-year chart published with an earlier discussion you will note that the recorded sales at that time were the lowest since 1904, indicating a market so narrow that manipulation would have been wasted even if it had been possible. But that charge is always made in a bear market and in the transition period between a major decline and its succeeding upward movement. If I had not already advanced so many arguments to prove what an inconsiderable factor manipulation really is, the volume of sales itself would be sufficient to make my point. But these sturdy protestants thought otherwise, and continued to fill my wastebasket with revilings for many months to come. For a time at least, a bull market was positively unpopular.

Relevance of the Volume of Trading

It is worth while to note here that the volume of trading is always larger in a bull market than in a bear market. It expands as prices go up and contracts as they decline. A moment's thought will reveal the reason. When the market has been under long depression many people have lost money, actually and on paper, and the fund for speculation or speculative investment is correspondingly contracted. On the advance, however, many people are making money, actually and on paper, and the well-nigh universal experience has been that in the last stages of a bull market they trade in stocks beyond their real resources. This is uniformly true of major bull swings, but is subject to great modification in the secondary movements. A sharp reaction in a bull market will often stimulate the volume of business. There is a picturesque example of this in the most spectacular reaction of the kind. The average monthly sales in May, 1901, have not been closely approached since. They were more than one million eight hundred thousand shares a day, including Saturdays, when there is only two hours of trading, and it was on the 9th of May that the Northern Pacific panic took place. There will be an opportunity to take up the secondary swing in some detail in a future discussion, and it is not necessary for our purpose to expand upon the subject now.

An Unbiased Mind

Not to be tedious, but to counter the charge of saying "I told you so," on ex post facto evidence, it has been necessary to offer these examples of the practical use of the stock market barometer. There is, indeed, little in these predictions to excite boasting. Any intelligent student of the averages who has once grasped the principle of the stock market barometer can draw such deductions for himself, provided he brings to the task a really unbiased mind. An interest in the stock market would be almost certain to weaken his judgment. It is only human to foresee what you hope and, indeed, what you expected when you bought stocks for the rise or sold them short. But the analyst of the price movement, writing for the guidance of others, must be absolutely disinterested. There are all sorts of traps to catch him if he is not, particularly if he has previously committed himself to inferences not clearly justified by the premises. Sheer pride of opinion has ruined more speculators in the stock market than all other causes put together.

An Unfortunate Guess

One of the shortest ways of going wrong is to accept an indication by one average which has not been clearly confirmed by the other. On May 10, 1921, the New York American ventured into prophecy on its financial page. To reinforce its prediction its forecaster published a reproduction of the Dow Jones chart. As the chart and the accompanying figures were taken without acknowledgment, altruists who believe that ill-gotten gains do not prosper will hear with satisfaction that the author of the Hearst American article did not even understand the meaning of what he had appropriated. He announced a bull movement for the industrial stocks, even prescribing its limits, a degree of prophecy hitherto unsuspected in the barometer; while the railroad stocks, as he expressed it, "marked time." It was a most unfortunate guess, for the industrials declined a further thirteen points, making their new low in June; while the railroads, so far from marking time, also showed a substantial reaction.

Averages Must Confirm Each Other

This was a case where the observer was misled by a bullish indication given in the industrial average which was not confirmed by the railroads. The former had been making what we have learned to call a line, and after a secondary rally in a bear market showed some strength, at a figure above the line and calculated to suggest accumulation if there had been any evidence of the same thing in the railroad stocks. But there was nothing of the kind, and it is to be hoped that the readers of the Hearst American article did not follow the tip; for the industrials, as shown by the averages, did not cross the closing figure of the day on which the bullish advice was given until the second trading day of December, seven months after.

It is possible, however, for us to assume charitably that this expounder of the barometer was not quite so superficial as he sounds. There may have been in his mind a recollection of the bull market of 1919, which the industrials made entirely off their own bat. If you will study the chart published with a later chapter, headed "An Exception to Prove the Rule," you will see that such an experience could not be repeated unless our railroad stocks returned to government ownership and guaranty—a condition which at that time took them entirely out of the speculative class and left them moving downward with bonds and other securities held for fixed income. These, as we know, inevitably decline in price with an advance in the cost of living, which was then in full flood.

This illustration serves to emphasize the fact that while the two averages may vary in strength they will not materially vary in direction, especially in a major movement. Throughout all the years in which both averages have been kept this rule has proved entirely dependable. It is not only true of the major swings of the market but it is approximately true of the secondary reactions and rallies. It would not be true of the daily fluctuation, and it might be utterly misleading so far as individual stocks are concerned. The indications of a single average can, and do, look seductively like the real thing, as I have discovered to my cost; for in that way I find, upon analysis of articles written long ago, that I more than once went wrong. It says much for the value of our barometer that error came from trusting it too little rather than too much.

Sticking to Our Text

It has been suggested that I should discuss the causes which were related to the major movements of the stock market—the depressions in business, the recoveries and the alleged or real overexpansion. I have my own opinion about the causes of the panic of 1907. I do not agree with writers rated as competent as myself, who ascribe it to Harriman and the "overexpansion" of the American railroads from 1901 to 1906; who choose to think that the advance in the Bank of England rate to the sufficiently startling figure of 7 percent at the end of 1906 was a direct result of gambling in railroad stocks by Mr. Roosevelt's "malefactors of great wealth." And by no stretch of faith can I believe that Harriman produced a panic in Alexandria, Egypt, in April, 1907; another in Japan within a month; what the London *Economist* called "the biggest financial disaster that had overtaken the city since 1857" in Hamburg in October; and still another in Chile—all preceding our own crisis at the end of October. It has seemed to me that the subsequent paralysis of railroad development, which should have gone on at the billion-dollar-a-year rate James J. Hill suggested in 1906, but was suspended almost entirely, was a much more serious matter for the country than the reciprocal ownership of railroad stocks of Harriman's plans. There could be no menace to the public there, with the Interstate Commerce Commission to protect us through the freight rates.

flour or bread at lower prices. It would be utterly impossible to synchronize the movements of wheat or cotton with those of stocks. These commodities often decline when securities are advancing. It is not the general opinion, but it seems to me that a bear of wheat who breaks a corner in that commodity, even if his end is selfish, is performing something in the nature of a public service.

Such an opinion as this, of course, will be unpopular with the farmer and still more unpopular with the farmer's political friends, to whom wheat at $5 a bushel looks like prosperity, with wealth beyond the dreams of avarice. It might well mean famine and widespread destitution. The farmer and his friends have become sensitive since their own wheat pool (not different morally from any other attempted corner in the staff of life), formed in 1919 to carry the price of wheat above $3 a bushel, collapsed under the futile leadership of the Non-Partisan League and the moral support of some of the members of what now constitutes the agricultural "bloc" in the U.S. Senate. That corner failed, and it is no unkindness to the farmer to say that it deserved to fail. The stock market of 1920 was warning him that such a pool could not succeed, in ample time for him to have realized all his wheat at prices well over $2 a bushel.

How the Barometer Adjusts Itself

We are not wandering from our text. Weakness in the cotton or grain markets may have much to do with secondary reactions in the stock market, if only for the financial commitments involved. Secondary movements, indeed, are influenced by much more transitory conditions than any of those which govern the major swing. The question is pertinently asked, "Do the averages predict a secondary reaction in any dependable way?" There would be such a prediction, naturally, if, in the course of a major bull swing, the market made a line in both averages, and then a price below the line to indicate that saturation point had been reached; and the converse would be true in a bear market. But experience tells us that when the line occurs it is, generally, not before but after a secondary break or rally. This line, then, is most useful to the speculator who has previously sold and wants to get into the market again, because a bull indication after a line of accumulation would point the way to a new figure higher than that from which the secondary decline took its origin. Such a new top would be conclusive evidence, on all our records, that the bull movement had been resumed. But these discussions are designed less for speculators than for those who wish to study the stock market barometer as a guide to the general business of the country. These students may well ask what is the real purpose and usefulness of the secondary movement. If we are allowed to mix our metaphor, it may be said that the secondary movement is not unlike a device sometimes used for adjusting compasses. Many of you have seen a ship's launch describing circles in the harbor, and wondered what it meant. I am well aware that the metaphor is anything but perfect, but it is clear that the secondary movement serves the valuable purpose of correcting our barometer. Our guide is, to that extent at least, self-adjusting. Remember that we are dealing with no such certain element as the mercury in the tube, whose properties we know all about. The stock market barometer is taking every conceivable thing into account, including that most fluid, inconstant and incalculable element, human nature itself. We cannot, therefore, expect the mechanical exactness of physical science.

Not Too Good to Be True

We might well be disposed to suspect our barometer if it were too exact. Our attitude would be that of a city magistrate toward police evidence, when every police witness tells exactly the same story in the same words. Such evidence is altogether too good to be true. I am repeatedly asked if I am quite sure about the low or high point of a given turning date; whether, for instance, the low of the bear market from which we are now emerging was really June, 21, or should not be considered in relation to the new low point, scored by the industrials alone, in the following August. It has been said that the averages must confirm each other, but if you like to take it that way and it suits your habit of mind, by all means allow yourself that much latitude. I cannot see that it makes any material difference. I have been shown figure charts where bear and bull movements, from the course of a single constantly active stock like U.S. Steel common, were professedly predicted with mathematical exactness. They have not inspired me, and I do not believe that they could stand the long years of test to which our barometer has been subjected.

There are other critics, far less kindly and with no real desire to help, who find no difficulty in picking holes in our theory because they do not wish to be convinced. They are merely contentious. They can, of course, find plenty of movements, especially secondary ones, which they think the barometer failed to forecast. What of it? An instrument of any such accuracy as they demand would be a human impossibility, and indeed, I do not think that any of us, in the present stage of man's moral development, could be trusted with such a certainty. One way to bring about a world smash would be for some thoroughly well-intentioned altruist to take the management of the planet out of the hands of its Creator.

Chapter XIV - 1909, and Some Defects of History

Since we have set the understanding of the stock market barometer as our goal, we are not to be discouraged by the real and fancied obstacles still remaining. We can always hearten ourselves by looking back and seeing how much we have already overcome. Perhaps the reward is in the race we run, not in the prize. This is not to say that the mere reading of this series of studies is any achievement if the reader has not, thereby, added to his mental bank balance. But if we look back we can see that we have not only established Dow's theory of the price movement, but constructed or deduced a workable barometer from it—a barometer with the invaluable quality of long distance forecast. We should know our theory by heart. It is that the stock market has three movements—its broad swing upward or downward, extending from a year to three years; its secondary reactions or rallies, as the case may be, lasting from a few days to many weeks; and the daily fluctuation. These movements are simultaneous, much as the advancing tide shows wave recessions, although each succeeding roller comes further up the beach. Perhaps it might be permissible to say that the secondary movement suspends for a time the great primary swing, although a natural law is still in force even when we counteract it. My pen would fall from my finders to the ground or the desk, by the attraction of gravitation, and that law continues operative, if not active. In a like way of putting it, the secondary movement can be regarded as simultaneous with the major swing, which still continues to govern.

That Unbalanced Equation

It has been necessary to refer in previous articles to business charts and records, and I would be the last to seek a quarrel with the compilers of such useful data. All I contend is that these charts and records are hardly, in a useful sense, barometers. They are hazy about the future, even where they make the assumption that they are based upon a great law of physics—that action and reaction are equal. They have still to show me that they have included all the factors of their equation. Certainly these business charts did not include the possibility of Germany winning the war in 1918. The bear market in stocks in 1901 took count of all that these tabulations ever formulated, and this overwhelming possibility besides. It is true that we can form little conception of what may happen in the future unless we are familiar with what has happened in the past, where like causes have produced like effects. But forecast may be mistaken or premature long enough to ruin any businessman, with no other guide than that. One of these business chart authorities not long ago advocated the purchase of a certain stock, on the basis of the earnings and dividends for a period of ten years past. There was a fundamental change in conditions, aggravated by an ill-judged change in policy, and the people who bought that stock suffered severe losses. How would a present holder of such a stock as American Sugar, for instance, have fared if he had bought the common stock in 1920 on its dividend record?

Insufficient Premises

Reasoning of that kind has too narrow a base. It lacks foresight. It is like saying that a patient will recover, irrespective of his symptoms, because he has enjoyed good health for ten years past. This is an example of reasoning from insufficient premises. No doubt the possibilities of changes in management and other things, which sometimes wreck concerns with a previously good dividend record, are averaged in the total of a recording agency's tables. But even when these things are averaged they are a record and not a barometer. The data of the Weather Bureau are of the highest value, but they do not pretend to predict a dry summer or a mild winter. You and I know from personal experience that the weather in N.Y. is likely to be cold in January and hot in July. We could infer that much without assistance from the Weather Bureau. That bureau can give us only an inadequately short view. It cannot tell us that there will be fine weather for our picnic the day after tomorrow. Still less can it tell the farmer that the temperature and humidity of the coming summer be such that he should plant potatoes instead of corn. It can show the records and probabilities; but the farmer must use his own judgment; while we take chances on the kind of weather that will make or mar our picnic.

How Little the Best Man Knows

We have seen that the stock market barometer does predict. It shows us what will happen to the general volume of business many months ahead. It even goes further and warns us of the danger of international events which could upset all ordinary calculations based on the course of business as inferred from the records. It cannot be too often repeated that the stock market barometer is acting upon all the knowledge available. I recently asked one of the greatest financiers in Wall Street, often credited, by sensation-loving journals, with the most searching knowledge of financial conditions and their influence upon coming events, what sort of percentage of the available knowledge he supposed he had. He said, "I have never worked that out but if I had 50 percent of all the knowledge which is reflected in the movement of stocks I am confident that I would be far better equipped than any other man in Wall Street." This was from a banker who handles the financing of great railroads and industrial corporations, whose foreign connections are of the very highest class. When he could confess this without false modesty to one he would not be foolish enough to deceive, how absurd must be the assumed omniscience of the "financial octopus" the politician is so fond of parading.

A Needless Accuracy

We have come a long way in the reading of the barometer based upon Dow's Theory. We have seen that a "line" in the average—a succession of closing prices, over a sufficient number of days for a fair volume of trading within a narrow range—must indicate either accumulation or distribution; and that a movement of the average price out of that line, downward or upward, will confidently indicate a change in the general market direction of at least a secondary and even a primary character, which we can depend upon where either average is confirmed by the other.

We have also satisfied ourselves that the averages must confirm each other, although they may not break out of their respective lines on the same day or in the same week. It is sufficient if they take the same direction. It is by no means necessary, as experience shows, that the low or the high point of a primary movement should be made in both averages on the same day. All we assume is that the market has turned, with the two averages confirming, even although one of the averages subsequently makes a new low point or a new high point, but is not confirmed by the other. The previous lows or highs made by both averages may best be taken as representing the turn of the market. This seems to be a difficulty which is still puzzling a number of people who expect an absolute mathematical accuracy from the averages, such as I would be the last to claim, if only for the reason that it is not needed. One critic believes that I am wrong in assuming that the low point of the last bear movement was in June, 1921, because the industrials made a lower point in the following August. But that lower point was not confirmed by the railroad average. Consequently, it is negligible from our point of view, although if it adds to the sum of that gentleman's certainty he will not go far wrong if he dates his upward movement from August and not from June.

A Double Top

In the present discussion it will be useful to show the turn of the market to the bear side in 1909. This is likely to be confusing to our meticulous critics, because the railroad stocks made their high for the preceding bull movement at 134.46 in August, 1909; while the industrials made a high of 100.12 at the end of the following September, 100.50 early in October, and 100.53, the highest of the year, at the beginning of November. The last high, taken with that preceding, is an example of what is called a double top. It is by no means infallible, but is often useful; and experience has shown that when the market makes a double top or a double bottom in the averages there is strong reason for suspecting that the rise or decline is over. If, however, I say that a bull market saw its top in August, 1909, and that the bear market set in from that date, somebody will tell me that the bear movement cannot be said to have set in until the beginning of November. What does it matter? If we combine the condition exhibited then with what we have learned from a study of the line of distribution or accumulation, we shall see that distribution preceding an important downward turn, possibly secondary but proving to be primary in this case, had been in progress and had established its inevitable consequences, at any rate before the completion of the first week's trading of November, 1909.

Bulls of Stocks Well Warned

That seems to me about as adequate a barometrical indication as we dare expect from a gauge which has to take into consideration all the fallibility of human nature itself. Never was the bull of stocks given such repeated chances as in 1909 to take profits at the top, or a few points below it. In a previous discussion I have said that the bull market which originated in December, 1907, was actually almost unpopular. The previous bear market had predicted an era of corporation baiting, originated by President Roosevelt, who could never have foreseen the absurd lengths to which his adversions upon "malefactors of great wealth" would be carried, or the devastating implications which would be drawn by people much more ignorant and far less sincere than himself.

To Criticize a Critic

The bull market of 1908-9 did not please a number of highly respectable and competent critics. I have appreciated and recommended elsewhere *Forty Years of American Finance,* by Alexander D. Noyes. His review appears to have been carried only to the beginning of 1909, to judge by his concluding paragraph. He seems to reprehend the bull market then in progress. He certainly failed to see that it would continue in force up to August, so far as the railroads were concerned, up to November as shown by the industrial average, and that, at the end of the year 1909, the railroads would be no lower than one hundred and thirty on December 31st, as against one hundred and thirty-four in the middle of August, and the industrials a bare point away from the top. Mr. Noyes says, in speaking of the bull market, with what can fairly be called a somewhat unsuccessful essay in prophecy:

"The end of this singular demonstration came with the opening of 1909, when facts were suddenly recognized, when prices for steel and other commodities came down, and when the Stock Exchange demonstrations ended. With the closing of the year 1908, this history may properly close; for it marked the ending of a chapter."

But we have seen, from the record of the averages, that the chapter was not closed so summarily as Mr. Noyes assumed. We may say, for convenience, that the bull market had spent its force in August, 1909— or in November, as we choose to look at it. But the bear market which foresaw the next period of depression did not begin to "hit on all cylinders" until January, 1910. Here again we see a profound and able observer influenced by accepting a record for a barometer.

A Record Too Brief

To a student of history—and the writer modestly claims to be something of the kind himself—it is a source of unceasing regret that there is relatively so little real history to study. Our table of averages is only truly effective for rather over a quarter of a century. When we say that the twenty active railroad stocks must confirm the twenty industrials it seems to me that this implies, at least in part, that less than forty stocks do not give a sufficiently inclusive picture of the market. I might, in some subsequent discussion, offer a partial and incomplete record of the years from 1860 to 1880, with an average high and low, month by month, of fifteen miscellaneous stocks. I may as well say now that I do not think that it has any conclusive teaching value; or that if it had been kept contemporaneously with the events of that time, and not compiled years after, it would have given business anything like the thoroughly trustworthy indications which we can read in the more perfect double-average barometer of today.

How History Records the Wrong Things

But my criticism of history goes much further than the mere records of which we are treating. It is that all available history, as far back as we can trace— from Egypt and the supposed cradle of the race in Asia Minor— records the wrong things. It tells us all about the dynasties of the Pharaohs, and nothing about those productive middle-class brains of management which made those dynasties rich—gave them a real people to rule over. We know that there were rulers and wars, slaves and industrial workers enjoying different degrees of freedom. We know now that, so far from labor creating everything—the preposterous major premise of Karl Marx—labor creates only a fraction of the sum of human wealth compared with the product of brains. Of the "people" of the past, in the sense that the Bolshevist demagogue uses the word, we know a good deal. Professor Thorold Rogers, of Oxford, many years ago compiled a tabulation of wages in England, from the time of the Tudors. But history seems to give something of the bottom and a great deal too much of the top. It tells us nothing, or next to nothing, of the middle class which must be the directing brain force of a nation with any commerce whatever.

Where Are the Business Records?

What do we really know about the Carthaginians? They were the greatest trading nation of their time. We might well afford to sacrifice the detailed accounts of the campaigns of Hannibal, to throw away most of what we know about the second Punic War, to scrap nearly all that part of history, in exchange for only one year's accounting of a typical Carthaginian merchant engaged in foreign trade. We would have more practical knowledge, applicable to the problems of today, from that single merchant's books of the year 250 B.C. than we can get from the *Decline and Fall of the Roman Empire,* and all it incidentally says about Carthage, to say nothing of the practical conduct of commerce in those days.

How did that merchant do his business? He dealt in tin from Cornwall and dyestuffs from Tyre. He had correspondents all over the known world, which then extended from Britain in the west to India in the east. Did he, or could he, for the tin or dyestuffs he received, pay exclusively in coined gold or silver? He may well have exchanged one of his commodities for another, or something else for both. How did he pay? How did he settle his balances? Did he have bills of exchange? I am inclined to think that he did, whatever form they may have taken, although no papyrus or parchment has survived. But history does not tell us the one thing we want to know. How did the Carthaginians adjust their international trade balances? They necessarily had them. The merchants of Joppa or Sidon or Alexandria kept books, or their equivalent. They had a record of what they imported from Carthage and what they exported there and elsewhere. Rome owed Carthage balances in account, in triangular transactions which must have required some knowledge of double entry, with more or less regular exchange quotations to balance one national coinage against another. What does history tell us about all this? Absolutely nothing. And yet that knowledge would be of infinitely greater value to us would save us more mistakes, than Xenophon's deathless story of the retreat of the ten thousand.

Who Financed Xerxes?

Heaven forbid that we should lose the inspiring lesson of Thermopylae. We have seen, in the Great War, that men are still capable of rising to the heroism of the fated three hundred. But what of the contractors who fed and clothed and armed the "five million men" in the army of the victorious Xerxes? "The mountains look on Marathon—and Marathon looks on the sea," and they may continue looking at each other, until the crack of doom, without telling us the cost of the ship's stores consumed in the fleet which transported the defeated Persians. "You have the Pyrrhic dance as yet, where is the Pyrrhic phalanx gone?" We could dispense with the dance if we knew how the Pyrrhic phalanx got its necessary three square meals a day, and from whence its food was imported. I am far from endorsing the Henry Ford criticism of history—it is not "bunk"; but what would we not give for a trustworthy analysis of the economic consequences of Diocletian's price-fixing edicts, in the year 301?

Where did the Greeks buy their naval stores? How were they assembled? How was the account settled? Was it in coined money, or in a draft written on parchment, transferring one merchant's debt to another in order to balance the books of a third? All this is left out of classical history, and is sadly lacking in modern history. It was not until the middle of the nineteenth century that Green wrote, not a history of the kings of England, but *A Short History of The English People.* It was all too short; and the most important part of the English people was loftily minimized—that respectable but inarticulate element which goes about attending to its own business and manages to "keep out of the papers." No one would belittle the record of the events which led up to the signing of Magna Charta. But if I am not greatly interested in King John, I want to know much more than history records about those useful mercantile and financial figures personified by Walter Scott in Isaac of York. The tortured Jew's extracted tooth outweighs, in real historical value, the sceptre of the Plantagenet king.

What of the Banking in the Middle Ages?

The more we search the work of the earlier historians, the more we are astonished at their inability to see a thing so self-evident, for they were almost invariably drawn from the class they failed to chronicle, except where it touched politics. Froude devotes chapters of a volume of his history to the divorce of Catherine of Aragon. He tells us nothing of value about the financial transactions involved in such a simple matter as the collection and payment of Queen Catherine's dowry to Henry VIII. I have heard experienced newspaper men say, "The most interesting news never gets into the papers." There is a good deal of cynical truth in that remark, and certainly the most instructive historical facts seldom get into the histories.

That is why the diary of Samuel Pepys, not written for publication, tells us more of the real things we want to know than anything which has ever been written, contemporaneously and since, about the period of the Restoration. It is almost from that date that we begin to get some familiar idea of what banking was like, and how it was conducted in the great city of London two and a half centuries ago. Our knowledge, so far as available records are concerned, hardly, in any real sense, antedates the incorporation of the Bank of England, at the end of the seventeenth century. The records of commerce and banking of the earlier financiers are almost hopelessly wanting. There must have been such records arising out of the colonial expansion of Holland, Spain and Portugal or, working back through the years, in the trade of the Genoese and the Venetians. But these highly respectable historians seemed to think that the birth of a king's bastard was more important than the opening of an avenue of trade, with the creation of the financial machinery necessary for its development.

How New Is Credit?

I am credibly informed that banking, and even branch banking, has been in use in China for at least two thousand years, with drafts, credits and the usual banking machinery, if in a much simplified form. It must also be admitted that the great structure of today's credit is essentially modern. But it would be absurd to assume that it is all modern, merely because we know so little about history. The trading of Carthage, Genoa and Venice was largely barter. But we may be sure that it was not all barter. Not only the Church canon law but the Bible itself and like works have many allusions to the sin of usury. But usury meant interest, and interest meant credit, just as coinage meant exchange. It was not all pawn-broking; nor was the banking of the Middle Ages. There is some evidence that the same people both received and paid interest. The merchant, then as now, probably had a good deal more practical sense than the theologian, and certainly a clearer idea of the line between legitimate interest and usury. The trouble is that historians, up to a late date, have been influenced by the ecclesiastical attitude toward money lending. They are exasperatingly dogmatic on the things they admit they don't know. I am inclined to suspect that it was not the early Middle Ages that were "dark" but only the historians. I am even disposed to agree with my friend Dr. James J. Walsh that, in point of real civilization and attainment, both artistic and literary, the thirteenth century in Europe compares favorably with our own. And even he has been unable to elicit anything of real usefulness about the mechanics of commerce.

And if this is the sum of our knowledge of the history of the most vital part of human affairs, the history of the men who paid the taxes and the men who made the taxes possible; the history of those who took the bare product of labor and fructified it tenfold—how difficult is it for us to gather together enough particulars to frame a trustworthy generalization from the wholly modern tabulation of the records of trade, industry and finance. There has recently been published a book by H. G. Wells, *The Outline of History,* which at least has had the excellent effect of persuading a number of people to read history who have done little serious reading in the course of their lives. But that "outline" is devoted to proving a fallacious assumption—that men are groping their way, rather blindly, in the direction of international socialism. Is there one single record in all the inadequate volumes of history, upon which Mr. Wells and we ourselves necessarily depend, which indicates anything of the kind? Everything points to the development of the efficient individual. There is nothing in the Wells inference which does not ignore the factor of management in production, dominant now and dominant always, from the time when man learned to save something out of his harvest, to keep himself and others through the coming winter, and exchange for what he could not produce.

A Sound and Conservative Forecast

With regard to the use of the barometer in the turn of the market in 1909, *The Wall Street Journal* on September 9th, a month after the railroads had recorded their high, said:

"The movement of the average on Thursday's break was one which has often marked the commencement of a downward swing. The indication as yet is not very authoritative, but whatever we may think about a resumption of the bull movement, 'now that all the bad news is out,' the averages undoubtedly look more bearish than they have done in a long period.

"Pessimism has never been the policy of this paper, but it published an earnest plea for conservatism when the market was at the top. Nothing has occurred since which has not emphasized the position taken."

From that time forward, although the market, as we have seen, was remarkably firm, showing only modified secondary downward swings practically up to the end of the year, *The Wall Street Journal* continued to draw lessons of warning from the averages. On October 28th it said, after pointing out the extent of the rally necessary to re-establish the old bull market:

"There is no pretense here to pass an opinion upon the market from any other point of view than a purely technical one, based upon the experience of the price movements as shown in the average record of many years, but the depression in the barometer, here evidenced, is well worthy of the consideration of thoughtful traders."

Growing Effectiveness of the Barometer

Remarking how widely the idea of a bull market in 1910 was then held *The Wall Street Journal* was unpopularly bearish on December 18, 1909, although both averages were within a very few points of the top. It is interesting to note that one of the bear arguments (other than that of the averages) discussed at that time was the high cost of living. On December 28th, any idea of a January boom—a movement always talked of at the beginning of the year—was rather cruelly discouraged. It would be easy to multiply examples. It is sufficient here to show, before taking up the discussion of the four years of somewhat indecisive market movements which preceded the war, how faithfully the stock market barometer, twelve years ago, was already serving its purpose.

Chapter XV - A "Line" and an Example

In past discussions of the stock market barometer— the record by daily averages of the closing "bid" prices of a number of selected industrial and railroad stocks, taken in two separate groups to check and confirm each other—emphasis has been laid upon what is called a "line." It is needless to say that no inference of value can be drawn from a single day's trading. However large the transactions may be, they cannot show the general trend. This daily fluctuation is merely the third and least important movement defined in Dow's theory of the averages. If we could imagine such a thing as an irregular daily tidal movement it is just that. The general level of the sea is not changed by an abnormally high tide in the Bay of Fundy or a tidal bore in the mouth of some Chinese river. The ocean's real encroachments and recessions take time.

A Definition

The line, therefore, may be considered as often preceding an appreciable recovery in a primary bear market or a well-defined reaction in a primary bull market, and, rarely, as the possible turning of a major movement. It can almost be set down as axiomatic for all our purposes that a line is and must necessarily be either one of accumulation or one of distribution. For a time the buying and selling power are in equilibrium. There are some most significant lines in the history of the averages to which reference has already been made.

Predicting the War

To show the special value of the averages as a barometer forecasting what even Wall Street itself does not know in any general sense or at any rate does not realize, the extraordinary line made by both averages, industrials and railroads, in the months of May, June and July, 1914, preceding the outbreak of the Great War, is here submitted. No severer test of the averages could be chosen. The war came as a surprise to the whole world. Did the stock market foresee it? It may be fairly claimed that it did, and had predicted it, or trouble of the most momentous character, before the end of July, while the German army crossed into Belgium on August 3rd-4th.

Let it be remembered that a primary bear movement had then been in progress in the stock market since October, 1912. In May, 1914, both averages started to make a line of unusual length. The fluctuations in the railroads were between one hundred and three and one hundred and one, and in the industrials between eighty-one and seventy-nine. Only once, on June 25th, did the railroads give a warning at one hundred. This was taken back the following day with a continuance of the line in both averages up to July 18th in the case of the railroads and July 24th in the case of the industrials. At the latter date, eight days before the German army invaded Belgium, the industrials confirmed the warning the railroads had given.

What Had Happened?

What had happened? German holders of American stocks and the best informed European bankers had sold in this market. If there had been no war all this would have been absorbed by the American investor at the unrepresentative low prices prevailing in a bear market which in July, 1914, had been operative for twenty-two months. All of it was absorbed by the American investor in the following year. The supply from Europe then, and subsequently, as the war forced foreign holders to realize, and war loans compelled the liquidation of other investments, took the place of the normal supply of new investment securities which it is the duty of Wall Street to create through concentration of opportunity and of savings and the bringing of the two things together. Over-regulation of the railroads, now recognized to have been an economic crime, had paralyzed their power to create new capital long before the war. The public attention had been diverted for five years before that calamity to industrial opportunity, some of it, like the shady oil promotions of our inflation period, of a dangerously speculative character. Without the foreign sales of American securities and the war, turning us in effect from a debtor to a creditor nation, there would have been a dearth of capital opportunity; and this is why after the all-revealing break late in July the market made only a relatively small decline on the reopening of the Stock Exchange, in December, immediately swinging into one of its great bull periods.

Relation to Volume

Knowledge is valuable not merely for telling us what to do but for telling us what to avoid. Inside information, so called, is a dangerous commodity in Wall Street, especially if you trade upon it, but at least it guards you against the rumors which cannot possibly be so. Diligent study of the averages will sufficiently show where a "line," having proved to be one of accumulation, has given definite information, not merely useful to the trader but valuable to those who look upon the stock market as a means of forecasting the trend of the country's general business.

Here is an appropriate opportunity for adding something about volume of sales. This volume is much less significant than is generally supposed. It is purely relative, and what would be a large volume in one state of the market supply might well be negligible in a greatly active market. If the line means absorption, this absorption sums up the market supply, whether it be three hundred thousand shares or three million Showers of rain vary in intensity, area and duration. But they all result from the moisture in the air reaching saturation point. Rain is rain whether it covers a county or a state, in five hours or five days.

How to Know a Bull Market

It might well be asked, how are we to tell when a secondary swing, upward for instance, has developed into a primary bull market? The result is seen in the averages in a succession of zig-zag steps. If the secondary swing reacts a little after what would ordinarily be its culmination in a primary bear market but does not decline to the old low figures, and subsequently recovers to points better than the new high established on the earlier rally, we may assume with confidence that a primary bull market of indefinite length has been established. It is, of course, impossible for the barometer to predict the duration of the movement, any more than the aneroid can tell us on October 30th what the weather will be on Election Day.

Barometrical Limitations

There is no need to expect omniscience from an aneroid barometer, which, as we know, frequently takes back its predictions and would be a most untrustworthy guide for the mariner if it did not. This is true of the stock market barometer, which must be intelligently read. Surgeons and physicians in our time have been greatly helped, to the lasting advantage of human life and comfort, by the X-ray photograph. But these medical men will tell you that the photograph itself must be read by an expert; that to the mere general practitioner not accustomed to its frequent use it may be unintelligible or misleading. The results of an X-ray to disclose, for instance, pyorrhea "pockets" at the roots of the teeth would be meaningless to the layman and perhaps even to some dentists. But any dentist could qualify himself to read those indications, and it is here submitted that any intelligent layman with a sympathetic interest in the stock market movement, by no means necessarily speculative, can read the stock market barometer.

Speculation's Necessity and Function

Wall Street is a mystery to many men who have unsuccessfully tried to speculate there without knowledge, only to become convinced that they have in some way been cheated in what is no better than a gambling game. It has not been the purpose of these chapters to discuss ethical questions; as, for instance, the morality of speculation or the line which divides speculation from gambling, or the place of gambling in the Ten Commandments, or the supposed special sinfulness of short selling. The personal opinion of the writer is that speculation within a man's means is unaffected by any question of morality. Perhaps this is only another way of saying that its morality is taken for granted, just as the lawful conduct of a man's business is assumed. If the man chooses to make speculation his business, or part of his business, the ethical question becomes purely academic. Speculation is one of the greatest essentials in the development of a nation. The spirit which inspires it can be called by prettier names, like adventure and enterprise. Certainly if no one had been willing to take a speculative risk for a larger profit than mere investment provided the railroads of the U.S. would have stopped at the eastern foothills of the Alleghenies, and what the maps of our childhood called "the great American desert," now our great wheat and corn-producing states, would have remained a desert for all we knew to the contrary. Rudyard Kipling once said that if the British army had always waited for supports the British Empire would have stopped at Margate beach. The speculator in the stock market, or any free market, is a fact and not a theory. He is the embryo investor who does not wait for supports. It will be a bad day for this country, and a sign that having ceased to grow it has begun to dwindle, when it abandons free markets and the free speculation which they necessarily entail.

Difficult But Not Unfair

It is not true to say that the outside speculator always loses money in Wall Street if he continues speculating long enough, as the present writer (who does not trade on margin himself) can testify from numerous instances to the contrary. But the man who means to hold his own in an encounter requiring capital, courage, judgment, caution, and arduously acquired information from study must devote the same attention to that business that he would to any other business. So far as Wall Street is concerned, the simile of a game of chance is always a bad and misleading one. But it may be said that to those who will not or cannot comply with the conditions of the game when playing against expert exponents of it, trading in Wall Street is a sheer gamble, with a deadly percentage in favor of the dealer (who does not need to be dishonest) and against such a player. No one would play auction bridge against scientific players without learning how to bid and how to draw correct inferences in the play. He would refrain, if only out of mercy for his prospective partner. But the man who will not risk his own and his partner's money in that way will not hesitate to speculate in Wall Street. Is it surprising that he loses his money?

Who Makes the Market?

This seems an appropriate place to answer a question which may be said to go to the root of the matter. "Who makes the market?" The manipulators? The great banking houses of issue with new securities to float? The professional traders on the floor of the Exchange? The large individual "operators" who talk to newspaper reporters of their profits and tell Congressional committees how they made them, but never say a word about their losses? Certainly not. The market is made by the saving, investing public of the whole U.S., first, last and all the time. There is no possible financial combination which can manipulate a bull market, by propaganda or in any other way, when the combined intelligence of the investing public sees that it is time to curtail their commitments in view of a coming decline in prices, earnings and the volume of trade. The most an expert manipulator can do is to stimulate activity in a particular stock, or a small group in a market which is already rising on its merits, with the approval of public sentiment. We hear about the successful manipulation of the market, in U.S. Steel or Amalgamated Copper, by the late James R. Keene in 1901 and 1902; but we hear nothing of almost innumerable attempts to manipulate for distribution abandoned because the general trend of the market made the operation profitless and dangerous. The great private financing houses are normally sellers of securities because it is their business to manufacture them, in the promotion of new enterprises, and the direction of the great reservoir of public capital into such channels. Individual Wall Street capitalists buy for private investment, and I could tell, from the wills filed for probate, of the unbelievable minor errors of judgment of this kind made by men so well informed as the late J. P. Morgan or the late E. H. Harriman, to name only two of many.

Speculation's Sound Basis

It has been said before that the stock market represents, in a crystallized form, the aggregate of all America knows about its own business, and, incidentally, about the business of its neighbors. When a man finds his jobbing trade or his factory showing a surplus he tends to invest that surplus in easily negotiable securities. If this improvement is general it is all reflected and anticipated in the market, for he can buy in July and carry on ample margin what he knows he can pay for outright when he divides profits at the end of the year. He does not wait till the end of the year, because he realizes that the knowledge he possesses in July will by that time have become common property, and will have been discounted in the price. He buys ahead just as he buys the raw materials for his factory ahead, at a time when the securities or the raw materials look cheap. It is important to note that this is, in the very best sense, sentiment, which comes from the Latin verb *sentire*—"to perceive by the senses and the mind, to feel, to think." This is anything but sentimentalism, which is not encouraged in Wall Street.

Sentiment

Wall Street knows what sentiment is. It is a thing of high emprise, of adventure, of noble effort to a worthy end. It carried Boone across the Appalachians, and the Argonauts of 1849 through the passes of the Rocky Mountains. It is something we inherit from our forefathers of Shakespeare's time. It is what they brought with them when they put out upon the trackless sea, defying the galleons of Spain, and named a plantation on an unknown continent after their Virgin Queen. Virginia is still here but, as Austin Dobson sings, and Admiral Dewey might have asked, where are the galleons of Spain? This sentiment is a life-giving principle in national growth, not to be confused with sentimental statutes for "an official state flower," with "smile weeks" and stop-over mothers' days." In the English-speaking race it is a perception which greatly survives for great occasions. It was sentiment which first gave a kingly funeral, and a memorial stone in Westminster Abbey, to the Unknown Soldier who had saved the race. It was sentiment which made all London still its voice and hold its breath, one year, to the minute, after the declaration of the armistice. I spent those exalted two minutes at the Mansion House Corner, in the City of London, in November, 1919. It was a moving sight, indeed, when it could bring tears to the eyes of the hardened newspaper reporter.

A great price movement is not the ordained outcome of enlightened individual choice, or even of individual leadership. It is a thing far greater and more impressive, at least to one who has learned, from personal contact, in Wall Street and out, "How very weak the very wise, How very small the very great are."

Chapter XVI - An Exception to Prove the Rule

A proverb has been called the wisdom of many and the wit of one. Sometimes, when the controversialist finds the proverb inconvenient, he calls it a glittering generality or a truism. A French philosopher told us that all generalizations are fallacious, "including this one." But a truism is presumably true, even if it is trite. It is said that there is no rule without an exception, but as a sufficient number of exceptions would make it necessary to formulate a new rule, especially in economics, the proverb which best suits our purpose is that which says that the exception proves the rule, although Coke's *"Exceptio probat regulam de rebus exceptis"* is not what we want. But the proverb is even startlingly true about what may be called the great exception in the stock market averages. Our two averages of railroad and industrial stocks must confirm each other to give weight to any inference drawn from the price movement. The history of the stock market as shown by these averages, going back many years, proves conclusively that the two averages move together. But there was one exception to this rule, and it is the more valuable for our purpose in that it is the exception which proves the rule we have set up.

Some Necessary History

It adds to the interest of the study of this subject that it is necessary to make excursions into contemporary history to explain the meaning of the price movement, often only fully apparent after the movement has been under way for many months. In 1918, for some nine months after we had entered the Great War, both averages showed a primary bull market with a strong secondary reaction over the end of that year. During that year the railroad stocks fully shared that upward swing but subsequently sold off, making almost a bear market of their own in 1919, when the industrials were strongest. Letters were written during the serial publication of these discussions, in which this well-known fact was adduced as a reason for rejecting the entire theory based upon the averages. But if ever an exception proved the rule this one does.

Movement of stock market averages

Remember that the industrial and railroad stocks used in the averages are essentially speculative. Only to a limited extent are they held for fixed income by people to whom safety of the principal should be the main consideration, and their holders are constantly changing. If they were not speculative they would be useless for a stock market barometer. The reason why railroad stocks during 1919 did not share the bull market in the industrials was that, through government ownership and government guaranty, they had in a real sense ceased, for the time at least, to be speculative. They could not advance in any market, bull or bear, more than enough to discount the estimated value of that guaranty.

An Impaired Barometer

Thus for a year or more the averages had half their usual value as a barometer, or indeed less than half, for the movement in the industrials lacked the essential confirmation of a corresponding movement in the speculative railroad stocks. It is made clear by the accompanying chart that during that period the railroads followed not the speculative market but the market for bonds. They had nothing to expect beyond the government guaranty, unless, indeed, far-sighted holders of them could have foreseen the destruction of earning capacity resulting from the colossal waste of government ownership and its subsequent collapse. It will be shown that the railroad stocks during the period of that ownership paralleled the speculative industrials accidentally and for different reasons, only so far as to discount the supposed value of a government guaranty; relapsed, and recovered with an ensuing price movement governed essentially by the totally different conditions which are compelling in the case of bonds.

An Important Distinction

There is some need to point out here the essential difference between a bond and a stock. The stock is a partnership obligation, while the bond is a debt, a mortgage, a liability ranking ahead of the stock. The stockholder is a partner in the business, while the bondholder is a creditor of the company. The bondholder has lent the concern his money on the fixed assets, such as the railroad's real estate or the manufacturer's mills. But the essence of the bond is that its speculative feature to the holder is subordinate, or even non-existent. It is held for its income return. The price fluctuates strictly according to the purchasing power of the income. The price of the bond will be high when the necessaries of life are low, and the investment bond will decline in price as the cost of necessaries advances. It would be easy, but constantly misleading, to say that the price of bonds is regulated by the value of money. The interest rate fluctuates from day to day, and only by the issue terms of longtime bonds can we get any idea of the quotation for money over a long period of years, which is at the best an estimate, and often wrong.

A Definition for the Layman

It is simplest to say that the price of securities held for fixed income is in inverse ratio to the cost of living. If the latter is high the price of bonds or other securities held for fixed income will be low and their apparent yield, measured in dollars, will be large. If the cost of living is low the price of securities held for fixed income will be high and the apparent income, represented by the yield in dollars, will be correspondingly less.

Effects of Government Guaranty

It is plain, then, that with a government guaranty of a minimum return, based upon the average earnings of three years ended June 30, 1917, the railroads entered the fixed income class. If they had continued speculative, with no government guaranty and no government ownership, their fluctuations would not have been governed by the cost of living but by their earning capacity, and chiefly by their prospective earning capacity; for it cannot be too often repeated that the stock market is not reflecting conditions as they are today but conditions as far ahead as the combined intelligence of the country there concentrated can foresee them.

Let us consider the history of the war period as it affected the railroad stocks. When we entered the war, in the spring of 1917, the arrangement between the government and the railroads was purely tentative. So far as the stockholders knew, their investments were still speculative, and these followed the speculative trend. It was not until late on the day after Christmas, 1917, that the announcement that the railroads would be definitely taken over by the government was made. The stock market had not time to discount the new ownership on that day, but on the following day, December 27th, the average price of the twenty active railroad stocks closed at 78.08—an advance of no less than 6.41 points from the closing Prices of the day before. For not more than two days previously was the idea that the roads would be permanently taken over considered seriously in the Street, although it had been expected for some time past that the government would advance the money for maturing obligations and capital improvements. On the morning of the day of the announcement one of the New York newspapers, in the confidence of the Wilson Administration, had a story to the effect that the plan was to take the roads over for a compensation based on the average of five years' net earnings. It is impossible to plumb the depths of Mr. Wilson's mind, but this new ownership was assumed, then and for long afterwards, to be permanent government ownership for all intents and purposes.

How the Averages Diverged

From the accompanying chart it will be seen that in the rally throughout 1918 from the bear swing which had followed the first bull market of the Great War—that culminating in October, 1916—the railroad averages had accompanied the industrials in a steady advance. But from the time when the fate of the stockholders became dominated by government management and guaranty the two averages parted company. The high point of the movement in railroads was made in October, 1918, while the bull market in the industrial stocks did not culminate until November, 1919. Toward midsummer of the latter year the railroads had made some recovery, after a break following the first impetuous buying on government guaranty. But from that point they steadily declined while the principal advance in the industrials was made, continuing to do so while the preliminary movement of the great decline of 1920 was in progress. In 1920 they ran counter to the falling industrials, on the way up actually crossing the industrials on the way down, in the autumn of 1920. There was simultaneously a confirmatory recovery in bonds.

The Esch-Cummins Act

It will be seen that the decline in the railroads in 1919 and the recovery in 1920 virtually paralleled the movement of the average daily prices of forty representative bonds in those years. It will be noticed how closely this corresponded to the inflation and subsequent deflation of the cost of living. During the spring and summer of 1919, while Mr. Wilson was absent in Europe, it was frequently reported that he was disappointed with the unexpected costliness and inefficiency of government ownership, and that he would seek an early opportunity for a return of the railroads to their private owners. There is reason to believe that he did expect, or at least hope, to return them about August 1, 1919, anticipating that Congress would have passed appropriate legislation by that time. Congress was working on the Esch-Cummins bill, now called the Transportation Act, which dragged through the summer and autumn until, on November 16th, the House of Representatives passed the measure. It was at that time, or early in December, that the President positively declared that he would return the roads on January 1st. But the Senate did not pass the Esch-Cummins bill until late in February, 1920; so that the President was compelled to extend the limit he had fixed by two months.

Selling "Ex-Control"

But more than nine months before, in May, 1919, when the railroad average was making the first figure of a "double top," completed in July, *The Wall Street Journal* said that the strength of these stocks in the face of discouraging reports of earnings might be due to the fact that they were beginning to sell "ex-control." There is no question that the decline from the point of the further (July) rally to the early low of 1920 was due to the appalling damage inflicted by government ownership, which actually, in most cases, had raised the operating cost above the operating revenue. The principal item, wages, had been advanced beyond all reason, by a management which was political rather than financial, and the cost of everything the railroads consumed had been multiplied. The war administration had actually bid up railroad ties in Maine against itself, the only buyer, from thirty-seven cents each to $1.40. It is noteworthy also that at that time the large but absolutely necessary increase in rates to render the railroads self-supporting under private operation was only being discussed. It was in fact not granted by the Interstate Commerce Commission until the time of its usefulness had passed.

A Difference of Kind

Federal control actually ended on February 28, 1920, two days after the signing of the Esch-Cummins act, which, however, extended federal compensation for another six months, created the Labor Board and gave the Interstate Commerce Commission the 6 percent net return as a rule of rate-making. Rates were not advanced until the following August, but Wall Street knew that they must necessarily be advanced, and, as usual, discounted that advantage as far ahead as it could see it—in this case nearly six months.

In considering the effect of the war upon business and production it is well to assure ourselves as to what extent the conditions it created are different, in kind or only in degree, from those following other wars. This was a difference in kind. Without help from other quarters the industrial stocks made a bull market off their own bat—a thing they had never done before. Stress is laid upon this fundamental difference here, and the causes which created it, because unless it is thoroughly explained and grasped it is inevitable that teachers and students of the future, to whom these discussions are intended to appeal quite as much as to the readers of the present, will become confused and discouraged, in the face of what might well be considered irreconcilable difficulties and discrepancies. Still another instance will be furnished of a like searching test.

A Sense of Proportion—and of Humor

There is no need for us to fall in love with our theory or to regard it in the false perspective of the enthusiast for any fad. If you hold a silver dollar at arm's length you can see it in its correct relation to surrounding objects. If you bring it too close to the eye its relation to those objects will become distorted and exaggerated, and you can hold it so close that you can see nothing else. Heaven forbid that I should attempt to found a school of economists prepared to die for the thesis that the world wabbles along on a theory of averages. There is no cry here for disciples. We can forgive a great deal to the founder of a school, but we can seldom forgive the school. Let us, therefore, hold the stock market barometer at such a readable distance from the eye that we shall not consider the barometer more important than the weather it predicts. We have sound theory to go upon, or this and the preceding chapters have been written in vain. Don't let us overwork it, as so many statisticians do. Scientists, even the greatest, are inclined to worship their hypotheses, with humiliating results. Herbert Spencer, the great synthetic philosopher, once said to the late Professor Huxley: "You may hardly believe it, but I, myself, wrote the beginning and at least the framework of a tragedy." "I can quite believe it," said Huxley. "I know the plot. It was how a perfectly beautiful theory was murdered by an ugly little fact."

Our Material Is Mostly Modern

Some disappointment has been expressed that Dow said so little that was definite upon his own theory of the market movement, or was able to draw so few of the inferences which were implicit in that theory, to say nothing of the practical and useful truths developed from its application. The wonder is that he got so far with the scanty materials then available. In the latter part of 1902, when Dow died, but six of the twenty industrial stocks now in the average were in the average then, and the number of such stocks used was only twelve. Ten years before, it would have been impossible to find a sufficient number of representative and consistently active industrial stocks to make an average at

conflicts compared with population and national wealth. There is one significant illustration which has not been offered elsewhere, so far as I know. It is that of the British national debt after the immense losses of the Napoleonic wars. Great Britain's debt at that time (1815-16) represented 3 1/2 percent of her estimated national wealth. Throughout the greater part of the century, and during the long reign of Queen Victoria, the debt was gradually paid off, until, previous to the Boer War (1899-1902) it amounted to not much more than 4 percent of the estimated wealth.

In round figures, the Boer War cost Great Britain about a billion dollars, and raised the proportion of debt to national wealth to over 6 percent. In the years between 1902 and 1914, in spite of the steady increase in the cost of living and the growth of taxation, the British national debt was again declining, although it did not reach the low proportion to national wealth of 1899. The British debt now is estimated at 33 percent of the national wealth, or a proportion of about 1 1/2 percent more than that at the conclusion of the Napoleonic wars, which had lasted, with a three-year interregnum, from 1793 to 1815. No doubt it is a formidably high proportion. But it is far from a hopeless proportion; and this is a basic reason why, of all the money units depreciated in the conflict, the British pound sterling approximates respectably in exchange credit to the American dollar.

One of Our Own Liabilities

In 1917 the stock market was asking itself what would happen to the pound sterling, and everything else if Germany won. If the German printing presses are working overtime to turn out paper marks, what sort of currencies would the allies be circulating now had the German drive in the spring of 1918 succeeded? We have satisfied ourselves by analysis that the essential quality of the stock market barometer is its foresight. Could there have been a more striking instance of the clarity of its vision than that salutary bear market, when we were deceiving ourselves with paper profits, inflation wages and inflation prices? In 1916 we had placed in the hands of the labor unions, through the Adamson Act, the power to inflate wages without guaranty of any corresponding productive return. Congress, with a presidential election in sight, had tried to buy votes, lulling the American consumer and taxpayer, who were to pay the bill, with professions of a philanthropic desire to inaugurate shorter hours with consequent greater safety for the railroad traveler. Of course the Adamson Act did not mean shorter hours but only earlier, and more, overtime. The hours of railroad labor were actually lengthened; for it was made strictly to the interest of the men, up to sixteen hours, to stretch their day to the legal limit. We know now what the demoralizing effect upon other labor was, in every department of industry. With such a precedent no wage demand was too preposterous after our own entry into the war, early in 1917, had fed our hands. There was hardly a single manufacturer in the country, and certainly not a consumer, who aid not reap the deadly consequences of that humiliating Congressional surrender.

What Watered Labor Means

In an earlier chapter, that on "Water in the Barometer," I have alluded to watered labor as being incomparably more deadly than watered capital. How many billions of our national debt might not have been deducted, as never incurred, if there had been no such dilution? Mr. Piez, director-general of the Emergency Fleet Corporation during the war, estimated that the efficiency of labor had been dangerously reduced through smaller individual output and larger wages, the latter only excused by the higher prices for commodities of which those wages themselves had been the automatic cause. He said: "Labor had been deliberately slack during the war. In the Atlantic Coast shipyards workmen received $2 for the same time that a year ago (1916) brought only $1, but that the individual output was only two-thirds of what it had been a year before."

Guy Morrison Walker, in *The Things That Are Caesar's,* quoting Director-General Piez, says that the unit of cost production during our share in the war was only one-third what it was at the beginning of hostilities. Estimating our national debt at $24,000,000,000 and deducting from it all, up to $11,000-,000,000, owed by the allied nations who borrowed from us, there remains $13,000,000,000, of which a large part, possibly half, constitutes watered labor. But we are to remember that in the advances to the allies, which were made not in cash but in the necessaries of war, of which labor was the costliest item, the water was also present in the same proportions. It was less the cash wages than the slacking, shirking and bad work. If we took all the water which has ever been squeezed out of corporation capitalization, by the remorseless stock market, we should not have a sum anything nearly approaching the shamelessly watered labor upon which we and our children and our children's children must continue to pay interest for half a century to come.

Paying for Bad Work

It has not been difficult to show the largely nominal character of "water" in capitalization. How relatively seldom has it represented any real loss, to anybody, compared with the irreparable losses from watered labor. How unsatisfying must seem the industrial and commercial activity, recorded of the five years of the war in graphic statistical tabulation, when we have deducted from it the triple price for that prosperity for which from henceforth we have to pay. Everyone of those sham dollars must be met in real dollars. Every wasted hour of bad work or shirked work has to be paid for in an hour of good work.

Secondary Inflation—And After

If I had to forecast the coming major bull swing in stocks, and the area of a possible secondary inflation, likely to be much less than that of the war but sufficiently obvious, I would compare it with the six years which followed the battle of Waterloo in Great Britain. It was in 1821 that the Bank of England went back upon a gold basis, and the premium upon gold disappeared. A self-deluded House of Commons admitted in 1819 that the famous *Bullion Report* was right, and that fiat money was wrong. And then followed the years in which the deflation of the war levels was taken in hand by a nation in which every sixth person was a registered pauper. Dare we suppose that we shall not pay our relatively lighter bill in some such way as this, sooner or later? It is less than four years since the armistice. The bull market in progress while this is written may or may not carry us to a date corresponding to that of 1821 in Europe. We are in no such desperate condition as Great Britain was then. But our foreign customers have an almost incalculably greater reckoning to meet. It is not a problem which can be solved by quack remedies. It can, indeed, be settled only by throwing the quack remedies out of the window, for the patient has been doped to the danger point.

Unsuspected Qualities of the Barometer

But sufficient unto the day is the evil thereof. The stock market barometer is enough for our purpose in that it records, well in advance, the periods of depression and prosperity alike, giving, as we have seen, the signal for a clear track ahead and the warning of danger. The averages are saying now that general business will be more active and more cheerful in the summer of 1922. The barometer does not profess to predict the duration of such prosperity, although on close scrutiny it seems to give tolerably clear indications of the character of the boom or depression which it forecasts. The business depression of 1908—9, predicted by the bear market of 1907, was deep rather than long. The period of prosperity of the latter part of 1909 and 1910 was more extended but much shallower; and the market bull movement which preceded it was also slower and longer than the bear market, while its range was correspondingly less. This is strikingly true of the narrower later fluctuations, both in business and in the stock market, with the latter characteristically preceding the former. It was only in the war years that the preceding major swings of the stock market became as vigorous as the developments in our trade.

It is also noteworthy that during those quiet years of narrow fluctuations before the war the volume of transactions in stocks, as shown in our twenty-five-year chart, contracted also. The average monthly transactions compare in volume, upon the whole, rather unfavorably with those preceding the re-election of McKinley in 1900. The years 1911-14 show a volume of trading below that recorded in the years 1897-00; and the year 1899 made a better showing in the average transactions than any one of the later years here taken for comparison.

Forecasting the War

We may say, therefore, that the stock market does foresee, although probably in a way not sufficiently definite to be of much practical usefulness, the character, and even the dimensions, of the thing it predicts. One thing it foresaw, so far as human knowledge could, was the war itself. Somebody knew that it was a lively possibility, and the bear market which preceded the war was no accident or mere coincidence. It will be remembered that in the latter part of 1912 a bear movement set in, of decidedly mild intensity compared with most of the bear movements of the past and especially those to which we have given particular consideration. There was an area of business depression of no great depth in 1914 which could be offered as partly convincing justification of the preceding major bear swing. But there can be little doubt that the decline was also influenced by liquidation of stock held by those who realized the dangerous possibilities in the German attitude toward other nations. This must have started somewhere about the opening of the Kiel Canal, strategically connecting the Baltic with the North Sea through German territory.

It may be justly claimed that the bear market, quite apart from predicting a contraction in business, was also discounting the possibilities of war. In a previous study, referring to the line of distribution made in 1914, before the outbreak of hostilities, it was shown that foreign liquidation was responsible for turning what would normally have been a line of accumulation into a line of distribution, during the period of almost three months of equilibrium so represented. To those who profess themselves dissatisfied that the major stock market movements are not always immediately adjustable to the various current business charts, it may be said that the fault is not in our barometer. That is universal, and takes note of international facts where those tabulations do not. If, therefore, they inadequately confirm our deductions, so much the worse for them. We have found that the more severe the test we apply to our barometer the more triumphantly does it vindicate its usefulness. It would be difficult to overestimate the value of its prescience both before the war and in the course of the conflict. What if the war had come at the top of a bull market?

Chapter XVIII - What Regulation Did to our Railroads

A sweeping assertion requiring no qualification would probably be one of two things. It would be an axiom, self-evident and containing its own proof; as, for instance, "the sum of the angles of any triangle is equal to two right angles." Or it would be a truism not greatly worth stating. I have said in previous necessary criticism that tabulated business records, however presented, are at best records, and only in a minor degree forecasts. But that is a statement which requires at least some qualification, because the youngest but most scientific of our business records embodies a quality of forecast. This is the service of Harvard University's Committee on Economic Research. Its index chart does offer a method of forecasting business, for the good reason that it adapts the idea of the stock market barometer, which has been in successful use by *The Wall Street Journal* and its allied publications for the past twenty years.

A Chart With a Forecast

Those familiar with the Harvard economic service will recollect that it uses three lines in its business chart —a line of speculation, a line of banking and a line of business. It commits itself to no floundering attempt to show that "action and reaction are equal." Its service dates from after the war; but it publishes a chart from 1903 to 1914 inclusive, which is a most valuable confirmation of what has been here laid down in the discussion of the stock market barometer. Its line of speculation, during those twelve years, uniformly precedes the lines of business and banking. In other words speculation anticipates the developments of business, which is exactly what these chapters have been directed to prove.

The Harvard Committee on Economic Research takes the average stock market prices for its line of speculation. It recognizes how completely the war threw many such calculations out of gear by breaking up the very foundations upon which they were based. Harvard, therefore, does not publish any chart of the years of the war. I find, in looking back over my records and newspaper comments, that conclusions upon the stock market movement and its prophetic relation to the business of the country were dropped almost entirely for the same reason. We have seen that when the government took over the railroads on a guaranty we had remaining merely the speculative movement of the industrial stocks, without any corresponding movement of the railroads to check and confirm it. We have seen also, in analyzing the war period which the Harvard service not unwisely ignores, that the stock market did, in a most valuable way, act as best it could in holding before the public mind the possibilities of the war itself, notably in the bear market of 1917, and that it also foreshadowed the war in the line of distribution for the three months preceding its outbreak.

Movement Greater Than the Major Swing

But there is another indication given by the averages which, while of the greatest importance today, has been largely unrecognized. We have seen that the railroad stocks, where there was a free market for them, in the years under private ownership, shared the major swings; and that we had a bull market culminating in 1909, a bear market determined in the following year, a greatly restricted and hesitating bull market, especially in the railroad stocks, carrying into the latter part of 1912, and another bear market culminating immediately after the reopening of the Stock Exchange in December, 1914, following eighteen weeks of war.

There is a historical significance—a lesson and warning of the very first importance—in the general trend downward of the prices of railroad stocks from 1906 to June, 1921. This is a movement not only wider than the major swings but even more considerable than any of these assumed cycle periods with which a previous discussion dealt. It has extended nearly sixteen years. It is not only likely but as nearly certain as anything merely human can be, that the railroad stocks on the average will improve in the coming year 1922. But there is a radical reason why they will not, in any near period of time, attain the old freedom and buoyancy which they enjoyed in the later lifetime of great railroad builders like J. J. Hill and E. H. Harriman. A condition for railroad enterprise has been established which has not only taken much of the speculative value out of the stocks but much of the permanent value as well. It is a condition which has left the railroads themselves emasculated and weak, with their virile creative power removed.

Roosevelt and the Railroads

If Theodore Roosevelt could have foreseen the deadly consequences of the agitation against railroad corporations which he inaugurated; if he could have realized that he was not applying temporary checks to temporary evils, that his policies, so called, carried to their logical conclusion, would cripple railroad enterprise for incalculable years to come, and perhaps forever, in order to punish a few who had abused the power which necessarily accrues to successful enterprise—we may be sure he would have acted far otherwise. The public power to reform has been construed, in the past fourteen years, as the power to destroy. Railroad development, which in the past has not only accompanied the increase in population but, on this continent at least, has preceded it, is now moribund or dead. No new capital has been forthcoming for the greatly needed extension of railroad facilities to parts of the country that do not enjoy them, to say nothing of greater terminal facilities. Lines of communication are the very arteries of civilization. But the adaptation of the Roosevelt theories—or rather the misconception of those theories, the ascription to Theodore Roosevelt of ideas he never held—has resulted in a hardening of those arteries, in a weakening of the great central heart which pumps the life-blood through them.

An Arrested Development

We can see the fact for ourselves in the mileage of the U.S. taken contemporaneously with each ten-year census. If we had two hundred and forty thousand eight hundred and thirty miles of railroad in 1910—an increase of nearly 25 percent since 1900 and more than double the railroad mileage in 1880— we should have had a continuing increase, shown in the census of 1920, of as much as ninety thousand miles. We have not had one-sixth of it. The increase has been less than fifteen thousand miles, the irreducible minimum, just enough to keep the railroads alive. A "craven fear of being great" has possessed our politicians. They have paralyzed the growth of our most important industry rather than permit a few conspicuous individuals to grow rich by the turning of great ideas to great needs. Harriman and Hill were rich when they died. I knew them both, and I know that their wealth was almost fortuitous. They were rich because they could have done nothing creative without the necessary financial strength to make them independent. But Harriman never controlled the stock of one of the railroads he directed. He was implicitly and deservedly trusted by the stockholders. He never had a voting majority in Southern Pacific, Union Pacific or even Chicago & Alton. He and Hill, incidentally to their own wealth, brought comfort, competence, affluence, to millions of Americans they never saw. The period of railroad development so clearly set forth in the record and chart of our barometer from 1897, the end of the reconstruction era, to 1907, the beginning of the destruction era, was

following year. Of all the contemporary comments on that disreputable exploit those of the *Boston News Bureau,* which flatly refused to be humbugged, were about the most vitriolic. Here is one of them, published less than a month after the fivefold "oversubscription." On June 1, 1899, the *Boston News Bureau* said:

"The drop in Amalgamated Copper stock which was the feature of the trading in outside securities yesterday, was particularly appropriate at this time when the general railway list is on the down grade. Many shrewd observers in Wall Street contend that the formation of the Amalgamated Copper Company was the red flag which warned conservative investors and speculators away from the security market; that a blind pool calling for a capital of $75,000,000 should be oversubscribed five times was an indication to the better element of speculators that the public lost its head and the crash would not be far distant.

"One of the worst features of the whole case is that the National City Bank, which is the largest institution of its kind in this country, should have stood sponsor for such a transaction," etc., etc.

Amalgamated Copper

It will be seen that, in spite of all the flubdub circulated about "over-subscription," the flotation had been a failure. The *Boston News Bureau* continued to comment upon "'The Amalgamated Fiasco," "Promises and Predictions Against Realities," "The Humor and Pathos of Copper Promises," in an acridly humorous vein. In the same month of June there were rumors that control of the Anaconda company had been purchased by the organizers of Amalgamated Copper, for something like $45 a share, though it was quoted at $70 a share by the time Amalgamated was floated, and was said to be going into the new Amalgamated company at $100 a share. The same Boston article points out that the $75,000,000 capital of Amalgamated Copper should have been sufficient to pay for the entire capital of the constituent companies, although only a control, presumably 51 percent was declared to have been acquired. The whole transaction was so raw that in the better Wall Street of today it seems almost unbelievable.

Keene's Part in Distribution

In the latter part of 1904, three years after the manipulated distribution of the stock by James R. Keene had taken place, that eminent operator wrote a letter, which became public, in which he admitted that he distributed, "for the account of Henry H. Rogers and associates," $22,000,000 of Amalgamated Copper (two hundred and twenty thousand shares) at prices ranging from ninety to ninety-six. In that letter he indicated the period of distribution with sufficient clearness. In the following January I published, in *The Wall Street Journal,* an analysis of what he had one, as shown by the recorded sales, under the title of "A Study in Manipulation." That analysis did not deal with the ethical question. You cannot say much about the ethics of people who seem to have none. By taking the sales of Amalgamated Copper stock, as recorded on the ticker, together with the names of the brokers executing orders as reported from the Stock Exchange, and by comparing periods of activity it seemed possible to dot Mr. Keene's "i's" and cross his "t's."

It had the result of making me some enemies in Wall Street, although, to do James R. Keene justice, I do not think he was one of them. I have said before that we were never intimate. But he made opportunities to see me at various times after that analysis was published, and nothing I could say seemed to convince him that I had not had some illicit access to his books. As he put it, "Somebody must have leaked." The Wall Street of that time, and the nature of his own business, made Keene habitually suspicious. His mentality was incomplete in the respect that he found it hard to believe a simple truth where it depended upon the unsupported word of anybody. Really great men, and some children, know when to believe—and whom. Keene was not a great man.

A Difference Between Steel and Copper

Leaving all questions of ethics apart, there was probably nothing more ably done in its day than the distribution of Amalgamated Copper in the stock market. Keene's handling of U.S. Steel common and preferred will remain an example of consummate generalship. But in that instance he had the enormous advantage of a public which wanted the stock he had to sell. It is not true that there was much real "water" in the capitalization of Steel. What was called watered capital was only intelligently anticipated growth. U.S. Steel was floated in 1901, and three years afterwards was showing a well-established surplus of 4.9 percent on the common stock sold to the public at fifty, which surplus had been more than doubled by 1905. In an earlier article I have pointed out the genuine book value of the stock now.

But Amalgamated Copper was an utterly different proposition. As a work of art the distribution, compared with that of Steel, bears about the relation of a Meissonier to one of the heroic battle pictures of De Neuville. Keene, in his subsequent statement, said that he was reluctant to take the matter in hand. It was not that he had to create a market, as in the case of U.S. Steel common and preferred; he had to begin his distribution in a market which others had done their stupid best to spoil.

Earlier Manipulation

On analysis of the sales, the first significant period seems to be that between December 3, 1900, and about the middle of January, 1901. Taking advantage of the general bull movement which set in shortly before the second election of McKinley, such members of the public as had really subscribed for Amalgamated Copper originally were unloading on the promoters of the enterprise. Certain "court circulars" of the time were talking boldly of "inside buying." They were right for once. Insiders were buying because they could not help themselves. They were "accumulating," much against their will, to judge from the downward movement of the stock. With a knowledge of the backs of the cards as well as the faces, the "Standard Oil crowd" which hatched the company could not conceal their crude and clumsy methods. We may here recapitulate the movements and total sales during the period: The opening price on Dec. 1900 was 96. Sales from Dec 3-13 were 160,000. The fluctuation in that period was from 96 to 90. Sales from Dec. 14-Jan.11 were 295,000. The fluctuation in that period was from 89 3/4 to 96. With all this stimulation the closing price on Jan. 11 was only 91 1/8.

Keene's First Appearance

Keene's first appearance seems to have been made then, and he was much too clever not to see that it would be necessary to break the market for the stock before he put it to a level which would attract the speculative public. The next record is: Opening price Jan. 1901 was 91. Sales from January 12-19 were 70,000. The fluctuation in that period was from 92 1/4 to 90 1/4. The closing price on Jan. 19 was 90 1/2. The sales from January 20-26 was 88,000. The fluctuation in the period was from 92 to 83 3/4. The closing price on January 26 was 89.

The closing price of January 26th was a tribute to Keene's ability. It was a much more real price than the ninety-six momentarily established by the fatuous "insiders" in the previous December. The beginning of Keene's operations is characteristic. There were transactions averaging from twenty thousand to thirty thousand shares daily in the third week of January, 1901, when, on the 20th of the month, the price was hammered to eighty-six, fluctuated between 83 and 89 on the following day, and tended to settle down stolidly at 88 on the day after. The gossip obtainable at the time was beneath contempt from a news point of view, but was well calculated to stimulate the avarice of the public. Everything tended to show that, if Keene was in the market at all, he was raiding the stock for a turn on the bear side. It is not venturing too far to say that he had previously taken no trouble to cover up his tracks, in order to create exactly that impression.

What a Major Bull Swing Made Possible

But the McKinley boom in the broadening market was well under way. Stocks were in that great swing, though violently interrupted, but not terminated, by the Northern Pacific corner and panic of the following May. Nothing could have suited Keene better than to have it believed that he was short of a "Standard Oil stock." He admits to having sold all the stock of the Rogers pool, at prices from ninety to ninety-six, shortly before the advance to one hundred and twenty-eight. That advance did not take place until the middle of the following April, but early in March the stock was already selling well above par. I assumed, when writing in 1905, that Keene meant that the $22,000,000 of stock was not credited to Rogers and his friends at one average price, but perhaps in a series of large blocks of stock averaging from ninety to ninety-six, after allowing for the cost of manipulation. Some of it was, of course, sold much higher, but we have already seen that some of it was sold below eighty-four.

Keene's Second Stage

Keene was not the man to press the market when it was going his way, and there followed a period where the stock was judiciously allowed to take care of itself, with occasional stimulus to cultivate bullish sentiment. Transactions were in relatively light volume. In the next period the extreme fluctuation was less than five points, but it is noteworthy that the higher figure was the prevailing price when we see Keene's hand again: Sales January 26 – February 23 were 110,000. The fluctuation in that period was from 92 3/8 to 87 3/4.

In this quiet period of a month he may have sold some real stock but certainly never forced it on the market. It is difficult to say how many shares he actually dealt in that he might distribute so large a quantity. It was possibly ultimately three times the stock he had to sell. In the early stages he was employing brokers on both sides of the market, even if they did not know that they were executing matched orders. That was, and is, against the Stock Exchange rules, and we can afford, at this distance of time, to give them the benefit of the doubt. As the market improved, manipulation of that kind probably grew less, and of course as the public took hold it disappeared altogether.

Keene's Final Distribution

What may be called the third movement shows the final distribution of the stock: The opening price Feb. 28 was 92 3/8. The sales Feb. 28 – April 3 was 780,000. The fluctuation in that period was from 92 to 103 3/4. The closing price on April 3 was 100 3/8.

It is in the final distribution period that Keene probably distributed the bulk of his two hundred and twenty thousand shares. He admitted that much to me, and was never satisfied with my answer to his question as to how I knew.

It is one of the discreditable facts of that period that throughout this trading Amalgamated Copper was practically on an 8 percent basis. It was declaring 1 1/2 percent quarterly, with a half percent extra; and its directors, with that extraordinary fatuity for which the public ultimately paid, were convinced that they could hold up the world price of the metal indefinitely. One of the items of gossip in the early part of the Keene movement was to the effect that the decline of the metal in London, then and now the world's free market for copper, had at last been checked effectually. It was not so. But it was as near the truth as any of the rumors of that curious time. It was some years before the competing copper magnate, Augustus Heinze, reached a settlement with the Amalgamated Copper people, but a settlement was among the rumors then exploited, and one of the principal bull arguments.

The Public's Own Boom

As a net result of the manipulation here detailed Keene had, in the first fortnight of April, 1901, created a market for the stock which may well have surprised himself. It was at least twice as broad as it had been in February or March, with daily transactions amounting to two hundred and fourteen thou-

averages was of barely half the extent of the preceding bear market in the panic year of 1907. The following bull market, if it attains quite that dignity, for it was anything but a boom, showed scarcely a third of the range of the preceding bull market which held from the autumn of 1907 to near the end of 1909. Altogether, in these instructive years, we can see a general dwindling movement. Examination of business records for those years will show that there was a corresponding slowing up of activity in trade, not amounting to depression but rather to a dull level of business; not without the improvement to be expected from the country's natural growth; but in no way conspicuous, or strong enough to stimulate any large volume of speculation.

Predicting Small as well as Large Movements

Here again we see another valuable function of our barometer. The major movements do, in this sense, forecast the extent and almost the duration of the coming improvement, or the depth, and even the severity, of the impending business depression. Our discussions of selected periods covered in our twenty-five-year chart have made this sufficiently clear, as anyone can see for himself by comparing the price movement analyses in previous articles with the subsequent developments in trade. It may be broadly said that business became dull in 1910 and that it did not recover its activity, in any sense greatly worth anticipating in the speculative market, until the boom created by the war.

Here is a period, then, which seems to raise a difficulty for the compilers of business charts, where a certain rhythm is postulated as a normal condition of business. Action and reaction can hardly be called equal in these instructive years, unless it may be the action and reaction of the pendulum of a clock which is running down. Perhaps that is not a bad simile of what took place before the war. It may be said that the demand for war material of all kinds wound up our business clock when it seemed to be slowing down. This is anything but accurate; but it gives a pictorial idea which is useful if not too rigidly applied.

But from the top of the stock market in 1909 we could plot what might be termed, with some show of justice, a bear market lasting nearly five years. I could be called, with a little latitude, a plausible instance of that five-year major swing which Dow so hastily assumed when he first formulated his theory. There had unquestionably been over-rapid development of the country's resources, and possibly of its railroad resources, which had culminated in the panic of 1907. We may, I think, cautiously infer that the effects of such major panics as that are not all dissipated by the subsequent and logical stock market rally; as, for instance, that recovery which culminated in 1909. We see that the business of readjustment took much longer.

Where the Cycle Becomes Useful

Here is a case where the "panic-cycle" theory becomes useful (and it has its proper place), even if it is altogether too vague for helpful application to daily affairs. It is immensely interesting historically, and teaches real lessons when seen in its true perspective. After the panic of 1873 there was some stock market rally, but a subsequent general dwindling of business, under entirely different conditions to those existing today but sufficiently like the period we are now discussing to afford a useful parallel. It might almost be said that it was not until the resumption of specie payments (1879) was well in sight that the business of the country picked up, going on to that broader development which was checked by the less severe panic of 1884.

In the same way, the panic of 1893 was followed by a period of depression much longer than that occupied in the break in stocks, although there were narrowing fluctuations up and down which, if charted, would look strikingly like those of the years following the strong stock market rally culminating in 1909. Here we have a uniformity which suggests at least similar laws, governing a movement broader than that of even the major swing which we have been able to deduce by the application of Dow's theory of the stock market movement. We can at least see that it is not a task of months but of years to restore confidence where it has once been successfully assailed.

Contracting Volume and Its Bearing

It has been pointed out already that business in stocks is always far lighter in a bear market than in a bull market. Our twenty-five-year chart, recording as it does the monthly average of daily stock trading, tells us that speculative business, in the years 1911 to 1914 inclusive, was very little if any better in volume than in the four years preceding the re-election of McKinley. The later period, here under our consideration, was followed by the war boom, an event which upset all calculations. The Harvard Committee on Economic Research does not even chart that period, representing as it does a set of world conditions as abnormal as an earthquake or some such natural phenomenon.

And since the war, and the culmination of what may be called the deflation bear market in June-August 1921, the volume of business has shown a marked contraction. We are experiencing one of the slowest and least spectacular bull movements of which we have any authentic record. Of the fact of the bull market, anticipated in more than one of these articles when published serially, there can be no manner of doubt. The recovery had extended in April, 1922, to twenty-nine points in the industrials and rather more than two-thirds as much in the railroads, with typical secondary movements. In a strong primary swing the secondary movement is correspondingly vigorous. It is noteworthy that neither the upward major swing nor the secondary movement of 1922 has shown a virility which is, as yet, prophetic of a boom in business, as distinguished from a conservative recovery. The barometer is saying that some recovery is due, but that it will come slowly and will take more than the usual time to establish itself. The prediction is rather of a bull market which will not carry prices to new high records, to put it mildly, than a spectacular movement which foreshadows a large and adventurous development of our industrial resources.

Throttling the Railroads

Readers of Chapter XVIII, in which the broad downward movement of railroad stocks over a period of sixteen years was considered, will easily recognize by the extreme conservatism of the stock market at present, even on its recovery, is justified. In our barometer at least, the twenty active railroad stocks represent one-half of our speculative material and record. Our railroads represent the largest single investment of capital in this country, exclusive of farming. The status of these railroads is anything but reassuring. There is nothing to show that more vexatious regulation may not still further restrict their wealth-creating capacity.

We have falsely and foolishly assumed, through our legislators, that 6 percent is the very maximum of earnings which should be permitted to a railroad stockholder; while he is to take the risk of anything less, down to a receivership. Obviously capital will never go into the development of transportation on any such terms as this. But we cannot establish such utterly discouraging conditions for one-half of the speculative field without injuriously affecting the other half. Who can foresee what politics may not bring forth if we are running into that populistic condition which marked the middle nineties? We are regulating capital out of public utilities of all kinds. Who is to say that this interference with the earning power of capital will not be extended to the great industrial corporations?

Politics in Industry

This is no idle surmise. It has been so extended. It certainly has not been so exercised with any gain to the public. But the action of the Department of Justice against the U.S Steel Corporation (now abandoned) shows what can be done if the dangerous theories of the demagogue are to be forced upon business. It is all very well to say that the tendency of modern production is toward concentration, and that commodities will ultimately be cheaper under one management, like that of the Steel Corporation, than under the score or more separate enterprises comprised in that great and beneficent organization. But if the politician's assumption that mere size is in itself an offense is accepted, as it has undoubtedly been accepted in responsible quarters in the past, we may well look upon the course of business in the next half-decade with serious misgiving.

Mr. Taft's Inherited Policies

It must have been in 1909 or early in 1910 that I saw President Taft at the White House. I pointed out to him how the unrelenting hostility toward the railroads, backed up as it had been by the Administration itself, was paralyzing railroad development, and how our regulatory bodies were adding to the business handicap. Mr. Taft was sympathetic, but cautious. He contended that we could no longer expect the rapid growth of the past, based though it had been upon speculative hope made true by great endeavor. But he said that he was inclined to believe that this was necessarily the price which must be paid for the security of the public through the regulation of these great corporations.

This was the "policy" he inherited from Roosevelt, and yet it did not satisfy the progressives in 1912! It was not a long interview, and that was the end of it. When Mr. Taft, with his unimpeachable honesty, could take that view, what was to be expected of all the little politicians, in the state legislatures and the state regulatory bodies, who were paying off old grudges against the railroads, regardless of the cost to the public?

Our Voluntary Fetters

What is the worth of these voluntary fetters we have assumed? Is it contended that railroad service has been improved by all this meddling? There is not a dining car today which gives meals as good as those provided by Harvey for the Atchison twenty years ago. The "standard railroad meal," established by Mr. McAdoo, is recalled like a nightmare by its victims. The railroads have not recovered the old level of service. Both the Pennsylvania and the New York Central once were able to cut the time between New York and Chicago to sixteen hours. But that time has now lengthened to twenty and twenty-two hours. Are the cars any more comfortable than they were? Are the railroad servants any more civil and obliging? When the railroads could discharge an employee for not keeping a car clean without risking an interminable inquiry before the Labor Board, the cars were kept clean. But we have legislated and regulated the spirit of service out of the railroads. Only in a half-hearted way are they competing in making their own route more attractive than that of their neighbors. What inducement is there for the railroads to spend capital in developing such attractions?

Congress has said that they will be robbed of any return from so wise an investment if it exceeds a purely arbitrary figure of 6 percent—one which makes no real provision for growth out of the earnings.

A True Psychological Condition

We are not wandering from the point. We are tracing one of the causes of the most significant movement shown in our averages. You cannot hit the railroads without hitting everything else, because the manufacturers of railroad supplies, as represented in the imposing list of the Railway Business Association, constitute a part of our national manufacturing industry so large that it swings all industry with it. If there is one word which has grown wearisome, from constant use and misuse in the era of quackery from which we are only slowly emerging, that word is "psychology." But here is a true psychological condition. We have lost trust in ourselves. We have meddled so disastrously with the law of supply and demand that we cannot bring ourselves to the radical step of letting it alone.

You cannot have real freedom in a country where you have no freedom in business. There is no tyranny so hard, because none so stupid, as that of bureaucracy. Take a single illustration: President Rea of the Pennsylvania, not so long ago, asked me how many reports supposed his railroad made to departments in Washington, principally the Interstate Commerce Commission, in a single year? Knowing how ample that railroad's reports are, I said that it might be safe to take five hundred a year, as all that were really needed, and multiply that figure by twenty; and ventured, on that basis, an estimate of ten thousand reports for a single year. Mr. Rea laughed ruefully. He said, "Last year we made one hundred and fourteen thousand reports for our lines east of Pittsburgh alone!"

A Reform or a Revolution?

And that was for part of one railroad! Multiply that by all the railroads in the country and see what bureaucratic red tape can do in tying up a great utility's service and impairing its efficiency. We have just begun, thanks to General Dawes, to import a little common sense into Washington business methods. But manifestly he has only scratched the surface. The reform which is needed almost amounts to a revolution, for we are to remember that the Department of Commerce and the Department of Labor, to name only two, are making their demands for more light and more figures, more stationery and more wasted time, upon the general business of the country.

One Handicap and Its Consequences

It is a self-imposed handicap. We have only ourselves to thank. Look at what I have recorded of President Taft's acceptance of the position twelve years ago. Who is to take the Old Man of the Sea off Sinbad's shoulders? How can we expect a general boom in business, or a restoration of the railroads to their old conditions of vigor and growth, so long as the politician can inflict such handicaps as these? We are all hit by it. It hits the farmer in Nebraska, who is burning corn because it works out cheaper per ton than coal. It is hitting our foreign trade. Ours are the largest coal resources in the world, but Great Britain is actually landing coal in this country. She has already supplanted us where we were able, through the war, to build up foreign trade. The attitude of Congress toward business is not merely a development of the insane prejudice against the railroads. It amounts, when analyzed, to the bolshevist idea of fettering success—of making large individual wealth impossible. Enterprise will be attacked in the legislatures, not because there is a speculative danger but because, in the development of the country, some individuals may grow rich. You cannot keep those individuals poor without keeping the country poor. Are we to try again the experiment which was made during the second Cleveland administration? Is that era of Populism and depression, of entire lack of confidence or trust in ourselves, what we shall run into when the present bull market culminates and begins to give signals on the bear side?

Chapter XXI - Running True to Form, 1922-1925

When *The Stock Market Barometer* first appeared serially in the columns of *Barron's,* mostly in the latter part of 1921, the order of the chapters adopted in the subsequent publication of the book was not used. Indeed, this study of Dow's theory of the price movement did not start out with the intention of making a book of itself. It was what an incurable newspaper man like myself would call a newspaper assignment. It partook, to some extent, of the character of contemporary criticism. This is curiously true of one of the most important chapters, the fifteenth, "A Line and an Example—1914." That article was submitted to the editor of *Barron's* with an entirely different line for illustration.

A "Line" in Illustration

All students of the averages will remember the broad rule that a "line" in the daily average indicates distribution or accumulation; and that after either saturation or scarcity has come about the movement of the averages above or below the line gives an important indication of the future movement of the market. Obviously, their advance above a "line" representing many days' trading and all within a range of three points or so indicates that the floating supply of stocks has been exhausted and that it is necessary to bid up in order to tempt a new volume of selling. Conversely, a movement below that line indicates the familiar saturation point, where the clouds resolve themselves into rain. There follows a marked recession in the market, to a point where stocks once more become attractive to buyers.

That fifteenth chapter was submitted to the editor of *Barron's* at the bottom of a major bear movement. The line first chosen for illustration was that which was then in the making. He considered such prediction altogether too daring, although I was willing enough to put Dow's theory and my conception of it to the hazard of such a test. The result would have been a remarkable vindication of the theory. But counsels of prudence prevailed and the illustrative line taken shows the action, or rather the inaction, of stocks during May, June and July of 1914, before the outbreak of the World War. There can be no question that the illustration chosen was the right one, both for historical purposes and for the subsequent authority of the book, which has, to my gratification, assumed a position of its own, with several times the circulation which the cautious publishers anticipated.

What is true enough to have become familiar and, therefore unimpressive, is that the book itself applied Dow's theory to an actual market and predicted, in the most positive way, the major bull movement which set in during the time of publication, serially, in the column's of Barron's. I have been asked to bring the topic down to date for this new edition, pointing out how the theory has been verified, or modified, in the three years which have elapsed since The Stock Market Barometer was first published. The topic should be interesting and useful, and I hope that a lifelong sense of humor will keep me from indulging in boasts about my inspiration as a prophet, even if it is necessary to furnish a few illustrations, from these columns and those of *The Wall Street Journal,* of the way in which the application of Dow's theory has been successfully made since 1922.

Some Successful Forecast

Since the publication of The Stock Market Barometer the market has experienced a major upward (bull) movement in which the industrials, between Aug. 24, 1921, and March 20, 1923, advanced over 61 points, while the railroads between June 20, 1921, advanced from 65.52 to 93.99 on Sept. 9th, 1922, or 28.47 points, and had only lost about three points of this when the high point of the industrials was recorded in the following March. *The Wall Street Journal* and *Barron's* were both entirely clear on this bull movement, the former saying, in Feb. 1922: "At present the major swing of the market is upwards." The final paragraph of that study is significant:

"The answer to inquirers, therefore, is that we are still in a bull market and that it should run much further, possibly well into 1923, and certainly for a time well beyond the improvement in general business which it forecasts."

That was sufficiently explicit, not merely as regards the movement of the stock market interpreted by the Dow theory but upon the improvement in general business which, in due course, followed the rise in the barometer. When the twenty industrials had advanced 26 points, or in the following June, it was said: "There is no reason to suppose that the present bull market is within months of its culmination." Remember that the bull movement really ran into March, 1923. The presence of a line was noted May 8, 1922, although no bearish inference was drawn. On the 22nd of May the resumption of the bull movement was noted, while its continuance "well into 1923" was again inferred. I note that in an interview given in Boston on June 16 I repeated the conviction that the stock market was likely to run further in the upward direction and that it would be all the better for the secondary reaction which had occurred about that time. A tendency to check in the railroad averages was noted in the "Study in the Price Movement" published July 8, but it was then said: "With this proviso it may be said that the indication of the averages is distinctly bullish" especially if he was wrong on the market, but at any rate on September 30 the industrials had reacted nearly six points from the high of the bull movement and the railroads more than four points. On October 18 the "Study in the Price Movement" said: "The stock market today, after a typical secondary reaction, is pointing clearly to the resumption of the major upward movement which developed in August, 1921."

It would be wearisome to recall all such predictions. I prefer to call them inferences. The bullish inference was again drawn on November 3. As late as Jan. 16, 1923, the "extended but by no means unprecedented secondary reaction" was discussed, but the primary upward movement was shown still to dominate.

A Short Bear Movement

For purposes of convenience the short major bear swing may be said to have set in after the top of the industrials was reached in March, 1923. On April 4 the "Study in the Price Movement" called attention to a bearish indication from the line of distribution. Taken all through, the bear market did not last long, and it is noteworthy that while the studies in "the Price Movement" were bearish they were slow to concede the primary reaction, evidently influenced by the fact that the previous bull movement had been decidedly slow. The decline continued to look rather like a secondary reaction in a bull market. The total recession worked out to 20 points in the industrials, culminating Oct. 27, 1923 as far as the industrials were concerned, while at that date the railroads were down rather more than 17 points, although the actual low had been early in the previous August. Rather for convenience of record this conspicuously short bear movement has been taken as primary, but a plausible case might be put up for dating the present bull market from the turn in 1921, when *The Stock Market Barometer* was appearing serially and was even charged with being indelicately bullish.

Influence of Taxes

What was unquestionably a new influence in the stock market had made itself felt in the averages. Congress had been in session all summer and on Aug. 29, 1923, *The Wall Street Journal* had a careful study of the way politics, by dangerous interference with business, had falsified, or to a large extent neutralized, the very barometers of business itself. Income tax and surtax were then at their highest points and *The Wall Street Journal* said:

"There is reason why the barometer in the past few months has been deflected by an influence not felt before in a major dull market. This influence undoubtedly is the cumulative effect of the income surtax.

Brokers can tell how steadily the dividend-paying common stocks, representing thirty out of the forty taken in the two averages, have been sold by large holders on any development of comparative strength. It is correct to call this a new factor, although it has been germinating since the bull market started autumn of 1921. The whole theory of the stock market barometer is based upon the assumption that pressure on stocks can only forecast coming liquidation of general business. But here, for the first time in the history of the averages, is a pressure of stock for sale which bears no reference to coming events.

"It is as though a hot coal or a lump of ice had been applied to the bulb of a thermometer. If it is too much to hope that Congress may see a return to sanity in taxation, this is a condition which will nevertheless cure itself, but only over a period of time beyond present calculation. That stage will be reached when every one of the twenty active railroad common stocks and the twenty industrials is as widely held as the stock of the Pennsylvania Railroad, where the average holding is round about fifty shares per stockholder.

"A rich man cannot afford to hold a common stock returning him six percent on its cost. Not only is he liable to see more than half of the return deducted by the tax-gatherer; such a holding pulls up the tax he must pay on all his other income. He, therefore, has been a steady seller for many months past, and this is 'inside' selling with a vengeance. It is well informed selling, in a way, but obviously it need not predict the general course of business. Congress, in imposing impossible taxes, has not merely laid a handicap on the country's business. It has falsified the very barometer of business."

That temporary influence is now in course of removal so far as Congress is concerned but the State taxes must have some not entirely negligible effect.

A New Bull Market

It would be hypocritical to say that I have really wished I had never written The Stock Market Barometer. It is true to say that I have witnessed with regret the way in which crude adaptations of Dow's complete theory have been taken by tipsters and market quacks to bolster up their unsound conclusions, drawn from an incomplete understanding of the principles involved in reading the averages. On Feb. 4, 1924, after refraining, in disgust at the clamor of tipsters, from discussing the price movement editorially, *The Wall Street Journal* said:

"On the method of reading the averages which is known as Dow's theory, the stock market is in a major bull movement, after the shortest major bear movement of record, one lasting barely eight months. So far as the low of the present movement is concerned, it would presumably date from November 1; but the bull point was given after both the industrial and railroad averages had made one of the most consistent lines of accumulation on record, emerging on the bull side last December (1923)"

It was noted there, as an eminently satisfactory reason for a bull market, that stocks were selling well below the line of values and had not discounted the possibilities of legitimate business expansion. Here again the barometer was right. The business expansion came in due course, slackening in the latter part of the year. This was curiously matched by a substantial secondary reaction in both averages from the high in the industrials of 105.57 on August 20 to the low of 99.18 recorded October 14, paralleled by a reaction of more than six points in the railroads, the averages having seen the low of that movement on October 14.

Since that time the bull movement has been in full swing, developing great activity immediately after the election, when a number of stock tipsters advised taking profits, and selling the market short, on the theory that the good news was out." As the real odds were something like forty to one that Coolidge would beat Davis,—they were openly twelve to one before the election— the "good news" was really the resumed expansion of general business which the market barometer had been predicting.

A Changed Technical Condition

There is a technical condition which has developed in the present bull market and one which did not exist before. Here is substantially what I have had to say about it in another place: Studies of the stock market, based upon Dow's well known theory of the triple market movement as disclosed by the average prices of the industrials and the railroads taken separately for comparison, have been astonishingly right in forecasting the broad upward movement of the stock market and indicating its continuance. The present major bull market, however, is subject to a condition which did not exist before, and it is important to consider the bearing of that limitation.

While the Stock Exchange Governing Committee has been strengthening its control over the conduct of business for a good many years past and certainly since the time when the unlisted department was abolished, the more

619

stringent regulation has been of entirely recent development. It has only been in the past year or two that the governors have assumed to tell the strongest brokerage houses how much of an account they may carry on their capital. In the not very old days a Stock Exchange house took all the sound business it could get, trusting to its own ingenuity to find a means of carrying an expanded account in a big bull market.

This has been drastically changed, and it is now an open secret that a considerable number of brokerage houses are carrying for customers all the stock the Exchange's law allows. Their position is eminently safe, but their policy is obviously changed. The way to make money in a bull market is to buy what you can afford when the upward movement is fairly assured, expand your bull account on the profits, hold on to the larger part of your interest, selling in periods of marked strength, and making up to the proportion you can afford in the inevitable secondary reactions.

But this is not the kind of customer a Stock Exchange house wants. It means the tying up of a substantial amount of capital, with commissions for purchases or sales only earned once in a few weeks. The broker likes the customer to pay commissions every day, although it is anything but profitable to the latter, because the attempt to guess the daily fluctuation is far more like gambling than speculation.

One result of the broker's new limitations is that stock in small quantities has been widely bought for cash and that wealthy customers are financing their own bull account through their own bankers in many Parts of the country outside New York. This leaves some uncertainty as to the real extent of the bull account, but also a hitherto unknown degree of stability, because there is less likelihood of a flood of selling orders all at one time. In the natural way of evolution the result will probably be to concentrate business among fewer houses, each with a much larger working capital than has hitherto been considered necessary. What is at least certain is that there is nothing in the new condition to change the rules for reading the stock market barometer.

Barometrical Indications

It would be timid to conclude this discussion without saying what I think of the barometrical indications writing in August, 1925. There is obviously a strong and well distributed bull account, and there is absolutely no indication in the averages that the bull market has culminated. Counting from the end of the short bear market in the latter part of 1923, the duration of the major swing has not been long and there are still many stocks which are demonstrably selling below the line of values. I think this assumption, if we could calculate an average line of values, would be true of the railroad and partly true of the industrial groups, in spite of their considerable advance.

All indications point to a further upward movement carrying into next year, although secondary reactions of substantial proportions would be very much in order.

Nothing has developed since the first publication of The Stock Market Barometer to shake my faith in the great utility of a common sense interpretation of the price movement. It may be valueless for individual stocks, except that these do not commonly make serious advances except when the general trend of the market is upwards. The one chosen by the speculator may lag behind and never catch up. I am not greatly interested in encouraging people to speculate in Wall Street, but I am humbly gratified that the business of the country has had its attention drawn to such a barometrical guide. It has been freely criticised by authorities of some weight, but has continued its useful service to the general business of the country.

Chapter XXII - Some Thoughts for Speculators

Many years ago one of the Southern states, which need not be otherwise identified, had a law which prohibited the playing of games of chance where any stake was involved. It need hardly be said that a law so foolish was "more honored in the breach than the observance." The sheriff of one of the smaller towns, however, determined to enforce the law and captured a party of young men playing euchre in a barn. Courts were not over-burdened with formalities in those days. It was not considered out of the way, or a departure from dignity, when counsel for the prisoners, while admitting that his "unfortunate clients" had been playing euchre, submitted that it was not a game of chance. As the court and the gentlemen of the jury habitually played the game themselves, the contention was received with incredulity. Nothing daunted, however, the counsel for the defense said: "If your honor will allow me to demonstrate the game to the jury for a short time I am sure I can convince them that euchre is not a game of chance."

Not a Game of Chance

This seemed eminently fair, and the jury and the lawyer were accordingly locked up together. In a short time various members of the jury sent out to borrow a little change from their friends. After an hour or so of "demonstration," the jury returned to court with the unanimous verdict that euchre was not a game of chance.

These articles would not be complete if I did not say something about speculation and, incidentally, give some practical counsel to the speculator. Speculation necessarily involves a large element of chance. It is the speculator himself who too often makes it a sheer gamble. I do not know what the Southern lawyer in the story did to convince the jury of the certainties underlying the game of euchre. But certainly, if the amateur is to come into Wall Street and "speculate" with the stupidity he so frequently exhibits, the professionals there can show him that his kind of speculation is not a game of chance, and they will not have to cheat to do so.

Real Protection in the Barometer

It cannot too often be said that Dow's theory of the stock market movement is not a "system" for beating the market—a get-rich-quick scheme which converts the Wall Street district into a sort of Tom Tiddler's ground, where any man with a few dollars for margin can pick up gold and silver. But if the intelligent speculator of today (who in many cases is or of tomorrow) cannot find himself in the stock market by an stock market barometer, these chapters have, in that respect, failed. He has already gained something tangible if he has correctly understood the major movement. If he comes into Wall Street on a mere tip from somebody he trusts about a stock of which he never heard before, without ascertaining whether the general market is in an upward or a downward major swing, he stands an excellent chance of losing all he brings in the way of margin, without a fair "run for his money." But if he has learned what the market movement means and appreciates the opportunity given to him in the dullness after a typical reaction in a bull market, he stands more than an even chance of making a profit. That profit will depend on a number of considerations which, apparently, do not enter into the minds of many people who come to Wall Street only to lose money, spending the rest of their lives denouncing the Stock Exchange as a gambling hell.

Speculation and Gambling

To these people all stocks look alike. But they are not alike. So far as well-protected speculation is concerned, there is all the difference in the world between such a stock as U.S. Steel common, with a well-established market— a stock well distributed and widely held—and the latest motor or oil proposition floated on the Curb for the purpose of distribution. The latter may be good, but it is at least untested, not only as regards the business the new company purposes doing, but in the market aspect of its stock.

It is a sound general rule that the outsider, when he buys a Curb stock, should do so outright. His purchase on margin is largely in the nature of a gamble. I am not laying down any law about the morality of gambling. Unless it comes under the head of covetousness, I do not know of any commandment against it, and, like an Episcopalian bishop of my acquaintance, with whom I have played auction bridge for small cash points, I am not in the business of inventing new sins. But margin trading in a security of which the amateur trader knows nothing that he has not had at second hand, in a market which only exists artificially by the manipulation of people who want to sell the stock, is the merest gambling. The man who chooses to speculate in it should regard his venture as on the same level with a bet on a horse race. He should see that his loss is limited to such amount as he could afford to lose on a bet.

Speculation is a different matter, and I hope the day will never come when the speculative instinct is not at least latent in an American's mind. If ever that day does come, if ever prohibition extends to the taking of a chance involving the risk of whole or partial loss, the result may be "good" Americans, but of a merely negative type of goodness. If as you enter Wall Street you will pause a moment in Broadway, to look through the railings of Trinity churchyard, you will see a place full of good Americans. When speculation is dead this country will be dead also.

Selecting a Stock

Let us suppose, then, that the outsider has considered the character of the major movement and tendency of the stock market. His next business is to select his stock. Here again the amateur, who wants quick action for his money, will not take the trouble to inform himself properly upon the stock in which he purposes to risk his small capital.

It is a good standing rule that in a stock for which no permanent market has been created—a new flotation or one which is still notoriously, by majority holdings, in control of the people who dictate the policies of the corporation—the small speculator should not trade on margin at all. This is, of course, a counsel of perfection, but at least he should make it a rule to take only a small risk in such a venture and to buy only what he can in some way finance himself if necessary.

By the time a stock is listed in the Stock Exchange there is generally a dependable market for it at most times although here the danger of too much ownership in few hands, as in the case of Stutz Motor, still exists. Such stocks are good to let alone; and only where the nature of the speculator's own business gives him access to special information should he embark his money in stocks of such a character, and even then his margin should be of the most ample kind.

On the Matter of Margin

This brings us to the question of margins. A complete misunderstanding of what constitutes a sufficient margin is responsible for many needless losses in Wall Street. Brokers are looking for business, and they tell the tyro that ten points margin is good enough if he can guarantee the firm that amount against fluctuations. This would mean $1000 on one hundred shares of stock at par. That margin is not enough, or nearly enough. Writing twenty-one years ago, Dow pointed out that "the man who buys a hundred shares on a 10 percent margin, and stops his loss at 2 percent, has lost (with commissions) nearly one-quarter of his capital." Obviously it does not take long to wipe him out. Dow was ultra-cautious, but he was not wide of the mark when he said that if such a man had begun with ten-share lots he would have been able to see a substantial loss and yet have averaged his purchases to yield him an ultimate profit, granting he was correct in his first surmise that the stock was selling much below its value. Certainly a trader with $1000, and no more, has no business to start with a hundred shares of stock unless it be something at a very low price. There was a time when Steel common could have been bought below $10 a share.

Little Traders and Large

Another delusion of the small trader is that he should buy part of the quantity he contemplates, adding to his holdings on each point of decline until he completes the amount he thinks he can carry. But why not buy it all at the last price? If he proposes to buy one hundred shares in twenty-share lots, and expects that there will be a decline of five points in the market, he is really contradicting the assumption upon which he originally decided to trade. He has not considered all the facts of the case. If the stock can go down five points the purchase is not so good a one as he supposed. It is quite true that great operators, like Jay Gould, did buy stock in that way. But they were not trading on margin, except in the respect that they financed their stocks mostly through their own banks. And they were buying upon considerations which would seem hopelessly remote to the small speculator who wishes to test his judgment in Wall Street. Such a man as Jay Gould, moreover, could himself give value to the things he purchased. He might well start to buy into a company during the course of a major bear swing, knowing that he could not get all the stock he wanted in a bull market.

The small speculator cannot afford to take any such view, unless he purposes to devote such exclusive attention to stock trading as he would give to any other business. There are plenty of people who do that, and I have in previous discussions given instances of their success. But we are talking now of the man who speculates on his judgment while interested in some other business. There is no reason why a speculator of this class should not have more than an even-money chance in the market if he would only bring a little common sense to bear. But if he will listen to the first casual friend who tells him to "buy a hundred shares of A.O.T., and ask no questions," and risks his only thousand dollars in doing so, he cannot complain if he loses. He is a gambler and not a speculator. He would have much more fun if he took his dollars to the races. He would have a healthy day in the open air and find the racehorse a much more amusing spectacle than the ticker.

A Quotation from Dow

In an editorial published in *The Wall Street Journal* on July 11, 1901, Dow said: "If people with either large or small capital would look upon trading in stocks as an attempt to get 12 percent per annum on their money instead of 50 percent weekly, they would come out a good deal better in the long run. Everybody knows this in its application to his private business, but the man who is prudent and careful in carrying on a store, a factory or a real estate business, seems to think that totally different methods should be employed in dealing in stocks. Nothing is further from the truth."

In the same article Dow went on to say that the speculator can avoid tying himself up in a financial knot at the outset by keeping his transactions down to a limit which, compared with his capital, leaves his judgment clear and affords ample ability to cut loss after loss short; to double up; to switch to some other stock, and generally to act easily and fearlessly instead of under the constraint which comes from a knowledge that his margin of safety is so small as to leave no room for anything except a few anxious gasps before we account is closed. This is as good sense now as on the day it was written. The speculator who comes into Wall Street must learn to take losses, and take them quickly. I have said before that more money has been lost in Wall Street from sheer pride of opinion than from any other single cause. If you buy a stock and find that it is falling rapidly, you have not considered all the facts of the case. You cannot consider them impartially so long as you are under the terror of losing all your capital. You cannot take a clear, unbiased view unless you get out and look at the thing objectively. When you are tied up in a losing speculation you are in the position of the man lost in the forest who cannot see the wood for the trees.

Avoiding Inactive Stocks

Readers will remember the story I told of the young man who refused a partnership offered to him by Jay Gould because, in executing Gould's orders on the floor of the Stock Exchange, Gould seemed to him to make nothing but losses. He was not broad enough to see that these unsuccessful attempts were merely testing purchases, and that Gould probably employed some other broker when he was quite sure that he had caught the turn of the market. Here is where the purchase of a stock only occasionally active becomes so dangerous. The broker may be able to carry it very well today, although inactive stocks are not looked upon with favor in bank loans.

But the broker himself does not know whether he can carry the stock so conveniently tomorrow. The peculiar circumstances which started the movement in that stock may be fully discounted in a few days' active trading, and the event will be a market without a single transaction for days together, where the seller is obliged to make concessions to find a buyer—generally a professional, who charges all the traffic will bear for such a service. Such a stock should not be carried on margin at all. But the man whose business is in some intimate connection with the steel trade or the textile industry may well take hold of Steel common or Bethlehem Steel or American Woolen, feeling that there is a permanent market if not always an active one.

A Word for the Consolidated Exchange

I have many friends in the N.Y. Stock Exchange, but I have also friends elsewhere in Wall Street. The odd-lot brokers, of whom there are fewer than ten firms specializing in that way, make the market in lots of less than a hundred shares. But the Consolidated Stock Exchange makes a regular market for those small quantities all the time. It is in every way a reputable institution, whose members are open to the same scrutiny the speculator ought to apply to any broker he employs. Our small amateur trader can do his business just as well on the Consolidated exchange, provided he chooses really active stocks. Such stocks are "seasoned" and thoroughly well disked, and this is not true of those which make up the list of the Curb Association. I am not saying one word against the latter, but the securities in which it deals are seldom popular in bank loans, and I should have the strongest suspicions of a Curb house which professed to trade for its customers indiscriminately on a 10 percent margin.

By all means get the idea of such a margin out of your head. The margin should be as good as you can make it. If you are engaged in business or living upon an income from investments with people dependent upon you, your losses in speculation should be limited to an amount which will not cause you serious compunction. It is probably heterodox to say so, but there is common sense in the proposition that gambling begins where we risk what we cannot really afford to gain something we have not earned.

A Glance at Short Selling

How can the stock market barometer help the speculator? In many ways. He cannot expect any stock, except under most unusual circumstances, to advance profitably against the general current of the market. He must be most unusually well informed, an almost instinctive reader of the market, if he can speculate successfully on the occasional rallies which take place in a major downward swing. I am saying little about short selling. The man who tries short selling in a bull market is merely guessing at the secondary reactions, and unless he is a trader on the floor or devoting all his attention to the business of speculation, he is certain to lose his money. I am not discussing the morality of short selling, because I do not believe the moral question enters into speculation at all, provided it does not degenerate into gambling with what is, in effect, other people's money. In every market in the world there is necessarily a great deal of short selling. The tourist in San Francisco whose stocks are locked up in his safe deposit box in New York cannot afford to miss his market by waiting until he returns across the continent. If he sells he is short of the market, and a borrower of stocks until he can make his delivery good. But on the law of averages, far more money has been made on the bull side than has ever been made on the bear side, if only for the reason that bull markets are generally much longer in their duration than bear markets. Short selling is an operation which may well be left to the professional, especially by the man who is only a student of the market learning the rules of the game.

Buying on Reactions

No knowledge of the stock market barometer will enable any of us to call the absolute turn from a bear market to a bull market. There may be weeks of narrow fluctuations before a definite trend is established, as we have seen in our previous studies of the market movement. All of these indecisive fluctuations eat up the speculator's capital, in broker's commissions and interest, to say nothing of the market turn. But when once the major bull swing is established the successful purchase of stocks for a rise becomes a feasible proposition. If on the completion of his purchase a stock reacts, carried down by a similar reversal of movement in the general market, the speculator should take his loss without hesitation and wait for that inevitable period of dullness which develops after a secondary reaction in a major bull swing. Here again he may buy his stock, and instead of purchasing on the way down, on the fallacious assumption I exposed earlier in this article, he may well add to his holdings as the market rises. Each advance adds to his margin of safety, and, provided he does not "pyramid" too much, and conceding that his holdings are not overextended so that his own account would be a tempting object of attack, the speculator may well, if he protects himself with "stop-loss" orders, make profits much more substantial than he at first expected. We hear a great deal about people who lost money in Wall Street but very little about those who made substantial profits there. The latter, as a class, are inarticulate, in my experience; and a man seldom cares to ascribe his prosperity to successful speculation. He prefers to call it judicious investment. There is little difference between a purchase of a house on mortgage and a purchase of stocks on margin, provided the purchaser can meet his contracts. In these great uplifting times, when everybody is minding everybody else's affairs, I am still disposed to say that it is nobody's business how our speculator carries his stocks so long as he does so out of his own resources which include his borrowing credit at the bank.

Ways of Losing Money

There is another class of speculator, all too common, who loses money by forgetting why he went into the market in the first place. Knowing me personally, he asks me my opinion of Atchison common. I tell him what the road's prospects are, what the earned margin may be over and above the dividend, and the general railroad outlook in that part of the country. He concludes that Atchison common (here chosen merely for example) is cheap, and buys himself some of it. If he would protect his broker with ample margin, or pay for the stock outright, and ignore fluctuations, he would probably make money.

But he listens to every bit of gossip, particularly stories of "traders selling," "Congressional investigation," "threatened strikes," "crop failures," and all the rest of it. He forgets that the market has made allowance for everything of the kind in the broad estimate of the prospective value of the stock. He becomes nervous on a minor fluctuation, takes a loss and decides never to ask my opinion again. At least I wish he would so decide; but, unfortunately, he does not. He comes to me again to see if I cannot say something to upset what he calls his judgment, based, this time, upon the opinion of somebody else.

Another Way of Losing Money

Take another easy way of losing money in Wall Street. The speculator is informed, correctly, of a coming quick movement, perhaps covering four points in a particular stock. He notices that the stock has been active, without paying much attention to the fact that a point and a half of the expected four points is already shown in the advance of the price. After some hesitation he buys, when the movement is almost completed. He sees a small profit, and then the stock becomes dull. The special movement is over. The attention of the professionals is turned to some other security, and his own stock sags with the market or eats its head off in interest. But he is still fatuously holding on instead of realizing that he has missed his opportunity and has had what, if he would look at it sensibly, is really a cheap and most instructive lesson.

Here again he forgets why he originally bought the stock, just as he did when he purchased on permanent value. If the special movement he anticipated fails to materialize he should take his loss, or his disappointingly small profit, and wait for another chance. But the trouble with most of the speculators of my acquaintance is that they lack not only memory but the virtue of patience. They must be dabbling all the time; and sooner or later they get tied up with an account, extended to their full resources, which seems to have run aground, with the general current of the market swinging past it.

"Where do the Gentiles Get It?"

It is a common mistake to suppose that the reputable broker makes his profits out of what his customer loses. The broker stays in business out of the commissions that his customers pay. He not only wants them to make money, but he does everything he can to help them do so, or, at the worst, to prevent them from losing money. It is only the bucket shop which wants a new customer every day, to fleece thoroughly before the market closes. All the reputable brokers of my acquaintance are proud to point to customers who have been employing them for many years, in good times and bad, extending in at least two instances I can recall, to nearly half a century.

In writing this I have necessarily outlined a patient, intelligent and level-headed speculator—in fact, a man of exceptional coolness and poise. But that is the kind of speculator for whom I am writing. I am certainly not drumming up business for the Stock Exchange. These stories of the continual losses of the outside public in Wall Street always remind me of the young Jew who said to his wealthy parent: "Father, where do the gentiles get all the money that we take away from them?" Where does the public get all this money which Wall Street is supposed to take from it in speculation? Is the broker's commission a sort of middleman's profit taken out of the whole business of the country? To a certain extent it is; but not to anything like the extent the people who do not love Wall Street assume. Wall Street is the great reservoir for small, trickling streams of capital. Great corporations would be impossible if there were not a free market for the interchange of their securities. The free market is in itself an element of value. If we could imagine two securities of exactly equal merit in every respect, the one with the free market would inevitably, and most properly, sell anything from five to ten points above the other. It is exactly this free market that Wall Street provides.

A Final Thought

This brings me to the conclusion of my discussions of the stock market barometer. I would not have it on my conscience that I had encouraged any weakling to gamble, or had expedited, by a day, the inevitable parting of a fool from his money. At least in that respect every man is a free agent. In spite of all sorts of personally regulatory legislation, he has still that much freedom allowed to him. We can imagine laws which would make speculation impossible, even if, as they certainly would, they paralyzed the business of the U.S. But we cannot imagine any law which would compel a man to trade in Wall Street if he did not choose to do so. All I have tried to do here is to show him how he can protect himself, and at least feel that not only has he had a fair run for his money but that he has earned the prize at the end of the run.